The Foodbook

The
Enriched, Fortified, Concentrated, Country-Fresh, Lip-Smacking, Finger-Licking, International, Unexpurgated
FOODBOOK

by James Trager

GROSSMAN PUBLISHERS *New York* 1970

For Toby, Mandy, Jamie
and others who won't
eat their spinach.

ᵒ₈⟦ *Preface* ⟧₈ᵒ

The shops are full of cookbooks. There are shelves of books on how to lose weight, or gain it, with proper diet. On how to eat your way to good health. And on the growing problem of hunger in the world.

This book is different. It contains no recipes, no revolutionary health diets or reducing diets, no panaceas.

It is a foodbook rather than a cookbook. Its purpose is to feed your appetite for knowledge. And to shed light on the most universally shared human experience, the one sensual pleasure we enjoy from our nonage to our dotage, yet strangely enough, a subject even most educated people know little about.

Food is the largest single item in most American family budgets (though people living in high-rent areas will find that hard to believe); yet a U.S. housewife will spend on a national average less than a fifth of her family's income to buy a ton of food for each adult and teen-aged member of her family. In other countries the percentage of income spent for food is higher, often much higher.

The world of foods is changing faster than most of us suspect. To understand the changes, for good and for bad, we need some background. Why do we eat what we eat? How did it all come about? Why don't we eat some of the perfectly edible things most of us never think of eating?

What we do know about foods we have learned largely in the last few hundred years of our history on earth. We still have a lot to learn. And to unlearn.

[vii]

We hear so much talk about the quality of life. Basic to that quality is the quality of our food, an intimate subject on which emotions run high. But both in the starving countries and in the lands of too, too solid flesh, lack of sound knowledge about food leads to errors of public policy and of private buying habits and eating habits, errors that are producing dismal effects.

The boundaries of some knowledge, notably of sex, have in recent years been rolled back to reveal more and more to increasing numbers of people. But on basic facts of life about food, most people are astonishingly ill-informed, inflexible, unimaginative. While most of the world is forced to live on monotonously limited diets, the scope of our own diets is limited by stale habit and familiarity. Our store of food information is full of false "facts."

We need to know more about food, about the sources of food and the roots of our eating patterns; about food taboos and food myths; about the techniques of producing and preserving food; about the additives used in so many present-day foods; about the most effective ways to get more for our food dollars.

Hence this foodbook. It is not a book about the niceties of *haute cuisine* (though it does deal with caviar, truffles and *pâté de foie gras* along with more basic victuals). It is about the nitty-gritty essentials of food, which is the nitty-gritty essential of life.

A study by the National Commission on Food Marketing shows that the U.S. food industry, or industries, spent $1.4 billion in 1966 to advertise foods. About $123 million was spent on research into promotional devices like package design; a paltry $12 million went into basic food research.

U.S. consumers spend about $90 billion a year on food and beverages (not counting the $25 billion we spend in restaurants), more than twice what we spent in 1950, and we'll probably keep spending more. With the exception of poultry, most foods have been rising in price.

The profusion of foods available to us creates a bewildering chaos. Advertising does little to guide the consumer through the supermarket, where some eighty per cent of U.S. grocery dollars are now spent; guidance is not considered to be advertising's function. Government agencies publish bulletins designed to inform the consumer and help him, or more usually her, to do the family marketing more intelligently and efficiently. But how many of us read the bulletins?

What fills the information gap is people's massive distrust of the food industry and its regulating agencies, a distrust that leads people to adopt foolish food fads. The purpose of this book is to fill the vacuum with more solid fare, to help dispel the pea soup murk.

There is, you must realize, no end to the subject of food. For most of the world there just isn't enough of it. For the rest, the attitude of poet Ogden Nash may be typical:

> Some singers sing of ladies' eyes,
> And some of ladies' lips
> Refined ones praise their ladylike ways,
> And coarse ones praise their hips.
> "The Oxford Book of English Verse"
> Is lush with lyrics tender;
> A poet, I guess, is more or less,
> Preoccupied with gender.
> Yet I, though custom call me crude,
> Prefer to sing in praise of food . . .
> Food,
> Just food,
> Just any old kind of food . . .
> Let it be sour
> Or let it be sweet
> As long as it's something to eat . . .
> If it's food,
> It's food;
> Never mind what kind of food.
> When I ponder my mind
> I consistently find
> It is glued
> On food.

Some of us may live to eat. All of us must eat to live. How we have eaten in the past and how we can eat better in the present and future are what The Foodbook is all about. It may help your family eat better. It will at least help satisfy a taste for information in an area now polluted by so much misinformation.

⸨ Bill of Fare ⸩

[xi]

History records the battlefields on which we lose our lives, but it disdains to tell us of the cultivated fields on which we live; it can tell us the names of the kings' bastards, but it cannot tell us the origin of wheat. Such is human folly.

—*Jean Henri Fabre,*
French entomologist,
1823–1915

The Foodbook

❦[*1*]❧

Maybe the proper study of mankind is food

For most of the earth's creatures, life is an unending and totally involving quest for food.

Animals, birds, fish, insects—all must eat to stay alive, and most spend their entire lives stalking, chewing, searching out or lying in wait for sources of nourishment.

Some animals (and some birds and fish) are strictly carnivorous; they eat only flesh. Others are herbivorous; they eat only plant matter. And a few, like bears and men, are, catholically or narrowly, omnivorous. Our foods are both animal and vegetable (with trace elements of mineral).

Early man must have lived the same sort of life as the lower animals. Before he discovered fire, he fed himself with the raw eggs of birds, with fish and animals he killed using primitive stone weapons, with nuts, fruits, berries, mushrooms, mosses, edible roots and seeds.

Prehistory you can sink your teeth into

Paleontologists distinguish the fossils of early humans from those of apes chiefly by the humans' lack of big overlapping canine teeth; man could grind his food from side to side instead of just chomping up and down. More than one observer, studying the skeletal remains of these first specimens of *homo sapiens,* has concluded that our primate progenitors were vegetarians. Teeth again. They lacked the powerful incisors of the carnivorous animals. Apes, after all, are herbivorous. This speculation is one of the bases of vegetarianism, which has had many adherents over the ages, and which we will examine in our next-to-last chapter. Since man was not meant by nature to eat meat, the argument goes, he imposes an unnatural burden on his digestive organs when he does eat meat.

The theory does not stand up. Chimpanzees, baboons and many of the monkeys supplement their plant diets with insects, birds' eggs and any small animals they catch. The late naturalist Fairfield Osborn conceded that many groups of primitive people were plant and fruit eaters, "especially those people living in tropical or subtropical regions."

> But [he concludes] the explosive, dominant groups, which appear to have made the strongest impact on the course of human civilization, particularly those living in the temperate zones, resorted in the earliest times to hunting, combat and killing.

So while gorillas may be vegetarians, man very early was not only bloodthirsty but meat-hungry. And while animals that are really herbivorous can break down the cellulose and raw starch in vegetables without much difficulty, man's digestive tract cannot deal with most vegetables unless they are cooked. We can, on the other hand, digest raw meat, fish and insects.

It may also be that over the centuries, human digestive organs adapted themselves to meat, just as man's teeth adapted themselves to meat eating when he was forced in winter to eat game for lack of plant food as he moved into the colder regions of the earth.

Much has been written in recent years about man's inborn aggressive instincts; his age-old territorial king-of-the-mountain games, it is said, mean that he is destined to destroy himself. But as someone has pointed out, no other animal—only man—invites his neighbors into his cave, his lair, his home to share his food.

While the need for food has obviously shaped man's history since the beginning of men, we can only guess about the early stages of that history. There were at first few men; they lived their short, brutish lives (in Thomas Hobbes' phrase) much like the lower animals, eating their food raw.

Millenniums, even eons, passed before stone weapons were improvised to kill game, more centuries before animal bones were fashioned into hooks to catch fish.

We have only our imaginations to tell us of man's trial and error progress in developing a body of knowledge of what could safely be eaten from nature's bounty; of which mushrooms could make him ill, or even kill him (and think how often the same mistakes must have been repeated), of how fire could be tamed and used, not only for bodily warmth but for making some foods edible and others more palatable. Since cooking breaks down the cellulose walls of plants and produces chemical changes in starch, partially digesting it, cooking enabled man to broaden his diet from fruits, nuts, berries and the animal foods that had previously supported it.

Again, we can only imagine how prehistoric man learned to harness the energy of fire: the dry grass or woodlands set ablaze by lightning, the coals kept alive, the fires extinguished by rain, the first fumbling efforts to start new fires with sparks from flintstones falling on dry tinder.

This discovery of man-made fire evidently goes back at least to 360,000 B.C., when man was a rare species on the earth, far outnumbered by other species, wandering in bands as he foraged constantly for food.

Peking man, the hominid whose fossil remains were found in caves at Choukoutien, near Peking, China, in the late 1920's and early 1930's, clearly cooked his meat. Along with the fossils of some thirty-eight individuals in those caves were the charred bones of many animal species, most of them now extinct. The charring of the bones indicates the flesh of the animals was roasted. And the hard-baked red and yellow clay under the carbonized bones shows that Peking man had hearth fires.

But who first discovered that cooking could make some foods taste better? Was a roasted carcass found in the wake of a forest fire? The roast pig story of Charles Lamb's famous "Dissertation" (Chapter 8) comes close to this hypothesis. Or was a piece of meat accidentally dropped in a fire built for warmth and for protection against hostile animals?

And why *did* early man like the flavor of warm meat? Was it, as Desmond Morris suggests in *The Naked Ape*, because of man's animal origins and his instinctive appetite for fresh-killed meat?

We can only theorize. The cave paintings found near the village of Aurignac in southern France, said to date back to the Paleolithic Age of 40,000 years ago, show bison and tigers and suggest that these animals were hunted for food by men of that era.

They show, too, that people even then cut off the more tender parts of meat, probably with chiseled stones, and wrapped meat in leaves to bake or steam in the ashes of fires. The people of Aurignac also, it seems, climbed trees to get bees' honey, caught fish which resemble salmon, and gathered wild fruit and nuts. Like earlier men, they ate human flesh on occasion. The charred remains of human bones in the area bear the marks of human teeth.

Until about 12,000 years ago, until what anthropologists call the Neolithic Revolution, man could use fire only for roasting, baking or, as at Aurignac, steaming foods in wet leaves. Cooking foods in pots came only with the invention of fireproof, watertight pottery, another step in the expansion of man's diet.

Excavations in the north of Europe show that the Neolithic people who lived there subsisted chiefly on seafood, including lobster. They evidently knew how to smoke fish to preserve it. And they brewed some sort of mead from honey and wild berry juice.

After perhaps another 2000 years, man began to keep herds and flocks of animals instead of depending entirely on wild game for meat and hides. Tribes of herdsmen began to replace the tribes of hunters which had comprised human society for hundreds of thousands of years.

The herdsmen moved to fresh pastures when their herds had eaten all the grass in one vicinity. Probably by observing how birds ate the seeds of wild grasses, some early men discovered they, too, could make good use of grasses gone to seed. Pounded with rocks, the seeds made a rough flour that someone mixed with water and baked into a crude, flat bread.

Cradles of civilization, and the hands that rocked them

The first men had raised no livestock; they had cultivated no crops. Food had been gathered from what existed in nature, and human existence had literally been hand to mouth.

Now, about 8000 B.C., some of the hunters or herdsmen learned to plant the seeds of grasses, probably millet and barley, scratching the surface of the soil with pointed sticks to soften it, covering the seeds with earth by dragging branches of trees across the fields. At harvest time, they beat the stalks to shake loose the grain. And as they came to live close to their fields, some men ceased to be hunters and tenders of flocks. They became farmers.

Except that it was almost certainly not *men* who developed this first agriculture, but rather *women*.

Associations between the fertility of the soil and fertility in women run deep in the folklore of almost every people. While Greek mythology assigned gods to some aspects of life and of nature, grain found female personification in the goddess Demeter and her daughter Persephone. We speak of virgin soil and of barren lands. Sophocles said Oedipus "tilled the field his father had tilled." And Sir James Frazer, in *The Golden Bough*, cited rituals which make a connection between the seeds of men and of nature.

Frazer wrote of a tribe in West Africa where "the night before a man sows earth-nuts [peanuts] he has intercourse with his wife for the purpose of promoting the growth of the earth-nuts which he will plant the next morning." Husbands and wives in parts of Java, said Frazer, did the same thing "at the season when the bloom will soon be on the rice."

He reported a festival held by the Indians of Peru in December, "when the alligator pears [avocados] begin to ripen," a little exercise designed "to make the fruit grow mellow."

> The festival lasted five days and five nights, and was preceded by a fast of five days during which they ate neither salt nor pepper and refrained from their wives. At the festival men and boys assembled stark naked in an open space among the orchards, and ran from there to a distant hill. Any woman they overtook on the way was violated.

Frazer gives many such instances. May festivals with their Queens of the May were polite refinements of more elemental rites.

If the rites and traditions do not altogether prove that Mother Earth was first tilled by women, two other pieces of evidence strongly suggest it.

One, a man's strength was not required to plant crops until the wooden plow was invented. The frailest woman could make a hole with a digging stick or hoe and plant a kernel of barley, millet or wheat.

Two, in primitive tribes which have still not emerged from their Stone Age culture, the men are still the hunters, the fishermen, the herdsmen; it is the women who dig the roots, till the soil, collect the seeds and vegetables, and a woman is valued more for her prowess as a field hand than for any other attractions she may have.

In our modern society it is generally the woman who concerns herself with procuring food, usually from the supermarket, and preparing it, while the man devotes himself to the chase. He may pursue money, blondes or golf balls, but the traditional forms of the chase are still with us, too: angling far exceeds any other participation sport (as many as 40 million Americans go fishing each year) and there are some 17 million U.S. hunters (a handful of whom comprise a highly vocal minority in opposition to sensible gun-control laws).

If indeed it was women who began the agricultural revolution—which has come only in the last one per cent of the time the human race has inhabited the earth—then civilization itself owes its existence to women.

Some of the earliest traces of civilization are the charred and petrified artifacts found in the remains of stilt houses built on lakes in what is now Switzerland. The evidence indicates that the Lake Dwellers had domesticated oxen which they hitched to crude plows made of tree branches. They cleared fields, planted grain and baked the first breads in the ashes of fires, mixing crushed millet, rye, barley, oat and wheat seeds mixed with water and flavored with caraway seeds. They ate cherries and apples, slicing and drying the apples to keep them through the winter. They also had dried peas and other legumes.

It is a measure of the frustration of historians that we have this much knowledge of the Lake Dwellers of 6000 B.C., yet we know comparatively little of what went into the stomachs of people in the so-called "Cradle of Civilization" at that time.

This "cradle" was supposedly the valleys of the Tigris and Euphrates Rivers in what is now Iraq, but there is evidence that civilization flowered even earlier in the Indus River valley farther to the east, and we know a little more about the foods of the people there.

The United Nations Educational, Scientific and Cultural Organization (UNESCO) is now trying to save from disintegration [1] the remains of the ancient city of Mohenjo-Daro, first excavated less than fifty years ago.

From these and later excavations it appears that as many as six different cities were built on that site in what is now Pakistan. As early as 4000 B.C., a thousand years before Babylon's zenith, Mohenjo-Daro was evidently a metropolis of brick houses with private wells, bathrooms and a sewage system under the streets. Its farmers used irrigation (which, as in so many early civilizations, eventually raised the saline and alkaline content of the soil and destroyed agriculture) and in their well-watered fields produced several crops each year of vegetables and cereal grains.

From here in the Indus Valley the Sumerians, Chaldeans, Mesopotamians and Babylonians got their first orange and lemon seeds. From here the Chinese got their first rice—5000 years ago by some accounts, not until the sixth or seventh century B.C. by others.

The first excavations of Mohenjo-Daro were made in 1922. What the archaeologists turned up there astonished the world. Inhabitants of that ancient city had evidently invented the mortar and pestle for crushing and blending spices. They had been the first to season foods. They had created the earliest curry powders, using the seeds of mustard, fennel, and most especially cumin and the rinds of tamarind pods, drying them in the sun and grinding them in their mortars. They had produced saffron from the stamens of the autumn crocus [2] and had used it both as a spice and as a yellow dye.

---

[1] The underground water table is rising due to a shift in the course of the Indus River. Less than ten feet below the surface, the water carries a high content of mineral salts that are drawn up into the ancient baked bricks, turning them to powder.

[2] Each blossom of the *Crocus sativus* has but three stamens, or stigmas, so it takes more than 4000 flowers to yield an ounce of commercial saffron, 225,000 hand-picked stamens to make a pound. This makes saffron the world's costliest spice (the U.S. price is now about $400 a pound). The Moslems introduced saffron to Spain in the eighth century A.D., along with rice and sugar; saffron rice is now popular throughout the Iberian peninsula and in northern Italy, where the Spanish introduced it, along with rice, in the fifteenth century. True, saffron is expensive, but a little goes a long way.

Citizens of Mohenjo-Daro were also probably the first people to eat anything much besides meat, raw fruit and crude unleavened bread.

They raised goats, sheep and cattle, but it is not clear whether they milked their animals. Except that it was sometime before 2000 B.C., nobody knows when man discovered he could squeeze a nourishing food from the udders of female goats, ewes, and later cows (or kine, to use the archaic plural). It began, perhaps, when a suckling infant was left motherless and milkless and some resourceful man used common sense and a placid she-animal. The animal milk may not have come, as in the old joke, from such cute containers as human milk, but in some respects it had more nutriments. While human milk is more digestible, cows' milk has more than three times as much protein, half as many carbohydrates, slightly less fat, almost four times as much calcium, more of some vitamins and less of others.

Whenever it happened, the discovery of animal milk was the first step in the liberation of woman. She was no longer the sole source of milk.

In Mohenjo-Daro, she raised vegetables. The women of that city were quite possibly the first to cook vegetables.

While people earlier had eaten plant food mostly indirectly, by eating meat and fish, the growth of agriculture brought a growth in direct consumption of crop plants.[3]

There were still hunters and herdsmen, but it was the farmers who produced most of the food that nourished those early civilizations of India's vast subcontinent, of Ur, Babylon, Nineveh, the Nile Valley and the distant, always aloof, rather mysterious Far East.

---

[3] All of life depends basically on green plant life, which uses energy from the sun, water and nutrients from the soil and carbon dioxide from the air to create a simple sugar, glucose, that sustains most animals. U.S. scientists have recently reported finding a way to duplicate the first step of this natural process (photosynthesis) using electrochemical energy instead of light. If the whole process could be duplicated on a practical basis, food could be produced in factories, using much less space than normal agriculture requires and without concern about all the hazards (like drought, blights, floods, rodents and insect pests) that have always impeded conventional agriculture.

Since the farmers could grow more than enough for their own families' needs, other people were freed to develop new arts and skills: pottery, metallurgy, the wheel, written language.

Society was based on co-operation. Prehistoric man had pooled his efforts to pursue and kill large animals. Farmers teamed up to harvest crops. And our whole pattern of inviting friends to dinner, our distinctively human act of hospitality, is based to an extent on the mutual advantages of sharing. When someone slaughtered a sheep or goat, or caught a great many fish, or killed a large game animal, he invited his friends and neighbors to share in the feast and nothing went to waste. When a neighbor slaughtered a pig or calf, or otherwise had food to spare, he invited the others in return; this way everybody enjoyed meat and fish more often.

There is archaeological evidence that the peoples who dwelt in the valleys of the Tigris and Euphrates enjoyed a considerable variety of meat. There was beef, lamb, mutton. There was fish, dried, salted and smoked as well as fresh. And there were vegetables, notably onions, lettuce, cucumbers and cabbage; and legumes—lentils, broad fava beans and chick-peas, or *garbanzo*, still mashed with sesame seed oil into the *hummous* that is a staple in Lebanon and other Mediterranean lands.

Fruits of the time included apples, apricots, dates and figs (both originally from Arabia), melons, pears and plums.

In the wedge-shaped cuneiform writing of the Sumerians, the oldest legend in history (older than any written language), "Gilgamesh," records that Enkidu ate ripe figs and stems, worms, a few leaves, wild cucumbers, cassia melons (a puzzlement, since no variety of cassia tree bears anything closer to a melon than a seed pod), grapes, caper buds, meat seasoned with herbs, honey and bread.

The bread was a kind of pancake, made of barley flour (also used for porridge) mixed with sesame seed flour and onions. Was? It still is the basic bread of peasants in present-day Iraq and it is delicious.

Another ancient dish still prized in those Mid-Eastern lands is lentil stew: onions and lentils slowly simmered in sesame seed oil.

Esau in the Old Testament sold his birthright for a mess of pottage, thought to have been this lentil stew of past and present.

Early Mesopotamians may have been the first to discover that meat could be cured (preserved from spoiling quickly) with salt. According to legend, a wounded pig ran squealing into the waters of what we now call the Persian Gulf. As he died of his wounds, he was washed with the salty brine. And someone noticed that this somehow kept the meat fresh and edible for much longer than usual.

The legend may be invention, but it was certainly through accidents like this that most such discoveries were made.

For the kings and nobles of Mesopotamia, the delicacies of the table were fried locusts served on skewers, roast partridge and hare, shellfish sprinkled with spices like cumin and coriander.

To celebrate important religious festivals or military victories, there were banquets at which scores of different cheeses were served, along with tens of thousands of bread discs and countless cakes, sweetened with honey and palm tree sugar. Oxen, sheep, goats, ducks and geese were roasted or boiled for the banquets.

Nobles and ministers ate little meat; they made up for it by feasting on cakes, yogurts and various fruits, notably grapes, apples, dates, figs and pears.

The cheeses and yogurts were made from the milk not of cows primarily but of sheep, goats, even camels. Soured milks, butterlike products and cheeses were common among the nomadic herdsmen long before they turned to farming. There are many references to milk in the Bible. To the men who wrote the good book about 1500 B.C., Canaan was "a land of milk and honey."

Pharaoh fare

South and west of Mesopotamia, a civilization flourished in Egypt 1500 years before the Bible.

Here as in Sumeria, systems of water control were developed, but mostly these early peoples were at the mercy of the natural floods and droughts. Until the Aswan High Dam was built in our own time, the June to September floods permitted only one crop a year. While the floods gave high fertility to the soil, at times they ravaged the land and all that grew on the land.

In Egypt's lush bottomland seedbed grew vast fields of grain: wheat, rye, barley. Vegetables grew, too: beans, parsley, radishes and, most especially, onions, leeks and garlic.

The Greek historian Herodotus wrote that the builders of Cheops' Great Pyramid at Giza, about 2900 B.C., lived mainly on garlic and onions. Egypt is still a major grower, consumer and exporter of onions.

While melons and grapes also flourished in the Nile delta, the Egyptians appear not to have cultivated the cucumber.

The subject of what crops were grown when has fascinated some historians. In 1883, Alphonse de Candolle in France pieced together the writings of ancient historians and archaeological evidences to publish *L'origine des plantes cultivées*. Some twenty-seven crop plants, said de Candolle, were cultivated in the Old World more than 4000 years ago:

almonds	mulberries
apples	olives
apricots	onions
bananas	peaches
barley	pears
broad beans	quinces
cabbage	rice
cucumbers	sorghum
dates	soybeans
eggplant	tea
figs	turnips
grapes	watermelon
mangoes	wheat
millet	

Another two dozen species, de Candolle said, were cultivated in the Old World at least 2000 years ago:

alfalfa	lime
asparagus	mustard
beets	nutmeg
breadfruit	oats
carrots	oranges
celery	pepper
cherries	plums
chestnuts	radishes
garden peas	rye
grapefruit	sugar cane
lemons	walnuts
lettuce	yams

Some fourteen species were listed as having been cultivated in the Old World (which included Africa and Asia, as well as Europe) for less than 2000 years:

artichokes	muskmelons
buckwheat	okra
coffee	parsley
currants	parsnips
endive	raspberries
gooseberries	rhubarb
horseradish	strawberries

Modern authorities, who tend to agree that date palms were probably cultivated before any other food plant, take exception to a number of de Candolle's entries; and of course not all the items were grown in the same place at the same time. The Egyptians, as we have noted (though the point is disputed), do not seem to have grown cucumbers, nor did they grow soy beans, rice or any number of other crops on de Candolle's pre-2000 B.C. list.

They did grow olives. Lila Perl says the Egyptians got olives—along with apples and pomegranates ("apples with grains" if we break the word down)—from the Hyksos, a nomadic Asian people who conquered Egypt in the eighteenth century B.C., using horse-drawn chariots to overpower the pedestrian Egyptians, and ruled for about 150 years.

But most sources say the Egyptians were using olive oil as early as 3000 B.C., and were the first people to cultivate the olive tree.

What makes this remarkable is that the wild olive is so bitter it is practically inedible unless preserved in brine or in a lime mixture. But long before written history, someone—and probably someone who lived along the Nile, that great river which kept flowing when other Bible land rivers dried up—discovered the beauty of olive oil.

From just one large olive tree, a family could obtain a year-round crop of ripe and unripened olives, both edible, and as much as half a ton of olive oil, all the fruit and oil a family could use. Oil from the first pressing was used to baste roast meats, dress vegetables and make sauces. The olives were pressed again to produce an oil used for moistening the skin and dressing the hair. A third pressing and a fourth yielded oil for lamps and to fuel stoves.

The Egyptians developed a less bitter olive for the table. Frescoes at the tomb of Ti, a royal official of the fifth dynasty, shows they force-fed geese to create *foie gras*.

But the great contribution of Egypt to food development was in bread making.

The value of cereal grains in the human diet had long been recognized. Even before agriculture, early man had probably chewed the seeds of grasses like millet, barley and wheat. Later he learned to crush the grains to make flour; the Egyptians were doing this well before 3000 B.C., milling barley (which grew in poor soil with little water) and wheat (which needed deep, moist soil and a longer growing season) with heavy grindstones, adding water to form a dough, shaping the dough into flat cakes, baking the cakes in an oven hollowed out of the ground and lined with clay, or on the outside of an earthenware jar heated from inside. Bread baked this way was coarse and heavy. It contained no leavening agent to make the dough rise and become light, airy and tender.

The early Hebrews used sour dough as a leaven; the Egyptians discovered that sour dough contains yeast. They isolated the yeast plant and became the first people to produce yeast-raised bread. This they produced in many varieties, from common flat pancake types to round, conical, spiral and triangular shapes. Egyptologists list forty variations.[4] At the Metropolitan Museum of Art in New York there is an eighteenth-dynasty Egyptian loaf from Thebes, buried more than 3400 years ago with an Egyptian princess named Meryet-Amum. The bread looks like a petrified disc with a hole in its center.

Herodotus wrote that the Egyptians "knead their dough with their feet but clay with their hands." He came along centuries after the Egyptian discovery of fermentation by yeast spores to leaven the dough. That discovery made Egyptian bread the envy of the ancient world.

Egypt's virtuosity at bread making came not only from using yeast to make bread rise, but also from using and blending various kinds of cereal grains to make breads of differing degrees of fineness or coarseness. And while the dough was not always embellished, the pharaoh's bakers as early as 4000 B.C. were mixing their finest bread dough with honey, sweet herbs, almonds, fruits and spices which included saffron and cinnamon.

The bread of the poor was made from papyrus reeds or bulrushes (now almost extinct in Egypt) and lotus plants. Herodotus found this poverty-class bread quite good. "Such as wish to enjoy the papyrus in full perfection," he wrote, "bake it first in a closed vessel, heated to a glow."

At the upper end of the social scale, nobles of the Nile Valley, sitting on chairs and eating at tables (both Egyptian inventions), were served at huge banquets by slaves or—if the evidence of old Egyptian wall paintings is accepted—by great hamadryas baboons trained to wait on table.

While naked dancing girls entertained them, these early plutocrats

---

[4] By comparison, about 200 kinds of bread are made today in the Soviet Union, 130 in the Moscow Central Bakeries alone. Russians are enormous bread eaters, more than a pound of bread (*khleb*) a day being the national average (in rural areas the average is probably even higher), though consumption has declined slightly in recent years. There are black breads and white breads, made of wheat, barley, rye and corn flour and the flour of several other cereal grains. There are even about twenty different kinds of dietetic breads. And they can all trace their ancestry back to ancient Egypt.

began with platters of tidbits to whet their thirsts and appetites: green cabbage (believed to delay drunkenness), pickled onions, sesame seeds, anise seeds, cumin seeds (like caraway seeds, but stronger).

Then they really fell to, eating roast geese, legs of small calves and gazelles adorned with lamb frills, grilled wild duck and quail, fish served raw or grilled, breads cut into various shapes, vegetables (including lettuce, endive, dried peas and cardoons—forerunners of artichokes—as well as onions, leeks, beans, parsley and radishes), all washed down with wine or, more usually, beer.

For sweets there were fruits, cakes oozing honey, and probably melons.

Historical events and important religious occasions were commemorated with feasts, following a tradition that goes back into prehistory. The Last Supper, for example, shared by Jesus with the Apostles, was the Passover meal at which Jews marked the reawakening of the earth with its fruits of grapes and grain, and the increase of domestic flocks and herds.

It was a sort of Jewish Thanksgiving, its roots buried in the primitive hunting culture in which an animal was sacrificed to propitiate the gods and assure good hunting. As the agricultural-pastoral civilization gradually replaced the hunting culture, the celebration tied in with the spring equinox which saw the start of a new growing season, the birth of baby lambs, calves and kids.

Knowing that the Last Supper was the Passover meal, we know something of what Jesus and the Apostles ate on that occasion. The meal is called the *Seder*. Its participants partake of wine ("the fruit of the vine"), roast lamb, and bowls of bitter herbs (lettuce, horseradish and parsley in today's service) which are dipped in a reddish sauce, *haroseth*, made of chopped apples, dates, figs and almonds ("the fruits of the earth") in wine and cinnamon.

Also eaten is unleavened bread, *matzoth*. Today, because the Passover meal has been given historical-nationalistic overtones and associated with the legend of Moses leading the Jews out of Egypt, where they had been enslaved by Ramses II late in the thirteenth century B.C., the *matzoth* is supposed to commemorate the story that the Jews, in their hurry to escape the Egyptians, did not have time to leaven the bread they carried on their journey. But in all probability, both the ceremony [5] and the unleavened bread derive from a time before the Jews were ever in Egypt, a time when leavened bread was still unknown.

Despite its frequent appearance in major Renaissance paintings of the Last Supper, one food *not* eaten at that gathering was the orange.

Crusaders returning from the holy lands reported having seen oranges there, which no doubt influenced Titian, Fra Angelico, Correggio, Botticelli and the rest. But the Crusades were more than a thousand years after the Crucifixion. During that millennium citrus fruits were introduced to the Mediterranean from China, by way of India.

The error of the Old Masters in their paintings is typical of the snares and misdirections that complicate efforts to trace the origins and history of foods.

The exotic East

Unlike the Egyptians, the people of ancient India seem to have abhorred garlic and onions. The strong-scented bulbs were forbidden in many places; anyone who wanted to eat them had to go out of town to do so.

In the Indus Valley, the farmers of Mohenjo-Daro grew wheat and six-rowed barley and field peas. They grew mangoes, sesame and dates. And they bred cattle, buffalo, camels, horses and asses, all of which they used for meat as well as for draft purposes.

---

[5] The Hebrew name for the Passover festival is *Pesah*, from which the English "paschal," as in the paschal lamb served at Easter, is derived. The verb root of *Pesah* is *psh*, "to be festive." *Pesah* means "the Feast of Feasts." *Psh* also means "to go leaping before," which relates *Pesah* (Passover) to the legend of the angel who spared (passed over) the houses inhabited by Hebrews during an Egyptian plague.

Mangoes probably originated in India (which still produces 7.5 million tons of mangoes a year, out of an estimated world total of 9.5 million). So, probably, did bananas, and lemons, limes and oranges; trading caravans carried their seeds or roots to Mesopotamia and to Africa. Pepper may also have been used for the first time in India.

The early civilizations of that great subcontinent were augmented by the ways of the Aryans, fierce warriors who overran the original inhabitants. These nomads from the steppes of Central Asia adopted some of the customs of the original peoples, like drinking wine extracted from flowers. But mostly they imposed their own ideas.

Foremost was shish kebab—chunks of meat skewered on a sword and broiled over a fire. It dates back to before 1000 B.C. and it is still called shish kebab (or *shashlik* in Russian, *souvlakia* in Greek).

The Hindus broke with the Aryan diet. Their first holy book, the Rig-Veda of the second millennium B.C., condemned eating meat and recommended a vegetarian diet for the best functioning of man's mind and body. This teaching, along with the age-old idea of non-violence (*shimsa*), made meat and fish taboo in orthodox Brahman families of India. Old epics and tales of early India, however, are full of references to hunters and fishermen; and ancient laws governing slaughterhouse operations are so detailed that there is no doubt members of the *Kshatriya* class (princely warriors and philosophers) and of the *Vaisya* (yeoman class) ate meat and fish regularly.

Bitter herbs and the juices of fruits (lemon, orange, pomegranate, tamarind) were used to flavor boiled meats, as were the juices of leaves.

Banquets, as described in epics like the *Ramayana*, could be lavish. Guests were offered whole animals roasted on the spit: young buffalo, whose juicy meat was basted with *ghee* (liquid clarified butter), was served floating in spicy sauces made of sour fruit and salt. Sometimes the meat was cut in slices and fried in *ghee*, sesame oil or mustard oil. Or a whole brisket (breast) of meat might be smeared with *ghee*, sprinkled with salt and pepper, and fried.

Birds were wrapped in bitter leaves, roasted, and served with thick sauces made of *ghee*, mango juice, salt and pepper. Succulent carp were cooked in curry sauces made of cardamom, cloves, cumin, salt and pepper.

And for dessert? Creamy cheeses, and balls of rice or wheat coated with sugar, either steam-boiled or fried in butter. Cane sugar, refined and molded into oval loaves, served as the base for dishes containing molasses, curds, *ghee* and pepper. The Indians doted on fruits, too, especially mangoes (which were pickled in slices in later centuries to make the chutney that accompanies curry dishes). Sweetened milk, flavored with spices, and camphor cooked with ripe bananas were Indian specialties. Honey was reserved for state occasions and major religious feasts.

Indian cooking still rests heavily on hot curry sauces. They come in many varieties and date back thousands of years. The earliest curries were made from the ground seeds of mustard, saffron, fennel and cumin, all mixed together; a sour spice from the rind of the acid tamarind fruit may have been added to some early curries.

The art of cooking, like all other arts, was considered a divine revelation in India. Among the famous cooks were numbered epic heroes and heroines, great kings and princes.

In ancient China, too, cooking skills were highly esteemed. Expert cooks ranked on the same social scale as talented painters and poets.

The Emperor Shen Nung, about 2700 B.C., tasted large numbers of plants and classified them according to their food and medicinal values. Distinguished scholars and philosophers composed recipes. More than a millennium later, the chief minister to Ch'eng T'ang, who founded the Shang or Yin dynasty about 1500 B.C., wrote a kind of geographical guide to good eating which has survived in a reconstructed form. His name was I Yin.

> Of meat dishes, [I Yin wrote] the best are orang-utan lips, . . . the tails of young swallows, . . . and the choice parts of yak and elephant. West of the wandering sand dunes, south of the cinnabar mountains, there are phoenix eggs which are eaten by the people of Wo. The finest fish are the turbot of Lake Tung-t'ing and the sardines of the Eastern Sea. In the Sweet Water River there is a kind of fish called "vermilion turtle" which has

six legs and pearls on its body like a hundred bits of jade. In the Huan River there is a fish called the flying fish which is shaped like a carp and has wings . . .

The tastiest vegetables are the duckweed of the K'un-lun Mountains and the flowers of the Tree of Long Life, . . . the parsley of Yang-hua, the cress of Yün-meng, the leeks of Chü-ch'ü, and a plant that grows in Chin-yüan called "earth blossom."

The best spices are Yang-p'u ginger, Chao-yao cinnamon, Yüeh-lo mushrooms, sauce made of bonito and sturgeon, and salt from Ta-hsia . . .

Among fruits, the best are sha-t'ang apples. North of the Ch'ang Mountains, above the Deeps of T'ou, there are a hundred kinds of fruit, fit for the gods to eat. East of Mount Ch'i, where the blue bird lives, grow sweet kumquats, and there are also the bitter oranges of Chiang-p'u and the citrons of Yün-meng. Lichens from Han-shang are best for bringing out the finest flavor . . .

Some translations of the passage, which appears in Chapter Fourteen of a work entitled *Lu-shih ch-un-ch'iu* and was compiled about 250 B.C., mention sweet oranges, mandarins and pomelos "from the Wan River. The fastest horses are required to fetch them." I Yin did not mention peaches, but the Chinese were enjoying that fruit as long ago as 2000 B.C.

China was very early a nation of farmers and perhaps the first range-grange battleground. Since dairy foods were associated with China's herdsmen enemies, the Tartars and Mongols, the Chinese did not use milk or milk products as did their neighbors in India. Instead, they developed derivatives of the soybean (*Glycine soja*), a legume which grows only in temperate climates. They made soy milk, soy pudding, soybean cheese.

Also unlike the Indians, the Chinese were generous users of garlic; it was their principal seasoning, though they also used soy sauce, sesame seed oil, scallions, ginger and such exotic spices as dry red blossoms from a now unknown Tibetan flower. Wild cinnamon, anise and pepper were also used.

The Chinese philosopher Confucius (550–478 B.C.) was devoted to good cooking. In his *Analects* he declared that food should not be

eaten stale or without taste, or when improperly blended. He insisted
that rice be polished white (an injunction fortunately not widely followed—those who did observe it, and whose diet was almost exclusively rice, often died of beriberi), that meat be finely minced and
properly marinated (soaked in brine or sauce).

A contemporary of Confucius was an Indian rajah's son, Siddhartha Gautama, who at the age of twenty-nine put aside his
princely finery, donned sackcloth and went into the jungle to ponder
the meaning of life. Gautama became venerated as the Buddha. Seeing
a family of insects destroyed by a farmer's plow, he wept. Buddhism
was founded on vegetarianism, based on a repugnance for taking life,
not far removed from the age-old ideas of *shimsa*, the aversion to
violence.

Legend says the Buddha lived for a time on one grain of rice a
day; history says he abandoned strict vegetarianism in his later years
and died (in 480 B.C.) at the age of eighty-four after feasting on pork.
His Buddhist disciples spread rice throughout southeast Asia, along
with cooking pots and mortars and pestles.

Another sixth-century B.C. philosopher was Lao-Tze, who told his
followers that the secret of long life was to be found in plants, the
foods closest to nature. Lao-Tze experimented with plants; he discovered the vitality of vegetables was destroyed by improper cooking.
So his followers, the Taoists, based their diet not merely on vegetables
but on raw or partially cooked vegetables, which they considered
nutritionally superior. The tradition persists in Chinese cooking today.

Tea was not common in the time of Lao-Tze, but the Taoists
made tea drinking an integral part of the quiet contemplation of life's
simple beauties.

Partly through the spread of Buddhism, rice became the basic dish
of China and of most of the Orient. The rice crop was important in
China possibly as long as 5000 years ago. The emperor and princes
used to plant the first rice each year. Little has changed. The Orient
still depends on rice more than we in the West depend on any single
food.

In the monsoon climates of the Far East, where 60 to 150 inches of rain fall during the six to seven months' rainy season and almost none the rest of the year, it is doubtful that any crop besides rice could have done what rice has done to support such dense populations.

Oriental tradition says rice is best when harvested by women's hands; so it is woman-hours—600 to 1000 per acre—more than man-hours that fill the rice bowls of East Asia. Without crop rotation, without fertilizers, without the soil being aerated, rice has grown continuously on the same land for century after century in these crowded lands of the Orient; yields have been maintained at fairly high levels, all things considered.

The ancient Chinese ate rice with dried fish, rice with eggs, rice with mushrooms, rice with ginger, rice with pickles, rice with barley cakes, rice with soybean gravy, rice with rice. And the Chinese do to this day.

The ancients also ate birds' nest soup, made from the lining of swifts' nests, a sort of jelly secreted by the birds' well-developed salivary glands (it looks like fluffy white wax). The nests are on steep cliffs high up and hard to reach. So birds' nest soup was enjoyed only at special feasts; and still is—it is monstrously expensive.

Other Chinese soups were made from deer heads, birds' tongues, fried wolf, deer kidneys, lambs' paws, sheep's heads, bear meat and lotus seeds. For meat the Chinese ate wild horse, wild camel, tiger, elephant, rhinoceros, wolf, rabbit, monkey, turtle and porcupine. They ate clams, crabs and snails. And they ate crow, not in any figurative sense but quite literally.

Over the centuries, half a dozen different Chinese cuisines developed: Shanghai, Peking, Manchuria, Szechwan, Fukien and Canton were the centers of the various cookeries, though most Americans are familiar only with the Cantonese. (In Japan, too, where Chinese restaurants abound, most are Cantonese.)

Except in the north, the Chinese never baked. Chinese "breads" (which are more like *Dim Sum* dumplings) are steamed. Wet steaming in a *jing loong*, in fact, is the traditional Chinese way of cooking almost everything. It is a gentle method; steamed foods do not get tough. As they steam, they are seasoned with herbs and spices. Chicken or fish prepared in the Chinese manner is put in rapidly boiling water for about thirty seconds, then left to steam for three hours.

From roughly 206 B.C. until 220 A.D., the Han Dynasty reigned in China. A document from that era, the Han Shu, recording the diet and life of the reigning classes, still exists. It lists all the edible plants grown in China then, including at least 365 items, among them cabbage and rice, eaten by the coolies who built the Great Wall.

Life for the great masses of Chinese peasantry was cruel in the vigorous period of the Han Dynasty, as it has been in almost all ages of history. Droughts, floods and wars during the first two centuries of the Dynasty brought at least twenty calamitous famines. Peasants were forced to sell their children into slavery and to kill their babies because there was no way to feed them. Instances of cannibalism are recorded.

In remote regions like Szechwan, the gentry often ate well, if a bit exotically by Western standards. Sculptured reliefs in Szechwan tombs suggest that feasts in those ancient times became so lavish and so wild the government finally had to restrict them to holiday festivals. At all other times it was illegal to have more than three guests to dinner.

Szechwan developed a cuisine noted for its fiery dishes, hot enough to bring tears to the eyes, but in ancient times its banquet specialties were snails preserved in vinegar, dog meat, turtle meat and sliced raw venison seasoned with ginger and topped with ant eggs.

Elsewhere in China, certain kinds of seaweed, stalks of water lilies and melon seeds were considered great treats. So were sharks' fins, used to thicken soups and to provide an unusual flavor. China's so-called 100-year-old (duck) eggs are really 100 days old; they taste something like good cheese (and they are as close to cheese as the non-dairy Chinese ever got).

Chinese cooks developed ingenious ideas: as early as 200 B.C. they were pickling cabbage in wine and using it as a green accompaniment to meals. Some 1400 years later, Genghis Khan substituted salt for the wine and, with his Mongol hordes, carried this "sauerkraut" (as it is now called) to the eastern edge of Europe.

The nearer East

The first Europeans whose diets we know much about were the Greeks and Romans. What is known about the menus of earlier cultures in the Near East is recorded mostly in terms of excesses.

Consider Solomon, king of the Jews. He lived in the tenth century, with 700 wives and 300 concubines. On an ordinary day, according to the Bible (Deuteronomy 14:5) his household consumed ten oxen, along with the "hart, and the roebuck, and the fallow deer, and the wild goat, and the pygarg," and some other mammals. Or so the Bible has been translated. But Peter Farb suggests that while the hart (and its female, the hind) was probably common in the Holy Land, the "roebuck" was most likely the gazelle and the "fallow deer" quite possibly the hartebeest, an antelope then widespread in the Bible lands though now it is found only in Africa.

For a feast, Solomon (it is written) would sacrifice 22,000 oxen and any number of fattened fowl. He had 12,000 horsemen roaming the countryside in search of "victual for all who came to Solomon's table."

The Assyrian King Ashurbanipal 300 years later (the Greeks called him Sardanapalus) established cooking contests, awarding as many as a thousand gold pieces to the winners and anticipating the baking contests run by today's big U.S. flour mills.

At Persepolis early in the fifth century B.C. the Persians' King Darius had 10,000 men traveling "over the whole world" (so said the Greek historian Xenophon about a century later) in quest of delectable foods and wines for the King's table.

Darius had a thousand animals slaughtered for the royal larder every day. Smoked camel hump was a dish favored by the Persians, who also dined on ox, zebra, gazelle, stag venison, Arabian ostrich, goose and gamecock.

Bowls of *pilaw*, rice steamed in meat or poultry broth (we call it pilaff), were popular with the Persians; they seasoned the dish with nuts, bits of chicken or lamb, spices, fruits and herbs. Like the Aryans of India, they ate kebabs, meat roasted on a spit or minced and baked into a meat loaf. The word *kebab* means meat, the word *shish* means sword or skewer; *shish kebab* is the ancient meal of Asian horsemen: chunks of mutton from fresh-killed sheep, skewered on swords and broiled in a wayside fire. Not only mutton and lamb were broiled this way, but also fish, poultry, duck and vegetables.

The Persians roasted whole baby lambs and chickens, first stuffing them with rice blended with raisins, peas or pine nuts. Sometimes they used a cracked wheat, bulgur, instead of rice. Bulgur and nuts cooked in olive oil, or a mixture of lamb meat, was used to stuff eggplant to make another Persian specialty.

The milk of goats, sheep and camels, all far more common than cows' milk among these Asian peoples, was made into yogurt, and spiced yogurt sauces were used on kebabs. (Some sources say the Persians also invented cheese.)

Darius, his son Artaxerxes and other Persian kings of the fifth and fourth centuries B.C. used sugar, brought by caravan from farther east and too costly for any but royalty.

While their enemies, the Greeks, were not big on sweets (neither were the Romans), the Persians gorged on them. They invented the thin, flaky pastry made with honey, nuts and syrup which we now call by its Turkish name, *baklava*. They drank fruit drinks. They mixed fruits (including apricots, which they called "sun eggs") with nuts, spices and honey. Persia's rulers became immensely fat, deeming obesity a mark of status. (Today it is the poor who tend to be obese, at least in our own culture, while the rich stay fashionably slim.)

As for the common people of Persia, they ate bread, a flat, sour-dough bread which is still the basic food for much of modern Iran. Half the daily calories of the average Iranian today come from the traditional flat bread of his ancestors.

A Milwaukee yeast company plans to change all that. It is building a plant to produce active dry yeast, made from sugar beets (grown in northern Iran) and sugar cane (grown in southeastern Iran). The traditional bread of the country, dating from antiquity, contains some yeast (from the fermented dough of the previous day's bread) which is used to leaven each new day's batch, but in the words of the American yeast company's international vice-president, "it also contains God knows what else. We've tested it and it has a garden of bacteria. Obviously, this is a dangerous sanitary condition."

So for at least some of Iran's 26 million citizens, bread will now mean high-rise American-style bread. It will, to quote the yeast man again, be "a more sanitary product whose quality can be standardized"; the Americans will "shorten the required time to manufacture bread and make new varieties of bread possible."

Things are changing. Most of the world still eats the same foods in the same ways it has for ages, but some old ways are yielding. The changes are slow. The new bread in Iran reportedly tastes little different from the old. It will still be eaten with rice, dipped in meat sauce and dunked in heavily sweetened tea.

Westward the course of appetite

Much of our knowledge of what Persia and Egypt ate in early times comes from Greek writing, since it was the Greeks and Romans who developed the art of written language.

As far back as 350 B.C., a Greek poet, Archestratus, wrote an entire work on "Gastrology." A little over a half-century later, the discriminating tastes of the Greek philosopher Epicurus created an approach to life that survives in our word "epicure," meaning someone with a refined taste for the better things in life.

To the Greeks, a professional cook was an artisan; he was paid better than any other hired worker. A new dish was as important to Greek intellectuals as a new poem.

If a good cook was respected in Athens, he was held in even higher regard by the citizens of the Greek city of Sybaris in the arch of the Italian boot. Cooks who came up with extraordinary dishes at banquets in Sybaris were crowned on a dais before all the populace.

The city was destroyed in 510 B.C., but it lived so well before it died that even today a sybarite is someone devoted to luxury and sensual pleasures. Under the laws of Sybaris, a cook was given a copyright on a particularly good recipe and could receive all profits from the sale of that recipe for a full year; nobody else could copy it during the year of his copyright.

But few Greeks could manage Sybaritic feasts. Greece is a rocky, barren land, and while it may have been more productive in ancient times than it is today, it was never a rich source of food. Less than a quarter of its land can be tilled. The area just north of Athens was called Boeotia, meaning "cow land," but few parts of Greece now have pasturelands lush enough to graze cows.

The ancient Greeks knew nothing about crop rotation. They sowed and harvested a field one year, let it lie fallow the next. They reaped wheat with sickles, having no scythes; they threshed their grain by driving their cattle over it.

From Homer's time to the classic period of sixth-, fifth- and fourth-century B.C. Greece, the quality of the land—and of the Greek diet—did not advance, but rather declined. Greek farmers never were able to feed the whole country; there was certainly never any food surplus.

Staple foods were olive oil, goat cheese, wine and bread, as they are today. Barley meal was commonly eaten in a kind of porridge; meat was rarely enjoyed except on special holidays.

The Greeks thrived on this lean fare. Euripides lived to age seventy-eight, Democritus to ninety, Hippocrates to eighty-three, Plato to eighty-seven, Solon to eighty, Sophocles to ninety-one.

There were apples, pears and quinces in ancient Greece. There were plums, introduced from Damascus (the Greek word for plum, to remind us of its source, is *damas'kinon*). There were no peaches yet, but there were currants, a variety of dried grape (the name comes from Corinth, a city to the west of Athens).

The first grapes probably came from Macedonia. At Photolivos, in the province of Drama in eastern Macedonia, archaeologists have unearthed tiny black seeds, the earliest known trace of the grape, dating back to 4000 B.C.

With olives and grain, grapes comprised the "Mediterranean triad" of Greek commerce. Greek wine, olive oil and wool as well were traded for food from other lands: cheese and pork from Sicily, grain and dried fish from the Crimea, more grain from Egypt.

The people of Athens were proud of their public bakers and the "fair-complexioned wheaten loaves" they made of native and imported grain. The Athenian baker Tearion is mentioned by both Plato and Aristophanes.

What meat the Greeks had was from goats and sheep, plus a little pork, the meager supply coming mainly from sacrificial offerings to the gods.

For the patricians of Athens, wealth consisted often of gnarled olive tree stands. Only the affluent could afford to wait sixteen years for an olive tree to mature, forty years until it reached full production. When the Spartans laid waste the countryside around Athens, as they did every year for a period in the fifth century B.C., they cut down olive trees along with orchards and grainfields. It took decades for the Athenians to recover from these losses. The conflict between Athens and Sparta assumes a sad and special poignancy when viewed in terms of food.

In good times, the Greeks ate little rolls of spicy chopped meat wrapped up in grape leaves, much like the *dolmathes* still found on Greek menus. The Greeks pursued the cruel Egyptian practice of force-feeding geese to make a pâté of their enlarged livers, though *pâté de foie gras* is now regarded as a classic dish of the Alsace.

Virtually everybody in ancient and classical times drank wine, though drinking was even then a matter of controversy. Lacedaemon (Sparta) fined citizens found to have partaken too heavily of the grape, even at the Bacchanalia, that festival dedicated to Bacchus, Greek god of wine.

Aristophanes called wine "the milk of Aphrodite," goddess of love, but Plato urged temperance. As "provocatives to drinking," the

Greeks ate caviar, roasted grasshoppers, cheeses, olives, oysters, tiny shrimp and pistachio nuts. At *tavernas* in Athens patrons are still offered pistachio nuts, mostly from the island of Aegina, to eat with *retsina* wine—or a martini.

Athenians ate little or no breakfast. They had a light lunch, then a heavier dinner late in the afternoon. Too often they simply didn't have enough to eat.

The Romans followed much the same pattern: practically no breakfast, the *prandium* (lunch) composed of leftovers from the previous day's big meal, and a late afternoon dinner, the *cena*. In earliest Roman times the *cena* was served at midday; later it became the fashion to dine later, and later. Ultimately the smart dinner hour in parts of the Mediterranean became 10 o'clock in the evening and later.

The first cookbook in the strict sense of the word, meaning a book of recipes, was Roman. It was *De Re Coquinaria*, or *De Re Culinaria*, "Of Culinary Matters," and was supposedly written by the merchant and gourmet Apicius who lived in the reign of Tiberius in the first century A.D.

Tiberius' son developed such a liking for Apicius' broiled broccoli, according to some sources, that the Emperor had to scold the boy. Apicius himself gluttonized on eggs with honey and pepper; he called them *ovemele*, "egg honey," which may be the origin of our word "omelette."

For poorer Romans, the staples were bread, olives and grapes (for wine), with honey the only sweetening.

There was little meat. A modern American breakfast-food maker advertised a few years ago that Roman legions "conquered the world" on a diet of grain. And it is true that Roman soldiers on a campaign once complained because they were issued rations of meat when grain supplies ran out. Rome's goddess of grain, equivalent to the Greeks' Demeter, was Ceres, whose name survives in our word "cereal."

Bread was so basic to most people's diets by Roman times that the word was a synonym for food. The Old Testament had used it that way in, "Man doth not live by bread alone" (Deuteronomy 8:4) about 650 B.C.; so did the New Testament (about 75 A.D.) in "Give us this day our daily bread" (Matthew 6:11) which became part of the Lord's Prayer.

At one point in Roman history as many as sixty-two kinds of bread were being baked. Bread was distributed free to the poor in times of need. Wealthy politicians won and maintained the favor of the populace with bribes of "bread and games." Juvenal first recorded the phrase *panem et circenses* in his *Satires*.[6]

Grain for Rome's bread came from the fertile farmlands of Egypt and North Africa, which became the breadbasket of the Empire. Aqueducts, along with roads, were the great engineering achievements of the Romans, who irrigated 2000 miles of North African coastlands with a vast system of waterworks. (Otherwise they advanced agricultural technology hardly at all.)

What meat the Romans ate was usually venison, mutton or pork. Suckling pig became so popular that pigs grew scarce; laws had to be passed forbidding the slaughter of virgin swine. Suckling pig after that became a rare holiday treat, as it still is in many cultures. Pork has always been the favored meat of agricultural societies; as the only meat which tastes better cured than fresh, it remained the most popular meat until the invention of refrigeration and modern preservation methods.

---

[6] The idea that "bread is the staff of life" comes from an English saying which has been traced to 1638 but is probably older. In recent times, the chief money earner in a family has been called the breadwinner, the economic depression of the 1930's produced breadlines, and in the "now" world "bread" has found a place in hippie vocabularies as a synonym for money. Slang is full of food words, but it would take a whole book to explain why a complaint is a beef, an argument a rhubarb, an unsubtle actor a ham, tired humor corn, poor quality cheesiness, a pretty girl a tomato, a woman of easy virtue a tart, or ambivalence by the U.S. Food and Drug Administration a waffle.

Imperial tastes and tables

Pushing up from the Mediterranean into the French and German lands they called Gaul, the Romans found primitive peoples who lived on wild game, berries and nuts, but who in some cases kept flocks and tilled the land.

In "Helvetia," Caesar's legions saw the tribesmen of the Alps making big-holed cheeses; great wheels of this "Swiss cheese" (now more properly called Emmenthal or Emmenthaler) were soon going back to Rome. In Britain, the legions found blue-painted Britons making Cheshire cheese, as the English still do.

As Rome grew, so grew her larder. Brillat-Savarin later remarked that the Romans "put the whole world to gastronomical use." In nearby Etruria, between Fiesole and Arezzo, fine wheat grew; more came from Egypt. Roman cooks made it into the first pasta.

From the herds of Tuscany the Romans got milk to make cheese of their own. From Campania, especially from Falernum, they got wine. They received game from the Laurentine forests, olive oil, rabbits and pickles (and more wine) from Spain, apricots from Armenia, peaches from Persia, apples and pears from Chios, dates and pomegranates from Libya, plums from Damascus, quinces from Sidon, cherries from the kingdom of Pontus, raspberries from Mt. Ida, pheasants from Greece, guinea fowl from Africa, pork sausage and venison from Gaul.

It was the Romans who discovered the merits of gelding a cock to create a capon, plumper and more meaty than an unaltered cock.

Like the Greeks, the Romans ranked good cooks with artists, an attitude found today only in France. The great French chef Antonin Carème,[7] who served Talleyrand, the Czar Alexander, Lord Castle-

---

[7] Called "the king of cooks and the cook of kings," Carème (1784–1832) codified French gastronomy in a twelve-volume work which formulated the principles of la haute cuisine.

reagh, Baron Rothschild, the prince regent who became England's George IV and France's Restoration King Louis XVIII, studied Roman cooking; he wrote that it was "fundamentally heavy and without refinement," and so it may have been.

Sausages and spicy meat loaves were distinctively Roman. The capital's cuisine included also lentil salad, eggs in wine sauce, baked leeks in cabbage leaves, shrimp (seafood was more common than meat on the tables of Rome); snails fattened on milk until they were too big to crawl back into their shells; stews of diced pork shoulder simmered in wine sauce and seasoned with chopped shallots, dill, apricots or mint—or with apples and leeks spiced with cumin and coriander.

Patricians enjoyed baked beans cooked .with bits of chicken, sausage, leeks and fennel.

The poor ate a boiled porridge of lentils, peas and beans called *pulmentarium*; they dined on salt fish or goat's meat, bread, olive oil and wine mixed with water.

Rich gourmands raised thrushes and chickens in small enclosures where the birds got no exercise except to waddle back and forth to the juniper berries in their feeding trays. Thrushes fattened on juniper berries (*geneproni*) are still sold in the street markets of Italy, and Italians still eat larks, sparrows and nightingales. (One writer has called Italy the land "where songbirds are regarded as delicatessen.")

Garlic had not been used much by the Greeks (and still isn't); their chief seasoning was basil, whose Greek name, *basilikon*, signifies royalty. Noble Romans, too, disliked the strong flavor and aroma of garlic. They fed it to their laborers with the idea that it made them strong, and to their soldiers, to give them courage, but they avoided it themselves. At one point, the Roman Senate passed a law, one of the first sumptuary laws, forbidding citizens to enter the sacred temple of Cybele after eating garlic. And even today, while garlic may be the dominant seasoning in Sicily and Calabria, most of Italy prefers basil, along with marjoram, thyme and oregano.

Imperial Rome used some garlic, but it seasoned its foods mostly with onions, salt and spices. There was a steady demand in the later

Empire for new, more piquant sauces and flavorings, and new inventions came along to satisfy the demand. One was *defrutum*, a dry wine boiled down to a thickened concentrate and used in making fruit preserves. A sweet wine concentrate was called *passum*; wine blended with honey was called *mulsum*.

For the ruling classes of Rome in the heyday of Empire, feasting was a high art. Like the Greeks, the Romans reclined on couches around a table when they ate, their heads just above the level of the table. They rested on their left arms and reached out with their right for food and wine. The Romans were the first to use napkins; the Greeks had used morsels of bread.

A "Roman banquet" even today means a lavish feast. We have it on the authority of Apicius,[8] author of the famous cookbook, that noble Romans banqueted on exotic fare indeed.

For appetizers, a banquet (which often included a drinking bout) might lead off with jellyfish and eggs, sows' udders stuffed with salted sea urchins, patina of brains cooked with milk and eggs, boiled tree fungi with peppered fish-fat sauce, and sea urchins prepared with a sauce of spices, honey, olive oil and eggs.

The main course that followed was any (or all!) of the following, depending on the number of guests: fallow deer (a small European deer with broad antlers) roasted with onion sauce, rue (a bitter herb Italians now call *arugala* and use in salads), Jericho dates, raisins, olive oil and honey; boiled ostrich with sweet sauce; turtle dove boiled in its feathers; roast parrot; dormice stuffed with pork and pine kernels; ham boiled with figs and bay leaves, rubbed with honey and baked in a pastry crust; flamingo boiled with dates.

Desserts ran to fricassee of roses with pastry, stoned dates stuffed

---

[8] The last banquet Apicius gave is said to have cost him 100 million sesterces. Left with only 10 million, not enough to go on entertaining in his customary style, Apicius poisoned himself. His book survived him, copied by monks on parchment, edited, revised and re-edited over many centuries. Apicius was by no means universally admired. The Roman philosopher Seneca said he had softened the fiber of the Romans with his recipes and "through his teachings corrupted the era."

with nuts and pine kernels and fried in honey, and hot African sweet-wine cakes with honey.

Fruits were a great favorite of the Romans. Pliny listed thirty-six different kinds of apples, more than forty varieties of pears, several kinds of plums and cherries (though some sources say the Romans did not plant cherry trees of their own until late in the seventh century A.D.).

A general returning from foreign campaigns on the borders of the Empire took pride in introducing exotic new fruit species to the tables of Roman senators (as Anastas Mikoyan a few years ago intro-duced American-style ice cream to the Russian people [9]).

One Roman general, Lucius Licinius Lucullus (110–57? B.C.) brought back cherries from Pontus, the Black Sea kingdom of north-ern Asia Minor that became a province of Rome. Lucullus spent vast sums entertaining his friends in the Hall of Apollo, serving dishes that cost as much as 25,000 sesterces per guest. One meal cost the equivalent of $2000. (We still call an extravagant meal a "Lu-cullan feast.")

When they had eaten their fill, the Romans had slaves tickle their throats so they could regurgitate and begin all over again. Men of more refined taste disapproved of the cycle of gorging and re-gorging (*"vomunt ut edant, edunt ut vomant"* in the phrase of poet-philosopher Seneca) and relieved the too-full feeling between courses with baths and massages.

But the Emperor Claudius, who ruled Rome between 41 and 54 A.D., was famous for resorting to the *vomitorium*.

In the Greek Stoic traditions of Zeno three centuries earlier, eat-ing and drinking had been minimized. Interest in such things was disparaged as base and unworthy. All oral, anal, genital and visceral

---

[9] Mikoyan fell in love with U.S. ice cream in the 1930's. The Soviet Union is still way behind the U.S. in ice cream consumption, but Moscow exceeds the U.S. rate with a per capita consumption of about fifteen pounds a year. The city has seven ice cream factories which produce as many as forty-five different items, including richly decorated ice cream cakes.

needs and appetites, in fact, were denied. And so through all of civilized history, while artists have often celebrated the body and gloried in the ribald joys of love and eating, philosophers and clerics have with few exceptions looked askance at orgies of either kind and seen them as vulgar, even obscene.

What is obscenity? A political science professor, in a 1969 book on the legal aspects of public morality, defined it in terms of making the private public, of exposing to public view certain intimate experiences of life where the viewers were not themselves "subject to the urgencies" of the act, whether it be defecation, watching a couple engaged in sexual intercourse or even "watching a solitary person eating."

The Romans did not do much watching, save for the storied occasions when Lucullus dined with Lucullus. They ate in company, if not with their women; and their banquets went on for eight or ten hours. Belching was considered a compliment to the host, as it still is among some Arab peoples.

The Emperor Vitellius, who ruled briefly in 69 A.D., probably never heard of Stoicism. He gluttonized on peacocks' brains and flamingoes' tongues, ate four big meals a day and so terrorized his nobles that nobody dared serve the emperor a banquet that cost less than the equivalent of $16,000.

The centuries that followed brought new glories to Rome, accompanied by cruelty, corruption and decay.

For Rome's neighbors, her role as spice merchant was vital and enviable. One of the first things the Romans did upon winning control of the Mediterranean was to take over the spice trade, though the sources of supply remained in Arab hands, the center being Sheba (now Yemen) whose queen had cut a wide swath in the days of King Solomon.

The cloves, ginger, nutmeg, pepper, cinnamon, calamus and cassia that made the Romans' half-spoiled meats edible and gave taste to their grain staples came from remote islands in the Indian Ocean, carried overland by Arab merchants in caravans to the ports of Tyre and Sidon. From there the Romans' slave-powered triremes took the precious sacks to outlying parts of the Empire.

By the third century, the Empire had begun to crumble. Alaric, king of the Visigoths, besieged Rome in 408 A.D.; a major part of the tribute he exacted from the city was 30,000 pounds of pepper.

⁘[2]⁘

How can you make history on an empty stomach?

With the fall of Rome's Empire, the art of cooking went into a decline, certainly in the West.

More affluent families walled themselves in against Vandals, Visigoths and other pillaging tribes; all over Europe, little feudal estates existed in isolated self-sufficiency. Milk from the cows of the manor was churned into sweet butter or cured in huge cheese vats; grain, cut with scythes, was gathered in sheaves and threshed with flails on barn floors, then ground between ponderous stones [1]; flour was baked into bread by communal bakers in the courtyards of the great manor houses.

---

[1] In prehistoric times, flour had been milled by pounding grains between two stones. In time the lower stone was hollowed out and the upper one rounded to make the mortar and pestle, or saddlestone. The rotary mill, or quern, was developed in about 300 B.C.; grain poured through a hole in the upper stone trickled down to a lower stone and a stick, serving as a lever, turned the upper stone against the lower. Slaves or draft animals or waterpower turned the larger millstones.

For these Thy gifts . . .

Religion was so dominant a force that the pleasures of the flesh, which include eating and drinking, were abjured as unworthy of good people's attentions, merely necessary bodily functions. While the pagans had reveled in gluttony, Christians taught and practiced an asceticism that regarded eating, like sex, as an unavoidable evil. It was back to Zeno and stoic self-denial.

Early Christians had used the fish as a symbol of Christ (the Greek word for fish, *ichthus*, is made up of the initial letters of Iesous Christos Theou Uios Soter, meaning Jesus Christ, Son of God, Saviour); it is still to be seen in the catacombs of Rome and elsewhere. For medieval Christians, meatless Fridays and Lenten fasting were acts of contrition for the sins of eating. Mother Nature and human nature, at least on the surface, took a back seat to the Kingdom of Heaven; entry into Paradise was supposed to be uppermost in every pious Christian mind and heart.

In eastern Europe, men of arts and letters who—in the old Hellenic tradition—were also good cooks, took refuge in monasteries from the oppressive Byzantine overlords of the seventh and eighth centuries. The black cap of the Greek Orthodox priests was adopted as a disguise by fugitive intellectuals; in time it somehow became the *toque blanche*, the white cap that still identifies the master chef. (The complete outfit traditionally includes, along with the white *toque*, a white shirt, checked trousers and an apron.)

Culinary arts that might otherwise have been lost in the disorder of wars and migrations in the dark centuries, were preserved in the tranquil monasteries, where despite the prevailing concern for keeping functions of the body apart from matters of the soul, some men still cherished the happier ways of keeping body and soul together.

The meager diet of monks included peas and beans, eaten also by peasants, but the "rude herbs and roots" we now accept as vegetables were mostly for the starving. Feudal lords ate venison, beef, mutton, pork, chickens and geese—and on Fridays, fish—all boiled or skewered over fires and eaten with knives and fingers. Vassals and serfs ate eggs and cheese, supplemented with an occasional hare or fowl.

In medieval France there were fruit trees, left from a time when river traffic had brought seeds and seedlings from the East up the Rhone and the Loire, but there were few fruits except apples until the Crusaders brought plum trees back from Damascus. Outside the feudal walls there were small strawberries and huge mushrooms. Hogs rooted in the woods for acorns (as they still do in Germany to make the famous Westphalian ham and bacon); they also turned up truffles.[2] Vegetables were rare, except for leeks and onions.

Wealth was measured by how many head of cattle a manor owned

---

[2] The truffle is a rather ugly, but delicious, fungus which grows from three inches to a foot underground in stony, porous soil near the roots of scrub oak or beech trees. Nobody has ever been able to cultivate truffles. The chief of vegetable production of France's Ministry of Agriculture said before the U.S. 1969 Moonshot, "There is still as much mystery about how the truffle grows as there is about life on the moon. All we can say is, the more oak trees you plant, the more truffles you are likely to find." The best truffle variety by most people's standards is black (*Tuber melanosporum*) and grows mostly in two districts of France, Quercy-Périgord due east of Bordeaux and Vaucluse-Gard due north of Marseilles. From these regions, and from Drôme and Ardèche, come two-thirds of France's truffles. The Périgord area alone produced as much as 300 tons a year before World War I; now the total French production is probably 100 tons, of which 17.6 tons are exported.

A truffle has an infectious aroma that permeates any food; it makes French *charcuterie* and *foie gras* distinctively French. Underground, the aroma is usually undetectable to the human nose, though some men say they can sniff out truffles and others claim to find them by observing the female truffle fly bore into the ground to lay her eggs. Animals can scent the odor (they also love the taste) and for centuries Europeans have trained pigs and, more recently, hounds to find truffles; the Russians have tried using bear cubs and the Sardinians have tried goats, but truffle hounds, or truffle terriers, and truffle pigs are in more general use.

Black truffles are shipped fresh to the U.S. in January and most of February; supplies were plentiful in early 1969, the rainy summer and fall (ruinous to wine grapes) being favorable to the growth of truffles. Even when the crop is large, French peasants get 60 cents an ounce for their truffles (versus close to $1 in a bad year); the price in Paris is $2 an ounce, in New York close to $3.

White "summer" truffles (*Tuber magnatum*) from Italy, many of them raised on the vast estate of the Urbani family in Umbria, northeast of Rome, are shipped fresh to the U.S. in autumn, but while some connoisseurs profess to (the word "capital" comes from the Latin *caput*, meaning head). The cows of the manors were not exactly prolific milk producers; a medieval cow did well to give enough milk in one week to make a single pound of butter. People did not drink milk, except for buttermilk. They drank ale and wine, the monks in the monasteries making most of the wine (and drinking a good deal of it, too, despite orders forbidding the practice).

In times of famine, the monks distributed stores of food to the peasants. They had plenty of opportunity. Wars more often than droughts brought hunger to western Europe many times through the dark centuries when the Vikings plundered the land. Some of the Norsemen stayed on. Rollo the Viking became the first duc d'Orleans in 911.

The spice trade, first in the hands of the Arabs, then of the Venetians, fell back into Arab hands again, though trade was inhibited by Europe's turmoil. Oriental spices did not reach England until about 900.

The spices of life

The English were a meat-eating people, as they are today. Because there was little fodder to keep animals alive through the winter, it was the English custom to slaughter all cattle except breeding stock each autumn and somehow try to store it through the long, cold months that followed. The annual feast of Michaelmas came after the late September slaughter. Some meat was salted down; but by midwinter even most of this was well on its way to being putrid. To make it halfway edible, Englishmen—and Europeans, too—used spices and seasonings, including the juice of bitter oranges.

The bitter orange was virtually the only orange known in Europe until after 1500. Its aromatic qualities made it a valuable seasoning

---

prefer them to French truffles, others call them tasteless (unscrupulous merchants sometimes dye them black).

Some forty varieties of truffles grow in the U.S. but none is good to eat; any truffles we use are imported, and are more costly even than caviar.

agent. Not until 1529 did Portuguese ships return from India with sweet oranges, which are still called "Portugals" in Greece, Albania, Rumania, part of Italy and in the Middle East.

The Chinese orange, even sweeter, reached Lisbon in 1635 and was enjoyed by Portugal's princess, Catherine da Braganza, before she went to England to marry the Restoration King Charles II in 1662.

The botanical name for the modern sweet orange, in fact, is *Citrus sinensis*, the second word being Latin for Chinese.

Spain grew oranges in the seventeenth century and exported Seville oranges (*Citrus aurantium*) to England where they were a luxury, despite their sourness. The "Orange Girls" sold them in theaters. One Orange Girl, Nell Gwynn, became an actress; she also became the mistress of Catherine da Braganza's faithless husband Charles.

But until the eighteenth century, when the rich bourgeoisie began eating them, oranges, certainly sweet oranges, were enjoyed almost exclusively by kings, emperors, prelates and aristocrats. Nobody else could afford them. By the nineteenth century they were common enough for the middle-class purse, though sweet oranges were mostly a special holiday treat until fairly late in the century and did not become the fruit of the people until the present century.

Like Chinese oranges, the spices of the Orient were only for the very rich in the Middle Ages and the Renaissance. Edward I spent 1600 pounds sterling each year for spices way back at the start of the fourteenth century. Spices were not merely grace notes to fundamental flavors as they are today. They made good meat taste better, true; but more importantly they made spoiled meat taste good enough to fool the palate. And in those times meat spoiled quickly.

Edward's English peasantry relied on onions and garlic to make unwholesome meats tolerable. They also used wild or home-grown herbs, most of them introduced over the centuries from the Continent, especially from the Mediterranean: angelica, basil, bay leaves, chervil, chives, costmary, dill (even more popular in Baltic and Scandinavian countries), fennel, juniper berries, marjoram and wild marjoram, mint leaves (scorned in France but used a lot in the Near East as well as in Britain), black and white mustard seeds (introduced by the Romans in 50 B.C.), oregano, pennyroyal, summer and winter savory, sorrel, tansy, tarragon, parsley, sage, rosemary (planted traditionally on graves "for remembrance") and thyme.[3] But these were less effective than the costly spices of India, China, Ceylon and the East Indies.

In the early part of the Middle Ages, dinner at a feudal castle might be at nine in the morning, with supper at four in the afternoon; breakfast consisted merely of bread and ale.

In later centuries, breakfast evolved into a formidable meal in England, though not in France or the Mediterranean countries. The idea of the day's first meal breaking a fast is a rather poetic notion the English language shares with the Spanish *desayuno* and the French *déjeuner*, though the latter word is used also for lunch (*petit déjeuner*, "little lunch," is the common French term for morning coffee with croissant or brioche). But nobody except of British stock shares in the tradition, now fading, of the classic English breakfast.[4] It is *sui generis.*

Medieval dinner, at least in times of plenty, included huge roasts, wild boar, deer venison, whole calves, game birds, domestic ducks, geese and chickens, fish if there was water nearby, cheeses, bread,

---

[3] The various herbaceous plants, shrubs, trees, menthaceous herbs and labiate herbs, whose variously aromatic, pungent, fragrant, sweetish and bitterish leaves, dried leaves, stalks, seeds and seedlike fruits have since ancient times been used in medicine and to season and flavor soups, meats, pickles and other foods, comprise a complicated subject. One complication is that some leaf vegetables, like spinach and lettuce, were once called collectively "salad herbs." Another is the fact that one familiar herb name may apply to any of several plants within a given botanical genus, or even of several genera.

[4] It dates to a time before the late 1880's when it was unfashionable to eat lunch. Thus breakfast often included items like kippers (split open, smoked herring, fried in butter), finnan haddie (smoked haddock; the name comes from a Scottish fishing port, Findhorn), kedgeree (rice mixed with fish, usually salmon, and hard-boiled egg; the word is a corruption of a Hindi word), cold roast beef, kidneys, bacon, sausages, snipe (in Scotland), porridge, scones (Scotland again), cold toast, butter, eggs and the inevitable tea—with milk. Oat cakes, marmalade and treacle are other English breakfast table staples, though wartime rationing, heated houses and the increase in luncheon eating has reduced the average Englishman's breakfast to a shadow of its former grandeur.

fruits and flowers preserved in honey, meat pies, sausages, blood puddings (sausages containing a good deal of blood, along with diced pork
fat and onions) and nuts—and sometimes all of these on the same
menu.

But the dishes, especially in the dead of winter, were often barely
palatable—until the spices of the Orient arrived. These included, in
addition to pepper, that foremost of spices, cloves (the dried flower
buds of the evergreen *Eugenia aromatica* tree), dried ginger roots,
nutmeg (the seeds of the *Myristica fragrans* tree), mace (the external
fibrous covering of nutmeg), cinnamon (the dried, ground bark of
the cassia tree, *Cinnamomum cassia*), the saffronlike powdered root
called turmeric, and the sweetish cardamom and aniselike coriander
seeds. These last three, along with cinnamon, pepper and caraway
seeds, were combined into a mild curry powder.

Medieval meat was commonly stewed in broth, though nobody
drank the broth until the twelfth century. Hunks of bread dipped in
the stew broth were called *sop*, a word eventually applied to the broth
itself and metamorphosed in time into our modern word, soup. The
French called it *pot-au-feu* and it became the basis of the French
peasant diet.

The estates were beginning to break up by the twelfth century.
Thousands of peasants were moving into the congested cities that
had begun to grow up. The streets of Paris were unpaved until Philip
II's time, and he did not take the throne until 1180. Salt and spices
were available in the marketplace, public bakeries sold bread in wide
variety. But sanitation was unspeakable: pigs in the gutters ate the
garbage thrown from windows, small ragamuffins competed with the
pigs for anything edible.

London was, if anything, worse. It was a village of thatched-roof
houses whose ruling class spoke French and whose people were
gradually adopting French words [5] for meat, words introduced by

---

[5] The English still use the word "gammon" (from the French *jambon*) for
what Americans call "ham," from the pre-1100 Old English word *hamm*,
meaning "bend of the knee." To the Saxons, killing veal calves was a Norman
act of wantonness; eating veal was not sanctioned in any English cookbook
until 1658.

the Normans under William the Conqueror beginning in 1066: beef (*boeuf*), mutton (*mouton*), veal (*veau*), pork (*porc*), poultry (*poularde*). While "beeves" was for years used to mean cattle, the Old English livestock names (cow, lamb, ox, pig, sheep) survived.

French cooking was little better than English; so when Eleanor of Aquitaine (who had been divorced by France's Louis VII), married England's Henry Plantagenet (later Henry II) in 1154, the French cooks she brought along to feed that lion in winter advanced the English culinary art no more than had the Norman conquerors of the previous century.

The Court of St. James made up in quantity for anything it may have lacked in the quality of its provender. For a weekend at the castle of Richard II, who became king in 1377, it took fifty swans, 110 geese, sixty dozen hens, five herons, six kids, seven dozen rabbits (called "coneys" at that time), 100 dozen peacocks, five dozen pullets (young hens, less than a year old) for jelly, eleven dozen pullets to roast, twenty dozen cranes and curlews and other "wilde fowle" to feed the crowd. The swans were served roasted whole in gilded plumage, the feathered skin first removed intact, then gilded and slipped back onto the cooked bird.

When Archbishop Neville was ordained at York in 1476, records show the feasting went on for several days; the celebrants consumed 1000 mutton sheep, 2000 geese, 1000 capons, 4000 pigeons, 5000 deer, 4000 meat pies, 1000 jellied dishes, 3000 cold baked custards, 300 tuns of ale (a tun usually equalled 252 wine gallons), 100 tuns of wine and a pipe (about 5000 quarts) of hippocras, an ancient spiced wine so named because it was clarified through a filter invented by Hipprocrates, the fourth-century B.C. Greek physician whose oath is still administered to doctors.

The basic sweetening through all these times had been honey. Sugar cane (*Saccharum officinarum*), native to China and imported to the Middle East before 300 B.C., was not introduced to Europe until the eighth century, when the Moors planted cane in Spain. Sugar was used to some extent in England and France by the late sixteenth century, but it remained a luxury, used at first solely as a medicine, even after the Crusaders brought it back to Western Europe in the thirteenth century.

Every manor house kept hives of honey bees, but because of the religious wars that swept Europe in the late Middle Ages, beehives were ruined and neglected as populations shifted in search of security. Manuscripts of the Renaissance speak of a great shortage of honey. And while old recipes call for honey earlier than 1600, from the mid-seventeenth century until the early part of our own there was little to be had.

One use for what honey there was, and there was always some at a price, was to make mead, a mildly alcoholic drink that was Queen Elizabeth's favorite tipple, and that of the Vikings before her. Made of honey and water boiled together with spices and herbs and lemons, left to stand for three months and then bottled, mead was considered ready to drink six weeks after bottling.[6]

The rude nature of cooking in those medieval times, the conditions that preceded the developing artistry of Italian cooks and French *cuisineurs*, can be seen in the language of a royal cookbook compiled about 1390 for cooks who served England's Richard II.

"Take rabbits," it says, "and smite them to pieces; seethe them in grease . . ." And "Take chickens and ram them together, serve them broken . . ."

The latter must have been a recipe for chicken hash. Interestingly, the book also contains a recipe for macaroni, adopted from the Italians.

Cookbooks were handwritten, first on parchment, then on paper after that Chinese invention was introduced in the twelfth century. Printing was not invented until the mid-fifteenth century. The first printed cookbook was published in Italy in 1475, though almost four centuries passed before a cookbook gave exact measurements for recipes, precise cooking times and the number of servings yielded.

---

[6] Other popular medieval drinks were posset (hot milk curdled with ale or wine and often spiced and sweetened) and punch, or "pauch," an Indian mixture of arrack (a distilled liquor), tea, lemon juice, water and sugar (or honey). The word *pauch* is an Indian word meaning "five" and reflects the five ingredients used to make punch.

The resourceful Mrs. M. F. K. Fisher has unearthed an obscure cook-book published in 1816 by an English eccentric which gave exact measures of ingredients—instead of "pinches," "dashes" and "dollops" —and their order of use. But while *The Cook's Oracle* (*Apicius Redivivus*) by Dr. William Kitchiner may have been first, Mrs. Isabella Beeton's *The Book of Household Management*, published in England in 1861, had far wider circulation and influence.

Cookbooks, along with Bibles, were among the earliest books printed and still outsell any other kind of book.

What people cooked from their Renaissance cookbooks was no large improvement over what they had cooked in the Middle Ages. But Europe was on the verge of a fabulous infusion of new foods, a revolution in eating habits and in the contents of people's diets.

We have seen the importance of spices in this old world of slow, creaky transport with its paucity of ways to keep food from spoiling.

Spices made meat not merely more tasty; they made it edible when it was long past its prime. Spices became as precious as gold and gem-stones to meat-eating Europeans. The lure of spice-market riches led Columbus to seek a passage to the Indies that would beat the long, hard overland journey across Asia.

His way was paved on the water by the Portuguese, particularly by Henry the Navigator, grandson of England's John of Gaunt and son of Portugal's John I of Avis. Henry, in the 1420's, gathered about him at Sagres some of the leading astronomers, map-makers, instrument-makers, pilots and scholars of the time. On a bleak promontory reaching out into the mysterious Atlantic, they pioneered a new science of navigation. And they invented a lateen-rigged ship, a caravel, designed to make headway against the winds on long sea voyages, and destined to change the course of history.

No spirit of adventure but simple economic incentive sent Columbus and other explorers venturing into the unknown.

Spices could be sold for enormous prices. Five years after Columbus found a new hemisphere while looking for the Spice Islands, Vasco da Gama sailed round Africa's Cape of Good Hope (despite the superstition then current that white men turned black if they proceeded too far south) and reached India. He returned to Portugal from the Malabar Coast with cloves, with cinnamon, with nutmeg and ginger roots, and with pepper bought at Calicut for only 3 ducats per hundredweight when the price in Venice was as much as 80 ducats.

On his second voyage, da Gama's cargo when he returned was worth sixty times what it had cost to outfit his fleet of thirteen merchant vessels.

Venture capital from Antwerp, Barcelona, Bristol, Florence, Genoa and Venice financed further Portuguese expeditions; four years after da Gama's first expedition, Portugal's maneuverable caravels imported 1300 tons of pepper. By the following year, 1504, the price of spices in Lisbon had dropped to a mere twenty per cent of the Venetian price and Venice's monopoly on the spice trade was broken.

But while low compared with the old Venetian rates, spice prices were still high enough to make the Portuguese spice business profitable. Immensely so.

Ferdinand Magellan sailed with a fleet of five ships in 1519. Just one ship, the *Vittoria*, commanded by Sebastian del Cano, completed the round-the-world trip and made it back to Seville three years later (Magellan himself perished in the Philippines in a fight with the natives there). But the spices carried by the eighteen men of the *Vittoria* more than paid the cost of the whole expedition.

A merchant underwriting a voyage to the Spice Islands was taking an enormous risk. But what a reward for success! To outfit and provision a ship for the two-year venture might cost $25,000 in today's terms; it could yield a return of well over $500,000, a twenty-fold profit. Nothing like da Gama's sixty-fold profit, but not bad.

Pepper was (and still is) the major spice. To the spice merchants of Europe, Columbus' venture was a failure; he brought back no pepper, no cloves, no cinnamon.

To others, more interested in expanding the existing repertoire of foods than in commercial gain, the Columbus expedition must have been a matter of some fascination. One, if he were still alive, would have been the Italian Alvise da Cadamosto, who had proudly described elephant meat [7] he had eaten on the Gambia River in Africa in 1456:

> I had a portion cut off, which, roasted and broiled, I ate on board ship . . . to be able to say that I had eaten the flesh of an animal which had never been previously eaten by any of my countrymen. The flesh, actually, is not very good, seeming tough and insipid to me.

A new larder for the world

When Columbus touched shore in the West Indies thirty-six years later, a vast new world opened up.

It was as if we were to land men today on a verdant new planet and have them return with a whole cornucopia of unfamiliar fruits, vegetables and poultry.

Columbus was disappointed in his quest for spices, gold and gemstones. What he and his successors found, however, far exceeded in value all the spices, gold, diamonds, emeralds and rubies of the then-known world.

If the Spaniards showed some trepidation in experimenting with novel foods in the islands they thought were the East Indies, a report from Columbus' personal physician, Diego Alvarez Chanca, may explain why:

> There were wild fruits of various kinds, some of which our men, not very prudently, tasted; and upon touching them with their tongues, their countenances became inflamed, and such great heat and pain followed, that they seemed mad.

---

[7] When elephant herds in South Africa's Kruger National Park are culled to avoid overcrowding, the meat is turned into dried strips called "biltong." Sold in butcher shops throughout the country, biltong is described as a delicacy, "tasty, but a little coarse." The herds number close to 8000 animals, nearly one per square mile. Many are fugitives from poachers in neighboring Mozambique and Rhodesia.

What stung the men's tongues was the fruit of the manzanillo, or manchineel, tree. Its deadly poison was used by Carib Indians to tip their arrows.

The Caribs practiced cannibalism (the word derives from the Arawak *Carib*). Columbus' men found emasculated boys being fattened for a feast and plump girls, captured from other tribes, being used to produce babies for the cooking spit. Dr. Chanca observed "the neck of a man, undergoing the process of cooking." He also saw Indians eating spiders and worms.

Exploring Cuba on a second voyage (this time with twelve caravels), the Castilians found the native delicacy was roast iguana (still a favorite in parts of Mexico, Central America and the West Indies). The men said they would sooner eat an alligator.

The Columbus expedition may have brought syphilis back to Europe; the explorers certainly brought home tobacco.

Mostly, however, they returned with new items of food. The list of those foods is quite amazing.

First and foremost was corn, not in the European sense (Europeans use the word to mean any kind of edible grain [8]) but more precisely *maize*. Columbus mentions maize in his journals of the year 1492. Until he brought back those first kernels to Spain, no European had ever known corn as we know it. For most Europeans, in fact, corn was still unknown more than a century later; when it finally arrived it came from the Levant and was thought of as Turkish. The Italians of Tuscany, Lombardy, the Piedmont and the Venetian provinces made it into a thick, coarse corn meal mush (*polenta*) as

---

[8] In England, a "corn" was a seed of grain, any grain. An ear of corn was the head of a stalk of wheat, rye, millet, oats or barley. Barleycorn survives as a word in the antique term, John Barleycorn, a personification of beverage alcohol (which was often based on fermented barleycorn mash). Barleycorn survives also as a unit of measurement in footwear. England's King Edward II decreed in 1324 that three barleycorns taken from the center of an ear and placed end to end equaled one inch. He also decreed that the longest normal human foot was thirty-nine barleycorns. King Edward's system was formally accepted by the U.S. shoe industry in 1888; shoes larger than size 13, thirty-nine barleycorns, have never been made in the U.S. except on a custom-order basis.

they made rice (introduced into Italy by the Spanish in the fifteenth century) into *risotto*.

Until Columbus and later Spanish explorers came home from America, nobody in Europe had tasted turkey. Or guinea fowl. Or turtle meat.

Or peanuts, cashew nuts, black walnuts, Brazil nuts or butternuts. Or cocoa. Or vanilla.

Or pineapple (though that fruit tasted not unlike the ancient and familiar quince). Or papaya.

Or potatoes or sweet potatoes.

Or tomatoes.

Or kidney beans, lima beans, navy beans or string (snap) beans (which are the immature pods of various kinds of kidney beans).

Or squashes, including pumpkins.

Or avocados, sometimes called alligator pears, those puzzling fruits that do not get soft or change color to show they are ripe (the Indians of Yucatan mashed them to make their *guacamole* sauce).

Or pimento. Or allspice, which comes from the *Pimenta offici-nalis* tree and smells like a combination of cinnamon, cloves and nutmeg.

Or peppers, by which we mean *Capsicums* [9]—the bell peppers,

---

[9] Chili and cayenne come from the *Capsicum frutescens* and the *Capsicum annuum* (Guinea pepper), paprika from the *Capsicum tetragonum*. The mild puffy green, or bell, pepper is the immature *Capsicum grossum* which, when it is ripe, is the hot red or yellow pepper. Capsicums vary in taste somewhat according to where they grow, hence the distinctive flavor of Hungarian paprika, the dried powder derived from the sweet red *tetragonum* pepper grown in Hungary.

None of these is any kin to *Piper nigrum*, whose fruit is the world's most important spice today as is Columbus' time. It is native to southwest India, whose Malabar Coast port of Tellicherry still ships the best peppercorns. The world uses about 175 million pounds of *Piper nigrum* a year; the U.S. uses some 50 million pounds, more than all other seasonings put together. Black pepper outsells white in the U.S.; in Europe it is the other way round. Both come from the same plant; white pepper, developed to avoid black specks in white sauces, is from peppercorns picked when fully ripe and stripped of their outer skins; black pepper, stronger than white, is from peppercorns picked earlier and then dried, usually in the sun.

bonnet peppers, pimiento peppers and Guinea peppers of chili, cayenne, paprika and tabasco sauce.

Not all of these came back to Europe with Columbus, of course. Some were not discovered until more than a century later.

Nor was every food plant discovered in the New World new. Grapes were one exception (though America had its own distinctive native varieties). Yams were another, for while sweet potatoes are native to the Western Hemisphere alone, yams are native to warm regions of both hemispheres.

Dr. Chanca is generally quoted as writing that the sailors of the *Niña*, the *Pinta* and the *Santa Maria* ate the first yams Europeans had ever seen. This could hardly have been so. Some Europeans must have been familiar with the yams of Africa and Asia. In any case, what Columbus' sailors ate were almost certainly sweet potatoes, not yams.

Many people think sweet potatoes and yams are the same thing. "Moist-fleshed" varieties of sweet potatoes are often called yams in the U.S. The Louisiana Sweet Potato Advertising and Development Commission is itself so confused it has declared January, February and March "Louisiana Yam Supper Season."

Botanically, yams and sweet potatoes are not even related. The sweet potato (*Ipomoea batatas*) belongs to the morning glory family; yams belong to a family of tropical and subtropical herbs or shrubs (*Dioscoreaceae* [10]) whose thick rhizomes often weigh thirty pounds or more.

One of the few varieties of yams cultivated in the U.S. is the *Dioscoreacea bulbifera*, the air potato yam; in other areas of the world, especially West Africa, the family yam patch is the mainstay of the family diet. But while yams are sweeter and juicier than sweet

---

[10] The name commemorates Dioscorides Pedanius, the Greek naturalist and physician of the first century A.D. There are nine or ten genera of yams and about 640 species, most of them in the genus *Dioscorea*. Only one species is native to North America. Progesterone extracted from wild Mexican yams is fermented to manufacture synthetic cortisone used to treat arthritis. Hormones based on extracts from the yams are also the bases of "The Pill" used for birth control. Dioscorides would have liked that.

potatoes, they are much less nutritious. They contain only a trace of yellow carotene, from which the body produces vitamin A, while the sweet potato is one of the richest sources of carotene. And sweet potatoes have about three times as much vitamin C. The reliance on starchy yams is one reason so many Africans are permanently under-nourished and have a life expectancy of barely forty years.

A more nutritious African staple is the peanut, or groundnut, which for years was thought to have originated in Africa and come into the Americas with African slaves. Peanuts are also called ground peas, monkey nuts and goober peas; goober (originally *nguba*) is one of the few African words still retained in the English language.

Goober peas, or goober nuts, may indeed have come westward in eighteenth- and nineteenth-century slave ships, but in an earlier century they evidently traveled in the other direction. Peanut seeds found in ancient Peruvian tombs and related wild legumes found growing in Brazil have established that goobers are native to South America; Indians in Virginia were raising the protein-rich peanut when the colonists arrived there early in the seventeenth century.[11]

It is remotely possible that peanuts are, like yams, native to both hemispheres. The picture is clearer in the case of the two fruits found by the explorers of the New World.

---

[11] Today's major peanut producers are India, Senegal, Nigeria, China and Indonesia. They produce the legumes (*Arachis hypogaea*) in as many as twenty different varieties, most of which are crushed for oil. Peanut oil is the common cooking oil of France. About twenty per cent of world trade in edible oils and oil-bearing materials derives from peanuts; the other eighty per cent comes from cottonseed, coconut, sesame seed (the favored seed for cooking oil in Japan), soybeans and sunflower seeds, all of which are called "oil seeds." The U.S. produces about one-tenth of the world's peanut crop, mostly in Georgia, Alabama, Texas, Oklahoma, Virginia, North Carolina and northern Florida. We produce about twelve times what we produced at the turn of the century and about fifty per cent more than we consume, though we do eat a lot of peanuts, salted and unsalted, roasted in oil and dry roasted. Peanuts have long been associated with circuses and sporting events, but relatively few people have experienced the sensation of opening a peanut shell, muching the kernels inside and discovering they are salty! Salted-in-the-shell peanuts, soaked in brine before they are roasted, are produced in St. Paul, Minnesota and in a few other places, but in much of the country they are unknown.

Because it looked to him like a giant pine cone, Columbus called the Indians' ananas "piña de Indes." The Guarani Indian name was *naná*, meaning excellent fruit. In most European languages the fruit is *ananas;* the Spanish still call it *piña*, the basis of our English word, pineapple.

The Incas in Peru and even their predecessor tribes cultivated this "excellent fruit"; natives of the West Indies put pineapples or pineapple tops at the entrance to their huts as a sign of welcome. The Spanish—and later the English and their colonists—picked up the tradition and carved pineapples on their gateposts and over their doorways.

The great Genoese mariner brought pineapples [12] back to Spain. But even two centuries later, in England, the pineapple was a "rare fruit." John Evelyn (1620–1706) wrote in his *Diary:*

> Standing by his Majesty at dinner in the presence, there was of that rare fruit called the King-pine, growing in Barbadoes and the West Indies; the first of them I had ever seen. His Majesty having cut it up, was pleased to give me a piece off his own plate to taste of; but, in my opinion, it falls short of those ravishing varieties of deliciousness described in Captain Ligon's History, and others, but possibly it might be, or certainly was, much impaired in coming so far; it has yet a graceful acidity, but tastes more like the quince and melon than of any other.

Pineapples have never traveled well. Another New World fruit, the papaya, won earlier and wider acceptance. By the mid-seventeenth century it was being grown in Asia, Africa, the South Pacific and the Mediterranean, though evidently the rest of the world did not use it, as had the Aztecs, to make meat more tender. Papaya extract is today the basis of papain, the enzyme used in our familiar "meat tenderizers."

---

[12] Not planted in the Hawaiian islands until 1790, pineapples were not widely cultivated there until the 1880's. The Islands now produce most of the world crop, though all but a tiny fraction of the vast Hawaiian crop goes into cans.

Meanwhile, back in the Renaissance . . .

The impact of all these new foods on the Old World was, in the beginning, almost nil. America's major importance to the world's cuisine at first was that some crops like sugar cane flourished in the New World as they never had in the Old, a fact which had effects we will discover presently.

The Spanish planted oranges in America, and wheat, as well as sugar. The English introduced walnuts, pears, peaches and apples into Virginia and Massachusetts.

But for the English who stayed home, little changed. The people were, as always, staunch meat eaters.

G.M. Trevelyan quotes Fynes Moryson, writing early in the seventeenth century:

> The English have abundance of white meats, of all kinds of flesh, fowl, and fish and of things good for food. In the seasons of the year the English eat fallow deer plentifully, as bucks in summer and does in winter, which they bake in pasties, and this venison pasty is a dainty, rarely found in any other kingdom. England, yea perhaps one County thereof, hath more fallow deer than all Europe that I have seen. No kingdom in the world hath so many dove-houses. Likewise brawn [boiled and pickled pork] is a proper meat to the English, not known to others. English cooks, in comparison with other nations, are most commended for roasted meats.

Moryson praised English beef and mutton as the best in Europe, and English bacon as better than any but Westphalian.

> The English inhabitants [he went on] eat almost no flesh commoner than hens, and for geese they eat them in two seasons, when they are fatted upon the stubble after harvest and when they are green about Whitsuntide [about two months after Easter]. And howsoever hares are thought to nourish melancholy, yet they are eaten as venison both roast and boiled. They have also great plenty

of conies [rabbits] the flesh whereof is fat, tender, and more delicate than any I have eaten in other parts. The German conies are
more like roasted cats than the English conies.

Despite strict laws and zealous gamekeepers, people of all classes
commonly poached deer and smaller game from the king's forests and
from the enclosures of lords and gentry.

Pigs, lambs and sides of beef were roasted over great open fires.
Beef and mutton were boiled in huge pots; in France such boiled
cookery is still *à l'Anglaise* (English style), a term not untinged with
scorn (it is applied also to meat breaded and cooked in a skillet).

The French, it seems, have always looked askance at the prodigious
English appetite for meat. Jean-Jacques Rousseau, as late as 1762,
wrote in *Emile:*

> It is a fact that great eaters of meat are in general more cruel and
> ferocious than other men; this observation holds good in all places
> and at all times; the barbarism of the English is well known.

Early English cookbooks show that Elizabethans, barbarous or
not, ate wild boar, swans (still served in their reapplied plumage as
ɪ Chaucer's day), peafowl, venison and such game birds as bittern,
soveler and puet, caught with falcon hawks, shot with bows or cross-
bows, or with "birding-pieces," but most commonly snared or trapped.

Candied violets and rose petals were, in the Elizabethan word,
"cates," meaning delicacies.

But the emphasis was on meat. And where meat was the mainstay
of diet, spices were important. Good English cooks knew the various
uses of pepper, coriander, cinnamon, aniseed, saffron, mace, cloves
and ginger, though few could afford them. First the Arabs, then the
Venetians and then the Portuguese held monopolies on the spice trade
and kept prices high. The Dutch took the lead from the Portuguese
early in the seventeenth century; it was a few years more before the
Honourable East India Company and the Levant Company were able
to make England self-sufficient in spices and even a dominant factor
in the Oriental spice trade.

Spices, like French wines, Spanish sugar and oranges, dates and the like had to be ordered months ahead by the lady of a manor house and often were enjoyed only at rare intervals. Vegetables and fruits were eaten in season and then simply disappeared from the market. Raisins from Greece, dried figs from Italy and Sicily came to England in great shiploads, but it was often months, even years, between ships.

Aside from spices, most food would seem inexpensive in terms of modern currency. A penny or two bought a good, substantial meal with many courses at a tavern or country inn; several pennies was the going price in London. Small game birds in the market fetched three cents a dozen. It was possible to buy a mallard duck for six cents, a r bbit for four cents, ten eggs for a penny, a peacock or pheasant for a Christmas feast for fourteen cents, a whole pig for eight cents a pound (high because pork was so popular).

Wages, however, were similarly small. A good cook might receive only 5 pounds (about $12.00) for a full year's work. A few pennies are a great deal when one is earning only $1.00 a month. The game poaching of the time was not for amusement; there were hungry bellies in England as the population, thinned two centuries earlier by the Black Plague, burgeoned to strain food supplies.

At better inns, and in the half-timbered houses of the rich and noble meat eaters, "cooked dishes" were the thing. Fish, game or meat was cut into very small pieces and mixed with heartily flavored ingredients—wine, spices and vegetable coloring—so a knight and his lady hardly knew what they were eating.

One reason for "cooked dishes," obviously, was the difficulty of keeping meat fresh over the winter. The English became accustomed to eating slightly spoiled meat ("high" game is still a tradition among the aristocracy), but some people must have choked on it. The great slaughtering season in the fall, traditionally at Michaelmas, September 29, produced a glut of pork, beef and young mutton. A great shortage of fresh meat set in after Christmas; Lent, with its strictures against meat eating, came none too soon.

Disguising the overripe meat in "cooked dishes" was considered a mark of sophistication; unusual combinations were given high marks. Cooks prepared oysters with sugar; sweets were cooked with sours, fish with fowl, meats with fruit, and a cook's skill was proved if the guests failed to identify what they had eaten.

England's traditional steak-kidney-mushroom-and-oyster pie is a carry-over from the cooked dish. So to an extent are Melton Mowbrays, the pies made of pork, game or lamb which originated in a market town in Leicestershire, and all the other English meat pies (which, in infinite varieties, are even more popular in present-day Australia).

Another vestige of the cooked dish, no doubt, is Scotland's famed haggis (oatmeal, onions, beef suet, beef lungs, intestines and pancreas, liver and heart, all cooked in a sheep's large stomach bag), a pudding— "Great chieftain o' the puddin'· race," poet Robert Burns called it— which loyal Scotsmen make a ritual of eating on St. Andrew's Day (November 30) and on January 25. The latter date is Robbie Burns's birthday and the less-than-poetic pudding is Scotland's national dish. Good Scotsmen profess to love it, served properly with neps (turnips) and nips (Scotch whisky); Sassenachs, as unreconstructed Highlanders still call the British, and other foreigners tend to find it repulsive and indigestible.

Another reason for the Elizabethans' cooked dishes was that many people simply did not have enough teeth to chew solid cuts of meat. The first metal dental fillings were installed in 1542, but older people often lacked all their teeth and the false teeth were primitive. Even in the mid-eighteenth century, as T.H. White says, "the lack of reliable artificial teeth, though this convenience did exist, produced the Punch-and-Judy profile in old age." Cooked dishes could be spooned up and eaten with virtually no chewing.

Large, long-handled spoons of the sort now used for stirring in the kitchen were, in fact, the table utensils of Elizabethan England, but while earlier they had been of wood, now they were increasingly of silver or tin. There were knives at every place to cut the meat if necessary. People ate off wooden trenchers or pewter dishes; there was no china.

Forks were ridiculed as fancy continental affectations, not for honest Englishmen. They had been mentioned in the Bible, and excavations show forks were used by Anglo-Saxons as far back as 796, but they evidently fell into disuse. Italians used forks in the eleventh century, and Thomas Becket, Chancellor of England under Henry II, introduced them to the royal court in the twelfth, but again we can only assume that either they never gained popularity or fell out of favor.

The first known picture of a fork is in an Italian book of 1570, Bartolomeo Scappi's *Cooking Secrets of Pope Pius V*. But in most countries people still ate with their fingers, which were invented before forks.

Marston Bates says France's Henry III discovered forks in Venice "in the seventeenth century and introduced them to the French court," but since that homosexual king was murdered by a monk in 1589, the statement has to be open to question. And while Queen Elizabeth may have owned three forks, two of them studded with jewels, most sources say she used her fingers when spoon and knife would not suffice.

Thomas Coryat, an English traveler, reintroduced forks to England from Italy toward the end of Elizabeth's reign, noting that "The Italian cannot by any means indure (sic) to have his dish touched with fingers, seeing all men's fingers are not alike cleane."

Forks were two-pronged until the end of the eighteenth century, when four-pronged forks became standard. By then even the lower classes in England had started to use forks.

Americans were later in adopting the fork. They mostly used their knives until after the Civil War, when special fish forks, oyster forks and dessert forks were fashionable and even ice cream was eaten with forks. In England and on the Continent today, proper dinnertable usage requires that peaches, pears and bananas be eaten with knife and fork; only picnickers, peasants and Americans pick up a piece of fruit and bite into it. Right-handed Englishmen and Europeans customarily keep their forks in their left hands; Americans put down their knives and switch their forks from left hand to right. No good reason for the custom: it is just one of our amusing American ways. Presumably all modern-day Americans above a certain age are accustomed to using forks. Presumably. Though a recent U.S. Air Force manual felt it necessary to explain that "The fork is used to lift, turn or move large or small pieces of food in a sanitary and practical manner."

The provender forked into Renaissance mouths could sometimes be quite exotic. One sixteenth-century cookbook recalls the old nursery rhyme:

> Sing a song of sixpence, a pocketful of rye,
> Four and twenty blackbirds, baked in a pie.
> When the pie was opened, the birds began to sing . . .

There was actually a cookbook in the 1500's with a recipe that began, "To make pies that the birds may be alive in and flie out when it is cut up. . ." It was, indeed, a dainty dish to set before the king.

In the preceding century, at the Feast of the Pheasant which was supposed to spark a final Crusade (it never came off) in 1454, France's Duke of Burgundy had had twenty-eight musicians play inside a giant pie to entertain the guests. The Feast lasted four days.

The business of entertainment at elaborate ceremonial meals was becoming important now. Not only musicians, but jugglers, acrobats and singers performed at the Feast of the Pheasant, and there were tableaux, a mystery play on a stage, even a falcon hunt with live birds inside the great hall of the Hôtel de la Salle.

Wives were coming out of retirement in the Renaissance and eating at the same table as their men—and enjoying the same entertainments, which in Italy were probably the beginnings of opera and ballet.

The great cooks of the time, perhaps of all time, were the French, though some say the French art of cooking began with the Italians—who, in turn, may have learned some things from the Chinese (via Marco Polo, who returned from the court of Kublai Khan in 1295). The Oriental tradition is still evident in some Italian dishes: the dumplings called *cappelletti* or *tortellini* are often cooked in a broth like Chinese wonton soup, and the way Italians cook greens is very much like the Chinese stir-fry *chow* technique.

But it is *not* true that the Venetian who opened a direct route to the Far East introduced Italy to the art of pasta-making. Several years before Marco's return there appeared a cookbook with recipes for making *vermicelli, tortelli* and *tortelletti,* not yet staples of Italy's diet but native inventions with innumerable variations of shape as they were developed over later centuries. In Rome and points north, Italian pasta is ribbon-shaped; from the Abruzzi south in the east, and from the Campania south in the west, it is tubular. The difference between noodles and spaghetti, or macaroni, is regional.

When Catharine de' Medici of Florence, whose family had prospered mightily in the spice trade, married the duc d'Orleans in 1533, she brought along her Italian chefs and confectioners as part of her dowry. The Duke later became Henri II of France;[13] cooking at the French court was cultivated and elevated to the level of elegant art.

But the French gastronomical tradition probably began earlier. A cook to the Valois dynasty (which ended with Charles VIII in 1498), one Guillaume Tirel (he was called Taillevent) penned a manuscript on the *haute cuisine* as early as 1480. The original is in the Vatican library.

Some of the French art conveyed itself across the Channel, but the English never achieved note for their culinary prowess, which by no means stopped them from eating enormous quantities of food.

---

[13] Henri's son-in-law (and second cousin) was the Henri IV who wished "there would not be a peasant so poor in all my realm who would not have a chicken in his pot every Sunday." Nearly four centuries later in the U.S., Al Smith claimed Herbert Hoover turned the statement into a political slogan, "A chicken in every pot and two cars in every garage," but Hoover actually said, "The slogan of progress is changing from the full dinner pail to the full garage." As for Henri IV, we are told by Raymond Oliver, owner of Le Grand Vefour restaurant in Paris, that Henri cracked garlic cloves in his teeth and had a breath that "could fell an ox at twenty paces." France was so torn by religious civil wars in the late sixteenth century that many peasants must have lacked chickens for their pots, even bits of chicken to flavor their gruel. Henri II? He was somewhat eclipsed by the splendor of his mistress, the celebrated Diane de Poitiers; he met his end in a joust.

That voracious victualizer Henry VIII gorged himself at great seven-hour banquets, becoming so grossly fat he had to be moved up and down stairs by special machinery.

Elizabethans, too, consumed food in rather awesome amounts. They ate four meals a day, though accounts vary as to the hours of those meals. All agree that the hour for the main meal advanced over the centuries. In thirteenth-century France it was evidently at nine in the morning, and this was probably true in England, too. Some historians say Henry VII dined at eleven in the morning, some say Henry VIII dined at ten. Some say the Elizabethans dined at ten in the morning, others say at eleven or at noon.[14]

If we take the 10 o'clock figure, then the other meals were break-fast at seven, supper at four, livery (a word now fallen into disuse in this sense) at eight in the evening. A "banquet" in Shakespeare's day meant an evening snack of sweetmeats (cakes or pastry).

The Elizabethan breakfast showed early portents of the substantial meal that started off the day in Victorian times: a whole loaf of bread washed down with a tankard of strong ale, four to six eggs, some cold meat or fish, usually herring.

The bread could be *pain-main* of fine wheat flour, or it could be barleymeal bread, branbread, peasebread, oatbread or oatcakes, hard-bread or unleavened bread.

Midday and evening meals ran to at least six or seven courses in the homes of the gentry, often with several pounds of roast meat for each guest. A whole roast chicken and a whole large loaf of bread was customarily served to each person at the table.

Though Voltaire two centuries later was to remark that the English had a hundred religions and only one sauce, it was hardly true even in Shakespeare's time. The most widely used sauces were a parsley sauce and a creamed garlic sauce; a score of others figured in Elizabethan cookery, but for most people it sufficed to splash a large dollop of vinegar on meat, poultry or fish.

---

[14] By the mid-1700's, the usual dinner hour had advanced to three in the after-noon. Horace Walpole, in 1789, wrote, "I am so antiquated as still to dine at four." And some forty years later, the fashionable hour was seven, though, as James Laver writes, "unpretentious folk like the Carlyles dined at six."

If the quality of meals in England was barely tolerable by most modern standards of cuisine, on English ships at sea, where that occupational disease of early sailors, scurvy, presented a major peril, the food was often quite intolerable. Shipboard menus consisted largely of dried or salted meat, salt fish, biscuit, rice, cheese, onions, garlic oil, vinegar, dried peas, wine and water. In good times, seamen ate about 3500 calories of food a day, but times were not always good. A chronicle of Magellan's Pacific crossing records some grim facts:

> We ate only old biscuits reduced to powder, and full of grubs, and stinking from the dirt which the rats had made on it when eating the good biscuit, and we drank water that was yellow and stinking. We also ate the ox hides which were under the main-yards so that the yard should not break the rigging . . . also the sawdust of wood, and rats.

Grain and ship's biscuit (hardtack) became sour and swarmed with weevils on many a ship, but even worse were the horrors of scurvy. With no refrigeration, it was virtually impossible to keep supplies of fresh fruit aboard ships for the weeks and months that sailing ships carried men out of sight of land.

Scurvy struck hardest on the route to India; on a passage to India it was considered lucky if only one out of five men died of the dread disease. One contemporary account, written by a survivor, pulls no punches:

> It rotted all my gums, which gave out a black and putrid blood. My thighs and lower legs were black and gangrenous, and I was forced to use my knife each day to cut into the flesh in order to release this black and foul blood. I also used my knife on my gums, which were livid and growing over my teeth. When I cut away this dead flesh and caused much black blood to flow, I rinsed my mouth and teeth with my urine, rubbing them very hard . . . And the unfortunate thing was that I could not eat, desiring more to swallow than to chew. Many of our people died of it every day, and we saw bodies thrown into the sea constantly, three or four at a time. For the most part they died with no aid given them, expiring behind some case or chest, their eyes and the soles of their feet gnawed away by the rats.

So while the Spanish and Portuguese planted citrus fields everywhere they landed, and the Dutch (and later James Cook) carried barrels of sauerkraut as an antiscorbutic, this nutritional deficiency disease for centuries proved as effective a barrier to sea exploration as gravity was to space exploration.

Nor was scurvy exclusively a nautical complaint. Because they lacked fresh greens, ate no potatoes and, for much of. the year, no fruit and no animal liver, almost everybody in medieval and Renaissance Europe developed what the English called "winter rash," a pre-scurvy symptom. (Seamen were on the verge of scurvy even before they left port, and the tendency to scurvy was a frequent cause of the toothlessness so widespread in these times.)

To combat winter rash, Elizabethans drank "verjuice," mentioned in antiquity by Lucius Apuleius in *The Golden Asse*. Made usually from grapes and crabapples, and from oranges if they were available, verjuice was a fermented drink (damask rose leaves were added prior to fermentation) often used in cooking winter dishes.

The staple food in Shakespeare's time was bread, and for all the variations listed earlier it was mostly white bread (though farmers preferred barley and rye breads). Wheat bread came in two basic varieties, white (called manchet) and dark (called cheat). Honey was the generally used sweetener, sugar being mostly too expensive, though some sugar was mixed with almond paste to make marchpane, as Elizabethans called the candy other people call marzipan. Water was often polluted, so people tended to drink cider, both fresh and aged, along with beer, ale and "small beer," a brew of low alcoholic content.

By our standards, these English were, if not barbarous, at least a rude, boisterous lot, even the "gentlefolk." Not only did they spurn forks, they wiped their mouths and hands on the tablecloth, if there was a tablecloth. It was a rough and ready crowd that sent its adventurers, renegades and religious rebels to colonize the New World and send back to England the bounty of the Americas.

One spoon or two?

While eventually it was the potato (Chapter 6) that proved to be America's greatest contribution to Europe's tables, low-cost sugar had a more important influence on European eating—and more especially—drinking habits in the seventeenth century.

Sugar was not native to the New World, but it was only when the Spaniards and Portuguese, and then the English and French, planted cane in the West Indies and Brazil that sugar grew so luxuriantly it became cheap enough for the average European household.

To most sixteenth-century tables, sugar was a new product, and far more useful than other newly introduced foods like corn, or even turkeys. But it was in the seventeenth century that sugar came into its own. England imported less than eighty-eight tons of sugar in 1665; by the end of the century it was importing an average of 10,000 tons a year.

Sugar opened the way to other things. Lemonade, for example, was invented in Paris in 1630 following a sudden drop in the price of sugar. Most importantly, the new abundance of sugar led to the popularity of coffee, tea and cocoa in the seventeenth century.

Tea was the older beverage, but coffee had earlier success in Europe and England.

Coffee is thought to have been discovered in Ethiopia in the middle of the ninth century. A goatherd, says the legend, saw his goats acting peculiarly frisky; he ate the berries of the evergreen bush the goats had been grazing on and felt a sense of exhilaration himself. Steeped in boiling water, the seeds (or berries) of wild coffee trees (*Coffea arabica*) produced a thicky, syrupy beverage someone called "the black enemy of sleep and copulation." The coffee bushes were cultivated in southern Arabia (they were cultivated in Africa only in comparatively recent times), and while strictly orthodox Moslem priests said coffee was an intoxicating beverage and forbade its use, other Moslem priests used it to keep their long religious services going and coffee drinking spread widely among Arabian Moslems.

Almost all coffee came from Yemen in southern Arabia until near the end of the seventeenth century. The most desirable coffees are still *arabicas*, though most of them are grown in Latin America.

Coffee was adopted by the Turks, who took to drinking ten or twenty cups of it a day, tiny cups of which only a thimbleful or two could be swallowed. The berries were not ground until about 1400. The first coffee house was probably the Kiva Han in Constantinople in about 1475.

Suleiman the Magnificent came to power in Constantinople in 1520 and Marco Memmo, the Venetian ambassador to the Sultan's court, brought coffee back to Venice; it found quick popularity. A German botanist took coffee from Constantinople back to Germany in 1575. The Dutch were early coffee drinkers. Then the Spanish and Italians took it up. Doctors prescribed it for various complaints.

By the end of the sixteenth century, coffee was important enough to draw the censure of the Roman Catholic Church, which condemned it as the wine of Islam, an infidel drink. But Pope Clement VIII tasted it and reputedly said, "This Satan's drink is too delicious to let the heathen have it all to themselves. We shall baptize it and make a Christian beverage of it."

Venice had dozens of coffee houses by 1675; the most famous was Caffe Florian, opened by a Venetian politician and diplomat and frequented by his followers. Florian's is still packing them in on the Piazza San Marco.

Fugitives from Turkish oppression introduced England to coffee. A student from Crete, a refugee from the Ottoman Empire, served coffee to his fellows at Oxford in 1637; another political refugee, this one an Armenian, opened England's first coffee house in St. Michael's Alley, in London, in 1652.

But what really seems to have given coffee drinking its great impetus in Europe was the lifting of the sixty-day siege of Vienna in 1683.

The Turks had often hammered on the doors of that city. In

1683 it appeared that they would finally gain their objective. The Turkish army, 300,000-strong, had the Viennese at the point of submission when a soldier of fortune, who was either a Serb, a Pole, a Hungarian or a Greek, and was named either Franz Kolschitzki, Franz Georg Kulczycki or Theodatos (accounts vary), got through the Turks' lines, reached Bavaria and brought back an army under John Sobieski, king of Poland. The Turks were routed just as they were about to breach Vienna's fortifications.

While acting as a spy behind the Turkish lines, Kolschitzki (if that was his name) had tasted the bitter black coffee of the Ottomans. In the wake of the enemy's retreat, he got hold of some bags of coffee beans and, in a tax-free building offered by Vienna's grateful city fathers, opened Central Europe's first coffee house,[15] *Zum Roten Kreuz* (At the Red Cross) near St. Stephen's Cathedral. The coffee was at first unsweetened. Later, quite by accident according to one story, syrup intended for some pastry was added. Still later, a mixture of milk and honey was used for sweetening. The Viennese still top their coffee with sweetened whip cream, or *schlag,* is short for *schlagobers.*

Vienna became a city of coffee houses, some of which developed

---

[15] Another consequence of the lifting of the Turkish siege was a crescent-shaped roll, the *kipfel,* echoing the crescent moon of the Turkish flag. The significance of the crescent goes back to 340 B.C. when Philip of Macedon besieged Byzantium. The siege failed, possibly because the moon, emerging from behind clouds, revealed Philip's army attempting a surprise attack, though that may be mere legend. The crescent moon was the symbol of the Byzantines' goddess, Hecate, and since they credited her with their success against Philip they adopted her emblem, which became Christian under Constantine and which the Turks adopted when they took Constantinople (once called Byzantium, now Istanbul) in 1453. Vienna's bakers in 1683 created the *kipfel* (the word means crescent) to ingratiate themselves with the Turks who, they thought, were about to take the city. This is still vehemently denied by Viennese bakers, but it is more reasonable than their story, that the *kipfel* was designed as a symbol of Vienna's finest hour. When the Austrian princess Marie Antoinette became queen to France's Louis XVI nearly a century later, she brought the *kipfel* recipe to Paris, where French chefs turned the roll into a flaky pastry, the *croissant* (French for crescent), the favorite breakfast roll—along with the *brioche*—of the French forever after.

into the "concert cafes" where composers like Franz Schubert wrote their music and where the waltz began. In London, too, the coffee house soon became the center of the city's social and political life of the early 1800's, when the clubs started up. The major vice of the time was drunkenness; until coffee, and later tea, became popular, there was little a man could safely drink (water and milk were hazardous) except beer and ale. Gin was becoming popular, too, though the extremes depicted in Hogarth's *Gin Lane* (a sign in the picture reads, "Drunk for a Penny, Dead drunk for two-pence") were not reached until well into the eighteenth century.

The coffee houses served no alcohol. Still, perhaps because society was strictly a stag affair, women circulated petitions attacking coffee as a cause of illness, even of death. To no avail: London had nearly 2000 coffee houses in 1725; her men, smoking Virginia tobacco in their clay pipes (the habit had become general by the time Elizabeth died in 1603), drank more coffee than the men of any other city in the world.

There were coffee houses for Whigs and coffee houses for Tories, coffee houses for the clergy, for Quakers, for papists, for Jacobites. Will's, near Covent Garden, catered to poets and critics. Samuel Johnson, a bit later, drank his coffee at the Turk's Head. So did Edmund Burke, David Garrick and James Boswell. One or two pence a cup was the usual price.

The Arabs, who would not let "infidels" see their coffee plantations on the mountain slopes of the Arabian peninsula, maintained a monopoly on the coffee trade, as earlier they had dominated the spice trade. They did permit foreigners to set up warehouses and offices in the port of Mocha, on the Red Sea. In 1740, the Dutch were able to smuggle coffee bushes out of Mocha and establish coffee estates in Java. Mocha and Java are still names synonymous with coffee, though Mocha is now grown in Yemen (it is no longer shipped out of Mocha) and very little coffee is still grown in Java, whose plantations were destroyed by the Japanese in World War II.

Earlier, in 1720, a Frenchman (the name Gabrielle de Clieu is sometimes cited) had stolen a single coffee bush from the Royal

Botanical Garden in Paris and taken it to the island of Martinique in the West Indies. The entire American coffee industry (Latin America now produces close to ninety per cent of the world crop) is said to stem from that one plant.

In Germany, coffee became almost a match for beer as the national drink. Frederick the Great, in 1775, took steps to reduce the flow of money to the foreign merchants who supplied Prussia with green coffee.

For the Germans, too, coffee drinking was at first largely a masculine pleasure. Johann Sebastian Bach wrote a "Coffee Cantata" expressing the emotions of women whose husbands neglected them to drink coffee with the boys. The German women solved their dilemma by inventing the *Kaffeeklatsch*, which became an important social occasion for both men and women, as tea time later became a high point in daily English social life.

It is hard to think of the English as being anything but tea drinkers, but tea did not become important in England until the eighteenth century and did not overtake coffee until the late nineteenth.

Even in China, tea became popular only in the eighth century. De Candolle listed it among the crops grown prior to 4000 B.C., but legend associates it with Bodhidharma, son of a sixth-century A.D. king of India. The prince traveled to China to preach his beliefs, vowing to stay awake for nine years to contemplate the virtues of Buddha. When he fell asleep after three years, the legend says, he cut off his eyelids, and where they fell, tea bushes sprang up. The caffeine in the tea (Chapter 8) helped keep Bodhidharma awake and has done the same for generations of people since.

In the beginning the Chinese drank their tea mixed with salt, ginger, even onions. (*Khat*, a drink made from the dark green leaves of Arabia's *Catha edulis*, may be older than tea.)

The name tea comes from a Chinese ideogram which is pronounced "chah" in Cantonese and "tay" in the dialect of Amoy. The "chah" pronunciation traveled to India, Persia, Russia and Japan; "tay" was brought to Europe via Java by the Dutch, and although it was spelled "tea" in 1660 it was generally pronounced "tay" until the middle of the eighteenth century, by which time England was importing 3 million tons of tea a year.

In Japan, tea was "chah"; it was not introduced to Japan until 805 and did not become popular there until the twelfth century. As with some other things Japanese, serving tea became an elaborate ceremonial ritual, the powdered tea leaves being brewed in a bowl, not a pot, and beaten into a foamy paste with a bamboo whisk, part of the Zen culture developed in the fifteenth century. The tea ceremony, *cha-no-yu*, which can last two hours, is designed (in the words of one Tea Master) "to cleanse the senses . . . so that the mind itself is cleansed from defilements." It takes about ten years to become a Tea Master; the masters are always men (the tea ceremony was invented by a man), but the 2 million or so students enrolled in the Urasenke tea ceremony schools in Japan are mostly women.

It was the Dutch East India Company that brought tea home to Europe in 1609; but England's East India Company, "The Governor and Merchants of London Trading into the East Indies," which Queen Elizabeth chartered in 1600, soon established a monopoly on tea.

The beverage was a slow starter in England. In September, 1658, the following advertisement appeared in London's "Mercurious Politicus":

> That excellent and by all Physitians approved China Drink called by the Chineans *Tcha*, by other nations *Tay*, alias *Tee*, is sold at the Sultaness Head, a cophee-house in Sweetings Rents, by the Royal Exchange, London.

Samuel Pepys, writing in his *Diary* two years later, recorded that "I did send for a cup of tea, a China drink of which I never had drunk before."

Most tea did come from China until the nineteenth century, and it came in increasing quantities in the three-masted "Tea Waggons" of the East India Company—Hyson tea, Bohea tea, Gunpowder tea, 10 million pounds of it a year by the late 1760's, all of it taxed to enrich the Crown.

In 1823, when an indigenous Indian tea was found in upper Assam (northern India), tea plantations were begun in that English colony. When Anna, wife of the seventh duke of Bedford, originated the institution of afternoon tea [16] and cakes (to provide sustenance during the long break between breakfast and 8 o'clock dinner) in about 1840, some of the tea the Duchess poured may have been Indian.

China remained the largest source of tea; the Great Tea Race of 1866, in which eleven clipper ships competed to cover 16,000 miles (speed was important because tea lost its flavor in the hot holds of the ships), left from Foochow, China. The winners reached London ninety-nine days later.

An early investor in the tea ships was a certain Earl Gray, who had a special blend made up for himself and later allowed it to be sold to the public under his name. The copyright on his name expired when he did; now any blend of teas may be called "Earl Gray," and while some may be good, the name is meaningless.

Tea shrubs, closely related to camellia bushes, yield the choicest leaves when grown at altitudes above 4,000 feet. Named after the districts in which they grow (like Assam and Darjeeling, provinces in India), the leaves are prepared in various ways to produce three basically different kinds of tea: black, green and oolong.

Leaves for all three are first withered by exposure to the sun or by heating in trays for eighteen to twenty-four hours until they are pliable. Oolong teas are partially fermented before being dried; they are more astringent than black teas, less astringent than green teas.

Teas are graded according to the age of the leaves used. The best grade is orange pekoe, made from the newest, youngest leaves and terminal buds (sometimes called flower pekoe). Lower grades, in descending order, are pekoe, pekoe Souchong and Souchong. And then there are almost endless varieties of jasmine teas (flavored with jasmine flowers), smokey teas and so forth.

What turned the English into tea drinkers in the nineteenth cen-

---

[16] Tea served at 11 A.M. in England is called "elevenses." Teatime is anywhere from 4 to 7 P.M. High tea, or early supper, may be at tea time, or later. Nobody orders tea at lunch except Americans.

tury was not the celestial, elevating esthetic experience cherished by the Japanese; it was rather a matter of economy. A pound of tea can produce about 300 cups of hot stimulation, a pound of Java only thirty to forty cups. Englishmen drank coffee and tea cup for cup until about 1850, but at that time most English coffee came from Ceylon. When rust [17] destroyed the Ceylon coffee bushes later in the century, coffee prices in England skyrocketed; coffee consumption dropped way off.

The average Englishman was using over two pounds of tea a year by the end of the eighteenth century. The figure climbed quickly toward the end of the nineteenth century: it is now eight pounds a year (versus less than two for coffee). Top quality Darjeeling tea, grown more than a mile high in the Himalayas, can sell for $20 a pound, but most tea today is cheap and over-plentiful.

The English, Scots, Welsh and Irish together use more than half the world's tea output (about 2.3 billion pounds, not counting the estimated 350 million pounds mainland China produces) and drink nine cups of tea for each cup of coffee.

Australians and New Zealanders average seven to eight pounds of tea a year (Australians in the bush make their tea in tin "billy" cans), but the highest consumption rate on the European continent (the Dutch have the record) is a mere two pounds. Tea, served in a glass and flavored with lemon or jam, is Russia's national drink. Bulgarians drink infusions of dried lime leaves.

While sugar from the New World encouraged the growth of tea and coffee usage in the Old, the original native beverage of the New World, cocoa, never achieved anywhere near the success of tea or coffee.

In the pre-Columbian markets of Chichen Itza in Yucatan, cacao beans, from the evergreen *Theobroma* (meaning "food of the gods") *cacao*, were used as currency. A rabbit cost ten beans, a pumpkin four, a live slave 100, the services of a prostitute eight or ten. Columbus evidently brought back some cacao beans to Spain from his

---

[17] *Hemileia vastatrix* appeared in Ceylon in 1869 and spread to destroy the coffee-growing industry throughout the Orient and Pacific islands.

fourth voyage in 1502. But most sources credit the introduction to Hernando Cortez, who invaded Mexico in 1518 with 400 men. In Tenochtitlán, the capital (now Mexico City), he found the Aztecs drinking something they called *cacaolatl* or *cacaohuatl*, prepared from roasted, husked cacao beans ground into a powder and mixed with water. The Indians mixed in vanilla, obtained from the pods of a native climbing orchid (*Vanilla fragrans*), and added red peppers, churning the mixture until it foamed. They drank it cold, chilled by snow brought down from the Sierras.

The Spaniards took cacao beans home, along with vanilla (both were long regarded as aphrodisiacs), and added sugar to make a chocolate drink that was an immediate success in Spain. When Maria Theresa, the Spanish Infanta, married France's Louis XIV, the Grand Monarch, in 1659, she introduced the drink to Versailles.

Two years earlier, a Frenchman had opened a shop in London to sell chocolate for making into a beverage, but his prices were too high for any but the well-to-do. Toffs and dandies comprised a big enough market, however, so that when coffee became popular in Queen Anne's time, early in the eighteenth century, it was to White's Chocolate House that the *beau monde* repaired for coffee, while Tories patronized the Cocoa Tree Chocolate House for theirs.

The cacao bean contains caffeine and theobromine which, along with theophylline, are also found in tea leaves. But hot chocolate, while a stimulant, is hardly as stimulating as hot coffee (Chapter 8). So while the page boy at the beginning of the opera *Der Rosenkavalier* serves morning chocolate to the Marschallin, morning chocolate never became the eye-opener coffee became.

In other forms, chocolate became immensely popular. The English added milk to it about 1700. Dutch and French processors late in the eighteenth century found ways to de-fat chocolate liquor and manufacture a powder, a process patented in 1828 by Conrad J. van Houten. By the middle of the nineteenth century finely ground sugar was being added to cocoa butter to make the first solid eating chocolate, which became popular in England after 1853, when the duty on cacao beans was lowered there.

Milk chocolate, introduced in Switzerland in 1876, became the dominant form of chocolate. (In the U.S. it must contain at least 12 per cent whole milk solids, though top quality chocolates contain 20 to 22 per cent. Sweet chocolate, bittersweet chocolate and baking, or bitter, chocolate contain no milk solids.)

Chocolate's appeal gradually spread, technology improved, and three centuries after the conquistadors found cacao and vanilla in Mexico, factories in the Alps and the Lowlands were producing the chocolate we know today in candy bars, chocolate cake, chocolate mousse, chocolate ice cream and the like. Per capita consumption of cocoa and chocolate is highest (three and a half pounds a year) in the U.S., which grinds twenty-one per cent of the 1.5 million tons of cacao bean grindings the world produces in a year. (West Germany accounts for eleven per cent; the Netherlands, about nine per cent; Britain, about eight per cent.)

Cacao beans now come mostly from hardy, high-yielding trees planted in Ghana, West Africa, and in Brazil, Nigeria and the Dominican Republic; these countries produce the base, or common, Forastero grade cacao that represents ninety per cent of the world crop. Fine, or flavor, grades—Criollos, Trinitarios and high Forasteros —come mostly from Venezuela, Ecuador, the West Indies, Ceylon and Java.

It takes a Mexican dish like *mole poblano*, turkey or chicken in a chile sauce that contains bitter chocolate, to remind us that chocolate, like the turkey, originated in America.

Cocoa took a while to win acceptance in the Old World; tomatoes and potatoes (Chapter 6) took even longer.

But sweet potatoes were an overnight success. Henry VIII, that glutton who came to power in England in 1509, imported sweet potatoes from Spain and had them made into heavily spiced and sweetened pies. (Sweet potatoes went on to become a staple food of the Pacific Islands; in places like New Guinea they now represent ninety per cent of the local diet.)

But nothing the explorers of the Americas brought home was more quickly adopted than the turkey. Like cocoa and corn, domesticated turkeys had evidently begun with the Aztecs. Cortez brought sweet potatoes back to Europe in 1519, and this may also be the first year turkeys were introduced.

These fifteenth-, sixteenth-, and seventeenth-century food dates are variously stated in various sources and are much harder to pin down than, say, dates of battles, treaties, marriages, coronations and deaths, the more usual events with which historians concern themselves.

The great mid-nineteenth-century chef of London's Reform Club, Alexis Soyer, wrote a *History of Food, and Its Preparation, From the Earliest Ages of the World*, which he called *The Pantropheon* and published in 1853. Soyer said the Portuguese had received the turkey from "Americus Vespucius" in 1504, but then Soyer said the Egyptians and Greeks ate "turkey-hens" and that the birds were introduced into Rome in about 115 A.D.

The history of the turkey is complicated by the fact that England had since the Middle Ages been receiving new foods from the Turks and used the word "turkey" to mean any big, edible fowl that was not familiar to them. Way back in the fourteenth century, long before the discovery of the Americas, a Devonshire man had on his coat of arms "three turkey-cocks in their pride proper." Perhaps the birds were peacocks; peafowl, wild and domesticated, were evidently called turkeys before anybody ever heard of a Western Hemisphere. Or perhaps the "turkey-cocks" were Chinese pheasants.

The French called turkey *coq d'Inde*, because America was thought of as the Western Indies, and even today the French word for turkey hen is *dinde*; a tom turkey is *dindon*.

Soyer's error-strewn book is typical of food histories in its carelessness with facts. This book will inevitably have mistakes of its own; if it has fewer than most it is because it has the advantages of more recent documentation.

Some histories say Miguel de Passomonte introduced the American turkey into Spain as early as 1511; some suggest the bird was first seen in Yucatan by Francisco de Cordoba's men in 1517; some credit the discovery to Cortez in 1519.

The exact year makes little difference; it may be that all the above-named were, at least in their own minds, the first to pioneer the turkey in Europe. Certainly the bird is native to the Americas. And we do know turkeys enjoyed enormous popularity in Europe right from the start. By the early seventeenth century, according to one contemporary account, farmers were "driving them from Languedoc [in France] to Spain in flocks, like sheep," just as geese had been driven since Roman times.

Anthelme Brillat-Savarin, the French gastronome, bowed gracefully to the turkey in 1825 when he wrote, "It is surely one of the prettiest presents the Old World has received from the New."

The early connoisseur of *la bonne table* who wrote *The Physiology of Taste* was a country doctor. A bachelor, he became mayor of his home town just after the French Revolution, an uprising provoked to no small extent by empty bellies.

Feasters and famines

In the centuries that preceded the storming of the Bastille prison in Paris in the long hot summer of 1789, there were many famines in France, all of them blandly ignored by royalty and aristocracy who ate like there was no tomorrow. For many, there *was* no tomorrow.

For seventy-two years, from 1643 to 1715, the Sun King Louis XIV had ruled and, after the death of his Prime Minister, Mazarin, ruled with a whim of iron. He isolated himself at Versailles, which he built at a cost of $325 million and 227 lives, and devoted himself to trivia, to personal glory, to *la gloire* of France, but hardly to the welfare of his people.

He did make one important contribution to the French diet and economy when he had sugar planted in Santo Domingo, in Guadeloupe and in Martinique (1654); the French became the world's leading supplier of sugar.

One of Louis' early mistresses, Madame de Montespan, received as a court favor a percentage of all the money paid for meat by the butchers of Paris at Les Halles,[18] the great central food market that Emile Zola later called "the belly of Paris."

For all its blatant corruption under *le roi-soleil,* France was the most powerful, cultured and civilized (if insensitive) country in the world. Its King was a gourmet. He was also an insatiable gourmand. One of Louis' followers wrote that he had often seen the King consume

> four full plates of different kinds of soup, a whole pheasant, a partridge, a large dish of salad, two great slices of ham, mutton served with gravy and garlic, a plate of sweet cakes and on top of that fruit and hard-boiled eggs.

Louis always ended a meal with a few hard-boiled eggs. His courtiers, who vied for the honor of serving him (and for the privilege of eating his leftovers), served eight courses, each one consisting of eight dishes, but not in any special order. From the sixty-four dishes presented, the King selected perhaps twenty, each of which had to be tasted by the attendant courtier before it could be eaten by *le roi.*

Louis ate, as a rule, three soups, five entrées, three fowls, two fish and vegetable dishes. He tasted various roasts, ate a few shellfish, had a few more entremets (usually vegetables), nibbled at some desserts and concluded with the usual hard-boiled eggs.

As a young man in Paris, Louis had been dined by the banker Nicolas Fouquet at Vaux-le-Comte Château near Fontainebleau, where 6000 banquet guests ate off gold and silver plates and won jewels and horses as door prizes. With his personal income of 29 *livres* ($10 million) a year, *le roi* could have outdone splendor even such as this; but that was not his style.

At Versailles, where he had over a thousand rare orange trees planted in silver tubs in the first *orangerie,* Louis usually ate alone in his bedroom (*au petit couvert*). When he dined *au public,* people drove out from Paris and lined up to file past the King as he ate: it was an entertainment, a happening. The King's food was usually cold. It had to be carried down long, drafty halls from distant kitchens, and it took time for it all to be tasted by the gentleman in waiting.

---

[18] Founded on the Right Bank of the Seine in 1137 by Louis VI, Louis the Fat, Les Halles was finally torn down early in 1969; the market was moved nine miles south of Paris to Rungis, near Orly Airport.

The King's teeth rotted; when he was forty, his doctors pulled the last ones remaining, and broke Louis' jaw in the process.

Still he ate. Madame de Maintenon, Louis' last mistress *en titre* and then his second wife, said she would be dead in a week if she ate half what the King put away.

This richest man of his time hated innovations; he did not drink tea, coffee or cocoa, and while forks were in use in Paris by 1648, fingers were good enough for *le roi* right up to the day he died.[19] Others in his realm adopted all sorts of new customs in eating, some of them exaggerated niceties, some the beginnings of today's basic table manners.

Beginning about 1660, each guest at a dinner party wore a napkin tied round his neck, and a good footman knew more than two dozen ways of folding the *serviette* into ships, birds, fruits and whatnot. Forks were coming into wide use by then, and plates were on tables where formerly slices of bread had served to hold food. The plates were mostly of earthenware, but in the homes of the rich at least some were of silver or even real china.[20]

---

[19] At Louis' autopsy, it was found that his intestines were twice as long as the average man's—and contained an oversized tapeworm.

[20] Porcelain was for centuries an arcane Chinese mystery; no European knew how to make it, though the Chinese had been doing it since the ninth century, using a pure aluminum silicate clay (*kaolin*) and a silicate of potassium and aluminum (*pai-tun-tzu* or *petuntse*). Portuguese, Dutch and English trading ships brought Chinese porcelain home with their tea in the seventeenth century, but true china remained a Chinese puzzle. A soft-paste, or artificial, porcelain was made in Italy at the end of the sixteenth century and in France in the seventeenth, but nobody began to use kaolin or petuntse until the early eighteenth, when Johann Friedrich Böttger, chemist to Saxony's Augustus the Strong, made some true, white, hard, translucent, crack-resistant porcelain in 1708. The Meissen pottery plant, which hard-fired its ware at high temperatures, was established at Dresden and by 1730 other European countries had porcelain factories. Handles appeared on cups in the 1730's, though they are still not used in the Orient, and were general by 1760. By the end of the century, England was making bone-china, adding the ashes of burned animal bones to the hard-paste body of clay before it went into the kiln. England was eating off Wedgewood by 1790, and off Spode, Staffordshire and Worcester by 1800. But the china of seventeenth-century France was not china unless it was from China.

Guests usually carried their own forks until the Duc de Montau-sier, in a lavish display of wealth, set the precedent of setting each place at his table with a silver fork. The same Duc de Montausier, in about 1695, invented the soup ladle. Before that, each guest had dipped into a common soup tureen with his own wooden or pewter spoon or, slightly earlier, had drunk from a two-handled porringer passed round the table.

The Sun King's courtiers who witnessed all these changes evi-dently did not eat lamb, which is still not a major *viande* in France.

One court favorite, Madame de Maintenon, opened a school for orphaned daughters of titled army officers. One subject taught was cookery, and the school in time became famous for its cooking lessons. Since each graduate wore a blue ribbon as part of her costume, the *"Cordon Bleu"* became the emblem of a good cook.[21]

While the English, as we saw earlier, were eating well by the seventeenth century, English life and English cooking were spare alongside the mannered extravagance of the French court.

Even the bourgeoisie in France was perhaps taking food a little too seriously. While the King ate only two meals a day (gargantuan meals, true, but only two of them), a rich Parisian by the end of the 1660's was having a *déjeuner* before his midday dinner and a *gouste* between that dinner and 8 o'clock supper.

When France was at war with England, the French army may have been on short rations and the common *citoyens* on the thin edge of starvation, but the feasting at Versailles went on undiminished.

At one banquet the table was decorated with a model of a besieged city, with fish ponds of jelly, siege guns of sugar, trenches of frozen cake. Tables at the court were covered not with linen but with baked dough. These "tablecloths" were tossed to beggars after a banquet; the hungry poor gathered at the palace gates waiting for the meal to end.

---

[21] When a school dedicated to *la haute cuisine* opened in Paris in 1895, it took the name *Cordon Bleu*. The *Grand Diplome* of the *Cordon Bleu* Cooking School is the highest credential a chef can have; even *le Cértificat Elémentaire* commands respect. The school is at 24 rue Champ de Mars in Paris's Seventh Arondissement; its classes are conducted entirely in French.

From 1705 to 1708, famine drove the people to eat the bark off trees. A million Frenchmen died, one out of every twenty; bodies were found along the roadsides, their mouths stuffed with weeds. Still the feasting went on at Versailles.

Louis XV, great-grandson of *le roi-soleil*, succeeded to the throne at age five, the same age at which Louis XIV began his reign, in 1715. This Louis acquired in time the knack of knocking the top off a boiled egg with one stroke of his fork (he did not maintain the royal tradition of eating with his fingers). He also possessed rare talents for making new kinds of omelettes, eating pâtés of larks and drinking champagne, at that time a still wine.

Louis' intimate little suppers for two or three couples were so intimate that the table was lowered through an opening in the floor to be reset below for the next course. In this way, according to a record of the time, "Guests are not annoyed by the importunate glances of servants. They are freed of all embarrassment and need not blush on being caught unawares."

One of Louis' courtiers, the Duc de Richelieu (grand-nephew of the Cardinal) invited some couples to dine in the nude.

Louis' father-in-law, the deposed King Stanislaus of Poland, started the Parisian craze for onion soup, so long a tradition—along with tripe and pigs' feet—at midnight snacks at Les Halles; he also invented *baba au rhum*, a spongelike cake, sometimes with raisins, soaked in a rum sauce.

French aristocrats sided with the American revolutionaries against the traditional "barbarous" English enemy; they symbolized their sympathies by eating roast turkey, the *dindons* stuffed with truffles (so costly they were called "the diamonds of gastronomy"). Alphonse Daudet, in his *Letters From My Mill*, quotes a gluttonous clergyman as saying, "Simply from having smelled those fine turkeys, the odor of the truffles follows me everywhere."

Along with turkey, France's nobility ate Indian pudding, though the American cornmeal and molasses mixture in France often contained cognac or calvados (apple brandy) and was topped with *crème de Chantilly* (whipped cream).

Outside the palaces and châteaux there were at least seven terrible famines before the eighteenth century ended. An Italian diplomat visiting Versailles called France a country where ninety per cent of the population was dying of hunger and ten per cent of indigestion.

One of the worst famines was occasioned by a drought in 1788, the year before the Revolution. In that Revolution, Louis XVI went to the guillotine. So did his queen, Marie Antoinette, she who had given France the *croissant*. The Queen may not have cared about the peasants' hunger, but it is not true that she suggested they eat cake. *Croissants*, maybe, but not cake. The "let them eat cake" line appeared in the sixth book of Jean Jacques Rousseau's *Confessions*, published in 1762—eight years before Marie Antoinette came to France.

Louis, who had sexual problems, compensated for his inadequacies in the boudoir by eating like a pig. Fleeing the Tuileries, he insisted on taking along a portable kitchen and giant food hampers. He stopped for three hours to lunch at Etoge; the revolutionaries caught him at Varennes. But for his gross appetite, Louis might have escaped with the Queen and the Dauphin.

The King was called a walking stomach. On his way to prison, the Temple, he seized a crust of bread from a bystander. The condemned monarch ate heartily in the years he awaited execution. His midday meal always included three soups, from two to four entrées, two or three roast dishes, four entremets (sweet courses), three loaves of bread and butter, several compotes, three dishes of fruit, a small carafe of Bordeaux, one of Malvoisie and one of Madeira, a bottle of champagne and four cups of coffee. His evening meal was similarly immoderate.

Brillat-Savarin, meanwhile, routed by the Paris Commune, had fled to the new United States where he spent two years of exile in New York and Hartford, Connecticut, giving French lessons, playing his violin and introducing his American friends to French ices and fondues.

Rise of the maitre d'

The chefs of the noble houses of France, scattered by the Revolution, opened restaurants.

Except for Tour d'Argent, which dates to 1533, there were no restaurants in Paris until 1765. Imagine Paris without restaurants!

Inns served meals to their wayfaring guests (the table of the host became the *table d'hôte*, or full meal, on French menus), but there were no eating establishments as such outside Tour d'Argent. Only the *traiteurs*, or caterers, were permitted by law to sell cooked meat to the public, and they sold it only for banquets, cooking whole carcasses. (The words "treat" and "entertain" derive from the French *traiteur*, a word which in France today still means restaurant proprietor.)

The great Paris restaurants of our time—Maxim's, Grand Vefour, Tour d'Argent and Lasserre [22]—are the legacy of a tavernkeeper named Boulanger (who was not a baker, though *boulanger* is French for baker).

M. Boulanger sold soups, which he called "restoratives," or "*restorantes*," at his tavern, an open-all-night place. In defiance of the *traiteurs*' monopoly, he made a "soup" of sheep's feet in a white sauce. The *traiteurs* sued and the case went to the French parliament. Leading gastronomes tasted the dish and said it was not meat. The King himself (Louis XV) took a taste and declared that it should not even

---

[22] The Guide Michelin, a directory published by an automobile tire manufacturer since 1900, rates French restaurants with one star, two stars or three stars. As Joseph Wechsberg writes, "Almost every Frenchman knows his country's celebrated restaurants, just as an American knows his baseball teams . . . The Guide Michelin's annual selection of three-star restaurants is awaited in France with as much suspense as the outcome of the World Series is in the United States." Only the four establishments listed above now carry Michelin's three-star rating in Paris, and in all the world there are but eight other three-star restaurants, all of them in France.

be called food. So Boulanger won his case and was soon serving stews at his place on the rue Bailleul.

In 1782 came a true restaurant,[23] the Grande Taverne de Londres on the rue de Richelieu, opened by one Beauvilliers, steward and chef to Monsieur the Comte de Provence, who became Louis XVIII after the Restoration of 1814 (he was Louis XVI's brother). Beauvilliers catered to the Paris elite whose heads were shortly to roll, and later to their survivors.

Three years before the Revolution, a restaurant called Aux Trois Frères Provençaux opened near the Palais-Royal, though its three proprietors, Messrs. Bathélemy, Maneille and Simon, were neither brothers (they were married to sisters) nor Provençal (they were from Marseilles).

New restaurants mushroomed: Badeleine was known for its fish dishes, the Véry Brothers for their truffled entrees, and Henneveu's both for its good food and, to quote Brillat-Savarin, "mysterious private little rooms on his fourth floor."

It was the beginning of a culinary tradition that led to such gastronomic shrines as the Hôtel de la Côte d'Or in Saulieu, and—holy of holies—the Restaurant de la Pyramide in Vienne. It also began a sociological tradition in which decor, and the haughtiness of head-waiters, has often surpassed the *haute*-ness of the cuisine.

By 1794, the year the Commune guillotined Antoine Lavoisier (who had founded the science of nutrition), Paris had 500 restaurants. The Reign of Terror sent some of the *ancien régime*'s ex-chefs to England, some to other parts of Europe, some even to the New World to open restaurants.

That New World, meantime, had been laying foundations of a culinary tradition all its own.

---

[23] Except for the German *gasthaus*, the Greek *estiatórion* and the Hungarian *étterem*, some version of the word is common to almost every language. A restaurant is a restaurant in French, English, Dutch, Danish, Norwegian and Romanian. In Spanish and Portuguese it has an "e" at the end of it. In Italian it is *ristorante*, in Swedish *restaurang*, in Polish *restauracja*, in Turkish and Serbo-Croatian *restoran*, in Russian *restauran*, in Czech *restaurace* and in Japanese *resutoran*.

⚬⟦ 3 ⟧⚬

Fruited plain,
amber fields of grain

All the traffic in food between New World and Old did not move from west to east.

Livestock and oranges came to America with Columbus. A friar from Grand Canary Island, sent to Santo Domingo as a missionary in 1516, brought with him banana roots, and evidently oats and "English grain" (or "Roman corn," meaning wheat), as well. Others introduced various trees, vegetables, grains, poultry and livestock.

But for the English who came to North America in the early 1600's, the most vital source of food turned out to be the corn of the Indians.

Foremost of those Englishmen was Captain John Smith, who not only founded the Virginia colony but charted the New England coast for later arrivals. The historian Henry Adams launched his career by discrediting Smith, who claimed to have been captured by the Indians [1] and saved by Pocahontas, but later historians have tended

---

[1] Smith also claimed he had fought the Turks at the battle of Red Mountain Pass in about 1601, had been one of the few Christians to survive the slaughter of that Romanian battle, had been sold into slavery and carried east of the Black Sea. "The Tymor and his friends [wrote Smith] fed upon Pillow, which is boyled Rice and Garnancis, with little bits of Mutton or Buckones, which is

to think Smith's wild adventures were more than mere inventions.

Guided by Smith's charts, the pioneers of "Plimouth," as Smith and Governor William Bradford spelled it, found New England teeming with wild game, wild ducks and gamebirds, fresh- and saltwater fish, and shellfish; nuts, roots and berries were everywhere.

But the Pilgrims were not hunters or anglers like Old England's aristocratic sportsmen; they were tradespeople, craftsmen, farmers. They had no fishing tackle or nets, what hooks they had were too large, they used the wrong bait. And they were miserable marksmen.

In time these original Yankees became superb hunters and fishermen. And they learned to slash sugar maples and, in the late 1630's, to cultivate black honeybees, introduced from Italy, for "tree sweetenin' and bee sweetenin'." But in their first years on the cold, bleak shores of Massachusetts Bay, they nearly starved to death.

It was the same in Jamestown, Virginia (founded in 1607 despite the fate of the Roanoke colony of the 1580's), as in the Plymouth Plantation in those grim early years of "The Starving Times."

The Pilgrims in Massachusetts—there were exactly 100 aboard the *Mayflower* when she left Southampton, England, and two more were born on the nine-week voyage—lost half their number to scurvy, starvation and illness in the terrible three months after they landed at Plymouth in December, 1620.

---

rost bits of Horse, Ulgry, or any Beast. Samboses and Muselbits are great dainties, and yet but round pies full of all sorts of flesh chopped, with varietie of Hearbs. Their best drink is Coffa, made of Graine, called Coava, boyled with water and Sherberke, which is onely Hony and Water. Mares Milke, or the Milke of any Beast, they hold restorative; but all the Comminaltie drinke pure Water. Their Bread is made of this Coava, which is a kind of blacke Wheate, and Cuscus a small white seed like Millet in Biskany. Our common victuall, was the Intrals and Offal of Horses and Ulgryes; of this cut in small pieces, they will fill a great Cauldron; which being boyled, and with Cuscus put in great bowles in the manner of Chafing-dishes, they sit about it on the ground; after they have raked it through as oft as they please with their fowle fists, the remainder was for the Christian Slaves." His master, "The Bassa . . . tooke occasion so to beate, spurne and revile him, that Smith forgetting all reason, beate out his braines with his [threshing] bat" and, stealing the master's clothes and horse, found his way back to England. And it may all have been true.

The corn in the cornucopia

What pulled them through was Indian corn, the maize developed through trial and error by Indians from a wild grass native to the highlands of southern Mexico. Corn had been carried north by generations of pre-Columbians.[2]

The colonists found a great store of corn left behind by some Indian tribe which had pulled up stakes and forgotten or forsaken a cache buried underground.

To grow their own corn, the Pilgrims learned agriculture Indian-style, which did not require felling trees or plowing the earth. The Indians simply cut a strip of bark all the way around each tree where they wanted to plant corn. The trees died, so no leaves grew to block the sun. Instead of plowing, the Indians made a few scratches in the soil with pointed sticks and dropped in their seeds (kernels left from the previous harvest). Nobody bothered much about weeds. As for pests, the Indian boys made whistles and hung them on poles; when the wind blew through the whistles, the sound frightened away any birds and mice which might eat the seeds.

From a friendly Indian, the Plymouth colonists learned how to plant corn. "When the oak trees' leaves are as big as mice ears," he said, "plant the kernels of corn. Put a small fish in between them. Round the soil into a little hill."

The fish, probably menhaden, decomposed and fertilized the soil. For forty days after planting, every dog in a plantation went around with one forepaw tied to its neck so it could not dig up the fish. Following the Indian's counsel, the Pilgrims planted four kernels close

---

[2] Pieces of "evidence" are brought forward from time to time to suggest that a handful of Phoenicians blundered into South America thousands of years before Columbus. If this were ever proved beyond doubt, it would invalidate a lot of thinking about some food origins, but thus far the evidence is far from convincing.

together in a circle. Plantings were in small hillocks a yard or more apart, the hillocks running in rows a yard apart.

Barley was planted, too, and did well enough; its harvest went into soups, cereals, bread and beer.

The colonists learned to time their plantings to get three crops of corn a year. Green peas, when planted early enough, grew better than they ever had in England.

Fields planted Indian-style in fact yielded over 200 bushels of food per acre, five times the amount grown in English fields. But it was some years before the harvests were bountiful enough to eliminate hunger. New groups of colonists arrived and had to be supported. In the fall of 1621, thirty-five new people arrived. Some sixty-seven came in 1622 and another large party in 1623. Each new arrival forced the earlier colonists to go on short rations.

In early spring of every year, food stores would be just about exhausted. What vegetables remained in root cellars were wilted or mildewed. It was the period the colonists called "the six weeks' want"; they turned of necessity to native weeds they found growing in the fields: milkweed and pokeweed shoots, marsh marigolds, Jerusalem artichoke roots, common nettles and others (Chapter 6).

The first corn was not ready for months. Several members of the Plymouth Colony were publicly whipped in the summer of 1622 for picking corn and eating it before it was ripe.

This Indian corn quickly became the mainstay of the colonies, both in Virginia and in Massachusetts.

Sir Walter Raleigh's men in Virginia had described the corn the Indians served them as "fair and well-tasted." They no doubt ate it roasted in a campfire's ashes or ground between stones and served in cakes that came to be called johnnycakes.

There were no milking animals in Plymouth until 1624, but a substitute milk was made from corn mixed with juices from boiled hickory nuts and chestnuts; hot or cold, it was "verie good" and must have nourished quite a few babies.

Corn was used in a great number of ways. A kind of sugar was obtained from fresh corn stalks. A porridge called samp, mush, hasty pudding, suppawn or loblolly, depending on where you lived, was made from coarsely ground unparched corn and provided the basis of many early diets.

The Indians taught the settlers to make simple corn breads, like corn pone and ashcake. Both were of corn flour, blended with water and shaped into flat, broad cakes on platters of wood, and then baked in a kind of oven (for corn pone) or in the ashes (ashcake) of a hearthfire. With salt added to the corn meal, the dough was baked on a hoe over an open fire to make hoecake.

Succotash, originally made of corn and kidney beans (today we use lima beans) and perhaps dog meat, all cooked in bear grease, was another Indian dish the Pilgrims adopted. The Narragansett called it *misickquatash.*

First feast of November's last Thursday

Most famous of early colonial meals was, of course, the Thanksgiving dinner shared by the Pilgrims with Massasoit and his tribe in 1621.

The chief dish, as everyone must know, was roast native turkey. On that memorable occasion in 1621, four men killed enough turkeys in a day to keep the company well-fed for almost a week. And those rugged colonists could eat! Their food was brought to the table on large wooden serving platters called trenchers; each diner had a smaller trencher of his own, hence the word "trencherman," meaning a hearty eater.

The first Thanksgiving dinner was really a breakfast. It ended with a surprise. When the Pilgrims and their ninety-two Indian guests had finished, Chief Massasoit's brother, a brave named Quadequina, disappeared into the woods and returned with a bushel of popped popcorn,[3] a startling novelty to the colonists.

---

[3] Popcorn was a distinct variety of corn, like dent corn or flour corn. It was cultivated by the Incas and used to decorate bodies for burial. Today it is the mainstay of the U.S. film industry. Without the profits of their concession stands, probably half the movie theaters in America would close down. (Movie

In times of abundance, seventeenth-century Americans enjoyed roast venison, roast turkey, fricassee of chicken, beef hash, boiled fish, stuffed cod, pigeons, roast goose stuffed with chestnuts, boiled eel, Indian pudding and succotash (both made of native corn), pumpkin pies, apple tarts and various kinds of vegetables. One colonial dinner might contain all these items and it took quite a trencherman to do justice to the feast. There was no regular order to how he approached the job as meals were not served in courses. Dinner might begin with pie and end with boiled eel, if that was the way someone wanted it.

As in Elizabethan England, prices for food sound astonishingly small: tuppence for a fresh codfish weighing twelve pounds, ninepence for a quarter of deer venison that would feed a large family for a week; a small turkey for a shilling. But a few shillings was the going wage for a hard day's work, so the prices were not really low at all.

A new food for the colonists was wild rice, which is not a true rice but rather the seed of a tall aquatic grass (*Zizania aquatica*) native to both North America and to Asia. It was an important food for the Indians—Sioux and Chippewa (Ojibway) braves fought over good stands of wild rice in what is now Northern Minnesota, which produces two-thirds of the world's crop.

True rice came from Madagascar, off the coast of South Africa. One of the founders of South Carolina, Dr. Henry Woodward, was given a small bag of rice by a sea captain back from an East Africa port in 1671. Dr. Woodward planted it in his garden where it thrived, but he didn't know how to clean it for use, and neither did anyone else, so for some years rice remained a garden curiosity. When the

---

exhibitors would rather run a John Wayne or Walt Disney movie, or a revival of *Gone with the Wind,* than an art movie: there will be more popcorn eaters in the audience.) Popcorn makers used to expand a kernel of popcorn fifteen times its original size; now they puff a kernel to forty times its size and even more, so a quart-size cup of popcorn, chewed with eyes glued to the Technicolor Cinerama screen, contains only about an ounce of corn. Popcorn consumption has doubled in the last ten years and now stands at 2.2 pounds per capita each year. The product has been made more tender, the hull content has been reduced and, even more than before, it is mostly air.

South Carolinians finally learned how to husk rice and prepare it for eating, rice became the state's principal crop; it did not yield that supremacy to cotton until the 1800's. (Today, with huge mechanized rice farms in Arkansas and Texas, the U.S. is a major rice exporter.)

Coffee, tea or milk? Or cider?

Apple seedlings were brought to Massachusetts by English colonists ten years after the Pilgrims landed. Apples were eaten raw and baked into pies. But their biggest importance was for cider.

Few people drank milk; it was generally viewed as a hazard. And it probably was. All milk was produced and sold under conditions we would now consider shockingly unsanitary (pasteurization and hygienic dairy food laws came much later); it was peddled from house to house in open buckets at a penny a quart.

In the rural South and Midwest, a disease called milk sickness, or "the milksick," was not uncommon even in the nineteenth century (the last recorded case was in 1938). Also known as the slows or the trembles, it came from drinking milk (or eating meat) from cows that had grazed on white snakeroot. Abraham Lincoln's mother died of the milksick.

Beer was also popular in the colonies. Even children drank it with their meals—breakfast, lunch and dinner—until about 1825.

But cider was the national beverage—not only apple cider, but pear cider (called "perry") and peach cider ("peachy").

As early as 1671, one orchard alone grew enough apples to make 500 hogsheads of cider. A single village of forty families in the 1720's made 3000 barrels of cider. Cider was cheap (about 3 shillings a barrel); it was plentiful; and it hardened into an intoxicating drink that fitted a hard-drinking society's needs (New Englanders sometimes mixed it with rum to make "Stonewall").

Before apples were pressed for juice, they went through a mill which chopped and bruised them into a pomace, or "cheese." This increased the sugar content and yielded a richer cider. The fermented juice contained from a half of one per cent to eight per cent alcohol.

Modern cider mills cannot legally sell anything alcoholic, so the apple juice they press, unless it is sold to a distiller to be made into cider brandy, or applejack, is usually pasteurized or dosed with preservatives to keep it from fermenting beyond a certain point. It is not, by English definition, cider at all, but merely apple juice.

Partly as a result of temperance pressures, which gathered force in America in the 1850's, our national drink today is coffee.

Coffee houses first appeared in colonial America about 1670, when Boston gave one Dorothy Jones a license to sell "Coffe and chuchaletto." Coffee houses were springing up in London then, too, and the colonists took their cues from London.

The word café, which means coffee in French, Spanish and Portuguese, derives from the old coffee house, though it is now used to denote a small restaurant or bar. In many unworldly parts of the U.S., the word is commonly pronounced to rhyme with safe, or waif (as Cairo is pronounced in Illinois to rhyme with faro, and Calais, in Maine, as if it were "callous"). Another word derived from coffee is "cafeteria," a combination of "café," meaning coffee, and "teria," meaning shop.

Hot chocolate, or "chuchaletto," was for years more popular in the colonies than coffee or tea.

Tea was introduced as early as 1690, when Daniel Vernon and Benjamin Harris were granted a license to sell it "in publique" in Boston. But even before it was taxed, tea was for years far too costly for the average colonial householder. (In Salem, the cooked tea leaves were salted, buttered and eaten on bread; the tea, boiled till it was strong and bitter, was drunk without sugar or milk, which might have turned any woman into a witch).

Wealthier colonists did drink tea in the eighteenth century, but oppressive taxes imposed by the Crown made the drink impossibly expensive and led, in December, 1773, to the Boston Tea Party and a boycott [4] of tea that was at least as effective in Virginia as it was in Massachusetts. In Boston, patriots gathered at the Union Street coffee house; tea became a dirty word.

In the War of Independence and thereafter, America's Tories, loyal to the English Crown, fled to Canada, where today tea is slightly more popular than coffee. (Canadians average three pounds of tea per capita each year, six times the U.S. average.)

In the years after the War, Boston drank, and still drinks, more tea than New York, which was Nieuw Amsterdam until Charles II's fleet sailed into its harbor in 1664. (England took formal possession of New Netherlands three years later when, in the Peace of Breda, it gave up all claims to the Spice Islands.)

Tea continued to outsell coffee throughout most of the nineteenth century in the United States. It was a retail tea store, opened by George H. Hartford in New York's Vesey Street in 1859, that led to the Great Atlantic and Pacific Tea Company, the A&P whose nearly 5000 retail grocery stores and supermarkets now comprise the nation's largest chain of food stores. [5]

What gave coffee its big boost in the U.S. was national Prohibition, imposed by the Volstead Act of 1919.

As Frederick Lewis Allen noted in *Only Yesterday*, food prices

---

[4] In eighteenth-century England, as well as in the colonies, tea taxes were offensive and people boycotted East India Company tea, often smuggling in untaxed tea from the Netherlands. The word boycott was not coined until a century later, in 1880, when Captain Charles Cunningham Boycott, in Ireland, refused to accept rents at the figures set by his tenant farmers. The tenants threatened Boycott's life, intercepted his mail, interfered with his food supplies. The Ulster Orangemen finally got in Captain Boycott's crops, but it took 900 soldiers to protect them. The boycott was part of the "Plan of Campaign" of the Irish Nationalist movement; the term "boycott" soon came into common usage to mean refusal, and inciting refusal by others, to have dealings with anyone as a means of bringing pressure.

[5] Hartford, a live-wire from Augusta, Maine, persuaded his boss, George F. Gilman, another down-easter, to give up the hide and leather business and go into tea. The partnership bought their tea directly at dockside, buying it by the clipper shipload and selling it at one-third the price other merchants charged. Their 31 Vesey Street store had flaked gold letters on a Chinese vermilion background, a color scheme still employed on A&P store fronts.

had skyrocketed in the five years from 1914 to 1919. Milk had gone from nine cents a quart to fifteen cents, sirloin steak from thirty-two cents a pound to sixty-one cents, fresh eggs from thirty-four cents a dozen to sixty-two cents. But for millions of Americans the unkindest cut was the Volstead Act.

You could still buy a cup of coffee for a nickel, and the ban on the sale of alcoholic beverages, which lasted until 1933, led millions to drink coffee, a drink that certainly does not have the same effects as alcohol, though it is not without physiological effects of its own (Chapter 8).

Until World War I, Europe had imported more than half the world's production of coffee. By 1934, the U.S. was importing about half, and six years later, with Europe at war, U.S. imports accounted for more than seventy per cent of the world crop. We still import about seventy per cent, most of it Brazil Santos, Colombia MAMS, El Salvador Central Standard, Guatemala Prime Washed and Mexican Prime Washed coffees. We also import Djimmas UGQ from Ethiopia, Ambriz No. 2AA from Portuguese West Africa, W&C No. 10 from Uganda and some coffees from Kenya, Hawaii, Jamaica, Haiti and elsewhere. Coffee is our single largest import of any kind.

Before World War I, average per capita consumption of coffee in the U.S. was only nine pounds a year. In the 1930's it was up to thirteen pounds; in 1941 it reached 15.7 pounds. The figure has fluctuated between 14.6 and 15.9 in the past decade, which is low compared to figures for Scandinavian countries (Swedes use close to thirty pounds of coffee per person a year) but much higher than figures for coffee consumption in most other countries.

We use only half a pound of tea per person a year; most tea consumption is in New England and the mid-Atlantic states, though a lot of tea is served iced in the South in summer. While the English drink five cups of tea to every cup of coffee, we drink twenty-five cups of coffee to every cup of tea. We make coffee in coffee pots and in saucepans, in drip pots, vacuum-type coffeemakers and in percolators. And because we do not measure both the coffee and the water accurately, or we do not time the coffee making carefully, or we do not keep the coffeemaker clean, or we boil the coffee, or overheat it, or do not serve it quickly enough after making it—or because of the poor quality of the chemically-treated water we use to make it— we drink a great deal of quite gruesome coffee.

As coffee and other beverages eclipsed cider in America, apple butter, a colonial invention, practically disappeared except as an antique curiosity. It took a bushel of peeled and quartered apples, a gallon of cider, three pounds of sugar, one eighth of a cup of allspice, a quarter cup of cloves, a half cup of cinnamon and seven or eight cups of continual stirring to make two gallons of apple butter. The J.M. Smucker Company of Orville, Ohio, biggest jelly and jam maker in the U.S. today, began by pressing apple butter in 1897.

Tree sugar and beaver tail

Some of the sugar used to sweeten coffee and to make apple butter was maple sugar, whose manufacture from the sap of sugar maple and black maple trees was one of the arts learned from the Indians. For while sugar cane thrived in the fetid lowlands of the Gulf Coast, maple sugar and bees' honey sweetened the bitter hardships of most seventeenth- and eighteenth-century Americans. The amount of maple sugar and syrup produced 200 years ago was four times the amount we produce today, even with all the population growth since those colonial days.

The French salesman-surveyor-explorer-farmer, St. John de Crève-coeur, who settled on a farm in New York late in 1769, described the production of tree sugar:

> In clearing his farm, my father very prudently saved all the maple trees he found, which fortunately are all placed together in the middle of our woodland . . . The common method [of tapping sugar maples] is to notch them with an axe. This operation, after a few years, destroys the tree entirely. That which my father followed is much easier and gives these trees wounds which are

almost imperceptible. The best time to make this sugar is between the months of March and April, according to the season. There must be snow on the ground, and it must freeze at night and thaw in the day. These three circumstances are absolutely requisite to make the sap run in abundance. . . . I previously provide myself with as many trays as I have trees. These I bore with a large gimlet. I then fix a pile made of elder, through which the sap runs into the trays. From them it is carried into the boiler, which is already fixed on the fire. If the evaporation is slow, we are provided with barrels to receive it. In a little time it becomes of the consistency of syrup. Then it is put into another vessel and made to granulate. . . . When the trees have ceased to run, we stop the holes with pegs made of the same wood. We cut them close to the bark, and in a little time the cicatrix becomes imperceptible. By these simple means our trees will afford sugar for a long time. They will run every year, according to the seasons, from six to fifteen days, until their buds fill. They do not yield every year the same quantity, but as I regularly bleed two hundred trees, which are all I have, I have commonly received six barrels of sap in twenty-four hours, which have yielded me from twelve to eighteen [pounds of sugar].

Farmer de Crèvecoeur noted that he also made sugar several times "with the sap of birch; though it seldom runs in any quantity, it is sweeter, richer, and makes stronger sugar. These trees, however, are so rare among us that they are never made use of for that purpose."

Maple trees, he might have added, take forty to fifty years to reach full production, one reason there has never been much selective breeding of sugar trees to increase their yields. One hole in a sugar maple at sugaring-off time (usually March) generally yields about fifteen gallons of sap; it takes thirty-five to forty gallons of sap, sometimes a bit more, boiled for hours, to produce one gallon of syrup. Cooked longer, the syrup crystallizes into sugar.

Until 1860, maple sugar was cheaper than white sugar in most of America, but in Vermont it remained cheaper much longer. Dorothy Canfield Fisher in her *Vermont Tradition* recalls being sent down as a child to her family's "treasure-packed cellar . . . with an old chisel and hammer, to chip off a week's supply of sweetenin' from the big barrel of dark crystallized maple sugar (white sugar was for company)."

Now maple sugar is many times costlier than white sugar, though a "reverse osmosis" method of making syrup, cheaper because it eliminates boiling sap, was tried successfully a few years ago and may lower the cost of both maple syrup and maple sugar.

About thirty-seven per cent of maple syrup and sugar is produced in New England today, one-third in New York State, the rest in less traditional states, mainly Ohio, Pennsylvania and Wisconsin. More than any other agricultural product, maple tree sweetening is retailed by its producers, who sell it at roadside stands and by mail order.

Along with the useful arts they learned from the Indians, the colonists learned wasteful habits.

Once they improved their shooting eyes, they found game meat plentiful. Rabbit, squirrel, bear and venison were everywhere for the taking with matchlock or, later, flintlock musket. But pioneer hunters often took the hide of a slain deer and left the carcass where it lay. No good way existed to keep the meat from spoiling in warm weather; salting, smoking and pickling kept it edible for just so long.

Some game was eaten only in winter, when other meat was not available. Though beaver pelts were the basic item of commerce [6] and a medium of exchange on the northern frontier, most people did not consider beaver very palatable. Some early Americans did eat beaver, as is evidenced by a notation in the secret diary kept by William Byrd of Westover, Virginia, who on February 20, 1712, "ate some beaver for dinner at the Governor's" in Williamsburg, capital of the Virginia colony.

In some early settlements, as at the trading posts of the Northwest, properly cooked beaver tail was a delicacy. The Earl of Southesk

---

[6] A Vermonter, George Perkins Marsh, who was probably the first ecologist, published a book, *Men and Nature*, in 1864 in which he related the invention of the silk hat in Paris to the comeback of the beaver in North America and the consequent creation of many small lakes and ponds by beaver dams. Before the silk hat, beaver pelts had been in great demand as a source of hat material and the beaver was almost wiped out.

supped on beaver tail at Edmonton, now capital of Alberta Province, in the latter part of the eighteenth century and reported it "tasted like fat pork sandwiched [7] between layers of finnan haddock."

The colonists used bear fat in place of olive oil; they cooked wild-cat and moose nose, pork cracklings made from connective tissue squeezed dry, and hams, bacons and pork shoulders smoked over hickory, sassafras, hard maple or corncob fires in little smokehouses.

The onions, parsnips, turnips and cabbages in colonial gardens helped ward off scurvy, though that was always a problem.

Baked specialties the colonists developed are still American classics. Biscuits, for example—little dough cakes, kneaded and baked in half an hour. On many menus they took the place of bread. What the English call "biscuits," we call cookies [8]—our own biscuits (the English

---

[7] "Sandwiched" must have been quite a hip word at the time. It derived from the contemporary (1718–92) John Montagu, fourth Earl of Sandwich, whose name is still applied to almost anything eaten between two slices of bread, toast, roll or bun.

[8] The difference between English and American English is nowhere better illustrated than in our differing terms for food and things pertaining to food.

English measures, liquid and dry, are larger than their American counter-parts: one British teaspoonful equals one and a half American teaspoons; one British dessert spoonful equals one U.S. tablespoon (and an English table-spoonful equals *two* U.S. tablespoons). A teacupful in England means half an American measuring cupful plus two tablespoons (American tablespoons); a breakfast cupful in England is equal to one and a quarter cups American.

The different food words we use suggest we speak different languages:

English English	*American English*
larder	pantry
sugar basin	sugar bowl
caster (or castor) sugar	granulated white sugar
demerara	dark brown sugar
loaf sugar	lump sugar
grilled	broiled
rump	sirloin
undercut or fillet	tenderloin
sirloin	porterhouse
offals	liver, kidneys, tongue, heart, etc.
kipper	smoked herring
tunny	tuna

would call them scones or tea cakes) are purely American, and our word "cookies" comes from the Dutch *koekjes* baked in colonial Nieuw Amsterdam.

The all-American grain

Nothing the colonists grew or cooked or ate was more truly American than the native corn and the many dishes it made.

Where the outer layer of other grains is removed by milling, the bran and the oil-rich germ of corn kernels was soaked off in a weak wood lye solution or crushed and sifted in a hulling machine. The horny, starchy part of the kernel that remained was washed and boiled until it was tender. It was called hominy—lye hominy or pearl hominy, depending on how it was made—from an Algonquin Indian word, *tackhummin*, meaning to grind corn or, more literally, to beat berry or fruit.

English English	American English
porridge	oatmeal
bramble	blackberry
dried currant	raisin
French bean	string bean or snap bean
treacle	molasses
Swede	rutabaga
monkey nut or groundnut	peanut
spring onions	scallions
endive	chicory
courgettes	zucchini
gammon	ham
mince	hash
crisp	potato chip
chips	French fries
shape	moulded pudding
made mustard	prepared mustard
vegetable marrow	squash (which in England means a noncarbonated soft drink, usually lemon or orange)
tin	can
greased paper	waxed paper

Hominy was often ground into grits—fragments slightly coarser than corn meal (which was made by grinding the entire kernel to produce "old-style" corn meal, or by grinding just the endosperm to produce "new-style" corn meal)—and eaten for breakfast with butter and milk, or made into breads and puddings. Hominy grits became a traditional Southern dish. Snow-white hominy was eaten with lumps of butter buried in it.

Another time-honored Southern use of corn was in hush puppies, bits of corn-meal batter fried in a fish pan. According to legend, these were fed to the hounds who yelped when they caught scent of their masters' fish frying for dinner. The men tossed the bits of fried corn meal to the dogs to hush them.

The corn of the settlers was not the sweet corn whose tender ears grace our tables today, and even now little of the corn our farmers grow is sweet corn. Most is what countryfolk call cow corn, or field corn; it may serve as a vegetable before it gets ripe and hard, but its chief use is to feed livestock and poultry, or to make corn meal, corn cereals, corn oil, corn syrup and cornstarch.

Until hybrid corn was developed in the 1920's, the corn grown in the U.S. corn belt (Iowa, Illinois, Indiana, Kansas, Minnesota, Missouri, Nebraska and Ohio) was dent corn, with orange, yellow, red [9] or white kernels, each with a dent or dimple in its top, that were larger than any other corn kernels; the ears were larger, too.

Farmers in the Northeast grew flint corn with hard, smooth kernels of golden-yellow, deep red or even blue.

But the corn the Indians grew was mostly soft flour corn, its kernels generally white, and this was the corn the Pilgrims grew; it continued to be the major variety in the South until hybrid corn.

Sweet corn was quite unknown until 1779, when Richard Bagnal, an officer in General John Sullivan's expedition against the Iroquois, found it grown by Indians along the Susquehanna River in western New York. Bagnal carried seeds of it back East, but it was not until

---

[9] At a corn husking bee, finding a red ear allowed a man to claim a kiss from any girl of his choice, "apparently a modification," as J.C. Furnas decorously puts it, "of a much less decorous Iroquois custom."

the 1850's that sweet corn began to replace field corn on American tables. It is still practically unknown in Europe, where great quantities of maize are grown, especially in Russia and Romania.

Recent research has revealed that sweet corn was grown in Peru in prehistoric times, and that a number of North American Indian tribes grew it, among them the Hidatasa, Iroquois, Mandan, Omaha, Pawnee and Ponca. But the first published mention of sweet corn was in 1801, and it did not come into wide use until shortly after the Civil War. Even today only a tiny fraction of America's total corn crop is the sweet corn we eat off the cob, out of cans, in corn fritters and in succotash.

Jeffersonian cuisine

For all its inventiveness, American cooking tended to be crude and provincial.

One who tried to make it more cosmopolitan by his example was our third president, Thomas Jefferson. He also had an influence on our early agriculture.

In Italy, where he traveled on diplomatic missions before his election to the presidency, Jefferson watched the making of Parmesan cheese at Parma. He smuggled rice that would grow in dry fields out of the Piedmont, this at a time when exporting the rice was forbidden on pain of death; Jefferson carried some grains in his pockets and introduced the rice to the Carolinas in 1787.

The Sage of Monticello imported Calcutta hogs. He came home from Europe with a waffle iron he had bought after tasting waffles in Holland.

He was the first to serve Neapolitan "maccaroni" (which was really spaghetti) at a formal dinner in America, and he was probably the first to serve "French fries" with beefsteak.

When he served French wines at the White House, he received a storm of abuse; Patrick Henry complained indignantly that the President "abjured his native victuals."

He did entertain on a grand scale, even when short of funds, serving elaborate meals ("sinful feasts," he called them) with as many as thirteen desserts, including macaroons, blancmange, meringues, *biscuits de savoye* and ice cream. Jefferson learned to make ice cream in France (he wrote the recipe down in his own hand) and he was one of the first to serve ice cream at a state banquet. On one occasion at the White House he served a crisp hot pastry with a center of frozen ice cream, a dish in later years called Baked Alaska.

Jefferson spent more than $2000 a year for imported wines, a big sum today and a much bigger one then. But he was equally enthusiastic about his "native victuals": Vermont maple sugar and Illinois "paccans," for example. Nor did he entirely give up Virginia ham and beaten biscuits; he just supplemented them with the good things prepared by his French chef, Julien Lemaire, often from items obtained by the U.S. chargé d'affaires in Paris or by Jefferson's maître d'hôtel—items like good vinegar, olive oil, anchovies, raisins, almonds, mustard, macaroni, Marseilles figs, Parmesan cheese and vanilla.

At his death, the author of the Declaration of Independence was $40,000 in debt.

A nation of trenchermen

Few of Jefferson's countrymen ate so well in the early years of the Republic. A particularly dim view of U.S. cuisine was given by Constantin François Chasseboeuf, Comte de Volney, whose *Tableau du climat et du sol des Etats-Unis d'Amérique*, published in Paris in 1803, was quoted by Benjamin Franklin in *Poor Richard's Almanac* and, later, by Henry Adams in his *History of the United States.*

> I will venture to say [wrote Volney] that if a prize were proposed for the scheme of a regimen most calculated to injure the stomach, the teeth, and the health in general, no better could be invented than that of the Americans. In the morning at breakfast, they deluge their stomach [sic] with a quart of hot water, impregnated with tea, or so slightly with coffee that it is mere

colored water; and they swallow, almost without chewing, hot bread, half baked, toast soaked in butter, cheese of the fattest kind, slices of salt or hung beef, ham, etc., all of which are nearly insoluble. At dinner they have boiled pastes under the name of puddings, and the fattest are deemed the most delicious; all their sauces, even for roast beef, are melted butter; their turnips and potatoes swim in hog's lard, butter or fat; under the name of pie or pumpkin, their pastry is nothing but a greasy paste, never sufficiently baked. To digest these viscous substances they take tea almost instantly after dinner, making it so strong that it is absolutely bitter to the taste, in which state it affects the nerves so powerfully that even the English find it brings on a more obstinate restlessness than coffee. Supper again introduces salt meats or oysters. As Chastellux says, the whole day passes in heaping indigestions on one another; and to give tone to the poor, relaxed and wearied stomach, they drink Madeira, rum, French brandy, gin, or malt spirits, which complete the ruin of the nervous system.

You did not have to be French to scorn American cooking. The American novelist James Fenimore Cooper was no less severe in his criticism:

The Americans [he wrote] are the grossest feeders of any civilized nation known. As a nation, their food is heavy, coarse, and indigestible, while it is taken in the least artificial forms that cookery will allow. The predominance of grease in the American kitchen, coupled with the habits of hearty eating, and of constant expectoration, are the causes of the diseases of the stomach which are so common in America.

In much of America, the staple meat was salt pork. A Southern frontier wife in Cooper's novel, The Chainbearer, called pork "the staff of life." "I hold a family to be in a desperate way," she said, "when the mother can see the bottom of the pork barrel."

The term "pork barrel" became American slang for a federal government appropriation secured by an elected official for local improvements to ingratiate himself with the voters. But the pork barrel in its literal sense remained a fixture on the rural scene well into our own century.

Henry Adams had written:

Indian corn was the national crop, and Indian corn was eaten three times a day in another form as salt pork. The rich alone could afford fresh meat. Ice-chests were hardly known. In the country fresh meat could not regularly be got, except in the shape of poultry or game; but the hog cost nothing to keep, and very little to kill and preserve. Thus the ordinary rural American was brought up on salt pork and Indian corn, or rye; and the effect of this diet showed itself in dyspepsia.

Dorothy Canfield Fisher, in Vermont late in the last century, still had, "disagreeable sloppy task for a child—to fish out a slippery chunk of salt pork from the brine in a barrel. It was pleasanter to reach down from its hook a flitch [side] of bacon, or a well-smoked shoulder of pork . . ."

Choicest meat from the hog was ham. There are Danish hams, Polish hams and Westphalian hams from Germany, French Bayonne hams, British York, or Cumberland, hams; there is Tennessee country ham with pickled peaches, Texas ham coated with corn meal, Georgia country ham glazed with sugar coating and champagne sauce, Kentucky ham fried with red gravy, Alabama ham loaf with mustard sauce and Florida ham with cayenne pepper; but Virginia ham from the Tidewater was always something special.

And the greatest prestige as a ham center has always belonged to Smithfield, named no doubt for London's venerable livestock center, called Smithfield even before Shakespeare's day.

Virginia's Smithfield was not founded as a town until 1752, but settlers in the area were exporting hams and bacons to England as early as 1639. Just over two centuries later Queen Victoria placed an order of six hams a week to come from Smithfield, Virginia.

So many imitation Smithfield hams were being sold by 1926 that the Virginia General Assembly was driven to enact a statute specifying that "genuine Smithfield hams [are those] cut from the carcasses of peanut-fed hogs, raised in the peanut-belt of the State of Virginia or the State of North Carolina, and which are cured, treated, smoked and processed in the town of Smithfield, in the State of Virginia."

An English visitor found the food a lot more palatable when he came to America in 1837. Captain Frederick Marryat, the naval officer-landowner-magazine editor-author (he wrote *Mr. Midshipman Easy*), observed:

> The cookery in the United States is exactly what it is and must be everywhere else—in a ratio with the degree of refinement of the population. In the principal cities you will meet with as good cookery in private houses as you will in London, or even Paris.

He noted that "in a new country, pork is more easily raised than any other meat, and the Americans eat a great deal of pork." City streets at the time were full of pigs, but Paul Gates has pointed out that most of the pork slaughtered in New York was shipped to Europe. Pork may have been the major meat in the South and the West (which was what we would now call the Midwest), but New York and New England ate mostly beef. They ate a lot of veal and lamb, too. The meat on American tables was, in fact, abundant in its variations.

> The meat in America [Marryat wrote] is equal to the best in England; Miss Martineau [Harriet Martineau, an Englishwoman who had visited America three years earlier] does indeed say that she never ate good beef during the whole time she was in the country; but she also says that an American stage-coach is the most delightful of all conveyances, and a great many other things, which . . . prove the idiosyncracy of the lady's disposition; . . . there is no accounting for taste. The American markets in the cities are well supplied. I have been in the game market at New York and seen at one time nearly three hundred head of deer, with quantities of bear, raccoons, wild turkeys, geese, ducks, and every variety of bird in countless profusion. Bear I abominate; raccoon is pretty good. The wild turkey is excellent; but the great delicacies in America are the terrapin, and the canvasback ducks. To like the first I consider as rather an acquired taste. I decidedly prefer the turtle, which are to be had in plenty, all the year round; but the canvasback duck is certainly worthy of its reputation.

Captain Marryat just was not describing the same Americans whose fare Cooper and Volney reported. He dined well in the private houses of our major cities, and he was impressed as well by the bill of fare at New York's Astor House and at Delmonico's. The list at the former (*"printed every day,"* Marryat emphasizes with astonishment) is certainly formidable:

ASTOR HOUSE, Wednesday, March 21, 1838

Table d'Hôte

Vermicelli Soup	Salade de Volaille
Boiled Cod Fish and Oysters	Ballon de Mouton au Tomato
" Corn'd Beef	Tête de Veau en Marinade
" Ham	Casserole de Pomme de Terre
" Tongue	garnie
" Turkey and Oysters	Compote de Pigeon
" Chickens and Pork	Rolleau de Veau à la Jardinière
" Leg of Mutton	Côtelettes de Veau Sauté
Oyster Pie	Filet de Mouton Piqué aux Oignons
Cuisse de Poulet Sauce Tomato	Ronde de Boeuf
Poitrine de Veau au Blanc	Roast Chickens
Fricandeau de Veau aux Epinards	" Wild Ducks
Côtelettes de Mouton Panée	" Wild Goose
Macaroni au Parmesan	" Guinea Fowl
Roast Beef	" Brandt
" Pig	Queen Pudding
" Veal	Mince Pie
" Leg of Mutton	Cream Puffs
" Goose	DESSERT
" Turkey	

Melting pot cookery

While many American foods were exported back to Europe, the exchange of recipes, as the French names on the Astor House menu suggest, went almost entirely the other way. Outside of the corn dishes, most American recipes came from the Old World along with the great waves of immigration that began in about 1820 and accelerated in volume for the next century.

Certain dishes became associated with certain cities and regions, not only because of the locally available provender, as in the case of Maine lobsters, but also because of the people who settled in various places.

The geographical distinctions that have existed from one part of American gastronomy to another are fast being blurred by the homogenization of the country through mass marketing, universal communications networks and jet travel. Someday perhaps only historians will remember that scrod and baked beans were originally New England dishes, scrapple a Pennsylvania Dutch dish, and so forth.

In Europe, not only every country but each of the various regions within a small country often has its distinct native specialties.

The United States, which eats the world's best food (as well as some of its worst), has a history not merely of geographic culinary distinctions but of cultural distinctions unique to its polyglot "melting pot" tradition.

The amazing diversity of American foods is based on transfusions from many sources. For example, from Scandinavia we have *knackebrod;* from Asia Minor, Euphrates bread. There are Russian pumpernickels, Polish ryes, Syrian round loaves, Jewish *challehs.*

We have the early Dutch to thank for doughnuts,[10] called "oily cakes" or *olykoeks* in Nieuw Amsterdam. Also introduced by the Dutch were waffles; a new bride in Nieuw Amsterdam was given a waffle iron with her initials and wedding date carved into it. (The fact that Jefferson did not discover waffles until he visited Holland illustrates the cloistered isolation of America's immigrant groups.)

Southern dishes had the benefit of the French touch. Baltimore

---

[10] Doughnuts were traditionally tossed in the air for children to catch on Fat Tuesday (Mardi Gras), the day before Lent began. Even people who know Mardi is French for Tuesday often forget that Mardi Gras has this literal translation, and that "carnival" is from the Old Italian *carnelevare,* which means "taking meat away." Americans have for three centuries fried doughnuts in deep fat, most traditionally on Fat Tuesday, or Shrove Tuesday, or Mardi Gras.

had many French planters who arrived from Hispaniola early in the nineteenth century when Henry Christophe led the slave revolt that established the Republic of Haiti on that island, once the source of half the world's sugar. Charleston, South Carolina, and New Orleans also had Frenchmen, mostly Huguenots.

Baltimore's major food was seafood; the city lay, in the words of native son H. L. Mencken, "very near the immense protein factory of Chesapeake Bay." Writing in the 1940's, Mencken recalled that English travel writers always said of Baltimore that "its indigenous victualry was unsurpassed in the Republic."

> . . . Out of the bay it ate divinely. I well recall the time when prime hard crabs of the channel species, blue in color, at least eight inches in length along the shell and with snow-white meat almost as firm as soap, were hawked in Hollins street of Summer mornings at ten cents a dozen. . . . Soft crabs, of course, were scarcer and harder to snare, and hence higher in price, but not much. More than once, hiding behind my mother's apron, I helped her buy them at the door for two-and-a-twelfth cents apiece. And there blazes in my memory . . . the day when she came home . . . complaining . . . that the fishmongers . . . had begun to *sell* shad roe. Hitherto . . . they had always thrown it in with the fish. [This was in the 1880's.]

While in Maryland there was terrapin soup (terrapin meat, said Mencken, was a man's dish; women did not like it), South Carolina had she-crab soup made with white crab meat and crab eggs. Other Southern specialties included the now much-abused Southern fried chicken, plump (a broiler, say purists, is too scrawny) and fried properly in half an inch of lard, or perhaps peanut oil (but never butter), in a heavy iron skillet. It may be fried with corn meal, maybe, but never with flour or an egg batter, and each piece should be taken out as it is done (some pieces take longer than others).

And then there was spoon bread, which began as Indian porridge, or suppawn (it still has the consistency of a pudding or porridge rather than what we think of as bread). And hot corn breads made from the soft flour corn Southern farmers always used to grow.

Other delights of good old Southern cooking were ham, black-eyed peas, turnip greens, fried catfish, deviled crabs, hot grits, bacon, coquina broth (made from the meat in conch shells), broiled red snapper, hush puppies, hot wheaten biscuits (related to Scottish scones), benne seed cookies (benne seeds are sesame seeds), candied sweet potatoes, relishes, baked bluefish and pompano (a fish Mark Twain called "as delicious as the less criminal forms of sin").

Pecan pie, Lady Baltimore cake and pralines, made of nuts cooked in brown sugar syrup, were traditional Southern desserts.

In New Orleans and its outlying parishes, French traditions mingled with those of Spain, England and the native Indian population to create a distinctive Creole cuisine, a cookery seasoned with thyme, bay leaf and sassafras filé, and based on local crabs, oysters, crayfish, shrimp, ham, salt pork, turkey, squirrel, rabbit, wild duck, okra, rice, and beans.

Pompano *en papillote* was a New Orleans invention. So was the poor-boy sandwich, served on a roll like the hero, the submarine and the grinder enjoyed elsewhere in America.

Exiled from Nova Scotia, the Acadians (of Longfellow's "Evangeline") introduced a Cajun strain to Louisiana's bayou country; combined with Creole cookery, it produced the dish of leftover rice and meat called jambalaya.

On the plains and in the Southwest, the mainstays were beans and chuck-wagon barbecued beef (the word comes either from the French *barbe à queue*, spitted from the whiskers to the tail, or from the Spanish *barbacoa*, the wooden grid on which meat was dried or roasted). Barbecues had been popular in colonial Virginia, where sturgeons and hogs were roasted over live wood coals, and turtles were barbecued in New York in the eighteenth and nineteenth centuries, but beef was the available meat of the West.

The beans, often refried in the Mexican manner, were usually pinto beans, the spotted or mottled variety of the common bean (*Phaseolus vulgaris*) that is sometimes called a kidney bean, navy bean or frijol bean.[11]

---

[11] Not to be confused with the lima bean (*Phaseolus limensis*), the scarlet runner bean (*P. coccineus*), whose thick, starchy root is eaten as well as its seed pods, or the Indian runner bean (*P. multiflorus*), though all are native to the Americas.

With their *frijoles* the Southwesterners ate warm Mexican *tortillas*—flat, very thin bread made of finely ground or powdered corn and used for other Mexican-style dishes like *tacos* and *enchiladas*. *Tacos* are usually fried and eaten warm or cold with a sauce; *enchiladas* are soft *tortillas* made with various fillings and sauces, and folded once or twice. Also popular in the Mexican borderlands were *tamales*, made from a more elaborate dough than *tortillas*. Steamed (usually in dried cornhusks), with or without a pork or poultry filling, *tamales* were eaten, and still are, as meals in themselves; unfilled they serve as bread, sweetened as a dessert, half-sized as appetizers.

These Mexican dishes, older than the Aztecs, acquired "Tex-Mex" versions: Texas *enchiladas*, for example, were richer and blander than Mexican, probably because that is how Texas' large German population liked them.

As for chili (sometimes spelled chile or chilli), there are an estimated sixty-one classified varieties of these peppers in Mexico alone and additional ones in New Mexico and California. Red chilies, except for the sweet red pimiento, are usually used dried; green chilies, and pimientos, are used fresh (though pimiento, imported from the Caribbean, is generally available only in cans or jars).

The commonest dried red chili is the *ancho*, quite large and rather mild. More pungent is the darker (almost brown) *mulato*. Even more pungent is the long, very dark *pasilla*. A very hot chili is the small *chipotle*, which is almost brick red. The tiny *pequin*, or *tepín*, is also very hot; so is the *cascabel*, which is somewhat larger.

Green chilies can be hot, too. Examples are the *serrano*, which is small and not widely available except canned; the larger *jalapeño* (though a deseeded, pickled "Mild Jalapeño" is also sold); the long, yellowish-green *largo*, sold in cans; and the dark green *poblano*. Any hot pepper can be cooled somewhat by removing the seeds, stem and veins and soaking it in cold water to which salt or vinegar (a tablespoon to two cups of water) has been added.

Dale Brown says it was a German in New Braunfels, Texas, who originated modern chili dishes by finding a way, in about 1902, to extract the pulp from chili pods and mix it with the right spices to create chili powder. The German built a successful *chili con carne* canning business in San Antonio. *Con carne* means "with meat." Originally called *carne con chili*, the dish was by some accounts invented by nuns in Mexico, using minced meat, beans and chilies.

Today, Texas has an International Chili Appreciation Society. Aficionados, called "chili heads," have included Will Rogers, who judged a town by the quality of its chili, and Jesse James, who refused to rob a bank in McKinney, Texas, because that is where his favorite chili parlor was located.

If Texas had Germans, Pennsylvania, Ohio and Wisconsin had many more, most of them from the Palatinate in southwest Germany. They settled on rich farmlands much like those they had left behind, and they maintained their old country cookery almost intact, even more so than the Dutch in Michigan, the Scandinavians in Minnesota, the Poles in Chicago or the Czechs in Iowa.

Many food favorites introduced by these immigrants remain part of the American scene. The pork, caraway and garlic sausage called *Kielbasa* by the Poles of Chicago is as distinctive to that city as to Warsaw; few Nebraskans give a thought to the Bohemian origin of the prune, apricot or poppy-seed pastries (*kolaches*) they eat with their coffee.

Every national group once had its particular chow, though assimilation has tended to homogenize American tastes. The word "chow" is pidgin English, imported by the Chinese who built America's western railways. Grant Avenue in San Francisco was the main drag of America's first Chinatown (still the largest center of Oriental population in the country). The inevitable Chinese restaurant in every American city can usually trace its ancestry back to San Francisco. Its inevitably Cantonese menu includes, in "column A" or "column B," Won Ton Soup, Egg Drop Soup, fried egg noodles, chow mein, egg rolls, spare ribs, bamboo shoots, rice, snow peas, hot tea and steamed mixtures of pork, chicken, beef, shrimp and lobster in various degrees of sophistication, all seasoned with soy sauce and monosodium glutamate (Chapter 9).

Fisherman's Wharf in San Francisco comprised the biggest Italian fishing village outside Italy, and still does.

Italian immigrants came chiefly from the south of Italy and were mostly people of small means, so cooking in every Little Italy ran to spaghetti and tomato sauce, garlic and olive oil, minestrone, pizza, spumone and other Neapolitan favorites instead of, say, saffron-flavored rice dishes or *polenta* of corn meal as favored by the better-heeled citizens of Milan, Turin and other northern Italian cities.

Pasta was not very popular until after the turn of the century, mostly because it was not very good. What improved it was, in large measure, the work of Mark Carleton, who introduced Russian durum wheat to make semolina and then campaigned to make macaroni popular. In time, the pasta got better, though most Americans still overcook it.

In time such things as the ham of Parma, known as *prosciutto* (taken from pigs fed on the whey by-product of Parmesan cheese, the one used for veal *parmigiana*) became a popular Italian-American accompaniment to melon. And today Italian restaurants regularly list Florentine dishes (*alla Fiorentina*) made with chopped or puréed spinach; the *lasagne, cannelloni, manicotti* and *tortellini* of Bologna (though the egg noodles for those pasta dishes are not always made fresh each day as in the old country) and Bologna's *bologna* sausage; the *gnocchi* (little dumplings of potato, farina or other flour) of Genoa; and other regional dishes including various salamis (the name may come from the ancient city of Salamis on the coast of Cyprus, destroyed in the fifth century B.C.)—all-pork Genoa and lola salami, the latter heavily-seasoned with garlic, all-pork Calabrese salami, the peppery-hot highly-seasoned pork-and-beef Cotto salami, hot and sweet pepperoni salamis.

Nineteenth-century America clung hard to its Old World cooking traditions; and the new Americans clung to each other. The interchange of cooking ideas was a long time in coming.

Clannishness, based to a considerable extent on distrust of unfamiliar foods, was in some cases based also on religious dietary laws. Orthodox Jews had to employ kosher methods of meat slaughtering (Chapter 4, 7), so Jewish peddlers, the patriarchs of *Our Crowd*, quite often lived vegetarian lives while on the road and ate meat only when they got home or were invited to dinner by fellow Jews in towns and cities along the way.

Many Jews remained vegetarians, and centers of Jewish population like New York City developed scores of lacto-vegetarian, or dairy, restaurants, along with kosher food stores and kosher butcher shops.

Dairy restaurants offered the *mavens* (experts) who patronized them such items as vegetarian chopped liver, made of hard-boiled eggs, onions fried in butter and Protose, a commercially-made combination of wheat protein, peanuts, salt, yeast, water and peanut oil. A vegetarian lamb chop was (and still is, for dairy restaurants are very much alive) made of green peas, carrots and stringbeans. Some dairy restaurants feature Protose steaks and mushroom roasts.

Mushroom and barley soup, made of imported dried mushrooms, (Chapter 7) is a Jewish favorite, as is potato soup. So are cold soups like *borscht*, a purée, hot or cold, of shredded (or finely sliced) beets with thick sour cream; *shav*, made from finely chopped sorrel (or sour grass) blended with sour cream; and fruit soup made of various fruits stewed in their own juices.

Sour cream is ubiquitous; modern Jews say with characteristic self-depreciation that "sour cream has killed more Jews than Hitler."

Jewish comedians on television have made the *bagel*, a hard, doughnut-shaped roll often eaten with cream cheese, familiar to most Americans.

Less well-known are *kasha*, a coarse cereal of buckwheat groats; carrot *tzimmes*, a sweet dish made with diced carrots, fat, salt, sugar, raisins and ginger that is traditional at Rosh ha-Shanah, the Jewish New Year; *falfel*, fried balls of chick-peas mixed with garlic and spices and popular, also, with Arabs; *pirogen*, mashed potatoes wrapped in a boiled or fried dough; *kreplach*, like *pirogen* but smaller and filled with sweetened pot cheese; *blintzes*, made of thin pastry dough filled with pot cheese, potatoes, *kasha* or blueberries; *latkas*, finely riced potatoes mixed with grated onions and fried into pancakes; stuffed derma or *kishka*, which are beef intestines stuffed with flour, onion and chicken fat; and *matzohbrei,* a thick pancake made of crumbled matzoh (unleavened bread) softened with water and mixed with eggs and milk and sometimes seasoned with salt and pepper.

Smoked fish, though older than history, is often identified with Jews. One of the first commercial smoked salmon companies was established in London in 1879; ninety per cent of its trade was with the local Jewish community. Today, smoked salmon from Nova Scotia, or saltier *lox* (Russian for salmon, which in German is *lachs*), is the most universal of luxury foods, served as an hors d'oeuvre at all the best cocktail parties, Jewish and Gentile. But smoked pike, sturgeon, carp and whitefish are also popular in Jewish households. So is *gefilte,* or *gefuelte,* fish, a dumpling stuffed with pike or white-fish ground with onions and spices, poached for several hours and served hot or cold in its own jelly.

An immigrant did not have to be Jewish to have his own pet dishes. Philadelphia, Baltimore, Cincinnati, Milwaukee and St. Louis in the nineteenth century all had a great many Germans, some of them former Hessian mercenaries who had fought for the British in the Revolution. The U.S. received 6.24 million immigrants from Germany, far more than from any other country, in the hundred and thirty years, 1820 to 1950, the peak year of German immigration being 1882. *Sauerbraten,* a pot roast of beef marinated in vinegar, sugar and seasonings, was—and still is—a typical dinner in those cities, along with wurst dishes of all sorts.

And while *knackwurst* (also called *knockwurst, knoblauch* or garlic sausage), *bratwurst* (a pork sausage seasoned with herbs and spices), liverwurst (or *Braunschweiger*[12]), *Thuringer* (a kind of summer sausage, or cervelat), potato dumplings, pretzels and coffee-cake or *schnecken* flourished in German-American kitchens, Austrian-Americans had their *wiener schnitzel* (breaded veal cutlets), their headcheese (scraps of meat in aspic; its German name is *sulze*) and

---

[12] From Braunschweig, or Brunswick, in Germany. Liverwurst is also called leberwurst, liver pudding and liver sausage.

their special pastry shops for ten-layer *Dobosch tortes, Sacher tortes, Pischinger tortes, Pressburger beugels* and other *bäckerei.*

Hungarian- and Bohemian-Americans had their sweet red paprika, their cold cherry soup (*cseresznyelevs*), their beef, veal, lamb or pork goulash (*gulyás*), depending on whether they were from Debrecen or the south or the west of Hungary or from Szeged, which mixed potatoes and sauerkraut with its pork. *Pörköolt*, another Hungarian dish, is not a pork stew but a veal stew with a concentrated paprika sauce.

Hungarians were known, too, for their black peppered *tokány* sauce, their pilsener beer and their *retés*—strudels (the strudel dough stretched so thin you could read a newspaper through it).

When Greek met Greek, they opened a restaurant and served an eggplant casserole called *moussaka*. And *dolmathes*. And *avgole-mono* soup of rice, eggs and lemon juice. To say nothing of feta cheese and black Calamata olives.

Earlier Americans, especially in the lower social orders, resented the foreign foods just as the Elizabethan English had spurned the cuisine of France. The more sophisticated among upper-class Americans quickly accepted French recipes in the Jeffersonian tradition, but the basic Anglo-Saxon stock refused to acquire tastes for new things and scoffed at politicians who made a show of eating *knishes* (mashed potato fried in dough, a Jewish specialty similar to *pirogen*) and corned beef and cabbage (the beef is cured with peppercorns and salt and kept in brine; with cabbage, it is as traditional among Irish-Americans as is "bubble and squeak"—sautéed leftover beef and cabbage—in England).

New England Yankees were particularly unaccepting of "furrin" ideas. Lucy Emerson, in her *New England Cookery* of 1808, said, "Gar-licks, though used by the French, are better adapted to medicine than [to] cookery."

In time, the foreign foods became less foreign. American onions are much milder than Italian onions; American Swiss cheese does not have the strong aroma of Swiss Swiss cheese.

And prejudices against foreign foods became less pronounced.

European cooks and nurses had an influence in introducing growing numbers of growingly-affluent Americans to the dishes of Italy, France, Germany, Ireland, Sweden, Scotland, Poland, the Balkans and Hungary. In the West and Southwest, Chinese and Mexican cooks left their marks.

Some "foreign" dishes had never been known outside the U.S.: Swiss steak, Russian dressing, chop suey, vichyssoise and cioppino, that savory fish stew of San Francisco's Fisherman's Wharf and the Monterey Peninsula—they are all as American as apple pie.

Scrapple was a Pennsylvania Dutch (originally *Deutsch*) invention, a thrifty way to use scraps of pork after the hogs had been slaughtered. While pig intestines were used for sausage casings and pigs' ears and snouts for headcheese, scrapple was made with pork shoulder, pork liver, corn meal, onions, cloves and herbs, all fried in shortening and "wonderful good" in Lancaster County parlance.

"Kissin' wears out, cookery don't," was a Pennsylvania Dutch expression, and some of the dishes of Lancaster, Lebanon, Ephrata, Bird-in-Hand, Blueball and Intercourse are as typical as hex signs: corn pie, wilted lettuce, homemade breads, freshly-churned butter, vegetable pies and the famous shoo-fly pie (a molasses cake baked in a pie shell) and apple pandowdy.

Another Pennsylvania Dutch specialty, an immigrant from the old country (like schmierkäse, or cottage cheese), was sauerkraut. When Robert E. Lee took Chambersburg on his way to Gettysburg, he demanded twenty-five barrels of "Saur-Kraut" for his triumphant Confederates.

Dietary traditions are still strong among what someone has called "hyphenated" Americans. And new arrivals continue to introduce new cookery such as that brought by the Puerto Ricans, who now number close to a million in New York City alone. *Pernil* (leg of pork), *empinadas* (meat fried in bread crumbs), *platanos* (plantain), *yames* (a root vegetable that turns purple when it is cooked), *pulpo* (octopus) and rice and beans are all Puerto Rican specialties. So is the classic Spanish *paella*, that one-dish meal of saffron rice, *chorizo* (Spanish sausage), and *camerones* (shrimp).

In immediate vogue today is "soul food," the current term for a variety of dishes favored by generations of black Americans and Southern whites. While the Pennsylvania Dutch used pig intestines for sausage casings, Southerners used them for chit'lins (an abbreviation of chitterlings). Sometimes called ruffle steak, chit'lins are usually cleaned and then boiled for about four hours with simple seasonings like an onion, celery and a bay leaf. They are served hot with vinegar, a hot sauce, or both. Or they are cooked until fairly tender and then fried.

Other items of soul food are fat back, which is the fat of salt pork with no lean meat on it; collie (collard [13]) greens and turnip greens, commonly served with fat back; pot likker, which is the liquid, rich in vitamins and minerals, from the kettle the collie greens or turnip greens have cooked in; black-eyed peas, a variety of cowpeas brought by slave traders from Africa to Jamaica about 1674; hoppin' John (black-eyed peas and rice cooked in pot likker with a bit of salt pork); whole grain hominy and fine grained hominy grits; candied yams (which are practically always sweet potatoes); sweet potato pies (like those so admired by Henry VIII in sixteenth-century England) and sweet potato biscuits, squirrel and 'possum; [14] fried mush; chicken fried in hog lard; mustard greens; pork chops coated with a mixture of flour, salt and pepper and then fried; pigs' feet (called "trotters") and pigs' knuckles, tails, ears, snouts, necks, backbones and stomachs (called "hog maw"); barbecued spareribs; black walnut pie; and watermelon (including pickled watermelon rind).

While many of these were parts discarded by the white folks on plantations and given to the slaves, only about ten per cent of Southern families ever had slaves. Many items of soul food were popular

---

[13] The name comes from the Anglo-Saxon "colewarts," meaning cabbage plants. Collards are similar to kale; both are cabbage forms older than history.
[14] Fat and tender, a baked opossum can taste almost like suckling pig. The animal, which weighs up to twelve pounds when mature, is native to the Americas. It is the only pouched animal (or marsupial, if you like) outside of Australia, where almost all wild mammals (the exceptions are a rat and the wild dog, or dingo) have pouches to carry their young.

in areas where there were no slaves at all, just as "fat back," under other names, is popular among Balkan peasants and pigs' knuckles are relished by Germans.

Many Negroes will not touch soul food. Chit'lins, even when "tender," are pretty tough; eating them has been compared to chewing on a football bladder. Soul food in general is fatty, overcooked and rather tasteless. The vegetables are often boiled so long they lose most of their taste and nutritive value (the pot likker is frequently thrown away).

Still, the current interest in black culture has given soul food, at least temporarily, a new respectability and wider use. It has also driven up the prices of things like chit'lins, which used to cost as little as seventy-nine cents for a ten-pound container that may now sell for five times that much.

If soul food has melancholy origins, so does Philadelphia Pepper Pot soup. According to one account, it started in the Revolution when a cook at Valley Forge, in the grim winter of 1777–78, was ordered by General Washington to provide a good meal to cheer the ragged troops. With nothing at hand but tripe (a "variety meat" from the first or second division of a cattle or sheep stomach), peppercorns and scraps, the cook improvised a soup and named it after his home town.

Americans did invent purely American dishes, but the U.S. diet reflected always the ethnic pluralism of the American people. And while the cafeteria may not have been a U.S. invention, it served the U.S. population well by enabling people to break a menu down into individual parts which could be reassembled according to their own particular traditions and tastes.

Mustard or catsup?

The hamburger, at least as served in a bun, is a native American idea and a national staple, though its name comes from Hamburg, the German city which once enjoyed a prosperous trade with Russia's

Baltic provinces. The people of those provinces ate shredded raw meat (we now call it steak tartare).

A hamburger was originally called a hamburg-steak; it was served like any other steak, not as a sandwich. By the start of the present century the hamburg-steak had become the hamburger-steak and this soon became simply the hamburger. The suffix "–burger" has since been attached to a great many other foods.

The U.S. hamburger, with or without relish, onion, mustard or catsup, has become so popular that while once it was made from scraps of beef, or from less desirable cuts, now whole carcasses are often butchered solely to keep up with the demand for hamburger. The hamburger is sometimes called a "Wimpy" after a character in the cartoon strip, "Popeye"; the protagonist of the strip wolfed down spinach—and is credited by spinach growers with boosting consumption of that vegetable; his side-kick Wimpy put away hamburger after hamburger, as do millions of real-life Americans. One, Philip Yazdzik, ate seventy-seven at one sitting (in Chicago, in 1955).

Without the bun, a hamburger is often called Salisbury steak. The name does not denote a place of origin; it comes from a Dr. J. H. Salisbury, who sometime about the turn of the century recommended ground steak three times a day for a whole list of ailments.

Hot dogs are just as American, or non-American, as hamburgers. Sausages date back at least to the Romans and the Gauls, who both used ground meat of one or several kinds, seasoned with spices and held together with an outer casing.[15] The name "wiener," often used for a hot dog, suggests a Viennese origin, but the frankfurter is called a frankfurter in Vienna and a wiener in Frankfurt, as if both cities were trying to disclaim it. Some accounts say it came to the U.S. from Frankfurt by way of a Bavarian-American immigrant, Antoine Feuchtwanger, who introduced it to St. Louis in the 1880's. He sold

---

[15] The meat may be pork or beef or a combination of several meats as described on the wrapper. Fresh sausage, like Bratwurst, Brockwurst, pork sausage and Weisswurst, usually must be cooked before you eat it; most smoked sausage, like Kielbasa (Polish for sausage), Berliner-style sausage and frankfurter, requires no cooking, though it will probably taste better if it is at least heated.

hot "franks" with cotton gloves so customers would not burn their fingers.

Some sources credit the introduction to Charles Feltman, another immigrant, who brought back the frankfurter after a visit to his homeland about the turn of the century and opened an establishment in Coney Island, New York. An employee, Nathan Handwerker, broke away from Feltman in 1916 and, with his wife Ida, started Nathan's Famous, Inc., which now calls itself the world's greatest hot dog purveyor.

Harry M. Stevens, a concessionaire at New York's Polo Grounds of fond memory, popularized frankfurters by telling his vendors one chilly day to shout, "Red hots! Get your red hots!" (Stevens is still the major concessionaire at New York and Florida ball parks, race tracks and other sporting arenas.)

But hot dogs were not called hot dogs until 1906, when a cartoonist, T.A. "Tad" Dorgan, showed a dachshund inside an elongated bun. If Dorgan was implying that hot dogs are made of dog meat, it was a canard. Hot dogs (or frankfurters, wieners or bologna) may, according to specifications of the U.S. Department of Agriculture's Consumer and Marketing Service, only be sold as such if they consist of beef, mutton, pork or goat meat, fat, and no more than three and a half per cent of cereal or similar filler.

How much fat? Let's wait until Chapter 11 to examine that and other controversial aspects of the hot dog, which is now such an important part of the national diet; we Americans eat 8.5 *billion* hot dogs a year, nearly 1.5 billion pounds of red hots.

We also eat extraordinary quantities of potato chips, another U.S. classic. Originally called Saratoga Chips, their invention is generally credited to a chef (an American Indian named George Crumb) at Moon's Lake House in Saratoga Springs. An upstate New York spa, Saratoga was especially fashionable in the late nineteenth century.

A fussy patron at the Lake House, the story goes, kept sending his French fried potatoes back to the kitchen, complaining that they were not thin enough. Crumb angrily sliced some potatoes thin as paper, dropped them in boiling fat and sent them out to the guest in a fury. The customer loved the thin, crisp chips and so have millions of people ever since. Fried now typically in cottonseed oil, potato chips have for years been the largest-selling U.S. snack food. Wisely or unwisely, Americans ate about ten pounds of potato chips each in 1969, more than twice as much as in 1957.

Potato chips are called "crisps" in Britain; the chips of fish and chips are really French fries.

Another famous "French" dish isn't French at all. *Crème vichyssoise glacé* or, as it is usually called, vichyssoise (the s's *should* be pronounced) is a cold potato and leek soup topped with chives, an adaptation of France's hot *soupe bonne femme*, though in vichyssoise the potatoes and leeks are puréed, not chopped. But vichyssoise is American; it was invented in 1910 to celebrate the opening of the roof garden at the old Ritz Carlton Hotel on Madison Avenue at 46th Street in New York. Its originator was Louis Diat, whose home town was near Vichy, the French spa, and it was served for the first time to the steel magnate Charles Schwab.

Boston's soup was not vichyssoise but rather clam chowder, which got its name from *la chaudière*, the enormous copper pot of early French coastal villages. Returning fishermen used to toss parts of their catch into *la chaudière* and the community would make a soup to feast the safe return of the men from the sea. The tradition—and the corruption of the word—came to New England by way of French Canada.

New England clam chowder is made of clams, salt pork or bacon, and milk. The runaway success of tomatoes after their long delayed acceptance (Chapter 6), a success which had millions of Americans squirting catsup, or ketchup, on almost everything they ate, led to Manhattan clam chowder, which employs water instead of milk and adds tomatoes. Feelings of loyalty to the New England version have been so strong that the Maine legislature once considered a bill that would have outlawed the mixing of clams and tomatoes.

Baked beans, another Boston contribution to our diet, are older than clam chowder. The Pilgrims found Indian squaws baking beans in 1620. The Indians soaked them first to make them swell and soften their skins, and then baked them overnight with deer fat and an onion in a clay pot stuck in a hole lined with hot stones. Since the Pilgrim women could not, for religious reasons, cook on Sunday, baked beans cooked the night before became a Sunday tradition. Later, when religious laws were less strict, baked beans were a Saturday night special, with pork replacing the deer fat of the Indians and brown sugar and seasonings added.

For years the beans were baked by bakers, who called each Saturday morning, took the family's bean pot to a community oven, usually in the cellar of a neighboring tavern, and returned the baked beans with a bit of brown bread for Saturday supper or Sunday breakfast. Boston became known as Beantown. (The community oven is still a fixture in many European towns, though pick-up and delivery service is not provided.)

Brown bread, served hot and steaming with baked beans, is still typically New England. Another Boston idea is the Parker House roll, most elegant of American dinner rolls. It got its name from The Parker House, a Beantown hostelry established in 1855. Corn bread, still a Southern specialty, long dominated American bread boxes because wheat was a luxury.

Wheat bread began its march to leadership when an American, Oliver Evans, pioneered in grinding flour with "bolting" devices instead of with ancient millstones. Evans' water-driven flour mill, the country's first "automated" factory, was established in 1787. The Evans process was covered by federal patents after 1790 and by 1837, 1200 automatic mills, using Evans' patent or infringing on it, were producing some 2 million barrels of flour a year in states west of the Alleghenies.

While corn, rye and whole wheat doughs will rise only slightly, white bread made of bolted flour can be light and airy, if somewhat deficient in B vitamins. The Hungarian Count Steven Szechenyi produced such a fine, aristocratic white flour in the 1870's that it captured a wide market, and in 1879 the Governor of Minnesota had Hungarian engineers come to Minneapolis to put up rolling mills on which Messrs. Crosby and Washburn established the General Mills Company.

Some Americans survived nicely on corn bread, or on sourdough bread, now associated with the prospectors of California, Alaska and the Yukon. Made of fermented dough, sourdough bread actually goes back to 4000 B.C. and may be the oldest of breads. Columbus had a sourdough started aboard ship when he reached the New World. The gold seekers carried starters (self-perpetuating yeast mixtures combining flour, sugar and water) in starter pots strapped to their backs; they were prepared to make bread anywhere they stopped to stake a claim. When they pulled up stakes and moved on, the sourdough starters and starter pots moved on with them.

Vanilla? Chocolate? Tutti-frutti?

Most of the world thinks of ice cream as an American dish. As we know it, perhaps it is, though the history is muddied by the different concoctions to which the term ice cream has been applied.

Italy had some kind of ice cream by about 1600, maybe earlier, but Italian water ices (*granita*) are not ice cream. Neither are Bavarian creams and other combinations of egg whites and custard that have been called "ice cream." We may love Italian *gelati*, but even *gelati* is a long way from what most Americans think of as ice cream.

It is hard to know exactly what was meant by ice cream in its early American developments. We do know Thomas Jefferson brought an ice cream recipe back from France (where the chef of the Duc de Chartres, by some accounts, invented it in 1774), that George Washington made ice cream, that Mrs. Alexander Hamilton served ice cream and that James Madison's wife, Dolly, made ice cream popular.

By the early 1900's, millions of Americans were eating ice cream in sodas, sundaes and out of bucket freezers. The old pot freezers, in which ice cream ingredients were beaten by hand and then shaken up and down in a pan of ice and salt until frozen, disappeared after 1846, the year Nancy Johnson invented a hand-cranked portable freezer.

Five years later, a milk dealer in Baltimore, Jacob Fussell, set up a large wholesale ice cream business, the first of its kind. The ice cream soda, it is said, was invented at the semicentennial of Philadelphia's Franklin Institute in 1874. And the ice cream cone supposedly came out of the St. Louis fair of 1904.[16]

Widespread use of refrigeration accelerated the use of ice cream and made the U.S. the world's biggest consumer of it. We now eat more than 750 million gallons of it a year, mostly low-grade, factory-packaged ice cream inflated with air, full of additives and artificial flavors, treated with emulsifiers (Appendix) so it will be stiff enough to retain the air, and with stabilizers (Appendix) to prevent the formation of coarse ice crystals. According to FDA standards, which took effect in 1966 after twenty-four years of industry-government wrangling, a gallon of ice cream must weigh at least four-and-a-half pounds. Low-grade ice cream, almost the only kind sold in supermarkets, can have its volume doubled by air, a gallon of mix being inflated to two gallons of ice cream that contains half again as much air as premium ice creams. The premium blends, sold largely in drugstores, confectionery shops and smaller food stores, contain up to 18 per cent butterfat, as against a low of 10 per cent, the federal minimum and the usual content of supermarket ice cream, which is often made with corn syrup instead of sugar, dried eggs instead of fresh, vanillin (Chapter 9) instead of vanilla. Downgraded it may be, but Americans still eat ice cream at the rate of about fifteen quarts a year per person.

The U.S. eating champ

The subject of American food usually brings up the name of Diamond Jim Brady, the railroad equipment salesman of the late nineteenth and early twentieth century who became immortal as the all-time classic trenchermen and *bon vivant*.

---

[16] An ice cream vendor at that centennial of the Louisiana Purchase ran out of dishes, so the story goes. A nearby merchant on the spur of the moment created a cone of the crisp, waferlike pastry known as Zalabia. Cones true to that original one are delicious; variations can taste like cardboard, though some children unaccountably prefer them to "sugar cones."

Brady's appetite and capacity defied belief. He was able to indulge that appetite by virtue of a lavish expense account.

For breakfast, Diamond Jim customarily had a gallon of orange juice (he had several beakers of it at every meal), hominy, eggs, corn bread, muffins, flapjacks, chops, fried potatoes and a beefsteak.

At eleven-thirty in the morning he had a snack: two to three dozen clams and oysters.

He lunched at twelve-thirty: more oysters and clams, two or three deviled crabs, a brace of broiled lobsters, a joint of beef, salad and several kinds of pie. And more orange juice.

An afternoon tea consisted of a platter heaped with seafood, washed down with a few bottles of lemon soda.

Charles Rector's (on Broadway between 43rd and 44th Streets) was a favorite place for dinner (Rector said Brady was the best twenty-five customers he had). A typical dinner for Diamond Jim began with two or three dozen Lynnhaven oysters, each six inches from tip to tail. Maryland dealers saved their choicest oysters for big Jim.

Crabs followed, six of them, eaten claws and all. Then came soup, green turtle soup as a rule, at least two bowls. Diamond Jim was just getting warmed up.

He went on to eat six or seven lobsters, two whole canvasback ducks, two portions of terrapin,[17] a sirloin steak, vegetables and dessert. And when Diamond Jim pointed to a platter of assorted dessert pastries, he did not mean any special one: he meant the whole platter. He followed this delicate repast with a two-pound box of candy.

After dinner, Jim might go to the theater. And after theater, how about a bird and a bottle? Only for Brady it had to be several birds (game birds, shorebirds or wild fowl) and several bottles—not of wine

---

[17] Turtlemeat, usually from the diamondback turtle (*Melaclemys terrapin*) still fairly common from Long Island Sound southward. Peter Matthiessen quotes the New York *Morning Telegraph* of May 7, 1912, as saying the terrapin "was never intended for vulgar palates." So while in some years 90,000 pounds of terrapin were taken from the Chesapeake Bay area alone, wholesaled at prices up to $1 per turtle (and served to customers like Diamond Jim Brady at up to ten times that much), the diamondback turtle species was saved from extinction by terrapin's fading popularity as its price rose.

(Jim Brady was abstemious) but of lemon soda. And maybe a little more orange juice.

His companions were prospective customers for the lightweight portable rail-sizing unit, draft gear, brake rigging, patent couplings and switch stands produced by Manning, Maxwell and Moore, the railroad supply house Brady so colorfully represented. While New York's elite dined at the Waldorf and Fifth Avenue hotels, or at conservative restaurants like Delmonico's and Sherry's, parvenus like Brady stood their out-of-town customers to big feeds at Rector's, Bustanoby's, Shanley's and Woodmanston (he also entertained lavishly at Manhattan Beach and Saratoga).

Diamond Jim lived his high life for years, sometimes in the company of singer-actress Lillian Russell, who matched him plate for plate and who weighed over 200 pounds (her ample charms attracted countless lovers and won her five husbands, including Brady's best friend, Jesse Lewisohn of *Our Crowd*).

Brady finally succumbed to stomach trouble at age fifty-six (Lucius Beebe suggests it was all that orange juice) and died five years later, in April, 1917, at the Shelburne Hotel in Atlantic City. At Johns Hopkins Hospital in Baltimore, a post-mortem showed his stomach was six times as large as any normal man's.

While admittedly a special case, Brady lived in an age of excess, even for a country whose people have historically eaten not wisely but too well. It was the era of the free lunch counter saloon (Brady's father ran one on New York's Lower West Side). Fashionable dinner parties at the turn of the century ran to fifteen or sixteen courses, from raw oysters or clams, to soup, cold hors d'oeuvres, fish, hot hors d'oeuvres, "releves" (substantial dishes like saddle of mutton, roast joint of beef or venison chops), Roman punch, the entrée (poultry, game *en coquille*, cutlets or the like), entremets (dressed vegetables served alone), *rôti* (game), *salade,* cheeses, sweet entremets, *glacés* (ice cream) and dessert cakes or biscuits (in the English sense of the word).

Even at staid Sherry's and Delmonico's, dinner parties sometimes created scandals.

In 1873, Henry Lukemeyer gave a $10,000 dinner at Delmonico's with a thirty-foot oval pond as a centerpiece. In the pond floated swans, four of them, shanghaied out of Brooklyn's Prospect Park under heavy sedation. The drugs wore off during the evening and the swans pecked furiously at each other. It was bedlam.

In December of 1896, Herbert Barnum Seeley, playboy grandson of circusman Phineas T. Barnum, gave a dinner for twenty at Louis Sherry's that was remembered for years as "The Awful Seeley Dinner." What made it "awful" was that Little Egypt, the exotic dancer who had been a sensation at the Columbian Exposition in Chicago in 1893, evidently danced on the table of a private dining room wearing nothing but a pair of black lace stockings and high-heeled slippers.

Sherry's was also the scene of the famous dinner on horseback, given in 1903 by C. K. G. Billings. Guests ate in the saddle, their mounts shod with pads to spare the sodded floor.

A monkey was the guest of honor at a dinner party given in Newport at the villa of Mrs. Stuyvesant Fish. Another millionaire gave a dinner for his dog, which wore a diamond collar worth $15,000.

Diamond Jim Brady, whose diamond set was worth over $87,000 and whose total collection of personal evening jewelry was worth more than $2 million, gave a dinner on the roof of New York's Hoffman House where fifty guests, honoring Jim's race horse Gold Heels, dined from 4 o'clock one afternoon until 9 o'clock the next morning, consuming over 500 bottles of Mumm's champagne along with the food. Counting $60,000 worth of diamond brooches for the ladies and diamond-studded watches for the gentlemen, the party cost Brady $100,000.

At another party, given by the swinging architect Stanford White, the gentlemen present pulled a long satin ribbon attached to a Jack Horner pie, which broke open to reveal a young showgirl clad only in a satin arm band; she danced down the table to Jim Brady, sat in his lap and fed him his dessert while eleven other young lovelies, similarly dressed, came in to minister to the other gentlemen.

The millionaires of Brady's time (the U.S. had over 40,000 millionaires in 1916, while in 1840 there had been fewer than twenty, in

1880 somewhere over 100 and in 1892 just over 4000) splurged shame-
lessly. And tastelessly.

Randolph Guggenheimer, president of New York's Municipal
Council, entertained forty of his Tammany Hall cronies at the Waldorf one February evening at a cost of $250 a plate. Oscar Tschirky
("Oscar of the Waldorf") served the men huge clusters of Hamburg
grapes, which cost $10 a bunch. The guests went on to consume
canapés, oysters, green turtle soup, broiled boned Delaware River
shad, a co. .nbine of larded fowl, a crown roast of mountain sheep
with marron (chestnut) purée. Pausing for a light refreshment of
sherbet flavored wit ·rème de menthe, the politicians resumed. They
put away canvasback duck, terrapin and fresh asparagus, an extravagant rarity then, and tapered off on fresh fruits, vanilla mousse, bon-
bons, walnuts, coffee and 1811 vintage cognac.

As callous as the kings of France to the poverty outside Versailles
(the U.S. had no European-style famines, but in 1892 well over 11
million American families had incomes of less than $400 a year), the
very rich gave "poverty socials" in their glass and marble palaces.
Guests dressed in rags and ate scraps from wooden plates, used newspapers for napkins and drank beer from old tin cans. What good times
they had in those days when the man in the White House (William
Howard Taft) never weighed less than 300 pounds.

The tradition of lavish entertaining continued in the 1920's and
even into the Depression. Star host was Henry Sell, who represented
the William Randolph Hearst newspaper and magazine empire and
was bankrolled by the legendary publisher. Sell, Hearst's editor of
Harper's Bazaar (he ran his own advertising agency on the side), kept
the nearly-bankrupt Waldorf-Astoria and Ritz-Carlton hotels alive
with his sybaritic blasts. He also invented a canned liver pâté which is
still sold under the name of Sell's.

Vanishing Americana

It would be an exaggeration, but only a small one, to say that American history is a history of food.

What brought Columbus to America in the first place was the demand for spices to season Europe's meat. British taxes on tea, sugar and molasses helped trigger the Revolution that won America's independence.

And while the English critic Denis Brogan slights the role of the farmer in America, saying it, "has been almost as important historically as it has been emotionally," the productive farms of the Northern Union were undoubtedly decisive in winning the Civil War which kept the states united. The army of northern Virginia was defeated less by force of arms than by hunger.

Plowed by John Deere's self-polishing plowshare, harvested by Cyrus McCormick's grain reaper, American wheatfields saved Europe from starvation when crops failed there during our Civil War (the U.S. has been exporting wheat ever since).

It was the vast farmlands of America that attracted the immigrants from the Old World, memories of famine years rattling in their heads, who enriched American cookery with everything from Appenzell cheese to Russian Zakouskie.

Early arrivals on American shores found here not merely an abundance of food but a superabundance. It is a sad, even tragic, footnote to history that this superabundance was, in so many of its forms, depleted and in others virtually destroyed.

Consider the wild pigeon (*Ectopistes migratorius*), the wood pigeon or turtledove we now remember as the passenger pigeon, "the most numerous bird [to quote Peter Matthiessen] ever to exist on earth." Jacques Cartier had marveled at the size of pigeon flocks he saw in Canada in the first half of the sixteenth century. Samuel de Champlain, who followed the New England coast south as far as

Cape Cod early in the seventeenth century, shot pigeons for food. The Pilgrims, though they viewed the birds as a menace to crops, especially in 1643, were saved from starvation in 1648 by eating pigeon when crops were poor.

Some estimates place the total number of passenger pigeons in North America at one time as high as 9 billion, twice the number of all land birds in America today. By 1672, John Josselyn observed that "of late they are much diminished, the English taking them with nets." (He also lamented the decline of the wild turkey, "the English and the Indians having now destroyed the breed, so that 'tis very rare to meet with a wild turkie in the woods.")

As late as 1736, you could still buy six pigeons for a penny in Boston, but the great flocks that migrated from the Gulf of Mexico north to Canada were beginning to disappear in the East. Still, there were an estimated 5 billion passenger pigeons in the country at the start of the nineteenth century. John James Audubon, who came to America in 1803, reported that some towns along the Ohio River lived on nothing but passenger pigeon for weeks on end. He saw a man in Pennsylvania kill 500 dozen in a clapnet in one day.[18]

A contemporary ornithologist, the Pennsylvania Scotsman Alexander Wilson, in 1810 reported sighting a flock of pigeons in Kentucky, between Frankfort and the Indiana Territory, which was a mile wide and 240 miles long. He guessed it contained more than 2.23 million birds, enough to consume well over 17 million bushels of mast (acorns and beechnuts, used for hog fodder). Other reports told of flocks which took hours to pass overhead, darkening the skies with their numbers.

Larger than the mourning doves which still exist in small numbers, passenger pigeons were succulent and easy to kill (someone in 1770 had described killing 120 or 130 with one shot of a blunderbuss); they were shipped to city markets by the cartload: 75,000 were sold in New

---

[18] Audubon preferred woodcock to pigeon, and blue-winged teal, he said, was "so tender and savoury . . . it would put . . . the celebrated Canvass-backed Duck in the shade." He once saw a friend kill eighty-four blue-winged teal by pulling both triggers of a double-barreled shotgun.

York in a single day. Farmers fed pigeons to their hogs; the birds could be bought dirt-cheap everywhere. But their natural habitats were destroyed as forests were cleared for farms and fuel and wetlands were drained. In the end, the multitudinous passenger pigeon was exterminated.

By 1848, pigeons were nesting only occasionally in the East; the Massachusetts state legislature that year passed a law to protect the birds from being molested on their nesting grounds. But in Ohio nine years later, a measure to control pigeon shooting was turned down by the state senate after a committee reported:

> The passenger pigeon needs no protection. Wonderfully prolific, having the vast forests of the North as its breeding grounds, traveling hundreds of miles in search of food, it is here to-day and elsewhere tomorrow, and no ordinary destruction can lessen them or be missed from the myriads that are yearly produced.

The view was understandable. In 1871, the pigeons were so numerous that their nesting in the sandy scrub oak barrens of south central Wisconsin occupied 750 square miles; thousands of white and Indian hunters and trappers, some alerted by the newly-invented telegraph, laid the area bare with nets, traps, fire and bird shot, shipping millions of birds to market by rail at a wholesale price of fifteen to twenty-five cents a dozen.

It was no "ordinary destruction"; yet some authorities think the pigeon was wiped out not by wholesale slaughter alone but by some ecological factor, exacerbated by the birds' habit of concentrating in such dense congregations. They may literally have fouled their own nest, much as man himself now seems bent on doing.

A Swiss zoologist, Dr. Vinzenz Ziswiler at the University of Zurich, suggests it may have been a peculiarity of the birds' mating habits that brought them to their end. When only a few thousand of the birds remained, widely scattered across the continent, it was harder for a bird to find a mate; and when a mate was found, something was still lacking: breeding communities had often included hundreds of birds on a single tree, all doing the same thing. Without the stimulus of some neighbors, the passenger pigeon was evidently unable to perform the mating function. Individual pairs were never bred successfully in captivity.

The final mass nesting ever observed was at Petoskey, Michigan, in 1878. The last wild pigeon in Wisconsin was shot in 1899 and a bird killed in Pike County, Ohio, the following year is thought to have been the last wild passenger pigeon ever taken, though a survivor of the extinction survived in the Cincinnati Zoo until 1914.

Another food was lost to Americans when a blight destroyed the native chestnut tree. Chestnuts had for years been used with meats, in cakes and bread, as a base for pudding and turkey stuffing, and just plain roasted. "There is no nut so well protected [by its shell]," Ernest Thompson Seton had said, "and there is no nut in our woods to compare with its food." American chestnuts were even sweeter than European varieties (mostly *Castanea sativa*), those *marrons* of France and *castagnas* of Italy, but the fungus disease *Endothia parasitica* that spread from a Japanese chestnut (*Castanea crenata*) exhibition at the New York Botanical Gardens in 1904 struck down virtually every American chestnut tree (*Castanea dentata*), proceeding at a rate much faster than the Dutch elm blight of our own time.

The loss of the chestnut may have been related to the final passing of the passenger pigeon, for which chestnuts were a basic food, but that bird's numbers were vastly diminished even before 1904.

Along with the passenger pigeon, some other game birds were driven to extinction: the Labrador duck, the Eskimo curlew, the Carolina paraquet, the heath hen. The latter, plentiful once throughout the East, existed even as early as 1839 only on Martha's Vineyard, off the coast of Massachusetts. In 1908, less than sixty of the birds were left, a number which had increased to 2000 by 1916. A fire that spring caught the females on their nests and by 1929 only one heath hen, a male (if it is possible to imagine a male hen!), survived. It was never seen after 1931.

Some of these birds had been staple food items. Many fell victim to overcrowding as millions of acres of marshes in the U.S. and Canada were drained to create croplands, but market hunters hastened the demise of some species. One professional hunter in March of 1821 killed 48,000 migrating golden plover. In the twenty years from 1867 to 1887, one Louisiana "sportsman" shot more than 69,000 snipe, along with several thousand other game birds.

Wild turkeys, once shot almost out of existence by market hunters, have been restocked since World War II and even introduced into new areas of the Middle and Far West. Hungarian partridge and chukar from India have been introduced, too (the "Hun" and the chukar are twice the size of bobwhite quail but smaller than ruffed grouse). But prairie chicken, another one-time food staple, Ross's goose and some species of quail are now considered endangered species, and canvasback duck, that pochard so admired by Captain Marryat and Jim Brady, rarely appears on the tables of any but actual hunters. The same may be said in general of most wild shore birds, upland game birds, quail, rail, woodcock and snipe,[19] though we still have open seasons in many places along the flyways of coots, scaup, brants and other waterfowl, and on many game birds as well. And we still have market hunters, who sell waterfowl at $1.00 to $2.00 per duck to restaurants and clubs.

In some of our great wheat-growing states, however, hunters in the autumn of 1969 were warned not to eat the pheasants and Hungarian partridges they shot; the pheasant season was called off altogether in Canada's Alberta Province. Organic mercury fungicides, used to treat seed wheat and other grains grown on the prairies, had left mercury residues in birds that ate them, residues which exceeded limits considered tolerable for humans.

While the passenger pigeon and some other bird species were extinguished, the American buffalo, or bison (a relative of the yak of Tibet and Siberia), barely managed to avoid extinction, though its decline was inevitable as America filled up with people.

---

[19] That the birds still exist at all can be credited to state conservation laws, some of them dating back to the early 18th century. Some New York counties declared a closed season on heath hens, grouse, quail and turkey as far back as 1708.

"The wildlife wonder of our continent," Stewart Udall has called the buffalo. At the time of the Louisiana Purchase, it is estimated that anywhere from 10 million to 100 million of the animals roamed the grasslands of the Far and not-so-Far West in what Peter Matthiessen says were "almost certainly the greatest animal congregations that ever existed on earth." A herd seen by the Indian fighter Colonel R.I. Dodge in Arkansas in the early 1870's may give the picture:

> From the top of Pawnee Rock I could see from six to ten miles in almost every direction. This whole vast space was covered with Buffalo, looking at a distance like a compact mass.

Poet Vachel Lindsay takes us inside that mass in "The Ghosts of the Buffaloes":

> Buffaloes, buffaloes, thousands abreast,
> A scourge and amazement, they swept to the west.
> With black bobbing noses, with red rolling tongues,
> Coughing forth steam from their leather-wrapped lungs,
> Cows with their calves, bulls big and vain,
> Goring the laggards, shaking the mane,
> Stamping flint feet, flashing moon eyes,
> Pompous and owlish, shaggy and wise.

The Plains Indians had set the prairies afire to drive the buffalo into ambushes; they stampeded the beasts off steep cliffs. But until the white man came with firearms and railroads, little dent was made in the buffalo population.

The big killing began after the Civil War. Market hunters like William "Buffalo Bill" Cody and Wild Bill Hickok wanted the animals for their "red rolling" tongues, considered a delicacy, and for their hides.

Railroad men wanted the buffalo destroyed to supply profitable freight in hides; the animals were wantonly shot by "sportsmen" from the platforms of moving trains.

Cattlemen wanted the buffalo out of the way to provide forage for livestock, though buffalo, according to Udall, is "more succulent by far than the steak of a longhorn steer.[20] The Indians had used the meat, wastefully at first (a redskin, said Colonel Dodge, had "contented himself with nothing but the very choicest portions of animal food,") then desperately ("now, pinched by hunger, [he] eats any and everything. Dogs, wolves, reptiles, half-decomposed horseflesh, even carrion birds, all go to appease the gnawings of his famished stomach.") The white man left the meat for the wolves and vultures; a good hunter brought in more than 1000 hides a year, but no meat except for the tongues.

The Army wanted the buffalo killed precisely to starve out the Plains Indians. Civil War General Phil Sheridan said the market hunters were doing more than the Army to subjugate the Indians. "Let them kill, skin and sell until the buffalo is exterminated," Sheridan told the Texas legislature, "as it is the only way to bring about lasting peace and allow civilization to advance."

A bill to protect the bison, the first measure ever passed by a U.S. Congress to protect a species of wildlife, was vetoed by President Grant in 1875. Grant shared the attitude of the market hunters, who saw themselves as patriots leading the march of progress.

The Union Pacific Railroad, for whom Cody killed 4280 buffalo in twelve months, cut the vast buffalo herd in two. Other lines followed.

> To the plains [writes Durward L. Allen] they brought white hunters and rifles, Dupont powder and Galena lead, Green River knives, tobacco and firewater. They carried tongues and hides, robes and finally bones, to Eastern markets.

Well over a million head were shot each year between 1872 and 1874, the last of the Southern herd falling in 1879 at Buffalo Springs, Texas. The remnants of the Northern herd, cut off from water in

---

[20] Cleophus Griffin, chef at New York City's Explorer's Club, agrees: "Bison is better than beef," he says. "Best roast I ever cooked." Pittari's restaurant in New Orleans serves pan-sautéed buffalo steak; Tommy's Joynt in San Francisco serves buffalo stew. When a beef carcass sold for $300, a buffalo carcass sold for about $500.

North Dakota, were mostly destroyed by white and Cree Indian hunters in 1883.

Stray survivors were rounded up in some cases, though a herd near Lost Park, Colorado, was destroyed for a taxidermist in 1897. By 1900, less than thirty buffalo were left. The species was saved, along with a scattering of prong-horned antelope, Dall sheep, mountain goats (which are really a variety of antelope related to the European chamois), American elk, or wapiti,[21] and bighorn sheep only by circumstance. Some stray bison in Canada and in the Yellowstone Valley of the Wyoming Rockies (where the first effective wildlife sanctuary in America had been established in 1872) escaped the general slaughter.

In 1909, conservationists established the National Bison Refuge, near Moiese, Montana, and today about 15,000 buffalo roam an 18,000-acre range there. The federal government has a 1200-head herd in Oklahoma; a private firm has a herd of 1400 in Wyoming. The total U.S. bison population is over 20,000, up from about 6000 in the early 1950's.

The disappearance of the buffalo did indeed mean starvation for the Indian tribes which had depended on the wild herds. The buffalo had supplied not only the Indians' meat, but also their clothing and tepees (made of buffalo hides), their farming implements (made of buffalo bones) and even their fuel (dried buffalo dung, called "buffalo chips," burned in Indian campfires). Killing the buffalo was part of the genocide that wiped out most of the Apache and the Arapaho, the Arikara and the Cheyenne, the Comanche and the Dakota, the Iowa, the Kansa, the Mandan, the Midatsa, the Omaha, the Osage, the Pawnee and the Ponca. Of those who survived starvation and massacre, most died of cholera or smallpox in the epidemics [22] that swept the prairies.

---

[21] Less lucky was the tule, or valley, elk, smaller than the wapiti, which survives only in captivity, and the Merriam elk, now extinct.

[22] A century earlier, Lord Jeffrey Amherst donated to the freezing Indians of New England blankets that had covered smallpox victims in hospitals. The slaughter of the buffalo was a late stage in the extermination of the noble savage in America.

Meanwhile, in the warm waters of the Atlantic Gulf Stream and the Caribbean, another American food source was being decimated.

The green turtle, so called because its edible fat has a greenish hue, was unknown until Columbus found it. Abundant in colonial times from Massachusetts south to Florida, the turtle, which reaches weights of 500 pounds and more, was a barbecue treat in eighteenth-century New York, a delicacy in England and a staple for the peoples of the West Indies. Georg Borgstrom has called it "the buffalo of the Caribbean"; in these "fish-poor, shark-infested waters," he says, it "played a role equal to that of the buffalo on the North American prairie."

But where once a man could catch 100 green turtles in a day off Cape Hatteras, now this turtle no longer breeds anywhere on the North American mainland. Peter Matthiessen calls the green turtle "one of the few large species to survive the Age of Reptiles"; how much longer it will survive may depend on efforts of people like Archie Carr, a University of Florida zoology professor who has for ten years been studying the sea turtle's habits, and a group which calls itself Mariculture, Limited, that has grown over 20,000 sea turtle hatchlings on the island of Grand Cayman, British West Indies, and hopes to raise them in a prototype sea-farming venture.

Aside from these programs, the turtle is in trouble; an occasional stray is found now and then, but the situation of the green turtle, a creature which inhabited the seas a million years before there were men or buffaloes, is not much better than that of the bison in the late 1890's.

It is late in the day now to ponder the fate of the passenger pigeon, but perhaps there is hope for the sea turtle, if not for the valley elk, the Merriam elk or the bison.

Where the buffalo had roamed, the praire grasslands became the province of farmers and ranchers, many of them completely ignorant of the special demands of operating in arid country. Before long the prairies were over-grazed and over-farmed. Zebulon Pike, of Pike's Peak fame, had found the Indians of the plains growing corn, pumpkins and watermelon on his westward trek of 1806 (the watermelon seeds must have been obtained from colonists), but he had called the high plains "incapable of cultivation," comparing them to "the sandy deserts of Africa."

Major Stephen H. Long, crossing the Nebraska plains fourteen years later, called the region that extended 500 to 600 miles east of the Rockies, "the Great American Desert." It was, he said, "uninhabitable by a people depending upon agriculture for their subsistence."

Such observations had a lot to do with the long delay in settling the plains, though the Kansas-Nebraska Act of 1854 opened lands previously reserved for the Indians, theirs for "as long as grass shall grow and the waters run." The Homestead Act of 1862 and the growth of the railroads (Chapter 8) after the Civil War brought in waves of homesteaders, few of whom knew anything of the importance of grass cover in a dry territory. The sod that held the soil intact was plowed under, barbed wire [23] fenced in the plains, and by 1930 much of the grasslands had deteriorated into the dust bowl celebrated by John Steinbeck in *The Grapes of Wrath.*

Though much of its topsoil has been irretrievably blown away in dust storms, the plains nevertheless became America's breadbasket; most of the corn, pork and wheat products in our diet today come from the plains states that once trembled beneath the pounding hooves of the buffalo.

For all their exploitation of native food resources, Americans by and large have always been well-fed. The quality of our cuisine may have dismayed men like Volney and Cooper, but in most times for most Americans, there has certainly been enough to eat.

How heartily later Americans, at least some Americans at the start of the twentieth century, could eat and did eat can be seen from a description John O'Hara gives in his novel, *A Rage to Live.* On a visit to the Pennsylvania Dutch home of his Yale classmate, Paul Reichelderfer, Sidney Tate is given a chicken-and-waffle supper at a farmer's hotel at which sixty young men and their female compan-

---

[23] Invented in 1873 by Joseph Glidden and Jacob Haish, each of whom had his own patented barb; in later years more than 600 different versions of the "devil's rope" were patented.

ions eat oysters on the half shell, thick chicken noodle soup, stewed chicken, mashed potatoes, candied sweet potatoes, string beans, lima beans, pickled (Harvard?) beets, creamed carrots, squash, endive salad, apple pie, cream pie, several kinds of cake and more waffles than one can easily believe. The women averaged five, but it "was not considered good form for a man to eat fewer than ten waffles, with chicken gravy or maple syrup. Sidney ate fourteen waffles, and Paul ate twenty."

The scene, with variations, has been played countless times in the history of America's amply-endowed middle class. It is still being played, though now with less abandon, less untroubled joy. Today's Americans have calorie-counting computers in .their heads.

"Some books are to be tasted . . ."

We Americans have always been enthusiastic eaters, and sometimes overenthusiastic in our food advertising and labeling. Until the federal Pure Food and Drug Act of 1906 (Chapter 11) clamped a lid on mis-branded and adulterated foods and beverages, the overenthusiasm got quite out of hand. Minced tripe dyed red was sold as deviled ham. Maine herring was labeled "imported French sardines" and put up in fancy boxes with labels in French. North Dakota alone consumed ten times as much "Vermont" maple syrup as the state of Vermont produced.

Worst offenders were the Chicago meat packers. To kill rats in the packing plants, they put out poisoned bread. Sometimes the dead rats, poisoned bread and all, went into the sausage-meat hoppers. And occasionally an employee slipped and fell into a vat of boiling meat-product oddments; by the time his bones were discovered, the rest of him had gone to market as pure lard or even bologna. Such stories hit the newspapers and reduced sales of meat and meat products (a spokesman for the packers told a Congressional committee that sales had fallen by more than half).

What inspired the Pure Food and Drug legislation was less the false labeling and advertising than the revelations of muckrakers, particularly those of the late Upton Sinclair, whose career ended only in November, 1968.

Sinclair's *The Jungle,* serialized in the Socialist press, turned down by five publishers, was finally published by Doubleday, Page and Company in 1905. Its exposure of conditions in the meat-packing industry shocked the nation.

[The carcass] had to pass a government inspector [read one passage], who sat in the doorway and felt of the glands in the neck for tuberculosis. This government inspector did not have the manner of a man who was worked to death; he was apparently not haunted by a fear that the hog might get by him before he had finished his testing. If you were a sociable person, he was quite willing to enter into conversation with you, and to explain to you the deadly nature of the ptomaines [24] which are found in tubercular pork; and while he was talking with you you could hardly be so ungrateful as to notice that a dozen carcasses were passing him untouched.

The Jungle was full of such reportage. Another example:

There were cattle which had been fed on "whiskey malt," the refuse of the breweries, and had become what the men called "steerly"—which means covered with boils. It was a nasty job killing these, for when you plunged your knife into them they would burst and splash foul-smelling stuff into your face; and when a man's sleeves were smeared with blood, and his hands steeped in it, how was he ever to wipe his face, or to clear his eyes so that he could see. It was stuff such as this that made the "embalmed beef" that had killed several times as many United States soldiers as all the bullets of the Spaniards [in the Spanish-American War]; only the army beef, besides, was not fresh canned, it was old stuff that had been lying for years in the cellars.

---

[24] Ptomaine, as Sinclair may or may not have known, is an unscientific term coined in 1870 by an Italian toxicologist for foul-smelling substances produced by decomposing food. Bacterial food poisoning, like staphylococcus infections and food infections, produced by salmonella and streptococcus bacteria, are both common, but there is no such thing as "ptomaine poisoning."

The Jungle had a wide impact, but its sales were small compared to those of cookbooks. Recipe collections have always been best-sellers in America. Someone has said that publishing houses are in business mainly to produce cookbooks; their sales generate the funds to publish all the less profitable books.

Of the top four all-time best-sellers (non-fiction) in the U.S., two have been cookbooks: *The Better Homes and Gardens Cookbook* of 1930 and *Betty Crocker's Picture Cookbook* of 1950. Of the top twenty, five have been cookbooks (add *The Pocket Cookbook*, 1942; Fannie Farmer's *Boston Cooking School Cookbook*, 1896; and *The American Cookbook*, 1939). *Diet and Health*, by one Lulu Hunt Peters, led the 1924 non-fiction list.

Some of the early cookbooks that became standards were really school texts. One was *The Settlement Cookbook* by Mrs. Simon Kander (Lizzie Black), published in Milwaukee in 1901 under the slogan, "The Way to a Man's Heart."

In recent years, large sales have been registered by a variety of crackpot nutrition books and various weight-reducing diet books.

The chief influence on early American cookery was English; and the first cookbook printed in America (in Williamsburg, Virginia, in 1742) was really just the leading cookbook in England at the time, Eliza Smith's *The Compleat Housewife*.

None of the early American cookbooks had recipes for native American foods like cranberries, terrapin, lobster, maple sugar or shad. There were no "receipts" for corn cakes or corn meal puddings.

First to introduce such things as Indian pudding, Indian slapjack (pancakes), johnnycake and pickled watermelon rind was Amelia Simmons in her *American Cookery*, published in Hartford in 1796. The book contained many standard English recipes, including one for that great English favorite, turtle meat, made from the green turtle of the Caribbean.

Today's cookbooks often glorify the traditional American regional specialties whose roots go back to Boston, Charleston, New Orleans, the Midwest, the Southwest and San Francisco. We have a sentimental attachment to those time-honored dishes.

But much of the writing about present-day American food is romantic. The Polyanna prose ignores changes in agriculture, in processing and packaging, in marketing and communications that have tended to standardize American foods. (When did you last eat Creole gumbo or baked beans with molasses and brown bread? Have you ever been to a real clambake or a chuck-wagon barbecue? How often do you go to a New England church supper for "home-cooked" ham and beans?)

The exceptions to standardization are becoming, like articles in an antique shop, rather self-conscious, precious exceptions.

We intend no jeremiad. But some of the aura of wholesome naturalness is disappearing from our menus—the runt potatoes, the wormholed apples. Cookbook authors and food columnists generally avoid any thought that something may have gone out of modern victuals. But even the easy convenience of being able to find almost any kind of food at any time of the year has taken a little of the joy out of eating. There was excitement in tasting the first strawberries of the season, or the first corn; they were occasions that brought people together and made events out of what we now take for granted.

For savory nostalgia, read Thomas Wolfe's description of an American pantry in his novel, *Of Time and the River*.

Everything was there, from the familiar staples of a cook's necessities to every rare and toothsome dainty that the climates and the markets of the earth produce. There was food in cans, and food in tins, and food in crocks, and food in bottles. There were —in addition to such staples of the canning art as corn, tomatoes, beans and peas, pears, plums and peaches, such rarer relishes, as herrings, sardines, olives, pickles, mustard, relishes, anchovies. There were boxes of glacéd crystalline fruits from California, and little wickered jars of sharp-spiced ginger fruit from China: there were expensive jellies green as emerald, red as rubies, smoother than whipped cream, there were fine oils and vinegars in bottles, and jars of pungent relishes of every sort, and boxes of assorted spices. There was everything that one could think of, and everywhere there was evident the same scrubbed and gleaming cleanliness with which the kitchen shone, but here there was as well, that pungent, haunting, spicy odor that pervades the atmosphere of pantries—a haunting and nostalgic fusion of delicious smells whose exact quality it is impossible to define, but which has in it the odors of cinnamon, pepper, cheese, smoked ham, and cloves.

And read his description of the inside of an icebox:

Even as the eye glistened and the mouth began to water at the sight of a noble roast of beef, all crisp and crackly in its cold brown succulence, the attention was diverted to a plump broiled chicken, whose brown and crackly tenderness fairly seemed to beg for the sweet and savory pillage of the tooth. But now a pungent and exciting fragrance would assail the nostrils: it was the smoked pink slices of an Austrian ham—should it be brawny bully beef, now, or the juicy breast of a white tender pullet, or should it be the smoky pungency, the half-nostalgic savor of the Austrian ham? Or that noble dish of green lima beans, now already beautifully congealed in their pervading film of melted butter; or that dish of tender stewed young cucumbers; or those tomato slices, red and thick and ripe, and heavy as a chop; or that dish of cold asparagus, say; or that dish of corn; or, say, one of those musty fragrant, deep-ribbed cantaloupes, chilled to the heart, now, in all their pink-fleshed taste and ripeness; or a round thick slab cut from the red ripe heart of that great watermelon; or a bowl of those red raspberries, most luscious and most rich with sugar, and a bottle of that thick, rich cream which filled one whole compartment of that treasure-chest of gluttony, or . . .

Sic transit. Only an age of large families could support such a display; we'd best not see its like again. We can live without gluttony, but must we lose the individual qualities of the items in that icebox? There used to be more point in saying grace before dinner; nature's bounty inspired genuine awe and gratitude. Somehow the cellophane-wrapped bounty of the supermarket commands less reverence.

The matter is often overstated. The weight of advertising for frozen foods and other convenience foods misleads us into thinking these account for the great bulk of what Americans eat. The facts are otherwise.

Foreigners are struck by the speed with which most Americans wolf their food, by the number of foods served simultaneously on the same plate, by the sweet jellies and conserves served with meats and vegetables, by the great quantities of dairy products on our tables.

But for the most part they can only envy the wide choice of foods available to Americans at relatively low prices.

Government inspection and the laws of the market place generally force U.S. food producers to maintain quality standards. The trouble with government inspectors is that they confine themselves to health considerations. There is a danger that standards of flavor and eating qualities are being allowed to decline, and here the consumer has no recourse but a refusal to buy.

This is not to say that American food commodities have lost their savor in any large over-all way; but in all things, quality is not static: it either rises or falls.

At the head of the world's table?

If we overlook the five per cent of Americans who are chronically hungry (and until recently they *have* been overlooked), the people of the United States are possibly the best-fed people on earth and the best-fed people in history.

The statement has to be qualified. France, Denmark, Uruguay, Canada, Australia, New Zealand and the United Kingdom are all listed ahead of the U.S. in the table of "Estimated Calories and Fat Content of National Average Food Supplies Per Caput" [25] issued by the United Nations' Food and Agricultural Organization. France, Canada, Greece, Hungary, Uruguay and New Zealand are listed ahead of us in the FAO's "Estimated Protein Content of National

---

[25] "So much a head, or per man, would not be *per capita* (any more than it would be '*per men*') but *per caput*," said H.W. Fowler in *A Dictionary of Modern English Usage*. He called the use of *per capita* "a modern blunder, encouraged by some recent dictionaries." The FAO starchily follows Fowler's 1926 rule, though in its bimonthly review *Ceres* it sometimes lapses into the generally accepted, if erroneous, term *per capita*.

Average Food Supplies Per Caput" table. And New Zealand and Uruguay are listed as having higher average animal protein content in their national diets.

We eat more of some things in the U.S. than people eat elsewhere; of some other things we eat less.

Most countries use more cereal per person than we do, whether the cereal be rice, wheat, rye, millet, corn or barley. The Japanese and the Greeks use about twice as much. Most countries eat more potatoes and other starchy foods, though the average Israeli consumes somewhat less.

We eat ten times more meat than the Japanese, but in Uruguay and New Zealand the average person eats more meat than the average American. Our average fish consumption is about three times what it is in Uruguay, but a Greek eats twice as much fish as we do, a Dane eats nearly five times as much and a Japanese six times as much.

An American will eat a lot more vegetables than a Briton or a Scandinavian, but a Frenchman, Spaniard, Italian or Greek will eat a lot more vegetables than an American.

U.S. egg consumption has declined, but it is still somewhat higher than in Britain and a good deal higher than in most countries (though an Israeli eats almost thirty per cent more eggs than an American. He also eats far more fruit, as does almost anyone in a warm country).

U.S. per capita consumption figures tend to conceal the regional differences in American eating. It is, after all, a big country. The average Southerner eats a lot more chicken and fish than the average Northerner or Westerner. He also eats somewhat more pork and eggs than the U.S. average—and about fifteen per cent less beef, turkey, dairy products and animal fats. While the South ranks higher than any other region in its consumption of vegetable oil, fresh vegetables, dry beans and peas and cereal products, it ranks lowest in fresh and processed fruits, processed vegetables, potatoes and sweet potatoes, peanuts and other nuts, and coffee.

Americans in the North Central states, on the other hand, rank highest in their consumption of potatoes and sweet potatoes, lowest in vegetable oil, fresh vegetables and cereal products.

Consumption of fresh fruits and nuts is highest in the West, of processed fruits and vegetables and coffee highest in the Northeast. Westerners rank slightly below average in their consumption of sugar and sweets.

The U.S. still has things to learn from the less well-fed countries, but where Old World eating habits historically influenced our food patterns, the influence is now turning circle; other countries are taking their cues from us. Someone has called it Coca-Colanization.

Not all American foods are processed foods, however, or all food-processing ideas American. Even in France, as Joseph Wechsberg has noted, younger people are adopting "sensible American eating habits, with their emphasis on fruit juice, salads and grilled meat." The latter evidently includes 18,000 Wimpy hamburgers which are sold in Paris every week.

In Japan, where Coca-Cola, introduced in 1961, has recently been attacked for alleged harmful effects on health, especially of children, food processors have developed their own factory-made food products. One is instant noodles (*Sokuseki ramon*) made of wheat, most of it from the U.S. (Japan imports about 250,000 tons of wheat a year). Cooked in lard oil for three or four minutes, the noodles, cut into individual servings, are turned into a hard, dry item that can be stored for months and later prepared in less than five minutes and served piping hot at a cost of about seven cents (twenty-five yen) per serving.

Instant noodles are a Japanese invention, but the idea sounds very American. And at the rate we export such ideas, a large part of the world's food may someday be homogenized, tenderized, pre-cooked, flavor-sealed, flash-dried, quick-frozen, dehydrated, polyunsaturated and ten cents off.

For the world at large, this would be a mixed blessing. And not every blessing can be made from a mix.

Again, the matter is too often hyperbolized. Processed foods are often very good. And they are not the whole story of the U.S. food scene by any means.

To appreciate American food, one has only to look at the

"greener" grass on the other side of the fence. Any American, especially one from a large, cosmopolitan U.S. city (where, ironically, the available food is likely to be better and more varied than in the country), who has tried to keep house in a foreign city has tales of woe. Even in London, Paris or Tokyo, favorite foods are generally available only at brief seasons of the year, if at all; prices are often prohibitive.

Try to buy a melon in Japan or an avocado in Britain or a jar of peanut butter in Rome and you come up against some hard truths. Until maybe fifteen years ago, salami was not sold in London, except in Soho; many items found in any U.S. supermarket are to be found in London only at shops like Jackson's in Piccadilly or at Fortnum and Mason's. Britons enjoy strawberries only in season; pineapples are an impossible luxury except for one fleeting month of the year—you eat "tinned" pineapple or none at all.

Americans, by contrast, have an almost limitless choice of foods, many of them at bargain prices. What Americans choose to eat is another matter. We often choose unwisely. And coming from many national backgrounds, we maintain many culinary traditions, some of them quite extreme. It is said that "there's no accounting for tastes," but America's cultural diversity accounts for at least some of its widely varied tastes. We do have one common dietary denominator: Americans are, above all else, meat-eaters.

ₒₒ[4]ₒₒ

Pregnant beasts and
fine-feathered friends

When Gertrude Stein wrote her famous line, "A rose is a rose is a rose," she was simply making a plea for honesty and simplicity in a poetic world that gilded lilies.

But is a rose just a rose just a rose?

One might as well say an asparagus is an onion. Both are members of the lily family.

All vegetables (and fruits, and nuts and what have you) are grouped by botanists into families.

Cabbages, cauliflowers, turnips, radishes and rutabagas belong to the mustard family.

The goosefoot family includes beets, spinach and chard.

This may seem academic. If one has a food allergy (and some experts guess that half of all Americans are at some time or other bothered by a food allergy) it is not at all academic. Anyone allergic to cabbage, will be allergic to all varieties of cabbage and to all other members of the mustard family. If one is allergic to peanuts, he will probably be allergic to other legumes but have no trouble with cashews, pecans, almonds or other nuts.

Potatoes and tomatoes are in the nightshade family, which has,

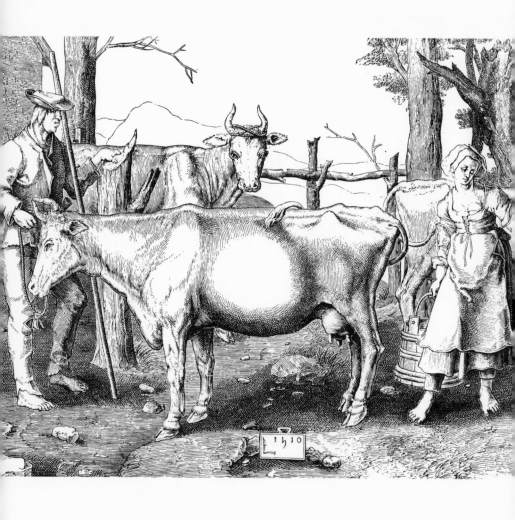

as well, some poisonous members,[1] one reason people remained for so long suspicious of potatoes and tomatoes. (Chapter 6)

Lettuce, endives and artichokes are in the thistle family; peas and beans in the pea family; carrots, parsnips, celery and parsley in the carrot family; gourds, pumpkins, watermelons, cucumbers, squashes and canteloupes in the gourd family; sweet potatoes in the morning glory family (which does not include yams or white potatoes).

The rose family, surprisingly, includes apples, pears, quinces, peaches, plums, cherries, apricots, blackberries and raspberries. It also includes strawberries, which are actually clusters of tiny plums.

While many of the items above appear on our tables, a larger share of a family's food dollar usually goes for meat and dairy products.

Animal life, like plant life, has infinite variety, which is precisely what has enabled these forms of life to survive drought, flood, disease and all other hazards. Different species, in fact, evolved to resist specific obstacles; less resistant species fell by the wayside.

But while most plant varieties are the results of natural mutations over the ages, most livestock and poultry variations have come out of deliberate and conscientious efforts by man to improve qualities (or more often quantities) of meat, milk, egg or wool production, hardiness or disease resistance through selective breeding or cross-breeding.

The improvement of the breeds

The source of all our steaks, hamburgers, roast beef and other cowboy-raised meat are, with few exceptions, descended from a cross between the long-legged, fierce and swift-running Great Ox, or aurochs, and the Celtic Shorthorn.

---

[1] Notably the mandrake, which contains an alkaloid similar to belladonna and can produce delirium. Many ancient superstitions were based on the mandrake root, but it did have valid medical uses. We have it on Pliny's authority that the root was given to patients to chew as an anaesthetic.

The Great Ox,[2] which of course was an ox only after it was castrated, stood more than six feet high at the shoulder; it had been in the forests of Germany back in Julius Caesar's time, though its domestication began as early as 2500 B.C. in Mesopotamia and Egypt. The unicorn of the Bible and of Greek mythology is actually the aurochs, whose black bull, striped with white or red down its back, had not one but two very long horns.

The Anglo-Saxons brought the aurochs into England and bred it with the smaller Celtic Shorthorn, the cow of Britain before 500 A.D.

America's first cows were Spanish, landed by Columbus in Santo Domingo on his second voyage in 1493; they were puny animals, weighing only eighty to 100 pounds full-grown; but they were enormous alongside the guinea pigs and low-slung "eating dogs" that had been the only livestock of pre-Columbian America.

Later breeding stock came from England, from Scotland, from Holland, from Sweden, from France (via the St. Lawrence River) and from Spain (by way of the West Indies, where Englishmen often stopped to buy cattle on their way to the Atlantic Coast settlements, and where the French stopped en route to Louisiana). But our most important breeds are of British origin.

When Mark Twain said that man was the only animal that could blush, or needed to, he may have been thinking of the vast manipulative sex programs used to improve the breed, not only of race horses, but of all manner of livestock and poultry.

This sexual side of meat and poultry production offended the sensibilities of Jacksonian Americans (the socially insecure often affect an excess of delicacy). The English found the American attitude amusing. James Laver cites a book, *Civilized America*, published

---

[2] Ox, like cow, pig and sheep, is an Anglo-Saxon word. Aurochs is from an obsolete German word, *Auerochs*. History books say the last surviving aurochs died in captivity in Poland in 1627, but an advertisement in the *Wall Street Journal* not long ago invited "sportsmen" to hunt for the "almost extinct" aurochs in Russia's Caucasus Mountains; and in the zoo at Cluj, in Transylvania, the Romanians have an animal they say is an aurochs, descended no doubt—like dozens of others in European zoos—from an aurochs scientifically "reconstructed" in 1921 by a German who crossbred domestic cattle which still possessed aurochs characteristics.

in London in 1859, which says that in America "a cock was called a rooster, 'a certain fowl' or a 'hen's husband.' " Mencken, in his discussion of "America's Golden Age of Euphemism," observes that in the 1830's and '40's words like bitch, ram, boar, buck and stallion virtually disappeared from polite usage. A stallion was called a "stable horse"; a bull was a "cow creature," a "male cow," a "Jonathan," even a "gentleman-cow," the term used when reciting Longfellow's "Wreck of the Hesperus."

Some of the taboo words are still considered "blushful" in parts of the Ozarks.

But in order to develop desired characteristics, unblushing breeders mate brothers with sisters (it is called "inbreeding") and mate second cousins ("line breeding") and never give a thought to the propriety or impropriety of it.

Out of inbreeding, line breeding and crossbreeding have come the most important breeds of beef cattle in America today: Hereford, shorthorn, Aberdeen-Angus and Galloway (all imported originally from the British Isles), Brahman (from India), Africander (from Africa), Charolais (from France) and Beefmaster, Braford, Brangus, Cattalo, Charbrais and Santa Gertrudis, all developed in the U.S.

One breed we have never imported, surprisingly, is Italy's Chianina of Tuscany, probably the tallest, heaviest breed of beef cattle on earth and the oldest—priests in ancient Rome more than 2000 years ago were sacrificing Chianina animals, burning their entrails to propitiate the gods and gluttonizing on their meat.

Chianinas reach enormous weights relatively quickly: a bull may weigh over 1000 pounds at one year, over a ton at two years. The meat has practically no fat, and a high percentage of it is concentrated in the preferred cuts.

But American beef derives mostly from breeds begun in England and Scotland in the eighteenth century, when a Leicestershire man, Robert Bakewell of Dishley, worked out theories of cattle breeding long before Mendelian laws of heredity.[3] On the premise that "like

---

[3] Developed by the Austrian monk Gregor Johann Mendel in the 1860's but not generally known and recognized until about 1900.

produces like," Bakewell often inbred his stock, selecting animals for blocky bodies low-set on short legs. The ideal beef cattle today is still generally short of leg with a deep wide body, short thick neck and heavy flesh over the hind quarters, ribs, loins and back.

Nine years after Bakewell's death in 1795, Charles Colling bred a famous sire named Comet. He also bred a beast called the Durham Ox, widely exhibited in England, which weighed 3024 pounds at the age of five and 3780 pounds at the age of ten, a monstrous size at that time. Charles's brother Robert bred a great white heifer in 1806, a 2300-pound creature, also considered a monstrosity and also widely shown.

The Colling brothers owed their successes in large measure to Viscount Townshend (whose grandson wrote the Townshend Acts of 1767 that taxed the American colonists and helped provoke the Revolution). Little had been done to increase the size of cattle before the end of the eighteenth century in England because little could be done: the breeding stock kept alive through the winters after the great fall slaughters had to survive on skimpy fodder. Then Viscount Townshend (he came to be called "Turnip" Townshend) introduced turnips from Holland as winter feed for English cattle. Keeping cattle through the winter became easier. Fresh meat could be bought in any season. And animals could be grown to great sizes, as the beasts of the Colling brothers demonstrated.

Durhams, as the Colling animals were called, were known as shorthorns on the Western range of the U.S., where they were introduced very early. Bigger than other beef breeds, they were often mated to Hereford cows in America.

Herefords were first imported into the U.S. in 1817, replacing the scrub-range stock common in Kentucky until that time. Because they thrived on range grass in a day when there were no supplementary feeds, Herefords became the favorites of the old-time cowboys. Along with the shorthorn, the red-bodied, white-faced Hereford became the basis of ranching in the old West, displacing the earliest range cattle, the Spanish longhorns whose meat was so tough it was passed up even by thieving Comanches who much preferred buffalo meat.

Longhorns had hornspreads that sometimes stretched seven feet from tip to tip; U.S. beef cattle today, except for the Africander, have short horns or no horns at all. Some small-horned breeds, like Herefords, have hornless strains; Polled Herefords, developed in the early 1900's, are easier to ship because they do not injure other animals on their way to market, or in feed lots. And they can be in the same pasturage as hogs or horses without endangering their companions.

Hornless Aberdeenshire cattle were known in Scotland as early as 1523, but the coal-black Aberdeen-Angus was not imported to America until 1873, when a retired London silk merchant, a Scotsman named George Grant, brought four bulls to his home in Victoria, Kansas. Bred to longhorns, the Aberdeen-Angus, while not so heavy as the Hereford or shorthorn, has become the most numerous breed in the East and South and has spread to the Far West.

Close cousin to the Aberdeen-Angus, though less important, is the Galloway, also Scottish and hornless, and also usually black, though it has a longer coat, often tinged with brown. Galloways were probably first brought to the U.S. about 1860.

Many U.S. cattlemen still buy pedigreed British stock, and this fact was indirectly responsible for the worst animal epidemic in British history, the hoof-and-mouth (the English say "foot-and-mouth") disease which infected thousands of cows, bulls, sheep and pigs in the autumn of 1967, nearly doubled the retail price of beef in Britain and led to the slaughter of hundreds of thousands of animals. (The Soviet Union experienced a plague of the disease at the same time.)

The vaccine against hoof-and-mouth disease in rare cases produces mild cases of the disease. The U.S., which wiped out hoof-and-mouth disease in the 1920's by a costly massive program of extermination, prohibits imports of meat and livestock from diseased areas (Argentina has been outlawed as a meat and livestock source for years for this reason). The British herdsmen refused to vaccinate on the ground that some mild cases might be produced which would scare off buyers from the U.S. and from Commonwealth countries (Australia, Canada, New Zealand and eleven other countries are also free of the infection).

British cattlemen will now, perhaps, change their ways. Many ways have changed in recent years in the production of meat and the improvement of the breeds that produce meat.

As beef cattle increased in size, natural mating procedures between gigantic bulls and hefty cows became positively hazardous; cattlemen had to develop ways to help the animals mate without the weight of the bull doing damage to the cow. The solution was artificial insemination, which not only took a load off cows' backs but enabled a superior bull to fertilize thousands of cows instead of twenty, the average in natural breeding operations.

The U.S. was late in using artificial insemination, employed (with dogs) as early as 1780 in Italy and developed in the Soviet Union between 1900 and 1930. Organized artificial insemination of dairy cattle was begun in the U.S. in 1938, the method being introduced from Denmark. About forty-five per cent of U.S. cows are now inseminated artificially,[4] the bulls being fooled by dummy cows into producing the necessary semen.

In the late 1950's it was discovered that glycerol could be used to deep-freeze sperm and preserve it almost indefinitely. When thawed, bull semen is almost as fertile as ordinary cooled liquid semen, though the technique is less successful with ram semen. It is also possible now to transplant the ovum from one cow or ewe to another. As Ritchie Calder says, "the ovary of a newborn calf contains some seventy thousand eggs, but rarely do even the best of our cows produce more than ten calves in their lifetime. By the use of hormones, more eggs can be produced and transplanted into other females. . . . It is possible to inseminate a pedigree cow and to transplant the ovum into a scrub animal which will give birth to a pedigree calf, unrelated to the animal which gave it birth."

This is the brave new world of "animal engineering," the logical outgrowth of decades of animal tinkering.

The King Ranch in Texas has been the center of other conventional breeding experiments, some of which produced the Santa Gertrudis breed whose most important sire was a Brahman-shorthorn

---

[4] Comparative figures: Denmark, 100 per cent; Japan, ninety-eight; England, Israel, the Netherlands, sixty-five; France, fifty-five; the USSR and West Germany, forty. Figures are much lower in Africa, Asia and South America.

named Monkey. Santa Gertrudis cattle are three-eighths Brahman, five-eighths shorthorn. They are usually red like shorthorns, have almost none of the Brahman hump and they do not grow thin when the Texas rangelands wither in times of drought.

The Brahman parent of the Santa Gertrudis is a strangely Oriental-looking breed which Marco Polo described in the thirteenth century; it is often called Zebu in Europe and South America. The name may come from the noise the Brahman makes, a sort of grunt quite unlike the lowing of other cattle. Or it may be a corruption of Cebu, an island in the central Philippines.

In their native India, some Brahman are sacred. Certain bulls are dedicated to Hindu deities by the Brahman caste; these animals wander freely about the countryside, siring unwanted native calves and devouring crops. In droughts, huge numbers of the half-starved animals perish, which is a relief to the peasants, whose Hindu religion does not permit them to kill the beasts for food.

India has nearly 200 million cattle and buffalo, one-third of all the cattle in the world and more than twice the number in the U.S. Some of the cows are milked (the taboo against killing cattle and buffalo, which goes back at least 3000 years, may have had the original purpose of protecting the milk supply), and some of the animals are used for draft purposes.

Most U.S. Brahmans are within a few hundred miles of the Gulf Coast, where heat discourages other breeds. Brahmans require no shade, thrive on sparse vegetation, have strong resistance to various insect pests and to drought and Texas fever. Most of our Brahmans can trace their ancestry either to a bull and cow imported to South Carolina in 1849 by Dr. James Bolton Davis [5] or to a couple of bulls given to Richard Barrow of Louisiana in 1854. They vary in color from light gray to brown and can always be recognized by their characteristic humps.

The hump is less pronounced in a close relative to the Brahman,

---

[5] Davis had been sent by President Polk as an agricultural adviser to Turkey. He brought the Brahmans back from the Royal Gardens in London. No Brahmans have been brought into the U.S. from India in more than forty years; quarantines against diseases like hoof-and-mouth have kept them out.

the red Africander breed developed by the Dutch in South Africa and imported for the King Ranch in 1931. Africanders have long horns that turn down and back. They have been mated with Herefords and shorthorns to develop crossbreeds.

One other breed developed to overcome heat and drought conditions on the Great Plains owes its existence to the survival of the American buffalo—and the determination of a Texan frontiersman, Charles Goodnight,[6] who crossed wild bison with European cows to produce (in the third cross) a hardy breed called Cattalo. Cattalo are resistant to certain diseases, are not easily disturbed by heel flies, mature quickly and have good beef configuration.

Four other breeds found in the Southwest are the huge, cream-colored Charolais, a relatively recent arrival from France where its meat has long been prized; the Charbray, a cross between the Charolais and the Brahman; the Brangus, a Louisiana development, three-eighths Brahman, five-eighths Angus; and the Beefmaster, which combines Brahman, Hereford and shorthorn strains. The latter two are esteemed for the quality of their beef, the first two more for the speed at which they grow and the economy with which they can be fed. The Charbray, Brangus and Beefmaster, along with the Santa Gertrudis, are more important U.S.-developed breeds than the Cattalo. So is the Braford, a Brahman-Hereford cross.

Crossbreeding in general produces heifers that reach puberty earlier, have higher sexual conception rates, deliver a higher percentage of calves during the first ten days of the calving season, and produce calves that are somewhat heavier at weaning time (and gain weight faster in the feed lots).

All good beef comes from steers fattened in feed lots. While few connoisseurs can tell whether their beef comes from a Hereford, a shorthorn, an Angus, a Brahman or a Charolais, if you eat beef fattened on grass instead of on grain, you will probably know it—and will not like it.

---

[6] Goodnight is credited with devising the first chuck wagons, using converted Army wagons in the 1850's to keep cowhands fed with stew and biscuits. Goodnight himself preferred buffalo meat and kept a wild herd until the day he died.

Before 1900, cattle generally matured five or six years before being marketed and were rarely fed much besides grass. After 1900, land in the West became too expensive to keep a steer even three or four years, much less five or six.

Today, only breeding stock live more than eighteen months. Most countries still do not slaughter beef until it is two years old or more (the *bistecca* of Florence is from Chianina steers killed at fifteen to seventeen months, but that is unusual—Chianinas fatten quickly); in the U.S. the demand is for baby beef, young corn-fattened animals from which small cuts of marbled, tender meat can be cut, the fat intermixed half and half with the lean. Fat slaughter calves are sent to the abattoirs for baby beef when they are eight months old or less.

"Stockers" and "feeders," including both steers and heifers (the latter are used only for inferior grades of beef) are sent either to feed lots, or to pasture, or are fed a mixture of grain and grass.

Fattening beef with corn before the slaughter [7] is a distinctively American contribution; U.S. beef—especially the "New York cut" (called shell steak in New York)—has become world-famous.

Aging beef is also an American idea. Elsewhere, meat is eaten immediately after it is slaughtered, before *rigor mortis* stiffens the animal's muscles; or it is eaten a few days later, after the muscles have softened, as pork is eaten even in the U.S. (pork fat easily becomes rancid and gives the meat an unpleasant flavor).

---

[7] A federal Humane Slaughter Law (1958) avoids needless cruelty in U.S. abattoirs. Most animals are knocked out electrically or with captive-bolt stunning pistols before they are bled. Kosher laws require animals (and poultry) to be bled first. The religious slaughterer, or *shochet*, must dispatch the animal with one clean slash of the throat; if his knife binds or sticks, even for a second, the animal is no longer kosher and cannot be stamped with the seal of the rabbinical supervisor, or *mashgiach*. In non-kosher packing plants, it sometimes takes two or three shots to knock the animal insensible. Which is more humane? It is a moot point, and a periodic source of controversy. There have been occasions, as in Switzerland in 1893, when kosher slaughtering was made illegal by popular vote—which may have been an expression of anti-Semitism rather than of humane sentiment. Of an estimated 115 million animals slaughtered in the U.S. each year, from 6 million to 10 million are slaughtered in the ritual of *Shechita* and declared kosher.

Unless it has enough outside fat, meat will deteriorate, even spoil, if held for more than five days or so. Veal and lamb generally lack the necessary fat covering and are not aged more than a few days. Higher grades of well-finished beef and mutton, meat with thick layers of outer fat, are made more tender by aging from five to eighteen days (and sometimes for up to six weeks) at a temperature of from 34° to 38° F. Enzymes in the meat evidently soften the muscle tissues, but few except gastronomes know that beef aged more than about two weeks, while very tender, either gets gamey or loses much of its flavor.

Calves fed mainly or entirely on their mothers' milk, and slaughtered at anywhere from four to fourteen weeks of age, are marketed as veal, which is especially abundant in late winter and spring. At other times of year, meat sold as "veal" may be darker in color, a sign it comes from an older animal than a true veal calf, probably a calf fourteen weeks to a year old. The ultimate grade of veal, raised in Wisconsin from Holstein stock and marked "plume de veau" on its outer skin, has a creamy white flesh and costs about twice what you ordinarily pay for the best standard veal roast.

Veal should be braised or roasted or, if cut thin enough, sautéed, as for *scaloppini;* it should never be broiled (it is too lean). Best cuts for roasting are the double loin, or saddle, and the loin, or tenderloin, though the rump of a young white veal also makes a good roast, as does a rolled shoulder. Veal has to be larded well with fat before it is roasted, and it should always be well-done.

In Italy, as in ancient Rome, veal is preferred to beef. North of Florence, Waverley Root [8] tells us, veal is *vitello;* it comes from a calf. South of Florence it is *vitella* and comes from a heifer. But friends in Rome disagree: *vitello,* they report, is the accepted word for veal. Italians eat *vitello* and *vitella* with tuna fish (*tonnato*), with a coating of melted Parmesan cheese (*parmigiana*), pounded into quarter-inch thin pieces (*scaloppini,* which the French call *escalope* and the Germans *Schnitzel*), in "veal birds" (*uccellini,* sometimes called *rollatine*),

---

[8] An emigré ex-newsman, Mr. Root has dined well on Europe's various cuisines for forty years. He has, in the process, become a noted food authority. And has increased his weight from 135 pounds to 230.

and many other ways. They averaged 15.4 pounds of veal apiece in 1968; if they ate a lot more beef (*manzo*), and they did average 48.4 pounds of beef, it was only because veal cost fifteen to twenty per cent more.

Not many Americans eat veal; our per capita consumption is only four pounds a year, down from 9.7 in the late Forties.

What we do eat is beef. Back in Shakespeare's England, eating a lot of beef was thought to cause stupidity and melancholy. Today, along with Canadians, Uruguayans and Argentinians, we Americans eat meat in quantities other people never begin to approach. And our favorite meat by far is beef.

In 1952 the average American ate sixty-two pounds of beef; by 1959 he was eating eighty-nine pounds; by 1960, ninety-nine pounds; and by 1970, 114 pounds.

Cattlemen, once plagued by overproduction and low prices, have increased supplies of beef, but not at a rate equal to the rate of U.S. population growth and, more especially, of personal income growth. While the mean family income in America is $1000 a year below the $9000 our government says is needed for a "comfortable" life (we are not so affluent as we think we are), American consumers have nonetheless bid up the price of beef, which has also been inflated by steep rises in distribution costs.

The result has been a sharp increase in beef prices, both wholesale and retail. Cattle feeders in the summer of 1969 were getting the highest prices they had received per hundredweight of Choice grade beef since the beef shortage of 1951. There were boycotts, organized and unorganized, by beefing consumers; Congress conducted inquiries. But demand remained high.

We are, it seems, creatures of habit. A Department of Agriculture survey of what was behind our 114-pound [9] beef consumption per

---

[9] Plus seventy-five pounds of other meat. Add poultry (over sixty pounds) and the average American eats more than 250 pounds of flesh a year. The average Briton by comparison eats perhaps 140 pounds, of which only twenty-eight is beef and veal. The average Frenchman in 1965 (latest figures available) ate thirty-nine pounds of beef, almost fifteen pounds of veal, and enough lamb, pork, chicken, rabbit and horsemeat (Chapter 7) to bring his total meat and poultry consumption to about 157 pounds.

capita found that despite high prices, ninety-three per cent of house-wives interviewed said they served their families beef at least once a week; only forty-one per cent served pork chops that often. Restaurants in many cases were serving smaller steaks to avoid raising prices; some proprietors instructed their waiters to push chicken, lamb—anything but beef—but still patrons ordered steak. And housewives still bought ground round at the butcher's, whatever the price.

Make friends with the butcher

Knowledgeable housewives save money by buying from friendly, helpful butchers—and by knowing as much as the butchers know.

It pays to know the anatomy of a steer, whose butchered carcass weighs anywhere from 600 to 750 pounds, depending on whether it is graded Good, Choice or Prime, a subject we will treat a few pages on. The carcass is divided up into two forequarters, each 155 to 190 pounds, and two hindquarters, each 145 to 180 pounds.

Each forequarter is split up into three primal cuts, each hind-quarter into four primal cuts.

These are further divided into smaller cuts which are sold under a bewildering variety of names, but are not really so hard to learn as first appears.

The best cuts, none of them kosher (Chapter 7), are from the hindquarters, whose primal cuts are whole round, which weighs seventy-five to ninety pounds; hip, twenty-five to thirty-five pounds; short loin, thirty-two to forty pounds; and flank, about twenty-two pounds.

From the whole round, which is the steer's hind leg and is mostly all lean meat, the butcher cuts top round, side of round and bottom round. The inside parts of the leg are tender and can be broiled; the outside has more connecting muscle tissue so it is tougher and must be moist-cooked or ground.

Top round yields round steaks, Swiss steak, butterfly steak, petite steak, minute steak, pepper steak, London broil top round, cuts suitable for pastrami and dry beef processing, top round roast and chopped round. Side of round, sometimes called veiny or knuckle roast, includes most of the same cuts as top round, along with some cuts called top sirloin (the French call it *contre-filet*) and sirloin tip, not to be confused with true sirloins from the hip, and tip steak. Cube steak can be from almost any cut, knitted together by a cubing machine in the processing plant or at the butcher's; the machine breaks down the muscles to make tough cuts tender. Bottom round is cut up into eye of round, heel of round and cuts sold as bottom rump, rump steak, standing rump and silver tip, the latter a cut which can be made into small minute steaks for pan-frying.

There's more for the money in bottom round than top round; it must be pot roasted, but that means less shrinkage, and a good pot roast is as fine a dish as anyone could want. Properly marinated as the Germans do it, pot roast is *sauerbraten*.

All the round cuts, being lean, are best prepared by roasting or pan-frying; they lack the necessary fat for broiling. Cook them on the rare side or they will be tough; and let them sit for fifteen or twenty minutes after cooking before they are carved. This should not make them too cold, but a hot gravy will always warm them up.

Moving forward to the steer's hip we come to the best cuts of beef, the sirloin steaks, which can certainly be broiled and should be, though they can be every bit as good pan-broiled as grilled. Years ago a housewife bought a three- or four-pound sirloin, complete with tail (from the flank) and fillet intact; she cut it up herself. Now sirloin is almost always sold minus the tail, which is less tender and cannot be broiled, and minus the fillet, which is sold separately. The individual sirloin steaks are mostly sold separately, too, in twelve-ounce to eighteen-ounce weights depending on thickness. The housewife pays less for waste the new way than the old way.

Sirloin should be pinkish red, have enough outside fat (one-half inch) to keep it from drying out or curling up when you broil it, have enough marbled fat to make it tender and juicy, not stringy or dry.

There are flat bone sirloins, wedge bone, pin bone and boneless sirloins; the latter, when the fillet is removed, is properly called shell hip in New York but may be called rump steak in another town. It should not, according to old timers, be called sirloin unless it contains some of the fillet.

Just forward of the hip is this prized filet mignon, which represents just seven to nine pounds out of the whole big steer; it lies between the hip and the short loin, the primal cut containing tenderloin steak (the French call it *Chateaubriand*), T-bone steak, porterhouse steak, shell steak, club steak and top loin steak. T-bone and porterhouse steaks both have a lot of waste.

Smallest of the hindquarter primal cuts is the flank, most of which is ground into hamburger. A little of it is cut on the bias and sold as London broil. Select a cut of at least two pounds of lean meat and nothing lighter for London broil.

Knowing one cut of meat from another can produce significant savings. Having a narrowly restricted range of meat cuts in her repertoire can cut a woman out of a lot of bargains; one cut of meat may be a good buy today, another cut a good buy tomorrow. There are seasonal variations: changing prices usually reveal what is in season. So do the newspapers, the radio and the TV: the Department of Agriculture issues bulletins to advise homemakers when certain meats (and other foods) are coming into the markets in enough abundance to sell at low, or at least relatively low, prices.

Heel of round is relatively economical at any season; so are some forequarter cuts.

The biggest forequarter primal cut is the chuck, ninety to 120 pounds; next is the brisket and plate, about thirty-five pounds; last is the rib, the best part of the forequarter, thirty-two to thirty-five pounds. Kosher butchers sell only meat from these cuts.

Brisket, in fact, while it may be a good buy in some cities, is the most desired cut in New York's kosher shops and commands a good price; at one time it was not even sold in gentile shops. Chuck and brisket cuts should be pinkish red; they will stay moist and tender and keep their flavor through the long, slow cooking needed to make pot roast. Corned beef is made from brisket, which is also sold fresh and used to make Romanian steak.

Skirt steak fillets, short ribs, plate beef and rolled plate all come from the brisket and plate cut, as do shank cross cuts and at least some stew beef. Shoulder steak comes from the chuck, and so does the little Collickle, the eye of the chuck, English (Boston) cut, short ribs, chuck blade (or blade chuck), arm pot roast (or arm steak), blade pot roast (or blade steak). Most of these can be pan-broiled. Other chuck cuts are sometimes glamorized as "skirt steak," "end of steak," "French roast," "California roast" (called New York chuck in California), "breakfast steak," "London Broil," "rib tips," "filet steak," "Braciola," "Swiss steak," and "TV steak." In some places, stores are required to identify the parent cut, but the word "chuck" in the ad is in small print.

Chuck steaks, say the experts, should be bought bone-in; boning ups the price more per pound than is saved by having the extra weight of the bone removed. Treated with a tenderizer, chuck steak is good broiled or baked. The chuck roast can be purchased and the flat bone from the outside edge removed, the large oval piece of meat at that side cut out and split into two one-inch steaks. Cut up the rest for beef stew.

Only the forequarter's rib cuts can rival the quality of the hindquarter's hip cuts, the regal sirloins. Fat is intermingled with lean better in these rib cuts than anywhere else in the forequarter. They include the standing rib roast, the rib steak, the boneless rib steak and the Delmonico (or rib eye) roast or steak, which gets its name from the New York restaurant so well patronized by Diamond Jim Brady.

Rib roast has a lot of waste, but it tastes so good it may well be worth whatever it costs. A roast sirloin may be a better buy than a rib roast, which is cheaper by the pound, but buying a standing rib of beef and having it cut into Delmonico steaks (*entrecôtes* in French) can save as much as twenty cents a pound.

In a few places it may still be good advice to have the butcher trim off the back fat, the back-strap, the feather-bone, the point of chine, the cracked chine bone and so forth, but packaged cuts of meat, sold out of refrigerator cases, are now replacing the personal butcher in so many locations that the advice has an increasingly antique sound.

It is still good advice to point out that some cuts of meat, while cheaper by the pound, contain so much bone or fat they end up costing more per serving. Short ribs, for example, usually have too much bone, and foreshank is rarely worth even its budget price.

Buying a side or quarter of beef may be thrifty, but only if all the cuts are used, and only if the steaks and roasts are used within eight to twelve months of freezer-storage time, and the ground beef within three to four months. It is usually better economics to buy what is available in the market from week to week, especially if the buying is done with a good working knowledge of the various cuts.

Hamburger, to be good, should be freshly ground and should contain no more than twenty-five per cent fat or suet; it needs close to twenty per cent to be juicy and flavorful. Hamburger should look rich and red, just slightly flecked with white. If it is light pink and has lots of white flecks, watch out: despite the legal maximum of thirty per cent fat, it may be as much as fifty per cent fat, only fifty per cent meat protein—bad for the heart, bad for the figure, bad for the budget.

Good hamburger is a medium-coarse grind of meat from flank, neck or parts of the shank (brisket is too tough-grained to make decent hamburger). For home-ground hamburger, buy chuck or stew meat instead of round steak; grinding makes all cuts about equal in tenderness. Put the meat through the grinder only once; its structure will be broken down and it will pack down too much and be dry and flavorless if it is twice-ground.

To freeze hamburger, remove it from the paper store bag and put it in an airtight container like a plastic bag. Hamburger is one of the few meats that can be taken out of the freezer hard as rock and immediately sautéed without losing any flavor.

Ground meat can be used in meat loaves, too, where it can be extended with such things as potatoes, rice and oatmeal, though the best extender is either nonfat milk powder or "Multi-Purpose Food" (MPF). Both serve to increase the protein value of the meat instead of diluting it, as fillers like potatoes and bread crumbs do.

MPF [10] was invented by Dr. Henry Borsook, a biochemistry professor at the California Institute of Technology in the 1940's. It is made up largely of soybean grits fortified with vitamins and minerals: two ounces of MPF powder, eaten with meat, potatoes or whatever three times a day, supply an adult's full requirement for protein, and all the vitamins, plus most of the minerals for which nutritional needs are known.

Half and sometimes more of the meat in some recipes can be replaced with MPF at a cost of less than ten cents per two-ounce portion. The bland-tasting powder assumes the taste of whatever it is cooked with.

"Variety" is good for you

One way to get more nutrition for the money is to buy liver of various sorts and other "variety" or organ cuts, all rich in nutritive values far beyond their cost and, if cooked properly, quite delicious.

Liver should hardly be cooked at all. Too much heat makes the meat tough and difficult to digest. It also destroys much of the vitamin content with which liver is so well endowed.

All liver is rich in vitamins A (our own liver contains ninety-five per cent of the body's vitamin A reserves), B and C. Veal liver, the tenderest of livers, also contains a good deal of iron. And so does calves' liver, slightly darker in color than veal liver but still tender.

One good method of cooking liver is to put it into a frying pan over a layer of sautéed onions, cover it, and heat it gently until the steam from the mixture has turned the liver from red to pinkish brown. Liver may also be broiled or braised, but just a little; it should be moist and soft as butter if done right.

Another economy meat is brains, usually calves' brains (*cervelles* on a French menu). They can be braised, or dipped in eggs and bread

---

[10] Available by mail from General Mills, Minneapolis, Minnesota, which produces it under license from Meals for Millions, Inc., MPF comes in four-pound-eight-ounce cans. A can sells for $3.00 postpaid, 6 cans for $15.00.

crumbs and then sautéed. Or cut them into bite-size pieces and put them into a strained lentil soup during the last fifteen minutes of cooking. But they are very perishable; use them promptly or pre-cook them.

Kidneys, heart, sweetbreads, tripe and tongue are other variety meats too often neglected or rejected without good cause. These "innards" are, like brains, quite perishable and should be used the day they are bought. If they must be kept a day or two, store them loosely wrapped in the refrigerator.

Brains are delicately flavored and extremely tender. Similar in texture are sweetbreads, the thymus gland of a calf, lamb or young steer (the gland disappears as the animal grows older). There are two lobes to the gland: the round heart sweetbreads and the elongated throat sweetbreads. Reddish sweetbreads are from a young steer, white and tender sweetbreads from a lamb or veal calf (*ris de veau*, say the French; Italians say *animelle*). Before cooking, sweetbreads should be blanched; they may then be braised, broiled or sautéed.

Tender veal and lamb kidneys (*rognon* on the *carte du jour*) may be broiled or sautéed, but tougher beef kidneys must be braised. Kidneys may come encased in their thick fat covering (the original basis of margarine) or they may be separated. All fat and membrane should be trimmed off, they should be seared in hot butter for no more than two minutes and, like liver, they should not be overcooked (the center will remain pink if you do them properly).

Heart, whether beef, calf or lamb, is fairly tough and must be braised or simmered until it is tender. The flavor is good. The size depends on the animal, ranging from about a quarter of a pound for a lamb heart to about three pounds for a beef heart.

Tripe, too, is rather tough until it is simmered; then it has a delicate flavor many people love. Tripe is the inner lining of a cow's stomach; it is sold fresh, canned or pickled (though even "fresh" tripe is partly cooked when we buy it).

Tongue is sold in various processed forms: canned, smoked, corned and pickled. Some forms are ready to eat, others require long cooking before they are tender. Beef tongue, often weighing from two to five pounds, and veal tongue, from three-quarters of a pound to a pound and a half, are sold fresh.

Americans who take their culinary cues from Europeans know the value of calves' cheeks, calves' feet and other items too often scorned without reason by so many of us. Foreign cookbooks can be instructive in opening eyes and minds to the many possibilities of low-cost "variety" meat dishes.

Prime, Choice and all that

As for the more conventional cuts of meat, the round purple USDA inspection stamp guarantees that the meat came from a healthy animal and was slaughtered and processed under sanitary conditions. We have come a long way since Upton Sinclair's time, and conditions are even more sanitary now that the federal meat inspection law, which took effect December 15, 1967, is being implemented.

Male feed lot animals in nine to eighteen months become "Prime" or "Choice" or at least "Good" or "Standard" grade beef; the grass lot animals become lower grades of beef.

These are official U.S. Department of Agriculture grades; [11] they are applied to beef, veal and lamb, all of which are stamped "U.S. Prime," "U.S. Choice," or Good, Standard, Commercial or Utility as the case may be. Choice is the top grade found in most retail stores, Commercial the lowest grade.

A big steak in a restaurant costs $1 in Buenos Aires or Montevideo, but it will not be up to the quality of Choice grade U.S. steak. It certainly will not be Prime grade. Even in the U.S., few steers are kept in pens and fed long and vigorously enough to produce Prime beef. A lot of waste is involved, and while Prime beef is exceptionally fine and tender, so much fat is produced in relation to lean red meat

---

[11] Swift, Armour and Wilson, the top U.S. meat packers, have their own terms for the top grades. Instead of Prime, Choice and Good, Swift uses Premium, Select and Arrow; Armour uses Star, Banner and Crescent; Wilson uses Certified, Special and Ideal. But the prices of the various grades speak for themselves.

that even the high price Prime fetches is hardly enough to offset the high cost of producing it. Most Prime beef goes to a relative handful of restaurants, clubs and hotels, mainly in the East.

The grades are accurate; a grader is a U.S. Department of Agriculture employee; the packer pays a fee for his services but has no control over what grades he stamps on meat.

The fat covering of Good and Standard grade beef may have a yellowish tinge instead of being creamy white, as in Prime and Choice beef. This merely shows the animal was fed more grass and less grain than the Choice or Prime grade steer; but yellowish fat has been found to have a higher vitamin A content than white fat, and the meat under the fat is usually richer in iron.

A doctor in Durban, South Africa, George Perling, claims he has developed a process for treating poor cuts of meat to make them taste like fillet. The tenderizing process, patented under the name "Tendaperl," is said to permit the use of seventy-five per cent of a steer's carcass for steak instead of the usual ten per cent.

Meanwhile, the U.S. Department of Agriculture says, "Low grades [of meat] take more cooking time, high grades take more money. Which do you have most of?"

Cooked long and slow in a casserole or stew, a lower grade of meat or a low-cost cut leaves nothing to be desired in tenderness, taste or nutritive value.

The milkshed

Protein-minded, calorie-counting Americans have been eating ever increasing amounts of meat in general, though raising livestock to produce meat is an extravagant way of converting plant protein into animal protein, a way most of the world just can not afford.

One of the most efficient converters—and the chief one in much of the world—is the milk (or milch) cow. About thirty per cent of the fodder a cow consumes becomes extremely nutritious food for man; dairy cattle produce that food at one-fourth the cost of producing beef.

In most countries, cattle breeds are not specialized. A milk cow in many places will be used to pull a wagon; her brother will be slaughtered for beef. But when a dairy breed milk cow in the U.S. calves a male, the animal is killed within ten days or two weeks and its meat sold to frankfurter makers.

We do have some dual breeds, raised partly for milk, partly for meat. Major breeds in this category are the Milking shorthorn, the Red Poll and the Devon. The latter, a hardy red cow, is perhaps the oldest to have pastured in colonial New England. Ships out of Plymouth, England, carrying supplies to the Pilgrims of Plymouth, Massachusetts, in 1624 had cows aboard; and although the Devon breed had not yet been registered, these Pilgrim cows were almost certainly of the type found in Devonshire where the Devon breed was later registered.

The eight major dairy breeds in America now are Holstein, Jersey, Guernsey, Ayrshire, Brown Swiss, Dutch Belted, Canadian and Dexter.

Dairymen keep careful records of milk production for each cow in their herds, measuring it not only in quarts or pounds but also in butterfat content. The average U.S. cow produces about 4000 pounds of milk a year; 190 pounds of it is butterfat.

Take only cows registered in the Dairy Herd Improvement Association and the average jumps to 9006 pounds a year (4189 quarts) of which 338 pounds are butterfat. In 1940 the average Wisconsin dairy cow yielded six quarts of milk a day; now, thanks to improved stock and special feeds, the average is ten quarts a day.

U.S. consumption of milk and cream is about 133 quarts a year per capita, down from 157 quarts in the late 1950's.

The decline is due largely to anxieties about weight and cholesterol, and to a small extent to worries about strontium-90, the long-lived radioactive fission product deposited by nuclear test fallouts and consumed by grazing animals. But while some Americans have fastened on milk as a strontium-90 hazard, "not drinking milk," in the words of ecologist Eugene P. Odom, "may not help because vegetables, fruit, or almost any food one might choose also may be contaminated [with strontium-90]."

Milk may also contain DDT, but legal limits for cows' milk keep DDT-content to 0.05 parts per million, whereas mother's milk, according to David Brower, former executive director of the Sierra Club, contains four times that much.

Testifying before the House Merchant Marine and Fisheries Committee in the spring of 1969, the conservationist said, "Some wit even suggested that if it were packaged in some other container, we wouldn't allow it across state lines."

The British have been urging their citizens to "Drinka Pinta Milka Day" for many years; they are still somewhat short of that goal on a per capita basis, but Britain now ranks fifth in the world in milk consumption per capita (three hundred pints per year). The French, despite the campaign of Pierre Mendès-France in the 1950's, drink barely 110 quarts each per year; most French adults drink none at all. Finland leads the world in milk drinking: the Finns may be big boozers, but they also average five hundred pints of milk a year.

Farmers generally milk their cows twice a day for a period of 305 days, or ten months, each year. (During the other two months, the cow goes dry prior to having her calf.) But some dairymen milk three times a day and others four times, 365 days a year.[12] Older cows produce more milk than younger ones, until they finally reach a mature age of from five to seven years.

Holsteins outnumber any other dairy breed in the U.S. Developed from a race of Dutch cows, the Holstein-Friesian breed first came to America in the early 1600's before there were recognized breeds; but it was a cow that came over in 1852 on a Dutch sailing vessel that had the most influence on our U.S. breed (which, incidentally, is now pronounced so the "stein" rhymes with wean instead of with wine as it used to be).

---

[12] With modern equipment, one man can take care of fifty cows, producing as much as 50,000 pounds of milk—enough for nearly 1400 Americans, or a great many more Frenchmen. The typical contented cow, usually a Holstein, eats about 120 pounds of hay, silage and grain a day and produces about sixty pounds of milk, sucked from the teats of her swollen udder by the four valves of an electric milking machine. While in Russia two-thirds of the cows are still milked by hand, milking is mechanized in most Western countries; a machine can milk fifty to sixty cows in an hour while a man can milk only four or five.

The champion Holstein was Carnation Ormsby Madcap Fayne. She produced 41,943 pounds (about 19,508 quarts) in 365 days. Holsteins are the most productive cows, but their milk has the lowest butterfat content of any dairy breed.

Jersey cows, on the other hand, rank highest in butterfat content of their milk; it averages 5.14 per cent butterfat, as compared with 3.45 for Holsteins. The little Jerseys, however, average only 5500 pounds of milk a year, versus 8000 for Holsteins.

Like their sister breed, the Guernseys, Jersey cows were originally bred in the Channel Islands between England and France. All cows from these islands were originally called Alderneys and were introduced into America under that name. Guernsey cows average 5500 pounds of milk a year with a five per cent butterfat content.

Halfway between Holsteins and the Channel Island breeds are Ayrshires, originally from the county of Ayr, in Scotland.

Brown Swiss cows, first imported in 1869, are blockier in build than other breeds, and average between 6000 and 7000 pounds of milk (four per cent butterfat) in 298 days of milking.

The Dutch Belted breed, which has rather startling markings, is said to have been developed by the Dutch nobility, probably from the same stock which produced the popular Holstein-Friesian. P.T. Barnum imported the first Dutch Belted cows into America in 1840 and showed them in his circus. The breed is not popular now, but one still sees a few in almost every state.

Our only native North American milk cow is the Canadian, developed by crossbreeding. Sometimes called Quebec Jerseys, Canadians are descended from cattle brought to New France from Normandy and Brittany by French settlers; they are probably related to the stock which produced the Channel Island breeds.

Most milk today is homogenized, pasteurized, irradiated with vitamin D and fairly expensive.

To cut milk bills by one-third, mix powdered milk half and half with whole milk. Dried skim milk, or nonfat milk solids, may not be so rich in protein as regular whole milk, but nothing is sacrificed by way of calcium or about 100 other normal milk nutrients. Dry milk is the least costly way to get those nutrients; it is also easy to carry, easy to store, long-lasting if kept in dry form in a tightly-closed container, convenient to mix, easy to use in cooking.

In late October, 1969, the Department of Agriculture announced that after fourteen years of research it had perfected a dried whole milk, packed in oxygen-free cans, which when "stirred into cold water . . . makes a beverage that most people cannot distinguish from fresh whole milk." Now ready for commercial development, the new powder will in some cases sell for less than fluid whole milk, in some cases for a bit more.

Do not, however, be fooled by imitation milk, which is not the same as filled milk (though filled milk must, by law, be called "imitation milk" in California). Filled milk (called "melloream" in New York State) uses a vegetable oil in place of butterfat. It looks, tastes and feels in the mouth pretty much like whole milk, it keeps better than whole milk, and it is five or six cents cheaper per quart than whole milk. The Armed Forces have used a lot of it overseas. But while filled milk has been made in quantity since at least 1916, it has been banned from interstate commerce since 1923 when Congress, under pressure from the dairy interests, said filled milk was adulterated and a menace to public health. It is not.

What *is* a menace to public health is the completely artificial milklike products that do move across state lines.

Coming on the heels of artificial whipped cream, which has captured eighty per cent of the whipped cream market, this ersatz milk, marketed under names like "Moo," "Farmer's Daughter" and "Country Cousin," are made from ingredients like corn-syrup solids, vegetable fat, sugar, salt, artificial thickeners, colors and flavors, sodium caseinate [13] and water.

---

[13] A milk derivative, sodium caseinate is also used in coffee whiteners, which the industry likes to call non-dairy creamers, even though sodium caseinate is a dairy product. It is non-kosher for Jews, who may not use it at meals where meat is served (Chapter 7), and it is potentially dangerous to as many as 12,000 infants born each year in the U.S. with an intolerance for the casein in milk. Soybean protein could be substituted for sodium caseinate with little loss in nutritive value and solve both problems.

One brand analyzed by the National Dairy Council a few years ago contained only twenty per cent of the calcium, fifteen per cent of the phosphorus and twenty-five per cent of the protein in whole milk.

The fact that imitation milk can be shipped across state lines means the FDA can set a standard of identity for imitation milk, as it does for other food products (see footnote, page 516). A good standard of identity will hopefully include adequate amounts of the above-named nutrients, plus vitamin B_{12}, pantothenic acid, pyridoxine (vitamin B_6), folic acid, biotin, choline, magnesium, chromium, cobalt, manganese, molybdenum and zinc, all of which are found in whole milk.

Mary, have a little lamb

Sheep outnumber any other kind of livestock in the world. For many countries, perhaps for most, the principal meat is lamb or mutton.

Not so for America. We Americans eat only about four pounds of lamb per person each year (Britons eat five times as much, counting both lamb and mutton, and they eat far more lamb than mutton; Frenchmen in 1965 ate 6.68 pounds of lamb on the average). The lamb Americans do eat is usually overcooked (it should be pink), and compared with beef or pork, lamb is not even in the running here. Of the billion-plus sheep in the world, we have only 19 million, and our sheep population keeps declining.

For most American tastes, mutton is too strong; one occasionally sees yearling mutton (one to two years old) in our stores, but more usually it is "Genuine Spring Lamb" (the USDA mark), which is three to six months old when it is slaughtered, or year-round lamb, five to eleven months old.

Costliest (it can sell for nearly $4 a pound) is baby lamb, or hothouse lamb, milk-fed like a baby for anywhere from three to nine weeks, but seldom for more than six. It is raised in New Jersey and Pennsylvania and is not available in the West at all, only in some

Eastern states. Alfred Hitchcock, the film director, used to send his private plane to New York to fetch baby lamb. While beef may have less flavor unless it is slaughtered at a more mature age, baby lamb is quite flavorsome, perhaps because it is packaged by tradition in hogsheads (large sixty-three-gallon casks) complete with hide and hooves.

Little lamb of any kind is eaten in the Western states, except in the coastal cities. With a distorted sense of "tradition" that keeps alive the old conflict between cattlemen and sheepmen, Westerners identify with Hollywood cowboys and scornfully call lamb "sheep," or even "goat" (as indeed it sometimes was before Upton Sinclair's *The Jungle* had its effect). Ironically, the beef sold in the West is inferior to what is available in the East; one can not get a sirloin steak with a bone in most places. Westerners are aware of the situation; they bluster about their marvelous barbecues, but they still prize "New York cut" steaks and one brand of pork is advertised as "Easternmost in quality."

For the more populous East, lamb chops (the French call them *côtelettes*, little ribs, *d'agneau*), crown roast of lamb, leg (*gigot*) of lamb, rack (rib section) of lamb, saddle (both loins) of lamb and baron of lamb (both loins or the saddle together with both legs) have some popularity, with or without mint jelly, but we eat little more than half as much lamb as we ate per capita early in the century, and we leave mutton chops to our English cousins (whose lamb chops are skewered around kidneys and broiled).

Some sheep are raised primarily for meat, some mostly for their wool; the latter include Merino sheep (developed in Spain from animals introduced there by the Romans in the reign of Claudius in the first century) and Rambouillets (developed in France from Spanish Merinos).

We will discuss America's Merino sheep presently, but while Merinos were an improvement over the "native" sheep American farmers had raised before Merinos were introduced (sheep were less subject to disease than hogs or dairy cattle), Merino meat does not taste like much and is dry. What gave lamb and mutton some popularity in late nineteenth- and early twentieth-century America was the importation of English breeds. Our big lamb and mutton producers today are the so-called Down breeds (Shropshires, Southdowns, Hampshires, Oxfords and Suffolks) and other medium-wool breeds from Britain like Dorset, Corriedale, Cheviot, Ryeland and Kerry Hill. For centuries these breeds not only supplied England with lamb and mutton but furnished the wool—the best in Europe—for the looms of Flanders and Italy and the worsted mills of Britain itself, wool for the woolsack, symbolic seat of the Lord Chancellor, wool that enriched the Crown and the people and enabled the English to build their Empire.

Only a fourth to a third of U.S. sheep are raised for wool; the rest are for food. We raise almost all the lamb we eat, though the "thin lamb" used in baby food is, according to the head of the Meat Importers Council of America, "almost unavailable from domestic sources and must be imported." The U.S. imported 23 million pounds of lamb in 1968, most of it from New Zealand and Australia, which upset the National Lamb Feeders Association and the National Wool Growers Association; they want Congress to set an import quota of 18 million pounds.[14] (Cattlemen, in turn, want imports of corned beef, cured ham and other cooked meats restricted; these and other meat imports amount to over a billion pounds a year, which helps keep prices down but miffs domestic producers.)

Most numerous of the Down breeds of sheep in America is the Shropshire, introduced here in 1855. Smallest and oldest of the Downs is the Southdown, which supplies the market for top-quality lamb.

Each breed has its adherents, each has special qualities. The largest animals are Lincolns, the next largest Cotswolds. A mature Lincoln ewe weighs about 225 pounds, while a mature Southdown weighs only 135 to 155 pounds. Biggest of the Downs is the Oxford, developed from the Hampshire, which is slightly smaller.

---

[14] Under the U.S. Meat Import Act of 1964, the President is required to invoke import quotas if receipts of certain meats are expected to exceed a "trigger point" level, but the quotas cannot be activated unless imports rise to 110 per cent of the base quota.

Cheviots, their faces bare of wool, the rams' noses distinctively Roman, eat rough fodder and do well in country where vegetation, while ample, is coarse. Cheviots were first brought to America by Scottish immigrants and have been popular in the Northeast and Midwest.

Hothouse lamb comes from Dorsets, raised mostly in the East. Dorsets, whose rams have handsome horns, heavy and spiral-shaped, mate earlier in the year than other breeds and produce their lambs in the fall.

Suffolks, with their black faces and stockings, are less common than the other Down breeds; they are found mostly on the Western ranges.

These Western sheep usually contain a strain of Merino blood. The reason is a matter of animal instinct. While the English breeds were traditionally raised in the confinement of small hedged or fenced fields, the Merinos in Spain customarily spent their winters in the South and were driven north to the high plateaus in the spring. In the Western United States, sheep follow the same dyed-in-the-wool pattern; it is important that they have no inclination to scatter when they make their long trips to and from their mountain pastures in Utah, Colorado, Wyoming and Montana. The trips take weeks; the sheep, often herded by a Basque from the northwest of Spain, working with a trained sheepdog, must stay together.

Back in the eighteenth century, the Spanish prohibited the export of their Merinos.[15] The controls were not strictly enforced in the case of Colonel David Humphreys, our first minister to Spain. A close friend of Washington and like Washington a farmer, Humphreys contrived to smuggle seventy-five Merino ewes and twenty-five rams across the border into Portugal when he stepped down from his post in Madrid. He had the sheep put aboard ship and taken to the Humphreys farm in Derby, Connecticut. It is said that he sold the coveted Merinos for as much as $1000 to $1500 each.

---

[15] Merinos were first introduced into Australia early in the nineteenth century; that country, whose 165 million sheep produce thirty per cent of the world's wool, prohibited export of Merino stud rams from 1929 to 1969. Export of Merino semen and fertilized Merino ova is still banned by the Australians.

Merinos were later imported on a large scale by William Jarvis, a Boston-born businessman who had a farm in Weatherfield, Vermont.

After Napoleon conquered Spain in 1808, restrictions against exporting sheep were eased; Jarvis, who was serving as U.S. consul in Lisbon, shipped nearly 4000 Merinos to a variety of American ports.

From September, 1810, to April, 1811, fifty-two vessels brought more than 9000 Merinos into New York from Spain, and eight more vessels landed an additional number that went unrecorded. Over 17,000 Merinos are estimated to have come into the United States through various ports at the time. New England (especially Vermont) and later Ohio became Merino breeding centers.

The Rambouillet, developed from a flock that France's Louis XVI kept on his estate at Rambouillet, is basically a Merino sheep grown larger. It was evidently first brought to America by Robert Livingston, the American diplomat who helped make the Louisiana Purchase in 1803 and who underwrote Robert Fulton's steamboat. Livingston brought Rambouillets to his Clermont estate on the Hudson.

An American breed, the Columbia, is a cross between some of the longer-wooled English breeds and the Rambouillet to create a sheep with a good weight of mutton and wool, a breed adaptable to rugged conditions on the Western range.

Two other American breeds are the Panama and the Romeldale. Not yet recognized as breeds but in the development stage are the Southdale and the Targhee.

English Leicesters were introduced to America early (George Washington had some) but they never became popular here.

Some of these sheep may be seen at state and county fairs, which are always more fun when something is known about livestock. Livestock judging has played a large part in the development of animals raised for meat in America; in some parts of the country the blue ribbons are still contested for as fiercely as ever.

And it all began with sheep: the first agricultural fair was organized about 1811 at Pittsfield, Massachusetts, by Elkanah Watson, a businessman who bred Merino sheep.

Billy, Nanny and the kids

The earliest animals domesticated by man may have been dogs, whose superior senses of smell and hearing helped first the hunter and later the herdsman.

Or they may have been goats: goatlike remains have been found in Swiss lake dwellings that date back to the Stone Age. The Egyptians drove domestic goats and sheep over the damp fields of the Nile Valley to trample seeds into the soil. Goats were certainly well-known in Biblical times for their milk, their hides and hair, and as sacrifices to Jehovah.

Virginia's first settlers brought milk goats with them, but while sheepmen in Texas (our biggest sheep-raising state) run goats with their sheep (to destroy thorns and prickles that can tear the fine wool of Merino sheep and, as "Judas goats," to decoy sheep into the slaughter pens), "the poor man's cow" has never been as popular in the U.S. and Canada as it is in Europe and Mexico.

Goats' milk is somewhat sweeter than cows' milk. Some people find its flavor and odor disagreeable; when the doe has been milked in unclean quarters, or the buck has been allowed to come near the milk, everybody finds it disagreeable. Buck goats do have a strong odor which is quickly absorbed by the warm milk. (Buck and doe are the proper words for what generations of children have called billy goat and nanny goat.)

Goats' milk is actually more digestible than cows' milk (it has smaller fat globules), so it is often prescribed for invalids, older people and children who cannot tolerate cows' milk.

The main breeds of goats are Toggenburgs (usually hornless and the most popular breed in America), Saanens, Spanish Maltese, Schwartzenburg-Guggisburgers, Nubians and French Alpines. The Saanen is the Holstein of the dairy goats; it produces the greatest quantity of milk, though no goat gives anything like the quantity a cow produces. A good milking doe will average two quarts a day for ten months, though some will average three and a few even four or five quarts. A Saanen doe holds the record with almost seven and a half quarts.

In Corsica, the Greek islands and a few other parts of the Mediterranean, young kid is prized as meat, roasted on a spit or cooked in a *ragout*, but Englishmen and Americans are prejudiced against goat meat as they are about so many foods (Chapter 7).

Everything but the oink

Cows, sheep and goats are sources of meat, milk, many milk products, leather, wool and some minor by-products (gelatine, for example, is made from parts of the hooves of young cattle. So is calf's foot jelly).

At least as many food and non-food items come from pigs.

Wild pigs were first domesticated more than 5000 years ago by the Chinese (the pig is still China's dominant livestock animal), though wild pigs even now roam the forests of Asia, Europe and the Pacific islands.[16] Mongol armies took pigs with them for meat and for cooking fat. The pigs were scavengers; they could generally feed themselves on whatever they could scrounge.

During the Middle Ages, some Chinese pigs were crossed with European pigs to produce lard pigs. Medieval pigs were greased and turned loose in enclosures, where they were chased by serfs to amuse the nobility. Later, in the eighteenth century, France's Louis XIV had pigs dressed in clothing to entertain the royal court.

America's first pigs were introduced by the Spanish explorer Hernando de Soto; he brought thirteen pigs with him when he landed in what is now Tampa, Florida, in 1542.

For most of history, pigs were pigs; little thought was given to improving the breeds. Not until the nineteenth century were medieval lard pigs broken up into different breeds in England.

---

[16] An authentic Hawaiian *luau* (outdoor feast) must, according to *kamaainas* (old-timers in the islands), include a *kalua* pig, roasted in an *imu* (underground oven) with bananas, breadfruit, sweet potatoes and such. Originally the pig was wild; now it is generally a domestic porker.

Most of our American breeds were developed here, though there is no native American pig unless you count the peccary, or javelina, of Mexico, now found also in parts of Texas and South America. The peccary is related to the pig, but so is the hippopotamus. The big prehistoric Entedelont had a piglike head and lived in North America before the Age of Man, as did the camel, but there is no American pig today that cannot trace its ancestry back to ancient China.

Wild razorback hogs found in the Great Smokies of Tennessee and North Carolina (there are also a few in Mississippi, California and New Hampshire) are not descended from either the peccary or the Entedelont; they stem from animals introduced by sportsmen for hunting. (Sportsmen also introduced the pheasant, the Hungarian partridge, the European hare, the Barbary sheep, the fallow deer and, for anglers, the brown trout.) Boar hunting is a big sport in Europe; it never gained much of a following here, but litters of razorback hogs, born to romantically-inclined runaway domestic gilts and sows, still roam some American woods to remind us of their sporting great-great-grandsires.

Lard pigs were the most popular kind in America until the late 1940's, when hydrogenated vegetable and seed oils began to replace lard in such products as shortening and margarine. As the demand for animals fats has declined, pigs have been raised primarily for ham, bacon [17] and pork chops. Improved breeding, feeding and marketing

---

[17] Bacon is an Old French word that meant pork and cured pork products. Pork was called "bacon" in England up through Shakespeare's (and Sir Francis Bacon's) day. What we call bacon the French now call *lard:* fried bacon is *lard frite,* a rasher of bacon is a *tranche de lard.* "Bacon" pigs are obviously used for many cuts of meat besides those extravagant strips (about four fifths of the strip is rendered into grease) which Americans use as a condiment for breakfast eggs, dinner salads and such. Top-quality bacon is rare today because it comes from the center bellies of small, lean hogs, slaughtered at 100 to 140 pounds, about 100 pounds less than the weight of most slaughter-gilts. English, Canadian and Danish farmers are encouraged to feed their hogs alfalfa, bran, oats and other fodder instead of fat-producing corn in order to yield better bacon. Danish bacon, exported in cans, is cured differently from U.S. bacon and is too salty for some tastes. Canadian bacon is boned loin of pork that has been cured and smoked. Irish bacon, more heavily smoked, includes both the loin and the strip or slice of pork we Americans know as bacon.

methods have reduced the average lard yield per slaughtered hog to about twenty-seven pounds, which is still a lot of lard. Demand remains low; so does the price of lard, which has led makers of margarine and shortening products to begin using more lard.

Breeders used to talk about lard pigs and bacon pigs (which were not developed until the twentieth century); now they look for "meat" pigs, which can be of almost any breed, even traditional lard breeds like Duroc (formerly called Duroc-Jersey), Poland China, Chester White, Hampshire, Spot, Berkshire, Hereford, Mulefoot and OIC.

The first five on the above list, despite their names, were developed in America. The Shakers (see footnote, page 281), who refrained from sexual intercourse themselves, created the Poland China by mating the white Big China breed with a rangy, half-wild backwoods hog.

There is considerable variation within any breed, as well as between breeds, in how much meat a carcass produces.

From traditional "bacon" breeds like Yorkshire and Tamworth, from England, and Landrace, from Scandinavia, a number of new swine breeds have been developed in the U.S. in the last twenty-five years, notably at the USDA Agricultural Research Center at Beltsville, Maryland.

In addition to the new breeds, inbred lines of existing breeds have been developed, the object always being to produce animals which will breed prolifically (livestock breeders try to achieve artificially what humans, through natural selection, have achieved over millenniums in terms of reproductivity), gain weight rapidly, use feed efficiently and produce a carcass that is high in lean cuts, low in fat cuts.

To develop good market hogs with broad backs, flat sides, good hams and not too much fat, pigs are fed largely on alfalfa, barley, skim milk and protein supplements, along with the traditional feed, corn, which is still the basic fodder of hogs.

The best Virginia hams are said to come from pigs fed on peanuts, but even these, you may be sure, are fattened chiefly on corn.

When a hog (or gilt) is slaughtered at five or six months of age, its weight is close to 220 pounds and, if it is U.S. No. 1 grade,[18] about forty-four per cent of the carcass is ham and loin.

Pork consumption, so high in early America, used to rival beef consumption in the U.S. But while beef consumption has nearly doubled, pork consumption remains about the same as it was sixty years ago. One reason is that people with farm backgrounds have always appreciated pork, the farmer's traditional meat, more than urban people, and today fewer and fewer people have roots in the soil. So while the average American now eats over 110 pounds of beef each year, he eats less than seventy pounds of pork, including ham, bacon, pork sausage and ham hocks, which is still more than twice the British average of less than twenty-five pounds. (Austrians are the champion pork eaters, averaging almost eighty-four pounds; West Germans average nearly seventy-four pounds; a Frenchman averages about sixty-one pounds, or did in 1965.)

Pork, when it is plentiful, is usually economical, especially cuts like pork shoulder, fresh shoulder butt, boneless smoked shoulder butt, smoked picnic pork, shoulder steaks, end-cut chops, ham shanks, hocks, pigs' feet and the organ cuts. Loin, leg and shoulder, in that order, are the most desirable cuts. Young pork is greyish pink with a covering of pure white fat; older pork, less desirable, is considerably redder.

Bacon is often the biggest meat expense for a family, though bacon has little nutritional value. Consumers Union suggests that since bacon deteriorates with age, it should stay in supermarket meat cases no more than a week or so and should be marked with a packing date so the buyer can know how long it has been in the store. No present law requires any such date marking, so we run a risk that the bacon we buy may have changed in color and flavor or even begun to turn rancid. Use the bacon within a week after opening the package or it may lose flavor or pick up foreign flavors from the refrigerator. Bacon keeps a little longer if rewrapped tightly in plastic; but do not freeze it unless it is impossible to buy fresh bacon once a week.

---

[18] Pork has fewer USDA grades than other meats, largely because there is less discrepancy in the ages at which hogs are butchered.

Slab bacon, sold with the rind on, keeps better than sliced bacon; buy it by the pound and slice it at home.

Hams are best bought canned because there is less waste; but be sure the can is refrigerated at the supermarket, and keep it refrigerated at home.

Fresh ham is a leg of pork, not cured or smoked; it is lovely roasted plain or stuffed with apple or cornbread stuffing, especially with a crisp skin (do not let the butcher skin it), but one has to buy at least half the leg—too much for a small family—and cook it long and slow.

Pork chops? Buy the whole center loin—the ends are cheaper but too often have big hidden pockets of fat—and have it cut into chops to get more for the same money. Instead of broiling or pan-frying them to death, as anxious Americans usually do, braise them and do them justice. Spareribs, once considered budget cuts, have become so popular they are now relatively high in price.

The pigsty is long gone. Pigs, which no longer "cost nothing to keep" as in the time Henry Adams wrote about, are now raised on the range and in clean, modern pig barns.

Years ago, problems of zoonoses (animal diseases) made it impossible to raise pigs and other livestock in close confinement. Infectious and non-infectious diseases, along with parasites, still take a heavy toll of cattle, sheep, swine and poultry and are mainly responsible for the low levels of livestock operations in Africa and Asia. Even in the U.S., animal diseases and parasites cost us close to $2 billion a year, despite the development of synthetic antibiotics [19] to control and eliminate most zoonoses.

---

[19] In April, 1968, the U.S. Food and Drug Administration proposed a ban on the use of injectable penicillin-streptomycin combinations which were shown by studies to persist in the bodies of food animals longer than had been suspected. Some people, said the FDA, might be allergic to the antibiotics. More important, they might favor the growth of drug-resistant bacteria communicable to humans. Subsequent evidence showed the residues of antibiotics to be far less than had earlier been suggested and in May, 1969, the FDA said the antibiotic injections could continue to be used except in the last thirty days before slaughter. They gave a trade group of veterinary drug-makers up to two years to prove that a residue of two parts per million poses no human health hazard.

In years to come, at least in some areas, livestock will have to be kept in barns. At this stage in history there is just under one head of livestock for every American man, woman and child; the countryside is full of grazing animals.

But urban sprawl is taking over at least a million and a half acres of open land every year, fifty per cent more than the rate ten years ago. Highways in America now cover with asphalt and concrete an area the size of Massachusetts, Connecticut, Vermont, Rhode Island and Delaware combined.

According to some observers, it is wasteful to use land to feed animals, anyway. It should be used to feed people directly. The indirect production of food via livestock wastes about ninety per cent of the food the animal consumes.

But the President's Science Advisory Committee has pointed out that "over sixty per cent of the world's agricultural land is nonarable and suited only for grazing. Animals are the only practical means of utilizing this resource for human food production." So raising more livestock and poultry may actually represent the world's best opportunity to feed more people and increase global nutrition levels.

People cannot eat grass. The polygastric ruminants (cattle, sheep, goats) can convert grass into protein. They can also, by virtue of having more than one stomach, convert the chemical compound urea into protein and are thus not dependent on grasses, or on feed grains.

Injections of penicillin, chlortetracycline, tetracycline, chloramphenicol and bacitracin are not permitted. U.S. meat packers are prohibited from slaughtering animals for thirty days after antibiotics have been injected; nor may the milk of cows given such injections be used for certain periods after treatment. In late November, 1969, Britain's Minister of Agriculture banned the use of penicillin and tetracycline in livestock feed and said, "We are the first country in the world to tackle this problem." Britain's National Farmers Union protested that the ban did not apply to imported food products. The British action was based on evidence of bacteria with R factors, resistant to antibiotics, being transferred from animals to humans. About $72.5 million worth of antibiotics are added to U.S. livestock feeds, though such feeds may not be used within three or five days of slaughter.

Urea, produced in giant factories, is used widely in dairy, beef and sheep feeding in the U.S. and other developed countries; a lot more would be used if prices of feed grains were to rise.

Thanks to the conversion powers of one-celled microbial organisms in the huge first stomachs, or rumens, of cattle and sheep, these animals can also be fed plant residues and mill wastes, rich sources of energy and protein for livestock though unsalvageable for human food. Examples include bagasse (crushed sugar cane or sugar beet wastes), molasses, bone meal, meat scraps, tankage (residues from tanks in which carcasses have been steamed and their fat rendered), spent brewers' grains and by-products of fruit, soybean, peanut, copra, palm nut, safflower, coconut and cottonseed processing. Even ground-up newspapers can be used for feed.

This may mean eventually that the hog, that "mortgage lifter" which converts feed into meat so quickly that it has helped generations of farmers pay off their mortgages, will lose favor in rural America. But as of now, the U.S. leads the world in pork production and our hog population fluctuates between 47 million and 60 million, depending mostly on the prices pork products fetch.

Milk cows have shown a consistent decline in numbers from almost 28 million in 1945 to 14.1 million at the beginning of 1969, despite the growth of population in those years. Increased productivity per cow and decreasing milk and cream consumption are the reasons.

Sheep have dropped in number somewhat less consistently, but there were only 18.2 million in the country at the start of 1969, down from nearly 29 million in January, 1960.

Beef cattle, on the other hand, have been on the increase. We had 47.8 million head in 1920, 54.6 million in 1950, 61.9 million in 1958, 76.7 million in 1960. Today we have close to 96 million.

The numbers sound big—until we look at the figures of America's poultry population.

Hens, eggs and chicken-feed

Poultry is such an efficient way to convert plant protein into animal protein that birds may become man's chief source of animal protein in the next half-century.

The Japanese, always short of land, have been raising poultry in multi-storied, circular houses open to the sun but shielded from the rain; such "fowl flats" may presage the future of husbandry in the more crowded parts of the world.

We Americans eat 12 billion pounds of poultry meat a year (some sixty pounds per capita, six times the British rate, about the same as the French). Chicken and turkey, once a special Sunday treat, are now generally about the lowest-priced meats the consumer can buy, mostly because of the enormous efficiencies achieved in poultry raising.

The discoveries of vitamins and their uses in feeding poultry in the mid-1920's, and the subsequent development of poultry health products, revolutionized poultry farming. Chickens and turkeys could be raised in confinement year-round. Diseases still wipe out flocks on occasion, but while every farmer's wife used to keep chickens, today the industry has become centered in huge concentrations like those on the Delmarva (Delaware-Maryland-Virginia) Peninsula and in Maine.

The growth of the industry has been far more rapid than that of livestock; per capita consumption has increased 600 per cent since World War II.[20] With six per cent of the world's people, the U.S. has about a third of all the world's chickens and turkeys. We produce more than 9 billion pounds of broilers a year, mostly in the South and the East: over two and a half billion birds, up from only 34 million in 1934.

On a modern American broiler farm, one man can take care of

---

[20] British poultry consumption, while still low by U.S. standards, has soared, too. Between 1956 and 1965 it quadrupled.

25,000 birds at a time, and since broilers are sold for market at eight weeks of age, he can raise more than 160,000 a year, more than twice what was possible for one man back in 1940.

Broiler production is a volatile, free-swinging business where factors like feed costs, consumer incomes, availability of pork and beef, supplies of hatching eggs, armed forces purchases, strikes and export shipments can cause thirty to forty per cent price swings within a given year.

The factor least considered, it seems, is taste.

Businessmen complain of the "rubber chicken" served at hotel luncheons and testimonial dinners; they exaggerate only a little. Housewives complain that chicken today is tasteless; they have a point. When chicken was killed at three or four months of age, it had time to develop some flavor; feeding chickens with supplements that fatten them to marketable size and weight in eight weeks may be efficient, but the efficiency is at the expense of flavor.

Smart shoppers look in October for "stewing fowl," broad-breasted hens close to a year old that egg farmers have sold off. No longer able to lay eggs at a pace to match younger hens, their meat is rich in flavor. It is too tough for anything but the stewpot, but it is chicken that tastes like chicken.

American broilers and fryers are no match for old hens.

The famous *poularde de Bresse*, in France, a breed praised for its table qualities since the sixteenth century, provides a shattering comparison. "The Bird with the Steel-Blue Legs," as it is advertised, must by law be fattened for three to four months before it is marketed; it is often fattened for ten months. Early in life the fowls roam freely in the fields near Lyon, eating insects, bran, wheat and barley. Then they are shut up in dark cells for two months or more and their gullets are crammed with a paste of corn and skimmed milk. Marketed from October to late March, this paragon of poultry (its only rival is the *poularde du Mans*) may weigh only three or four pounds (as much as a U.S. broiler weighs at eight weeks) or it may reach fourteen pounds—all solid meat, not fat, and very little bone.

Expensive? *Bien sûr.* But nothing like the *poularde de Bresse* is available in the U.S. at any price. Agriculture Department researchers are trying to cross U.S. chickens with quail [21] to give chicken more flavor. Perhaps there is hope. But thus far the poultry industry is too concerned with the economics of producing a pound of meat from 2.25 pounds of feed (versus 4.5 pounds back in 1941). It is all very efficient, but it takes a lot of herbs and spices to make chicken taste like anything.

In addition to efficiently specialized broiler and pullet farms, we have developed farms that specialize in turkeys, in ducks, in game hens, and in eggs.

Which came first?

A hen will lay twelve eggs for every four pounds of feed it consumes, more than 200 eggs a year on the average—which is not enough to satisfy the average American appetite. With over 372 million hens a-laying, we ate an average of 314 eggs each in 1969, down from 356 in the 1957–59 period but up from the 300 average of the late 1930's. (The British, by comparison, have been increasing their consumption of eggs as consistently as we in America have been decreasing ours: from eighty-five eggs each in 1880, Britons moved up to 116 in the 1920's, to 228 in the late 1950's and to over 270 today, the highest egg-consumption rate in Europe.)

Eggs have throughout history been symbols of fertility. Slavic and German peasants used to smear egg on their plows to ensure good crops. French brides used to break an egg when they crossed the threshold of a new home, and the Easter egg not only celebrates the end of Lenten abstinence but represents a Christianization of pagan egg ceremonies linking human sexuality with spring planting, a connection we observed in Chapter 1.

While the average American hen lays 217 eggs a year (versus 203 for the average British hen), an English Rhode Island Red laid 353

---

[21] Called partridge in the South, though in England quail and partridge are two distinct species of small birds.

eggs in 1957 and ten Japanese Leghorns that year laid 3611, an average of 361 per bird. As for size, the record is a sixteen-ounce double-
yoked egg an American Leghorn laid in 1956.

Eggs that become chickens take twenty-one days at a warm temperature to hatch their wet, chirping chicks (duck and turkey eggs
take twenty-eight days); just how much warmth is required came in
for some debate in England late in 1969 when Anthony Armstrong-
Jones, Lord Snowden, produced a BBC TV documentary which pur-
ported to show a live chick hatched from a fertilized egg incubated
between the breasts of a sixty-year-old housewife.

A knight from the Isle of Anglesey objected that "it takes twenty-
one days at 104 degrees Fahrenheit to hatch an egg and from my
experience of ladies' bosoms this is rarely attainable." But Britain's
National Institute of Poultry Husbandry countered that "if you tried
to hatch eggs at 104° you would cook them"; eggs, it said, were usually
incubated at about 99°, close to body temperature.

The affair occupied acres of newsprint and hours of BBC television time. Historians cited the fact that Livia, wife of the Roman
Emperor Augustus, had hatched an egg in her corsage on the advice
of an oracle to determine the sex of her unborn child (the chick was
a male, and so was the child, who grew up to be the Emperor Tiberius). Students of the English novel recalled Arabella Donn, in
Thomas Hardy's *Jude the Obscure,* who asks the hero to keep his
hands off her because she is incubating a Cochin's egg in her cleavage.

However it is incubated, an egg must be fertile to produce a chick.
But few hens today receive the attentions of ardent cocks. The in-
tricate ovum, the small womb with its fetus and protecting sea of
albumen, hardly ever turns into another egg-producing bird. Most of
the eighty billion chicken yolks and whites produced in North
America each year are broken out of their brown or white shells
(speckled shells are now scarce as hen's teeth) and fried, scrambled,
boiled, poached, shirred, coddled, deviled, made into omelettes and
soufflés, used in recipes (eggs serve as binders and leavening agents
in baking, they enrich icings, sauces, candies, custards, ice cream and
mayonnaise) or dried into powder.

Egg producers promote the egg as the original packaged food and boast legitimately of the egg's high protein, vitamin and mineral content, soft-pedaling the fact that an egg's fat-content is equal to that of a tablespoon of heavy cream, which makes cholesterol-conscious Americans unhappy and has led to our decrease in egg consumption.

Most hens start producing eggs at five or six months and keep it up for twelve or fifteen months, after which they are slaughtered. To extend the egg-laying life of hens, many farmers today follow a "recycling" process called force-molting. When a hen molts naturally, she loses her feathers and stops laying eggs for a month or so. By inducing molt (achieved by removing the bird's water supply for a day and her feed for three or four days), the egg farmer can put a hen back in production after a six- to eight-week layoff and she will lay eggs for another nine or ten months. It is cheaper than buying new birds, but it leads at times to overproduction, which lowers prices— good for consumers, bad for egg farmers. Most recently, the problem has been underproduction. Americans were using 64 billion eggs a year, U.S. egg farmers were unable to meet the demand, and despite imports from Denmark, Holland and Spain, retail egg prices went up to nearly a dollar a dozen in early 1970.

Eggs were hatched by artificial means in ancient China (the Chinese had domestic chickens as early as 1400 B.C.) and in Egypt, but the modern incubator is less than 100 years old. It controls temperature, ventilation and humidity to approximate natural hatching conditions in the nest. Some incubators rock to simulate the movements of the mother hen setting on her eggs. Much of today's U.S. egg industry depends on such artifices as the incubator and force-molting.

Hens introduced to England from Asia in the sixteenth century laid brown eggs, which are still preferred to white eggs in Britain and on the Continent. Brown eggs command a premium price in New England, too, while white eggs cost more than brown in other sections of the country. Inside the shell there is no difference if the grade is the same. It is silly to pay more on account of color prejudice, but thousands of housewives do it. (Sykes International, Britain's biggest poultry breeders, spent $625,000 to have a team of geneticists, using a $150,000 computer, develop a hen, the Sykes Brown, which lays uniformly large brown eggs; the success of this effort was announced late in 1969.)

Some eggs break more easily than others; their shells are thinner. Younger hens lay eggs with stronger shells; so do hens whose feed contains special vitamins and minerals, including ground-up oyster shells. The harder shell is often less porous, too, so it keeps the egg fresh longer.

Watch the sizes of eggs. If medium-sized eggs are an eighth cheaper than large eggs, save money by buying medium-sized eggs. If small eggs are a fourth cheaper than large eggs, buy the *small* economy size.

Eggs are graded AA, A, B and C, the grades being determined by candlers, who no longer use candles and who, in addition to grading the eggs, weed out fertilized eggs which cannot be sold as kosher (Chapter 7). Eggs should be fresh. Because of our fetish for cleanliness, alas, they are now washed in hot water before they reach the store, so they taste less fresh than the spattered eggs of yore.

Grade AA or Fresh Fancy eggs have good thick whites which stand up well when fried sunny side up. The yolk is round and firm and stays in the center of the egg when it is boiled. The white is thinner in Grade A eggs, the yolk is slightly lower and less well-centered, but both A and AA eggs are recommended for frying, boiling or poaching and to look most appetizing and taste best. B and C grades are perfectly good for scrambling, baking or using in recipes; they are particularly good buys in summer.

As for what comes out of the eggs allowed to hatch, it was all a matter of chance through most of history; the surprise when Hans Christian Andersen's "ugly duckling" turned out to be a cygnet, or baby swan, reflects the general confusion that existed before scientific poultry breeding, a relatively modern phenomenon.

Wild jungle fowl (*Gallus bankiva*) have been traced back to 3000 B.C., but while they were domesticated early in China, nobody did much to improve the original wild stock until about 200 years ago. Since then, improvements have been vast: while the little two-pound jungle hen laid only a few eggs a year, the big thirteen-pound Jersey Giant may lay 300.

Many medieval superstitions centered around chickens, which probably reached western Europe about 600 B.C. As a symbol of courage, the cock became an emblem of France.

One thing that helped develop the vitality of poultry and gave domestic fowl wide distribution was the ancient sport of cockfighting, a test of courage.

In many countries, including the U.S., the cruel matching of fighting cocks has been outlawed for years for humanitarian reasons (though it was estimated in the 1950's that Texas had more cockpits than movie theaters, and this may still be the case). For all its bloody savagery, cockfighting did speed up the old Darwinian survival-of-the-fittest process of natural selection; and as the sport spread throughout the world, so did sturdy chickens.

Chickens came to the New World with Columbus and the colonists; they became the focus of voodoo rituals performed by *houngans* (voodoo priests) in Haiti and the focal point of many an American Sunday dinner.

Our domestic chickens today are of four basic classes: Mediterraneans, Asiatics, English and Americans. Mediterraneans include Leghorns, from Livorno in Tuscany, Minorcas, Anconas and some minor breeds.

Asiatics, descended from jungle fowl and Malay fowl, were not interbred until they reached England and America in the nineteenth century. Cochins, Brahmas and Langshans were so exotic-looking that people who saw them at shows (the "Golden Era" of livestock and poultry shows was from 1870 to 1920) became chicken breeders. Show breeding, however, aimed at appearance (a profusion of loose feathers was the prime desideratum); qualities of non-broodiness and egg production were hardly considered. Selectively bred for the wrong reasons, Asiatics suffered. While they made valuable contributions to the development of American crossbreeds, none is a major pure breed in America today.

Of the English breeds, only the Buff Orpington, which lays brown-shelled eggs, has wide distribution in the U.S. now, though the Cornish, which is a poor layer but meaty, with well-developed breasts, has increased enormously in popularity.

American Class poultry has yellow skin, preferred in many markets to the white skin of English breeds, though chicken that is too yellow has too much fat. American Class poultry also lays brown-shelled eggs,[22] unpopular in most markets.

Rhode Island Reds, Wyandottes, Barred Plymouth Rocks and White Plymouth Rocks are all American Class breeds. Farmers of the Little Compton district of Rhode Island developed the Rhode Island Red originally by crossing Malay game fowl with reddish-colored Shanghais (or Cochins, as they were later called). Subsequent crossings introduced blood of other breeds like Brown Leghorn, Cornish and Wyandotte.

Oldest of the Plymouth Rocks, the favorite of broiler producers, is the Barred variety started in Connecticut in 1865 with a cross between a Dominique and a Black Cochin. Other American Class breeds (though some do not sound very American) are Dominiques, New Hampshires, Javas, Chantecleers, Jersey Giants and Lamonas.

There are, as well, newer breeds. The U.S. Department of Agriculture, at its great Beltsville, Maryland research center, has developed chickens that are virtually all white meat, and turkeys small enough to be practical for small families. Spring chicken and autumn turkey are now available at any time of year, fresh as well as frozen.

The only daughter of Benjamin Franklin, that founding father who said we should have chosen the turkey, not the bald eagle, as our national bird, married an Englishman, Richard Bache. It was Bache who introduced the English pheasant to America and tried to raise them on his New Jersey estate. But while pheasants raised today on state game farms are about twenty-four weeks old when they are set free at the start of the annual hunting season, the chicken we buy

---

[22] The only exception is the little-known Lamona breed, whose hens lay white eggs.

at the store is only eight weeks old when it is sent to market—which is why it does not taste like France's *poularde de Bresse*.

The gobblers

A chicken is not just a chicken, a turkey is not just a turkey. The bird Ben Franklin admired did start, remember, in America. The seven varieties we now raise in America are all descended from the ocellated turkey of Yucatan and the North American turkey (which has five subspecies), though the foundation stock of our present breeds came to America by way of Europe, where the Spanish (Chapter 2) had introduced turkeys, possibly as early as 1498.

The commonest and handsomest U.S. turkey today is the Broad-breasted Bronze with its mixture of black, bronze and yellow or orange feathers with white tips. We also raise Narragansetts, White Hollands, Bourbon Reds and Beltsville Small Whites, Blacks and Slates, killing them at three to six months of age (they used to live to eight or twelve) when they weigh at least five pounds each.

Turkeys are the hardest of all poultry to raise. The young ones catch cold if their feet get wet; the older ones sometimes panic and suffocate themselves, pressing together in their fear. But the great amount of meat per bird outweighs any disadvantages of turkey raising; U.S. growers will send close to 110 million turkeys to market in 1970. The record year was 1967, with 126.4 million of the big birds depressing prices and lowering future output. Per capita consumption of turkey in 1969 was 8.4 pounds.

Ten years ago, eighty per cent of turkey meat was eaten at Thanksgiving and Christmas; now the year-end holiday season accounts for only fifty per cent of our 1.4 billion pound consumption of turkey meat; often listed as "chicken" on restaurant menus, turkey is a year-round staple.

Web-footed flocks and gaggles

America's twelve major breeds of ducks are, with one exception, all descended from the common mallard, the wild duck of the Northern Hemisphere. The exception is the Muscovy duck, originally found from Mexico to southern Brazil. The other breeds include the Rouen from France, the Aylesbury from Britain, the Pekin (introduced to Long Island from China by a mid-nineteenth-century sea captain), the Cayuga, the Indian Runner and the Khaki Campbell, all of which are kept for meat or eggs or both; and the Black, the East India, the Mandarin and the Call Duck, which are kept purely for show.

The ancient Chinese, Japanese and Romans kept ducks in a semi-wild state. Columella, the Roman agriculturist, described netted enclosures in which Rome's farmers kept ducks to prevent their flying away; the Romans sometimes took wild duck eggs and put them under setting hens until they hatched, which led to domesticated ducks.

Today's Long Island duckling industry is based largely on Pekin ducks, killed when eight or nine weeks old, mostly from April 1 to November 15, and shipped frozen all over the country. Most fresh-killed duckling is sold within easy shipping of Long Island, though Wisconsin and the Far West now raise some ducklings, too.

Geese, whose meat is lean in the wild "honker" state but fat in domesticity, are more common to poor countries than to countries like ours, though we do raise big three-pound Toulouse and Embden geese. For eastern Europe, the goose, like the pig, is a source of cooking fat. This is true as well of Alsace-Lorraine and the central plateau region of France, notably Périgord. Strasbourg in Alsace and Périgueux in Périgord are famous for their *pâté de foie gras*, goose liver enlarged by force feeding the goose (or often a Rouen or Barbary duck) after the practice of ancient Egypt.

In recent years, *foie gras* (literally, fat liver) has become increasingly scarce and increasingly expensive. Younger farm wives, it is reported, are refusing to fatten the geese. They understandably balk at poking a funnel down a bird's throat, pouring mash down the funnel, and working the mash down with a milking motion so the bird can not cough it up. The goose may be a twenty-five-pound gray goose with a white belly, or any of fourteen other species; it will have nearly seventy pounds of cooked, salted and mashed corn forced down its gullet; and when it is slaughtered its liver will weigh a pound or a pound and a half, though some weigh over four pounds.

Given a flock of ten or twenty six-month-old geese, which must be force fed three times a day for three to five weeks, there is a lot of work involved, even if one is not squeamish about the inhumanity of it, and even if one gets sixty cents an ounce for the *foie gras*.

The price increases several times before the product reaches the consumer; undiluted, unseasoned *pâté de foie gras* costs about $24 a pound in a Paris supermarket, much more if it is flavored with port wine and seasoned with truffles down the center, following the practice originated by Doyen, cook to the first president of France's parliament, in 1772 at Bordeaux.

France's leading woman's magazine, *Elle*, said in December, 1969, that the price of *foie gras* had tripled in the past six years, though this was disputed at Fauchon, the *épicerie* in the Place de la Madeleine in Paris which is the world's largest retailer of *foie gras*. Fauchon's chief taster and buyer told a UPI reporter that the increase had been more like eleven or twelve per cent in the last five years.

France produces 660 tons of *foie gras* a year, most of it in the southwest, and consumes at least three times that much, importing it from Austria, Bulgaria, Czechoslovakia, Hungary, Israel and Luxembourg. Budget watchers, who can not afford goose *foie gras*, buy duck *foie gras*—less fat, very flavorful, but inclined to break down in cooking. A rich, creamy slice of *pâté* of some bird's *foie gras* is still a tradition of Christmas feasting in France, as obligatory as turkey with stuffing in the United States.

One in every pot

Aside from variety meats, the best buy in animal protein these days is likely to be chicken or turkey.

One can buy a whole roasting chicken (three and a half to six pounds), or a whole turkey (five to sixteen pounds frozen stuffed, four to twenty-four pounds fresh-chilled or frozen unstuffed). Some unstuffed turkeys come pre-basted with butter or fat inserted into the meat. Some come with stuffing clamps. Others have cooking indicators set in the meat, ready to pop out when the turkey is done. Chickens, whether fresh-chilled or frozen, usually have their giblets (heart, liver, neck, gizzard, etc.) wrapped up inside to be removed and cooked separately.

Broiler-fryers (which may be roasted or braised, if preferred) run from one and a half to four pounds, stewing fowls (less tender, but fine for a fricassee, stew or creamed dish) from two and a half to eight pounds, capons, usually roasted (very tender, with lots of white meat), from six to eight pounds.

Rock Cornish hens, usually sold frozen, can be broiled, fried or roasted. A one- to one-and-a-quarter-pound bird is enough for just one serving, a two-pound hen can be cut in half to serve two.

Boneless rolled turkey roasts, from two to five pounds, are a new convenience form; some permit a choice of white meat, dark meat or a mixture; some even mix half breast of turkey and half ham.

As a rule, allow between three-quarters of a pound to one pound of chicken or turkey per serving when you buy poultry in conventional forms. With duckling or goose, allow one to one and a half pounds per serving.

Just as they eat more goose than we do, Europeans also eat more small birds. Figpeckers, swallows and larks are caught by taking the leaves off small trees, liming the branches and plucking off the birds whose feet are stuck in the lime like flies on flypaper (the practice was once common in England, too). Whole flocks of wild birds are trapped in nets as they migrate through mountain passes. Italy now forbids netting, but 1.5 million Italian hunters shoot an estimated 100 birds each in the season that extends from September through March.

Americans no longer eat robin pie, popular in the early part of the nineteenth century, and our passenger pigeons (Chapter 3) are gone forever, but we do eat squab, which are young, commercially raised pigeons. The breeds in this class, none native to America, are the Carneaux, King Hungarian and Mondain. They are all descended from one species, the Rock pigeon; when mature, they are all too tough to eat, which is why even hungry hippies in the park leave the pigeons alone.

Rabbit is more popular in Europe than in the U.S.,[23] but we Americans, believe it or not, consume more than 50 million pounds of rabbit meat a year, *not* counting wild rabbits shot by hunters. Rabbit is mostly white meat, mild in flavor, and can be cooked in many of the same ways as chicken. Wild jack rabbits and cottontails (*Sylvillagus floridanus*, America's number one game animals) often have a disease called tularemia, or rabbit fever, which can be fatal in up to eight per cent of infected humans and can lead to chronic after-effects. The bacteria are killed by heat in cooking, but it is a good idea to wear rubber gloves when handling uncooked wild rabbits, and to bleed and eviscerate them right after they are killed.

Rabbits are probably 100 times more widely shot than game birds, waterfowl or deer by U.S. hunters, few of whom ever think of eating rabbit any other way than fried.

In addition to their wild varieties, rabbits come in many domestic breeds and crossbreeds.

---

[23] The average Frenchman in 1965 ate practically as much rabbit as lamb—6.6 pounds versus 6.68 pounds. Europeans who know their rabbits look for the "three-quarter" hare, one from a litter dropped at the beginning of the year which has reached full growth and has not yet mated. While old hares reach seven or eight pounds, the "three-quarter" weighs no more than five. It is best when "jugged." Jugged hare, a stew cooked in a stone or earthenware pot, is a classic English dish, but thickening the sauce with the rabbit's blood makes it more than an ordinary stew.

So, as we have seen, do all the animals and birds whose meat we consume. Plainly, any growing thing we eat is produced by nature, with or without the help of man, in unending variations of life—animal and vegetable.

Man left animal life pretty much to its own development until about 200 years ago. The plow ox of the Middle Ages was essentially the same animal that roamed wild in Stone Age Europe.

Scientific breeding methods came only late in the nineteenth century following the discoveries of the Moravian monk Mendel, whose botanical experiments with peas in Austria showed that some genes pass on their traits more readily than others. Mendel established the difference between dominant characteristics and recessive characteristics and charted their significance. Male pollen and female seed, he found, both contain "life-atoms" or genes which help determine the nature of a new plant (or animal).

As a result of Mendelian laws, animal breeders have been able to improve their livestock and poultry significantly: modern cows give up to ten times more milk [24] than cows of a century ago; hens lay up to four times more eggs; beef is ready for market some three years sooner than it used to be. The progress is partly a result of improved feeds, but it owes much to the improvement of the breeds.

Man has not been content with these improvements. We go right on interfering with nature, deceiving ewes with artificial darkness in summer to make them produce spring lambs in late summer and autumn, flashing lights in henhouses in the middle of the night to fool the hens into laying more eggs. Thus do we exploit our fertile animals and fine-feathered friends.

---

[24] The average annual yield per milking cow (in kilograms) varies from a high of 4180 in the Netherlands to a low of 200 in India, says the FAO. The U.S. average for registered cows in 1968 was 9006 lbs., higher than in Britain or France, lower than in Belgium or Denmark.

How doth the busy little bee . . .

We started this chapter with a suggestion of nature's great diversity of plant and animal forms. It should be obvious that Noah in the Old Testament would have needed an ark the size, say, of *Queen Elizabeth II* to carry two by two all the various breeds of domestic livestock and poultry, along with all the multiple breeds of wildlife of jungle, plain and tundra, on the crest of the Flood.

But we have strayed a long way from the rose.

To return, consider that ancient flower-power food, honey. Honey is about forty per cent levulose, a monosaccharide, or simple sugar, which turns into glucose without any digestive change; it is therefore the quickest source of human power, or energy. Honey also contains about thirty-four per cent dextrose (grape sugar), two per cent sucrose (cane sugar), eighteen per cent water and significant amounts of minerals, B-complex vitamins, amino acids (the building blocks of protein) and enzymes; at least it does unless it is pasteurized.[25]

Honeybees were probably native to southern Asia. They were introduced into New England sometime between 1638 and 1640 (the Indians called the honeybee "the white man's fly"). Swarms of honeybees escaped and established hives in the wilderness, along with ordinary wild bees which were native to this continent but produced no honey. (Out of 10,000 or 12,000 varieties of bees that have been identified in the world, only four or five varieties of *Apis mellifica* store honey.) Honeybees had crossed the Mississippi by 1800; Stephen F. Austin, on his first trip to Texas in 1821, recorded in his diary that

---

[25] The only reason to pasteurize honey is to prevent it from granulating into crystals, which some people mistakenly take as a sign the honey is spoiling. Granulation actually proves the honey is high in quality and is unpasteurized. To restore granulated honey to liquid form, just immerse the jar in hot—*not* boiling—water until the crystals disappear.

his party had discovered a bee tree and obtained a gallon and a half of sweet honey.

Honey is not just honey. Its color varies according to its botanical source. Different native plants give honey their own particular flavors, and names, as the bees use the nectar from those plants to make their viscid contribution to man's diet.

While American honeybees use as raw materials mostly the nectar of clover and alfalfa, the bees of other countries have varied tastes. So do their honeys.

Bavarian pine-blossom honey is thick and strong. Norwegian honey is a sparkling variety, full of bubbles. Acacia honey from Hungary is often regarded as the world's finest, but it has many rivals for that distinction. France's rosemary honey from Narbonne, crystal white and granular, has been called the world's oldest honey (Julius Caesar mentioned it in his dispatches from Gaul), but wild thyme honey from Mount Hymettus, the honey of the Greek gods on Olympus, must be older.

There is lotus honey from India and eucalyptus honey from Australia. There are black honeys from Brazil, snow-white honeys from Siberia, dogwood honeys from Jamaica, leatherwood honey from Tasmania, dogwood ulmo honey from Chile. There is black-locust honey from Italy, lolitza honey from Mexico, coffee-tree honey from Guatemala, Buckwheat Abbey moorland heather honey from England and other heather honeys from Scotland, Holland and Norway (they stay liquid for only a short time after stirring, turning quickly to a jellylike consistency).

Some unusual American honeys are orange-blossom honey from Florida, raspberry honey and strong buckwheat honey from New Jersey, chewy dandelion honey from Colorado, tupelo honey from the swamps of Florida and Georgia, fireweed honey (pale-gold and molasses-thick) from Oregon and Washington, river-willow honey from the banks of the Mississippi. There are also manzanita honey from California, sage-blossom honey from Arizona, gallberry honey from Georgia, heartsease honey from Illinois, tulip-tree honey from Maryland, linden honey from New York, anise-hyssop honey from

Iowa, spearmint honey from Indiana, milky-white guajillo honey from Texas and alergoba honey from Hawaii.

The honeybee who manufactures all this mellifluous sweetness lives for only four to six weeks. In this brief span it can collect only a teaspoonful of nectar. To produce one pound of honey takes close to four pounds of nectar, from upwards of 2 million flowers. Some 80,000 bees are needed to bring in that much nectar, another 80,000 to evaporate the nectar into honey by fanning it with their wings in the hive. So it takes an estimated 160,000 bees to produce one pound of honey, which the bees store in ingeniously strong hexagonal cells called honeycombs (often provided in prefabricated form by apiarists to save the bees' valuable time, though the original designers were the bees themselves).

More than a third of the bees' honey is left in the hive for the manufacturers to eat over the winter; the surplus is removed from the combs, now usually by centrifugal extractors, and marketed as liquid (strained) honey, though some is sold comb and all. The fresh crop generally begins arriving in stores in October, when flavors are at their peak of intensity.

Because it is hygroscopic (it absorbs and retains moisture), honey is used by the baking industry to keep its goods fresh and moist. Tobaccomen use honey for the same purpose. Honey does not freeze, but unless it is kept in a dry place it will ferment, as it did in Viking and Elizabethan times to make mead.

Just as livestock and poultry manufacture meat protein from plant matter, honeybees make their product from the nectar of buckwheat, star thistle, cotton, sage, heartsease, spearmint, raspberry, borage and from countless varieties of flowers—including, of course, roses.

ॱ⟦ 5 ⟧॰

Denizens of the deep

At least seventy per cent of the earth's surface is water, four-fifths of it a mile or more deep.

More than one paleontologist has theorized, and produced evidence in support of the theory, that the human species evolved as a riparian creature, living on the banks of streams, rivers, lakes and oceans.

As the geographer Carl Sauer has noted:

> It is a curious fact that no other primates appear to have taken to living on seashores, though certain Asiatic macaques do come to them for crabs and other shellfish, and are able to swim. Most primates seem not to forage in water, and some do not swim at all.

Sauer hazards the possibility that modern man's physiological need for iodine and salts, his "inclination" to high protein intake and his greater tolerance for unsaturated fats than for saturated may trace back to his origins as a seaside resident.

In some dim periods of prehistory, as in the late Ice Age 10,000 to 12,000 years ago here on the North American continent, encroaching glaciers may have forced men either to find sustenance at the edge of the sea or to perish. And it was along the seacoasts that the races of men fanned out to populate the earth.

The ancient Greeks panned the seas for salt. They fished in the Ionian for tuna, mullet, squid, octopus, sardines and anchovies. But the clear waters of the Aegean and of the eastern Mediterranean are scant of plankton, which makes for a dearth of fish. Greek boats often returned to port with little to show for the fishermen's efforts. Eating fish in Homeric Greece was a sign of poverty; in later ages— as the population swelled—fish, or at least fresh fish, became a luxury. Aristotle was reputedly a connoisseur of fresh fish.

As for dried fish, it was, along with wheat bread, Athens' chief source of nourishment; both came principally from the Crimea, which made the Dardanelles a major concern of Greek statesmen and warriors.

In local waters the Greeks found oysters—and used their shells as ballots. Votes were inscribed with styluses; when early Athenians voted to banish a citizen from the community, the citizen was "oyster-shelled," or ostracized.

The Romans ate more seafood than meat. Like the Greeks, they admired oysters. Athenaeus, an Egyptian Greek of the third century A.D., wrote that the Romans ate their oysters raw and sometimes roasted, and stewed them with mallows [1] and docks (both wild potherbs) or with fish (cod's head and oyster sauce was a favorite dish) and "esteemed them very nourishing."

Oyster herds

But while the Greeks had collected oysters as they found them, the Romans as early as 100 B.C. established oyster beds to safeguard a reliable source of supply. They cultivated oysters at what is now Taranto and in salt ponds around Baiae (near Naples). This was the first instance in history of men farming the seas, a concept novel even

---

[1] Mallows are related to hollyhocks. The roots of the marshmallow yield a sticky juice once used to make the confection toasted over Boy Scout campfires, but the juice was replaced first by gum arabic and then by gelatin, both of which are cheaper. Now all that is left of the marshmallow as a food is its name.

today. We still pursue the wild game of the seas as ancient men pursued game in the forest.

While they later found great natural beds of oysters in the estuaries of Britain's East Anglia, the Romans were far ahead of their time in their cultivation of oysters.

Breeding oysters is not like breeding livestock or poultry. British oysters and round-shelled French *plate* oysters belong to the *Ostrea* group, which is sensitive to changes in water temperatures and salinity and which keeps its eggs inside its shell for a week after fertilization. Portuguese oysters belong to the oviparous *Crassostrea* group which is more tolerant of water changes. Both groups are hermaphrodites; they change their sex, sometimes several times a year.

Oysters became popular in Europe in the eighteenth century; it was not uncommon for an oyster lover to go through thirty *dozen* oysters as a preface to dinner. As transportation improved in the nineteenth century, and the middle classes became more affluent, demand for oysters increased to the point where, by the mid-nineteenth century, French oystermen had dragged up all the wild oysters off the coasts of Brittany. A French marine biologist, Coste, stumbled on the old oyster cultivations at Lake Fusaro, near Naples, and introduced artificial oyster beds to France. At Loqmariaquer, in Brittany, oystermen learned to move the bivalves from place to place as they grew, so they would gain flavor in one place and put on flesh in another. They drained the beds twice a day to deprive the mature oysters of water, thus educating them to remain closed to survive their journey to market out of water.

Today, baby oysters, or *naissain*, are shipped from Brittany to Britain, Norway, the Mediterranean and North America. Some are bred in *claires*, or fattening ponds, in old salt marshes on the Atlantic coast to become French *Claires* oysters, greenish in color. (Like *Marennes* oysters, they get their color and delicate flavor from the sea algae they ingest; the *naissain* sent abroad develop quite different flavors and colors.) *St. Vaast-la-Hougue* oysters are bred in latticed cages immersed in the tidal current of the English Channel (or *La Manche*, as the French call it).

Eventually, France's natural oyster beds recovered and oyster-dragging for Brittany's *Belon* oysters and Mont St. Michel's *Cancale* oysters, once forbidden, is now permitted again, though with definite restrictions. (Natural oysters are said to be more pungent in taste than the blander oysters raised artificially, though that taste often has an iodine quality many people dislike.) Oyster-culture is still a thriving heritage of ancient Rome.

The modern use of anchovies in sauces and meat dishes may date back to a sauce the Romans used in place of salt. They called it *liquamen* and they made it in factories, taking small fish and the entrails of larger fish, and often oysters as well, covering them with salt and letting them sit in the sun a few days until the mixture had putrefied. The liquid they then drained off was called *garum*. It was sometimes blended with wine, honey, vinegar, oil, spices and herbs to mask its overpowering odor, and it probably had an anchovylike tang. *Garum* has been called the soy sauce of Rome, though it was vastly more costly than soy sauce. The best of it was reputed to come from Spain, where it was made from mackerel. A small jar of *garum* was found in the ruins of Pompeii.

One well-remembered Roman seafood glutton was the Emperor Heliogabalus (also called Elagabalus). He entered Rome from Syria in 218 A.D. in a chariot drawn by naked women. During his brief reign, in which he often dressed as a woman himself, wearing the tiara of the priests of the sun god and surrounded by eunuchs, courtesans and clowns, Heliogabalus maintained a fleet of fishing boats to catch eels, whose roe was prized as modern emperors have prized caviar from Russia's sturgeon.

Not that sturgeon roe—nor sturgeon flesh—itself was any stranger to the tables of Imperial Rome. While the fish had earlier been found in the Po and the Rhône, in later centuries it came from the distant Caspian Sea, kept alive in tubs on the decks of ships and carried live in water by relays of slaves from the port of Ostia into Rome. It was customary to display such large fish on marble slabs so everyone could admire them before they were cooked.

Eels, however, were a more particular favorite of Heliogabalus.

He fattened conger eels in tubs, feeding them the flesh of Christian slaves killed in the Coliseum. Heliogabalus sent hunters to Libya to look for the phoenix bird, he had 600 ostriches killed to make ostrich brain pies for one meal and—well, there was no limit to his excesses. He served meals that cost $10,000 each, emptying the treasury of Rome.

Ichthus

In the ages that followed the fall of Rome, the seafood-loving Vikings ran riot over Europe, whose people were in ever increasing numbers ruled by the Holy See in Rome, which made abstinence from meat eating an obligatory act of penance and self-denial.

To observe the influence of Lent on Renaissance feasting, especially on a Friday during Lent, consider a bill of fare from the year 1571. The occasion was a banquet, offered by the city of Paris to receive Elizabeth of Austria, bride to Charles IX, a young man of twenty-one who had been titular king since age ten. (His mother, Catherine de' Medici, no doubt pulled the strings.)

Obliged to forgo meat, the royal party and its horde of courtiers went through two barrels of Brittany oysters, fifty pounds of whale meat, 200 crayfish, great platters of broiled lobster and steamed mussels, 400 herring (half of them fresh, the other half salted), eighteen brill, twenty-eight salmon, ten turbot, fifty carp and 1000 pairs of frogs' legs.

The herring were from the North Sea, by now a great herring fishery. Earlier, in the thirteenth, fourteenth and fifteenth centuries, the sun, moon and earth had been in relative positions which (Rachel Carson tells us) occur only about every eighteen centuries and which exerted such force on the tides that submarine waves carried great schools of herring up the narrow Sund and Belts passageways into the Baltic. The great Hanseatic herring fisheries of Scandinavia prospered, especially during the winter solstice. But by the sixteenth century the tide had weakened:

These herrings [wrote a contemporary English chronicler quoted by G. M. Trevelyan], which in the times of our grandfathers swarmed only about Norway, now in our times by the bounty of Providence swim in great shoals round our coasts every year.

So while Swedish and Norwegian nets came up empty, Dutch, French and English fishermen grew rich on the silver bounty of the herring run.

Under Elizabeth I, Englishmen ate whale meat, seal, porpoise, and grampus (a kind of dolphin) along with their mutton, pork and beef.

"Fish days" were enforced by stiff laws. An innkeeper served no meat on Fridays (and sometimes Wednesdays) or during Lent or risked being pilloried. Religion had little to do with it; the Crown was encouraging the fisheries whose men crewed the royal navy and mercantile fleets that Britannia might rule the waves (and incidentally safeguard her access to food sources).

For the poor, almost every day was fish day. "Poor-John," mentioned early in the first scene of *Romeo and Juliet*, was dried, salted hake or cod, the cheap food of England's poverty class. Hake, sole, plaice (the poor man's sole), salmon, whiting, trout and turbot were also popular on fish days. Oysters, shrimp, mussels, whelk (from conch shells) and cockles (but not lobsters) were widely used, but seafood in Elizabethan times was mostly for fast days and for the poor.

Later, no doubt because they were an island nation, the English came to eat quantities of fish. Not so their neighbors across the Channel. In France, too, fasting in Lent was enforced by law. A 1648 ordinance forbade hotels and restaurants, such as existed, to serve meat on fast days or during Lent, though the French law and its enforcement may have been inspired more by the clergy than by economic and military considerations. Clergymen did not abide by the law in all cases: the Paris police raided a monastery in 1659 and found the monks violating the Lenten strictures with a dinner of partridges, pies, hams and wine; a dozen monks went to jail. In 1671 the police were given the right to search houses during Lent and to give any forbidden articles of diet to hospitals. Hospital authorities operated the only five shops licensed to sell meat in Paris during Lent.

The French in the time of Louis XIV ate sardines to bring out the flavor of their wine; they ate oysters, both raw and grilled in their shells with butter and pepper; and they ate salmon. But otherwise they avoided fish and fast days were a hard burden.

English royalty felt differently. It doted on herring pies and on stewed lamprey. The lamprey is a fatty, rather indigestible eellike creature which sucks the blood of other fish. This in no way prejudiced the first Elizabeth, who loved lamprey ("one of my passions," said Good Queen Bess) even though a surfeit of stewed lamprey had finished off both Henry I, grandson of William the Conqueror, and King John, he who signed the Magna Charta in 1215. Another victim of the lamprey, or at least of eel pies,[2] was Charles V, king of Spain and emperor of the Holy Roman Empire. Charles ate one eel pie too many in 1558.

For the Elizabethans who voyaged across to Virginia and New England, as for the poor back home in England, seafood was an almost daily staple. The colonists would have been lost without the bounty of the seas and were far more dependent on fish and shellfish than either their countrymen or their American descendants.

"The aboundance of Sea-Fish"

Massachusetts Bay teemed with mackerel, bass, "Heering, Turbot, Sturgion, Cuskes, Haddocks, Mullets, Eeles, Crabs, Muskles and Oysters," but the dominant fish was cod.

The above spellings are those of Francis Higginson, who in 1630 wrote, "The aboundance of Sea-Fish are almost beyond beleeuing, and sure I whould scarce haue baleeued it except I had seene it with mine owne Eyes."

---

[2] Eel pies seasoned with Worcestershire sauce are still a popular snack sold in the streets of London's East End. The English call them "green pies" (and call Worcestershire simply "Worcester," pronouncing it Wooster just as we do). An even bigger favorite is jellied eel, small pieces of eel in pale green aspic, served in thick, handleless china mugs or paper cups and sprinkled with chili vinegar.

Scrod, a young filleted cod, was one of the first distinctly New England dishes; cod in its many forms, including sautéed codfish tongues and cheeks, sustained generations of Bay Staters.

As far back as 1640, Massachusetts sent 300,000 dried codfish to market. While Southerners exported a lot of pickled fish, Yankees established a virtual monopoly on dried fish.

Peter Faneuil, a Boston merchant who made a fortune shipping New England codfish to distant markets, expressed his gratitude for all his prosperity by presenting the city of Boston with Faneuil Hall, which became a gathering place for Revolutionists. Daniel Webster called it "the cradle of American liberty."

Boston's George Cabot, founder of a still-great family fortune, skippered a codfishing boat at age eighteen.

Fish and shellfish were available in almost unlimited quantities. Visiting Nantucket, thirty miles off the coast of Massachusetts, de Crèvecoeur wrote:

> The shores of this island abound with the soft-shelled, the hard-shelled, and the great sea clams, a most nutritious shellfish. Their sands, their shallows, are covered with them; they multiply so fast that they are a never-failing resource. These and the great variety of fish they catch constitute the principal food of the inhabitants.

Nantucket was not yet the great whaling center it became in the nineteenth century, but whales were an important source of oil and were plentiful in the coastal waters of the North Atlantic, and even in rivers.

In the St. Lawrence, according to de Crèvecoeur, there was a seventy-five foot variety "which . . . produces 180 barrels of oil: I once saw sixteen boiled out of the tongue alone." The oil was valuable for lighting, but whales were not a significant source of food. Europeans of the Middle Ages and the Renaissance ate whale meat and fat, sometimes with peas (*craspois*), and whale steak enjoys an occasional fad as an exotic meat today, but few people except Eskimos have ever eaten it as a regular thing.

Even Eskimos are now hard pressed for whale meat. Herman

Melville, author of *Moby Dick*, wondered whether "Leviathan can long endure so wide a chase, and so remorseless a havoc"; and that was before there were harpoon guns to fire projectiles with explosive heads.

In the last sixty years, more than 325,000 blue whales have been slaughtered in the Antarctic. Caught with the help of helicopters and sonar (the British call it asdic), the blue whale catch declined from 6908 in 1958 to just one in 1965, when blue whales were last hunted. It is estimated that not more than 1000 survive. Fin and sei whales are still caught by the thousands; their edible oil is used for margarine and other food. But sperm whales, whose oil is used for industrial purposes, are a threatened species. After 29,000 were killed in 1964, the International Whaling Commission tried to set limits, but its recommendations have been ignored by the Japanese and Russians (the Norwegians have abandoned the chase).

By de Crèvecoeur's time, the New England fisheries were at their peak. The Revolution diverted seamen to privateering. To obtain extensive fishing rights for the new Republic after the Revolution, John Adams used the slogan, "Fisheries or no peace," but New England fishermen never brought home as many catches, or as large, as they had netted before the Revolution. The great shoals of baccalo (as cod were called by the "savages" Sebastian Cabot found in America) presumably moved out to the edge of the continental shelf, the Grand Banks off Newfoundland which Breton fishermen had been visiting annually at least since 1497, and possibly since before Columbus.

Even at a reduced level, the American codfishing industry was still tremendous. In 1784, a Mr. John Rowe moved in the Massachusetts House of Representatives that "leave might be given to hang the representation of a Cod Fish in the room where the House sit, as a memorial to the importance of the Cod Fishery to the welfare of this Commonwealth."

A four-foot-eleven-inch "representation," the Sacred Cod, was hung that same year. The South American soldier and revolutionist, Francisco de Miranda, visited Boston in the fall of 1784 and wrote that he had seen hanging in the Statehouse the "figure of a cod-fish of natural size made of wood and in bad taste." Exiled from Venezuela, de Miranda was a connoisseur; J. C. Furnas says he "liked American girls in his bed but not male strangers or [bed-] bugs," so he slept on the floor at the inns where he stayed.

The Sacred Cod was moved to a new Statehouse in 1798, and moved again in 1895 to a spot opposite the Speaker's desk in the House Chamber, where at last report it still hung.

Today the Grand Banks are dominated by foreign fishing vessels, most of them from the U.S.S.R., Poland and East and West Germany. Gorton's of Gloucester, founded in 1755, imports blocks of frozen, compressed, filleted fish slabs (used to make fish sticks and other pre-pared fish products) from the Polish, who sell them at prices well below what Gloucester fishermen must charge. The Poles catch the fish as close as fifty miles to the Gloucester factory.

Upstream to die

While cod was the mainstay of New England, anadramous fishes (which inhabit salt water until they ascend fresh-water rivers and streams to spawn, and rarely taste salt water again) were more im-portant elsewhere: salmon, shad, striped bass and sturgeon brightened meals up and down the Atlantic Coast.

America's salmon were larger than those in the old country—"larger salmon than they had ever seen before" in the words of Eric the Red's Viking chronicle. The Atlantic salmon extended at least as far south as the Connecticut River, swimming up the Aroostook, the Penobscot, the Kennebec, the St. Croix, the Machias and other rivers just as it swam up Scottish, English, Irish, Welsh, Norwegian, Icelandic, French and Russian rivers. But our salmon were bigger.

At least thirty-three Atlantic Coast American rivers had regular salmon runs. But thwarted by dams and pollution, the Atlantic salmon has long since ceased to have any commercial importance in U.S. rivers. Our biggest salmon canner is the New England Fish

Company, but it is in Seattle, not New England. Artificial stocking provides salmon for anglers, but from a Maine coast salmon catch of 150,000 pounds in 1889, the figure declined to less than 1000 in 1950. Only eighty-two salmon were landed in Maine that year. In 1962, a good year, 485 salmon were "killed," but at least 2000 anglers were trying for the fish, most of them without success.

We depend now for our Atlantic salmon [3] on the deep-water fisheries of the northeast, and even these fisheries are now threatened by over-fishing. Commercial fishermen in 1964 discovered a major salmon feeding ground off the southwest coast of Greenland. The total Greenland catch had been only 127 tons in 1961; it was 2,000 tons in 1969, about 1100 tons coming from the Dauls Strait where the fishermen, mostly from Denmark and the Faroe Islands, took fish that averaged seven pounds. Fully mature salmon can weigh three times that. In May, 1969, the Northeast Atlantic Fisheries Commission, an international body, urged a ban on salmon fishing outside national fishing limits (it also suggested that member nations consider a quota plan limiting cod and haddock catches). British Prime Minister Harold Wilson subsequently made a personal appeal for a ten-year ban on ocean salmon fishing.

Denmark and West Germany, which have virtually no salmon-spawning rivers, have generally opposed any restrictions on access to

---

[3] Pacific salmon have fared somewhat better than salmon in the East. King salmon (which weigh up to 100 pounds) chinooks, silver salmon, chum salmon, pink salmon (the most plentiful) and sockeyes still head up the Columbia, the Sacramento, the Klamath, the Rogue, the Snohomish and thirty other rivers and streams in California, Oregon and Washington (plus eighteen rivers in Alaska). But their survival has depended on manmade stairs, called fish ladders, to help the fish bypass dams, and on artificial propagation. Some 17 million pounds of salmon are still caught on the Columbia every year, a far cry from the record 49 million caught in 1911 but still a catch worth $20 million. Most salmon is canned, and while the U.S. canned-salmon pack dropped from 4.3 million cases (of forty-eight one-pound cans) in 1950 to 3.4 million in 1968, catches are now increasing. Federal agencies co-operated to save a resource in the West that has been lost in the East, though a five-year, $25 million program of andramous conservation, enacted by Congress in 1965, may help bring the salmon back to Maine.

the deep-water fisheries. But dams and pollution have so reduced the salmon runs in the Rhine, the Volga, England's River Tees, Scotland's Spey and other streams that in most countries they are about as bad as Denmark and Germany.

Scotsmen, who rent fishing rights on their government-stocked salmon and trout streams to rich Sassenachs, Americans and Canadians, threaten to boycott Danish butter and bacon; but the Danes blame disease and pollution for the reduced catches in rivers and resist efforts to ban high-seas salmon trawling, saying it is all a plot by British aristocrats and North American millionaires. The British and Canadians counter that the Danes, Swedes and West Germans are taking fish artificially bred in hopes that the baby salmon will return as ten-pound beauties to spawn in the streams where millions of dollars were spent to stock them. (Less than 15 per cent live to make more than one spawning run and become prize catches.) Quotas have been set for yellowfin tuna and may soon be set for giant bluefin tuna; if quotas are not quickly set, and enforced, for the Atlantic salmon, that fish may become as rare as the green turtle (Chapter 3) or the blue whale. The angry controversy over salmon highlights the need for a powerful world body to protect our earthly resources.

If America's salmon were larger than Europeans had ever seen, her sea sturgeon were more multitudinous. "We had more Sturgeon, than could be devoured by Dog and Man," wrote John Smith. Enormous numbers of the giant fish were still ascending Smith's Virginia rivers 150 years later. In the Hudson in the eighteenth and nineteenth centuries, the big, sluggish bottom fish provided the basis of a considerable industry. Children on New York waterfront streets bounced rubberlike sturgeon snouts like balls, their parents ate the black or golden-brown sturgeon eggs as caviar, but the big business was in the flesh. "Albany beef," it was called; sample the beefy taste and texture of fresh broiled sturgeon to learn why.

Some 1.2 million pounds of sturgeon was landed in New York and New Jersey in 1897. Pollution killed the "Albany beef" industry (a mere 25,000 pounds was landed in 1961), but just how many sturgeon are left in the Hudson is a matter of dispute. After Congress passed the "Endangered Species Act" in early 1967, the Department of the Interior classified the big sea sturgeon (*Acipenser oxyrhynchus*) as "rare," meaning (officially) that it "is in such small numbers throughout its range that it may be endangered if its environment worsens." The much smaller short-nosed or round-nosed sturgeon (*A. brevirostrum*) and the white sturgeon (*A. transmontanus*) was classified as "endangered," meaning (officially, again) that its "prospects of survival and reproduction are in immediate jeopardy . . . [It] must have help, or extinction will probably follow." [4]

But according to Robert Boyle, fishermen in the area of Peekskill say the Hudson is still thick with sturgeon, despite the pollution, and though none is as big as the twenty-six-foot sea sturgeon, weighing a ton and a half, which have been taken in Russian rivers, a seven-and-a-half-foot specimen whose roe alone weighed fifty pounds was caught in early 1968.

Another native American fish, the shad, is still commercially important, though not in the Hudson where once the fish was so abundant in early spring that 3000 were taken at a single haul. To the early Dutch of Nieuw Amsterdam, shad was known as *elft*, the eleven fish, because the first shad in the Hudson was traditionally caught on the 11th of March. Probably for the reason that it was so easily come by, shad was disdained. It was never served to guests in the 1600's, and while plenty of delicious shad were caught and eaten, few people admitted they ate it, as if eating anything so common were a social gaffe.

By a century later, attitudes had changed. Baked shad was one of George Washington's favorite dishes and, in the early days of the Republic, congressmen sailed down the Potomac to enjoy great feasts of fresh-caught shad in the spring.

Captain Marryat mentioned shad in his account of his 1837 visit to America:

---

[4] Also on the endangered list is the primitive lake sturgeon, our biggest freshwater fish; it still reaches eight feet in length and 300 pounds in weight where it survives, but it is practically extinct in U.S. lakes and rivers as a result of overfishing.

Fish [he wrote] is well supplied. They [the Americans] have the sheep's head, shad and one or two others, which we have not. Their salmon is not equal to ours, and they have no turbot.

By 1849, as Thoreau noted in *A Week on the Concord and Merrimack Rivers*, the shad, "formerly abundant here and taken in weirs by the Indians, who taught this method to the whites by whom they were used as food and as manure," were disappearing as "the dam, and afterward the canal at Billerica and the factories at Lowell, put an end to their migrations hitherward."

Shad [Thoreau wrote] are still taken in the basin of Concord River at Lowell, where they are said to be a month earlier than the Merrimack shad, on account of the warmth of the water. Still patiently, almost pathetically, with instinct not to be discouraged, not to be *reasoned* with, revisiting their old haunts as if their stern fates would relent, and still met by the corporation with its dam. Poor shad! where is thy redress? When Nature gave thee instinct, gave she thee the heart to bear thy fate?

Henry David Thoreau himself was all heart. And a sharp-eyed reporter. Elsewhere he writes:

It is said, to account for the destruction of the [shad] fishery, that those who at that time represented the interests of the fishermen and the fishes, remembering between what dates they were accustomed to take the grown shad, stipulated that the dams should be left open for that season only, and the fry, which go down a month later, were consequently stopped and destroyed by myriads. Others saw that the fishways were not properly constructed. Perchance, after a few thousands of years, if the fishes will be patient and pass their summers elsewhere meanwhile, Nature will have leveled the Billerica dam and the Lowell factories, and the Grass-ground River run clear again, to be explored by new migratory shoals . . .

How like he sounds to the frustrated conservationists of our own time.

Eastern shad (sometimes called American shad or white shad)

were introduced into the Pacific in 1871 and are now common there, though few Westerners, curiously, eat shad; the roe is frozen or canned for shipment East, and the fish itself is turned into cat food, instead of being stuffed with crab meat and properly baked on a wooden plank.

In the East, this large but delicate variety of herring so favored by early Americans still enters Chesapeake Bay, generally in March when the water warms up enough to encourage the spawning run. Buck and roe shad are caught until June 5, when Maryland law forbids netting the fish. Boned shad fillets are usually from female fish, which are fatter and juicier; left whole, but minus her roe, the female is sold as "cut shad." The male, left whole, complete with milch, is sold as "buck shad."

While the shad have not returned to those New England rivers of Thoreau, have vanished from the Delaware and are no longer of any great commercial value in the Hudson,[5] shad catches in Maryland and Virginia have remained fairly healthy, if variable; and while catches in the Potomac have ranged from a high of 1.3 million pounds in 1947 to a low of 113,000 in 1961, more shad was caught in that highly polluted river in 1968 (376,000 pounds) than in 1967 (323,000).

---

[5] From more than 3.8 million pounds caught in 1944, the Hudson catch, according to the Department of the Interior's Bureau of Commercial Fisheries, fell to 724,000 pounds in 1958, to 238,000 in 1965, and to 116,000 in 1966, when the Bureau stopped keeping any record. One might conclude that the river so "clear, blue and wonderful to taste" when Henry Hudson found it in 1609 is now too filthy to support the poor shad. But Robert Boyle in his new book on the Hudson points out that the river's shad catch has "had violent ups and downs" and there may be hope in the lack of any consistent downward direction. The all-time high was in 1889, when 4.33 million pounds was landed; the catch then declined to the low point of just over 40,000 pounds in 1916, was up to almost 375,000 pounds in 1919, down to 94,369 in 1924, up to 2.47 million in 1936, nearly always above a million pounds for the next twenty-three years, up to 4.25 million in 1942. It is "now down to about 100,000 pounds annually," says Boyle. Lockwood & Winant, a venerable Fulton Fish Market firm, for several years took Hudson shad only for its roe, selling the flesh—contaminated with oil—for crab bait at one cent a pound. The 1969 catch was a little cleaner, but the good shad sold by Lockwood & Winant now comes largely from the coastal rivermouths of Georgia, not from the Hudson.

Still, our total shad catch is now a mere one-tenth of the 49 million pounds landed between Maine and Florida in 1897; and the quality of the fish can hardly be compared.

Not just on Friday

Americans are not big fish eaters, but we are eating more and more of it. We actually eat more now than we did before the end of 1966, when the Roman Catholic Church rescinded its rule forbidding U.S. Catholics to eat meat on Fridays and liberalized restrictions against eating meat during the Lenten season.[6]

Instead of dropping thirty per cent as had been feared at the time, fish sales dropped only about ten per cent in areas of heavy Catholic population (the U.S. has more than 47 million Roman Catholics, up from less than 12 million in 1904). The lost ground had been regained by the end of 1967, and fish consumption has been climbing steadily ever since.

The average American ate eleven pounds of fish in 1969, the highest amount since the mid-1950's. (Britons, by comparison, average about nineteen pounds, slightly less than they used to, though they still eat as much prepared fish and fish cakes as ever. "Fish and chips" is popular among lower-class Britons, but fish consumption is much higher as you move up the economic ladder. Frenchmen average about thirteen pounds of fish a year; Danes average over fifty pounds and Japanese over sixty-five.)

All fish is relatively expensive these days, partly because water pollution and over-fishing have reduced the size of catches (rough seas can produce shortages and raise prices from time to time, too), but mostly because of increased demand.

---

[6] Catholics in Spanish-speaking countries had centuries earlier been relieved by Church dispensation from the obligation to abstain from meat on Fridays and during Lent. Fasting and abstinence for U.S. Catholics are still voluntary acts of penitence encouraged by bishops, but violations are no longer serious sins of disobedience as they once were.

American fishermen cannot keep up with American appetites for fish. The catch of U.S. fisheries has, in fact, declined alarmingly since World War II, though tuna catches are still high and the 1968 shrimp catch set a record. By 1950 world fisheries had regained their prewar level of 20 million tons per year, doubled this by 1960 and still continue to grow. But the U.S. now catches at least half a billion pounds less than we used to. The port of Gloucester, founded in 1623, lands less than 100 million pounds of fish annually, while it used to land about 350 million. We have become the world's major fish importer, bringing in annually over a billion pounds of fish, including shellfish. While 41.4 per cent of our food fish [7] was imported in 1960, fifty-eight per cent was imported in 1968.

Persistent pesticides like DDT are blamed for much of the loss of fish life in the seabed of the American continental shelf, though U.S. fishermen are inclined to put more blame on foreign trawlers, which use nets of finer mesh than Americans are permitted, and pay their men what Americans would call starvation wages.

Whatever the reasons, fish is expensive. Chicken, once much costlier, is now generally cheaper and often much cheaper, though seasonal influxes, like the flood of spring mackerel in East Coast ports in May, can make specific kinds of fish cheaper than chicken.

But high prices are not the only reason more people do not eat fish. Some people just do not like it. Some eat it only because they think it is brain food. While fish is rich in protein and mineral elements that promote good health and mental alertness, and it is rich in vitamins and low in saturated fats, eating fish will not make a dullard any brighter.

Some people are discouraged from buying fish simply by lack of knowledge. Frozen fish portions and fish sticks are easy enough to buy and prepare; fresh fish is another matter. The very names are confusing: the same fish may be called by one name in one part of the U.S., by a completely different name somewhere else. The geographi-

---

[7] The leading variety of fish we catch is not a food fish: it is menhaden, caught off the coasts of our mid-Atlantic and Gulf states and used for oil and fertilizer as the Algonquin Indians had used it to fertilize corn.

cal confusion of ichthyological nomenclature gets worse when you go abroad and encounter new species of fish like *loup de mer*, that great Mediterranean prize, and *roucou*, Saint-Pierre, gurnard, chapon, dory, *rascasse*, weever, *baudroie*—but never mind those. We have enough trouble sorting out our own kettle of fish.

Cod, that basic fish of so many fisheries, is known as Atlantic cod, grouper, black snapper, common cod or, in the Pacific, true cod, gray cod or sea bass.

Sea bass may be called common sea bass, rock bass, bluefish, black-will, hannahill, humpback or, in the Pacific, giant sea bass, black sea bass, grouper bass or seabass.

Bluefish may be sold as tailor, skipjack, fatback, snapping mackerel; butterfish may go as harvestfish, hardhead or tomcod. You may see red hake labeled mud hake and white hake called common hake or squirrel hake.

King mackerel may be sold as cero, silver cero, black salmon, cavalla or kingfish; but kingfish may also mean king whiting, which is sold as well under the names ground mullet, whiting, gulf king whiting, surf whiting, southern whiting, sand whiting and silver whiting. Just plain whiting, though, may be called silver hake.

Striped bass (*Morone saxatilis*), the game-fish prized by surf anglers but threatened now by commercial beach seiners and gill netters, who take up to 40 tons of stripers a day in the fall migration off Long Island, is sometimes called striper, greenhead, squidhound, rock bass or rockfish. Actual rockfish (the Pacific Coast has about fifty varieties) is often called rock cod, sea bass, rosefish, grouper, red snapper, Pacific ocean perch or red cod. Ocean perch goes as redfish, rose fish or red perch.[8]

Pollock, a good substitute for haddock (which used to be New England's favorite food fish, but is now nearly fished out), is sold as

---

[8] A fish cutter in 1935 discovered that ocean perch, caught in the Atlantic from southern Labrador south to the Gulf of Maine, and in the Pacific from the Bering Sea south to lower California, yield a small white fillet much like that of fresh-water perch in taste and texture; the discovery created a boom in the fishing industry.

Boston bluefish, pollack, silver cod, green cod, green salmon, queddy salmon and sea salmon, though it certainly is not a salmon, a bluefish or a cod. Lingcod, sometimes called cultus cod, is not a cod either.

Swellfish, blowfish, globefish, puffer and swell toad are all the same fish (they may appear on a menu as "sea squab"). So are shad, American shad and white shad.

Flounder comes in many variations, but various names—gray sole, lemon sole, fluke, blackback (the correct name), dab and sand dab—are often used interchangeably for the same fish. Fluke is from the Atlantic, dab from the New England and Pacific coasts. Rex sole is sometimes called petrale, rex, sand sole, flounder or turbot (though true turbot is strictly a European fish); it comes from the Pacific waters off California. Dover, or English, sole must be imported from the English Channel on ice to be the authentic article. Of all these, gray sole is the most delectable, but try to buy it whole, not filleted. As Roy de Groot says, the head keeps the juices sealed in and the backbone transmits the oven or grill heat through the center of the fish, so it cooks faster and tastes much better.

The fish named so varyingly above are all salt-water fish. They can be caught without a fishing license; and at today's prices, some skill and a little luck can save a lot of money.

Among fresh-water fish, the same confusion of names applies. Rainbow trout may be called brook trout (or vice versa, though in many places true rainbow trout has replaced brook trout, which was eaten up by perch, which is now being eaten by rainbows).

Pickerel may be called chain pickerel or grass pickerel. Walleye pike or pike perch may mean yellow pike; lake perch may mean yellow perch.

The whole glossary of fish names would make a book in itself. But instead of writing a book, the fishing industry would do better to agree on universal names, thus doing itself and the consumer a service.

If it is good and fresh, fish has no strong "fishy" odor. Its flesh is firm and elastic and does not pull away from the bones easily. Its eyes are bright and bulging, its gills are red and clean and its skin is shiny and iridescent. If the eyes are clouded and sunk into their sockets and the gills are covered with slime, the fish has been out of the water too long.

Be on guard in some places against unscrupulous fishmongers who try to sell thawed-out frozen fish as fresh. Such fish are not only drained of much of their nutritive value but they may also be a health hazard. Defrosted, or "slacked," for more than a few hours, fish lose up to twenty per cent of their weight; fluid containing vitamins and minerals is lost with the melt water. A broken tail, dull eyes, dull, loose scales, brown gills and soft flesh that is inelastic and separated from the bone are all signs that a fish may have been "slacked."

Cook fish soon after buying it—and do not overcook it. Many people who "don't like fish" have simply never tasted properly cooked fish, but only overcooked fish (which not only suffers in taste but stinks up the house).

Fish is naturally tender; cooking it a little may bring out more flavor, but it will not make it more tender, only tougher.

Some fish are fat, some lean. Fat fish lose some fat when cooked; add little or no fat in cooking them.

Relatively fat fish are:

albacore	sablefish
butterfish	(or black cod)
chub	salmon
eel	sardines
herring	shad
mackerel	smelt
pompano	tuna
(or permi	trout
or Carolina permi)	whitefish

The lean fish (below) may require some fat during the cooking, especially if broiled.

bluefish   porgy
blue runner   rockfish
carp   scup
cod   sea bass
croaker   sea trout
dab   snapper
flounder   sole
fluke   striped bass
grouper   swellfish
haddock   swordfish
hake   (or broadbill)
halibut   whiting
lake herring   wolf fish
mullet   (or ocean catfish)
perch   yellowtail
pickerel   (or rusty dab
pike   or yellowtail flounder)
pollock   shellfish

To store fish briefly, wrap it in waxed paper or polyethylene, handle it gently, and put it in the coldest part of the refrigerator, but *not* in the freezer compartment.

Shellfish, too, deteriorates quickly when stored at temperatures above the freezing mark—and suffers in taste when frozen. It is well to cook it and use it promptly.

You do have to shell out

If fish is expensive these days, shellfish is more so.

Our most popular shellfish is shrimp. Americans now eat close to 400 million pounds of shrimp, fresh and frozen, per year—1.41 pounds per capita, up from less than one pound ten years ago.

We have to import shrimp from all parts of the world to supplement our domestic catches, but while supplies increase fifteen to twenty per cent each year, demand increases thirty to thirty-five per cent. Upwardly mobile Americans have made the shrimp cocktail a standard overture to the expense-account luncheon and an obligatory status appetizer to the rubber chicken at catered banquets.

The shrimp is a ten-legged crustacean; but the front part, the thorax with the ten legs, is removed and, except in New Orleans and thereabouts, so is the head with its feelers and stalked eyes; we eat only the tail and the abdomen. Except in the South, and in July and August up North, all our shrimp is sold frozen. And while expensive, it is less so than in shrimp-loving Japan, which must import most of its *ebi*.

Large shrimp are often called prawns (though the famed Dublin Bay prawn is really a species of lobster and not a shrimp at all) or, in Italian, *scampi*. Shrimp in Europe are generally much smaller [9] than our Gulf of Mexico shrimp, though we have some diminutive shrimp ourselves; the French call the little shrimp *crevettes*; Italians call them *gamberi*. (Spanish for prawns is *camerones*, for little shrimp *gambaros*, or *gambis*.) Scampi run about seven to a pound, colossal size shrimp (for frying) sixteen to twenty per pound, jumbo size (for shrimp cocktail) about two dozen to a pound, medium size (for shrimp salad) from forty to fifty to a pound. Fresh or frozen shrimp should still have its shiny shell on when you buy it.

Next to shrimp, our favorite shellfish is crab.

We eat king crabs and tanner crabs from the North Pacific off Alaska, big Dungeness (soft "g," please) crabs (found all the way from Alaska south to Baja California in Mexico, though named after an area in Washington state), red crabs and rock crabs from the Pacific, rock crabs and Jonah crabs from New England and California (they are closely related to Dungeness crabs), stone crabs mostly

---

[9] Small people are sometimes called shrimps, but not because they're like the shellfish. It's the other way round: the name of the shellfish derives from *shrimpe*, which meant a puny person in Middle English; the Middle English word came from *schrimpfen*, which meant "shrink" in Middle High German. Today's Germans call the shellfish *Garnelen* or *Krabben*).

from Florida (though they range from North Carolina round the Florida peninsula to the Texas Gulf Coast), green crabs from southern Maine to New Jersey (they are also found on the Atlantic coasts of England and France), lady crabs (also called sand crabs or calico crabs) from Cape Cod to Florida, buster crabs from the Gulf of Mexico, Samoan crabs and Kona crabs from Hawaii and blue or hard crabs from both the East and Gulf Coasts.

We eat lump meat (whole lumps from the large body muscles), flake meat (small pieces of white meat), flake and lump (a combination of the two) and claw meat (brownish colored), all from blue crabs.

The soft-shell crab is a blue crab that has shed its shell. Its peak season is July and August. When a crabber sees a blue crab about to molt, he puts the "peeler" in a special float until it sheds its shell. He leaves it in the water an extra hour until the new shell hardens enough so the crab can be shipped, keeping a fairly close watch for the full six to eight hours the whole business requires.

Dungeness crabs are in season from November to June around San Francisco, from December 1 to mid-July around Crescent City. In the mid-1950's, crab fishermen out of San Francisco were catching close to 9 million pounds of crabs a year. Now the catch is down to between 1 million and 2 million pounds, and in 1966–67 only 400,000 pounds were landed. But the Crescent City fishermen still get around 8 million pounds a year. Back in the days of the big catches, a three-pound crab sold for sixty-five cents. Now crab fetches about $1 a pound retail in San Francisco, except when competition from Crescent City forces the prices down.

If crabs are popular on the West Coast, they are even more so in the Southeast, where they go into she-crab soup in Charleston, gumbo in New Orleans, fish stuffings in Savannah, pilau in Norfolk and crab cakes in Baltimore (whose native son H. L. Mencken said there were supposed to be at least fifty ways of preparing crab meat).

For those who can afford the price of crabs, be sure when buying them alive that they can move their legs. Live crabs can be refrigerated, but not for more than twenty-four hours. As a rule, dead shellfish should not be used, though lobsters and crabs may be safe enough if they smell all right and their flesh is still pretty firm.

"Maine" lobster

Governor William Bradford of the Plymouth Plantation was shame-faced in 1622 that the only "dish they could presente their friends [sixty-seven colonists who just arrived] with was a lobster . . . without bread or anything els but a cupp of fair water."

The Plymouth colonists could scarcely bring themselves to eat the great, formidable-looking clawed lobsters flung up on their beaches.

It took until the mid-nineteenth century for people to overcome their lobster phobia and for *Homarus americanus* [10] to become the delicacy of robber barons and businessmen on expense accounts. Then the surging demand almost knocked out the lobster beds. From an all-time high of 130 million pounds in 1885, the lobster catch dropped to a low of 33 million in 1918. With conservation laws, catches have been brought back to between 70 and 80 million pounds a year, though two out of three "Maine" lobsters now come from Quebec, Newfoundland and Canada's Maritime Provinces. Canada sells about 40 million pounds of lobster a year versus 20 million pounds from Maine waters. We get another 20 million pounds from South Africa, South America, Australia and Mexico, but these are spiny lobsters, not *homards*, as the French call North Atlantic lobsters. (Some people call clawless lobsters "crayfish"; they are wrong: crayfish, or crawfish, are fresh-water crustaceans.)

Most canned lobster is also from Canada, which permits canners to cook baby lobsters below the minimum size specified in the Maine

---

[10] *Homarus vulgaris*, found off England, Scotland and Norway, is bright blue with orange joints and is smaller. Smaller still are the lady lobsters, Dublin Bay prawns or *scampi* (*Nephrops norvegicus*) of the North Sea and the Mediterranean. Spiny lobsters, or *langoustes*, are clawless and not even comparable, though a brisk business is done in "lobster tails" from *langoustes*.

conservation law, a size not reached until a lobster is seven or eight years old. About ninety per cent of lobsters are caught at that age; few live to reach the immense sizes *Homarus americanus* can reach in fifty years if left undisturbed.

Commercial lobsters come in four sizes, from chicken lobsters (about one pound) through medium and large to jumbo (about four pounds), and the big ones are just as tender as the small ones. Average size is one and a quarter pounds. The record is a forty-two-pound monster caught off Virginia in 1935; its shell hangs in Boston's Museum of Science.

When buying live lobster, try *not* to buy it out of a tank but rather from a retailer who keeps it on cracked ice; lobsters out of tanks contain two or three ounces of water, expensive ounces at today's prices. The legs of the lobster should move and its tail should curl under when it is picked up. Keep lobsters in the coldest part of the refrigerator for a few hours, but not much longer. And do not try to keep lobsters fresh by putting them in salted water; the salt content will not be right and the water not cold enough.

Lobsters should be cooked soon after they are bought. In inland sections people seem to prefer their lobsters broiled, which makes for a rather dried-out dish. True *homarus*-philes boil or steam lobsters by dropping them live into boiling water.

Canadian biologists say a lobster feels no pain because it does not have the necessary nervous equipment. But if boiling alive still seems too brutal, follow the advice of the Massachusetts Society for the Prevention of Cruelty to Animals: soak the live crustacean first in a mixture of two quarts of cold water, one pound of salt; this "anaesthetizes" the lobster so he can be boiled within the next five minutes without "visible signs of discomfort."

Objections to the drop into boiling water do not come only from tender hearts. Some cooks say it makes the lobster stiffen its muscles (a reflex action), which toughens its meat fibers. So they put their lobsters into salt water in a covered pot, turn up the heat till the water reaches a rolling boil and keep it there for ten to twelve minutes, regardless of the lobster's size. Other cooks say to plunge the lobster headfirst into boiling salted water (one tablespoon to a quart), cover the pot, bring the water up to the simmering point and let the lobster simmer for exactly five minutes, plus one minute for each quarter-pound over the first pound. Still others advise putting the lobster into *cold* salted water and then immediately placing the pot over the highest heat on the range. When the lobster is red, it is dead and should lickety-split be plunged into cold water.

Any part of the lobster except its shell can be safely eaten, provided the lobster is healthy and not too long dead. The greenish liver, or tomalley, is perfectly good. And if there is any coral roe, do not throw it away—it is the female lobster's ovaries and quite a delicacy. Some people prefer tail meat, others claw [11] meat, but whichever, do not waste a bit.

Shellfish prices today are reducing the popularity of lobsters, crabs and such. At the root of the exorbitant price increases is the mounting price of hand labor, along with the growing scarcity of the shellfish themselves. Tending crab and lobster pots, picking the meat out of crabs for canning, sorting shellfish in general—they are all tough jobs, jobs no machine can do as well as a man. And good men, strong enough to work at times in sub-freezing weather, are scarce and getting scarcer.

Clambake time

The most affordable shellfish are the clams and mussels we can dig up ourselves at low tide along any unpolluted sand or mud flats.

New England's clambakes, at which clams, lobster, corn and sometimes other things are steamed over wet seaweed in stone-lined pits, go back to Indian times.

Live clams, dug up or store-bought, can be kept in the coldest part of the refrigerator for several days (so can oysters, mussels and

---

[11] Lobsters' claws are not equal in size; if the right claw is larger, the lobster is "right-handed." If one claw is lost in battle or by accident, the lobster can grow another, a knack that DNA researchers talk of transferring to humans.

scallops). If a clamshell is not tightly closed, or does not snap shut when tapped, the clam is dead; and the same goes for oysters. With mussels, running cold water over the shell for a minute or two should close it; if not, the mussel is dead—do not eat it. Do not eat Pacific Coast mussels from May to October in any case; in those months they can be poisonous, and their poison (saxitoxin) is 150,000 times more lethal than curare, the plant poison some South American Indians put on the tips of their arrows.

Mollusks are as safe as the waters they are found in; if the water is polluted (check with the local authorities), avoid them; if the water is clean, enjoy them.

Safest of the mollusks, at least in the East, are mussels, because they are never eaten raw as are clams and oysters. But while the French prize and even cultivate mussels, the abundant blue mussel (*Mytilus edulis*) found on our shores from the Arctic south to Cape Hatteras is mostly unappreciated in this country. It is exactly the same species beloved as *moules* by the more knowledgeable French and as *cozze* by the Italians, many of whom prize it above any other mollusk, steaming it with thyme, bay leaf, chopped scallions or shallots and a little white wine to make *moules marinière* or *cozze alla marinara*.

We do eat clams in America, and have ever since we found the Indians eating them. New England prides itself on its "quahogs" (the white man's version of an Indian name), which are actually the same roundish hard-shell clams (*Venus merceneria* [12]) found up and down the East Coast. They are eaten when young and small as littlenecks or, when even younger, as cherry stones on the half-shell; bigger and older, they go into chowders.

For clambakes, the preferred clam is the soft-shell, longneck or steamer clam (*Mya arenaria*), even more common in New England

---

[12] One edge of a quahog shell is usually a deep purple and there are sometimes splotches of purple elsewhere. The Indians used these purple parts to make bead money, or wampum; purple wampum was worth twice the value of white wampum, made from conch shells. This monetary usage no doubt explains the Linnaean *merceneria*, but the *Venus* is a puzzler.

than the quahog but found only as far south as North Carolina. Introduced on the West Coast in the 1880's, it is now found from Monterey north to Alaska and is the leading clam in California markets.

Another Eastern clam, the long fragile-shelled razor clam (*Ensis directus*), which really looks like an old-fashioned bone-handled straight razor, should be eaten (steamed, fried or in a chowder) the day it is dug up.

The Atlantic Coast has other clams, like the surf clam or hen clam (*Spisula* or *Mactra solidissima*), whose giant shells are the cliché ash tray souvenirs of seaside vacationers, but hard-shell, soft-shell and razor clam are the most common.

Off Long Island, clams cluster in huge mounds along the path of the transatlantic cable on the floor of Great South Bay, attracted to the cable as pompano off Louisiana's Gulf Coast are attracted to oil rig structures.

New Jersey leads all other states in clam production, accounting for more than 40 million pounds a year. A clam dredge skipper off the Jersey coast can make $30,000 a year if he can stand the pace and the often bitter weather. A major factory in Great South Bay is the Doxsee family's Long Island Sea Clam Corporation; the family has been supplying the market for more than a century.

The Pacific Coast has, in addition to soft-shells, its own varieties of clams.

One is the highly esteemed and increasingly rare Pismo clam (*Trivela stultorum*), which must measure five inches across to be of legal size, a size it takes from four to seven years to attain. It is usually sautéed, baked or made into a chowder. Once so common it was plowed from ebb-tide beaches by local farmers and fed to pigs and chickens, the Pismo is now almost impossible to find, except perhaps on beaches along Baja California (it hardly exists now on Pismo Beach, Oceano or Morro Bay, though it originally thrived from Half-Moon Bay north of San Francisco south to southern Mexico's Socorro Island).

The big geoduck (pronounced "gooey-duck," *Panope generosa*), probably the largest of inter-tidal bivalves, is supposedly found from

Northern California to southern Alaska, but one is not likely to find
it except during the extraordinarily low tides of spring and fall, and
even then it is not easy. Digging geoducks is a two-man job and the
bag limit in the state of Washington is two per man per day. Sliced
and fried, it is delicious; its "neck" or siphon is ground up for
chowder.

Another large West Coast clam is the horse clam (*Schizothaerus
nuttallii*), also called the gaper or otter shell, which is often mistaken
for the geoduck, though the latter is so meaty it can never close its
shell at any point without bulging, whereas the horse clam bulges
out of its ugly shell only at its siphon end (which is really its tail,
not its neck).

There are several other West Coast clams of lesser importance,
but only the tender little butter clam (*Saxidomus giganteus* and *S.
nuttallii*), also called the Washington clam or money clam, is commonly eaten raw. (It is also good fried, stuffed or in chowder.) Despite the name Washington clam, this clam is dug all along the coast
from Southern California to Alaska.

One shellfish found only in the Pacific, mostly in Mexican and
California waters, is the abalone, a large sea snail up to a foot in
diameter whose firm white "foot" (which abalone hunters pry loose
with tire irons) is subtly flavored but tough and rubbery. Some abalone lovers say baking gets the toughness out, but most abalone is
fried in butter after first being filleted, marinated and pounded with
a wooden mallet.

Perhaps because it needs so much preliminary tenderizing, abalone
years ago was despised as a coarse, common shellfish. Japanese immigrants opened American eyes to the trove they had on their offshore
rocks, and abalone steaks can now fetch over $4 a pound. Like shad
on the East Coast, abalone was once abundant on the West Coast,
which may also help explain its erstwhile low status. Now it is
growing rare, despite California laws against shipping fresh abalone
out of the state. The scarcity certainly explains the current high price.
(But "Who buys?" asks a San Francisco skin-diving enthusiast.)

A smaller industry than clams, shrimp, crabs or lobsters is scallops. As with the huge surf or hen clams of the northern Atlantic Coast, only the large cylindrical adductor muscle and the coral of the scallop is edible. In Europe, scallops are sold in their shells, alive; the red tongue, or coral, is prized as the best part. In America, scallops are usually dead when bought (though they are quite safe if they do not stink); the coral has been thrown away.

Bay scallops—pinkish, light tan or creamy white—are sweet, tender morsels sold only from November through February (the season used to be much shorter, but the scallop beds off Long Island and New Jersey have grown with good conservation laws). These baby bay scallops, the basis of *Coquille St. Jacques*, are smaller and more delicate than sea scallops, which are marshmallow-shaped, range in color from white to orange or pink, and are sold all year round. The Pacific rock scallop is gone, a victim of starfish.

Nostalgia on the half-shell

Oysters, like clams, vary from one coast to another. East Coast oysters —notably the American or Eastern oysters that are variously called Blue Points, Chincoteagues, Cotuits, Cape Cods and other names, and the little mangrove, or coon, oyster—are scarce today, so scarce that this gastronomical treat carries an astronomical price tag.

Early Americans found the shores of New York well laden with oysters—mangrove oysters in the Virginia Colony, big Eastern oysters from far north of the Plymouth Colony on down to the Florida Keys. The Indians were eating oysters when the English arrived; the colonists made them an important part of their own diet.

Oysters grew in popularity until by the mid-nineteenth century they had become a national mania. Even before the railroads, there were oyster expresses from Baltimore that carried big six-inch and even eight-inch Chesapeake Bay oysters across the Alleghenies and deep into inland settlements. The Lincolns, when they lived in Springfield, Illinois, gave oyster feasts where people ate the bivalves by the dozens.

There were oyster houses in every Eastern city, oyster peddlers in the streets. In 1877, 50,000 oysters a day went down the hatch at New York's Fulton Fish Market, which even then was fifty-six years old (it was finally torn down in 1969). Earlier, in the 1840's, there were places that offered all the oysters you could eat for six cents, though it was said the proprietors usually slipped a bad oyster onto your plate to keep you from eating too many.

Americans ate Blue Points, Cotuits, Chincoteagues, Cape Cods, Lynnhavens, Chicatics and tiny Olympias from the Pacific. They ate oysters both raw and baked on the pearly half-shell, oyster stew, pickled oysters, pan-fried oysters, scalloped oysters and oysters Rockefeller, a dish baked with spinach and bacon which originated in 1899 at Antoine's, the famous New Orleans restaurant. A customer, so one story goes, tasted the dish and said, "It's as rich as Rockefeller."

Some critics have said that while American oysters are enormous (the English novelist Thackeray said eating one was like swallowing a baby), they were no match in flavor for northern European oysters like France's *Malpeques* or *huîtres de Courseulles*. Captain Marryat, before Thackeray, wrote:

> Oysters are very plentiful, very large, and, to an English palate, rather insipid. As the Americans assert that the English and French oysters taste of copper, and that therefore they cannot eat them, I presume they do; and that's the reason why we do not like American oysters, copper being better than no flavor at all.

American oysters, it was charged, needed all the benefits of heavy batter, rich sauces and cream stews to make up for their lack of taste. But for most people they were quite flavorful enough.

The Oyster Bar in Grand Central Station, New York, opened on May 22, 1912. It still serves an oyster stew made according to its old 1912 recipe to remind us of the oyster's glory days. The stew costs vastly more than it did in 1912, a reminder that the glorious oyster may be passing into memory.

At its peak in the late 1880's and early 1900's, the U.S. oyster catch was as much as 150 million pounds, counting only the meat, not the shell. Now the figure is between 50 and 60 million pounds, and relatively little of that comes from the New England and Middle Atlantic states whose shores once yielded most of our oysters, and our best.

Changing biological and ecological conditions reduced the production of oyster grounds from Connecticut to New Jersey from 3.3 million bushels in 1950 to less than 160,000 bushels in 1966.

Chesapeake Bay has been known as a bountiful source of oysters since John Smith came to Virginia in 1607. In 1885, the Maryland oyster catch was nearly 15 million bushels; in some years since 1930, only a tenth that amount has been raked or dredged out of the Bay.

Under Maryland law, dredging under power is permitted only on Mondays and Tuesdays, and only from November 1 to March 15. On other days only sailing dredges are permitted. Some of the big skipjacks used for the work are over seventy feet from bowsprit to stern; they are the last commercial ships still working under sail in the United States.

But the oyster fishery the skipjacks work is a fraction of its former size; despite efforts to conserve it, that fishery is still being depleted. The state of Maryland each year dumps 5 million bushels of clean shell near the brood oysters; the spats, or newborn oysters, attach themselves to the shells. At the end of the season, the state employs oystermen to dredge up the shells, now covered with little seed oysters, and move them out into open water where, in three or four years, the seed oysters can grow to edible three-inch size.

Unfortunately, oystermen often harvest the oysters when they are only two and a half years old. Restaurant patrons, who may pay as much as $1.75 for half a dozen oysters, grumble that the oysters are too small and tough. The best American oysters are now probably the big Malpeques we import from Canada.

Says the *Wall Street Journal*, "The oyster has about had it." Water pollution, over-dredging and a mysterious parasite called MSX are all blamed for thinning out the nation's oyster beds though different factors are responsible in different areas. In the Delaware River Basin, a predatory snail called the oyster drill is the major menace.

In Long Island Sound, Long Island ducklings nearly finished off the industry. A variety of plankton which is nourished by duck manure, but which oysters cannot digest, became dominant before State and County Health Departments put pressure on 33 Suffolk county duck farms to build sewage-treatment plants. It was a matter of ecology. Other environmental changes in Long Island Sound have encouraged invasions of starfish, which prey on oysters. Whatever the reason, the Sound's Oyster Bay was practically bereft of oysters in the late 1960's. Progress has been made: about half the shell-fishing beds in Moriches and Bellport Bays reopened in 1970.

Rutgers University maintains an Oyster Investigation Laboratory at Bivalve, New Jersey, which is trying to develop a parasite-resistant oyster strain. The state of Maryland is spending $1.3 million a year on artificial oyster beds in Chesapeake Bay. The University of Delaware is experimenting with an off-bottom system, developed in Japan, which suspends young oysters from rafts in the bay water—on racks, in bags, or on strings threaded through their shells—to keep them out of reach of the oyster drills. The system makes use of the full depth of the water instead of just the bottom surface. Within the last ten years, annual oyster production in Delaware Bay fell from 4.2 million pounds to 34,000 pounds.

Perhaps the new efforts will revive the dying industry. Meanwhile, the oyster has begun to price itself in the direction of caviar.

Somewhat more abundant and more affordable are the tiny Olympia oysters (it takes 1400 of them to make a gallon) native to the West Coast, and the larger Pacific oyster (which was introduced from Japan).

East Coast oyster fanciers get a break when Pacific King oysters are flown in from the West Coast. These are cultivated by thirty producers along the Coast from Eureka, California, north to Puget Sound.

King oysters are seeded in oyster beds, much as the ancient Romans seeded oysters in the Mediterranean; but the cold Pacific water kills the spawn (a three- or four-degree drop in water temperature can be fatal) and a "commercial" set is possible only about once in every three or four years, even though the "seed" is planted during the summer months when water temperatures are generally above 65°.

It takes about three years for the seed oysters to reach maturity; during that time the beds are harrowed to keep the oysters spread out and to weed out starfish, the oysters' natural enemy. At harvest time, the oysters are shucked, washed and packed for fresh marketing or freezing. They are sold ready to cook, packed in their own liquor in eight- and twelve-ounce containers.

Westerners eat the big King oysters "Western style," which means dropped in boiling water and simmered for five minutes before being put in a stew or casserole. King oysters are also good raw; many people prefer them to other varieties. A narrow, dark frill along the lip edge usually means the oyster is extra rich in flavor.

As with other shellfish, the price of labor is a major factor in the high price of oysters. Oyster beds have to be combed, oysters have to be shucked. The average age of oyster shuckers in Maryland is over fifty and rising; young people are hard to recruit. A shucker can usually shuck two gallons of oysters an hour at $1.60 a gallon; good pay, but he averages only six hours a day, four days a week, thirty weeks a year. If an oyster-shucking machine could be devised that would shuck sixty oysters a minute, cost $5 an hour to operate and last five years, it would be a bargain for oyster-packing houses, even if it cost $50,000—so says a study made by the University of Maryland.

The oysters, of course, would have to do their part by reproducing themselves in quantities to keep up with the appetites of the machines.

Troubled waters

While even the Romans saw the need to farm the sea and conserve its food resources, modern man has directed his efforts toward primitive exploitation of oceans, lakes, rivers and streams, using them as dumps for industrial wastes, municipal sewage and the run-off of agricultural chemicals, and plundering their diminishing marine-life populations.

The results have been horrendous. The Michigan grayling, the San Gorgonio trout and at least four other species have gone the way of the passenger pigeon. Other marine species, like the green turtle of the Caribbean, are in peril at a time when the human species is faced with the problem of satisfying the most enormous appetite for food in all of man's history.

Some 15 million U.S. fish, two-thirds of them commercial varieties and nine per cent "sport fish," are estimated by the Interior Department to have been killed by water pollution in 1968.[13] Chesapeake Bay, source of Maryland's oysters, is threatened with thermal pollution by a projected atomic energy plant. By heating the waters around them, such plants change the ecology of the aquatic environment. The changes affect the multiplication of plankton organisms, hatching of eggs deposited by fish and insects, continuance or stoppage of parthenogenic reproduction, spawning of both fish and invertebrates. Aquatic organisms have narrower ranges of temperature tolerance than do most land creatures. So while raising water temperatures encourages spawning by oysters and other mollusks, a continued elevation in the temperatures could have a disastrous effect on the aquatic life used by the mollusks for food.

Atomic power can mean cleaner air than power produced from fossil fuels, but the discharge of nuclear plants can and must be controlled to avoid the destruction of marine life, as has happened on Florida's Biscayne Bay and as happened in 1963 when Consolidated Edison opened its nuclear power station at Indian Point on the Hudson River. An estimated 2 million striped bass were killed at Indian

---

[13] The figure seems low; some 40 million fish were estimated to have been killed in just five days in June, 1969, when a large quantity of endosulfan, a chemical insecticide closely related to DDT, spilled from a barge and polluted the Rhine River between Bingen, central Germany, and the Rhine's North Sea estuary in Holland. The U.S. 1968 figure of 15,236,000 poisoned fish, based on reports from forty-two states, was exceeded in 1964 when 18,387,000 fish were estimated to have died from pollutants.

Point before a fine-mesh screen was erected to keep the spawning bass, attracted by the warm water, out of harm's way. Smaller fish-kills have ensued at Indian Point despite the screen.

Insecticide and pesticide run-offs from our farms and orchards can—and do—kill fish and shellfish as surely as industrial wastes and the raw sewage of our cities and towns; so do run-offs of fertilizer phosphates and nitrates, which have ecological effects at least as great as those of thermal pollution.

Our dilemma is that fertilizers and weed-killers and insect sprays have made U.S. agriculture enormously productive; without them, crop yields would be much smaller, food prices much higher. We would hardly, in fact, be able to feed ourselves.

It is not a dilemma we can solve simply by banning DDT, though for non-malarial areas at least that would seem not only a sensible step but one we urgently need. When DDT was first sold back in the early 1940's, its price was $1.19 a pound; now it sells for seventeen cents a pound, which helps explain its popularity. Most of the DDT used in U.S. agriculture is used in the cotton states, and far more is used in urban areas (against termites, bedbugs, cockroaches, lice and garden pests) than on croplands. Research at Michigan State University has shown streams from urban areas carry much higher pesticide residues than do streams from rural areas.

The short-term effect of raw sewage from urban centers has been far more devastating to marine life than have pesticide, herbicide or fertilizer residues. Safe fishing waters should not have a fecal coliform count in excess of 1000 per 100 milliliters; a count of seventy per 100 milliliters is standard in shellfishing areas. But counts as high as 24,000 per 100 milliliters have been recorded in the Potomac, as high as 27,000 in the worst parts of Long Island Sound and up to 36,000 in the James River below Richmond.

Fish need dissolved oxygen in order to breathe; the normal minimum is four milligrams per liter. At some points in the James River oxygen concentrations are below three milligrams per liter, and this is true also in parts of the Potomac and other polluted rivers.

Conditions of high bacteriological count and low oxygen concentration are for the most part worsening, not only in this country but everywhere, even in the open sea. One of the most polluted sea areas is the Baltic. The narrow Danish sounds mentioned by Rachel Carson are now practically stagnant, and the concentration of poisonous hydrogen sulphite in the deep Baltic waters is rising, making that sea in many places as dead as America's Lake Erie, which produced 75 million pounds of fish as recently as 1954 but now produces almost none.

Steel mill wastes, laundry detergents [13] and raw sewage were the culprits in Lake Erie; paper factories have poisoned the Baltic. For while the gases produced by the Kraft method of paper making do not pollute the air as sulphite process effluents pollute the water, the gases smell so bad that a lot of paper is still made by the sulphite process.

If sewage and industrial wastes kill fish populations, so do oil spills. The wreck of the tanker *Torrey Canyon* off the coast of southern England in 1967, the blowout of an offshore oil well in California's Santa Barbara Channel in 1969 and the disasters of the early 1970's in Nova Scotia's Chedabucto Bay, in Florida's Tampa Bay, and off the Louisiana Gulf Coast are dramatic examples of oil spill, but most oil wastes in the sea are produced by routine washing of tankers' cargo tanks with salt water after each load. Other ships often fill empty fuel tanks with water for ballast, pumping out the contaminated mixture before they enter port to refuel. Ocean shipments of oil are increasing rapidly, offshore petroleum production is expanding at a rate of ten per cent a year. Seepage is chronic; it goes almost unnoticed, except by fish and wildlife.

The U.S. Coast Guard says the U.S. alone had 714 major oil spills in 1968, up from 371 in 1966. There are no world-wide figures.

---

[14] "Non-biodegradable" phosphorous in detergents promotes the growth of undesirable algae beyond the ability of marine animals to consume it. As the plants die and decay they consume dissolved oxygen which fish need to live, a process called "eutrophication." Detergents depend on phosphates for their heavy-duty cleaning power; so far the industry has found nothing to replace them.

But while sewage, industrial wastes and oil spills are present horrors, run-offs of chemical pesticides jeopardize future generations of fish—and of fish eaters.

While the federal limit on DDT-content in cows' milk (Chapter 4) is 0.05 parts per million, the limit in fish is five parts. This, like the seven parts per million limit for many fruits and vegetables, and for the fat of animal meat, is based on concerns that DDT may produce cancer in humans.

Early in 1969, the Food and Drug Administration noted that ninety per cent of the fish sold in the U.S. has less than one part DDT per million, but a vocal minority says the tolerance level should be zero. A spokesman for mackerel fishermen, who operate out of Los Angeles's San Pedro harbor but had to suspend fishing when shipments of their fish were found to contain up to ten parts per million of DDT derivatives, has asked that the safety maximum be raised.

The U.S. and Canada are now sharply reducing their use of DDT and similar compounds, but the FAO has urged that developing countries, whose insecticides are made up fifty to seventy-five per cent of DDT and its chemical relatives, continue to use such compounds on a controlled basis, the benefits being considered greater than the risks.

Growing numbers of Americans are more concerned with DDT's effects on fish, and on the birds and wildlife which eat fish, than on its dangers for humans. There is some evidence that humans eliminate DDT once it reaches a level of ten or twelve parts per million, although one study has shown an average of 147 parts per million among men who had worked in a DDT factory for nineteen years, and one man had 648 parts per million. Another study shows that the average in the general U.S. population has declined from about five parts per million to 1.46 parts per million today.

In lower forms of life DDT concentrations build up by what scientists call "biological magnification" in the food chain. Some sea birds have been found to have DDT concentrations of ninety-nine parts per million after eating large quantities of fish; the fish had concentrations of three to six parts after eating tiny amphipods with concentrations of 0.41 parts. The high DDT concentrations in the birds interfered with their ability to reproduce: DDT causes some bird livers to produce enzymes which attack hormones that control calcium production. That means thinner eggshells, more broken eggs, fewer baby herring gulls, baby ospreys, baby mallard ducklings, baby pelicans, peregrine falcons. And fewer bald eagles, the birds that have been the symbols of this land of the free, despite Ben Franklin's preference for the turkey.

Farmers, exterminators, gardeners and housewives have been free to use DDT for nearly three decades, though it has been under attack by concerned ecologists at least since 1948, when Fairfield Osborn published *Our Plundered Planet*. DDT's terrors were spelled out more frighteningly in 1962 by Rachel Carson's widely-read *Silent Spring*.

But the bird lovers' lobby is not a political force muscular enough to push lawmakers into action.

Arizona ordered a one-year moratorium on the use of DDT early in 1969 when milk in that state was found to have high DDT levels; it had nothing to do with birds.

Michigan restricted spraying crops with DDT after the seizure by the FDA in April, 1969, of 28,000 pounds of coho salmon. Interstate shipments of fish caught in the fall of 1968 were found to have DDT concentrations of twenty parts per million. The fate of birds was not at issue.

What moved the Michigan authorities was the fear of losing its sportsman-tourist trade. Fishermen poured into the state each fall to battle fifteen- and twenty-pound coho salmon—and spent close to $100 million on motel rooms, boats, gasoline, fishing tackle, licenses and bait.

But the coho had grown fat feeding on alewives, small fish which concentrated DDT in their bodies from what they themselves ate. Even before the FDA seizure, the Michigan Department of Agriculture had opened some cans of coho salmon and found the contents contained high levels of dieldrin, another chlorinated hydrocarbon pesticide which is more toxic than DDT but is used less widely.

Officials of the World Health Organization, more concerned about malaria and encephalitis than about birdlife or fishlife, have said that DDT is not harmful to humans. In terms of direct danger to health, they may be right, though it is too early to say what effect DDT and its ilk may have on future generations of humans, who even now have higher concentrations of DDT in their bodies than the levels permitted for meat in interstate commerce.

Indirect effects of DDT are now clear enough to alarm most people who are worried about our environment and our continued ability to feed ourselves as our numbers increase on the earth.

There are still far more crop-devouring insects than people, and we must contend with those insects if we are to grow food.

But more states and more countries are deciding that we can survive without persistent pesticides like DDT and its close relatives, DDD, dieldrin, aldrin, chlordane and lindane. Michigan still permits use of DDT against bedbugs and some other insect pests, but California and some other states have now restricted use of at least some chlorinated hydrocarbon pesticides. Sweden has declared a two-year moratorium on home use of DDT and on all use of its related chemicals. Canada, which used to permit spraying DDT on sixty-two cultivated food crops, now permits it on only twelve; and Canadian fruits and vegetables, which formerly could have DDT levels of seven parts per million, may now have only one part (though apples, pears and celery may have 3.5 parts).

Ironically, in the U.S. it is the southern states, where fish and shellfish compose a higher percentage of the diet than anywhere else in the country, that are most affected by restrictions on the use of DDT, restrictions whose environmental effects will not be felt for years.

Perhaps it is not too late. Perhaps the "hard" pesticides will be universally outlawed, raw sewage chemically treated, phosphate-content of detergents limited (the "enzyme" detergents are the worst offenders), industrial wastes controlled and petroleum leakages and discharges minimized before irreparable damage is done to one of our major food resources.

The dilemma is complex, global and very frightening: it requires a variety of solutions, all of which arouse conflicts of opposing interests (including the conflict between East and West which aborts co-operative efforts to save the Baltic from pollution and the Grand Banks from over-fishing).

Prospects are not bright; as Harvard's Professor George Wald has remarked in another connection, when the possibilities for disaster reach a certain point, disaster becomes a probability.

Meanwhile, DDT in fish eggs is stopping the reproduction of trout in New York's Lake George, stores of war chemicals have been dumped in the North Sea and the North Atlantic; the poor shad and its fellow creatures of the deep are bearing the brunt of man's progress, proliferation and reckless short-sightedness.

As for mankind itself, it may soon be time for some philosopher to echo Thoreau and say, "Poor man! where is thy redress?"

⚬⟦ 6 ⟧⚬

The flowering earth deflowered

The apple in the Garden of Eden, says the Koran, was not an apple; it was a banana.

This Darwinian idea recalls the conjecture that the first men were vegetarians. But whether or not our ancestors restricted themselves to fruits, nuts, berries, roots, seeds and other products of growing plants, these must certainly have figured importantly in their diets.

It is generally thought that the crop plants grown by the initial agriculturists were the grasses whose seeds were crushed to make flour. Those early farmers did little to violate the earth's surface. But their digging sticks led to the plows that began the rape of the virgin soil, and in time turned forests into Saharas and prairie pasture lands into dust bowls. Their irrigation ditches eventually raised the saline levels of the land; croplands degenerated into salt flats, destroying the civilizations which had created them.

Our major crop plants today are, with one exception, still the grasses. But what of all the fruits and vegetables we now enjoy? For Britons, Scandinavians and others in the north, and for people brought up in the cultural traditions of northerly countries with relatively short growing seasons, fruits—and more especially vegetables—have

not bulked large in diets. But they have been important diet components of peoples in southerly climes and of heirs to their traditions.

Going back to de Candolle, we find that such fruits as apples, apricots, bananas, dates, figs, grapes, mangoes, peaches, pears, quinces and watermelons were cultivated more than 4000 years ago. So were many vegetables: broad beans, cabbages, cucumbers, eggplants, olives, sorghums, soybeans and turnips (we will omit for the moment fruits and vegetables cultivated by the Indians of the New World).

By the start of the Christian era, said de Candolle, cherries, grapefruit, lemons, limes, oranges and plums were being cultivated in the Old World. So were asparagus, beets, carrots, celery, garden peas, lettuce, mustard, radishes and yams.

We have dealt earlier with the prominence of onions in some of the earlier civilizations' diets, and with the varying attitudes toward garlic. As for other vegetables which today appear fresh and frozen in the world's market places and supermarkets, it may be well to remember that all vegetables in their original forms grew wild.

Beginning with fig leaves

Early man, living close to nature, had more knowledge of the growing things about him than most of us do today.

Anthropologist Claude Lévi-Strauss, a latter-day James Frazer, tells us that a desert region in Southern California, apparently a completely barren area on which a bare handful of white families subsist today, once supported several thousand Coahuila Indians. They were familiar with at least sixty different edible plants, and they did not begin to exhaust the natural food resources of the territory.

"Uncivilized" peoples have often had amazing knowledge of plant life. In the words they use for various plants, they frequently group plants together in ways which show an instinctive knowledge of the plants' chemical content as well as other values shared by vegetation forms which are ostensibly quite different.

America's Great Lakes Indians used 130 species of plants for food (they used 275 for medicinal purposes, and twenty-seven for smoking).

Negrito pygmies in the Philippine uplands know much more about the plant life of their environment than do the Christian lowlanders. Most Negrito men, trained by acute observation, know the names (specific or descriptive) of at least 450 plants. Before a Negrito will announce that he knows or does not know a particular plant, he smells the leaves, tastes the fruit or root, breaks the stem and examines it.

A backward people in the Tyukyu archipelago, Lévi-Strauss tells us, can even as children take a tiny wood fragment and tell what kind of tree it came from—and be absolutely right.

Most travelers who observe native agriculture methods get the wrong idea, says Lévi-Strauss. The natives they see live near big highways and cities; their ancient cultures have broken down and they have become careless. The true primitives, he says, are fanatical about adhering to ideal plant types.

But long before people cultivated crop plants they ate plant foods found in the wild—green herbs at first, according to Ovid, then acorns. Plutarch said that in primitive times when men "had by chance tasted or eaten an acorn, they danced for joy about some oak or aesculus, calling it by the name of life-giver, mother and nourisher. And this was the only festival that these times were acquainted with; upon all other occasions all things were full of anguish and dismal sadness." Acorns, some of which are sweet (though even bitter ones can be eaten if cooked in several changes of water), could be squirreled away to be eaten when other foods were not available. Great stores of acorns have been found buried in prehistoric village sites in Switzerland and the north of Italy.

The whole history of vegetables and fruits is a story of people gingerly trying new things, taming wild foods to improve them, developing desirable characteristics and routing out undesirable ones, though the premises of desirability have not always been the same.

Botanists have identified more than 250,000 species of plants; over 1500, wild and cultivated, are used by man; only about 300 are commercially grown (and some of these, like cotton and flax, are not raised primarily for food).

George Washington Carver, famous for championing the peanut in his great career at Tuskegee Institute, once remarked that a weed was only a vegetable growing in the wrong place. Of the billions of weed seeds cast to the autumn winds, he pointed out, only the sturdiest survived; and this quality of survival usually gave a weed more vitality and succulence than vegetables coddled in kitchen gardens.

Carver introduced dandelions, pepper grass, watercress, chicory and chickweed to the dining hall at Tuskegee. As an old man in the early part of World War II, he wrote a government bulletin which introduced some people to the flavor and economy of chicory coffee (popular for centuries in France), "rhubarb" pie made from curled dock, "asparagus tips" of common pokeweed shoots and close to 100 other nourishing dishes made from weeds and wild flowers.

Our leading modern enthusiast for wild foods is Euell Gibbons, who wrote in one of his many books that "ridiculous as it sounds, we might be better off nutritionally if we threw away the crops we so laboriously grow in our fields and gardens and ate the weeds instead."

The weeds, he says, echoing Carver, often taste good. They grow with no encouragement whatever, even resisting strenuous efforts with cultivators and herbicides to eradicate them. And in many cases they are extremely nutritious, containing more vitamins and minerals than commercially-grown vegetables, all of which in some form or other, once grew wild.

Cabbage, lettuce, chard, spinach and parsley are the leaves of plants. So are Brussels sprouts and artichokes.

Cauliflower and broccoli are the flowers of plants.

Peas, beans, sweet corn and popcorn are the seeds of plants (though some beans are seed *pods*).

Cucumbers, eggplants, pumpkins, squashes[1] and tomatoes are the fruits of plants.

---

[1] The English call squash "vegetable marrow," perhaps because in medieval and Renaissance England, the word "squash" meant an unripe pea pod. Mature peas were called peascod.

Asparagus and rhubarb are the stalks or stems of plants (rhubarb leaves and roots contain oxalic acid which can be poisonous).

Carrots, beets, parsnips, sweet potatoes, turnips and radishes are the roots of plants.

White potatoes are tubers which grow on the roots of plants.

Onions are bulbs. Little roots reach out from the bulbs, but we do not eat the roots, only the bulbs.

And if all these leaves, flowers, seeds, roots, tubers and bulbs, many of which we will explore in this chapter, make good food, why not other leaves, flowers, seeds, roots, tubers and bulbs?

Beware. But at least be aware

Some plants, like rhubarb leaves and roots, are to be sure poisonous.

Jimson weed (a corruption of Jamestown weed, *Datura stramonium*, found originally in the Jamestown settlement) is notoriously poisonous, and its seeds have hallucinogenic powers, as some American Indian tribes well knew. Jimson weed grows wild throughout North America.

Also poisonous is the fruit of the horse nettle, the one that looks like a yellow cherry tomato.

Daisies are not harmful, but *please* don't eat the sweet peas. Do not eat buttercups or tulip bulbs either, or the rootstock or pip of lily of the valley, the bark or seeds of the black locust, pokeweed roots or berries (sometimes called pigeonberries because birds, including robins, grackles and waxwings, eat them with immunity), the leaves of the mountain laurel or rhododendron, Jack-in-the-pulpit berries, privet leaves or yew needles, mistletoe, baneberry (*Actaea rubra*), fool's parsley (*Aethusa cynapium*), bleeding heart, dogbane (or Indian hemp, *Apocynum cannabium*), buckeyes, water hemlock roots (*Cicuta maculata*), poison hemlock (*Conium maculatum*), snow-on-the-mountain (*Euphorbia corollata*) or peach tree leaves. The medicine digitalis comes from the leaves and seeds of foxglove (*digi-*

talis purpurea) which, if eaten, can overstimulate the heart to the point of cardiac arrest.

The hemlocks have parsleylike foliage and could be mistaken for wild parsnips or carrots (about which we will speak in a moment), though much larger. Eating water hemlock roots can produce violent convulsions; the poison hemlock, Socrates' death potion, can paralyze the nervous system almost instantly and be fatal, as it was for the Greek philosopher.

Two poisonous species of milkweed occur in the southeastern U.S. and on the Gulf Coast, but three other species, which occur in these same areas and almost everywhere else in the U.S. (though not on the West Coast) are quite edible if boiled in water, drained, covered again with fresh boiling water and the process repeated at least three times to get the bitterness out. Treated this way, says Euell Gibbons, the young shoots in spring can be cooked like asparagus, the unopened buds like broccoli, the young pods like okra and the newly opened leaves like spinach (though he warns they do not taste like asparagus, broccoli, okra or spinach; good, but different).

Others warn against confusing dogbane with milkweed; dogbane stems are tougher and forked in their branching, which is not true of milkweed.

Given these warnings, and a few more we will get to presently, there is still plenty of room for productive foraging.

Some wild plants can be eaten raw: watercress, for example, and sheep sorrel and the crisp roots of Indian cucumbers.

The leaves of dandelions, jagged like the teeth of lions (*dents de lion* in French), are good in salads and can be cooked as well. Pigweed, also called wild spinach or lamb's quarters, can be cooked just like spinach; so can sorrel, or sour grass (which is blended with sour cream to make *shav* in Jewish dairy restaurants). Some people like cooked dandelion leaves, pigweed and sorrel even better than spinach; the weeds are generally at least as rich in vitamins and minerals. Amaranth, a type of pigweed, makes a good cooked dish, too, especially when mixed with cress or chicory.

Purslane can be eaten raw or cooked—stems, leaves and all, and the seeds can be ground into a flour that is fine for pancakes.

Why bother [Euell Gibbons asks] with wild food plants in a country which produces a surplus of many domestic food products? With as much reason, one might ask, why go fishing for mountain trout when codfish fillets are for sale in any supermarket? Or why bother with hunting and game cookery when unlimited quantities of fine meat can be purchased at every butcher counter?

The answer, he says, is that there is a trace of the primitive in all of us. And an excitement in "reaping where you did not sow." Many children who "do not like to eat" change their minds, he observes, when they get interested in gathering and preparing wild foods.

Mountains and dense forests are poor places to look for wild plant foods. Much better are abandoned farmsteads, old fields, fence rows, burned-off lands; there is good picking along streams and dirt roads, in wood lots, around farm ponds, in swampy areas, even in the vacant lots of cities and suburbs.

Plantain, the common weed of the *Plantago* genus, not to be confused with the bananalike *Musa paradisiaca* of the tropics, includes among its many species some whose young leaves can be eaten raw in salads, brewed into tea or cooked into an appetizing and nutritious soup.

Most wild foods—nuts, berries, greens, fruits or whatever—are seasonal. If one is in need of food and lucky enough to be in the right season, fine. But the most dependable year-round sources of plant food in the wilds are roots and tubers.

A number of these can be peeled and eaten raw, but they are better if boiled or roasted in the coals of a campfire.

Queen Anne's Lace is botanically so close to the cultivated carrot that taxonomists make no distinction between the two, and while its root is not so well developed (it has not, after all, been selectively bred) it certainly tastes carroty enough to fool anyone. (But do not be fooled by water hemlock or poison hemlock; the first grows only near shallow water, in swamplands and wet meadows; the second usually along roadsides, around old dumps and in waste lands.)

Other plants with roots or tubers edible at virtually any time of year are the arrowhead, cattail, prairie apple, groundnut,[2] hog peanut, wild potato vine, chufa grass, floating spatterdock, sweet water lily and Jerusalem artichoke. It can be useful to learn how to recognize all of these.

The rather sweet starch in the roots of the Jerusalem artichoke, native to the Americas, made the plant popular with early settlers who found the Indians cultivating it. The colonists called it the Canadian potato and in 1616 sent samples back to Europe (where it is now widely grown and enjoyed—the French call the roots *topinambours*; Jerusalem artichoke soup is *potage Palestine*).

Jerusalem artichokes have nothing to do with Jerusalem or Palestine, and they are not artichokes. They are quite unrelated, at least, to the French globe artichoke. The Jerusalem artichoke is a misnomer for a kind of sunflower, *Helianthus tuberosus*. (The other sunflower, the immensely taller-growing one native to the western U.S.,[3] is *Helianthus annuus*.) The Spanish word for sunflower is *girasol*, "turn to the sun," based on the mistaken notion of long standing that sunflower blossoms do indeed turn all day to keep facing the sun; they do not. It is easy to see how *girasol* came to be tortured into "Jerusalem," but how the root came to be called an artichoke is anybody's guess.

Root, tuber, rhizome—the terms are all related, though some are actually enlarged or thickened underground stems or their out-

---

[2] *Apios tuberosa*, as distinguished from *Arachis hypogaea*, which we commonly call a peanut but is called a groundnut in England. American Indians ate the *Apios tuberosa*. Sagaponack, out near the eastern tip of Long Island, is a Shinnecock Indian word meaning "place of the groundnuts." The "Sag" in Sag Harbor, just to the north, is short for sagaponack.

[3] Sunflowers grow twelve feet high in their wild state and may reach seventeen feet under cultivation (Jerusalem artichoke stalks grow six or seven feet tall). Not much used by America's colonists, sunflowers are now a valuable commercial crop grown in the U.S. and quite widely in Soviet Russia and eastern Europe; their seeds are used as poultry feed, pressed for use as cooking oil and in margarine production, or made into oilcake for both livestock and poultry feed. The stalks are used for fodder and ensilage in America and for fuel in parts of Europe.

growths. Suffice it that roots and such were probably the basic food of early man, always available even when fish or game was scarce and fruits and berries not in season. Many foods are ripe for the picking in summer, but fall, winter and spring are good times to gather Jerusalem artichoke roots. The colonists used to pickle them.

American Indians, and colonists, too, ate the roots of common cattails (*Typha latifolia* and *Typha angustifolia*), which had been brought to North America from Central Asia in prehistoric times.

Roots must have saved Stone Age man from starvation many times (root foods are often more nutritious than food crops grown above ground) and they were the saving of more than a few of North America's explorers.

Père Marquette, the Jesuit missionary who ventured into the Northwest in the 1670's, wrote of surviving on wild onions.

Meriwether Lewis, of the Lewis and Clark partnership, had the bitterroot (which is not bitter when peeled) of the Rocky Mountain foothills named after him (*Lewisia rediviva*). On their two-and-a-half-year journey across the continent between 1804 and 1806, Captain Lewis and Second Lieutenant Clark, with forty men and a congressional appropriation of $2500, had no choice but to live off the land. They had several occasions to be grateful for wild roots, though the bulbous camas root gave them severe dysentery.

On the Snake River in what is now Idaho, the expeditionary force ate biscuit root, or Indian biscuit (*Lomatium geyeri*, also known as cowas or cous); it tastes something like fresh celery, and the Indians of that area still eat a lot of it, sometimes in a flour.

The explorers made "yellow loaf bread" from the root of the wild sweet potato (*Ipomoea pandurata*) which grows over nearly half of North America. Lewis mentioned the prairie apple, or bread root (*Psoralea esculenta*) in his *Journals*. It has always been a staple food of the Sioux and other tribes of the Great Plains.

Lewis mentioned also the Jerusalem artichoke. And his party survived the hard winter of 1805–06 on wapatoo (*Sagittaria latifolia*), another Indian root.

They are never out of season [Lewis wrote]. . . . They are nearly equal in flavor to the Irish potato and afford a very good substitute for bread.

Arriving a few decades later in Deseret, Utah, the Mormons (whose Church of Jesus Christ of Latter-Day Saints was organized in 1830) escaped starvation by eating the corms (enlarged bulblike stems) of sego lilies. Today, the sego lily is the state flower of Utah. And *Lewisia rediviva* is Montana's state flower.

Only a few of the many, many edible roots which grow widely over Europe, Asia and North America are cultivated. Some, like the Jerusalem artichoke and the German rampion, sometimes called the evening primrose (*Oenothera biennis*), are grown commercially in Europe but not in America. The French grew the rampion for centuries for its big perennial roots and its young green shoots (they make good salad greens). They introduced it to New France; but who grows it here or in Canada today?

Some of these wild roots, or marginally cultivated roots, have potential for development into major food crops. Meanwhile they are known only to primitive peoples and to some outdoorsmen.

For anyone faced with a problem of wilderness survival, the most versatile—and certainly the most easily identifiable—source of food is probably the cattail, also called elephant grass or reed mace; it usually grows in damp areas and along the edges of fresh-water lakes and streams.

The cattail's rootstalk, the core or marrow of the young plant, the flower spikes and even the pollen are edible. From autumn to early spring, the rootstalk is full of stored starch and is quite nutritious. Peel it and then boil or bake it. The inner stems of young plants can be eaten raw or boiled in early spring. The flowering spikes, before they develop pollen, can be eaten raw, boiled as a vegetable or made into a soup. And the pollen can be boiled as a porridge or made into a dough and baked as a kind of bread.

To roast roots or tubers, whether of cattails, Jerusalem artichokes or of almost anything (except rhubarb, lily of the valley, pokeweed

or tulips, whose bulbs or rootstocks are poisonous), follow the advice
of the Boy Scout Handbook. First wrap the roots in several layers of
large leaves that have been soaked in water. The wet leaves will first
steam the roots; then, as the leaves dry out, the roots will be roasted.

The easiest thing a resourceful outdoorsman can make is a cup of
hot tea. A lack of tea leaves is no problem. Pouring boiled water over
green spearmint, peppermint or wild Bergamot [4] leaves, over spicebush
twigs, over elderberry or basswood flowers produces quite agreeable
varieties of tea. So does boiled water poured over the dried leaves of
wild strawberry, sweetbriar, black birch or wintergreen.

For dessert, the time of year makes all the difference. With luck,
it is possible to find wild strawberries, red raspberries, blackcaps,
dewberries, huckleberries, blueberries, cranberries, wild grapes and
prickly pears. Some people like the ripe fruit of the May apple. Persimmons are good after the first frost. So is pawpaw, also called
custard apple (and not to be confused with the tropical pawpaw, or
papaya, which is called *fruta bomba* in Cuba, where papaya is an
uncouth slang word with sexual connotations conveyed in the U.S.
by a feline term).

In the fall there are nuts: black walnuts, butternuts, hazelnuts,
hickory nuts, beechnuts, chestnuts (from blight-resistant trees introduced here from the Orient) and, in the West, Indian nuts which
cluster by the score inside the cones of piñon pines. In Utah, the
Navajos and Utes go after piñon nuts; so do the Goshiutes of Nevada,
the Shoshones of Idaho and members of most other tribes in the high
plateau country between the Rockies and the Sierras. Digger pine
nuts are good, too, and easy enough to harvest and to roast. With some
of the others it is often troublesome getting to the edible kernel.

To repeat, do be careful about wild foods. Do not eat anything
unrecognizable. U.S. Public Health Service figures show 15,000
people get ill from eating poisonous plants in a typical year; about

---

[4] The Oswego Indians made "Oswego tea" from Bergamot leaves, and Bergamot
tea is said to have been popular among rebellious American patriots who refused to drink English tea. Wild bergamot is a kind of bee balm or horsemint
which grows in damp places. Its flowers are bright scarlet.

seventy-five die. Plant poisoning is listed as the sixth leading kind of poisoning among children under five.

No figures are kept on the number of livestock and pet animals killed by poisonous plants, but it is much larger than the number of humans, who do not ordinarily make a practice of eating raw wild vegetation. Snakeroot, larkspur, loco weed, water hemlock, milkweed and cocklebur will all poison cattle if consumed in large enough quantities. Even sweet clover hay or silage can be toxic if not properly preserved. And in conditions of extreme drought or frost, Sudan grass and other sorghum grasses, Johnson grass, chokecherry, black cherry, arrow grass, velvet grass and Christmas berry can develop prussic acid and kill foraging livestock within a few minutes.

Members of the New York Mycological Society recall the time their founder, composer John Cage, went into a coma and had to be rushed to a hospital after eating white hellebore (*Veratrum viride*) which he had mistaken for the edible marsh marigold (both look something like skunk cabbage, whose roots, cooked and dried, make a flour of sorts).

Gathering dandelions, purslane or other "weeds" along a busy highway is not recommended: the natural foods may be full of unnatural lead from automobile exhausts.

Experts at the New York State College of Agriculture at Cornell have a further warning: meat skewered on an oleander branch can kill; the poison in the wood contaminates the meat. Oleander leaves are extremely toxic: just two can be fatal if eaten.

It may be enjoyable to go wild food foraging as a sport, but the possibilities of our having to survive on wilderness weeds are remote; our concern with wild foods here is really with their relevance to the vegetables sold at the store.

Euell Gibbons is hardly realistic in his ideas about raising "weeds" instead of the plant crops we now grow. He does, however, make a good case for conservation: the wild plants of today could in some cases conceivably be the food crops of tomorrow, which makes the phrase "conservation for conservation's sake" meaningless and dangerous. We cannot yet know all the values of keeping our wilds wild.

Our civilized plants

The history of the more conventional vegetables we eat is complicated by the geographical and cultural variations in that history. While the Chinese were growing soybeans and rice, the Egyptians, who raised neither, were cultivating olives, though they did not raise cucumbers, which earlier peoples in the "Cradle of Civilization" had been growing for centuries.

By the time of Athens' flowering, broad beans, dried peas, cabbages, lettuce and lentils were staple vegetables [5] in their seasons (and were in some cases dried for use out of season).

For both the Greeks and the Romans, vegetables assumed increasing importance. They ate peas, but only dried peas. The Egyptians had eaten no peas at all, but the Greeks learned of them from the Aryans of the East, who also ate them only in dried form (it was the Chinese who first ate peas green).

Cucumbers were popular in Rome. The Emperor Tiberius liked them so much he had his gardeners devise artificial methods for growing them out of season. (When someone used vinegar to make pickles out of cucumbers, every man could enjoy them in all seasons.)

Radishes, edible sooner after planting than any other vegetable, were prized by Greeks and Romans alike. An ancient Greek physician wrote a book about the radish plant. And while Athenian artisans made replicas of beets in silver, and of turnips in lead, gold was used for

---

[5] Peas, beans, soybeans and lentils are actually legumes, which is the French word for vegetables but which in English has a stricter definition. Peanuts, chick-peas and cowpeas are legumes. So are lima beans and garden beans (or kidney beans). The young pods of garden beans are called string beans or snap beans or wax beans; the unripe seeds are called shell beans; and the dried ripe seeds are called garden or kidney beans. There are also forage legumes: alfalfa, clover, kudzu, the lespedezas and the vetches. Legumes in general absorb nitrogen from the air, which makes them rich sources of protein and gives them a useful role in maintaining the fertility of the soil.

replicas of radishes. The Greeks called radishes *raphanos*, meaning "easily reared." The Romans, who had many kinds of radishes—small ones, mild ones, early ones, round ones, long ones and big, late-maturing ones that weighed several pounds each—called the radish *radix*, meaning root; it is the root of our English word.

Leeks, like onions except that they form cylindrical bulbs instead of round ones, were known in Egypt from earliest Biblical times. The Romans regarded Egyptian leeks as the best; one Roman, the Emperor Nero, was so fond of them (he thought they improved his singing voice) he was nicknamed *Porrophagus* (*porrum* is Latin for leek). Roman legions took the leek to Britain, where it became the national emblem of Wales, worn like a flower in buttonholes on Saint David's Day, March 1, and served in leek broth (*Cawl Cennin*) and in chicken-and-leek pie (though Scotsmen, with their cock-a-leekie soup, consume even more leeks than the Welsh).

Beets were used by the Greeks only for their leaves; the large fleshy edible roots were unknown as food until the first century A.D. The leaf beet, which we call chard, grew wild in several varieties over wide areas of the Mediterranean, Asia Minor, the Caucasus and the Near East. Aristotle wrote of red chard in the fourth century B.C.; Theophrastus, half a century later, mentioned light green and dark green varieties.

But the root of the wild beet was used only for medicinal purposes until the later centuries of the Roman Empire. Recipes for cooking the root of *Beta vulgaris* are found in the records of the second and third centuries A.D., and some Roman epicures claimed the beet root was a better vegetable than the cabbage.

Nutritionally, there is no comparison. Cabbage is so rich in vitamins and minerals it has been called man's best friend in the vegetable kingdom. And it comes in more variations than any other vegetable.

To the Greeks and Romans, cabbage did not mean what it usually means today. The forms tolerant to warm climates were leafy, non-heading varieties, the kinds we now call kale and collards. The Greeks made little distinction between these varieties. Aristotle, among others, followed the Egyptian practice of eating cabbage before banquets in the belief it would keep the wine from fuddling his wise philosopher head.

Hard-heading cabbages are thought to have come into Europe with the Celts about 600 B.C. but were developed only in the cooler parts of the continent. The word "cabbage" comes from the Latin word *caput*, meaning head. There is no word for cabbage in Sanskrit or other ancient Eastern languages, which leads plant historians to think that Eastern peoples did not have cabbages—not even for kings.

Some sources say the more advanced forms of cabbage, like broccoli and cauliflower, were not developed until the Middle Ages, but Pliny wrote about both in the first century A.D. if the translations are correct. And remember the penchant Tiberius' son had for the boiled broccoli of Apicius. The word "broccoli" comes from the Latin *bracchium*, meaning arm, or branch.

A vegetable the Greeks collected from the wild but never cultivated was the asparagus, native to the eastern Mediterranean region. A fourth-century B.C. writer warned that asparagus caused blindness, but the Romans as early as 200 B.C. were following detailed gardening rules for the cultivation of the stalks. Some grown at Ravenna had stems that weighed three pounds. In the Getulia plains of Africa, the Romans found asparagus growing twelve feet high.

Not only did the Romans eat asparagus in season (the season being spring), they also dried asparagus shoots for later use. Boiling the dried asparagus shoots produced a quick dish (it never did do to cook asparagus more than eight minutes). The Emperor Augustus was fond of asparagus and is reported to have originated a saying, "Quicker than you can cook asparagus."

While lettuce, called *tridax* by the Greeks, was said by Herodotus to have been served on the tables of Persian kings of the sixth century B.C., Romans evidently waited until the first century A.D. to eat lettuce. Roman writers described a dozen different varieties, some evidently quite common. Romaine lettuce, developed in a moderately warm climate, may be Roman in origin, as its name suggests. The word "lettuce" has a Latin root in *lactuca*.

Both Greeks and Romans ate wild parsnips, though neither people cultivated them. Tiberius was supposedly so fond of parsnips he had them imported from Germany, where they grew in abundance along the Rhine.

The Romans also knew many distinct types of turnips, some of them with Greek place names which suggest earlier development by the Greeks. Pliny described long turnips, flat turnips, round turnips. He used the names *rapa* and *napus*; the latter term became *nepe* in Middle English and *naep* in Anglo-Saxon. Put together with the word *turn*, meaning "make round," *naep* became "turnip."

Pliny called artichokes "monstrous productions of the earth" and pointed out that "four-footed beasts instinctively refuse to touch them." But in Rome in the second century A.D. no other garden vegetable fetched such a high price.

This artichoke enjoyed by the Greeks and Romans was not the globe (or French) artichoke (*Cynara scolymus*), that thistle flower head whose petal bases and "heart" we eat so laboriously [6] today. The ancients, Carthaginians as well as Greeks and Romans, ate the cardoon (*Cynara cardumculus*), whose edible portions are its young leaves and undeveloped stalks, grown in the dark to keep them white and tender.

Parsley was well-known as a flavoring and a garnish by most of the ancient world. Festive garlands were made of parsley which, like cabbage, had a reputation also for staving off the effects of too much wine.

Of all these vegetables, the ones most honored, perhaps, were the broad bean, or *faba*, and the chick-pea, *cicer arietinum*, from which the noble Fabius and Cicero families took their names.

---

[6] Richard Armour has written that "the artichoke is the only vegetable if vegetable it is, of which there is more after it has been eaten." He says, "the most astonishing thing about the artichoke is how it looks when one has finished eating it. In place of the tightly balled flower head is a large dish filled with bracts, each bearing teeth marks so plainly that a dentist could identify the eater if a crime had been committed and he were called to testify in a court of law."

Melons were popular in Rome, including cantaloupes, honeydews, casabas and Persian melons, which are all muskmelons. Muskmelons were known to the Greeks in the third century B.C., described as something new in the first century A.D. by Pliny, but have been identified by some observers in pictures of Egypt of 2400 B.C. The Greek physician Galen wrote of the melon's medicinal virtues in the second century A.D., and Romans of the third century were giving directions for growing melons.

As all these food plants came to be cultivated in garden patch concentrations that expanded to become vast fields, problems of insect and fungus depredations were created that had not existed while the plants grew scattered in the wild. And as the problems became more acute, farmers who had selected fruits and vegetables for size and flavor began to select them more with an eye to their resistance to disease or to pest damage.

In cold climates, hardiness to extremes of weather was the major consideration. But as we noted earlier, people in the north did not take readily to eating vegetables and resisted accepting many new, unfamiliar vegetables.

A greengrocer could have starved

The English were obstinate in their resistance. A manuscript of 1440 (it still exists) which lists seventy-eight plants suitable for cultivation in England suggests that the English under Henry VI ate few vegetables beyond radishes, spinach, cabbage and lettuce, but even on these there is no agreement. Some sources say spinach (*Spinacia oleracea*, introduced to Europe by the Moors) was "known" to English botanists in 1538 and that monks ate spinach on fast days. And there are sources that say lettuce was not introduced into England until 1562. In any case, neither was common to English tables in the fifteenth and early sixteenth centuries, and this must have been largely true of other peoples living in similar climates.

By Elizabethan times, people were eating broad beans, dried peas, beets and turnips, but onions and leeks [7] suited them best.

By one account, peas (*pisum satinus*) helped the peasants of England survive a famine in 1555:

> Pease, which by their great increase did such good to the poore, without doubt grew there for many years before but were not observed till hunger made them take notice of them and quickened their invention, which commonly in our people is very dull.

The syntax is rough, but the idea is clear; and it suggests that peas were not cultivated, but only gathered in the wild. By another account, peas were unknown in England until the reign of Henry VIII, meaning after 1509.

The English, according to the nursery rhyme, ate "pease porridge hot," cold and even nine days old. But dried peas, not green.

Green peas were still a novelty at the end of the seventeenth century. W. H. Lewis, in *The Splendid Century*, quotes Madame de Maintenon writing from Marly in 1696 that "impatience to eat [peas], the pleasure of having eaten them, and the anticipation of eating them again are the three subjects I have heard very thoroughly dealt with. . . Some women, having supped, and supped well at the King's [Louis XIV] table, have peas waiting for them in their rooms to eat before going to bed."

Cooking green peas is no great art, but a good sauce is something else. This was the Age of the Sauce for France's *ancien régime*. "Hunger is the best sauce," said Cicero, and for the mass of Frenchmen under the Sun King it was the only one, but aristocrats dipped their peas, pod and all, into a sauce and ate them from the shells.

Louis XIV's contemporary across the Channel was William III, who ruled England with his wife Mary. Lunching on one occasion with his wife's sister, Princess Anne, William grabbed all the green peas on the table and wolfed them down without offering any to

---

[7] Chaucer's Pardoner, the most unpleasant of his pilgrims, "well loved the garlic, onions, aye and leeks."

anyone else. William was, as the Duchess of Marlborough said, no gentleman.

All this was close to a century after Elizabeth, whose subjects—especially in the lower orders of society—were considerably less enthusiastic about vegetables, green or yellow.

Eggplant (*Solanum Melongena*) was introduced into England in 1587. At least there is a record of its being introduced then, though it may have been planted earlier. And it may not have been used much as food until quite a bit later. John Gerard, in his *Herball* (1597), said:

> But I rather wifh Englifh men to content themfelues with the meate and sauce of our owne country than with fruit and sauce eaten with such perill; for doubtleffe thefe apples have a mifchievous quality; the ufe whereof is utterly to be forfaken.

Which sounds like similar warnings issued against the "love apples" and other food items brought back to Europe by explorers of the New World.

The eggplant, in fact, is related to the tomato, and to the potato, the capsicums and tobacco, but it is native to Arabia rather than to the Americas. The name *melongena* antedates Linnaeus, who laid down his rules of binomial taxonomy in 1737, and may be related to the Greek word for apple. Called the *aubergine* by the French and Germans (and by many present-day Englishmen), *melanzana* by the Italians and *berenjena* by the Spanish, the fruit of the eggplant is usually a purple color, but one of its rarer species is small, white and looks a good deal like a hen's egg, which explains its English name.

Like the eggplant, many of today's common vegetables have changed radically from their original forms, which were often barely edible, or were not considered safe to eat.

The same is true of our fruits. Oranges, as they originally grew in China, were not much larger than big marbles, and were not very sweet. (The Chinese orange that came into Europe in 1635 was sweet by virtue of botanical development.)

Only through long, painstaking selection and improvement in the plants themselves, and through changes in public attitude, did such things as eggplants, potatoes and tomatoes grow as we grow them today and become popularly acceptable.

"Love apples" and earth apples

Tomatoes probably grew first in Mexico and Peru (the name is derived from the Aztec *xitomate* or *xtomatle*, depending on whose transliteration of Aztec you accept), though the picture is muddled by a 200 A.D. description by the Greek physician Galen of an Egyptian fruit which sounds very much like a tomato. Most authorities, however, concede the tomato its South American origin.

Why was it called a "love apple?" There are various theories. The Spaniards called it *manzana*, or apple, at first because it looked like an apple. The Italian word for apple is *pomo*, the French word *pomme*. Since the first tomatoes were yellow, the Italians called the tomato *pomo d'oro*, golden apple. To other Europeans of the sixteenth century, Spaniards were known as Moors. According to one story, a Frenchman visited an Italian, asked about the funny "apples" he was served and was told they were *"Pomi dei Moro,"* or Moor's Apples, which sounded to the Frenchman like *"pommes d'amour,"* apples of love.

The rumor that tomatoes were aphrodisiac (Chapter 10) may be based on that misunderstanding.

The idea that tomatoes were dangerous is more likely based on their being listed among the narcotic herbs in the deadly nightshade family by Pierandrea Mattioli, the Italian herbalist, in his *Commentaries on the Six Books of Dioscorides* first published in 1544. Mattioli called the tomato *mala aurea*, or golden apple, and associated it with belladonna, henbane and mandrake.

Tomatoes were introduced into England in 1596 but only as ornamental plants. The vines were patiently trained to grow on trellises where their bright colored fruit could be admired, but nobody ate the fruit.

Earlier, in Spain, a chef at the royal court had combined tomatoes with olive oil and onions to make the first tomato sauce. It was enthusiastically received and tomatoes were widely adopted by the "Moors." But while Othello may have eaten tomatoes, it is doubtful that Shakespeare ever did. Elizabethans viewed the tomato with a certain horror. Gerard, in his *Herball*, said with his characteristically inconsistent spelling:

> In Spaine and thofe hot regions they vse to eate the Apples prepared and boiled with pepper, salt and oyle: but they yeeld very little nourifhment to the body and the fame naught and corrupt.
>
> Likewife they doe eat the apples with oile, vinegare and pepper mixed together for fauce to their meat, even as we in thefe cold countrief doe Muftard.

The English were still uneasy about tomatoes more than 150 years later, in 1752, when a friend of Carolus Linneaus, horticulturist Philip Miller, "Gardener to the Worshipful Company of Apothecaries at their Botanick Garden in Chelsea," published *The Gardener's Dictionary*. Under "Lycopersicon Love Apples or Wolf's Peach," Miller wrote:

> The Italians and Spaniards eat these apples as we do cucumbers with pepper, oil, and salt, and some eat them in sauces, etc., and in Soups they are now much used in England, especially the second Sort which is preferred to all the other. This fruit gives an agreeable Acid to the Soup; though there are some persons who think them wholesome from their great Moisture and Coldness not and that the nourishment they afford must be bad.

The language is almost unreadable, but the passage is hardly a rousing endorsement.

During the Battle of Marengo in Lombardy (1800), Napoleon's chef Dunand could not find any butter for cooking; being in what Gerard called "thofe hot regions," he fried a chicken in olive oil and added a sauce of Marsala wine, herbs, mushrooms and tomatoes; it is still called Sauce Marengo.

But the French, or at least the Parisians, did not take much to tomatoes until Napoleon III's Empress Eugénie, daughter of a Spanish grandee, introduced Spanish tomato dishes into France in the 1850's. By then, tomatoes were grown widely in the hot, dry Mediterranean countries where they slaked thirsty throats as melons and fruits had done for so many millenniums past. Tomatoes became essentials of Neapolitan cooking. And even today, anything on a French menu identified as *provençale* or *à la portugaise* is a dish made with tomatoes.

Much more important, ultimately, to European menus than the tomato, though similar to the tomato in geographical origin and in the slowness of its acceptance, was the potato.

Potatoes were unknown in the world until the Spanish conquistadors found the Inca eating them in South America.[8]

A Spaniard, Gonzalo Jiminèz de Quesada, found potatoes being used for food in the Andes in 1530. (No doubt other Spaniards did, too, but Quesada's name comes down through the chronicles and while the history is shaky, the temptation to use a name is irresistible.) The Inca word for the white tuber was *papa*.

Those early South American potatoes were usually about the size of peanuts, and shaped like peanuts, though some were as big as plums. To the soldiers of Spain, they seemed a kind of truffle, which seems somewhat incredible, but there is no other way to explain why the conquistadors called the potato a *tartuffo*. In northern Germany the potato is still a *Kartoffel;* the Russian word is *Kartófel,* the Romanian *cartof.*

The Indians ate the largest potatoes and planted the tiniest, so each year, through this unnatural selection, their *papas* grew smaller and smaller. They soaked the potatoes in water and let them freeze in the cold air of the altiplano; then they dried them in the sun and rubbed off the skins by walking on them with their bare feet. The potatoes turned black and hard as stones (and lost much of their

---

[8] The Inca also ate guinea pigs, which were reared on scraps and greens right in the kitchen. Though duck was eaten as a rare delicacy, guinea pigs were the Inca's main source of meat. There were perhaps 15 million people in Latin America when the Spanish arrived (today there are more than 250 million), and nobody knows how many guinea pigs.

nutritive value along with their skins). Before they could be cooked, they had to be soaked again for three or four days.

The Indians called the potatoes they prepared this way *chuño*, pronounced choon-yo. *Chuño* is still an important food in the Andes. It is used to make soup, and sometimes to make a kind of flour for bread.

The conquistadors brought the potato (*Solanum tuberosum*) to Spain from Quito, Ecuador, in about 1539. White potatoes were grown and sold in public markets, but the Spanish much preferred that other South American tuber, the sweet potato, which they called *batata*. The white potato got its Spanish name *patata* from *batata*.

Potatoes were introduced into France in 1540. Like tomatoes, they were regarded at first purely as ornamental plants. The French called the potato a *pomme de terre*—apple of the earth (in Holland it is an *aardappel*, or earth apple; in Bavaria, an *Erdapfel*), not because the crisp texture of a raw potato is somewhat like that of a fresh apple, but rather because, as we saw with eggplants and tomatoes, many different fruits were called "apples" in the Middle Ages, including the fruit of the tree of knowledge in Eden.

Darwin is no longer doubted; the biblical Garden was a fig leaf of imagination. But if there had been a Garden of Eden its "apple" would certainly not have been an apple, but most likely an apricot. Lemons in medieval times were "Persian apples," dates were "finger apples," pomegranates "apples of Carthage."

Pedro de León mentioned the potato in his *Crónica del Perú* of 1553, the first known written reference. Folklore credits Sir Walter Raleigh with giving England the potato, and possibly he did grow the tubers on his estates at Youghal, near Cork, in Ireland, but the history is not clear. Certainly potatoes were not widely accepted in England, even when the Royal Society urged their planting in 1663 to prevent famine; they did not become the basis of the Irish diet until late in the eighteenth century.

The first illustration of a potato plant is apparently the one in Gerard's *Herball*, but Gerard erroneously called it the Virginia potato. Three decades later, the Parliament of Besançon, in France, forbade the cultivation of potatoes, which were viewed with as much suspicion as tomatoes (it was said they produced leprosy).

Even as late as 1771, by which time potatoes were becoming a staple in the rest of Europe, the French still had their doubts. Maybe potatoes did not cause leprosy, but were they fit for human consumption? Were they not weakening?

Antoine-Auguste Parmentier, the agriculturist-botanist who was later to champion the potato, originally listed it along with horse-chestnuts, acorns and roots of iris and gladioli as something to be used only in times of famine.

Europe's first big potato eaters were the Germans. *Ein Neu Kochbuch*, published in 1581, contains what must be the earliest recipes for potato dishes. A century later, Frederick William saw in potatoes a solution to the recurrent crop failures in his native Brandenburg; he ordered the country's peasants to plant potatoes on pain of having their ears cut off, and their noses, too. In Prussia, fifty years after the Brandenburg decree, Frederick the Great distributed seed potatoes and cultivating instructions among his peasantry.

England and France were less enlightened. Queen Elizabeth and her English court evidently had some acquaintance with potatoes, but England did not grow enough of them for public sale until 1770. Even then, some of the Presbyterian clergy in Scotland maintained that potatoes, since they were not mentioned in the Bible, were not safe to eat.

By that time, the French were beginning to come round. Parmentier, who learned to like potatoes while a prisoner of war in Prussia during the Seven Years' War, came home and persuaded his countrymen to put aside their fears. The name "Parmentier" still appears on French menus in connection with potato soup.

Once it was accepted, the potato grew in size, in quality and in popularity. It became before too long a major source of food in Europe. The world potato crop is second now only to the world wheat crop, and it runs a very close second. Of the nearly 293 million metric tons of potatoes grown in the world in 1967, some eighty-five per cent were grown in Europe.

Some observers have associated the population explosion which began in the eighteenth century with the efficiency of potato culture. Thanks to the potato, enormous quantities of food could be produced at small cost from a tiny plot of land. An acre [9] and a half could feed a family of five or six for a full year. It took four to six times that much land to yield a comparable amount of food in grain crops. Having more food made it feasible to have larger families.

And potatoes were so easy to plant. For the primitive method of potato culture used in Ireland, it was not even necessary to plow; all that was needed was a spade to dig trenches. (The word "spade," through a mixture of Gaelic and cockney English, became "spud," which is what the Irish called potatoes, and which many people call potatoes even now. The term "Irish potatoes" is so well established that many think Ireland is where potatoes originated.)

The Irish laid potato sets (the "eyes" of the tubers) on the ground, covered them over with earth from the trenches they had spaded, then covered them with more earth when the green shoots appeared. The trenches provided ample drainage, so potatoes could be grown in the wet ground of Ireland, even in bogs and up mountainsides where nothing else would grow.[10]

Potatoes have one serious drawback: they cannot be stored from

---

[9] An acre originally meant any field, whatever its size. It comes from the Anglo-Saxon word *aecer*, meaning land that has been sown. Until the thirteenth century, an acre in England meant as much land as a yoke of oxen could plow in a day. Under Edward I, the able "Longshanks," the word acre became more definitive, but it was only in the nineteenth century that an act of George IV reduced varying measures of an acre to one uniform standard for the whole kingdom. Even today Scottish and Irish acres may vary from the English 43,560 square feet (or 1/640th of a square mile). Countries using the metric system measure land in hectares, a hectare being 10,000 square meters, or 2.47 acres.

[10] Some tubers which grow only in tropical soils are more nutritious than the potato. Yautias, closely related to the taro root of Southeast Asia and the Pacific, grow only in tropical America and have about twice the nutritive value of potatoes. They are probably the oldest of root crop plants. Yautias are sometimes available in the *grocerias* of New York's Puerto Rican *barrio*. Another tuber with more protein (and more carbohydrates) then the potato is the dasheen, grown commercially in the U.S. South since 1913.

one year to another as can many grain crops. When potato crops failed, as they did in Ireland, Germany, Russia and even in America in the 1840's, people starved. There had been previous failures, but those in the 1840's were the most serious and widespread. The failure of the potato crops was, in fact, the root of much of the political unrest of the late 1840's.

"Arise, ye prisoners of starvation," began the Communist anthem, the "Internationale." Those who listened often *were* prisoners of starvation.

In Shakespeare's words (*Coriolanus*):

> They said they were an-hungry; sigh'd forth proverbs,
> That hunger broke stone walls, that dogs must eat,
> That meat was made for mouths, that the gods sent not
> Corn for rich men only: with these shreds
> They vented their complainings.

All that meat and no potatoes

England in Shakespeare's day evidently knew the potato as a small, finger-size thing of no great importance. The line, "Let the sky rain potatoes," appears in *The Merry Wives of Windsor* (Act V, Scene 5). In *Troilus and Cressida* (Act V, Scene 2) there is the bawdy innuendo, "How the devil Luxury, with his fat rump and potato-finger, tickles these together."

Most authorities, however, think the reference in both cases is to the sweet potato, not the white potato. The English were not yet the meat-and-potatoes people they later became. Nor were the Elizabethans who struggled for survival in the New World.

Captain John Smith was familiar with potatoes. The Indians he found in Virginia were eating something else: the tuckahoe (*tock-awhoughe*, as Smith transliterated the Indian term). "It groweth like a flag in marshes," he wrote. "In one day a savage will gather sufficient for a week. These roots are much of the greatness and taste of potatoes." But whether of white potatoes or sweet potatoes he does not make clear.

Tuckahoes, now sometimes called Indian bread, are not roots at all (though some sources still call them roots and use a botanical term, *Peltundra virginica*); they are the hard, enlarged mycelia of sclerotia, large mushrooms often attached to pine roots. The Indians did use them to make a kind of bread. But it is doubtful the white potato ever reached the Virginia colony (one source says it came by way of Bermuda in 1621).

What is generally accepted is that some Irish Presbyterian settlers brought "Irish" potatoes (which came to be called "mickeys" or "murphys") into Boston in 1719. These descendants of the Incas' *papa* found a permanent home the following year in Londonderry (now simply Derry), New Hampshire. But as in Europe, potatoes were not widely eaten in America until the start of the nineteenth century.

When potato crops failed in Ireland in the middle of that century, the resulting famine led to a wholesale emigration of Irish to America,[11] a notable instance of hunger influencing population movements.

If the colonists ate no potatoes, they ate no more green vegetables than they had back home. Fresh vegetables were, in fact, considered unwholesome and were used chiefly to make sauces and soups.

The Pilgrims did grow vegetables. Beans were planted between corn rows, the vines climbing the cornstalks to reach sunlight. They also planted "peaze," but the first year they planted them too late and saw them withered by the summer heat.

Some things grown in Pilgrim fields had never been known at home: pumpkins ("pompions"), squash and sunflowers, whose seeds were used to make a bread and a soup but whose other uses were unknown.

---

[11] The passage cost between 4 and 5 pounds sterling and was made in small sailing vessels, unregulated, not inspected and often not seaworthy. The emigrants provided their own food, but supplies were often inadequate. Crammed with emigrants in all stages of poverty and hunger, the "coffin ships" were as heavily laden with human misery as with hope.

The berries

Grapes grew wild and were plentiful, just as they had been when Leif Ericson had found them in Nova Scotia nearly 500 years before Columbus. Hadn't the Viking called his landfall Vinland? The word means "wine land."

But while forty species of grapes, more than anywhere else in the world, grew in North America, none, alas, was a good wine variety. Lord Baltimore tried as early as 1616 to grow the European, or wine, grape (*Vita vinifera*) on his lands. So, later, did Thomas Jefferson. No luck: the vines died.

Not until 1769, when the Mission Fathers under Junípero Serra introduced *Vita vinifera* at their missions of San Diego, San Gabriel and Santa Clara, did wine grapes flourish in America. The Mission variety was the country's leading wine grape until 1861, when the California State Legislature commissioned Agoston Haraszthy de Mokcsa, a Hungarian nobleman, to bring the choicest grape varieties over from Europe. Count Haraszthy selected 100,000 cuttings, representing 300 varieties, and these provided the basis for California's vineyards, whose fruit was picked in the beginning by $8-a-month Chinese laborers.

But except under glass, the European grape has never been successfully grown east of the Rockies. And ninety per cent of the U.S. grape crop now grows in California.

Eastern grapes like the northern fox grape (*Vitis Labrusca*), which has less sugar and more acidity than *Vita vinifera*, and the muscadine (*Vitis rotundiflora*) gave rise to many now-famous varieties of table grapes. The muscadine grape (sometimes called the Southern fox grape) was best known for a variety called the scuppernong. The Northern fox grape was the dominant parent of the Catawba grape, first developed by John Adlum in his vineyard near Georgetown (now part of Washington, D.C.) in 1820 and planted a few years later in the Finger Lakes District of New York State by the Reverend William Bostwick. By 1860, nine-tenths of the grapes grown east of the Rockies were Catawbas.

But the Concord grape, perfected about 1850 by Ephraim Bull in the Middlesex County town where Thoreau lived beside Walden Pond, became the leading native American grape. It marked the beginning of commercial table grape cultivation in the U.S. The source of the Concord was the Northern fox grape, which was the dominant parent also of Delaware, Niagara, Iona, Diana, Brighton and Isabella, all important table grape varieties.

American grapes in general were larger and more hardy than European grapes. Their flesh was more watery; their thin skins easier to slip off. They were, as we used to say, the berries.

Grapes, in fact, are technically a form of berry. But strawberries and other berries were the true glories of the colonists' adopted land.

Roger Williams, founder of Providence (in 1636), wrote that the strawberry, bigger than any ever seen in Europe, was "the wonder of all the Fruits growing naturally in these parts. The Indians bruise them in a Morter, and mix them with meale and make strawberry bread." There were strawberry fields forever. The colonists invented strawberry shortcake.

The big *Fragaria virginiana* was sent to France in 1624 for cross-breeding with the tiny *fraise des bois,* the wild wood strawberry which had been planted in European home gardens as early as 1300.

In 1712, the French explorer-spy Amédé Frézier, checking Spanish fortifications on South America's west coast, stumbled on the big wild beach strawberry of Chile, *Fragaria chiloensis,* and brought it back to Europe. But all five of his plants were female, none male (Frézier, an amateur botanist, should have known better). Later, some French growers found the Chilean strawberries would bear fruit if planted next to Virginia strawberries; they called the resulting cross-breed a pineapple strawberry (*Fragaria ananassa*).

In England, at the end of the eighteenth century, Thomas Knight, the pioneer of scientific fruit breeding, developed this pineapple strawberry into the beginnings of the big, sweet strawberries now grown commercially.

Americans continued to eat mostly wild strawberries until the latter half of the nineteenth century. James Wilson in New York State developed the hardy, adaptable, productive Wilson strawberry in 1851 and this led commercial strawberry acreage in the U.S. to jump from 1400 acres in 1800 to 100,000 acres in 1880. Today every state grows strawberries; North America's total strawberry acreage is still only 130,000 acres (out of a world total of 300,000), but the Lassen and Shasta varieties, grown on a mere 8000 acres in California, account for a quarter of the world's strawberry crop.

More than a third of California's strawberries are shipped by air and sold as far away as Frankfurt, Germany, where a basket sells for eighty cents in the spring. And they taste almost as good as *fraises des bois*, or as the wild strawberries of colonial Virginia.

Along with the strawberry, early Americans cultivated the raspberry (introduced from Europe, where the French call it *framboise*), and the blueberry; they also cultivated the blackberry, not considered worth the trouble anywhere else. At first it was called a brambleberry or bramble (as it still is in England) and was regarded as a nuisance, even in the new United States. Beginning in the 1830's, however, it became quite popular and went into many a pie [12] and flummery. (A flummery was a molded dessert made of gelatin, milk, wine or fruit juice, and sugar. The gelatin could be isinglass, made from the air bladders of certain fish, or it could be a jelly made by boiling calves' feet, straining the liquid, allowing it to set, skimming off the fat next day, letting the rest liquefy, sweetening and flavoring it, and then

---

[12] Purely American developments are the boysenberry (named after botanist R. Boysen) and the loganberry (named for horticulturist James H. Logan); both are twentieth-century variations on the genus *Rubus*, the same genus as the raspberry and the blackberry. Pie making flourished in America when more efficient sugar-processing machinery and larger plantations in Louisiana reduced sugar prices. Lard shortening made flaky pie crusts, pricked with designs that vented steam during baking.

letting it set again in molds. Later a few tablespoons of cornstarch were found to do the job almost as well as gelatin with much less trouble.)

Less important for pies than for turkey sauce were the cranberries (*Vaccinium macrocarpus*) the Pilgrims found growing in New England. Like American strawberries, the cranberries were much bigger (*macro* is Greek for "large") than any European cranberries. The Indians used them for food, for medicine and as a dye. These "bounce-berries" (their ability to bounce was the test of their ripeness) helped protect the first New Englanders from scurvy.

Today, New Jersey, Wisconsin, Oregon and Washington all produce cranberries, but the traditional accompaniment to roast turkey is still produced mostly in New England. Two-thirds of the nation's crop comes from the sandy bogs of Cape Cod.

Ripe, red, green, yellow and juicy

Most of the country's pies—deep-dish like English fruit tarts in New England, shallow in the pie belt across the Alleghenies—were apple pies. The memory of Mom's apple pie may not have inspired American fighting men in World War II, but sentimental folklore said it did, and the folklore was based on centuries of pie eating.

Apples have always been this country's favorite domestic fruit (though our commercial apple crop is not as big as France's).

While English colonists introduced apple seedlings to North America, many distinct American varieties were originated here, beginning probably with the Sweet Rhode Island Greening; it was grown by a clergyman, William Blaston, who moved from his farm on Beacon Hill, in Boston, to a farm in Rhode Island in 1635.

In the early days of the country, New England could hardly have survived without its apples. The fruit has almost no nutritional value, but it can sweeten up a meal that is otherwise dreary. According to tradition, Yalemen were served apple pie at supper every evening for 100 years. New Englanders ate apple pie for breakfast, along with a bit of cheese (which contained more nutriments than the pie). As a saying of the era put it, "Apple pie without the cheese is like a kiss without a squeeze."

What helped to propagate apples across America was the zeal of Johnny Appleseed. There really was a Johnny Appleseed. His true name was John Chapman and he was born in Leominster, Massachusetts, in 1775. Chapman collected appleseeds from cider mills, dried them, put them up in little bags (following the Shaker [13] idea of labeled paper garden seed packets) and pressed them on everyone he met who was headed West.

The best apples are developed by grafting superior scions onto existing trees, but Johnny Appleseed stuck stubbornly to planting from seed as the good Swedenborgian Lord intended. For forty years he traveled through Ohio, Indiana, parts of Illinois, even to Iowa, planting seeds in what he considered likely spots. Going by horse and wagon, sometimes by canoe, Chapman was an eccentric—a ragged, bearded hippie with a wild-eyed passion, or obsession, for planting orchards. He was welcomed everywhere, especially after he saved the people of Mansfield, Ohio, from being massacred in the War of 1812.

Fruits of Chapman's work can still be found. He never made it all the way to what is now Washington state, where America's biggest apple crop grows, or to California, another big apple-growing state. But apples of trees descended from seeds Johnny Appleseed planted still go into apple pies and turnovers on American tables.

---

[13] Shakers, so-called because of their shuffling ritual holy dance, were "Believers in Christ's Second Appearance," members of the Millennial Church, a branch of Quakerism introduced to the U.S. in 1774 by an English blacksmith's daughter, Sister Ann Lee. The Shakers avoided the "generative lust," believing that physical passions prevented people from fulfilling their abilities. They celibately generated a wealth of food ideas: corn "oysters," cider-baked ham (from Poland China hogs bred originally by the Shakers, as we saw in Chapter 4), oyster pie (baked in round pie ovens of Shaker invention), gravies enriched with the water that vegetables had baked in, fancy breads. The cult grew by adopting orphan children; in the thirty years before the Civil War, as many as 6000 Shakers lived from New England west to the Ohio Basin in communal "families" of thirty to 125, all meekly, honestly, religiously avoiding "filthy gratification." And eating high off the Poland China hog.

At one time there were probably more than a thousand different American apple varieties; most have now disappeared.[14] Some succumbed to insects and disease for which no controls existed, others were left to die out because they had russet skins, natural spots or unusual colors that did not sell, or because they did not ship or store well. Some trees were cut down by temperance workers fighting the evils of cider and applejack. Quite a few were felled during the 1930's Depression when it was thought they harbored insects and diseases that menaced commercial orchards.

Many of the more valuable old varieties were saved from extinction by an experimental orchard established in 1952 by the Worcester County (Massachusetts) Horticulture Society.

Among the many apples still grown commercially are the mellow Baldwin from New York, New England and the Midwest, the Ben Davis, the delicately-textured Cortland from New York and New Jersey whose white flesh resists browning after it is cut open, the yellow Golden Delicious whose firm sweet flesh also resists browning (though covering any apple slices with water to which has been added a little lemon or lime juice, draining and patting them dry will keep them from turning brown) and the Red Delicious, now the world's leading apple variety.

There are also the soft-skinned Gravenstein used for applesauce, the crisp, tart Greening of Michigan and New York used for apple pie, the sweet Grimes Golden, the Jonathan of the Northwest (named after Jonathan Hasbrouck, an American judge who died in 1846) and the small Red Lady, which the French call the *api* after Apicius, that cookbook author of ancient Rome who produced this apple by grafting.

Also popular are the McCoom, the McIntosh (named after an Ontario farmer, John McIntosh, who first cultivated the variety in

---

[14] Including the King, the Bellflower, the Fallawater, the King Tomkins, the Famense and Johnny Appleseed's favorite, the Rambo, which originated in Pennsylvania in about 1800. It is almost gone from Ohio, where it once grew on every farm, but is still seen sometimes on small farms in the Appalachians, along with Stark, Black Twig, Grimes Golden and a few other minor varieties.

1796), the Missouri Pippin and the crisp Northern Spy of New York, Michigan and New England.

Dorothy Canfield Fisher, recalling girlhood days in Vermont, mentioned "the sound, red-cheeked Northern Spies which

> polished to brilliance, would light up the side-table in the dining room. Their presence would go far beyond the dining room, and pervade the house with an aroma which . . . became the characteristic odor of home, bringing back childhood with [an] actual . . . presence.

Others, recalling the apples of their youth, would mention the big Rome Beauty baking apple, the Newton (or Newtown) Pippin (or Albemarle) still found in Virginia but grown now mainly on the West Coast (as are Gravensteins and some others) and used mostly for cooking, the Snow, the Stayman from New Jersey, the Twenty-Ounce, the Wealthy (which makes a good pie when it is green), the tart, spicy Winesap, the Winter Banana, the York Imperial from Pennsylvania and points South, the Duchess, the Red Astrachan and the Yellow Transparent.

These last three were among the 300 varieties the U.S. Department of Agriculture imported from Russia in 1870; most of the other 297 have fallen by the wayside. While the Newton Pippin is sometimes called the Albemarle Pippin (Queen Victoria imported Albemarle Pippins from an orchard, now called Royal Orchard, in Albemarle County, Virginia), most apple variety names were standardized by the American Pomological Society beginning in 1848. Before then, a single variety might have gone, like fish, by any number of names.

The U.S. produces about 100 million bushels of apples a year, out of a world total of 700 million; our top apple-growing state is Washington, whose Yakima Valley first grew apples in 1875. New York ranks second, followed by Virginia, Michigan and Pennsylvania, not always in that order.

About seventy-five per cent of the apples grown in New England today are McIntosh, and this variety, given the go-by in bygone days because it made a watery cider, accounts for about half the apples grown in New York State, too. Great eating apples like the Pound

Sweet are rare now. The ubiquitous, if somewhat lackluster, Red Delicious and Golden Delicious are increasing in popularity with orchardmen in New England and New York; in most of the country they are, sad to say, the dominant varieties, accounting for about one-fifth the national crop, versus ten per cent for McIntosh. (Winesaps, Jonathans, Rome Beauties and Staymans rank third, fourth, fifth and sixth in order of importance.)

Farmer Jefferson

Johnny Appleseed was not the only American fascinated with the idea of spreading seeds and agricultural knowledge across the new Republic.

No less a personage than Thomas Jefferson shared the enthusiasm. As a boy at Shadwell, the family plantation in Virginia, young Tom began garden books and kept meticulous records, which he continued to do for half a century. Jefferson was intensely curious about every vegetable, exotic or ordinary. On his 10,000 acres, tended by 150 slaves (though in his first draft of the Declaration of Independence Jefferson favored abolition), he grew chicory (which he called "succory"), endive, Spanish onions, savoy (a cabbage with a compact head of curled and wrinkled leaves), turnips, peas (his favorite vegetable), beans of various kinds and some of the first sugar beets. He experimented with cucumbers, salsify (sometimes called oyster plant because its root tastes like oysters), squash, eggplant, artichokes, lettuce, cauliflower, sprouts and spinach, though he failed with olive trees and wine grapes.

He also had potatoes, which by this time had begun to emerge from the doubts that had overhung them in America as in Europe. Like tomatoes, they had been considered a powerful sex stimulant. They had also been accused of shortening men's lives. So even after they became the second-ranking crop in America's farm economy (a position now held by soybeans), potatoes were used mainly as animal fodder, like corn. As late as the mid-nineteenth century, the

Farmer's Manual suggested that potatoes "be grown near the hog-pens as a convenience toward feeding the hogs."

Jefferson was one of the first Americans to eat tomatoes, which were slower even than potatoes in gaining acceptance.

A Frenchman in Philadelphia had made efforts to get people to eat tomatoes in 1788; he had little luck. By the time of Jefferson's presidency, between 1801 and 1809, some tomatoes were being marketed; the President noted the seasonal arrival of fresh tomatoes at produce stalls in the nation's capital. Tomatoes were being sold in the New Orleans markets on a regular basis by 1812, the customers being mostly enlightened French immigrants.

In the North, the tomato was the target of Puritan pronouncements. And while the Quincy Hall market in Boston was selling tomatoes by 1835, an incident five years earlier illustrates that popular suspicion of the juicy red fruit was still rampant. A Colonel Robert Gibbon Johnson stood on the steps of the courthouse in Salem, New Jersey, and ate a "poisonous" raw, red tomato to the horror of spectators, who predicted he would be dead before morning.

Johnson survived, of course, but there were still doubters. *Godey's Lady's Book,* published in Philadelphia (it was the first of the "women's magazines"), said in 1860 that tomatoes should "always be cooked for three hours." Sarah Hale, the editor, observed that if tomatoes were cooked for only one hour, the result would be just a "sour porridge."

Not all Americans were so timid. Many, led by the French, ate tomatoes raw, in salads, and cooked in meat and game stews. By shortly after the Civil War, tomatoes were being consumed in huge quantities, but not in Jefferson's day.

Few of Jefferson's countrymen thought as freely as did our third president. Not many could match his active, venturesome mind. Wherever the man traveled, he kept up his interest in fruits and vegetables. In France (where he served as our first ambassador), he made note of strawberries at Castres, seedless grapes at Marseilles, wild gooseberries at Beaujolais and blooming almonds at Lyons. He compared the tastes of various oranges in the south of France.

And he came home loaded with plants. In his greenhouses at Monticello, Jefferson grew vegetables from imported seeds, among them asparagus and broccoli. In his late years he was still constantly exchanging plants, roots and cuttings with other interested agrarians, and scattering seed broadcast throughout his state of Virginia.

The Burbank strain

The Jeffersonian tradition was picked up by men like the aforementioned George Washington Carver and even more notably by Luther Burbank, though men like Charles Hovey, who originated the Hovey strawberry in Cambridge, Massachusetts, in 1838 made valuable botanical contributions well before Burbank.

The "plant wizard," as Burbank was often called, was born in Lancaster, Massachusetts, in 1849. After only a year of higher education (at the Lancaster Academy), he started breeding plants on a seventeen-acre plot near Lunenberg, Massachusetts, and two years later developed his famous Burbank potato, more by luck and intuition than anything else. He sold the potato to a nurseryman for $150 and used the money to move out to the Santa Rosa Valley of California.

While that original potato was Burbank's most important achievement, he went on to create a white blackberry, stoneless cherries, new kinds of apples, peaches and tomatoes, plums larger than any before known, a seedless plum, a blackberry with no prickles on its stem. He introduced sixty-six new kinds of fruit which grow on trees, twelve new fruits which grow on bushes, nine new vegetables, seven new tree nuts and a new groundnut.

Nature, aided by bees and other insects, has many times over the ages crossed pollen and created new plants. Men like Burbank sped up the process, and made a science out of what in nature comes only by freakish accident.

Developing new plant strains is often achieved not by cross-pollinating but by budding, grafting and such. Most citrus trees, for example, have an upper framework, the scion, which may be of one variety, and a rootstock—the roots and trunk of the tree—which may be of another kind.

A faint horizontal line, the bud union, appears around the trunk of a mature tree to show where scion and rootstock come together. Citrus trees planted from seed take about fifteen years before they bear much fruit, and they are thorny. Budded trees have practically no thorns and start bearing fruit after five years.

Most Florida orange trees have lemon-tree roots. Almost all California lemon trees have orange-tree roots. One citrus tree, in fact, can with a botanist's help have lemons, limes, oranges, tangerines,[15] kumquats and grapefruit growing on its branches at the same time.

On one rootstock or another, some of them stemming from stock planted in Florida by Ponce de Léon in 1513, the U.S. now grows 25 billion oranges in a typical year, more than the next three countries (Spain, Italy and Mexico) combined.

While only two per cent of Spain's oranges are Valencias, almost all California oranges and half of Florida's are of this variety. We also grow Parson Browns (named after Nathan L. Brown, a Florida clergyman), Pineapple oranges and Hamlins, all early-maturing varieties. Natural hybrids often grown in Florida are the tangors (half orange, half tangerine), the Temple orange and the Murcott Honey orange, named respectively after William Chase Temple and Charles Murcott Smith, two growers who propagated them early in the game.

But we grow more than two dozen other orange varieties, including a few of Spain's Blood oranges, streaked inside with red and much sought-after in Europe, though American women are put off by the color and will not buy them.

About eighty-five per cent of Florida's juicy orange crop today is processed, more than two-thirds of it into orange juice concentrate. Some connoisseurs say that oranges grown from Sour Orange rootstocks taste better than oranges from Rough Lemon rootstocks, which

---

[15] When they first reached Europe, evidently not until 1805, tangerines arrived from Tangier, in Morocco; hence their name.

are less susceptible to virus diseases and produce faster-growing oranges. The critics blame the swing to Rough Lemon rootstocks on the burgeoning of orange concentrate (Chapter 8).

Much of the variety in orange development owes at least a conceptual debt to Burbank. His kind of work is frustrating. It usually took him from five to ten years from the time a seed was planted or a graft made before a new fruit was ready for introduction; thousands of unsatisfactory trees were destroyed along the way. And only a small fraction of his experiments were successful: he grew half a million strawberry plants to produce one prize plant, though the naturalist John Burroughs called it the best strawberry in the world.

What makes a fruit or vegetable "best," however, will depend on whether one is a grower, a processor, a shipper, a retailer or a consumer. Considerations of taste often take a back seat to criteria of transportability, shelf-life and so forth, something to bear in mind when going marketing. Knowing more about fruits and vegetables can help anyone market more intelligently.

The fruits of experience

Before World War I, eighty-seven per cent of the fruit sold in the U.S. was sold fresh. By World War II the percentage was down to seventy-four per cent. Now it is less than fifty per cent.

Some people are timorous about buying fresh fruit. They may profit by the experience of veteran shoppers, whose first rule is to put taste ahead of appearance.

Some fruit is grown in hothouses; it looks lovely on the dining room table, but it cannot match the taste of the same fruit grown naturally in fields and orchards. Some fruits continue to ripen after being picked; others, if picked prematurely, may be almost tasteless. The grocer will not let the customer taste before buying, but there are often other ways to choose for taste.

Bananas should be bought green or just barely yellow and allowed to ripen at home. Pears and some melons can be bought before they are quite ripe, too; pears allowed to ripen on the tree, in fact, have a coarser texture than pears picked just before they are fully ripe.

But most fruit should be ripe when it is bought, and finding tree-ripened (or vine-ripened) fruit is not always easy.

Picking ripe melons at the store is particularly tricky. No other fruit is so difficult to select. If a melon is ripe, it should give under a little pressure around the stem-end "button" or "eye."

This is especially true of canteloupe, which, like watermelon, does not improve in flavor or sweetness after it is picked. Unless it is well-ripened, in fact, it is reminiscent of that other *Cucumis*, the cucumber, and no more sweet. If the stem-end is rough, the cantaloupe was probably cut off the vine prematurely; do not buy it.

The cantaloupe is a kind of muskmelon; it is named after the castle of Cantalupo, in Italy, where this Armenian melon was first cultivated in Europe at the country seat of a sixteenth-century pope outside Rome.

Ripe cantaloupes [16] have a definite, and delicious, musky-sweet fragrance. The veining on the rind stands out clearly against the melon's yellowish-gray background.

Honeydew melons, which do get sweeter after they are picked, are descended from an old French variety called "White Antibes Winter"; they were not introduced into the U.S. until about 1900. Honeydews should have rather smooth rinds, either creamy-white or creamy-yellow.

A Casaba melon's rind should be yellow with deep lengthwise furrows; it should *not* have any aroma.

Persian melons are like large cantaloupes but have a later season (into November). All these melons actually originated in Persia, now Iran, as did other muskmelons like Cranshaw, Spanish, Santa Claus, Montreal and banana melons.

Watermelon is something else. Mark Twain called it "chief of

---

[16] The U.S. cantaloupe is really the netted, or nutmeg, muskmelon—true cantaloupes are grown only in Europe. California's Imperial Valley is our big "cantaloupe" producer; the melons come from special strains of plants developed to resist powdery mildew.

this world's luxuries . . . When one has tasted it, he knows what angels eat." Watermelon is related to the muskmelons, but only as a member of the gourd family, which includes cucumbers and squash in addition to melons.

Watermelons originated in Africa, but they have been grown in the Middle East and the warmer parts of Russia for thousands of years. They reached southern Europe with the Moors early in the Christian era, arrived in China about a thousand years ago and came to the Western Hemisphere and the Pacific Islands with European colonists.

Some watermelons are very small, some very large; the pulp may vary in color from pale pink to deep red. Watermelons are often cut into halves or quarters so the pulp can be seen, but a farmer always tests a watermelon's ripeness by thumping it: if it has a metallic sound, 't ain't ripe.

Pears, as we have said, are best ripened *after* being picked. They should be fairly firm when bought; as with bananas (Chapter 8), they can ripen in the fruit bowl at home. The ancient Chinese used to leave green pears to ripen in a closed room filled with burning incense.

Our most commonly available pear (it represents seventy per cent of our 713,000-ton crop) is the Bartlett, first introduced by Enoch Bartlett of Dorchester, Massachusetts. He brought it over from England, where it is called the William Bon Chrétien. Bartletts today are grown almost entirely in Oregon and Washington, where they are less susceptible to blight than in the East, though we import some from Capetown, South Africa, along with those wonderfully green, crisp, tart Granny Smith apples [17] we get in May. American Bartletts are in season from July into November; in winter they come to us also from Australia, Argentina and Chile. When ripe, the Bartlett is clear yellow or slightly blushed.

The little Seckel pear, in season from September to November,

---

[17] First grown in Australia in 1867, Granny Smiths are well-known in Europe and the Far East. They are in season from late spring through July—autumn in the Southern Hemisphere.

is named after a farmer who grew the variety outside Philadelphia just after the Revolution.

Bartletts and Seckels represent the two basically different classes of pears, the "European" type (like the Bartlett) with a soft consistency, the "Asian" type (like the Seckel) with a hard flesh and a gritty consistency. "Asian" types are sometimes called "sand pears."

Other "European" types are the big juicy Comice (originally *Coyenne du Comice,* grown now primarily in Oregon's Hood River Valley and in season from November to late May), which may be entirely green or slightly blushed when ripe, and the chunky green or yellowish-green Anjou, in season at the same time. Other "Asian" types are the Bosc, also a winter pear, and the very pretty Ferelle, freckled with red spots (it is the fancy pear packed in bon voyage baskets). The skins of Bosc and Anjou pears, especially the Bosc, may show a roughening (called russeting) which does not affect their taste.

Our U.S. pear crop is now one-fourth the size of our gigantic apple crop. And a good proportion is sold fresh for the table.

Table grapes, at the fruit counter, should be plump and firmly attached to their stems. Shake the bunch gently; few if any grapes should drop off.

Almost all our table grapes come from California. The earliest variety, coming to market in June, are the Perlettes, followed by the Cardinals in mid-June and then by the Thompson Seedless, all of them European varieties. Ribiers arrive in August, Tokays in September and Emperors in October.

White and green grapes, like delicate Niagara Whites, Finger Grapes, Perlettes and Thompson Seedless, are usually ripe when they begin to turn slightly amber. Purple or black grapes, like blue Concords, Emperors, Malagas, Muscats, flame Tokays and Ribiers (all European varieties except Concords, which are usually only available locally), have to be tasted to know if they are ripe. Americans have yet to experience seedless purple grapes, though Europe now enjoys a seedless Italian Cardinal variety.

Grapes should be refrigerated as soon as they are brought home. Instead of washing them, it is a good idea to eat them European style, serving them with a bowl of water into which each grape is dipped before it is eaten.

Michigan, a major U.S. table-grape producer, is also a leading cherry grower, but most of its varieties are sour cherries. Sour cherries, in fact, outnumber sweet cherries two to one in the U.S. Used mostly for pies and tarts, they are grown in New York and Wisconsin, as well as in Michigan; those three states account for more than ninety per cent of sour, or tart, cherry production.

About eighty-five per cent of our sweet cherries are raised under irrigation in California, Washington, Utah, Oregon and Idaho. The major sweet varieties are Bing (named after a Chinese who developed them in Oregon in 1875), Lambert and Windsor. Others are Chapman, Republican (or Lewelling, named after an Oregon pioneer who founded that state's cherry industry in 1847), Royal Ann (or Napoleon), Sweets and Tartarian. Buy sweet cherries in May, June and July; they keep for two or three weeks in plastic bags in the refrigerator.

Blueberries are sometimes called huckleberries, though true huckleberries grow only in the wild and are smaller, less sweet and have large bony seeds. Blueberry seeds are so small you barely notice them in your mouth. More than sixty per cent of the 1969 U.S. blueberry crop, largest in history, was picked by machine. Little more than a third were marketed fresh of the eighteen varieties that stem from crossbreeds developed by a U.S. Department of Agriculture botanist beginning in 1909. Concord, Jersey, Stanley and Dixi are the major cultivated varieties.

Cranberries are cultivated in drained bogs with acid subsoils; they do best where the bogs can be flooded at will to control temperatures and certain pests. Early Blacks and Howes are among the important varieties. Cranberries may be fairly large, bright red and slightly sour, or smaller, darker red and sweeter. But most are processed into cranberry sauce.

Very small strawberries, the famous *fraises des bois* of France, are marvelous in France; larger strawberries are usually better buys in this country. In winter and early spring, Missionary and Klonmore varieties are available. Blakemore and Temple varieties (and, from California, Lassen and Shasta berries) come in mid-spring, Catskill and Sparkle in late spring. They should be free of moisture and their bright green caps should be attached—do not remove the caps until after the berries have been washed or they will absorb water. Avoid boxes containing small, misshapen berries or berries with little hard green spots. Stained boxes are a sign of leaky berries; do not buy them. Refrigerate strawberries, but serve them at room temperature.

Aside from strawberries, berries should be free of leaves or stem caps, either of which indicates the fruit is not mature. Both berries and cherries should be dry and clean when bought; moisture and dirt make them vulnerable to quick spoiling. Do not wash them or remove the berry hulls until just before using the berries.

Like bananas, our fresh pineapple is imported; like bananas, it is picked before it is fully ripe (it will ripen after buying, but do not refrigerate it). We get our pineapple mostly from Mexico, Central America, Bermuda, the Bahamas and the Caribbean, though some comes from Hawaii (most of the Hawaiian crop is canned). But no fresh pineapple available in the continental U.S. ever seems to have the sweetness and tenderness of the naturally-ripened article eaten where it grows.

Puerto Rican Red Spanish pineapples range in color from golden yellow to pale red; they ripen evenly. If the center barbed spikes have separated and pull apart easily, it is usually a sign the fruit has reached full maturity. The smooth Cayenne pineapple from Puerto Rico and Hawaii may vary from light yellow to deep golden yellow. Like the Sugar Loaf from Mexico, it has a smooth-leafed "crown" and usually ripens from the bottom up. Any fresh pineapple should be heavy for its size, firm; when ripe, it should have a strong, fresh pineapple aroma. Pineapples will shrink and deepen in color if stored where the air is too dry. A soft, dark area near the base of the fruit means the pineapple is decaying. March through June is the best time to look for pineapples, but they are available in all seasons.

Drupe fruits

Second only to the apple in commercial importance among the fruits we eat in America is the peach.

James Fenimore Cooper, in *The Travelling Bachelor*, wrote,

A French peach is juicy, and, when you first bring it in contact with your palate, sweet, but it leaves behind it a cold, watery, and almost sour taste. It is for this reason so often eaten with sugar. An American is exceedingly apt to laugh if he sees ripe fruit of any sort eaten with anything sweet. The peaches here leave behind a warm, rich and delicious taste, that I can only liken in its effects to that which you call the *bouquet* of a glass of Romanee.

It was not an Elberta peach which Cooper was describing; that most widely sold of our freestone peaches was, according to most sources, imported from Shanghai in 1850, though one source says it was named after the wife of Samuel Rumpf of Marshalville, Georgia, who first grew the variety in 1870.

While some Elbertas are canned, peaches used for canning, freezing, pie making, cooking and pickling are mostly clingstones, not freestones.

The species name *persica* suggests a Persian origin, but most authorities think peaches originated in China.

Other important freestone varieties are Dixired, Redhaven, Triogem, Halehaven, Sunhigh (all of which mature earlier than the Elberta) and Rio Osa Gem (which matures later). One of the newer cross-strains will probably supplant the Elberta as the dominant peach in the next few years.

Peaches are more sensitive to pressure than any other fruit, even before they are ripe, and certainly after. Most peaches grown for shipment to fruiterers and supermarkets have to be picked before they are fully ripe; they mature en route or in the store. Skin punctures and oozing syrup on a peach are signs that worms have already gotten to the fruit. For the best flavor, choose well-ripened peaches; fully-ripe ones have an unmistakable fragrance. Another test of ripeness is to hold the peach and press it, gently, but do not pinch it with thumb and finger—this will leave a mushy bruise. Avoid peaches with brown spots or shriveled skins.

Peaches and cherries are what botanists call "drupe" fruits; all such fruits have an outer skin called the epicarp, a pulpy succulent layer called the mesocarp and a woody inner shell, the endocarp, which usually encloses a single seed.

The most widely varied drupe fruit is the plum, introduced to Greece from Damascus, cultivated by the Romans, reintroduced from Damascus by the Crusaders, but eaten, at least in its cruder varieties, by the prehistoric Swiss lake dwellers in whose ruins plum stones have been found.

The closest thing to a plum that is native to America is the wild persimmon, terribly bitter if not properly ripe and rarely used by the colonists except as a pudding ingredient in the Carolinas and on the Western frontier. Persimmons did not become popular at all in America until Commodore Matthew C. Perry introduced the Japanese persimmon in 1855 after his expedition to open the Nipponese door.

True plums were introduced by the colonists and grown throughout the early colonies. Today, dozens of varieties are cultivated in the U.S., while Europe has only three or four.

Some of the better known plums grown commercially are greengages,[18] damsons (named for Damascus) and egg plums. All are European varieties raised mostly for canning and for drying into prunes.

Any plum is a potential prune, provided it can be dried without having its stone removed and has firm, long-keeping qualities after it is dried. Our U.S. prune industry is based largely on the Agen plum,

---

[18] The French call them *Reine-Claude*, after Claudia, queen to Francis I (1515–47); they were brought to England in about 1725 by a Sir William Gage, hence the English name greengage.

introduced to California by a Frenchman, Pierre Pellier, in 1856, and named after a district in France known for its prunes. The Santa Clara Valley, where Pellier planted plum trees, is still a big prune source.

But the mainstay of the California industry, which grows over ninety per cent of U.S. plums, are derivatives of a Chinese plum, domesticated in Japan and introduced to California in 1870. (Outside the U.S., Yugoslavia, Germany, Turkey and Japan are the leading plum producers, though much of the Yugoslavian crop is used to make a plum brandy, *slivovitz.*)

Plums, which the French, confusingly, call *prunes* and growers often call Italian prunes or Japanese plums, range in color from yellow-green to deep purple (though the California Fresh Plum Promotion Advisory Board likes to say the colors are red, white and blue), and in size from that of a small cherry to a hen's egg. Flavor, season of ripening and duration of ripening also vary widely.

The dozen-plus varieties we grow, mostly in the West, run into more than 200 different names.

Leading varieties, in order of ripening, are the Texas Beauty, Abundance, Burbank (the great botanist developed some sixty varieties of plums), Formosa, Santa Rosa, American Mirabelle, Grand Duke, Stanley, Imperial, Epinence, Reine Claude, Italian Prune, French damson and Albion. Some come to market in June and July, others in September.

Santa Rosa, Beauty and Formosa plums are red to crimson, with yellow to amber flesh; Italian Prune (which is not Italian and is not used for prunes) is a small, blue-purple freestone, strongly flavored; Kelsey and Wickson plums are pale yellow-green with yellow flesh. Nubiana, or Cherrystone, is heart-shaped and reddish-purple. Sugar-plum, oval and blushing-red, is very juicy but bland. Also heart-shaped is the Eldorado with its reddish-purple skin, the same color as the Empress. Tragedy, Laroda, Queen Ann, Standard and President plums are all dark purple to black with yellow-green to amber flesh.

Ripe plums are just soft enough to give with slight pressure. They are picked and shipped just before they are fully mature, and they turn ripe to overripe faster than any other fruit. Do not buy any that are sticky or too soft, and store them in a cool, dry place or, if they are fully ripe, in the refrigerator.

Nectarines, a cross between plums and peaches, have smooth skins instead of the fuzzy skins characteristic of peaches. If it is ripe, a nectarine is plump and firm (but not hard) and the "seam" along its side shows a slight softening.

More fruits. And a non-fruit

More than any other fruit, the grapefruit owes its popularity to botanists.

Various varieties of grapefruit are grown in tropical and subtropical countries under names like *pomelo, pummelo* and *pompelmous*; the name on a French menu is *pamplemousse*. The parent species is the pomelo (*Citrus grandis*), native to Indonesia and mentioned by that ancient Chinese Baedeker of foods, I Yin (Chapter 1); but American grapefruit (*Citrus paradisi*) is probably a native North American plant originating, it is thought, in Jamaica. The history, as with so many foods, especially plant foods, is somewhat obscure; some sources say the Spanish introduced grapefruit into the West Indies.

We do know grapefruit was called "shaddock" in England for many years, being confused with another fruit taken from the East Indies to Barbados by a Captain Shaddock in 1696. In the eighteenth century, merchant ships are said to have used "shaddock" for ballast and for cleaning their decks.

In his *Hortus Jamaicensis* of 1814, John Lunan mentioned a variety of "shaddock" which was "known by the name of 'grapefruit' on account of its resemblance in flavour to the grape" but not nearly so large as other shaddock. Grapefruit hardly tastes like grape. The word "grapefruit" more probably derives from the fact that the fruit, though ordinarily scattered about on a tree like oranges or lemons, may appear as a huge cluster on a heavily-laden tree, with forty or fifty grapefruits on a single stem.

But if I Yin liked "pomelos from the Wan River," he must have used a lot of sugar on them. Grapefruit was once much too bitter to be sweetened by any but heaping amounts of sugar, which is why it did not become an important food in the U.S. (which now produces ninety per cent of the world crop) until 1900. And that importance came only as a result of improvements in the fruit by U.S. botanists, who made grapefruit much sweeter than its original varieties.

Grapefruit is at its best from January through May, which is also when it is cheapest, though there is a "summer" grapefruit from California which pinch-hits for the desert grapefruit of California and Arizona, sold from October to July.

Best for squeezing is the Florida Duncan, which has more character—and a lot more seeds—than the Marsh Seedless variety usually seen in the market. The seedless varieties (another is the Thompson or Pink seedless) dominate the market simply because housewives do not like seeds, though no grapefruit is absolutely seedless (nor is any orange; citrus fruit is called seedless if it has five seeds or less).

Seedless and pink varieties cost more. The pink is natural, but the juice is not pink unless it is from the Florida Burgundy variety. Do not be put off by rust spots or green tinges on the outside of a grapefruit; they have no effect on the meat inside. The biggest grapefruits are not always the best; look for fruit that is firm, compact, springy to the touch, well-shaped and heavy for its size. Avoid coarse-skinned, puffy fruit; it is not as juicy as heavy, thin-skinned grapefruit.

California oranges have more natural sugar in them than do Florida oranges; they are the ones to buy for eating. Florida oranges are the best for squeezing. As with grapefruits, the best oranges are firm ones that are heavy for their size. Citrus fruits do not ripen any further after they are picked; neither do apples.

Apples, even with the thinning of their ranks, still come in so many varieties one can never taste them all, but do learn the difference between the eating varieties, like Jonathans and Red or Golden Delicious, and cooking varieties, like Greenings and Northern Spies. Some, like McIntoshes and Winesaps, star in both roles. Rome Beauties are the apples for baked apple.

Rhubarb is not a fruit at all, though it is eaten as one (often with strawberries). Rhubarb is really a vegetable, like asparagus. It was known to the Greeks (its name comes from the Greek *rheon barbaron* which translates freely into something that comes from the barbarous country of the Rha, the Greek name for the Volga. Rhubarb grew extensively along the banks of that river and the first rhubarb imported into England came straight from the Volga).

Rhubarb stalks should not be too big. Look for small, immature leaves, a sign of tender stalks. A crisp, fresh look is a good sign, too.

Garden-fresh savvy

Where you buy fresh vegetables can be as important as *how* you buy them. The best place is a store with quick turnover, especially one where the produce is kept on crushed ice or on refrigerator shelves. The general rule with green vegetables is that the youngest are the tenderest and will taste the best.

Leaves of cooking greens (chard, kale, collards and spinach) and salad greens (arugala, chicory, endive, escarole, leaf-type lettuce and watercress) should be clean and look fresh. Avoid greens with wilted leaves, discolorations or sprouting (which means the greens are too old and may be tough).

Lettuce at the store is most often iceberg or Simpson lettuce, the variety most easily packed and shipped. Buy the heaviest, hardiest head you can find. Boston (or butter) lettuce has more character, but it is tender. It may be either red or green. Also fragile (and liable to bruise and brown quickly) are Bibb lettuce, field lettuce, oak-leaf lettuce, red and green curly lettuce, corn salad (or lambs') lettuce and limestone lettuce. These are less widely available; if they are around, buy them—but use them promptly and treat them gently.

Next to iceberg, most widespread is romaine (buy the heaviest, fullest head). Any lettuce leaves should be bright-colored, crisp and have a firm-shaped head. Beware of small brown spots on the inner leaves. Romaine, head lettuce, endive and escarole are all fairly solid and can be stored for as long as a week.

Do not worry if there is browning at the core-end of lettuce: it does not mean the lettuce is old. When lettuce is cut in the field, a milky substance appears at its core-end and the air immediately turns it brown, a natural sealing of the wound.

All lettuce should be washed carefully on both sides under running water; run a thumb down inside to get out all the dirt (though iceberg lettuce is usually pretty clean). After the lettuce is washed (just rinse it lightly if it will be kept a few days), drain it in a colander; then wrap it in a towel and store it, towel and all, in a plastic bag in the refrigerator. This is the only way to keep it fresh.

Most of our celery is now Pascal celery, a green variety, while a few years ago celery was all blanched. Serve the hearts of celery fresh and the big outer ribs cooked. The leaves are good in a stock pot and make a nice garnish for meat or poultry; do not let the grocer cut them off. Celery should have fresh, crisp clean heads. Break a rib to make sure it is not soft or too hard; it should snap cleanly.

The snap test works well with snap beans or green beans, too (the French call them *haricots verts*; we used to call them string beans, but they have been stringless for years). Some snap beans have green pods, some yellow; some pods are flat, some oval, some round. They are available all year round, and they are fresh if they snap easily.

Tomatoes, strictly speaking, are a fruit (as are avocados [19]), but we eat them as vegetables. If the tomatoes are still hard when bought, ripen them at home. But do it at room temperature, preferably in the dark. Do not buy tomatoes with cracks or scars in their skins; look for ones with a plump shape and a good red color.

Be warned, however, that the color may be deceptive. A tomato

---

[19] The horticulturist Henry Perrine introduced avocados into Florida from Mexico in 1833 (they were already growing in Africa, Polynesia and Hawaii by then); the Florida Lula variety has a smooth, or slightly corrugated, skin dotted with yellow, but the leading variety is California's fuerte which has a leatherlike "alligator pear" skin. Avocados ripen off the tree; they're plentiful from January to April.

will not get very red if it is grown in weather that is too hot. And while it should at least have begun to turn red before it is packed and shipped, it may well have been picked and packed while still green. Shipping tomatoes at low temperatures, instead of making them keep longer, makes them ripen prematurely. Shippers may use ethylene gas to turn green tomatoes red; it does not hurt them, but they do not taste as good as vine-ripened tomatoes.

A ripe, firm tomato can be kept for about a week at room temperature, or for two or three days in a refrigerator. Beyond that point it will start to lose its vitamin C content.

Summer tomatoes are best. Winter ones come from Florida and from Mexico, which has moved out ahead of California and Texas as a supplier of winter fruits and vegetables to U.S. tables and may pass Florida. Mexican shipments quintupled between 1956 and 1967; tomatoes account for more than seventy per cent of those shipments. The Mexican tomatoes, produced at about forty per cent of the cost in Florida, undersell Florida tomatoes in U.S. markets west of Chicago. About ninety per cent of them are vine-ripened, while eighty-five per cent of the Florida crop is picked green.

Early in 1969, the Florida Tomato Committee, which has authority under federal law to draw up size, maturity and grade requirements for the Department of Agriculture, decided that green tomatoes could be sold at 2 9/32 inches in diameter, while vine-ripened tomatoes would have to be at least 2 17/32 inches in diameter. The ruling affected only fifteen to twenty per cent of the Florida crop, but it barred from thirty to fifty per cent of the Mexican crop from U.S. markets. Result: tomato prices in U.S. stores rose as much as thirty per cent, there were more tasteless green tomatoes, and the Mexicans were understandably furious.

The Floridians had got the Secretary of Agriculture to raise the minimum size on two previous occasions. Since seventy-five per cent of Mexican winter tomatoes are small to medium size, as compared to thirty-eight per cent of Florida's winter tomatoes, tomatoes coming in through Nogales, Arizona, and a few other points were pretty clearly the target of Florida's action. Arizona's merchants were as angry as the Mexicans. The Agriculture Department said the Mexicans were having a great year despite the new regulations, that Mexican tomatoes had now captured more than half the U.S. market, and that "imports from Mexico are now declining. Thus the impact of the regulations will be principally on Florida tomato producers." How is that for sophistry?

We have gone on at some length about winter tomatoes to illustrate the point that political actions can and do affect the prices and qualities of the foods you buy.

To return to our primer on vegetable buying, celery should have crisp, clean, brittle stalks, not too big and not discolored around the heart or leaves.

There is not much point in saying that pea pods should be light green, firm and crisp in texture and filled with well-developed peas. Hardly any U.S. housewives still shell their own peas. In 1933, per capita consumption of fresh peas was one pound; now the figure is well under one-tenth of that. Those in the dwindling minority should uses the peas (and lima beans) right after shelling or the legumes will quickly lose their flavor and tenderness.

Of cabbages and kings

The chief source of vitamin C and a rich source of other nutrients for ancient kings and commoners was cabbage.

Cabbages belong to the mustard family, one of whose wild members is thought to have developed into both green and red cabbages, though red cabbage and kohlrabi were not known until the Middle Ages, which may be true, also, of broccoli and cauliflower.

The French call cauliflower *choux-fleur*, or cabbage-flower, but while anything *Parisienne* on a menu means a dish made with broccoli (just as *Florentine* means it is made with spinach), the French have no word for "broccoli," good evidence the vegetable came late to France. Turnips and rutabagas, the roots and tubers of two other cabbages, are much older. Brussels sprouts, which are tiny cabbages, were not developed until the sixteenth or seventeenth century.

When buying cabbage, look for solid heads relatively heavy for their size, with the stems trimmed close and little or no discoloration in the leaves. Cabbage (called *kraut* or *kohl* by the Germans, who eat a great deal of it), is available all year round, since it stores well. It comes, as we have seen, in many varieties.

Pointed or "new" cabbage is greener than winter types (like Danish and Domestic) but less solid. Wrinkled green savoy has a somewhat mellower flavor. Red cabbage, rather loose-leaved, is common in New York and Wisconsin. Collard, or colewort, is grown mostly in the Southern states (for collie greens). Kale, closely related to collard, is a handsome curly-leaved cabbage.

Brussels sprouts should have a bright green color and be firm to the touch. Belgium has been exporting them for nearly two centuries, but we raise plenty ourselves.

Kohlrabi is a combination of *kohl* and turnip; the edible part is the bulb, which tastes like a sweet and tender turnip.

With cauliflower, the queen of the cabbage clan (Mark Twain defined it as "a cabbage with a college education"), the flower clusters should be compact and firm, not dried out. Outer leaves should be fresh and green, the flowers white or creamy-white.

Chinese cabbage, or Pe tsai, is really a mustard; its blanched center makes a beautiful salad, especially when chopped up with bits of fresh apple.

One cabbage form, broccoli, was not introduced into America until a generation ago (it came in from Calabria, Italy, and is often called Calabrese). Broccoli bud clusters may range from dark green to purple green. The stalks should be firm but tender.

Like the cabbages, every vegetable has criteria to look for when marketing.

Peppers, both sweet and hot, should be fairly firm and should have a strong color, red or green according to variety.

Sweet corn should have fresh-looking green husks, moist enough to fit snugly around the cob. The kernels inside should be milky and either small or well-developed, according to taste. Corn with brown, mushy kernels at the tip of the ear should be avoided.

Unhusked corn, as well as unshelled peas and lima beans in the pod and ripe tomatoes,[20] should be refrigerated *uncovered*. Most other fresh vegetables should be kept in the vegetable drawer or compartment of the refrigerator, or covered over and stored in the lower part of the refrigerator.

Before storing, even briefly, sort vegetables and discard any that show signs of decay; clean the rest with a dry cloth. If the vegetables are washed, be sure to dry them well before putting them in the refrigerator, or they will lose their crispness.

Summer squash, including zucchini (the French, and the English, say *courgettes*) and white bush scallop, are best when their rinds are soft, which means they are not too mature. Other summer squashes are crookneck, straightneck and cocozelle. Be sure they are heavy for their size and not bruised or discolored. And be sure to store them in the refrigerator; they tend to spoil easily. See that the rinds are free of soft spots, too.

Winter squashes, like butternut, hubbard, Turk's-neck and acorn, should have hard rinds and need not be refrigerated. Eggplant, dry onions, turnips, parsnips and potatoes can also be stored in a dry place without refrigeration.

Pick dark purple eggplants that feel firm and heavy. Do not take any with bruises or cuts on their smooth skins.

Onions may be green or dry. Green onions, leeks and scallions [21] should have green fresh tops and their necks should be white two or three inches up from the root. Store them in the refrigerator, well-wrapped. Dry, mature onions should be globular and bright and

---

[20] Tomatoes will taste better if not refrigerated (most flavors are more intense warm than cold), but do not delay using them.

[21] The name comes from the Latin *caepa Ascalonia*, onion of Ashkelon, that Biblical city in David's lament for Jonathan (2 Samuel 1:20) when he bade the people of Judah to "publish it [the news] not in the streets of Ashkelon; lest the daughters of the Philistines rejoice, lest the daughters of the uncircumcised exult."

perfectly dry; if there is moisture at the neck or on the outer skin, the onion has probably begun to decay. Onions will sprout if stored at temperatures much above 60° F. Store them in a loosely-woven bag. Without the right kind of storage space, buy onions only in small quantities.

Turnip and beet tops can be cooked and eaten just like spinach. Young peas can be cooked in their pods and eaten pod and all (as the Chinese eat "snow peas"). Older peas can be cooked the same way; the soft peas are then removed from the pods with a knife and the pods themselves made into a pea-pod purée.

Wilted vegetables can be made into a delicious broth, along with a week's vegetable parings, all combined and chopped finely (or put through a meat grinder or blender). Put them in a pot of boiling water, boil for half an hour, let them cool and drain them through a strainer or colander. In addition to being nutritious, waste scraps can be a gastronomic triumph.

One potato, two potato

Potatoes should be smooth and clean when bought. Do not buy any that show the slightest amount of green; they are likely to be bitter. Do not buy any that have sprouted; the eyes should be mere dimples. Get shallow-eyed, regular-shaped ones. Dark brown spots can mean the potatoes have been scarred or bruised and may be decayed. Small, black-lined holes mean wireworms have been at work. Over-size potatoes may be hollow at the center.

Pinch potatoes to make sure they are firm, not leathery or spongy, two signs they have been frozen or improperly stored, which will make them lose flavor, color and mineral values, and make them spongy when cooked.

A late crop mature potato should stay firm and usable for up to three months, but be sure to store it in a cool, dark, moist place where the average temperature is between 50° and 60° F.—not near the furnace or oil burner. Do not store defective potatoes; they will spoil the good ones.

Even under the best circumstances, a potato will change in chemical content while it is stored; the starch will diminish and the sugar increase. To remedy this, take potatoes out of storage and keep them at room temperature for a week or so before using them, right up to the point where tiny white sprouts appear. This waiting period brings up the starch content and restores the potato to just about the nutritional value it had when it was dug out of the ground.

There are about 160 varieties of potatoes grown in the U.S. Our biggest producer (surprise!) is California. But the grocer will probably have just three or four.

For boiling, the best potatoes are Chippewas from Maine and Michigan, Irish Cobblers from Maine, Katahdins from Maine and Pennsylvania, Russet Rurals from Michigan, Sebagos from Maine and Wisconsin, and Triumphs from Nebraska.

For baking, Russet Burbanks and White Rose potatoes from Idaho, Green Mountains from New York, Irish Cobblers from Wisconsin and Sebagos from Washington State are the choices. Red River Reds from Minnesota and North Dakota, though uncommon, are also uncommonly good.

"New" potatoes bruise easily and do not keep well. More durable are "late" and "old" potatoes, but do not take any scarred or mottled ones.

Like meat and eggs, vegetables have USDA grades, but these are rarely seen except sometimes on potatoes. And with potatoes "U.S. No. 1" means second-grade; first-grade are marked "U.S. Fancy." The grading system is based on wholesaler usage, now a century old; food processors resist any compulsory grading (the present system, which is voluntary, was established to make army food procurement easier in World War II) because it pulls the rug out from under brand names in which they have invested enormous advertising monies.

For mashing, the preferred potatoes are Russet Burbanks, White Roses and Green Mountains from Maine and New York, and Irish Cobblers from Maine.

But powdered mashed potatoes made from Idaho and Washington potatoes are good, too, and they save a lot of time.

The *Wall Street Journal* says home-mashed potatoes may some day become "as rare in American homes as home-made noodles." More and more women are buying processed potatoes, which include not only flakes for mashed potatoes but also prepared hashed browns, potato puffs, French fries, cottage fries, potato pancakes, potatoes au gratin and diced potatoes. Frozen baked potatoes, complete with cheese or sour cream toppings, are sold in some places.

Prepared French fries comprise the leading form of processed potatoes. Plants that prepare them use nearly 35 million 100-pound bags of potatoes a year. To improve the flavor of prepared French fries (and also of potato chips), researchers are experimenting with the addition of amino acids during processing.

Per capita consumption of processed potatoes was only 6.3 pounds in 1950; in 1969 it was 49.4 pounds. Of all the potatoes produced in the U.S. in 1966, only 56 per cent were served fresh-cooked.

Potato processors cite the average twenty per cent loss in peeling fresh potatoes at home and claim their dehydrated potato flakes are usually cheaper for mashed potatoes than do-it-yourself mashed potatoes. If a sixteen-and-one-half ounce package of flakes sells for fifty-five cents, the package yields thirty-three three-ounce servings (each ounce of flakes, reconstituted with hot milk or water, makes about six ounces of mashed potatoes) at 1.6 cents per serving. Fresh Idaho russet potatoes, given the usual loss in peeling, may cost more than two cents a serving. And with the potato flakes there is no chance of getting potatoes that have been damaged in handling or have deteriorated in storage. Unprocessed potatoes, however, are much richer in vitamins.

Potato consumption in the U.S., which had fallen in the 1950's because housewives were watching their weight (though potatoes are not fattening unless cooked in butter or something similarly calorie-adding) and because nobody likes to peel potatoes, were back up to 110 pounds per person on the average in 1969. The increase was ascribed to wide use of dehydrated and frozen potato products, which reversed the downward trend.

Potato chips made from dehydrated potatoes were test marketed in 1969 by General Mills and by Procter & Gamble, much to the chagrin of traditional potato chip makers, who claim the "synthetics" should not be allowed to call themselves potato chips. About fifteen per cent of the U.S. potato crop goes into potato chips, regular or newfangled, marketed mostly by small companies serving local markets.

As for dehydrated mashed potatoes, restaurants are big users of them; they say the reconstituted flakes are less quick to turn dark on steam tables than are freshly-mashed spuds.

Got a green thumb?

Some vegetables are much better grown fresh in a backyard garden than bought in any store.

Whether the home gardener saves any money raising his own produce will depend on a number of factors, but the grow-it-yourselfer will certainly have the advantage of being able to enjoy choice varieties not generally available at any supermarket. He may even raise uncommon vegetables rarely encountered except among dedicated vegetable gardeners.

Sweet corn is the prime example of a vegetable never tasted properly unless cooked within five minutes of picking it. To do that, grow the corn at home or live next door to someone who grows it. Most of the sugar in commercial sweet corn hybrids is transformed into insoluble, non-sweet carbohydrates long before the ears reach the table. Plant geneticists at the U.S. Department of Agriculture have been trying to alter the gene pattern of commercial sweet corn to make it stay sweet longer. Before their work is ever translated into commercial realities, though, they will have to combine the qualities of longer-lasting sweetness with high yield, sturdiness and other qualities.

To enjoy sweet corn here and now, plant it at home. The best-tasting variety is probably Seneca Chief, though Wonderful lives up to its name. Some good early-maturing varieties are Seneca Beauty and Spring Gold. The All-America Selections [22] are hybrid Golden Beauty for early corn and hybrid Iochief for later. Smart gardeners plant their corn every five to seven days so they will have fresh corn ripening straight through from late July to mid-October (the dates are for low altitudes within a few degrees of the 40th parallel).

Garden-fresh lettuce is another example of something much better grown at home than store-bought. Some good varieties are Summer Bibb (named for John B. Bibb, an amateur horticulturist who developed the variety in his garden in Frankfort, Kentucky), Buttercrunch, Salad Bowl and (in midsummer) Cos, a Romaine lettuce. Buttercrunch and Salad Bowl are both All-America selections.

Some good varieties of other vegetables are Champion and Cherry Belle (A.A.S.) radishes, Detroit Dark Red and Ruby Queen (A.A.S.) beets (best when they are picked small), Tendercrop and Executive (A.A.S.) bush snap beans (or Kentucky Wonder if poles or a trellis are available).

Tomatoes come in many varieties, including some that are resistant to verticillium wilt, a fungus disease that attacks the plants through the roots, especially in soils that have been used for growing vegetables several years in a row. Common types like Big Boy, Moreton Hybrid, Rutgers, Glamour, Cardinal and Fireball are all susceptible to verticillium wilt. They may do well the first or second year; later, for better yields (and better tomatoes) plant new varieties like Gardener 67, New Yorker and Fireball VR. Springset and Spring Giant (A.A.S.) are other resistant varieties, maturing early. Superman and Jet Star resist verticillium wilt but mature later.

What vegetables a family likes best, and what vegetables are costliest to buy or hardest to obtain, will determine which ones to plant. The 1970 All-America selections for some were as follows:

---

[22] A.A.S. judges evaluate the results of field trials at twenty-six test gardens, comparing the vegetables with the best commercially-grown varieties. These are the only recognized ratings of new vegetable varieties grown in North America.

Bush lima beans: Fordhook 242
Broccoli: hybrid Green Comet
Brussels sprouts: hybrid Jade Cross
Cabbage: hybrid Stonehead
Cabbage (savoy): hybrid Savoy King
Cantaloupe: hybrid Samson
Carrots: Gold Pak
Cauliflower: Snow King
Cucumbers: hybrid Spartan Valor
Endive (Batavian): Full Heart
Okra: Clemson Spineless
Onions (Sweet Spanish): Utah strain Yellow Valencia
Parsley: Paramount
Peas: Freezonian
Peppers: hybrid Bell Boy
Spinach: America
Squash: hybrid zucchini Chefini
    Early Prolific Straightneck
    hybrid St. Pat Scallop
    winter Waltham Buternut
    winter Kindred
Tomatoes: hybrid cherry Small Fry
Turnips: hybrid Tokyo Cross

Some vegetables, like asparagus, yield much more quickly if roots are planted instead of seeds. Two-year-old roots produce harvestable asparagus stalks after a year, but one-year-old roots are more likely to transplant safely. To grow pale stalks, the kind preferred in Europe, plant seeds or roots in deep trenches.

Green thumb or not, grow some fresh culinary herbs in the garden or a window box. Sage, rosemary, thyme, oregano, tarragon and chives are all perennials. Basil, chervil and parsley should be planted from seed each year. Herbs in general need less water, less fertilizer (none after the start of the season, and even then no peat moss or acidy plant food) and less insect protection than most plants, though mulching the perennials in the fall helps bring them back more vigorously the following spring.

Most herbs do best in a neutral soil. Some, like chives, grow readily indoors.

There is no end to the list of wild and cultivated garden herbs used to flavor the world's foods: borage, hyssop, lovage—many are quite unfamiliar to most Americans, who more and more buy commercial dry or powdered versions of the more common herbs, which are pale shadows of the fresh herbs themselves (though dry bay leaf is quite acceptable).

When housewives do use herbs, they frequently use them without subtlety. Strong herbs, or "potherbs" (like bay leaf, basil, dill, marjoram, mint, oregano, rosemary, sage, tarragon and thyme), can drown out any other flavor, as can too much garlic. A single bay leaf can be too much bay leaf for a given dish.[23]

Milder herbs, like chervil, chives, parsley and savory, can be used more liberally, but potherbs require a delicate hand.

The phrase "bouquet garni" means a combination of parsley, thyme and bay leaf. "Fines herbes" means any of three combinations: chervil, chives, parsley and tarragon; basil, chives and parsley; or burnet, parsley and thyme.

But grow the herbs at home. Once tasted, they put to shame the stuff sold in jars.

"For everything there is a season..."

The year-round availability of many foods makes some housewives forget that there are still seasons when it is just not smart to buy any particular meat, fish or produce item because its price is bound to be out of line and its quality probably not up to snuff.

Europeans are much more season-oriented. The French wait eagerly for their *primeurs*—winter and early spring vegetables, mostly from the lower Rhone valley. In May they gorge on *fraises de bois* and on wild asparagus from Majorca (scorned by the Spanish

---

[23] Saffron, too, can take over a dish unless limited to a minuscule pinch. But saffron is not considered an herb: it is a spice, as are sesame seed, paprika, mustard and, of course, pepper, cayenne pepper, allspice, cloves, curry powder, ginger, mace, juniper berries and nutmeg.

but prized in Paris), while Italians flock to *ristorantes* and *trattorias* for the first *piselli* (green peas) and *prosciutto*.

Come June and there are May Duke cherries in Holland and long, mauve-colored radishes in Portugal's seacoast towns of Estoril and Cascais.

Italian and Greek melons and green figs come into season in July, red figs in August, the month when the English eat ripe fruit from Devon.

Seedless red Cardinal grapes come to market in Italy and Greece in September; the Italians eat white truffles in October, and so it goes.

Seasonal variations are still a reality in America, and seasonal price differences are often extreme. But quick-frozen, canned and processed foods have so increased their shares of the consumer food dollar that many shoppers must be reminded that the price of spinach is not the same in December as it was in May.

While fresh asparagus in February may not be quite so unobtainable now as when Oscar of the Waldorf served it to those Tammany politicians early in the century (Chapter 3), some foods even today are scarce and costly out of season unless they are canned or frozen.

More than eighty-one per cent of fresh asparagus sold in the U.S. is sold in March, April and May. More than half the artichoke crop is sold in the same period, while eighty per cent of our sweet corn and nearly sixty per cent of our cucumbers are sold from May to September.

Fresh fruits are even more seasonal than fresh vegetables. More than ninety-four per cent of fresh apricots, more than eighty-eight per cent of sweet cherries are sold in June and July. Nearly seventy per cent of the strawberry crop is sold in April, May and June. More than eighty-three per cent of fresh peaches and nearly seventy per cent of cantaloupes are sold in June, July and August. More than ninety per cent of tangerines and tangelos are sold in November, December and January; more than ninety per cent of persimmons are sold in October, November and December; ninety per cent of pomegranates are sold in October and November; ninety-seven per cent of plums are sold from June to September.

Some items, like cabbage, carrots, celery, endive, escarole, lettuce and bananas are available at a fairly even pace the year round. And at a price, one can buy almost any fruit or vegetable at almost any time of year in our major cities. And buy it fresh, not canned or frozen. But the price may be high—double the price out of season, or even more, than at the peak of the natural season.

More and more fruits and vegetables are being sold pre-packaged. Of the $104 billion Americans spent on food in 1969, about ten per cent went for fresh produce; about one-third of this was pre-packaged at the retail level. Now that percentage has more than doubled: ninety per cent of some vegetables (e.g. radishes and carrots) are found this way, and the general average is at least seventy-five per cent. Wrapping produce in plastic on a modern assembly line at the warehouse instead of at the grocery store can lower food costs, according to an Agricultural Research Service survey. But it is getting harder and harder to press the peaches and smell the cantaloupes.

The lost innocence

Efforts of men like Luther Burbank and his successors have borne some fruit that is, if not bitter, of questionable value.

When Europeans criticize our American foods, the criticism is often just sour grapes. But occasionally a story comes to light that gives credence to the scorn of U.S. foods by European gastronomes. One recent story, ironically, involves grapes—not sour grapes, but tasteless ones.

From more than five pounds a year, per capita consumption of table grapes in the U.S. declined in the last two decades to less than three pounds. When our housewives cut down further on their purchases of grapes (this was before the boycott of California grapes in support of Cesar Chavez's migrant grape workers), an investigation revealed that California grapes were, indeed, declining in taste values.

California is our leading table-grape producer (its 1967 crop was 415,000 tons, worth more than $40 million). Standards for California grapes were once very high, so high that many growers could not meet them and quit the market. In ten years, table-grape acreage in California went down from a million acres to half a million.

But recently standards have fallen. There are not enough inspectors, there is no approved device for measuring sugar content of grapes. San Joaquin Valley growers, hoping to avoid a mid-season glut, harvest their grapes too green.

What is more, investigation revealed that a Japanese plant hormone, gibberellic acid, which stimulates plant growth, was being used on about eight per cent of the California grape crop, increasing the size of the grapes by twenty to sixty per cent. The plant hormone, a triumph of science, gives the grapes great "eye appeal," but the beautiful grapes do not taste like anything. The Japanese, whose fruits are extraordinarily tasty, can hardly use much gibberellic acid themselves.

The laws of the market place theoretically force food producers to maintain quality standards, but those laws must realistically be backed up by legal statutes, by effective inspection and by discriminating buyers.

In the case of the tasteless grapes, economic pressure will probably force the growers to mend their ways. But consumers too often tend to accept inferior taste and eating qualities for lack of anything better. It is the penalty of apathy.

And because so many of our fruits and vegetables have been selectively bred for size, hardiness, color, shelf-life and almost every characteristic except the ones that matter to the eater, because they are often picked green for reasons of efficient marketing, and because they are protected from weeds and insect pests by herbicides and persistent chlorinated hydrocarbon pesticides, we pay other penalties as well.

❧ 7 ❧

What's wrong with eating the daisies?

What people will and will not eat, what they chew and what they eschew, is often determined by age-old prejudices, habits, family customs, myths, taboos and religious rules handed down, usually without thought, from generation to generation.

Sometimes a prejudice is just negativism, as in the classic cartoon Carl Rose drew for *The New Yorker* magazine in 1928. Perhaps you remember the child refusing his broccoli. "I say it's spinach," he declared in E.B. White's caption, "and I say the hell with it."

Some long-standing customs of diet are based on sound, sensible reasons, or at least reasons that originally made sense. But often, while the reasons may no longer be appropriate, the habits, prejudices, rules and taboos are so firmly entrenched that there are people who will quite literally starve to death before they will change their dietary ways.

The United Nations has found that starving peoples will actively resent and resist attempts to make innovations in their diet; in times of rice famine in Asia, wheat and millet have been angrily rejected by emaciated Indians and Orientals who could easily have been saved from starvation if they had only been able to unbend and adapt them-

selves to unfamiliar foods. (Part of the problem was that some Asians tried to cook grains of wheat the way they cooked rice, just as English women have tried to brew coffee beans the same way as tea leaves.)

Breadfruit and flint corn

This phenomenon of rigidity in diet, observed years ago by Rudyard Kipling, is well illustrated by two bits of history. The first concerns breadfruit, and Captain William Bligh of *Mutiny on the Bounty* fame.

Bligh had served as sailing master board the *Resolution* on the second expedition (1772–74) of Captain James Cook; he was called "Breadfruit Bligh" after he discovered the virtues of the melon-sized fruit that served as a staple food in Tahiti (breadfruit had actually been described earlier, in 1688, by Captain William Dampier, the English pirate-explorer-navigator, who found it growing in Guam).

Natives of Polynesia and Malaysia had been eating breadfruit for as long as anyone could remember, gathering it before it was ripe, when it was full of starch, and preparing it in various ways. *Rima*, as they called it, was often baked whole in the hot embers of a fire; its flesh, when scooped out, tasted like boiled potatoes and sweet milk.

Bligh's mission on the *Bounty* in 1787 was to bring specimens of the breadfruit tree (*Artocarpus incisa*) to the West Indies as a new source of food for England's colonies in the Caribbean. His purpose was foiled by the mutiny in 1789, but Bligh, if cold-hearted, was also indefatigable. Set adrift in a small boat by the mutineers, he reached land after a long voyage, got back to England and, in 1791, set sail once again, this time aboard the *Providence* (accompanied by a tender aptly named *Assistant*).

In 1792, Bligh once again loaded his decks with breadfruit plants in Tahiti. This time he completed his mission, planting ten of the saplings in St. Helena in the South Atlantic (later the last place of exile for Napoleon) and hundreds on the islands of St. Vincent (in the Grenadines) and Jamaica. The young trees had to be watered daily on the long sea voyage, even when it meant that the men went thirsty.

Yet after all that, breadfruit was not a great success in the West Indies. The trees thrived in their new homes, but the West Indians' staple starch was plantain; and while breadfruit is used to a certain extent in the Antilles, plantain (which ripens all year round while breadfruit is seasonal) is still the preferred starch. It is as basic to the diet of Jamaica as ackee (called botanically *Blighia sapida* after Captain Bligh, who may have introduced it along with breadfruit), a native fruit, poisonous until ripe, that looks and tastes, when it is prepared, like scrambled eggs. Other Jamaican staples are "garden eggs" (eggplant), mangoes, papaya (or "pawpaw" as Jamaicans call it), fish, lobster (the clawless kind), coconut, naseberries (sapodillas), pineapples, otaheite apples (also introduced from Tahiti, which was originally called Otaheite) and citrus fruits, but very little breadfruit.

Our other bit of history has to do with the Irish potato famine of 1845–46.

To help relieve that famine, the Prime Minister of England, Sir Robert Peel, acted on his own responsibility to import Indian corn (as the Irish called American maize). Corn was then virtually unknown in Ireland. Peel's relief program ran into political difficulties and problems of misunderstanding; the U.S. chargé d'affaires at Brussels wrote to the British purchasing agents to warn them that "flint" corn was very hard and could not be ground with ordinary millstones.

The major obstacle to corn was lack of knowledge, paired with the narrowness of people so accustomed to boiling potatoes that they knew practically no other food. In the backward areas of Clare, West Cork, Donegal and Mayo, the peasants evidently did not even realize that the wheat, oats and barley they grew for their landlords could be made into bread. They did not eat bread. They ate potatoes. And when the potatoes rotted in the fields, the poor Irish starved.

Incomprehensible? Incomprehensible. But take away hamburger

and many Americans would be almost equally bewildered, so slavish is their dependence on the familiar chopped round.

Hang-ups of pride and of bias

Food snobberies have always compounded the problem of human in-adaptability to new foods. Citizens of the early United States were loath to admit they ate anything so common as shad. Caviar, on the other hand, now has such prestige value as a status symbol that fresh caviar can sell for as much as $60 a pound. And people will force themselves to acquire a taste for it.

This sort of pretension is harmless up to a point. It is related socio-logically to the terms for food cited by H.L. Mencken in *The American Language*. During what Mencken called "The Golden Age of Euphemism" in America in the 1830's and 1840's, nice people called a cock a rooster, and "leg" was used only by the vulgar, "first joint" being the socially acceptable term for a chicken leg (and "second joint" was substituted for thigh). Americans, who had earlier been plain-spoken enough, were now more distressed by indelicacies of speech than distinguished for the delicacies of their tables.

In the 1920's, under President Warren Gamaliel Harding, Americans (who had called sauerkraut "liberty cabbage" and German toast "French toast" during World War I) were again asking for a first joint or second joint, or for "white meat" (it was *infra dig* to say "breast"; the word "brisket" was used at the butcher shop). Mencken called this excess of nicety "Gamalielese." Some of it is still with us.

Snobbery is self-penalizing. While the French prize small, wild fruits and vegetables, the Portuguese regard wild strawberries and asparagus as food only for the very poor. The English, and many Americans, think good manners dictate that one leave something on the plate, while the Germans, and many others, think it impolite not to polish the plate bare.

It is all very amusing. It becomes serious only when a food is disdained because it is associated with poverty and, as a consequence, people's health is jeopardized by the distortion of nutritional truth.

Back in ancient Greece, a character in Aristophanes' play *Plutus* remarked of a newly-rich acquaintance, "Now he doesn't eat lentils anymore." The phrase became a proverb, applied to anyone risen from rags to affluence.

But lentils are legumes (also called "pulses") and, like other legumes, are rich in protein. Dry legumes have, in fact, been called "the poor man's meat"; the term goes back far beyond any knowledge of proteins as such.

Yet the contempt for legumes survives in an English-language booklet I picked up recently in Bulgaria. The booklet hails the progress Bulgaria has made under socialism, which has been considerable; but at one point its author boasts that "in Bulgaria the consumption of pulses, which are comparatively indigestible and not very valuable foodstuffs, is falling, while in Turkey it is going up, and in Greece it has remained at the former level." He makes no mention of Bulgaria's high consumption of eggplant, a food that is nutritionally almost worthless.

Old food prejudices, however unfounded, do not die easily. But times change, and so do some popular attitudes.

Taboo

At one time in ancient Rome it was forbidden to eat eggs; the egg was regarded as a potential chicken and therefore too valuable to be eaten, an attitude not unlike the opposition to legal abortion in our so-called modern world. Fortunately, the Romans discarded their proscription and enjoyed eggs mixed with everything from rose petals to fowl's brains.

Abortion is a religious issue; the notion of taboo is also a religious idea. Captain Cook first encountered the word in Polynesia and used it initially in a description of his third voyage (1776–79):

The people of Atooi [1] . . . resemble those of Otaheite [Tahiti] in the slovenly state of their religious places, and in offering vegetables and animals to their gods. The *taboo* also prevails in Atooi, in its full extent, and seemingly with much more rigour than even at Tongataboo. For the people here always asked, with great eagerness and signs of fear to offend, whether any particular thing . . . was *taboo*, or as they pronounced the word, *tafoo?*

Cook and his men were charmed by the Polynesian girls, who had no inhibitions about showing their delicious naked bodies or even about making love in public; but the English were struck by the taboos against a woman eating in the company of men, and against a member of the ruling family helping himself to food, to name but two Polynesian taboos. (The word rapidly came into popular use in England; it was often spelled *tabu* and it lost its original religious connotations.)

The taboos against various foods in various cultures and societies form a long, long list, though some avoidances are perhaps better described as prejudices; an aversion based on misinformation, on taste or on family tradition is not the same as one based on symbolic value.

Forbidden fruit and sacred cows

In Puerto Rico, many people living on the edge of starvation will not eat fruit that grows wild, regarding it as dangerous or indigestible, even when it is there for the picking. Some Puerto Ricans will not eat pineapple in combination with any other food, an idea reminiscent of Hayism and other U.S. food fads (Chapter 10).

In parts of West Africa, older people think it is undignified to eat oranges; they discourage their children from eating the fruit lest it make them soft. Raw food generally is seen in West Africa as fit only for cattle.

---

[1] Atui, one of the Hawaiian Islands, which at that time were called the Sandwich Islands after John Montagu, fourth Earl of Sandwich (see footnote to page 101).

Maize, the "corn" of America, is in northern Europe considered suitable solely as chicken feed.

Greeks insist that cucumbers be eaten only raw, but they will eat zucchini squash, green beans and peas only if they are cooked. Raw cauliflower is considered inedible in Greece, though raw cabbage is quite acceptable.

Carrots were for years thought in England to be no more than a treat for horses (the carrot in front of the nose has been a classic symbol of incentive). Only after World War I did the English begin to serve carrots to any great extent on their own tables.

And so it goes.

Navaho Indians will not eat fish, and Apaches will not touch bear venison. Some American Indian tribes consider milk disgusting. Some African groups, on the contrary, prize milk as a precious food and reserve it for adult men, though in Senegal the women think drinking milk will make them barren.

The reason dairy products have never been important in Far Eastern diets may *not* be the cultural fact of enmity between China and the nomad herdsmen who were her neighbors. Recent studies by U.S. and Australian scientists suggest that most non-white adults develop an intolerance to milk. The intolerance, which often begins during adolescence, is linked to the lack of an intestinal enzyme, lactase, which is needed to digest the milk sugar, lactose, splitting it into glucose and galactose, which the body absorbs. With insufficient lactase, a person drinking more than a single glass of milk may suffer abdominal bloating, cramps or diarrhea; the symptoms vary from person to person.

The studies have been cited by those who question shipping powdered milk to some of the nutritionally deprived countries of Africa and Asia, but most young people of all races seem to have enough lactase. The Japanese drink twenty times more milk than they did twenty years ago and thrive on it.

An earlier study at Johns Hopkins University Medical School indicated that seventy per cent of adult American Negroes could not digest milk; African Negroes in Uganda showed a similar percentage of intolerance. A Nigerian health official commented, "It's not we who have a deficiency of lactase, it's you who have an excess. Adults are not supposed to drink milk."

Many U.S. servicemen, returning from Viet Nam, have encountered problems from drinking more milk than their lactase could digest. Europeans often ridicule Americans, calling us babies because we drink so much milk as adults.

Romanians abstain completely from milk and butter during long fasting periods, but not for reasons of insufficient lactase in their small intestines.

Hindus use milk and milk products like *ghee* but do not eat meat (their religion forbids the taking of life). Some cows, though not all, are sacred among the Hindus.

Laws and taboos involving foods, the preparation of foods and the serving of foods were probably of major importance in many early societies. They are still strong in countries like India, where the caste system is based to some extent on variations in cooking and dining customs.

Underlying the stratification of castes is the idea that food has magic qualities, that it can transmit spiritual infection and pollute the soul. Natural grasses and cereal grains, according to this belief, can be handled by anybody without contamination, but once the seeds are pressed for oil, or the grain is softened by cooking, the *mana*, or "soul stuff," of the person preparing the food can be absorbed by the food itself.

As a protection, an Indian of a certain caste may not share his food with anyone outside that caste. Each caste has its own set of rules governing who shall cook the food, who serve the water, and so forth. A high-caste Brahman, if he is orthodox, must have his grain cooked only by another Brahman. He may eat vegetables cooked in ghee by cooks who belong to castes just below the Brahman caste, but he cannot eat with members of these castes.

Some Indians will eat nothing that grows under the ground, which rules out potatoes, carrots, beets, peanuts and many other common foods. Members of some castes will eat fish but not meat. In other castes, eggs may be eaten, provided they are unfertile, but neither fish nor meat (fertile eggs are considered full of meat). The highest castes are generally limited to purely vegetarian diets.

Giving a dinner party in India can be tricky, like serving a group of people, each of whom has a different food allergy. And the complexity of dietary laws makes intermarriage among castes extraordinarily difficult, thus helping to perpetuate the caste system. There are some castes where marriage can take place only among fifteen families.

Many major religions have at least some dietary laws. Until the end of 1966, Roman Catholics were forbidden by the Church to eat meat on Fridays; dietary prohibitions are still observed during the Lenten season, from Ash Wednesday until Easter Sunday.

Strictly kosher

Mohammedans,[2] along with Laplanders, Navaho Indians, the Indians of Guiana, the Yakuts of Turkey and the natives of Borneo, do not eat pork; neither do Orthodox Jews. But for Orthodox Jews, and even for some Conservative and Reform Jews, that is just the beginning.

Kosher dietary laws are spelled out, along with other laws, in a Scripture-based code called the *halakhah*, the "way," which is based on passages in Leviticus and Deuteronomy in the Old Testament.

Oriental philosophers of the sixth century B.C., as we saw in Chapter 1, urged their followers to be vegetarians. Genesis, the first book of the Old Testament, which dates back two centuries earlier, saw vegetarianism as a spiritual ideal (Adam, in the Garden of Eden, was limited to fruits and vegetables) but conceded to reality (to Noah and his sons, God said, "Every moving thing that liveth shall be for

---

[2] Because their overlords, the Mohammedan Turks, would not touch pork, the people of the Balkans, whose traditional meat is lamb and mutton, raised swine during the centuries of their occupation by the Turks. And they still do.

you; as the green herb have I given you all. Only flesh with the life thereof, which is the blood thereof, shall ye not eat!" Genesis 9:1–4).

Deuteronomy and Leviticus, however, severely limited the number of "moving things" which might be eaten. Before we examine them, consider the words, "Only the flesh with the life thereof, which is the blood thereof." Reverence for life underlies most of the kosher laws, the same sort of reverence that has kept the Vatican so staunchly and sadly opposed to artificial methods of birth control.

A hen's egg is kosher, but not if it has the dark spot "which is the blood thereof" that shows the egg has been fertilized.

Ideas of kindness and avoidance of suffering dictated kosher rules for slaughtering animals (Chapter 4). The Hebrew words (from right to left) *basar kasher* on a kosher meat store means the meat (*basar*) sold is kosher. If requested in advance by the customer, it has been thoroughly rinsed with water, soaked for a half hour, placed on an inclined or perforated surface for the blood to drain off, spread with coarse salt to further purge it of blood, then rinsed three times in clear, cold water. But most customers do all this themselves at home. Special procedures are used for the heart and liver, which contain extraordinary amounts of blood.

Most of the dietary laws embodied in the Kashrut are in Chapter 11 of Leviticus. They proscribe the flesh of birds and animals of prey (as the Babylonian laws of Mani had proscribed birds of prey), reptiles, creeping insects, animal blood, any animals except those which "chew the cud and have cloven hoofs," and meat from the hind quarters of any animal.

Sirloin steak, porterhouse, T-bone, flank, loin and round steak, rump steak and rump roast, leg of lamb, loin lamb chops, leg (round) of veal, veal cutlets (from the center of a calf's hind leg) and loin roast of veal are all from the hind quarters. All are non-kosher.

And it is not enough that an animal chew its cud or have cloven hooves; it must *both* chew its cud *and* have cloven hooves.

> The camel, because it chews the cud but does not part the hoof, is unclean to you. And the rock badger, because it chews the cud but does not part the hoof, is unclean to you. And the hare, because

it chews the cud but does not part the hoof, is unclean to you. And the swine, because it parts the hoof and is cloven-footed but does not chew the cud, is unclean to you. Of their flesh you shall not eat, and their carcasses you shall not touch. They are unclean to you.

Popular belief has it that these "shall not's" are based on ancient health wisdom, dating from a time when there was no refrigeration. People think about trichinosis (tapeworm), which comes from eating undercooked pork, and marvel at the medical knowledge of the ancients. It is also widely believed that the tabooed animals (and, as we shall see, birds and fish and shellfish) are tabooed because of their eating habits; many are scavengers. The use of the word "unclean" seems to support the belief. But certainly no animal is unclean *because* it does not chew the cud or have cloven hooves. The taboo against eating pork has been explained in various ways, none of them having to do with cleanliness or health. (Chickens, as Marston Bates points out, have eating habits just as filthy to our eyes as pigs' habits.)

One explanation is that pigs were associated with religious cults that antedated Indo-European culture. Another is that the pig was identified with the Egyptian god of evil, Set. There is even a theory based on the fact that some primitive peoples shunned the meat of certain animals lest they take on the characteristics of those animals. The Carib Indians were afraid they would get little pigs' eyes if they ate pork.

To us the most reasonable explanation is that the pork taboo was a vestige of the cultural conflict between range and grange. Swine were the domestic animals of farmers; early Jews were herdsmen. (Cain in the Book of Genesis, son of Adam and Eve, was "a tiller of the ground," but his brother Abel was "a keeper of sheep"; the "mark on Cain" after he slew his brother was to keep him from being killed in vengeance, which sounds like an effort by the Scripture writers to make range-grange adversaries cool it.) Just as the Chinese may have avoided milk products because they were the foods of their herdsmen enemy, Jews and Mohammedans and others avoided the meat of their farmer antagonists.

The prohibition in Jewish dietary law against mixing meat and dairy products stems from the injunction in Deuteronomy (14:21): "Thou shalt not seethe ["boil" in the Revised Standard Version], a kid in its mother's milk."

Moses Maimonides, the Jewish scholar of the twelfth century, said the origin of this was the cooking of a kid in its mother's milk as part of a fertility rite practiced by pagan cults in ancient Canaan. Other scholars ascribe it simply to feelings of humanitarianism and kindness to animals.

Such feelings turn up everywhere. The Jews did not hook fish, they netted them.

Certain seafood is excluded from kosher diets: "Everything in the waters that has not fins and scales is an abomination to you."

The Jews are not alone in this. The people of Iran will not eat finless or scaleless fish, nor would the ancient Romans offer the gods such fish in their sacrifices. Eel is taboo in many of the South Sea islands.

Among the water creatures denied to Orthodox Jews, along with eels, are sharks, oysters, clams, lobsters, shrimp and mussels. The roe of any fish without fins is also non-kosher. In the summer of 1968, two caviar firms in New York City (which has more than 1,800,000 Jews, double the number in Jerusalem, Haifa and Tel Aviv combined, making it the world's largest center of Jewish population) were fined $250 each in Manhattan Criminal Court. Their crime: they sold lumpfish caviar as "kosher." The lumpfish has spiny protrusions on its skin, but no true scales.

Fish that Orthodox Jews *may* eat is *parve*, or neutral; it may be eaten with meat (if not cooked with butter or with non-kosher margarine) or with dairy products.

But the effect of the rule against seething the kid in the milk of its mother is that an observant Orthodox housewife must have separate sets of dishes, silverware and kitchen accessories, one for meat (*fleishedig*, in Yiddish), one for dairy dishes (*milchedig*); she must not get them mixed up; she must certainly never use cream or butter at the same meal she serves meat. To avoid contamination, meat and dairy dishes and utensils must be washed and dried separately. And there must be two glass containers for the blender, two sets of parts for the mixer and enough storage space for everything. Some Orthodox households even use two separate kitchen sinks and two separate dishwashers.

Chicken—and nice hot chicken soup, sometimes called "Jewish penicillin"—are, along with most other poultry, basic to kosher cuisine. But both Leviticus and Deuteronomy forbid the eating of certain birds, namely:

> the eagle, the carrion vulture, the osprey, the kite, the falcon according to its kind, every raven according to its kind, the ostrich, the nighthawk, the sea gull, the hawk according to its kind, the owl, the cormorant, the ibis, the water hen, the pelican, the carrion vulture, the stork, the heron according to its kind, the hoopoe and the bat.

The bat, though its flesh may be inedible, has no particularly unclean eating habits. Nor, for that matter, is it a bird at all; it is a flying mammal.

As for the other items, the list is the one given in at least one edition of the Revised Standard Version of the Bible. Different versions [3] vary in their lists; so do different editions of the same version. There are twenty items in each list, but since there are many species of falcons, of ravens, of hawks and of herons, many more than twenty birds are forbidden. Some versions list, in place of some of the birds on the Revised Standard list, the sea-mew, the little owl, the great owl, the horned owl, and the glede.

"The carrion vulture" appears twice on the Revised Standard list (otherwise there would be nineteen items). In the Authorized Version, the first "carrion vulture" is usually given as the "ossifrage," a

---

[3] Hundreds of versions of the Bible have been published, including a vegetarian version and some that eliminated all references to sex. The most widely sold is the King James Version, commissioned early in the sixteenth century by England's James I (Scotland's James VI) because other Bibles of the time had marginal notes questioning the divine right of kings. Publishers prefer it for the beauty of its language and because it is not copyrighted, they can reprint it without paying royalties.

bird called also the bearded vulture, or lammergeier (meaning lamb vulture). This vulture feeds on the carcasses of lambs, swallowing the small bones whole, dropping the large ones from great heights onto rocks to shatter them and get the marrow (*ossifrage* is Latin for broken bones) after other vultures have picked the carcass clean. Aeschylus, the Greek playwright, is said to have been killed by a tortoise dropped on his bald head by a lammergeier; the bird mistook Aeschylus's pate for a white rock.

The second "carrion vulture" is, in the Authorized Version, "the gier eagle." The Hebrew word in the first instance, transliterated, is *peres* and in the second instance *racham*. Does *peres* mean the lammergeier? Does *racham* mean the gier eagle? The fact is, nobody knows exactly how the original Hebrew should be translated (the Dead Sea Scrolls shed no light on the question). Very observant Jews are nervous about eating *any* wild fowl lest it be a forbidden one.

If a Jew observed *all* the "shall not's" of Deuteronomy, he would resist military service for the first year of his marriage (and drop out of business for that year, as well); he would have his rebellious sons stoned to death by all the men of his city; he would cancel all debts owed him by his neighbors every seven years; he would practice many other curious customs. Few of those customs have survived, but dietary laws have lived on in the Kashrut.

Aside from the additional costs of all the extra crockery [4] and utensils required to "keep kosher," kosher food itself tends to be more expensive. An Orthodox mother in Brooklyn recently applied to the State Supreme Court to require New York state to authorize a New York City relief allowance to cover the higher cost of kosher food. She lost her case.

Commercial airlines make special provisions for Orthodox passengers to help them eat without violating their dietary laws. This can

---

[4] In addition to *fleishedig* and *milchedig*, an Orthodox household must have two other sets of dishes for use on Passover, though the everyday glassware may be used if soaked first for seventy-two hours, the water being changed every twenty-four hours. Everyday silverware may be used only if first thoroughly scoured and then immersed in boiling water.

have its amusing aspects, as when a stewardess on Japan Air Lines is confronted with the baffling request of the lady in seat 7C who must have her after-dinner coffee in a paper cup, please, directly from the coffee urn and not from the carafe (which may have been used for milk or cream, forbidden after a meal which included meat).

There are funny sidelights to dietary laws. Jewish planters in Dutch Guiana (now Surinam), South America, in the seventeenth and eighteenth centuries had Negro house slaves, many of whom escaped and established villages up the jungle rivers of the country. A friend who visited one of these Bushnegro villages tells us that inside a native hut, hanging on two separate walls, he saw two separate sets of dishes and cooking utensils, one for meat, one for dairy products. The descendants of the escaped slaves were still observing the dietary law of their ancestors' masters.

Then there is the grim side of dietary laws: the Maccabean revolt (168 B.C.) of the Jews of Judea when their conqueror, the Seleucid King Antiochus, ordered them to sacrifice pigs on their altars; the martyrdom of the aged scribe Eleazar, who submitted to death rather than eat pork; the defiance of the Inquisition's laws against kosher [5] meat by the Marranos of Spain; and similar stories of Jews who defied Russian czars and Nazi Gauleiters rather than abandon their tradition. It is a tradition freighted with emotion and galvanized with determination. It is what keeps the *hălakhah* alive and sacred.

But at least one Jewish cleric has proposed that "we . . . reconsider the traditional laws." As quoted in the *New York Times*, Rabbi Arthur Green, of Cambridge, Massachusetts, said in June, 1969, "I believe that eating should be a sacred act, but I'm not sure that eating beef is more sacred than eating pork. Maybe in our day keeping

---

[5] In the U.S., food acceptable under Jewish dietary laws is called "kosher," meaning fit or proper; kosher foods are often marked with a K, alone or in a circle, which means the food is guaranteed kosher by an endorsing agency. The largest such agency is the Union of Orthodox Jewish Congregations of America, whose mark of endorsement is a U in a circle. Some foods are marked P or *parve*, meaning they are "neutral" and may be eaten with both meat and dairy dishes.

kosher should mean eating natural foods and keeping away from cellophane and TV dinners. Certainly something like the refusal to eat grapes in support of the migrant workers' strike is a religious act."

Rabbi Green's position raises questions of relevancy. To most Americans, kosher laws seem curious and quite irrelevant to modern life. Yet each of us has his own unwritten laws about what may properly be regarded as good food, as do all people.

The Japanese prejudice

Until the American diplomat Townsend Harris went to Japan in 1856, no Japanese ever ate beef. A Portuguese Jesuit, Luis Frois, had remarked that "we are horrified at the killing of human beings but don't mind killing cows or chickens; the Japanese are horrified at seeing animals killed whereas killing people with them is common usage."

Japan's cattle were used only as beasts of burden. The historian Shibusawa says, "People who had cows and oxen regarded them virtually as members of the family." It was as basic as Buddhism.

What changed the Japanese, or at least began the change, was the slaughter of a beef animal by Townsend Harris, sent by Franklin Pierce as the first U.S. consul general to Japan. While waiting to be recognized by the ruler of Japan, Harris spent most of two years in the village of Hamasaki at the southern end of Izu Peninsula, close to the little fishing town of Shimoda where Commodore Perry had landed in 1854 on his second expedition to Japan.

A dyspeptic New York merchant, Harris recorded in his journal for October 30, 1856, that "This P.M. they brought me a leg of *real venison*. It is excellent, tender, juicy and well flavored."

Two weeks later he wrote, "The Japanese brought me this evening the finest specimen of a male golden pheasant I ever saw."

Harris had trouble breeding chickens in face of the inroads by cats, rats, foxes, weasels, hawks, owls and crows. His unusual diet or the tension of waiting played hob with his stomach.

I have brought down my diet to plain boiled rice and a little fowl [he wrote on May 31, 1857]. I tried fish for some days, but that was worse than the fowls. I cannot eat bread, either fresh or of the American biscuit. I have taken any quantity of the blue pill, but all is of no avail. I suffer horribly from acid stomach and am getting leaner day by day. What is very singular is that my appetite is uncommonly good; but, my digestion being so much out of order, my food does not do me much good.

The Japanese promised the homesick Harris *itsigo*, or strawberries, but they turned out to be rather "insipid" raspberries.

Hardest to bear was the lack of familiar kinds of meat. Writing to the fifteen-year-old daughter of a man he had known in Canton and Macao, Harris in November, 1856, wrote,

I am now supplied with Wild Boars [sic] flesh, which animal abounds in the Hills.—The flesh is peculiar; quite different from the Boars flesh of Java, India, or the Straits of Malacca [in his Journal entry of October 22 he had identified the Japanese wild hog as the "baibarossa, or *hog deer* of India and the Indian Archipelago"];—it is very tender, juicy, and of an excellent flavor; the taste is between delicate veal, and the tender-loin of pork:—I am promised a supply of it during the Winter season: In addition to this, I am occasionally furnished with some delicate Venison; fine large Hares, and Golden Pheasants equal to any in the world.—It seems impertinent to note such small affairs, but you must bear in mind that the only animal food used by the Japanese is Fish and Poultry.—There is not a sheep or Goat in all Nippon, and the few Bullocks that are kept are used for burden or the plough only; they are never eaten, No milk can be had,—Pigs are raised by the Dutch at Nagasaki—and some are now kept at Hakodadi for foreigners.

The elders of Shimoda spied on Harris [6] and wrote an eight-

---

[6] A New York City merchant in his early fifties, Harris' Victorian sensibilities were shaken up by Japan's public bath houses, in which both sexes bathe together in the nude. "I cannot account for so indelicate a proceeding on the part of a people so generally correct," he wrote in his journal in late October, 1856. "I am assured, however, that it is not considered as dangerous to the chastity of their females; on the contrary, they urge that this very exposure lessens the desire that owes much of its power to mystery and difficulty."

volume diary of his activities, but neither that diary nor Townsend Harris' journal nor any other document gives any clues to the incident marked by a stone which stands in the temple yard across from the stone commemorating the first raising of the U.S. flag on Japanese soil. The inscription reads:

> This monument
> erected by the butchers of Tokyo in 1931,
> marks the spot on which the first cow in Japan
> was slaughtered for human consumption
> (Eaten by Harris and Heusken)

Heusken was Harris' secretary. The date of the event is not given, but it was 1856. Some sixteen years later, the Emperor Meiji himself ate some beef and the country went on a beef binge. For those who could afford it, beef eating (in the words of one Japanese historian) was "regarded as a sign of advanced state of civilization."

The Japanese dish, *sukiyaki* (pronounced "skee-*yak*-kee") had been introduced by the Portuguese or Dutch in the sixteenth or early seventeenth century,[7] but the pan-broiled meat (beef or chicken) and vegetable (bamboo shoots, watercress or chrysanthemum tops, the ubiquitous bean curd, black Japanese mushrooms, and the yam noodles called "spring rain" in Japan) specialty, now often overdosed with sugar, was something served only to foreigners until the Japanese accepted beef.

Today Japan is America's biggest export customer for meat, though the Japanese are famous for their own Kobe beef (which is not produced in Kobe, but used to be shipped out of that port on the Inland Sea); it comes from cattle fattened on beer and *New York Times* editor Craig Claiborne says it "may be the tastiest and best textured beef in the world." But even costlier is Wadakin or Matsu-

---

[7] Another Japanese idea imported from Europe in the sixteenth century is *tempura*, which is deep-fried fish, vegetables or even fruit. Unlike deep-fried U.S. food, like fritters, *tempura* is fried in a mixture of sesame seed oil and vegetable oil or peanut oil flavored with sesame seeds. Sitting on their straw mats, *tatami*, the Japanese eat thin slices of lotus root, gingko nuts and slivers of eggplant, all fried *tempura* style.

zaka beef, produced in Mie Prefecture, not far from Nagoya and Mt. Fuji; it comes from animals raised individually in dark sheds at the backs of farmers' houses, given hot feed (usually beer mash) in winter and massaged daily to distribute their weight.

The Japanese are by no means big meat eaters. They eat about five times as much fish as we do, per capita, and about forty times as much rice, but only a tenth as much meat.[8]

An extraordinary thing about the acceptance of beef in Japan—at least by affluent Japanese—was that it meant overcoming a distaste for the smell of people who eat meat.

Orientals have a superior perception of smells and tastes (Chapter 9) which applies even to table hardware. Metal forks and spoons may not appear to have any detectible taste to a Westerner, but as Bernard Rudofsky points out in *The Kimono Mind*, when a piece of tinfoil gets in your mouth while eating cheese, "you may perceive its nauseating sweetness. Yet the taste of tinfoil differs from the taste of other metals only in degree." Juxtaposed to chocolate, tinfoil is not sweet, but it has an unsettling flat taste that makes Rudofsky's point just as well.

Chinese and Japanese eating utensils have for countless centuries been of wood, whose organic taste is closer to that of foods. The word "chopsticks" is pidgin English for heavy Chinese eating sticks (*fie-gee* in Cantonese, *kwaidze* in the north); the light Japanese kind are called *hashi*.

Koreans, it would seem, have less discriminating tastes. They use metal eating sticks which look something like knitting needles. Korea's national dish is *kimchi*, shredded cabbage which is pickled and spiced

---

[8] The Japanese also eat a lot more sweet potatoes and radishes than we do; some seventy per cent of Japan's acreage in little market gardens is planted in radishes, especially the large white sweet radish, *daikon;* about ten per cent of her tilled land is used to grow sweet potatoes, *satsuma-imo*. Before 1860, when Japan was still ruled by the Tokugawa shogunate and Tokyo was still called Edo, the island of Kyushu was called *Satsuma*. *Satsuma-imo* means Kyushu potato; in Kyushu the sweet potato is *kara-imo*, or foreign potato. Japan got sweet potatoes from China, though they came originally (Chapter 2) from the Americas. They have been a staple in Japan for centuries and a lifesaver when rice crops are ruined by autumn typhoons, as sometimes happens.

with garlic, stored in huge vats sunk into the ground, and sometimes augmented with bits of shredded fish. Meat is as scarce in Korea as it is everywhere in the Orient.

Eating any animal fat produces butyric acid, which gives the eater a definite odor; we do not notice it, but the Japanese, until they became accustomed to it, definitely did. In the late nineteenth century they called Westerners *"bata-kusai,"* or *"butter-stinkers."* One Japanese wrote, "Westerners have a strong body odor which is quite nauseating. The body odor of the average American or Englishman is undoubtedly the result of a heavy meat diet." Of course only the rich Japanese could afford meat, which may suggest the origin of the term, "stinking rich."

The prejudice works both ways: a friend who frequently visits Japan on business complains that Japanese girls, because of their diet, have an unpleasantly fishy odor.

Prejudices, racial and national, which fester in all parts of the world, not just in the United States, and social discriminations, too, may be rooted more than we suspect in people's aversion to other people's distinctive body and breath odors which stem from distinctive diets. Wurst eaters, cabbage eaters and garlic eaters all have their detractors, and this was certainly a factor in the hostility Anglo-Saxon immigrants to America exhibited toward later immigrants from southern and eastern Europe.

Economic factors were involved too, naturally; nor did the dark fears and suspicions that infect many Americans and affect their acceptance of commercially available foods (Chapter 10) begin with the later immigrations from Europe. They are as old as Salem "witches."

But wurst eaters, cabbage eaters and garlic eaters [9] met with a

---

[9] Someone has called garlic the catsup of intellectuals, but only those who emulate France's Henri IV (see footnote to page 63) eat garlic raw. Members of society considerate to their fellows and to their own digestive tracts use garlic, as in a Provencal or Catalan dish, with subtlety, employing it to season what is cooked but never as something to be eaten, even in shreds, of itself. Salad bowls may be *rubbed* with garlic, but for actual salad components shallots are recommended to satisfy the palate without antagonizing one's companions. This advice has saved friendships, love affairs, marriages and careers.

xenophobia as intense, almost, as that of the Japanese under the shoguns (whom Westerners called tycoons), and with social barriers nearly as high as those which still confront black Americans. Denied opportunity in the Establishment business structure, the later arrivals reacted with understandable hostilities and prejudices of their own, withdrawing into ghettoes, sometimes retaliating against ostracism with criminality, and perpetuating a divisiveness that still pervades American society and reflects itself in borderline paranoid actions even by our national leaders.

Mmm, grasshoppers

Western society abhors the idea of eating insects (though we do not hesitate to eat honey, an insect-manufactured food) and regards insect eating almost as an unnatural act. Arabs, and other Africans and Asians who do eat insects, for their part can scarcely believe Westerners would eat shellfish which, like insects, are invertebrate arthropods. (Put a lobster beside a grasshopper and note the similarity of construction.)

We eat lobsters, crabs and shrimp, but how about land crabs? They are a great delicacy at Las Croabas, in Puerto Rico, but in Florida, where land crabs abound, nobody will touch them. North Americans will evidently eat arthropods, but only if they come out of the water.

St. John the Baptist is supposed to have lived in the wilderness of Judea on "locusts and wild honey" (to quote the Gospel according to Matthew). Some authorities claim these "locusts" were really carob beans (a tree legume, *Ceratoria siliqua*, native to Syria and cultivated in Mediterranean countries since ancient times).

Sometimes called St. John's bread, carob beans served as forage for the cavalry of Wellington in his Peninsula campaign and for Allenby's cavalry in Palestine. The beans are imported into the U.S. to flavor chewing tobacco and dog biscuits, as a chocolate substitute for people who cannot tolerate chocolate, and as a thickener-additive for foods (Appendix).

But long before John the Baptist, fried locusts were a delicacy in ancient Mesopotamia; the Greeks ate roasted grasshoppers; and the ancient Jews, who would eat no shellfish, ate several kinds of insects. Moses named four of them (Leviticus 11:21-22) in his list of animals that the tribes of Israel were permitted to eat. In St. Jerome's Latin translation, these were *locusta*, *bruchus*, *ophimachus* and *attacus*. Naturalists are not sure about the last three (often translated as the bald locust, the cricket and the grasshopper), but the first is clear enough—and it is not carob beans.

The locust is, strictly speaking, a grasshopper (*Schistocerca gregaria*) in its migratory phase. This grasshopper is all too plentiful in the Near East and in parts of Africa; only smaller varieties, less suitable for eating, are found in Western Europe and the eastern parts of North America.[10]

The Greeks were not plagued with locusts, but they did eat cicadas (which Americans sometimes call locusts, though locusts are actually quite a different insect). Aristotle wrote in his *History of Animals* that cicada nymphs tasted best when they first came out of the ground, before they shed their skins. He also admired the taste of adult male cicadas and of females big with eggs. But Plutarch regarded cicadas as sacred and musical; he disapproved of eating them.

Greek historians and geographers referred to grasshopper eaters (*Acridophagi*) living in what is now Ethiopia. Ethiopians still eat grasshoppers and sometimes, because they neglect to remove the legs and wings, suffer severe intestinal obstructions.

Moslems may not eat pork, but locusts are quite permissible. Mohammed is said to have received trays of them as gifts from his wives. Some Moslem theologians maintain that locusts should not be eaten if they have died of cold; others say they may be eaten only if

---

[10] A swarming species of grasshopper in the Rockies were once important in the diets of North American Indian tribes in the area.

the heads are cut off. There is also disagreement as to whether locusts should be classed as land animals or sea animals.

The locust, popular also in Japan, is only one of many insects esteemed as perfectly respectable food. Nice fat crickets are offered for sale in Bangkok at the Sunday market. The Chinese eat the chrysalis of the silkworm.

During the Nigerian-Biafran war, when thousands of Biafrans were dying of starvation, a London group in the summer of 1968 appealed for funds to aid the hungry Biafrans. Their full-page advertisement in the *Manchester Guardian* showed a large winged insect and carried the ironic headline, "Fresh food is now flying in to Biafra."

> Good nourishing stuff it is, too [said the copy].
> Sausage-flies are full of protein.
> So Biafran mothers feed them to their children. It's the only way to keep them alive.
> And if they can't stomach sausage-flies, there are always rats and lizards.
> But sausage-flies are the easiest meat. At night they flock to any bright light they see.
> Which is more than can be said of relief planes.

It was an effective ad for a just cause, but its strength lay in the shock with which its readers must have regarded eating insects. African readers would not have been so shocked.

Most Westerners shy away from eating insects or their larvae. Rugged Australians eat the Bardi worm, a fat slug found in trees, but this is atypical.

In Malawi and Rhodesia, however, sun-dried termites are such a delicacy they fetch seven cents a tablespoonful. The *Macrotermes goliath* termites are potentially a rich source of protein for African diets and some research is being conducted toward creating a food staple out of the "white ants," which swarm in mounds as big as twelve feet high and thirty feet in diameter.

African pygmies eat ants (and caterpillars) both dried and roasted.

They also eat roasted monkey and field mouse, boiled elephant foot, crocodile meat, various kinds of beetles, grasshoppers and lizards.

Ants are a favorite of the Jivaro headhunters of Peru and Ecuador, who eat their parasol ants raw. The Jicaques of Central America stew their ants. Amazon River and Honduran Indians pull off the ants' heads, wings and legs and eat the bodies, toasted.

The ancient and eternal cockroach is a gourmet delight in parts of China, Thailand, among Australian aborigines and in French Guiana.

But the only insects in American supermarkets, at least the only kinds offered for sale, are fried grasshoppers, Japanese ants, bees and silkworm pupae, and Mexican maguey worms (the larva of a butterfly, *Aegiale hersperialis* [11]). All are sold in cans, ostensibly as cocktail snacks but basically for their entertainment value. Americans' propensity for "impulse purchases" is prodigious.

Insects are only the beginning of what most "civilized" people refuse to eat. And the reasons for refusal are not based on religious admonitions.

Roast saddle of horse

One flesh forbidden by Mosaic law was horse meat. The Tartars have always eaten horse meat; so have the gauchos of South America, and so, for many years, have the French. But most Indo-Europeans have always tabooed horse meat: the Romans would not touch it, nor would the Scandinavians or the English.

The poet-scholar Robert Graves has related the taboo to a primitive sacramental October "horse feast," which he claims was the greatest holiday of the year for Saxons, Danes and, earlier, Romans. Graves' account is confusing; he says horse meat was taboo even to the horse feast participants except on the occasion of the feast, which

---

[11] The larva bores in the maguey, or agave, plant. Maguey sap is the source of *pulque*, Mexico's national drink; maguey spikes are used to flavor Mexican *Barbacoa de Carnero* (barbecued mutton or lamb).

the Church in later ages forbade as idolatrous (though they turned other pagan festivals into religious holidays like Christmas and Easter). From that point on the Graves' explanation is clearer, and is as good as any. The ban on the horse feast made horseflesh taboo. Teutonic tribes saw nothing wrong with eating horse meat until they were converted to Christianity. But all through the Middle Ages and the Renaissance, accounts of sieges always reported that people ate rats or even leather jerkins before they would slaughter their horses.

"The Danish authorities," says Graves, "even made forcible eating of horseflesh a deterrent to crime: by 1860, no other meat could be provided for felons in gaol."

Horse steaks were available ration-free at special horse meat shops in England during both world wars, but the English gave them a wide berth. Americans have for the most part followed in the Anglo-Saxon tradition. We have used horse meat largely for dog food, though it has been a traditional fixture on the Harvard Faculty Club menu since World War II.

The French taste for horse meat is a story in itself. Never mind the age of the horse slaughtered, never mind whether it is a colt, a filly, a stallion, a mare or a gelding, *cheval* has long been a staple in Paris, despite police ordinances in the eighteenth and nineteenth centuries forbidding its sale.

Though plenty of Frenchmen ate horse meat during the Revolution and the Reign of Terror, sale of the meat was prohibited in 1803 and again in 1811. Restrictions were removed in about 1830 after Parmentier, the potato promoter, and others published reports of an event that had occurred during the Napoleonic wars. The event concerned a certain Baron Larrey. In 1807, after the Battle of Eylau, the Baron had been cut off with his men and isolated on the isle of Lobau. To feed his wounded troops, the Baron made soup out of horse meat, using the breastplates of the dismounted cavalry as cooking pots and seasoning the soup with gunpowder in the absence of salt.

Horse meat grew steadily in consumer acceptance. The rising demand, combined with the increasing scarcity of horses, imported largely from West Germany, forced the price of horse meat above the price of beef. Horse meat had originally been much cheaper than beef, and in fact had carried a stigma of poverty, but by the summer of 1967 one could pay $1.20 a pound for chopped horse meat in a leading horse butcher shop while a nearby *boucherie* was selling chopped beef for ninety cents a pound. Horse filet could run $2.30 a pound.

Then, in the fall of 1967, something happened to drop the demand—and the price. Girls at a school in southern France became ill with salmonellosis, a form of food infection. The contamination was traced to chopped horse meat the girls had eaten at lunch. One of the girls died, and on the same day three girls in a Paris suburb became ill after eating chopped horse meat. The publicity following these events dropped horse meat consumption a drastic sixty to eighty per cent. In 1965, the average Frenchman ate 3.52 pounds of horse meat— almost as much horse meat as the average American ate of lamb or veal. Recent figures are not available.

Until the 1967 episodes, the municipal slaughterhouse in Vaugirard, near Montparnasse, had killed fifty horses a day for the horse meat Parisians bought at their *boucheries de cheval* and ate in steaks, roasts, mixed with pork or beef in sausages, but most commonly as chopped meat simply eaten raw with onions or other seasonings, or perhaps heated briefly (the French eat almost all meat "bloody" or *bleu*, and what an American calls "rare" is well-done by French standards).

It is forbidden by French law for a butcher to stock chopped meat; he must chop it fresh for each customer. The suburban butcher who sold the tainted horse meat confessed he had mixed old scraps with fresh-chopped meat, and he was put in jail. But while salmonella bacteria can occur in many different foods (poultry products are frequent sources of salmonella gastroenteritis), horse meat got a black eye in 1967 and it may take years for it to regain its position in the minds and eating habits of French consumers.

"Brain food," R months, Dr. Dolittle and elephant trunk

Misconceptions about food (Chapter 10) can be so firmly ingrained that they affect patterns of eating just as strongly as do any legitimate truths.

Many people, as we noted in Chapter 5, staunchly believe that fish is "brain food" and will actually help develop intelligence or at the least clear thinking.

The idea that oysters are edible only in months whose names include the letter "R" is just as soundly based, yet except on the Pacific Coast, where oysters are sold all year round, the bivalve mollusks are hardly to be found in most U.S. stores from May through August.

It is true that in England, where the round oyster, *Ostrea edulis*, keeps its young within its mantle cavity for a considerable period, oysters taste gritty during the summer months. But the American oyster, *Crassostrea virginica*, discharges its eggs directly into the water, the larvae attaching themselves to debris on the bottom.

The "R"-month tradition has had the positive effect of protecting oysters during the spawning months, and it may be as Roy de Groot says that oysters do not taste their best until October (the French eat oysters only from October through March), but there is no truth in the fancy that oysters are harmful in May, June, July or August.

Another oyster myth, that they contribute to male virility (a subject we will examine further in Chapter 10), is so well established that a waitress in Minneapolis once stared in astonishment when my female dinner companion ordered oysters as an appetizer. She said she had never heard a *woman* order oysters before. Calf testicles are served on Western U.S. tables under the name "mountain oysters" or "prairie oysters," though the latter term is also used to mean those mixtures of raw eggs, salt, pepper and Worcestershire sauce employed as hangover remedies.

To clear-thinking unsentimental people, taboos and religious injunctions against various foods seem about as scientific as the common run of hangover remedies. They are mostly regarded as unworthy of enlightened intelligence—until, that is, we run into the strongest food taboo of all.

Just short of this "ultimate taboo" is what might be called the "Dr. Dolittle taboo." The hero of the Hugh Lofting stories was a vegetarian because he could not bear the idea of eating the flesh of his friends the animals.

This is not entirely a fictional proscription. Someone has said, "Man is the only animal that eats its friends"; but early agrarian societies tended to avoid eating the flesh of the plow cattle which were their working companions, and this may lie behind India's sacred cows and the age-old avoidance of beef in Japan.

Most Westerners shudder at the thought of eating dog or cat meat probably because of associations with a beloved pet. Such feelings ran high in December, 1871, when animals in the Paris zoo were slaughtered for food during the siege of the city in the Franco-Prussian War. The animals were not just animals. They had names. Still, when firing squads dispatched the dear familiar elephants Castor and Pollux, butchers sold cuts of elephant trunk at forty francs a pound and some unsentimental Parisians ate elephant with béarnaise sauce. Others ate spaniel, or rat, all no doubt cooked in rich sauces. Horse meat, previously eaten only by poor Parisians, suddenly became socially acceptable.

The ancient Phoenicians had no squeamishness about eating man's best friend. Roast puppy was, in fact, a delicacy of classical antiquity. Dogs are still raised for food in many parts of the world [12], as they

---

[12] The sale and consumption of dog meat is illegal in Hong Kong, but when restaurants and food stalls put out red-lettered signs announcing the arrival of fresh supplies of "goat meat" or "special beef," the meat is usually dog, which is especially popular, along with snake meat, in the fall and winter. There are few arrests or prosecutions, despite the efforts of the Hong Kong Society for the Prevention of Cruelty to Animals, whose officers are British. Britons do not eat dog, but Hong Kong's Chinese love it.

were by the Indians Columbus found in the Caribbean and by the Tahitians Captain Cook encountered in the Pacific. Alan Moorehead tells us that "Cook and his companions fell back a little when they were offered roast dog for dinner one day. Yet when they tried it they found it delicious, no doubt because the animals [unlike dogs in Europe or England] were vegetarians. There were few, Cook wrote, 'but allowed that a South Sea dog was next to an English lamb.' "

Perhaps, as Carl Sauer has suggested, our Western taboo against dog meat is related to the cultural taboo against pork. Because their superior senses of hearing and smell helped early man hunt for meat, dogs were the earliest domesticated animals. In time, says Sauer, the dog "came to be an object of sacrifice, and of ceremonial consumption." In later ages the religious connotations were forgotten and "the dog became a food item, especially at feasts." But where dogs were venerated in one culture, they became "objects of antipathy in neighbor cultures of other ceremonial and religious orientations" just as had pigs.

Dogs and other animals have always, or at least in modern times, been most venerated by the English, who baited bears in Elizabethan days but are now famous for their soft-hearted emotional displays toward our animal friends. Anthony Lewis, in the *New York Times*, suggests the possibility that the British upper class, which "can be the most controlled people in the world," may "in expressing their emotion toward dogs and cats and horses, . . . [be] letting go what they so often suppress in human relationships. That is, they come right out and admit they have feelings."

Certainly the English who followed Cook to Tahiti were somewhat obtuse about the feelings and best interests of the Tahitians, however much they may have balked at eating dog. The herbivorous dog of the island was bred out of existence by the larger species Europeans introduced; it was extinct within a few decades of Cook's visit.

But the practice of eating dog meat is no more extinct than that of eating snake meat or insects, or that of *not* eating pork or shellfish.

De gustibus, said the Romans, *non disputandum*.

For everyone in the world who will not eat dog meat, or snake meat, there is someone who will not eat beef, or pork. And for everyone who will not eat beef or pork, there is someone who will not eat chicken. Many African tribes prohibit their women from eating poultry; some tribes do not let anyone at all eat it, others permit only members of certain ages or social status to eat bird meat.

Roast loin of man

Early man had no hesitation about eating anything edible, including the flesh of human friends and foes.

Fossil bones believed to be the oldest remains of man ever found in the Western Hemisphere were unearthed by a bulldozer in the State of Washington in the spring of 1968. The bones, those of a young pre-Indian nomad, date back between 11,500 and 13,000 years. They indicate the man's enemies or fellow tribesmen split his bones to eat the marrow, just as they did with animal bones.

In the Caucasus Mountains of Europe in the fifth century B.C., while Rome and Greece and the Middle East had quite advanced civilizations, the Massagetae ate their grandfathers. Eating grandpa, it was thought, made him immortal: he lived on in the persons of descendants who ate the old man's roasted flesh. If a man died of disease and could not be eaten, the family was disgraced.

Eating human brains, according to primitive ideas of homeopathic magic, gave a man wisdom. Human liver gave him courage, though it had to be eaten raw lest the magic be cooked away (as some vitamins are destroyed by cooking). African tribesmen even now eat the livers of their human victims, though otherwise they are not cannibals.

The Stoics of the third century B.C., as Montaigne tells us in his essay "On Cannibals" (1580):

did indeed consider that there was no harm in using a dead body for any need of our own, or in consuming it either, as our own ancestors did during Caesar's blockade of the city of Alesia, when they resolved to relieve the hunger of the siege with the bodies of the old men, women, and other persons who were incapable of fighting.

When Hannibal, during the Punic Wars of the third century B.C., besieged the Spanish town of Sagunto in Valencia, the people turned cannibal and ate their own dead rather than surrender. (When defeat became inevitable, they set fire to their town and committed mass suicide.)

Early Vikings drank the blood of their foes at victory feasts. The toast *Skol!* may derive from the human skull used as a drinking vessel. When Scandinavians became more civilized and human skulls hard to come by, drinking horns took their place.

The Crusaders, a few centuries later, were known on occasion to have cooked and eaten the flesh of their infidel victims. The meat, in the words of one chronicle, tasted "better than spiced peacock."

In the seventeenth century, on the Upper Congo in Africa, men, women and children were blatantly bought and sold, not only as slave labor for the Americas but as potential food.

In the eighteenth century, human meat was reported in butcher stalls along with animal flesh on the South Pacific island of New Britain, while savages in the Solomon Island group fattened women for their feasts. Human eyes, cheeks and brains were considered especially choice. So were the rump and calf; the rest was tossed to the dogs. (In New Guinea even now there is no large wild game and only a few domestic pigs; meat, except for human meat, is hard to come by and cannibalism, though supposedly suppressed by the government and by white missionaries, is still practiced. Two missionaries were reportedly cooked and eaten in 1968 by a tribe in West Irian, formerly western New Guinea, an area where eighty-five per cent of the local diet is supplied by sago, a starch pounded out of the insides of trunks of various palm trees and made into a kind of pudding.)

Commodore Perry, who opened Japan to commerce with the West, encountered cannibalism in Sumatra and observed its niceties: palms of hands and soles of feet were considered tidbits; V.I.P.'s were served ears, seasoned with lime juice, salt and pepper.

Neighboring Java was no different. Sir Thomas Raffles, namesake of the famous Raffles Hotel in Singapore, wrote as British Governor of Java in 1820 that "the Bataks are not a bad people, and I still think so, not withstanding they eat one another, and relish the flesh of a man better than that of an ox or pig. You must merely consider that I am giving you an account of a novel state of society. The Bataks are not savages, for they write and read, and think full as much, and more than those who are brought up at our Lancastrian and National Schools."

By the end of the nineteenth century, seventy to eighty years after Raffles made this observation, some cannibals were complaining that human flesh had lost its savor. One said that tobacco smoking had ruined the flavor of "long pig," as the Maori and Polynesians called cooked man; men raised on tropical plants, it was claimed, tasted better than meat-fed men. A Fiji Islander is said to have declared that white flesh was tough, and European sailors so tough they were not worth the trouble of cutting up.

But Pierre Loti, the French novelist who died in 1923, said a Tahitian had told him, "The white man, when well roasted, tastes like a ripe banana."

The word "cannibalism," as we saw in Chapter 2, came from the Carib Indians found in the New World. In their wars with the Arawaks, the Caribs took captives and broke their legs so they could not escape; in due course, the captives were eaten. Some wars were evidently fought for the express purpose of taking edible captives.

Cannibal traditions were still strong in eighteenth-century Brazil. A native chief there said to an explorer, "When I have slain an enemy, it is surely better to eat him than to let him go to waste. You whites are too dainty."

In the "Starving Times" from the fall of 1609 to the spring of 1610 in Jamestown, Virginia, Indian arrows, sickness and starvation reduced the colonists' population from 500 to perhaps sixty—and may have reduced the people to cannibalism, though an account of a man who killed his wife, "powdered [salted] her, and had eaten part of her before it was known," was denied as a fabrication by Sir Thomas Gates.

Better documented is the classic instance of cannibalism in American history, the case of the Donner Party, ten men and five women snow-bound in the Sierra Nevada en route to California in the winter of 1846–47. After four days without food (in what is still called Donner Pass), someone suggested drawing lots, the loser to be killed in order to keep the others alive. The group balked at that. But then a Mexican in the party died. And a bad snowstorm killed four more men. When the snow let up, the five men and five women who remained alive roasted some of the flesh of their dead companions. When that meat gave out, there was talk of killing the two Indians with the party, but they escaped. A couple of days later one of the starving whites found the Indians close to death and shot them. Their flesh kept the group alive. In the end, all five women but only two men reached a settlement at the edge of the Sacramento Valley, a little over a month after they had been trapped by the snow.

The explorer Vilhjalmur Stefansson pooh-poohed most stories of cannibalism. He drew a line of distinction between killing people to eat them and killing them for unsocial conduct and then eating them.

Bradford Angier, the outdoorsman who quotes Stefansson on the subjects of cannibalism, himself raises the cool scientific point that "animal proteins are desirable in direct ration with their chemical similarity to the eating organism, [thus] for the fullest and easiest assimilation of flesh materials, human meat can hardly be equaled." He does not recommend cannibalism; he merely cites the abstract point that objections to it are "psychological and sociological."

Some of the darker pages of history suggest that Angier and Stefansson are too detached. When plagues of locusts and mice wiped out supplies of food in the Sudan in 1889, emaciated bodies lined the streets and floated down the Nile. People in Omdurman became so desperate they ate young children, though possibly not their own. Certainly there was cannibalism in Leningrad in the winter of 1941–42, when 3 million people were besieged by the Nazis. There may even have been some commercial trade in human flesh, though no real proof of that exists.

In the capital of one African country, the law at last report still requires that meat in the public markets be sold with some of the hide attached as evidence that the meat is not human flesh.[13]

The taboo against eating people has always been a powerful one in most cultures. Extremes of hunger, however, can drive people to extraordinary behavior.

Pakistan's Ayub Khan, when he was president in 1964, is supposed to have said sadly, "In ten years' time, human beings will eat human beings in Pakistan."

His country has since then come closer to balancing its food-population equation; Pakistan's grain production, thanks to good weather and to new strains of dwarf wheat, increased by twenty-three per cent in 1968 over the year before. The country's population, however, keeps growing, especially in crowded East Pakistan where rice fields were ruined in disastrous floods in the summer of 1968. That raises a grim question as to which will die out first—the 3000-year-old taboo against eating cattle meat in neighboring India, or the taboo against cannibalism in Pakistan.

Many vegetarians regard all meat eating as a kind of cannibalism. Moral outrage of this sort has many degrees. Most food taboos cannot stand the light of unemotional, objective analysis. But the almost universal horror of true cannibalism makes the smaller horrors of *traif* (non-kosher food) and similar off-limit foods less difficult to comprehend.

What people regard as good to eat is determined less by individual experience than by traditions and cultural institutions. The decisive

---

[13] All countries have had deceptive practices in food merchandising. In Spanish markets, rabbit is often displayed with the furry paws intact to prove the meat is not cat. In the nineteenth century, Spanish inns were suspected of passing cat off as rabbit; the phrase *vender gato por liebre*, to sell a cat for a hare, is still a common term for deception in Spain.

influences and prejudices often have no more basis in fact than the suspicions which for so long kept people from eating potatoes and tomatoes.

As we have seen, many food restrictions are rooted in religious laws. Jewish dietary rules are often maintained as a defense against assimilation more than for any other reason (though their grip on the unconscious is sometimes so strong that an Orthodox Jew may become physically ill upon discovering that he has eaten *traif*). The Roman Catholic rule against eating meat on Fridays, on the other hand, has been rather blithely abandoned, at least officially. (Many Catholics— and non-Catholics, too—continue to eat fish on Fridays for sentimental reasons, or from habit, or just because supermarket fish is freshest on Fridays.)

In time, perhaps, many ideas of what constitutes proper food may undergo radical change.

What, for example, is wrong with eating daisies?

Nature's wild cupboard

In our last chapter we discussed the many "weeds" which are perfectly edible and even nutritious.

A professor at Cornell University, E. Laurence Palmer, has written that the young green leaves of daisy plants are very good to nibble in early summer, though "as the season advances they lose some of their desirable qualities."

If eating daisy leaves sounds peculiar, how about roses? Not the flowers (though they have been fricasseed and candied by older societies and candied rose petals are still a specialty of Toulouse, France) but the rose hips, those swellings at the ends of the stems which reach up and enclose the seeds. Usually green in summer, rose hips turn orange and finally bright red in fall, which is when they can be gathered for food, though be careful not to take any from bushes treated with systemic pesticides or fungicides.

In England during World War II, seeds from rose hips were

pressed into vitamin C pills and sold in drugstores. Collecting wild rose hips as a source of ascorbic acid (vitamin C) is a big industry in the Soviet Union, which has almost no citrus trees and suffers a shortage of the vitamin. A cup of pared rose hips may contain as much vitamin C as ten or twelve *dozen* oranges. Rose hip jam—popular in some U.S. communities—is made without cooking the rose hips, so none of the volatile vitamin is lost.

Foraging for wild foods Euell Gibbons style (Chapter 6) can be good sport. Living off the land can also become a vital necessity, as it has been in cases where people have survived airplane crashes in desolate places, or have landed on deserted islands, or have simply gotten lost and had to find food in order to remain alive.

American soldiers being trained to fight in Viet Nam have been given a five-day "preparation for Overseas Replacement course" which includes a film on jungle survival. The film shows infantry and field artillery personnel how to kill a snake, clean it, slice it into chunks and mix it with roots of water lilies to make a stew.

Smooth caterpillars and grasshoppers (minus their wings and legs) are not only perfectly edible, they are good sources of protein, the G.I.'s are told; but not fuzzy caterpillars—their fuzz can be as rough on a man's stomach as fiberglass splinters. (So can bamboo shoots, eaten fresh in the Far East, if they are not properly prepared.)

Air Force men are given similar training, usually more complex and extensive since a flyer may have to survive in widely varying terrain in the event of an emergency landing.

History is full of cases of people who have had to live off the country; and grim necessity has sometimes introduced valuable new ideas to our larders.

Fish and birds' eggs are obvious sources of survival food. So are such slow-moving animals as porcupines, fairly easily caught without traps or weapons.

Mushrooms take savvy

Since 1945, the word "mushroom" has been linked with the cloud of the atomic explosions that destroyed Hiroshima and Nagasaki. Mushrooms themselves have always been under a cloud of suspicion. The doubts are well-founded. A few pounds of muscaria, the alkaloid poison found in some of the Amanita mushrooms, could kill as many people as any nuclear explosion.

There are about 38,000 kinds of mushrooms in the world, roughly 1000 of them in the U.S. The nutritional value of any of them is dubious, though some are delicious. A few are unquestionably poisonous; they will cause anything from an upset stomach to violent death, and not even modern science has any antidote for certain fungus toxins.

Some mushrooms are classified as poisonous when their real effect is hallucinogenic. The classification is justified, perhaps; eating such mushrooms may be as devastating as taking a trip with LSD (which is itself based on a fungus: *Claviceps purpurea*, or ergot). Not enough is known to make a judgment on the safety of such mushrooms. But while "poisonous" in one sense, they hardly have the appalling effects of some Amanita varieties.

In ancient Egypt, mushrooms were reserved as food for the pharaohs. In later ages, eating the delicate fungi has been associated with royalty and with aristocrats, common people needing more nutritious fare (since nearly ninety-one per cent of a mushroom's flesh is water, its food value is thought to be low—there is little research on the subject; but nutrition is not everything). Thus the incidence of death by mistaken mushroom poisoning has throughout history been notably high among the rich and noble.

In the essay, "Centaur's Food," Robert Graves has speculated that various hallucinogenic mushrooms were the legendary "ambrosia" of the gods, forbidden to mortals for their own good; that the feasts of

Dionysus, divine half-brother of Alexander the Great, were mush-room orgies rather than drinking bouts; and that Alexander, with his phalanx and his ships and cavalry, could have destroyed the early Romans and created a Greek empire if he had not tried to outdo Dionysus. Others have suggested that the "Soma" of the Hindu *Rig-Veda* (Chapter 1) was the fly agaric mushroom, *Amanita muscaria*.

Whether or not Alexander died of mushroom poisoning (he may simply have drunk himself to death or been a victim of lead poison-ing), the Greek dramatist Euripides lost his wife, daughter and two sons to the deadly Amanita. The Roman emperors Tiberius and Claudius are both said to have succumbed to mushroom poisoning, though other factors (a poisoned feather in the case of Claudius, suf-focation in Tiberius' case) may also have been involved.

Alexander I, perhaps the greatest of Russian gastronomes (he employed the founder of *la grande cuisine*, the French chef Carème), definitely died after eating poisonous mushrooms in 1825.

Pope Clement VII and France's Charles V were also prominent mushroom victims.

And as millions of children know, the royal father of Babar, king of the elephants in the now classic picture books of Jean de Brunhoff, turned green and died after dining on poisonous mushrooms.

As for hallucinogenic mushrooms, the ancient Aztecs called more than twenty different mushroom varieties *Teonanactl*, meaning "food of the gods," which fits Graves' theory neatly. A cult of divine hallucinogenic mushroom eaters has been traced back to about 1500 B.C. Some unusual indole alkaloids, notably psilocybine, used in psychological experiments, have been isolated from mushrooms like the *Psilocybe mexicana*. Though driven into hiding by early Christian ecclesiastics, the mushroom cultists still survive in remote mountain areas, especially in Oaxaca.

As food, mushrooms have been cultivated only since the seven-teenth century. They are feared and avoided in their wild state by most Americans (though we now lead the world in producing commer-cially-grown mushrooms) and are usually mishandled when they get to the kitchen.

Europeans tend to be less timid than Americans about wild mushrooms. Whole villages empty out when the *cèpe* (as the French call *Boletus edulis;* Germans call it *Stein-Pilz* or *Herren-Pilz*) is reported in the woods. Restaurants in Europe regularly offer a large variety of mushrooms (more than twenty different varieties are cultivated in France). Street vendors in Java sell a *Volvaria* mushroom grown on rice straw. Mexican markets display many different varieties, including a black fungus that grows on ears of corn during the rainy season.

Here in the U.S. it is virtually impossible to buy fresh anything but the field mushroom, *Agericus campestris*, *Agericus bisporus* or *Agericus hortensis*, small versions of which are sold as button mushrooms. They can be grown in anyone's cool basement from commercially pre-packaged materials based on a culture method developed in Louis XIV's France and described by de Tournefort in a publication of 1707. The French were growing champignons in quarries around Paris by about 1800 and the English, by the end of the nineteenth century, were exporting mushroom spawn to Germany, Denmark, Australia and the U.S., where the spores were planted in stable-manure compost underground.

Some brown *Agericus* varieties are sold in California markets, but white mushrooms have dominated the U.S. industry since 1926, when Lewis Downing, in Downington, Pennsylvania, found some mild-tasting albino "sports" among his cream-colored fungi; he was able to propagate them and U.S. mushroom sales mushroomed. The commercial industry for years centered in Kennett Square, Pennsylvania, not far from Downington, southwest of Philadelphia, but the biggest commercial mushroom-growing area now is in Pennsylvania's Butler and Armstrong counties, northeast of Pittsburgh, where millions of pounds are grown in the cool (56° F.), dark galleries and corridors of abandoned limestone mines.

But the *Agericus* mushrooms, while good varieties, hardly compare by gastronomic standards with the morel and some of the other more strongly-flavored mushrooms found only in the wild. And while commercial mushrooms are sold the year round, they are not always available in spring and summer.

There is no single guide to wild mushrooms that anyone can recommend, any more than there is one good cookbook. Some guides are better in certain respects, other guides in different respects.

Mycologists, as mushroom hunters are called, suggest the morel, the sulphur polypore, the puffball and the shaggymane as four varieties every amateur woodsman should know and be able to identify, though there are actually some fifty mushrooms that may be eaten with perfect safety, and often with perfect delight.

Clyde Christensen has called the above-named varieties the "foolproof four," though it is always well to have an experienced mushroom hunter along when hunting even these.

The morel, which is occasionally listed fresh on the menu of some elegant U.S. restaurants, appears only for a brief two-week period, any time from February in the South up through late May in the northern states. The morel is not rare, but it is elusive, often not appearing in the same place two years in a row.

Georg Borgstrom has written in *The Hungry Planet* that "factory production of morels has been tested and is technically feasible," but most sources say they cannot be grown commercially or even as a private hobby. The threadlike growths, or hyphae, can be collected in a culture bed, but nobody knows how to make them develop into fruiting bodies. Until somebody finds a way, we have to go out and find the morel—and we have to go at the right time. The morel is a small mushroom with an unmistakable pitted and ridged spongey cap surface, reminiscent of brain coral. It is never more than six inches tall and sometimes only two. It varies in color from tan to a rich brown and it is shaped very much like a pine cone. (There is a so-called "false morel," but its shape is different; with the help of a few field guides, there should not be much confusion.) The best way to prepare morels is to sauté them in butter. But first find the morel: it may be easy to identify, but it is damned hard to find.

Even easier to identify is the big puffball, which appears in the summer and autumn in open fields. The puffball looks like a round white to brownish ball which narrows toward its base; its stem is practically invisible. The flesh, when it is sliced open, is firm and white in its immature stage (when it is old it is full of brown powder that emits in puffs when squeezed). Puffballs, young and fresh, can be eaten in puffball steaks, breaded puffball cutlets, raw sliced puffball salad or creamed purée of puffball soup.

Another summer and fall mushroom is the sulphur polypore, or chicken mushroom, which the uninitiated probably would not touch. A luridly sulphurous orange or yellow, polypores do not look like any common mushrooms. They grow in rows of fan-shaped shelves out of the sides of trees or dead logs. A row can be several feet long and one series of shelves can yield six pounds of meat, which will have the texture and taste of bland breast of chicken. It can be seasoned and then fried, baked or stewed; it is also good as polypore fricassee, polypore soup or polypore croquettes.

Most fleeting of the "foolproof four" is the shaggymane, which must be eaten almost as soon as it is picked. The cap dissolves into an inky black fluid within a few hours after the shaggymane reaches maturity; just before then, the cap looks like the bearskin hat of a guardsman, except white instead of black. It is usually from four to six inches tall, though it can be taller. The usual way to prepare it is to steam it for five minutes, adding cream or melted butter, or baking it with a mild cheese sauce.

Experienced mycologists and mycophogists (mushroom eaters), who stick to Latin names to avoid any confusion, sniff at Christensen's limited list, tend to scorn the puffball, and avidly collect *Armillaria mellea* (honey mushrooms), *Collybria velutipes, Boletus edulis, Coprinus atramentarius,* chanterelles, *Clitopilus abortivus, Pholiota squarrosoides, Tricholoma sejunctum, Hydnum caput-ursi, Hydnum repandum, Pleurotus serotinus, Hygrophorus russula,* various *Laccaria* varieties, *Hypholoma incertum, Hypholoma perplexum* and *Amanita caesarea.*

They recognize and positively identify all these by their caps, stems, rings, veils, gills, spores and teeth, but the names "Uncertain Hypholoma" and "Perplexing Hypholoma" and the fact that the Caesar's mushroom is edible while other *Amanitas* can kill you, suggest the vital importance of expertise in picking mushrooms. And even the "experts" are inclined toward cautious hesitation. The agile, indefatigable Guy Nearing, a Ramsey, New Jersey, rhododendron breeder who often leads the New York Mycological Society on its forays, says, "It's the 'experts' who die of poisoning." Just turned eighty, Mr. Nearing takes no chances.

Endless legends and myths have grown up about the mushroom and its "supernatural" origins (in the stories of ancient India, Greece, Rome and Mexico, mushrooms—often in "fairy rings"—sprang up from a bolt of lightning). Mushrooms were thought to have magical powers. Alice in Wonderland shrank when she nibbled one side of a mushroom, grew bigger when she took a bite from the other side.

Mushrooms change color so often as they mature, are called by so many names and come in so many subtle variations, it is no wonder people steer clear of them. Some of the fears, however, are misplaced. The French call *Craterellus cornucopioides*, an inconspicuous dark brown or violet trumpet-shaped mushroom, the *trompette de mort* (trumpet of death), though there is nothing the least deadly or even sick-making about it; it is, in fact, delicious and much sought after.

And while the fly agaric, *Amanita muscaria*, can be fatal if eaten in quantity, some tribes in northeastern Siberia are still said to eat it for its hallucinogenic effects. The modern users urinate into a pot after digesting the mushrooms and drink the pot's filtered but intoxicating contents to whoop it up at weddings and other festive occasions.

But there is no question about the poisonous properties of some mushrooms, especially some of the *Amanita* varieties, though they are not the only killer fungi. While *Paneolus* species and others may lead to a bad trip of the LSD variety, the *Amanita verna* (which is pure white and sometimes called the "Angel of Death" or "Destroying Angel"), the "Death Cup" (*Amanita phalloides*) whose cap may be any color from oyster white to ochre-brown to smokey-olive, and possibly *Pholiota autumnalis* and *Hygrophorus conicus* can kill you as dead as arsenic or cyanide.

Muscaria poisoning, also frequently mortal, can result from eating *Amanita muscaria, Amanita pantherina,* some of the Inocybes and *Clitocybe illudens.*

The *Amanitas* are agarics and used to include *Aminitopsis* mushrooms, which are not poisonous, and still include *Amanitopsis vaginata,* which is eminently edible, though nobody eats them because they look too much like the *Amanitas.*

Amanita mushrooms may range in color from a soft delicate green to a cheerful orange, from a creamy white to a flaming red spotted with white dots. Their poison cannot be destroyed by cooking, freezing or drying. One mouthful can produce agony and death, though the effects may not occur until after the victim has complimented the chef and even enjoyed a good night's sleep. There is no antidote [14] for the poison in the doctor's little black bag.

Lucy Kavaler in her book *Mushrooms, Molds and Miracles* describes the grisly fate that may await the *Amanita* eater:

> Then, usually about ten to twelve hours later, comes the seizure of violent cramps, nausea, diarrhea, convulsions, intense thirst and delirium. Seizures are interspersed with periods of prostration during which the victim's eyes are sunken and staring, his skin tight and dry and his nose pinched. This appearance is typical of all such cases of poisoning.
>
> Several years ago workmen were moving a group of early fifteenth-century mummies from a medieval cemetery in France to a new resting place. The men crossed themselves and muttered to one another with horror about the expression of unendurable pain on the faces of one family of seven. Doctors came to look and diagnosed the cause of death: the dread Death Cap [more correctly called Death Cup] had done its work all those hundreds of

---

[14] The medical center of each Department of France is required by law to have a supply of an anti-phallinic serum, but U.S. doctors doubt its efficacy and it is rarely available here. Atropine injections are used for muscaria poisoning, which is somewhat less deadly than the phallin toxin, but atropine is not an antidote.

years ago and left its record of suffering. Even today, with the best of medical care, the chances of survival are not much better than even. An antitoxin produced by the Pasteur Institute in Paris is helpful [see footnote 14], if it can be given in time. Aside from this, little can be done besides relieving the pain and injecting glucose to restore the sugar level in the blood, sharply lowered by the poisoning. Death if it comes, occurs within five to ten days, welcomed by the despairing victim.

Poisonous mushrooms used to be called "toadstools," but this dates back to a time when people thought they could tell the safe mushrooms from the poisonous varieties by methods now known to be old wives' tales.

Poisonous mushrooms may or may not tarnish silverware, *do not* turn dark in a salt-water solution, *do not* turn milky in vinegar. And whether a mushroom is easy or hard to peel has nothing to do with whether or not it is poisonous.

Experts frown on peeling mushrooms, anyway, and discourage soaking them. They do not even recommend thorough washing. If the fungi seem very dirty, give them a quick rinse in cold water and dry them immediately; otherwise just wipe them with a damp cloth. To store mushrooms, pack them loosely, unwashed, in an uncovered plastic container; they can keep for a full week in the refrigerator. Or dry them and then, months later, soak them in water and they will be as good as fresh, or almost. Several New York City firms sell dried mushrooms, mostly *Boleti*, chanterelles and parasol mushrooms (*Lepiota procera*), imported largely from eastern Europe and Russia.

Euell Gibbons, on a foraging trip with *The New Yorker* magazine writer John McPhee, found some oyster mushrooms, *Pleurotus ostreatus*. "When they steam," he said, "they smell like oysters."

"How do you tell the difference between an edible mushroom and a poisonous mushroom?" McPhee asked him.

"You can't," replied Gibbons. "A family in New Jersey died two weeks ago from eating *Amanita verna*—you know, the death angel. A reporter at the Philadelphia "Inquirer" called me up and said, 'How do you tell the difference between mushrooms and toadstools?' You don't. There are too many of them. Some are neither edible nor poisonous. You learn to recognize edible species. It is exactly like recognizing someone's face; once you know a person, you know that person from all people. Oyster mushrooms, meadow mushrooms, chanterelles, shaggymanes, puffballs—you get to know each one, and you never forget them. I don't go out, find a mushroom, eat it, and see if it's going to kill me. I know what I'm looking for."

Few Americans are about to follow the lead of Euell Gibbons. We are an adventurous people, but only in certain areas; and eating is not one of them. Look at our history. Our colonial forebears shrank from eating their big lobsters. Wild rice now sells at fancy prices (as much as $10 a pound retail) while once it was considered a poor substitute for the polished rice cultivated in fields and processed in factories.

Maple sugar, too, commands steep prices, though one of the earliest reports on maple sugar, as made by the American Indians, a report written about 1700, stated that maple sugar "lacks the pleasing, delicate taste of cane sugar."

Narrowmindedness in matters of eating has been called a form of infantilism. Children develop distastes for certain foods and form attachments to others; in many cases they never lose the likes and dislikes of childhood. Only rather late in life, if at all, are the majority of us able to acquire tastes for foods and drinks different from the ones we grew up with.

A savory (and unsavory) salmagundi

There are many people in this world, and some surprising food preferences exist among them.

Australians, even in childhood, like kangaroo soup, made from the flesh of the marsupial found and named (the word "kangaroo" has never turned up in any native language or dialect) by Captain Cook, who introduced his countrymen to the word "taboo."

The French enjoy frogs'[15] legs (*cuisses de grenouilles*) and so do some people who are French only by cuisine.

Eskimos eat musk oxen, arctic hare, wild birds (like ptarmigan) caught in nets, the kidneys and livers of seals (their main source of vitamin C), the raw soft outer skins of whales (*mutuk*), the eyes of fish.

Sheep's eyes are an Arab delicacy.

Italians and other Mediterraneans admire the taste of squid and octopus (*calamari*), which can be delicious but which an English girl once described to me as "fried rubber bands." Italians are also partial to the meat of the whelk, that large spiral-shelled marine gastropod you may call conch (pronounced "konk"). In Italy it is called *scungilli*, a dialect corruption of *conchiglia*, meaning shell; Italians eat the bland, light gray meat in chunks, steamed and served with hot sauce.

The Japanese, like the ancient Romans, eat the gonads of prickly sea urchins (so do Peruvians, Chileans and many Mediterraneans, including the French, who call them *oursins*). The Japanese also eat crunchy pickled jellyfish, cut like spaghetti. They eat live, wriggling shrimp; hot pickled ginger; artfully cut slices of raw octopus, abalone, sea bass, tuna, clams and shrimp (called collectively *sashimi*); cuttlefish; sea slugs; sugared beans; candied flower petals; seaweed;[16] lots

---

[15] Frogs, like some people, are finicky eaters, which makes them hard to raise domestically. The French get theirs from a variety of sources, including the Danube Delta. The U.S. gets its frogs mostly from Japan. Back in 1938, Louisiana bullfrogs sold for two and a half cents a pound, but demand for frogs by research laboratories has bid the price up to about eighty cents. The decline in swamps, drained by irrigation projects, has dried up supplies. Louisiana sold more than 1260 tons of frogs for frogs' legs in 1936; in 1967 it sold less than twenty-one tons. Prices have doubled just in the past five years. Some bullfrogs weigh as much as five pounds, but the average is about one pound. Japan exports 900 tons of frogs a year (frog exports brought the Japanese $1.6 million in revenue in 1967). Like snails (*escargots*), frogs' legs are largely a vehicle for eating garlic; unseasoned, they are much like chicken legs.

[16] About twenty species are used, most of them cultivated, and the Japanese consume about 5000 tons (dry) of seaweed a year. *Nori* is pressed into cellophanelike sheets or eaten like a paste with soy sauce. *Wakame* is eaten fresh in salads but is used mostly for soups. *Hijiki* is cooked with soy sauce and served as a side dish. So is *konbu*, or *kombu*, the costliest kelp (the best comes from the northerly waters off Hokkaido), which is also used as stock for soup.

of radishes and sweet potatoes and of course, rice, along with rice wine (*sake*), warm or on the rocks, and tea. Raw tuna (*maguro*), which tastes like beef, is popular. For wealthy Japanese gastronomes, the muscle of the giant three- to four-foot tridacna clam is an expensive luxury.

Nowadays Japanese, whose diets contain enough vitamin C but who take pills to make up for deficiencies of ten to forty per cent in other vitamins, drink increasing quantities of milk, coffee, hot chocolate and Coca-Cola. They eat hamburgers, spaghetti (with forks, not *hashi*), pre-sliced bread,[17] chops and French-fried potatoes (the Yankee influence). But traditional dishes still predominate: *shushoku*, or "main food" (rice), bean curd, radishes, sweet potatoes, *miso shiru* (a soup made of fermented soybean paste), bean sprouts (*moyashi*), pickled vegetables, seaweed and fish, either baked, deep-fried or raw.

Other people eat raw fish, too. For the Dutch, young fresh herring, eaten raw (the taste is described as being not unlike that of fresh caviar), is a treat; "green herring," it is called. Raw fish, pickled in lime juice and called *seviche*, is popular on the west coast of South America.

Garden snails, taken out of their shells, cooked in garlic butter and served, honestly, *en pots* or forced back inside shells which are usually not their own, are prized as *escargots* in France, while Belgians eat tiny *karicollen*, which may come either from the vineyards or, like the periwinkles of Scotland, from the sea.

In Botswana, South Africa, !Kung Bushmen in the Kalahari Desert (now being mined for diamonds) have for years now dug up a kind of truffle which they eat by the bucketful (worth $28) for dessert. European restaurants are eager to buy the truffles; the bushmen are dubious about selling. Their main food items are snakes, lizards and ground grubs, but they like their truffles.

---

[17] No Japanese ate bread of any kind until some shipwrecked Portuguese sailors introduced it into the country in 1543. And almost no Japanese ate bread until the end of World War II, when large amounts of U.S. wheat were shipped into the country, whose own wheat is better suited to making noodles (it lacks the viscosity needed for bread).

Chacun, say the French, *à son goût.*

But please do not leave this chapter thinking Arabs eat only sheep's eyes and Ethiopians only grasshoppers; they do not, any more than Irishmen eat only potatoes. Ireland is famous for its fat Dublin prawns, its County Down lamb, its Antrim ham. In many Arab countries, barbecued lamb, *mechoui,* and semolina wheat soaked with lamb soup and vegetables (a dish called *couscous*) are staples. Ethiopians feast on *injara,* a pancake made from their chief cereal grain, *tef,* and on a meat or vegetable stew they call *wat.* The *wat* is dished out onto layers of thin, yard-wide *injara,* then folded into strips and eaten.

There are, none the less, some extraordinary food tastes in the world. Some are hardly explainable in terms of history, religion or anything else.

Why do Austrians generally avoid lamb? If it is because their traditional enemies, the Turks, are big lamb eaters, then why do other traditional enemies, like the Greeks and Turks, eat so similarly? And how can we explain why the Czechs and the Russians eat so few vegetables? Or why Danes disdain not only vegetables, but salads and eggs as well?

Chacun à son goût. One Frenchman, Napoleon, while in exile on St. Helena (where he may have tasted Bligh's breadfruit), told a friend, "A man's palate can, in time, become accustomed to anything."

Perhaps. But while all men share a common need for food, the disparity in food preferences divides nations and contributes to discord in the family of man. It may even be at the root of some prejudices: from having an aversion to eating tripe, ham hocks, rabbit, sweetbreads, raw fish, horse meat or insects, it is but a short step to despising people who do eat such things, as Jean Jacques Rousseau despised the "barbarous" meat-eating English.

In America we pay through the nose for steaks and chops, yet turn up our noses at the visceral organ meats [18]—*abats de boucherie,*

---

[18] The prejudice goes back to medieval England, where the heart, liver and entrails were called "umbles" and were baked into big pies. Eating umble pie was for social inferiors.

the French call them—which are richer in nutrients and often much lower in price. (U.S. butchers used to give them away; now they are mostly exported to the Common Market or turned into tankage and used as livestock feed.) We shoot rabbits wholesale where they menace crops—and bury them by the thousands instead of using them for food, a complete waste. When giant African snails as big as a man's fist appeared in Florida in the summer of 1969, they were viewed only as a problem. One snail could eat an entire head of lettuce, and the mollusks threatened a variety of Florida fruits and vegetables. But almost nobody thought of eating the snails.

The psychologist-philosopher William James wrote, "Few of us are adventurous in the matter of food; in fact, most of us think there is something disgusting in a bill of fare to which we are unused."

So while many of the world's bellies go unsatisfied, most of the world's palates are satisfied with an eternal sameness of bill of fare. Jam yesterday, jam tomorrow and, yes, jam—or more likely yams or rice or fish or plantain or potatoes or hamburger—today. People seem to like it that way, which in most cases is just as well (it is no good having a taste for variety when the range of foods available is limited).

But some affluent Americans, with almost every kind of food at their command, are malnourished, or obese, or continually eating saturated fats that menace their hearts, simply because rigidity of eating habits keeps them from widening their horizons and eating the foods they should. And the difficulty of getting acceptance for new and unfamiliar foods poses a major problem in a world beset by starvation.

⚜[8]⚜

The fertile minds of men

In eating meat and honey, men showed no advance over baser animals. Neither food needs cooking or any other processing. The wax of the honeycomb may not do much for the taste of honey, but it has never interfered with bears' enjoyment of the bees' larder (few bears get their honey from the jar as did Winnie the Pooh).

Africans even now often eat honeycomb along with honey—and ingest a few live bees in the process. The savagery of the carnivore is not far beneath the veneer of human civilization.

Superficially, however, we have come a long way from the raw animal behavior witnessed by the English explorer James Bruce in 1768. In Ethiopia, when he saw steaks hacked from the living flesh of cattle, he wrote, "The prodigious noise the animal makes is a signal for the company to sit down to table."

An orgy of eating and drinking followed, the women joining the men, and a wild scene ensued as the dinner party proceeded:

Love lights all its fires [wrote Bruce] and everything is permitted with absolute freedom. There is no coyness, no delays, no need of appointments or retirement to gratify their wishes; there are no rooms but one, in which they sacrifice to both Bacchus and Venus. The two men nearest the vacuum a pair have made on the bench by leaving their seats, hold their upper garments like a screen before the two that have left the bench; and, if we may judge by sound,

they seem to think it as great a shame to make love in silence as to eat. Replaced in their seats again, the company drink the happy couple's health; and their example is followed at different ends of the table, as each couple is disposed. All this passes without remark or scandal, not a licentious word is uttered, nor the most distant joke upon the transaction.

Apes can't cook

Man is still in many ways as close to his unveneered animal nature as he ever was. His successes at improving on nature, using the advantages of his enlarged cortex, his reasoning mind and his thumb-opposed hands, began with his mastery of fire, a great turning point in history, according to Claude Lévi-Strauss.

With hearth fires came cooked food. In his roast pig "Dissertation" written in the first part of the nineteenth century, Charles Lamb showed the influence of James Bruce's observations in the eighteenth. He began:

> Mankind, says a Chinese manuscript, . . . for the first seventy thousand ages ate their meat raw, clawing or biting it from the living animal, just as they do in Abyssinia to this day.

Fire that could roast pigs could also permit eating such complicated ancient foods as poi, that staple dish of Polynesian islanders. A thin, pasty mass of starch taken from the taro root, poi is often baked into cakes. The ancient Romans used taro root as a food for a time, but later gave it up, perhaps after some bad experience.

In their natural state, taro roots contain acrid crystals of calcium oxylate, which make the roots inedible unless they are baked or boiled. Sometime in prehistory, the people of southeast Asia and the Pacific Islands (settled long before European navigators ever ventured abroad in the open sea) learned that cooking destroys the calcium oxylate crystals. Poi has long been basic to diets of many Asian and Oceanic countries. It is perfectly digestible (the Kanaka language used in so many poi-eating lands contains no word for indigestion) and according to some travelers even quite palatable, though others are less complimentary.

A staple in many other tropical countries is derived from another poisonous root, bitter cassava (also called manioc, yuca or the tapioca plant). There are two cassavas, bitter cassava and sweet. Both are species of *Manihot*, a Brazilian plant (the native name is *Man-ihot*) which has nearly 150 species, some of which yield a variety of rubber. The starch from the roots of sweet cassava, or aipi, is quite safe. But the starch of the bitter cassava contains a glucoside related to prussic acid, or hydrocyanic acid.

It might be expected that sweet cassava would be cultivated and bitter cassava avoided. In fact, bitter cassava is much more important commercially than the sweet, partly because it has bigger roots (they weigh up to thirty pounds) and therefore yields more starch.

Bitter cassava, or manioc, is one of the two most productive plants for forestland cultivation (the other is plantain, which requires more water), but so far not much research has been done on it. It is now being studied at a new tropical agricultural research station near Cali, Colombia, with the help of Ford, Rockefeller and Kellogg Foundation money and expertise.

Legend says the food value of the manioc root was discovered by a Spanish explorer lost in the jungles of Brazil. He had heard from Indians that the sap of the cassava was highly poisonous. Rather than die a slow, lingering death from fever and starvation, he elected suicide. So he boiled cassava plant roots in water and made a soup. Instead of being poisoned, he was nourished (the volatile acid in manioc is driven off by even a slight amount of heat) and lived to tell the world how bitter cassava had saved him.

But at least some of Brazil's Indians knew how to process manioc roots long before the white man ever set foot in South America.

The flourlike meal modern Brazilians call *farinha* [1] and the trans-

---

[1] The word comes from *far*, a dough originally made of buckwheat or spelt (another wheat native to western Asia and southern Europe) and a staple of the ancient Phoenicians, other early Mediterranean peoples and, later, of the Brittany French.

lucent granules they call tapioca are staples of the country. *Farinha* is sprinkled lavishly on Brazil's national dish, *feijoada*, made of rice, black beans, spicy Portuguese sausages, pork chops, Tabasco-soaked onions, rum-soaked bananas and chilled orange slices.

Latin America produces more than 7000 tons of manioc-derived food a year. The plant is also cultivated widely in Africa and in the Pacific Islands (it is the most important tropical root crop next to the yam and the sweet potato, but while it yields at least ten times as much food per acre as corn or wheat, it is mostly starch: corn has at least twice as much protein content).

Taro roots, too, have spread far beyond their Pacific base; they are grown throughout tropical America and Africa, wherever there is wet soil and a long growing season.

All the milky ways

Overcoming the obstacles to using manioc and taro roots as food sources are most likely achievements of early man, possibly older even than the discovery of animal milk and the inventions of products made from animal milk: butter, yogurt, cheese and the like.

Butter, like some other foods, was originally used not as food but as medicine. The Greeks and Romans did not eat butter; they employed it as a remedy for skin injuries (as we still use it for burns).

The few people who did eat butter in early times did not eat it fresh. As late as 300 years ago in Spain, butter was available only as a medicine. It was probably the Scandinavians who first made wide use of butter as food and introduced it as food to the rest of Europe.

A doctor in Paris, writing in 1648, advised eating bread with fresh olive oil, not butter. Butter, he said, produced leprosy, a disease widespread in medieval and Renaissance Europe. Leprosy was mistakenly thought to come from eating spoiled meat or fish; any butter found in a city like Paris in the mid-seventeenth century was likely to be rancid. The Parisian doctor, given the circumstances and the science of the time, was drawing a logical conclusion.

Every family used to make its own butter, using cream a day or two old, whipping it until it was full of little lumps, whipping it some more until it was one big lump.[2] Churned butter still has some milk in it; to make it keep well and taste right, all the milk must be pressed out of it and washed away. It takes an average of nearly nine quarts of whole milk to make one pound of butter; connoisseurs can tell by tasting whether the milk was separated on the farm or at a plant.

All U.S. butter is eighty per cent butterfat; that is a government minimum, and for economic reasons it is also a practical maximum. There are government grades of butter: AA, A, B and C, the first being equivalent to the term "93-score" still used in the trade. It goes back to a time when butter was rated on various quality points. Few people can taste the difference between AA grade butter and B grade, but C grade, equivalent to "89-score," is used only in baking and food processing plants.

Butter is often used to symbolize peacetime production ("guns or butter" was the classic polarity enunciated by the Nazi Hermann Göring). In peacetime Europe today, butter production has become an economic monster, farmers being subsidized to churn out far more of the stuff than anyone will ever eat.

In many countries, as in the Mediterranean region, almost nobody eats butter (olive oil is more available and much cheaper). In India, while butter is made fresh every day, usually from buffalo milk, it is melted and clarified into a liquid called *ghee* (Chapter 1) which is also found widely in Africa. American visitors usually loathe *ghee*, but the Indians prefer it to solid butter; and it keeps better in India's heat.

Because milk spoils so quickly, people in many countries have for uncounted centuries clabbered (soured) and fermented milk—mares' milk, ewes' milk, goats' milk and camels' milk (which contains no

---

[2] When the lumps of butter are removed from the churned cream, what is left is buttermilk, though most buttermilk sold today is a cultured milk: skim milk, partly skimmed milk or reconstituted nonfat dry milk is cultured with *Streptococcus lactis* and incubated. Salt is generally added to bring out the flavor.

butterfat) as well as cows' milk—to make various kinds of yogurt, which last much longer than plain milk. Some milks are used in combination: a cows' milk-ewes' milk yogurt marketed in Greece is especially good.

Ordinary sour milk is curdled by any old wild bacteria (*not* by thunder, despite the myth; electrical storms are common in hot humid weather, the kind of weather in which bacteria multiply fastest); true yogurt is turned to curd by two specific beneficial bacteria cultures, *Lactobacillus bulgaricus* and *Streptococcus lactis*. They were isolated about the turn of the century by Dr. Elie Metchnikoff, the Russian bacteriologist and Nobel Prize winner (1908) who headed the Pasteur Institute in Paris.

For millenniums before Metchnikoff, Mongolians, Armenians, Arabs and Persians, as well as Bulgarians, had been fermenting milk into yogurt, which is called *mast* in Iran and the Middle East, *laban* by the Arabs, *kumyss* or *kefir* in Russian and *matzoon* in Armenian. Abraham in the Old Testament ate a goats'-milk yogurt; Genghis Khan ate a yogurt of mares' milk and yaks' milk.

Bulgarians claim that only the mountains of their country can produce the *Bacillus bulgaricus,* and that only this bacillus can curdle milk the right way for good yogurt. They say, too, that the milk must properly be goats' milk and water buffalo milk, a brew twice as rich in butterfat as cows' milk. Bulgarians eat as much as six pounds of yogurt a day and claim that yogurt made elsewhere is a disgrace. Yogurt in Bulgaria is very good, but it would take a connoisseur, which I am not, to single it out as the world's best.

Only recently has yogurt become important in the United States. It was sold here originally as a health food (it has all the vitamin and mineral content of pasteurized whole milk with somewhat fewer calories). But yogurt did not find a broad market in America until it was sold with strawberry preserves added. Now, thickened beyond a point European or Mid-Eastern yogurt lovers would tolerate, it is made in a variety of flavors and Americans eat some 110 million cups of it a year, more than ninety per cent of it on our North Atlantic or Pacific coasts.

U.S. yogurt is made with clarified, homogenized, pasteurized cows' milk from which half the butterfat has been removed and protein and other supplements added. Because the butterfat content is reduced by half, yogurt is believed by many to have half the calories of milk. Not so. It has half the *fat* calories, but there are calories in its protein and carbohydrates, too. So while a glass of milk has 170 calories, an equal amount of yogurt, *plain* yogurt, has 125. Buttermilk, made of cultured skim milk and much cheaper than yogurt, is much lower in calories.

Americans who know their yogurt, and are dissatisfied with the yogurts available in the store, make their own. It is not hard. Boil a quart of fresh milk, which may be homogenized or skim milk, let it cool to lukewarm, and add two or three tablespoons of any commercial yogurt (which contains the necessary bacillus) which has been mixed in a cup with some of the warm milk. The mixture must be kept uniformly warm (about 77° F.) for anywhere from eight to eighteen hours in glass or crockery, well covered, while the culture incubates. The result is yogurt that is yogurt.

While yogurt is of ancient origin, the first man-made dairy food, cheese, was probably a more widely used product.

The original cheese, if we can believe legend, was discovered by an Arab merchant who stopped in the desert for lunch (dried dates and goats' milk, probably). The jolting of the merchant's camel had turned the goats' milk, carried in a saddle bag made typically of animal intestine, into a kind of cheese.

Women used to make their own cheeses at home, just as they churned their own butter. There is still some "farmhouse" cheese, but most cheese today is made in factories, using sweet milk whose casein is curdled with rennet.

Rennet is a combination of two inorganic ferments or enzymes, rennin and pepsin. There are two kinds of rennet: animal rennet comes from the membrane of the abomasum, or fourth stomach, of unweaned calves, lambs and kids; vegetable rennet is contained in thistle, yellow bedstraw, common figs and other plants. Most cheese makers use an extract of animal rennet marketed commercially as a liquid or thick paste.

Given a certain amount of rennet and heat, milk thickens; the liquid part, or whey, is drained off and the solid part, or curd, is left to cure. (Little Miss Muffet in the nursery rhyme [3] ate both curds and whey, but most children today have no idea what those are.)

It can take 2500 pounds of milk to make 200 pounds of some cheese. There are perhaps 350 basically different kinds of cheeses made today. Some of the big cheese-producing countries and their major cheeses are the following:

Belgium: Limburger (and Hervé, which is even stronger).

Canada: Oka, Canadian Cheddar, Canadian blue cheeses.

Denmark: Creme Danica, Danbo, Danish blue cheeses, Danish Camembert, Elbo, Esrom, Fynbo, Havarti, Maribo, Molbo, Samsoe, Tybo.

France: Roquefort, Brie, Camembert, Pont-l'Evêque, Neufchâtel, Gervais, Petit-Gervais, Petit-Suisse, Münster, Port Salut, Livarot, Cantal, Boursault, Boursin, Triple-Crèmes, Maroilles, Baby Bel, Bon-bel, Mimolette, Reblochon (like Camembert) and La Vache Qui Rit.

Germany: Bierkäse, Hand Cheese, Tilsit and Romadur.

Great Britain: Cheddar, Stilton, Cheshire, Blue Cheshire (not available in the U.S.), Gloucester and Double-Gloucester (the second is twice as big and aged twice as long), Lancashire, Leicester, Caerphilly (from Wales), Dunlop (from Ayr, in Scotland) and Wensleydale (from a valley in the Pennine Mountains of Yorkshire).

Greece: Feta, Kasseri, Kefalotyrie.

Italy: Gorgonzola, Parmesan (from Parma, aged at least two years), Provolone (popular in southern Italy), Romano, Ricotta, Bel Paese, Taleggio (aged in caves in the northern plains of Lombardy), Fontina, Mozzarella, Cacciocavallo (more properly Cacio a Cavallo,

---

[3] A tradition dating back to 1805 says the little miss was Patience, daughter of a Dr. Thomas Muffet (1533–1604) whose book, published in 1655, was one of the first books relating food and health. It was called *Health's Improvement, or RULES Comprizing and Discovering the Nature, Method and Manner of Preparing all sorts of FOOD used in this NATION.* Dr. Muffet was also an entomologist with a passion for spiders, which his daughter quite possibly hated and feared. Many nursery rhymes concern food: Jack Sprat and his wife, Little Jack Horner, Little Tommy Tucker, The Old Woman who lived in a shoe, the baker's man, hot cross buns and pease porridge hot, to name a few.

a round version of Provolone), Crescenza, Stracchino, Sardo (from Sardinia), Asiago and Pecorino Pepato (from Sicily).

The Netherlands: young and old Edam or Edammer (which in Holland is a natural yellow-brown; the red paraffin coating is only for export cheese), both round as cannon balls, and the flattened Gouda, Leyden.

Norway: Jarlsberg, Norwegian Tilsit, Bifrost, Gjetost, Norwegian blue cheese.

Portugal: Quejo de Serra.

Spain: Queso Manchego.

Sweden: Hable Crème Chantilly, Herrgård, Sveciaost.

Switzerland: Emmenthaler or Emmenthal, Gruyère and Appenzell, all of which Americans call simply "Swiss Cheese," though Gruyère—no relation to the processed cheese sold as "Gruyère" in the U.S.—has a more pronounced flavor and smaller holes than Emmenthaler, and Appenzell, or Appenzeller, is stronger than the other two; Raclette, Saanen, Sapsago, Sbrinz, Beckenried.

United States: Liederkranz, brick, Colby, cottage cheese, Monterey Jack from California, New York cheddar, Vermont cheddar and Vermont Sage.

There are cows'-milk cheeses, goats'-milk cheeses (like Feta, Saanen, Le Banon) and sheep-milk cheeses (like Roquefort, Queso Manchego, Kaseri and Pecorino Romano); sharp cheeses, strong cheeses and bland cheeses; fresh cheeses, fermented cheeses and processed, or "process," cheeses.

Fresh cheeses are made with very little rennet; they have a slightly acid flavor because the lactic acids have not been entirely fermented out of them. Some familiar fresh cheeses are cream cheese, Neufchâtel, cottage cheese, farmer cheese, Ricotta and factory-made Mozzarella, the cheese used for pizzas [4] and mixed with Ricotta in *lasagna*.

The classic cheeses are the fermented ones. There are four basic

---

[4] A "pizza cheese" made specifically for U.S. pizzas is manufactured in the Midwest. It is even drier than factory-made Mozzarella, but when melted and mixed with tomato paste in the oven it does a satisfactory job. It is a far cry, however, from the Mozzarella of Italy's Campania, made from water buffalo milk (*latte di bufalo*).

varieties of these. Some (like English Cheddar, French Cantal, German Tilsit, Dutch Edam and Swiss Emmenthaler) are hard-pressed but not cooked.

Some (like Swiss Gruyère and Italian Parmesan) are hard-pressed and cooked.

Some—the great after-dinner cheeses—are soft and get their flavor mostly from bacterial growth; these include Brie and Camembert (the latter invented, it is said, by a Norman peasant woman, Marie Harel of the town of Vimoutiers, in 1781), which take about a month to mature, and slightly stronger cheeses, like Livarot and Maroilles, which take longer. Connoisseurs try to eat these cheeses *à point*, which means at just the point of ripeness where they are soft enough to be runny but have not yet spoiled. These have to be eaten in Europe; U.S. Department of Agriculture laws forbid entry to "soft, freshly ripened" cheeses because they are made from unpasteurized milk; pasteurizing kills the benign bacteria which bring the cheeses to their proper ripeness. Sometimes, as Mr. Bumble said in Dickens's *Oliver Twist*, "The law is a ass, a idiot."

We do import the most prized of fermented cheeses, the blue-veined varieties like English Stilton (originated, it is thought, in Stilton, Huntingdonshire, early in the eighteenth century), green-veined Italian Gorgonzola, French Blue (or *Bleu*) and French Roquefort. The latter must by French law be made entirely of rich ewes' milk in the Roquefort area, as it has been for centuries.

Then there are the "process" cheeses or, as the English critic T.A. Layton calls them, the "packet" cheeses. Some of these, he concedes, are quite good, but his example is Philadelphia brand cream cheese, which is not typical.

Many "process" cheeses are made abroad, but such a large number are made in the United States that Layton defers to an American, writer Clifton Fadiman, whom he quotes on the subject. So shall we. In an introduction to an earlier book, Fadiman wrote,

> . . . no matter what the law may say I refuse to call this stuff cheese. For me (though it's only fair to say that millions like the stuff) the processed cheeses belong to the same family as ordinary commercial white bread, powdered coffee, cellophaned cake and

our more popular carbonated beverages. The most I can say for it is that it is non-poisonous; the worst, that it represents the triumph of technology of science over conscience.

In preparation of this solidified floor wax—of the product of emulsification with sodium citrate, sodium phosphate or rochelle salts; of steaming and blending odd lots of cheese; of paralyzing whatever germs might result either in loss of profit or gain of flavor—every problem but one is solved: that of making cheese.

To put it less fervently, processed cheese is made from one or more natural cheeses—ground, pasteurized, stirred with an emulsifier (Appendix) and water into a smooth, homogeneous fluid which is poured into foil or foil-lined containers. Its ripening is arrested so it keeps well. Processed "cheese *food*" is made the same way except it need contain only fifty-one per cent cheese (milk, nonfat dry milk, cream, whey solids, water and also fruit, vegetables, meat, spices and flavorings may be added).

As Fadiman says, millions *do* like the stuff. The Borden Company tells me some thirty-five per cent of all cheese sold in the U.S. is processed cheese; Roy de Groot says the percentage is sixty-seven. Leaving out cottage cheese and pot cheese, but including cheddar, Colby (like cheddar but softer and milder) and young brick along with foreign types produced in the U.S. or abroad, the percentage of processed cheese, says Borden, rises to forty-two. Much of it goes into cheeseburgers, grilled cheese sandwiches, Welsh rabbit, potatoes *au gratin* and the like.

While consumption of milk, cream and butter has declined per capita in the U.S. in the last forty years, cheese consumption (if, unlike Mr. Fadiman, we "call this stuff cheese,") has increased by some fifty per cent, though the eleven pounds of cheese the average American eats in a year hardly compares to the figures in countries like Denmark, Holland, Norway and Israel where it is standard procedure to serve cheese at breakfast. The average Swiss eats eighteen pounds of cheese a year, the Norwegian seventeen, the Dane, Swede and Dutchman sixteen pounds.

The American figure looks even smaller when you consider that so much of the cheese an American eats is hardly cheese by standards of people like Mr. Fadiman.

The percentage of processed cheese, however, is not increasing; if anything, it is declining. And while the U.S. imports enough low-priced Edam, Gouda, Emmenthaler and Gruyère-process to worry domestic producers and create political problems, this country now leads the world in cheese production. About fifteen per cent of our milk goes into cheese, and the two billion pounds of it we make each year is twice as much as France, the runner-up, produces. We turn out some creditable versions of foreign cheeses. Our Kasseri is said to be better than the original Greek Kasseri; some of our New York, Vermont, Wisconsin and Oregon cheddars compare favorably with English cheddars; our Münster, while far milder than French or German Münster, melts better (and Wisconsin's Fundutta, similar to Münster, is softer and more buttery).

Many cheeses have been popular for centuries or even since antiquity. Others, just as well-known, are comparatively modern inventions.

Port Salut, or Port du Salut as it was originally called, first appeared on tables in Paris in 1873. It was invented by the monks of l'Abbaye de Notre-Dame, who registered the name at the Tribunal de Commerce in Laval in 1878.

An Italian cheese similar in texture to Port Salut (and to Münster) is Bel Paese, a trade name for an uncooked, sweet, semi-soft, mild, fast-ripening cheese made from fresh whole cows' milk, usually pasteurized. Bel Paese was first marketed in Italy in 1921 by cheese maker Egidio Galbani, whose firm now makes Bel Paese in Brazil and Wisconsin, as well as in Italy. Pennsylvania Bel Paese, made by someone else, is very much like the Italian.

Liederkranz, to the surprise of many Americans, is as American as Vichyssoise. It is a trade name (the Borden Company owns it) for an improvement on the strong-smelling soft Belgian cheese, Limburger (or on German Bismarck Schlosskäse—accounts vary). An apprentice cheese maker, Emil (or Emile) Frey, stumbled on the art of making Liederkranz in Monroe, New York, in 1892. The name means "wreath of song"; Liederkranz Hall, which stood until a few years ago on New York's East 58th Street, was named not for the cheese but for a singing society to which Frey's employer belonged. The cheese also was named after the singing society.

Liederkranz is strong cheese. So, at least when it is aged a little, is brick cheese, another U.S. invention. Here the originator was a Wisconsin cheese maker, John Jossi, who made his firmer, more elastic and slightly milder version of Limburger in 1877, fifteen years before Frey's Liederkranz. Brick became popular in the Midwest and, while it is practically unknown on the East and West Coasts, it is still popular on sour rye and pumpernickel, with beer, throughout the Midwest.

We have noted some exceptions but basically, cheese—like poi, tapioca, butter and yogurt—is a food of ancient origin, even older than agriculture. It is contemporaneous, perhaps, with the invention of carding and spinning flax, wool and cotton fibers and weaving them into cloth.

Cheese was evidently an achievement of men. Women may have invented agriculture, but innovations in foods have come mostly from men. This inventiveness embraces everything from the development of dairy products and new plant foods to mechanical cultivation and harvesting equipment, from better ways of transporting foods to improved preservation techniques, synthesized flavorings, advances in food preparation, more efficient marketing methods, even botanical improvements.

The sweet with the bitter

One of the most dramatic examples of human innovation in basic foodstuffs is the sugar beet, developed from the mangel, or mangel-wurzel, which in turn was developed from the oldest type of beet, chard.

As we saw earlier, sugar was a rare luxury in Europe until sugar cane, originally from India, was grown cheaply in the New World. Sugar brought back from the Near East by the Crusaders was sold by the ounce and was mostly for the rich and wellborn; common housewives had to be content with honey, or with no sweetening at all, until the end of the eighteenth century.

By then, importation of sugar from the West Indies and Brazil was well established and sugar was no longer such a rarity in Europe. But the Napoleonic wars cut Europe off from much of this imported sugar.

More than half a century before Napoleon, in 1747, a Prussian chemist, Andreas Sigismund Marggraf, had discovered sugar in beet juice. In 1793, a Berlin man of French origin, François Achard, perfected a process for producing sugar from beets; he revealed the process that year at Kunern, in Silesia.

Benjamin Delessert, head of the Bank of France, saw the possibilities in beet sugar for blockaded, sugar-starved Frenchmen. He set up huge factories for producing the sugar at Passy about 1810. Delessert installed modern steam engines (invented by James Watt only forty years before) and developed ways to strain the molasses and crystallize the sugar.

Napoleon visited the factories, honored Delessert and ordered sugar beets planted in great stretches of land in the north of France. Delessert's factories turned out more than 4 million kilos of sugar in two years, but when Napoleon's empire fell after Waterloo and cane sugar came in from Martinique, Guadeloupe and Brazil, the price of sugar dropped by a third. Beet sugar was not commercially practical until the late 1870's, when a new production process and more efficient mills were developed. When these were demonstrated at the Paris World's Fair of 1878, almost every European country hurried to plant sugar beets and build facilities for sugar making.

In terms of botany, the development of the sugar beet surpasses any other achievement of human ingenuity in food creation. Every other major food crop plant has been known for uncounted generations; the sugar beet stands alone as a crop developed by modern man. It frees countries in the temperate zone from complete dependence on tropical cane. And it has made the Soviet Union the world's largest sugar producer (Russia grows about a third of the world's sugar beet crop).

Beet sugar was scorned at first as having a bad taste and being less sweetening than cane sugar; after it was shown by experiment that the two sugars were absolutely identical in every way, beet sugar gradually won general acceptance. Its use increased when the difference in size between cane sugar granules and beet sugar granules was eliminated. Today, about 33½ million short tons of the world's nearly 74½ million short tons of raw sugar are derived from beets.

Sugar beets were first planted on a commercial scale in many U.S. states in 1880; they are now raised mainly in California, Colorado, the Red River Valley (Minnesota, North Dakota, Nebraska, Wyoming) and Texas, though Utah, Michigan and Maine are factors, too.

The rise of the sugar beet was a blow to the economies of the Caribbean islands which had produced so much wealth for eighteenth- and early nineteenth-century France, England and Spain.

Cane sugar production has increased enormously in the continental U.S. in recent years, but it is still nowhere near the volume of our beet industry. Beets got a big impetus in World War II; Fidel Castro gave them another push. Now we produce more than 3.5 short tons of beet sugar for every 1.4 short tons of cane sugar. Total U.S. sugar production still falls short of our sugar consumption; next to coffee and meat, sugar is our largest food import item.[5]

Peanut butter and substitute butter

While fair goers in Chicago in 1893 were sampling their first grapefruit (Chapter 6), another botanical achievement of man, a St. Louis doctor was promoting the world's first peanut butter. He had developed peanut butter in 1890 as an easily digested high-protein food.

Started thus as a health food, peanut butter was an instant success. Grocers ladled it out to their customers from big tubs or pails (after first stirring it to make its consistency uniform). Today peanut butter

---

[5] Before the Castro revolution, three fourths of U.S. sugar imports came from Cuba, which exported three fifths of its crop to this country. Most nations could import sugar at less cost than raising it themselves, but many raise it lest they be cut off from sugar supplies by war or unfavorable trade balances.

is stabilized so the oils do not separate out. Dextrose is sometimes added to absorb oil; extra protein is sometimes added as well (peanuts are lacking in methionine, lysine and threonine, important amino acid components of protein).

Peanut butter comes in both a smooth, creamy form and a crunchy form which contains bits of roasted, blanched nuts. There is a jar of peanut butter in four out of five American homes; we eat over 235,000 tons of it a year and consumption is increasing: Americans ate sixty per cent more peanut butter in 1966 than in 1955. The product is rich in phosphorus, niacin and thiamine, as well as in protein, and, after some bitter fighting, its peanut content has been regulated at ninety per cent.

Not only peanut butter but, as we have seen, true butter churned from "soured" cream is also a man-made food. Butter, however, is today not half so important in the U.S. as margarine, a more recent invention of man.

When the Illinois and Wisconsin Dairymen's Association was founded in 1867, the dairy farmers could have had no idea that in France that year a man was beginning to work on a product that would one day threaten their livelihood and demand the marshalling of all their powers to resist its inroads.

The man was a chemist, Hypolite Mège-Mouriès. Napoleon III offered him a handsome prize if he could "produce a cheap butter for the Army, Navy and needy classes of the population." After a sojourn of work at the Emperor's farm, Bon Ouvrage, Mège-Mouriès won the prize with a pearly-white product made of suet, or animal kidney fat, melted down and clarified, freed of its softer fats, or stearin components, under pressure, mixed with milk and churned into solid fat.[6]

---

[6] The method was later simplified: the animal fats were gently heated and pressed; the oil fraction separated out was called "oleine," the solid part "stearin" or "margarine"; the hard fat was sold as "butterine." By 1890 it was found that margarine could be given a melting point like that of real butter by blending in vegetable oils like arachis oil (from peanuts) and palm oil. After 1910, when the liquid oleine was hardened by hydrogenation (discovered by the English chemist William Normann in 1901), margarine production increased enormously.

Mège-Mouriès named the lustrous butter substitute after the Greek word "margarites," meaning pearly. The process was patented in England in 1869. It was soon taken over by American meat packers. Two Dutch companies, Van den Bergh and Juergens, made margarine a commercial success after the Franco-Prussian War, beginning production in 1871. By 1880, some fifty factories were producing the "butter of the poor" in dairy-rich Holland. Juergens, Europe's biggest butter dealers, were shipping 40,000 tons of margarine to England, their biggest customer, by 1883. Later, they teamed up with Van den Bergh, their biggest competitor, and with the Levers in England to form Unilever, whose Lord Leverhulme said in 1918 that his company had "drifted" into the margarine business "because of its close connection with oils and fats for the soap kettle."

Margarine has been made from whale oil; it is still made from palm oil, coconut oil and peanut oil. A major ingredient today is soybean oil. Soybeans were an insignificant commodity in the U.S. before World War II; now they are the nation's second biggest farm crop. American margarine producers use almost 1.3 billion pounds of soybean oil a year (more than twice the amount of corn oil, cottonseed oil, safflower oil, other vegetable oils, animal fats and nonfat dry milk they use).

Before World War II, Americans ate six times more butter than margarine. Despite protective legislation to impede it, margarine use has grown every year since 1934. While "pure creamery butter" is often "color added," the sale of yellow margarine was outlawed for years in our dairy states. The last holdout, Wisconsin, finally yielded in 1967, fifteen years after New York state repealed its law against the yellow peril. Under the old state laws, margarine was sold white; the package included a capsule of yellow vegetable coloring material —one colored his margarine or ate it white. The Dakotas, Minnesota and Utah, as well as Wisconsin, still impose special taxes on yellow margarine, which is colored at the factory.

The average American today uses close to eleven pounds of margarine a year and less than half that much butter (4.8 pounds in 1967, down from 5.4 pounds the year before).

Federal price supports have kept the price of butter well above the price of even top-quality margarine. But that alone does not explain the fall of butter and the rise of oleo. It is hard to avoid the conclusion that fewer and fewer Americans can tell the difference between butter and margarine, which is partly a tribute to the improved quality of U.S. margarine but more a reflection on the lack of discernment in popular taste.

The British, quite the other way, eat more than twice as much butter as margarine. Despite the huge surplus of the "Butterberg" across the Channel in France and Germany, most of Britain's butter is imported from her "private dairy" (New Zealand) and from Denmark, Australia, Poland, Holland and Ireland. Margarine consumption has actually been on the decline in the U.K., mostly because British margarine has not tasted enough like butter to fool anyone. U.S. and Scandinavian margarines have been much better, though one British margarine brand has lately advertised itself as being equal in quality to American margarine. Britons are hardly rolling in money nowadays, but the low prices of margarines have not attracted many converts. In 1954, the average Briton consumed over eighteen pounds of margarine; now he is using only nine. Add butter and margarine figures together and the Britisher eats about twice as much as the cholesterol-conscious American.

Margarine in France? You jest, *mon vieux*. Well, the French *do* use margarine (which they pronounce with a hard "g"), but only a little over four pounds per person, as compared with twenty pounds of butter, and certainly not for things like croissants and pastries, which would be disasters if made with anything but *le vrai beurre*.

Margarine is only one of many man-devised foods now in common use that came into being late in the nineteenth century and early in the twentieth. Conspicuous on the list are breakfast foods, cola drinks, tea bags, iced tea and gelatin desserts.

Grape-Nuts and Coca-Cola

At the Battle Creek Sanitarium in Michigan (about which more in
Chapter 10), the patient-guests ate no meat, drank no tea, coffee or
alcohol, used no tobacco. An ulcer patient, Charles W. Post, created
there a cereal beverage, Postum. He also developed a dry breakfast
food he called "Elijah's Manna." The Biblical name ran into trouble
with grocers so it was changed to Grape-Nuts. The two products
were the basis of today's mighty General Foods Corporation.

To help a patient who had broken her false teeth on a piece of
zwieback (a special egg bread made into rusks and, to take its German name literally, twice baked), a surgeon at the sanitarium created
a breakfast cereal made from thin flakes of corn. His name was Dr.
Harvey Kellogg; his corn flakes began a giant health food industry
which at one point saw forty different breakfast food companies
struggling for survival in Battle Creek.

Grape-Nuts contains neither grapes nor nuts, a point once made
in court to defend another man-made food invention of the late nineteenth century, Coca-Cola. Its inventor was John S. Pemberton, a
Georgia-born pharmacist who settled in Atlanta in 1869 and, in
1886, produced a syrup he called Coca-Cola. Mixed with water,
it made (he claimed) a useful remedy for headaches and hang-
overs.

Another pharmacist, Asa G. Candler, bought ownership of Coca-
Cola in about 1891. Candler was a chronic dyspeptic and suffered
from chronic headaches, but he did not see Coca-Cola as a therapeutic drink. Ever since 1833, when John Matthews introduced carbonated water, soda water had been a growing American passion. A
Frenchman added syrups a few years after Matthews' invention and
Americans were soon drinking root beer, spruce beer, birch beer and
various orange-, lemon-, cherry-, lime- and berry-flavored concoctions.

By 1891, when Candler bought Coca-Cola, *Harper's Weekly* was saying, "Soda water is an American drink." New York City that year had more soda fountains per capita than bars, though the soda fountains were patronized mainly by women. A few years after he organized The Coca-Cola Company in 1892, Candler began promoting the drink for its refreshing qualities.

Pemberton had included in his original mixture some extract of cola nuts, along with a pinch of caffeine. The Coca-Cola letterhead in 1900 mentioned "the tonic properties of the wonderful COCA PLANT and the famous COLA NUT." Early advertising claimed that Stanley had reached Livingstone because his bearers chewed cola nuts. In West Africa, where the cola tree (*Cola heterophylla*) grows, cola nuts *are* valued as strength-builders. The Surgeon General of the U.S. Army in the 1890's said that chewing cola beans (which contain caffeine and another stimulant, kolanin) enabled infantrymen to perform well on forced marches.

Coca leaves are chewed by Indians on the altiplano of the Andes to reduce hunger pangs, fight fatigue and dull sensitivity to cold. Coca is, in fact, a drug.

None of this, however, has much to do with Coca-Cola. In its early days it did contain a minute quantity of cocaine which was not removed from the coca leaves. The company now calls whatever trace amounts of coca it contains "a non-narcotic extract from de-cocainized coca leaves."

And if there is practically no coca, there is even less cola, perhaps because the nut has a very bitter taste. The cola content of Coca-Cola is only one-third the coca content; the amount is so small (perhaps 1/100 of one per cent) that it does not show up in any laboratory analysis. Diet-Rite Cola's recent advertising about African cola beans is as meaningless as most food advertising.

After the Pure Food and Drug Act was passed in 1906, Coca-Cola was attacked for misbranding. The famous case of United States v. Forty Barrels and Twenty Kegs of Coca-Cola came to trial in 1909. It dragged on for nine years. Coca-Cola said there was no mislabeling involved in its name; after all, it said, there were no grapes or nuts in

Grape-Nuts and no butter in butternuts. Charles Evans Hughes, in the U.S. Supreme Court, decided against the company. If Coca-Cola were upheld, said Hughes in the last opinion he wrote before he ran for the presidency in 1916, somebody could put out a product called "Chocolate-Vanilla" which contained neither chocolate nor vanilla. As a result, Coca-Cola has had to put at least trace amounts of coca and cola in its product to maintain its trademark.

The trademark "Coke" was registered in 1945, though it was never used by the company until 1955. More than four-fifths of Coca-Cola is sold in bottles, the famous bottle shape dating back to 1916; it is beyond doubt the most distinctive and best known commercial food product package in the world.

The exact ingredients of Coke are kept secret, though Cubans, deprived of Coca-Cola syrup from the U.S. for some years, make a soft drink they call Coca-Cola which reportedly tastes pretty much like the real thing. The authentic article is ninety-nine per cent sugar and water; the other one per cent includes caramel (for coloring), caffeine, phosphoric acid, the aforementioned traces of coca and cola and about eight other ingredients which may number among them cinnamon, nutmeg, vanilla, lavender, lime juice, various citrus oils, glycerine (derived from vegetable matter because animal glycerine would make the product non-kosher) and a secret ingredient the Coca-Cola people call 7X (it may be a combination of some of the above-named ingredients).

There are between eighty-one and eighty-six calories in a six-and-a-half-ounce bottle of Coke, as compared to 138 calories in six and a half ounces of milk and 84.5 calories in a six-and-a-half-ounce glass of beer. Since Coca-Cola's calories come almost entirely from sugar, a small size Coke bottle contains about five teaspoons of sugar.

The caffeine content of Coke is one basis of the product's "adult image," an image which helps keep it popular with youngsters. The Coca-Cola company used to defend the caffeine content in its promotional literature. An early advertisement said, rather defensively, "You Don't Taboo Coffee, Do You?" A 1916 promotional booklet said that "the nations that lead the world in thought and in action are

the nations that rely most fully upon the caffeine beverages for refreshment of mind and body."

But "The Pause That Refreshes," as Coca-Cola was for so long
advertised, contains less caffeine than either coffee or tea, even less
than some cocoa, and its promotion now makes no mention of any
caffeine.[7]

Coke has been attacked as a cause of cancer, ulcers, heart disease,
sterility and impotence. Classroom demonstrations have been used to
show that a piece of meat left in Coca-Cola will gradually dissolve.
"See that, children? It will rot your stomach." But the demonstra-
tion simply shows that the acids in Coke are like human digestive
juices, which will also dissolve meat. As do other sugar-heavy soft
drinks, Coca-Cola wreaks considerable havoc on children's teeth, but
its only other ill effect, at least for adults, is the negative one of taking
the place of nutritive foods and beverages in the diet.

For a food with no value beyond the energy its sugar supplies,
Coca-Cola is consumed in gigantic quantities. The company estimates
that the world drinks 90 million Cokes a day. (Annual per capita consumption in Coca-Cola's home town, Atlanta, has been over 265, and
in Rome, Georgia, it has been as high as 300. Some individuals drink
twenty and more Cokes a day.)

Pepsi-Cola challenged Coke with a "twice-as-much-for-a-nickel"
twelve-ounce bottle in the 1930's; Coke sued for trademark infringe-
ment. The court ruled that since "Trade Mark Reg. U.S. Pat. Off."
appeared only in the bottom of the "C" in "Coca-," anyone could
use "Cola."

---

[7] The FDA in 1966 ruled that cola drinks did not have to list caffeine as an
ingredient on bottle labels, which Ralph Nader's people (Chapter 11) suggest
was influenced by political pressures. When caffeine was scarce during World
War II, chemists proposed that uric acid, a close chemical relative to caffeine
and easily converted into caffeine, might solve the Coca-Cola Company's problem of caffeine supply. They proposed the use of bat guano as a source of uric
acid. Bats, like birds, do not urinate; their solid excrement contains a high percentage of uric acid. But someone at Coca-Cola realized what might happen if
people discovered bat guano was being used as a raw material for the world's
leading soft drink. The plan was quashed.

Coca-Cola outsells Pepsi by roughly two to one; add all the other brands of soft drinks America gurgles down each year and the total U.S. soft drink consumption figure for 1968 was 3.83 billion cases— 8½ billion gallons.

So let's have another cup of coffee

If 8½ billion gallons sounds like a lot, hear this: we Americans drink three times that much coffee.

According to the Pan American Coffee Bureau, almost seven out of ten Americans over ten years of age drank coffee on a typical winter day in 1969. The percentage was 68.7, down from 74.7 in 1950 but still well above the figure for any other beverage (52.5 per cent drank milk or a milk drink, 44.6 drank fruit or vegetable juice, 43.9 drank a soft drink, 25 drank tea. Only 3.2 per cent drank cocoa).

Decaffeinated coffee accounts for only five or six per cent of total coffee sales, but this represents a four-fold increase in the past ten years. (Decaffeinated cola drinks appear to be the next major development in the soft drink market, sixty-six per cent of which was in cola drinks in 1969.)

Caffeine has long been a source of concern, especially in coffee. Brillat-Savarin, back in 1825, said:

> Coffee is a far more powerful liquor than is commonly believed. A man of sound constitution may drink two bottles of wine a day, and live long; the same man would not so long sustain a like quantity of coffee; he would become imbecile or die of consumption. . . . It is the duty of all papas and mamas to forbid their children coffee, unless they wish to have little dried-up machines, stunted and old at the age of twenty.

Dr. Irwin Ross, in *Science Digest*, has written that the caffeine in one or two cups of coffee can increase your stomach temperature ten or fifteen degrees, make your stomach secrete up to 400 per cent more hydrochloric acid, make your heart beat fifteen per cent faster and make your lungs work thirteen times harder. Many doctors link caffeine with stomach ulcers; some link it to coronary thrombosis; it has even been associated with cell breakage and chromosome damage (Chapter 9).[8] Temperance organizations used to campaign against the use of coffee (it was considered an aphrodisiac) as well as against alcohol.

Adult Americans have nevertheless thrived on coffee and enjoy its stimulating effects. The average American drinks nearly three cups of coffee a day. (The average for milk and milk drinks is about 1.1 glasses, for soda pop about 1.17 small bottles, for juice .63 glasses. As for tea, the average American drinks only .48 cups of tea—or, in some neighborhoods, "glasses tea.")

So pervasive is the U.S. coffee habit that in some American restaurants the waitress asks if the customer would like a cup of coffee even before she gives him a menu.

---

[8] Caffeine, like theobromine and theophylline, is a purine or xanthine derivative. A stimulant to the cortex, especially to the psychic and sensory functions, caffeine allays drowsiness and fatigue; it also has diuretic effects, causing diarrhea in some people. Caffeine keeps some people awake at night, has little or no effect on others. It occurs in coffee beans, cocoa beans, tea leaves and kola nuts. Caffeine content varies from one coffee to another; Brazilian coffee has more caffeine than Colombian or Central American, Philippine coffee has more than any American. A South American drink, *guarana*, made from the seeds of a large woody climbing plant native to the Amazon valley, has three times as much caffeine as most coffee.

Tea leaves have a higher caffeine content than coffee beans, but as a prepared beverage tea has no more caffeine than coffee and usually much less. How much caffeine there is in a cup of tea or coffee depends on variables like the strength of the brew; some sources say a six-ounce cup of coffee contains seventy-two to ninety-six milligrams of caffeine, others say 100 to 150. Some sources say a six-ounce cup of tea will have thirty-six to forty-eight milligrams of caffeine, some say it will have as much as a cup of coffee—and that a cup of cocoa may have fifty milligrams. (Cocoa also contains theobromine, also found in tea; it has some caffeinelike effects but has little effect on the central nervous system.)

Coca-Cola contains caffeine, but only about four milligrams per fluid ounce which, the company tells me, is "about one-fourth the amount present in an equal volume of coffee; one-third that of tea. Therefore, there would be approximately twenty-six milligrams of caffeine in a regular six-and-a-half-ounce bottle of Coca-Cola."

Instant (or soluble) coffee is nothing new; "coffee-powder" was offered for sale in the American colonies in the eighteenth century. But instant coffee was improved in the late 1940's and now accounts for slightly more than twenty-five per cent of all the cups of coffee Americans drink at home, up from 7.2 per cent in 1951. (In the United Kingdom, nearly seventy-five per cent of all coffee sold is instant coffee. The average Briton uses 0.35 ounces of instant coffee a week, as compared with 2.5 ounces of tea. Coffee consumption in total is three to four times the prewar level in Britain, partly because of a fad for Italian *espresso* coffee. The English in the past have tended to make coffee as they made tea, dropping the grounds in a pot and adding boiling water; instant coffee had to be an improvement on that. The 2.5 ounce figure for tea is a record low; tea consumption is slipping a bit in Britain.)

Growth of soluble coffee sales has leveled off in the U.S.; freeze-dried instants may give it a new stimulus. More expensive than spray-dried instants, freeze-drieds have been quite successful in Europe; they have more flavor. Spray-dried coffee is evaporated at high temperatures, which destroy taste values. Freeze-drieds start, as do spray-drieds, with extremely strong brewed coffee. Then, at least according to one patented process, the brewed coffee is chilled to a mixture of coffee and slush ice. The ice is removed from the liquid and the concentrated liquid coffee is dried at temperatures below zero. Innovation triumphs again.

Tea bags, iced tea and Jell-O

What tea Americans drink comes mostly from tea bags.[9] Their history goes back to 1904, when a tea merchant, Thomas Sullivan, sent samples of his various tea blends out to customers in little hand-

---

[9] Almost fifty-three per cent of the tea sold in the U.S. in 1969 was sold in tea bags; less than fourteen per cent was sold "loose." Over thirty-eight per cent was instant tea, a form which in 1960 had accounted for only five per cent of tea sales.

sewn bags. The customers found they could brew tea simply by pouring boiling water over a tea bag in a cup. To Sullivan's surprise, they sent in hundreds of orders for tea put up in bags. (Today even the English are brewing more and more of their tea with tea bags, filled largely with grades of broken leaves; some even use instant tea.)

According to legend, iced tea began that same year, 1904. The oft told tale has it that an English tea salesman, Richard Blechynden, was promoting his product at the St. Louis International Exposition, the same Louisiana Purchase Centennial celebration which saw the birth of the ice cream cone (Chapter 3). Blechynden's tea, steaming hot, got little play from the sweltering July fair goers. In desperation, he put a chunk of ice in the tea urn. His iced tea created a sensation, partly because most cold drinks at the time were alcoholic and the temperance movement was booming in the Midwest.

The story may be true, but J.C. Furnas reminds us that a staff writer on Horace Greeley's *Tribune*, one Solon Robinson, had recommended ice tea in 1860, and that Owen Wister, author of *The Virginian*, had enjoyed iced tea in 1894 at the Can Can Saloon in Benson, Arizona.

Blechynden's iced tea may have started the drink on its path of popularity; as we have seen so often, long years often elapse between discoveries or inventions of food items and widespread acceptance of those items.

Gelatin desserts began their popularity in the 1890's. Charles B. Knox, a salesman in Johnston, New York, watched his wife make calf's-foot jelly and remembered hearing about powdered gelatin which could make her job easier. Knox packaged the powder in easy to use forms and, at his wife's suggestion, had salesmen go from door to door to show women how easily the gelatin sheets could be dissolved in water to make aspics, molds and desserts.

Peter Cooper, inventor of the "Tom Thumb" locomotive, had invented a mixture of powdered gelatin, sugar and artificial fruit flavors as far back as the 1840's, but it was not until Jell-O came along half a century later that people were ready for such a short-cut dessert, or that advertising and merchandising apparatus—and the icebox—existed to exploit their readiness. The growth of mechanical home refrigeration a few decades later elevated gelatin desserts into the staple category in American diets.

Mechanical refrigeration, as we will see presently, had an enormous influence on the supplies, varieties and qualities of foods available to the public. So did the development of improved methods of transportation.

To market, to market

While nine out of ten Americans were engaged in farming, as was true in 1789, the remaining one tenth of the population did not represent much of a market. But the proportion of farmers to non-farmers declined rapidly. By 1826, eighty-three per cent of Americans were still farming; ten years later the figure was down to seventy-five per cent.

Getting his crop to market was a problem for a farmer. The rise of the whiskey industry in Kentucky dates to a time when it was easier and more profitable for a farmer to ship his corn East over the mountains in the form of whiskey rather than in sacks of grain.

By the 1850's, less than one half of Americans were employed on farms.

The growing numbers of non-farmers created a growing market for farm products; getting those products to market presented a growing problem.

The first great solution was the Erie Canal, DeWitt Clinton's Ditch that went 363 miles from Buffalo, on Lake Erie, to Troy, on the Hudson River. Begun in 1817, the Ditch was finished in 1825. Western farmers could ship their corn, wheat and salt pork to the Eastern cities in barges; manufactured goods had a low-cost entry to the West. And New York began the growth that led to its becoming the country's biggest city.

Seeing the success of the Erie Canal, Ohio dug a canal from Lake Erie to the Ohio River. Indiana and Ohio together dug one 452 miles up the Maumee River from Lake Erie and down the Wabash to reach the Ohio River near Evansville, Indiana.

Railroads were cheaper to build than canals, and faster, and they did not freeze up in winter, but American railroads did not really begin until 1829 and did not get as far west as Chicago until 1852. The iron rails reached the Mississippi in 1854; they got to Council Bluffs on the Missouri in 1866.

Before the stock cars came, Texas steers were driven 600 miles overland "Coma Ti Yi Yippi Yippi Yay, Yippi Yay" on the famed Chisholm Trail; they lost millions of pounds of meat as they hoofed it for two months and more on their way to market. Some Texas cattle as late as 1855 were herded all the way to New York.

More than 4 million Texas longhorns were trailed north to Abilene and the other railheads, or "cow towns," in 1880, and while railroad tracks met with a golden [10] spike (near Ogden, Utah) to span the American continent in 1869, it was not until about 1885, when the Missouri, Kansas and Texas rails reached into the heart of Texas cow country, that the great cattle drives ended.

The first refrigerated railway car had been put into service in 1863; by 1867, George Pullman's "hotel cars" were bringing luxury to American rail travel.

Dining car menus in 1870 offered seventy-five-cent meals of oysters on the half-shell, porterhouse steak, quail, antelope, plover, fresh trout and terrapin, with second helpings on the house. There was champagne at every meal, including breakfast, and passengers ate in the splendor of Turkish carpets, French mirrors, fringed portieres and rare inlaid woods. The Denver and Rio Grande made a specialty of mountain trout, the Union Pacific was famous for its antelope steaks, the Northern Pacific for its grouse and salmon. It was the Golden Age of railroading.

---

[10] The spike may really have been of polished iron. When Leland Stanford, president of the Central Pacific, swung his sledge hammer to drive the final spike home, he missed. He handed the sledge to Thomas C. Durant, a vice-president of the Union Pacific, who also missed, possibly to be polite. The condition of the two men is not recorded.

The main effect of the rails, however, was to change the livestock industry.

As the first Henry Wallace put it, "The railroad shortened the hogs' noses, shortened the legs, done away with the bristles, and put a more lovely kink in the tail. . . . And now, instead of cattle of indeterminant breed, Shorthorns were being introduced in our neighborhood." Before the railroads, according to "Uncle Henry," in the time of the great droves, "there was no baby beef; for the steer could not travel over the mountains unless he had length of limb. Hogs were not bred exactly for speed, but for ability to walk to market." Since meat is animal muscle (hind and forequarters, while the most flavorful parts of an animal, also have more connective tissue—and are tougher—because the muscles in those parts get more exercise), the rails had the effect of making American meat more tender.

Another railroad contribution was grain-fed meat, rare before the rails brought cattle to the Corn Belt, where cattle-finishing centers readied livestock for market. Today, instead of the cattle coming to the Corn Belt, the corn is going to the cattle: packers are building plants in the Plains States and the Southwest and short-circuiting the old rail terminals and stockyards.

Even slower to improve than overland freight was water transport. Most cargo ships in 1800 were still tiny sailing craft of from 100 to 500 tons.[11] The biggest were the East Indiamen, which carried up to 1500 tons. Faster, more graceful clipper ships appeared in the 1840's, but it still took three months to sail from China to Europe; the clipper ships' cargoes were mostly luxury goods, like tea.

Steel-plated, steam-powered freighters, capable of carrying huge foodstuff cargoes, did not come until the late nineteenth century. As

---

[11] Columbus' *Santa Maria* is thought to have been a 100-ton craft, meaning she could carry 100 "tuns," or double hogsheads, of wine. In shipping terms today, a "register ton" is a measurement of the internal capacity of a ship; it is equal to 100 cubic feet. A "displacement ton" is the amount of sea water, in long tons (2240 pounds) equal to thirty-five cubic feet, which the ship displaces. Cargo capacity is also measured in "deadweight tons" (weight) and in "gross tons" (volume).

late as 1870, only sixteen per cent of world shipping was in steamships, and these often were slower than wind-driven craft. The log of the clipper *Cutty Sark*, namesake of the scotch whisky brand, records that in 1889, en route to Sydney, Australia, she passed the new P. & O. steamer *Britannia* which was making sixteen knots. Even in 1900, steamships accounted for only sixty-two per cent of world shipping.

What made spices so costly in medieval Europe and Britain was the low state of transportation at the time, which also made oranges a rare Christmas treat instead of the commodity they are today. In much of the world, transportation is still primitive; food rots because it cannot be carried to market. This is certainly not the basis of the world hunger problem, but in many places it is a significant factor. Even in the U.S. transport limitations force us to use quantities of additives (Appendix) in our foods to keep them from spoiling between producer and consumer.

What flexibility we do have in our food marketing, and much of the year-round variety in our diet, must be credited to the passenger automobile. Cars led to the building of highways, which now carry truck-loads of food. Special trucks carry nothing else but milk, refrigerated trucks carry foods consumed locally, trucks link "truck farms," poultry farms and orchards to city markets.

Foods move faster by truck than by train, partly because freight cars have to wait to be assembled into trains before they can move. Thus it takes citrus from Florida three days to reach New York by rail, only thirty-six hours by truck.

On a global basis, refrigerated ships are responsible for things like the New Zealand sheep industry. That country has 80 million sheep—twenty for every human inhabitant—mostly because refrigerated cargo space has enabled the islanders to raise more lamb and mutton for overseas markets, which also take large quantities of New Zealand butter.

Some goods even go by air. A large transport plane today carries more food than the cargo of spices carried back by Magellan's *Vittoria* in 1522. Planes put fresh seafood on the tables of our Midwest; they carry fish and shellfish into inland areas everywhere. We have come a long way from the days when Inca kings, in their mountain capital of Cuzco, received fresh fish carried 130 miles up from the Pacific by relays of runners climbing the stone stairs of that marvel of the ancient Americas, the Inca highway.

More than ninety per cent of the world's food is consumed in the countries where it is grown; the balance, however, is so large it accounts for more international trade than oil, steel, timber or anything else. A country like Iceland depends on its fish exports for ninety per cent of its economy. Oil-rich desert countries and most island nations must import the major part of what they eat. The U.S. is mostly self-sufficient, but in the crates outside the Royal Opera House in London's Covent Garden, for centuries the city's produce market (the market is soon to be moved south of the Thames), there are grapes from Spain, oranges from Israel, peaches and onions from Italy, everything from everywhere. Britain has for nearly 100 years imported about half of what she eats, though latest statistics show 52.4 per cent of the U.K.'s food is home-produced (just over forty-two per cent of the country's calories, nearly sixty-two per cent of its protein).

And still there are foods which are virtually never exported, not even to rich America. To enjoy highly perishable tropical fruits like the sapodilla,[12] the sour-sop (or *guanábana*), the *pitaya*, the custard apple (or *chirimoya*), the *granadilla*, the *curuva* and some others, there is little alternative but to visit Central or South America or the Caribbean islands.

---

[12] Sapodillas, from the same tree that yields chicle for chewing gum, are occasionally available in some New York City markets. So are Chinese gooseberries, or "kiwi fruit," imported from New Zealand (they're an unprepossessing fuzzy brown on the outside, bright green—and quite delicious—inside). Also seen, especially in late winter, is the Ugli from Jamaica, said to be a blend of tangerine, grapefruit and Seville orange and discovered in 1915 or 1916 by F.G. Sharp, owner of Jamaica's Trout Hall estates. For most Americans, these fruits are as unknown as tomatoes, pineapples and papayas were to fifteenth century-Europe.

Banana boats and bananas

This brings us to the banana, a fruit whose pleasures we savor largely by virtue of improved transportation. When the International Longshoremen's Association struck East and Gulf Coast docks for more than six weeks early in 1969, the A&P raised banana prices in the New York area from fourteen and a half cents a pound to seventeen cents. Without ships, and men to unload them, we would not eat bananas.

Botanists say the banana plant, the most prolific of food plants,[13] dates back to the Pliocene era, a million years ago. The Koran says the forbidden fruit in the Garden of Eden was a banana, not an apple. Alexander the Great found the wise men (*homines sapientes*, in Latin) of India eating bananas when he crossed the Indus in 327 B.C., which is the alleged reason for the banana's botanical name, *Musa sapientum*.

The Arabs grew bananas in northern Egypt and the Holy Land in the seventh century. Eight centuries later, in 1482, Portuguese explorers found the fruit growing on Africa's west coast and picked up the name Guinea natives used for it, a name that sounded to Portuguese ears like "banana."

At one time it was thought that bananas were native to the Americas as well as to the East Indies, southern India and the Malay Peninsula; now it is believed that Spanish explorers who mentioned finding bananas in the New World were talking about the plantain (*Musa paradisiaca*), that staple starch of the West Indies which breadfruit

---

[13] In three months, a banana plant, grown from an "eye" set in a deep, wide hole, grows as high as a man's head. In another three months the plant is twice as tall as a man. Six months later the fruit begins to form, and in another three or four months it is ready to be cut. The plant bears just one bunch of fruit, which usually has about ninety bananas in nine clusters (but may have as many as 140). When the one bunch is cut, the whole plant is chopped down and another one planted. Planted in a favored commercial variety of banana, one acre can yield from 600 to 800 bunches in a year—some 9 million calories, more digestible calories than any other major above-ground crop. But to subsist entirely on bananas, a person would have to eat five pounds a day.

(Chapter 7) has never displaced. Plantain, sometimes called a "cooking banana," is larger and starchier than the *Musa sapientum*, and less sweet. To be palatable, it has to be baked, boiled or fried.

Today's great banana plantations of the West Indies and of Latin America's "banana republics" are not based on plantains; they probably can be traced to a few banana roots planted in Santo Domingo by Friar Tomás de Berlanga in 1516.

Today these Caribbean and Latin countries are the major banana exporters, though they are by no means the biggest banana producers. Africa grows about nineteen billion pounds of bananas a year (a bunch, or stem, weighs upward of sixty pounds), versus about 13 billion in the Americas; but the Africans themselves consume ninety per cent of the bananas they grow.

As for the bananas we consume in the U.S., they are all imported, and were almost unknown here until the development of improved transportation.

Back in the eighteenth century, New England sea captains used to come home with descriptions of bananas they had enjoyed in the tropics. But how can you describe the taste of a banana? It is unique.

Few North Americans had ever tasted a banana in 1804, when Captain John Chester brought about thirty stems of green bananas (there are ten to fifteen bananas to a "hand," seven to twelve hands to a stem) into New York from Cuba aboard his schooner *Reynard*. New York waited another twenty-six years before a full cargo of 1500 stems arrived aboard John Pearsall's schooner *Harriet Smith*.

James Fenimore Cooper, who died in 1851, said "bannanas" were common in New York in his time:

> Owing to the facility and constancy of intercourse with the Southern States [he wrote in *The Travelling Bachelor*], the fruits of the tropics are found here, not quite as fresh, certainly, as when first culled from the plant itself, but well flavored, and in absolute contact with the products of the temperate zones. Pine-apples, large, rich, golden, and good, are sold from twelve to twenty-five sous; delicious oranges are hawked in the streets much cheaper than a tolerable apple can be bought in the streets of Paris, and bannanas, yams, water-melons, &c. are as common as need be in markets.

But large-scale traffic in bananas did not start until 1870; it was the schooner *Telegraph* out of Boston, skippered by Captain Lorenzo D. Baker, that started it. Baker, unable to get more "worthwhile" cargo at Kingston, Jamaica, loaded bananas on the open deck of his ship and, with favorable winds, made the passage to Boston in just fourteen days. The fruit, a great novelty, sold out quickly.

A clerk in the Boston fruit brokerage firm of Seaverns Company, one Andrew Preston, saw the opportunity in bananas and went into partnership with Captain Baker. Their Boston Fruit Company acquired other ships. It introduced bananas, individually wrapped in tinfoil, at ten cents apiece at the Philadelphia Centennial Exposition of 1876, giving thousands of people their first exposure to the fruit. (It is interesting how large a role fairs and expositions have played in America's food history.) Not until some years later were bananas imported in large tonnages, and then it was through the introduction of refrigerated cargo ships. Today, Americans eat more bananas than any other fruit—18 pounds per year for every man, woman and child—and while the state of Hawaii grows 6 or 7 million pounds, we import about 3.6 billion pounds a year in banana boats.

The banana story is a story of resisting the ravages of lead spot, Panama disease and banana wilt; of the Boston Fruit Company, merged by Samuel Zemurray and Minor Keith into the United Fruit Company in 1899; of revolutions fomented by soldiers of fortune like Lee Christmas and his lieutenant Jerry Murphy, both in the pay of Zemurray; of railroads built at great loss of life to deadly fevers in the jungles of Central America; of a commodity transformed into a brand-name specialty through the talents of an animated banana named Chiquita (and the marketing talents of the men who made her the top banana).

But mostly it is a story of transportation; or more specifically, of refrigerated cargo vessels.

Chiquita Banana, in her famous song of the 1940's, told housewives never, never, never to put bananas in the refrigerator. The 40° temperature inside a household refrigerator will make a banana turn brown, which dismays consumers though it does no harm to the fruit inside the peel. To avoid spoilage, however, bananas must not get too hot. They must be maintained at a temperature between 55° and 65° F. when they are shipped, which is possible only with refrigeration.

We virtually never see the red banana, which is inclined to break off the stalk, or the very small fig (or lady-finger) banana [14] so much esteemed in the tropics, but without refrigerated banana boats we would have almost no bananas at all, Chiquita would never have sung her song, and America would still be singing, "Yes, we have no bananas."

The spoilers and the anti-spoilers

Refrigeration is a relatively recent invention. Until about 150 years ago, there were only a very few known ways to preserve foods from spoilage—ways that could be applied to only a limited range of foods, ways that left some foods with unpleasant tastes or undesirable characteristics.

One way of food preservation, used for fish since time immemorial, is salting. Just as salt butter keeps longer than fresh "sweet" butter, other foods are kept edible longer by being salted.

In prehistoric times, the only method known for preserving meat was to dry it; this process is still used in Spain for *jamon serrano*, a sun-cured mountain ham, in the Vallais of Switzerland for *viande sechée*, which is beef or pork dried in the airy Alpine barns, and in the crisp mountain air of the Grisons where *Bündnerfleisch*, a thin-sliced sun-cured meat, is a specialty.

American Indians dried some of their buffalo meat by cutting it into wide slices, folding the slices over poles and hanging them in the sun and wind until they were brown and hard. The early settlers of the West called this dried meat "jerky," from the Spanish *charqui* or

---

[14] For years, the Gros Michel ("Big Mike") banana dominated the banana trade; since 1962 it has been increasingly replaced by the disease-resistant, stronger-stemmed Cavendish or Valery variety which grows on a lower plant and is less vulnerable to wind damage.

charki, a word derived in turn from a South American Indian term for the dried strips and slices of meat which in Mexico are called *tasayo.* The Indians also packed meat in holes in the ground which they lined with dry grass and covered with branches and earth, a practice still followed in parts of South America.

Beef jerky, despite its leathery texture, has become a popular snack food in the U.S., with retail sales estimated to run between $8 million and $10 million a year and growing fast. It is made mostly from round steak that has been stripped of fat and gristle, cut in strips, dried in ovens and sold in cellophane for ten cents a quarter-ounce, $5.50 for a fourteen-ounce jar. Cowboys and Eskimos have carried jerky in their saddlebags and parkas for years. Its current popularity is credited to its use by GI's in Viet Nam.

Another Indian meat-preservation idea was pemmican, a mixture of dried meat (commonly venison) pounded into a powder, mixed with bone-marrow fat (usually from a bear) which had been melted into a buttery consistency, dried berries and dried vegetables. Arctic explorers have carried something very much like pemmican—made of dried meat and raisins—on their expeditions.

Fish is still commonly preserved by drying, as well as by salting; both methods were once applied to vegetables and even to fruit. Colonial Americans dried great quantities of apples which, de Crèvecoeur tells us, was "one of those rural occupations which most amply reward us."

> The neighboring women are invited to spend the evening at our house. A basket of apples is given to each of them, which they peel, quarter and core. . .
> Next day a great stage is erected, either in our grass plots or anywhere else where cattle can't come. Strong crotches are planted in the ground. Poles are horizontally fixed on these, and boards laid close together . . . When the scaffold is thus erected, the apples are thinly spread over it. They are soon covered with all the bees and wasps and sucking flies of the neighborhood. This accelerates the operation of drying. Now and then they are turned. At night they are covered with blankets. If it is likely to rain, they are gathered and brought into the house. This is repeated until they

are perfectly dried. It is astonishing to what small size they will shrink. . .

The method of using them is this: we put a small handful in warm water overnight; next morning they are swelled to their former size; and when cooked either in pies or dumplings, it is difficult to discover by the taste whether they are fresh or not.[15]

Farmer de Crèvecoeur dried peaches and plums and also pumpkins. Some dried apples were shipped by the colonists to the West Indies.

Food preservation became more sophisticated with the advent of smoked meats. The microorganisms which help plants and animals live efficiently also speed up the decomposition of these plants and animals after death; smoking meats kills or arrests the growth of many of these microorganisms and delays spoilage. Wood smoke contains such things as formaldehyde, tars, alcohols and creosote—not enough to hurt anybody, just enough to stop bacteria. And to give the meat an interesting flavor.

Using salt, sugar and smoke to make meat "keep" and not spoil is called "curing," as if untreated meat suffered from a disease. The presence of bacteria is common both to untreated meat and to most diseases, but the use of the word "cure" as applied to meat preservation precedes any knowledge of bacteria as such.

As noted earlier, spices have been used since early times to help preserve meat (and to disguise the effects of spoiling). There are more effective ways today to preserve meat than by smoking it or spicing it. Still we continue to enjoy smoked hams, smoked bacon, smoked salmon, corned beef, hams studded with cloves and countless other spiced and smoked products. Why? Because we like the taste, though in many cases the "smoky" flavor comes from a liquid "smoke" used in packing houses. Most ham and bacon is now cured in a few days where it used to take up to six months.

The ancient Egyptians knew nothing about microorganisms, yet

---

[15] Apple pies and dumplings were thus available almost all year round. Dried skins and cores were also used to brew a kind of beer whose barm (de Crèvecoeur spells it "bawm") or yeast was used to raise bread.

they developed a variety of primitive, but fairly effective, methods of preserving foods, many of which are still in wide use. They kept some foods dry in cool storehouses. Fish and meat were salted and dried in the sun.

Later preservation techniques included such basic ideas as adding sugar to jam and vinegar to pickles. The effect, in every case, was to create an atmosphere in which decay agents could not live.

Vinegar, incidentally, is an ancient invention, much older than the Old Testament (which has Ruth dipping a bit of bread into vinegar). The name comes from *vin aigre*, French for "sour wine," which is what vinegar is, or what it was originally. The bacteria *Acetobacter* sours the wine, dissipates the alcohol and leaves a mixture of four per cent acetic acid and water. Roman legions put wine vinegar into their drinking water to purify it. And Cleopatra once dissolved a perfect pearl in vinegar as a put-down to Mark Antony. Vinegar was a by-product of wine makers and brewers until about the seventeenth century when vinegar making was established as a separate industry in France. The English still turn their sour beer and ale into malt vinegar. America makes cider vinegar out of fermented apple juice.

Pickling, a preservative method used by the ancient Chinese, the Babylonians and other early civilizations, can mean keeping food in brine (salt) solutions, sugar, acid liquids like vinegar or combinations of these.

The Romans preserved meat in brine, soaking it later in milk to remove most of the salt. The wine in Roman wine jars was covered with a film of olive oil to keep it from turning sour (cork stoppers, made from the thick outer bark of a Mediterranean oak,[16] were not used until the late 1600's).

To keep food from spoiling, people have at various times in history tried almost everything. At one point it was solemnly believed that plain water, reduced to one-third its volume by boiling, was somehow effective as a preservative. Some foods were preserved in wine or

---

[16] The cork oak (*Quercus suber*) of Spain and Portugal lives as long as 500 years. It is a broad-leafed evergreen and its outer bark can be removed every nine years beginning when the tree is fifteen to twenty years old.

honey. Oysters and green vegetables were stored in vessels treated with pitch.

Enveloping food in fat, an early European method, is still used to preserve some meat. *Pâté de foie gras* has traditionally been preserved by putting it in stoneware pots (*terrines*) and covering it with fat, which congeals to make an almost airtight cover, like the paraffin used to seal jelly jars.

Dawn of the can opener

Tin cans, when they became important near the middle of the nineteenth century, revolutionized food preservation. Frozen foods, eighty years later, began a further revolution, still in its early stages.

The canning industry, based on a process of hermetically sealing food, dates back to 1809 when a French confectioner, Nicholas Appert, was awarded a prize [17] by Napoleon Bonaparte for his invention of a process to keep foodstuffs edible. Appert extracted the air from glass jars and heated food inside the hermetically-sealed jars.

French sailors tested the food aboard ship and found Appert's idea worked. Provisioning ships was revolutionized. In the days before Appert, travelers and seamen had resorted to elaborate measures to feed themselves at sea. A Frenchman sailing to the Far East in 1690 recorded that "the ship is a farmyard." In cages and pens on deck were two cows, eight bullocks, six calves, twelve pigs, twelve geese, twenty-four sheep, twenty-four turkeys, thirty-six pigeons, forty-eight ducks and 500 hens.

Because it freed men from dependence on any one harvest, the

---

[17] The prize was 12,000 francs, nearly a quarter of a million dollars in modern exchange. Military reasons motivated the French to offer so much. In the wars of the 1790's after the French Revolution, Napoleon's armies were depleted as much by starvation and deficiency diseases as by battle wounds. Appert worked fourteen years to develop his process, which was for a while a French military secret.

invention of canning (to which many men besides Appert contributed) has been ranked with the great inventions of man—fire, agriculture and the wheel—and the only one, except for Pasteur's microorganism discoveries, made during recorded history. (The evaluation was made prior to more recent discoveries like DNA.) It was said that Napoleon, if he could have kept food canning exclusively French, might have conquered the world.

Like atomic secrets, however, canning knowledge leaked. An Englishman, Bryan Donkin, obtained a patent for a canning process in 1810, using tins [18] instead of Appert's glass jars. Neither Donkin nor Appert understood they were killing decay bacteria with the high temperatures they used in their processes; that knowledge came with Pasteur's findings.

Tin cans, which are really steel cans coated inside with a thin film of tin, moved quickly to America, where lobster and salmon were the first foods canned. An American, Thomas Kensett, invented a tin can for packing meat, poultry, fish, vegetables and fruit, but not until 1847 was a stamping process invented which made tin cans cheap enough for wide sale of canned goods.

Perhaps the greatest effect of canning was to introduce many people to foods they had never tasted fresh. Even today, with so many foods available frozen, most people have never tasted some foods any way but canned: anchovies, most chilies, hominy, mincemeat, plum pudding, tamales, sardines, tuna fish, many soups, tomato juice, and pineapple juice. Only a tiny percentage of the world's pineapple crop is sold fresh; most is canned. And this is true of a good many other fruits and vegetables, though some foods are adversely affected by plain tin plate (which slightly bleaches canned sauerkraut, grapefruit sections, peaches, pears and fruit juices) and require tin can linings

---

[18] The uses of tin to line cooking and drinking vessels, and thus avoid lead poisoning, were known as early as 23 A.D. Bohemian tin was used for tin plate in Germany in 1575. Cornwall produced tin for a British tin-plate industry established between 1720 and 1730 and remained the major source of tin until 1870, when Malayan tin surpassed it. Tin is also mined in Central Africa and in Bolivia, and is recovered from used tin cans.

coated with oleoresins, vinyl plastics, phenolic plastics or (in the case of beer) special waxes.

Most American housewives were once familiar with the quart jars of Indiana's Ball Brothers and Oklahoma's Kerr Glass Manufacturing Company, still the major factors in the home canning industry. Women boiled, stirred, poured paraffin and "put up" vegetables, fruits, jams and jellies by the ton.

Commercial canning has now far outdistanced the do-it-your-selfers, though home canning has had a surprising resurgence in recent years. The Glass Container Manufacturers Institute in Washington estimates that U.S. homemakers now put up more than a billion jars of fruits, vegetables and preserves a year.

Modern housewives are generally advised not to keep even commercial canned goods for more than a year. It would seem an excess of caution. Canned food is remarkably safe; it has been for years. Back in the late 1930's, someone discovered a four-pound can of roast veal put up back in 1824. It was gingerly opened. Nobody quite dared eat the contents, so it was fed to a dozen rats over a period of ten days, and did them no harm at all.

Canned food by modern methods is sealed into its container and then placed in a pressure cooker that holds temperatures as high as 250° F. for as long as three hours, completely sterilizing the contents of the can, and incidentally cooking it to save work for housewives.

Captain Robert Falcon Scott, on his ill-starred 1910–11 South Pole expedition, carried along canned pemmican, which sounds a little like wearing both a belt and suspenders. When an expedition forty-five years later searched Scott's abandoned camp, the canned pemmican was found to be quite edible.

A more significant canned item is condensed milk, first manufactured in 1858 following the 1856 patent granted to its inventor, Gail Borden. Borden was an experimental dairyman of Litchfield, Connecticut, the son of a frontiersman. In 1852 he went to London to interest fair goers at the International Exposition there in a dehydrated biscuit he had developed. His funds exhausted, Borden was forced to return home in steerage, traveling with immigrant families from southern and eastern Europe. En route, he saw infants, sickened by raw milk from infected cows carried aboard ship (just as cows had been in 1690), die in their mothers' arms.

Louis Pasteur had tried to find ways of preserving milk, but it took Borden to turn the trick. Perfecting his process and convincing skeptics was a four-year job, but condensed milk proved a godsend to the shattered South after the Civil War, a conflict in which both armies made wide use of canned foods.

A decade before that war, the U.S. landscape was already blighted with the tin can scourge. J.C. Furnas quotes from the letters of a woman, a gold rusher's wife, who wrote that in the 1850's Rich Bar in the Feather River country of California was "thickly peppered with empty bottles, oyster cans, sardine boxes . . ." And he quotes Owen Wister's *The Virginian*, in which a cowhand loads his saddlebags with canned sardines, canned chicken and canned tomatoes before riding out past the "ramparts of Medicine Bow—thick heaps and fringes of tin cans . . . that civilization had dropped upon Wyoming's virgin soil . . . the wind has blown away the ashes of the [cowboy's] campfires; but the empty sardine box lies rusting over the face of the Western earth."

In the wild west of Colorado in 1865, corn, tomatoes, beans, pineapple, strawberries, cherries, peaches, oysters and lobster were all available in cans; for a price, of course: $12 to $15 for a case of twelve cans, each about two quarts (in Montana the price was $27 a case).

By 1870, sales of canned foods in America were up to about 30 million cans a year. Canning methods were not always perfect, and most housewives still viewed canned food with suspicion. But canning techniques improved, and the Pure Food and Drug Act of 1906 helped allay the widespread distrust of canned goods (though millions of people still believe mistakenly that an opened can should not be used to store food in the refrigerator).

Before World War I, the can opener had become a fixture in most U.S. kitchens. About twenty-six billion cans and jars of food are now opened in those kitchens every year, sweet corn, green beans, tomatoes and peas being, in that order, our favorite canned vegetables and peaches, applesauce, pineapple and fruit cocktail our favorite canned fruits.

Frozen foods have replaced a considerable number of canned (the English say "tinned") goods, but canned fruits and vegetables, tuna fish and sardines are still American staples; and where people do not have home freezers, meaning most of the world, plenty of canned meat and poultry is still sold.

A question of degrees (F.)

Freezing as a means of preserving food has prehistoric origins. Modern freezing techniques date back at least as far as 1877, when 5500 frozen mutton carcasses left Argentina aboard the *S.S. Paraguay* and were delivered at Le Havre, France, over six months later (the ship had a collision en route) in perfectly good condition. This marked the start of today's great trade in meat between producers in South America, Australia and New Zealand, and consumers in Europe.

Freezing does not kill bacteria; it merely arrests their growth. It affects the flavor of some foods (fish tastes much better shipped in ice than frozen), but less so than does canning.

Many people have tried to preserve foods by freezing them. Sir Francis Bacon, back in seventeenth-century England, got fatal pneumonia while attempting to freeze chickens by stuffing them with snow.

But until quick freezing came along in the last half century, results were poor: slow freezing changed the flavor and texture of foods, while quick freezing did not. The pioneer of quick-frozen foods was Clarence Birdseye, a scientist from Brooklyn. On an expedition to Labrador for the U.S. Fish and Wildlife Service in 1914, Birdseye noticed something Eskimos had always known: the fish he caught through the ice froze stiff the instant they were exposed to the air. Defrosted and cooked weeks later, they still tasted fresh-caught; at least they met Birdseye's taste standards. Quick freezing worked well with caribou steaks, too.

After World War I, Birdseye went into the fishery business in Gloucester, Massachusetts, experimenting all the time with quick freezing of fish and other foods in temperatures well below the zero mark. He froze raw meats, vegetables, fruits, cooked foods, cakes, pies and breads in lockers he designed for the purpose. With Wall Street backing, he offered freezer cabinets free to stores willing to stock his frozen foods.

The first Birdseye packages went on sale in 1930. They cost a lot more than fresh foods, and the country was hardly enjoying boom times. Frozen foods required special handling in the kitchen; housewives had to learn how to use them. Despite all the obstacles, in less than ten years the whole gamut of foodstuffs was being marketed in quick-frozen versions across America.

Frozen foods not only brought convenience and relief from the sameness of canned foods whose flavors were often unnatural, they also introduced new variety to U.S. tables. Shrimp, once enjoyed only by people along the seacoast or near Gulf ports, became common in inland cities. By 1960, Americans were eating 10 million pounds of South African rock lobster tails, taken from spiny lobsters out of the icy Benguela Current that moves from the Antarctic past the Cape of Good Hope. In 1969, almost thirteen million pounds of the lobster tails arrived in the U.S. by refrigerator ship.

The biggest impact of quick freezing was, in fact, on the fishing industry. Blocks of fillets and frozen whole fish, now increasingly processed and frozen at sea in factory ships, made fish a commodity in international trade rather than a simple perishable food resource.

About thirty-three per cent of all seafood sold in the U.S. is now sold frozen (as compared with twenty per cent of poultry, only three per cent of red meat), even though Morris Kaplan, technical director of Consumers Union, has said, "Frozen fish has been lousy for a long time and is still lousy; the quality is abominable."

Even that purist Mrs. M. F. K. Fisher does not go so far. "I do use frozen fish [she says in her *Bold Knife and Fork*], which I . . . pick up like bleak logs now and then in the markets. They tease my inventiveness."

Less inventive Americans consumed nearly 70 pounds of frozen foods each in 1968 (compared with 1967 figures of nearly 67 pounds for the U.S., 10.3 pounds for Britain, eight for West Germany and 0.5 for Italy, though figures for all countries have been rising rapidly and must have been much higher for 1969).

Latest reports show that over 14 billion pounds of frozen foods —$7 billion worth—are sold in the U.S. each year, with frozen prepared convenience foods like TV dinners gaining on frozen vegetables, the leading category of frozen food. Restaurants and institutions like schools and hospitals are using more and more frozen dishes to reduce their kitchen staffs. Biggest frozen food packer is Consolidated Foods Corporation, which owns Sara Lee, Booth Fisheries, Ocoma Foods and other companies; the Birds Eye division of General Foods Corporation is a close second.

Frozen foods have improved enormously in recent years. Frozen peas, spinach, asparagus, candied sweet potatoes, fordhook lima beans, winter squash, berries (especially in new quick-thawing versions) and cherries are particularly successful; summer squash, French beans, zucchini and melon are rather less successful in quality, even when not permitted to thaw and refreeze in the course of marketing.

Even the microscopic ice crystals of quick freezing are destructive to the textures of some foods, like tomatoes and raw salad vegetables and the freezing process softens fruits. A new DuPont process, announced early in 1969, which sprays liquid Freon freezant directly on foods, may add tomatoes, tropical fruits and other items to the list of foods available frozen. And it may improve the quality of frozen fish.

The frozen food section

While frozen foods may be more costly than fresh foods in some instances (in other cases they are actually cheaper, and just as good), they do represent a great step forward in convenience.

More than a quarter of U.S. homes now have home freezers, which first became commercially important in 1937. Many home freezers are bought with the justification of economy, but their real benefit is convenience. Between the early 1930's and 1951, thousands of commercial frozen food locker plants were built in the U.S. The number has been declining rapidly since 1951 because Americans will not bother going to the locker plants when they can have a freezer right at home.

For most urban Americans, the supermarket is close enough to make a home freezer quite unnecessary. Modern refrigerators have freezer compartments big enough to hold a week's supply of frozen foods for most families.

But there are things to know about buying foods in the supermarket's frozen food section, and most housewives do not know them.

The display cabinet at the store should, for example, have a dial thermometer to show the storage temperature. The Department of Agriculture has released studies which show a wide variation in quality between frozen food stored, say, at 20° F. and food stored at zero degrees. Frozen string beans may last only a week at 30°, a month or so at 20°, six months at 10° and one to three years at zero. Just under zero? Indefinitely.

As soon as a frozen food package starts to thaw, its contents begins to deteriorate. The thawing can be stopped by refreezing the package, which stops the deterioration; but some damage has been done and cannot be undone. When the food thaws again, deterioration begins again where it left off.

So it is smart to pick frozen food packages from below the top of the stack and close to the sides of the freezer; to make them the last foods selected at the supermarket; to ask the clerk to put them in a separate, insulated bag (lots of luck) or wrap them tightly in newspapers; to get them home as fast as possible; to keep home freezer temperature close to zero, or even below zero if possible; and to use up the oldest packages first.

It is also a good idea to ask the store manager how his frozen foods are handled and delivered. Do they come in by refrigerator trucks?

Does the store have a "first in, first out" policy for freezer case products so no packages can remain in the cabinet for too long?

Ideally, frozen food tastes more like fresh food and keeps its nutritional values better than canned or dried food. But it often falls short of the ideal. It may be transported in insulated containers in an unrefrigerated truck and left for twelve hours or more while its temperature climbs up to 20° or higher. It may be unloaded in the hot sun. It may be left in a back room until it is practically thawed before it is put in the display case. The temperature in the display case may be too high. Or the temperature may be zero but some packages may be stacked above the "load line," where it is warmer.

All these various factors can make frozen foods vary in taste, color, freshness and food value. A can of frozen orange juice may lose half its vitamin C content before it gets into breakfast glasses.

The way frozen food is defrosted at home is a critical factor, too. Take frozen meats. Less than three per cent of the fresh beef, pork and lamb we eat in the U.S. is now sold frozen, but the figure is growing slightly. Usually frozen meats can be cooked without thawing them first; simply allow a little more cooking time. A large roast, for instance, may require fifty per cent more cooking time than the same roast cooked unfrozen.

For foods normally eaten chilled, like fruits, cooked shrimp and cream pies, the best procedure is to move the unopened frozen package from the freezer into the refrigerator. Leave it there long enough —six hours per pound is the general rule—and it will be ready to serve without any of those little ice crystals found in food that has been improperly defrosted.

Leaving frozen food at room temperature may be a faster way to thaw it, but it is a bad idea because it gives harmful bacteria a chance to develop. Letting the frozen food package sit immersed in water is a little safer, because it is quicker, but it still exposes the food to bacteria development for too long a period; salmonella and streptococcus food infections are a real and present danger.

Some baked goods can be defrosted by heating them slightly in an oven at a moderate setting.

Vegetables should be thoroughly defrosted before cooking. Prior to being frozen, they were blanched—that is, plunged briefly into boiling water, then into cold water to stop their cooking. To cook defrosted peas and spinach, heat them for just a few minutes with a little butter in a covered saucepan, season and serve promptly. Most other defrosted vegetables must be brought to a boil in water or chicken stock, the pan covered and the vegetable then cooked with a tablespoon or so of butter until barely tender; then boil away any residual liquid with the pan uncovered, shaking to keep the vegetable from burning or sticking. Avoid aluminum or iron pans, which can give some vegetables a metallic taste and may badly discolor asparagus and artichokes.

The iceman cameth

Frozen foods would have been impossible without mechanical refrigeration, itself a relatively recent development even in our "developed" countries, and still practically unknown in most of the world.

To combat heat, which encourages the growth of food-spoiling bacteria, men have for centuries used dark caves, running water and ice.

The Chinese were cutting and storing ice as early as 1000 B.C. The Caesars brought ice down from the Apennines. French kings imported ice from Sonnefjord, in Norway, and built special ice storage rooms in their castle cellars.

Ice refrigerates because it absorbs heat as it melts. This heat-transfer principle is basic to all refrigeration; it follows the second law of thermodynamics, that heat cannot pass from a colder body to a warmer body, only from a warmer body to a colder body.

Michael Faraday, the English physicist and chemist, discovered in 1823 that certain gases under constant pressure will condense until they cool. Just eleven years later, a Massachusetts inventor living in London, Jacob Perkins, produced the first continuously acting compression refrigerating machine on which all home refrigerators are still based; it pumped away the vapor and condensed it under pressure so it could be used again and again. A French engineer, Edmund C. Carré, developed the first absorption system in the early 1850's, and a German, Carl P.G. von Linde, introduced the first successful compression system using ammonia in 1873.

But it was 1918 before the first practical automatic home refrigerator was put on sale in America.

Early Americans kept their milk and butter downcellar, hung it down the well or stored it in the cool running water of a springhouse, but for a century before the first home refrigerator, and for long after, the iceman with his rubber shoulder pad and his sixty-pound block of ice was a familiar visitor in American homes, and the sound of melting ice, dripping into a pan beneath the icebox in the kitchen, was familiar to American ears.

Cutting giant blocks of ice from the country's northern lakes and rivers developed as a big domestic and export industry beginning with the efforts of Boston's Frederic Tudor in 1805.

The energetic Tudor secured rights to build icehouses in Charleston, South Carolina, in the West Indies and in Havana. He obtained monopolies to the ice of New England ponds. He sold iced beverages at the same price as unchilled beverages to encourage a taste for cold drinks. And he developed efficient ice depots for tropical climates that reduced melting from over sixty per cent to less than eight per cent.

Tudor's father had gone to Harvard; young Frederic preferred business. Harvard, he said, was "a place for loafers." Another Harvardman's son, Nathaniel Jarvis Wyeth, felt the same way. He became manager of Tudor's ice company and in 1825 devised a machine that revolutionized ice harvesting.

Wyeth's horse-drawn hoist, which lifted blocks of ice out of the water and up to a chute, which slid them into the icehouse beside a pond, lowered the cost of harvesting ice from thirty cents a ton to ten cents. (Wyeth also discovered the value of sawdust to prevent blocks from melting together in transit, thus creating a demand for the previously useless by-product of Maine's lumber mills.)

Tudor remained the Ice King. In 1833 he sent his ship *Tuscany* to Calcutta with 180 tons of ice that remained unmelted for four months, though the *Tuscany* crossed the equator twice on her voyage. Tudor built a big ice depot in Calcutta and tried to get Anglo-Indians to eat apples, butter and cheese, all of which he shipped out of Boston.

By 1846, Boston was exporting 65,000 tons of ice to more than fifty destinations in the U.S. and the farther reaches of the tropical and subtropical world.

Some of that ice came from Henry Thoreau's Walden Pond. Thoreau wrote in the winter of 1846–47:

> An hundred Irishmen, with Yankee overseers, came from Cambridge every day to get the ice. They divided it into cakes by methods [invented by Wyeth] too well known to require description, and these, being sledded to the shore, were rapidly hauled off on to an ice platform, and raised by grappling irons and block and tackle, worked by horses, on to a stack, as surely as so many barrels of flour, and there placed evenly side by side, and row upon row, as if they formed the solid base of an obelisk designed to pierce the clouds. They told me that in a good day they could get out a thousand tons, which was the yield of about one acre . . . They told me that they had some in the ice-houses at Fresh Pond five years old which was as good as ever . . . The sweltering inhabitants of Charleston and New Orleans, of Madras and Bombay and Calcutta, drink at my well . . . The pure Walden water is mingled with the sacred water of the Ganges.

Ice from Walden Pond went as well to the Caribbean, to South America, to Persia, China, the Philippines, the East Indies and Australia.

By 1856, Boston was exporting more than 130,000 tons of ice. And by 1860, American cookbooks assumed their readers had iceboxes (the word had been coined in America a few years earlier) in their kitchens.

Ice harvesting remained a big industry in America until well into the 1930's, but an extraordinarily mild winter in 1889–90 created a severe ice shortage and gave impetus to the development of artificial ice-making plants.

Today more than 99.6 [19] per cent of electrified American homes have refrigerators, all of which owe a debt to a couple of Swedish undergraduates who developed the Electrolux absorption system in the early 1920's. This system takes the refrigerant around the refrigeration cycle without using any machinery with moving parts. The two engineers who discovered it, Carl Munters and Baltzar von Platen, were still at Stockholm's Royal Institute of Technology when they pioneered the system.

Ether was the original refrigerant gas; it was dangerously flammable. Various other gases, including ammonia, carbon dioxide and sulphur dioxide, were tried as replacements for ether. A search for a safer refrigerant (safe meaning nontoxic, nonflammable, nonexplosive, stable, noncorrosive and easily detectable in case of leaks) undertaken in 1931 resulted in the development of Freon 12 (dichlorodifluoromethane) which is probably the most commonly used refrigerant today—the most commonly used *mechanical* refrigerant, that is.

Good old ice, or just plain cold water, is still used far more often than is any gas in most of the world. Refrigerated ships and trains still depend heavily on ice, as they did when a few tons of butter were shipped from Ogdensburg, New York, to Boston in a sawdust-insulated iced wooden boxcar back in 1851. C. C. Palmer designed the first modern refrigerated car in 1888, but both water ice and dry ice (solidified carbon dioxide) are still used extensively in refrigerated transport.

A cold store opened by the Western Cold Storage Company in Chicago in 1878 was cooled with blocks of ice at first, but from 1886 on it was machine cooled. Today the frozen food storage capital of the U.S. (and of the world) is Kansas City, which has a capacity fifty per cent greater than that of runner-up city Chicago.

---

[19] Up from 89.2 per cent in 1953. About sixty per cent of British homes now have refrigerators, up from only eight per cent in 1956, but of course the English climate makes refrigeration less imperative than do the extreme temperatures of American summers. On the Continent, refrigerator ownership has grown even faster than in Britain. While only seven per cent of French homes had refrigerators in 1954, seventy per cent have them today. But refrigeration is most lacking where it is most needed: in Mexico, for example, only thirteen per cent of homes have refrigerators.

It is not mechanical refrigeration that gives the honors to Kansas City; a half-dozen great underground caves in the strata of limestone bluffs around the city never get warmer than 56° to 60° F., which reduces by about two-thirds the cost of air-conditioning them to any desired degree of cold.

Lack of any means of refrigeration, natural or mechanical, dictates much of the world's diet, and some of the world's food shortages. In many places fish not cooked the day it is caught is simply thrown away. India and Africa use ghee instead of butter because butter, without refrigeration, spoils too fast. The highly spiced foods basic to so many national diets, especially in warm climates, derive from efforts to retard spoilage or conceal evidences of spoilage. So do marinades, smoked and salted meat and fish, and countless other commonly accepted food items and preparation methods.

Only in America is refrigeration so widespread as to permit the development of a frozen-food industry. The U.S. had over 2 million refrigerators in use by 1937.[20] Today, more than a quarter of U.S. homes have home freezers, which first became commercially important in 1937. Freezers, like the freezing compartments in refrigerators, maintain temperatures of from 0° to 10° F. (as compared to 35° to 45° in the rest of a refrigerator).

Frozen o. j.

An outgrowth of quick freezing has been the orange concentrate boom in Florida since World War II.

Concentrating orange juice by removing most of its water content sounds easy enough, but most of the flavor goes out with the water— or did until Dr. Louis Gardner MacDowell got the idea of *over*-concentrating the juice and then adding fresh juice to it. Along with

---

[20] Selling refrigerators to Eskimos was once regarded as the classic comic impossibility. Now the U.S. Department of Labor sponsors a course in Alaska to train Eskimos to repair mechanical refrigerators, but for most Eskimos a pit dug in the ground and filled with ice suffices to preserve seal meat all summer, even when temperatures occasionally get into the sixties.

C. D. Atkins and Dr. E. L. Moore, MacDowell evolved the technique of "cutback" concentrating in the late 1940's. It quadrupled the demand for oranges, which in 1948 were a drug on the market (the Florida growers cut down trees and planted avocados as they saw prices for oranges drop to unprofitable levels).

Fresh orange juice is an uncertain product, varying widely in sweetness, tartness, acidity and flavor. Reconstituted juice, prepared by adding three cans of water to one can of orange concentrate, is predictably uniform in its quality (though connoisseurs maintain that concentrates have vintage years, like wine, as a result of freezes and other variables. The 'sixty's and 'sixty three's were poor, the 'fifty-eight's worse, they say, while the 'fifty-five's and 'fifty-nine's were outstanding and the 'sixty-four's memorable).

Orange juice concentrate plants (one plant can use 8 million oranges a day) reduce the juice to a super-thick viscosity and add a "cutback" which consists of fresh juice and other flavoring elements, notably d-limonene from peel oil. Peel oil is also used in Coca-Cola (which owns Minute Maid, the leading orange juice concentrator); the lemony smell from an empty Coke bottle is d-limonene.

Old-fashioned canned orange juice, so-called single-strength juice, suffered a sixty-five per cent sales decline between 1950 and 1965 as people turned to the concentrates and the "chilled juices." Per capita consumption of fresh oranges, which people used to eat in greater numbers than all other fresh fruits combined, has dropped seventy-five per cent in the twenty years since the advent of the concentrates, and while more oranges used to be grown in California than in Florida (California oranges are for eating, not juice), now it is the other way round.

Chilled juices are not concentrated but are merely extracted and flash heated to a temperature of nearly 200° F. to kill enzymes. Federal standards of identity require the producers to label their chilled juices "pasteurized," which can be misleading. If the juice were really pasteurized by dairy standards, it would lose most of its vitamin C content. The loss from flash heating is nil. Orange juice contains about forty-five milligrams of vitamin C per 100 milliliters; it loses no more than five or six per cent of this through processing and distribution, if kept cold. The Bureau of Standards permits no addition of vitamin C to orange juice, though the vitamin is added to the diluted juice beverages.

In the most recent development, completely synthetic "orange" drinks have appeared with vitamin C added. They have grabbed off an important share of the market, scaring the daylights out of orange growers.

Quick orange juice crystals are the industry's answer. They have been used by the armed services for several years and promise to be the first real "instant" orange juice.

Irradiation

In the past ten years or so, the U.S. Government has spent more than $15 million to develop safe methods of preserving foods by a method which could have advantages over both canning and freezing—namely irradiation with gamma ray treatment from cobalt 60 or cesium 137.

Private research on irradiation was begun in 1946 by M.I.T., Electronized Chemicals Corporation and General Electric. Swift, the meat packer, did pioneering work on radiation preservation of foods beginning in 1949. After spending more than $750,000 on its radiation studies, Swift has curtailed its work, citing problems of off-flavors, impaired colors and textures, and high costs. Besides, says Swift, most American homes today have plenty of refrigeration space; foods that can be stored without refrigeration have no great commercial market.

Such foods would, however, be of great value to the armed forces and to people in primitive areas or in underdeveloped countries where spoilage contributes substantially to world hunger problems.

The great proponent of irradiation has been the U.S. Atomic Energy Commission, though some seventy-six other countries have conducted research programs in food irradiation. The U.S. Food and Drug Administration has been cautious about approving food irradiation. The agency has approved an irradiation process which retards sprouting in white potatoes for at least sixteen months. It has approved a process which kills insects that infest wheat and wheat flour (chemical pesticides kill the adult insects, but the eggs remain and hatch when temperatures rise, causing great damage). These processes require relatively small doses of radiation—.005 to .05 megerads. The FDA had also approved radiation-sterilized canned bacon, but here the dose was 4.5 to 5.6 megerads and the approval was withdrawn in the summer of 1969.

In the spring of 1968, the FDA rejected the Army's application for approval of irradiated canned ham. The Army had planned between 1968 and 1972 to request approval of many other irradiated foods, including pork sausage, chicken, beef, hamburger, shrimp, codfish cakes and tuna.

Strictly speaking, the Army, which in fourteen years had given 26,000 guinea-pig servicemen more than fifteen tons of irradiated bacon, is exempt from the federal food additives law, but in this case at least it voluntarily submitted itself to that law, which insists that irradiated foods be proved wholesome, microbiologically safe, free from toxicity and nutritionally adequate. The Army conducted extensive animal tests at its Natick, Massachusetts, Laboratory, but the FDA questioned the validity of these tests.

The FDA does not say irradiation does anything to the vitamins and minerals in foods. It does not say irradiation kills beneficial microorganisms as well as the ones that cause spoilage. Nor does it say eating irradiated foods over a period of years can increase the chances of cancer or can make a man sterile. It simply says the Army's research does not positively rule out all of these dangers.

Enormous controversy surrounds the whole question of irradiation. Lack of proper storage has meant monumental losses of crops in many countries, and many hopes have been pinned on the development of safe procedures for preservation of foods by irradiation. Hopefully the doubts raised by the FDA will be allayed by further research, or improved processes will be completely safe. Early problems of color, odor and flavor in irradiated foods have, according to the AEC, been mostly solved or substantially reduced "by irradiation at very low temperatures, application of adsorbents as odor scavengers, skillful uses of spices and condiments and appropriate cooking practices."

CA

While the fate of irradiation hangs in the balance, another way of keeping food—or at least fruit—fresher longer is coming into wider use.

Apple growers used to have to "dump" their fast-spoiling fruit in February and March. Prices dropped ruinously; the growers took a beating. Then, in 1940, a Cornell University professor, Robert M. Smock, got two apple growers and a cold storage company to try his controlled atmosphere, or CA, storage method. They stored McIntosh apples in a gastight room in which the oxygen content of the atmosphere was reduced. Removing oxygen slows down the ripening process of the apples, which normally breathe in oxygen and give off carbon dioxide, just as animals and humans do.

About ten per cent of America's 140-million bushel apple crop now goes into CA storage. Finer grades of apples can be marketed for twice as long a period as they formerly could, even into late summer.

Since 1966, some of the strawberry and lettuce crops have also gone to market under controlled atmosphere conditions. Fresh apricots keep for six weeks instead of ten days and sweet cherries four weeks instead of seven days when natural gas is used to brake the natural ripening process and stave off spoilage.

At last count, some 5000 railroad cars, 1000 piggy-back trailers, 150 highway trailers and 500 shipboard containers had been equipped with the sealed joints and atmosphere ports necessary for CA shipping.

One California company ships strawberries in plastic "sleeping bags" injected with low-oxygen atmosphere. The berries go by air to points in the U.S. and Europe. Chiquita Banana goes the CA way to Europe and to Japan, which is now the fifth largest importer of bananas.

The ingenuity of man's fertile mind has enabled men not only to keep foods fresh longer, but to increase the efficiency of agriculture, to broaden the human diet, to multiply the world's store of food. In every conceivable aspect of food, men keep innovating. More and more it is the hand of man, not of Mother Nature, which determines what the world shall eat. If that hand has been turned sometimes too much in the direction of efficiency, and taste values have suffered accordingly, still it is man's triumph—and his burden of responsibility —that he can now determine how well the world shall eat, and whether some of it shall eat at all.

⁜[9]⁝

All a matter of taste

"And then we run it through some organoleptic tests," said the food company product development chief, "to see . . ."

The organo—what?

"Organoleptic" is not in the Random House Dictionary of the English Language. Dictionaries that do include it are not too clear in their definitions. Yet most importers, buyers, processors and packagers of foods employ professional tasters to make organoleptic tests, which are basically subjective taste evaluations.

No machine or instrument has yet been developed to match the human tongue and olfactory membrane for registering sensory perception of taste. Top creative tasters can earn more than $30,000 a year;[1] major marketing decisions are based on their judgments.

The common sense of taste

As Anthony Smith writes in *The Body*, touch receptors are concentrated in just a few parts of our bodies; "the tip of the penis, the clitoris, the tongue, the lips and the fingertips are all highly sensitive to

---

[1] It takes time to develop the art of tasting, but it can be taught. One company alone, Arthur D. Little, Inc., a research firm headquartered in Cambridge, Massachusetts, has trained more than 1000 tasters in the last twenty years.

BEST & CHEAPEST COOKED FOOD

" FrameFood" DIET

TRADE MARK

16 OZ. for 1s

Compare Price, Weight, and Value of other Foods.

for INFANTS, INVALIDS & EVERYBODY

Contains   Extracted   Wheat   Phosphates

"FRAME FOOD" DIET supplies the PHOSPHATES, ALBUMINOIDS, and other constituents necessary to the full development of the bones and muscles of the growing CHILD; it builds up the strength of the INVALID wasted by disease. To expectant and nursing mothers it is invaluable, as it helps to replace the loss in the maternal system, and adds largely to the value of the milk as a food; and as "FRAME FOOD" DIET is composed of all the constituents forming a perfect food, it should be taken by all who seek to preserve their health. **¼-lb. Sample Free on receipt of 3d. for Postage.** *Sold everywhere in Tins, 1 lb. at 1s., 4 lb. at 3s. 9d.; or sent carriage paid by the* **FRAME FOOD CO., Ltd., Lombard Road, Battersea, LONDON, S.W.**

touch." But while smell and taste are almost indivisible in most people's minds, only the tongue is well equipped with taste receptors, or taste buds, though there are some taste buds on the palate, the pharynx and the tonsils.

The surface of the tongue is covered with tiny projections, called papillae, which are in turn covered with the taste buds. Smith says we each have about 3000 taste buds (and a pig has twice as many). Desmond Morris says we each have 10,000, though they decline in number and lose their sensitivity as we grow older, which is one reason old people complain that things do not taste as good as they used to. (Queen Victoria, at fifty-seven, bewailed the fact that strawberries did not taste as good as the strawberries of her girlhood.)

There are only four fundamental taste properties: sweet, salty, bitter and sour (or acid). Our taste buds register the proportions of these properties in everything we eat and drink. The tip of the tongue is especially responsive to sweetness and saltiness, the sides to sourness and the back of the tongue, where some of the taste buds are raised up on long nodules, to bitterness.[2] There are practically no taste buds on the tongue's center.

The tongue, being sensitive to touch, can also register the textures of foods and their temperatures, but the subtle aspects of flavor are not really tasted at all—they are smelled as aromas of foods drift up into the nasal cavity and register on the olfactory membrane, which is literally millions of times more sensitive and discerning than the

---

[2] A biochemist in Boston claims it is a protein that enables the tongue to detect bitter tastes. He says he has isolated this protein and hopes to identify its chemical structure. If he is successful, food chemists will be able to find tasteless "dummy" substances which will combine with the bitter-sensitive protein and thus disguise the bitterness in such foods as cassava and fish flour. Previously, a sweet-sensitive protein had been isolated from the tip of the tongue and sour-sensitive and salty-sensitive proteins may be isolated in the future. Two substances known to change man's ability to taste are contained in a tropical berry used by West Indians to enhance sweetness (they chew the berries before eating sour bread, or drinking sour wine), and in the leaves of an Asian plant, *Gymnema sylvestre*, which blocks sweetness. Nobody knows exactly how these substances work, but they may combine with proteins of the tongue.

tongue. The tongue can detect sweetness at a dilution of one part in 200, of saltiness at one in 400, of sourness at one in 130,000 and of bitterness at one in 2 million, but odors can be detected at a dilution of one part in a billion or more.

Hence bread never tastes as good as the bakery's aroma, the taste of coffee never lives up to the promise of the perking pot's fragrance and high game and cheese that stinks to high heaven are quite palatable to the less critical tongue.

With exceptions like high game, smelly cheese and the durian fruit of the East Indies (which is delicious but has an offensive odor), to taste good something must also smell good. Anyone whose nasal passages are blocked by a head cold, sinus trouble, an allergy or some other form of anosmia knows how "tasteless" food can be, though there is nothing the matter with his tongue.

"Certain tongues," said Brillat-Savarin, "are ill-provided with the nervous fibers whose function it is to absorb and appreciate savors. They can convey to their unhappy owners none but a dim sensation, and are to taste what blind eyes are to light." We know much more today about the physiology of taste than did the man who wrote the book, but are our tongues more discerning than Brillat-Savarin's? Or are we perhaps less able to "appreciate savors"?

Quotations abound to the effect that taste is a matter of individual preference. It is true that tastes vary [3] (Chapter 7) as widely as do individual abilities to discriminate among tastes. But it is also true that virtually all people share certain basic tastes, albeit in varying degrees. The sweet tooth is common to all men as among all primates, especially in the young of the species. The taste for salt is instinctive in man and in virtually all herbivorous animals (which in the wild

---

[3] Europeans and Americans generally have less sensitive tastes than do non-European peoples. U.S. chemist Arthur L. Fox found about twenty years ago that to some tongues the crystals of PTC (phenylthiocarbamide) have a bitter taste, and to other tongues no taste at all. About a third of Europeans and Americans are "non-tasters" by PTC tests; the proportion is much lower in many non-European peoples. Both genetic and psychological factors may be involved in the differences in ability to taste. There may be environmental factors as well.

gather at salt licks), though people who eat mainly animal protein need little salt (Eskimos have a positive aversion to it) and neither do beasts of prey.[4]

The salt of the Earth

A salt-rich (high sodium) diet has been associated with high blood pressure, a precursor to stroke. It has been suggested that the higher incidence of stroke fatalities in the Southern U.S. (the rate in Georgia and the Carolinas is two to three times that of the rest of the country) may be connected with the fact that Southerners generally eat more salt than do other Americans.

There has been criticism, also, of heavily salted baby foods on the grounds that high sodium intake may be related to early development of hypertension, the most common type of high blood pressure. If a baby's kidney function is normal, and he drinks enough water, he will probably excrete any excess sodium. If, however, he has a genetic predisposition to hypertension, too much salt can be a hazard. (In any case, the salt in baby foods is to make them attractive to the mothers

---

[4] The sense of taste in animals is a subject of some dispute. Many U.S. state laws forbid the use of any concept of flavor in advertisements for pet foods on the premise that animals cannot taste, but many companies now promote "gourmet" pet foods for America's 25–30 million dogs and 20–30 million cats (estimates are rough, but well over forty per cent of U.S. homes have a dog, a cat or both). Sales of pet foods in the U.S. are as large as sales of all cereals and instant items combined. They equal the combined sales of all frozen foods. They are surpassed only by coffee and canned vegetables. Americans spent nearly $900 million for pet foods (canned, dry and semi-moist) in 1968, more than two thirds of it for dog food, up from a total of about $600 million for all pet foods in 1965. New pet foods introduced since 1957 accounted for seventy-eight per cent of 1968 sales. There is speculation that as much as twenty per cent of dog food is sold to people who eat it themselves. A supermarket in Chicago sells a lot of pet food to residents of a public housing project where pets are forbidden. More certain is the point made by Howard J. Samuels who, as Under Secretary of Commerce in the Johnson Administration, said, "We spend more on pet food than on food stamps for the poor."

who buy them. Just as people tend to lose their sense of taste as they grow old, taste perception in infancy is quite undeveloped.)

Most salt comes from mines, the fossil remains of salt lakes which once covered many land areas. The salt from the lakes was pressed into rocks and pushed underground as the water dried up and the earth heaved during its millenniums of aging. So salt is extracted from the brine of rock-salt deposits, or mined like an ore; or it is dried by solar evaporation of salt water or pumped from natural brine.

The salt mines of Hallstatt in upper Austria were exploited by the Illyrians as far back as 1000 B.C. The Romans came into the territory about 100 B.C. and their military camp of Juvavum became Salzburg, or salt mountain. The medieval German city of Lübeck on the Baltic owed its existence to near-by deposits of salt, used to preserve the herring catch. The rock-salt mines of Wieliczka in Poland have tunnels that wander for more than sixty-five miles underground; chapels, ballrooms, statues, shops and restaurants there have been carved out of the rock salt 800 feet underground.

In some places salt is so scarce it is considered a treat, as children in our own culture regard sugar candy. Little cakes of salt, each stamped with a likeness of the emperor, were once used as money in China. Roman soldiers were sometimes paid in salt (the word salary derives from the Latin *sal*, meaning salt); but long before the Romans, Europe was crisscrossed with routes used by salt traders.

A salt tax, the *gabelle*, was levied in France beginning in 1341, and salt has throughout history been a focus of political agitation and a factor in warfare. A lack of salt for his horses and men was a major reason for Napoleon's retreat from the snows of "General Winter" in Russia. Secret deals arranged by Benjamin Franklin kept the American colonies supplied with salt from Bermuda during the Revolution. Salt shortages contributed to the defeat of the Confederacy in the Civil War. African nations have fought wars over possession of salt deposits. And in India in 1930, Mahatma Gandhi led a famous 165-mile march to the Arabian Sea to get ocean salt and break the British salt monopoly that had for so long taxed India's poor (much as the

English sugar and tea taxes had burdened American colonists). Even today, camel caravans cross a thousand miles of Sahara wasteland at 2.5 miles an hour to carry salt from an ancient pit at Bilma to central Niger.

This commodity that has figured in so much of history is thirty-nine per cent sodium and sixty-one per cent chlorine. Dissolve it in a liquid and it breaks up into ions, the chloride ion having the salty flavor. Only five per cent of the salt produced in America is used for flavoring food, however; the rest goes into chemicals. Our chemical industry uses more salt than any other substance next to water, air, coal and sulphur. As a seventeenth-century French philosopher put it, "This mineral is like unto the four elements—earth, air, fire and water. So universal, so necessary to life." Yet a quarter-pound dose of salt can kill a man (normal intake for a healthy adult is one-third of an ounce per day).

Who was it who said, "Kissing a man without a moustache is like eating an egg without salt?" Many flavors have synthetic substitutes, as we will soon see, but there is no substitute for salt.

Saltiness, sweetness and other tastes are less apparent in very cold foods than in foods (and beverages) consumed warm, or at least unchilled. Taste buds are evidently numbed by cold. The flavor of beer is certainly less pronounced when the beer is chilled; the British, who drink their many varieties of malt beverages at room temperature,[5] are astonished at the American insistence on ice-cold drinks.

How sweet it is

Americans, in their turn, are amazed at the British capacity for "sweets," as Britons call candy.

To the upper classes, the notorious English sweet tooth is a lower-class aberration. But the aristocracy is a dwindling minority. The rest

---

[5] One *can* get ice-cold beer in Britain. Ask for "lager."

of the population, from John o'Groat's to Land's End, puts away bulls' eyes, toffees, sherbet dabs, jelly babies and licorice bootlaces at a rate no other nation can rival.

More than half the sweets the British eat now are chocolates, though boiled sweets (hard candies) used to predominate. Average per capita consumption of the two combined is between seven and eight ounces a week in the United Kingdom, though it was up to nine in 1954. (Americans by comparison average barely six ounces a week, which adds up to twenty pounds of Hershey bars, Milky Ways, M&M's, Baby Ruths, Life-Savers, Almond Joys, fudge, peanut brittle, licorice whips and such per year.)

Tooth decay, caused by acids which bacteria in the mouth produce from starch and sugar, is the most widespread diet disease in the U.S.; it is even more common in Britain (less than five per cent of Britain's 48 million people have fluoridated water supplies). One large survey showed that over eighty per cent of five-year-old Britons had tooth decay. Sticky sweets, like toffees, are the chief offender: they produce acids that erode enamel surfaces.

"Behind their mythologically stiff upper lips," a dentist wrote in the London *Times* about his fellow Englishmen, "hang some of the sweetest and rottenest teeth in the world."

Including what they buy in their sweet shops, the English consume 111 pounds of sugar per capita each year (tooth decay dropped off sharply in Britain during World War II when sugar was rationed). U.S. sugar consumption, according to New York sugar brokers Farr, Whitlock, Dixon and Co., is ninety-nine pounds, which comes to more than a quarter pound a day per man, woman, child and infant. The United Kingdom figure is topped by Australia, with 115 pounds, Holland with 120, and Ireland with 127; annual sugar consumption in France is only seventy-six pounds per capita, in Japan only thirty-eight and in India only ten.

The British use a lot of sugar in tea and in custard. Warm, liquid and sweet, custard is served in England with fruit pies (called tarts), gelatin desserts (called jelly), puddings, tapioca, sponge cake (the combination of sponge cake and custard is called "trifle") and fruit salad (which comes out of a tin).[6]

Britain's poor balance-of-trade situation is not due to any great extent to food imports, which represent only a sixth of her total import bill; but along with tea, butter and beef, sugar figures large among those food imports.

Unlike salt, which has always come from natural deposits—either recent or fossil—of evaporated salt water, sweetening has seen an historical evolution.

The Moslem Moors brought sugar cane, the "honey-bearing reed," to Spain, along with rice, spinach and saffron. As early as the eighth century, there were cane plantations in the southern part of the Iberian peninsula.

No other European country enjoyed cane sugar until the Crusaders brought cane, which was native to India, home from the Near East. Up to that time, Europe used only honey or enjoyed no sweetening at all beyond that of natural fruits, melons and berries. Most Europeans continued to use only these natural sweetenings until the cane fields planted in the New World brought sugar prices down to affordable levels (Chapter 2).

Maple sugar was important in the American colonies (the colonists resisted the tax imposed by the British Sugar Act). Beet sugar (as we saw in Chapter 8) became significant only late in the nineteenth century.

Some great American fortunes were made in sugar. Claus Spreckels made his in West Coast sugar. Spreckels, who came to the U.S. from

---

[6] It should in fairness be noted that many Englishmen eat "savouries" in place of sweet desserts. Examples: "Scotch Woodcock" (no relation to any game-bird, it is scrambled eggs with anchovies and capers), "Devil on Horseback" (prune wrapped in bacon), "Ivanhoe" (creamed smoked haddock topped with a walnut), "Canape Diane" (liver and bacon), soft herring roes, mushroom and bacon and, most popular, Welsh rabbit (only Americans say "rarebit"), made with Cheddar cheese, paprika, cayenne pepper, mustard (always hot in England), flour, butter, eggs and sometimes beer or ale. All savouries are served on a square of toast.

Germany in 1846 and entered the sugar business in San Francisco seventeen years later, invented and patented (in 1868) a method that reduced the time it took to refine cane sugar from three weeks to a mere eight hours; using sugar he grew in Hawaii, he obtained a virtual monopoly of the Pacific Coast sugar trade. Spreckels introduced the sugar cube to America before he sold out to the Havemeyers and their American Sugar Refining Company. By 1900, this early trust was refining virtually all the sugar used in the United States.

Cane and beet sugars are still by all odds the dominant sweetening agents; but in 1879 there occurred a little accident which not only affected the sweetening of many foods but, since it gave rise to the first important synthetic food additive, had a bearing on almost all the food now sold at the corner grocery store or supermarket.

The surrogate sugars

Working in a laboratory at Johns Hopkins University in Baltimore, a young German chemist, Dr. Constantin Fahlberg, accidentally discovered a white, crystalline powder, $C_6H_4COSO_2NH$, 500 times sweeter in dilute solution than sugar, 300 times sweeter, pound for pound, than sucrose (the crystalline disaccharide, $C_{12}H_{22}O_{11}$, which is found in cane sugar, beet sugar and sorghum and comprises the major part of maple sugar).

Dr. Fahlberg, removing a shred of tobacco from his tongue one evening, discovered that his fingers tasted extraordinarily sweet. He rushed back to his lab, examined the chemicals he had been using, and found what had produced the sweetness.

What he discovered was later given the name, "saccharin."

The same sort of happenstance nearly half a century later led a University of Illinois graduate student, Michael Sveda, to discover another artificial sweetener, sodium cyclamate, in 1937.

The cyclamates (calcium cyclamate was developed for people on low-sodium diets) are thirty times sweeter than sucrose, but they have much less of the bitter, metallic or astringent aftertaste left by saccharin, and fewer people can detect the aftertaste. Cyclamates can be used in cooking, too, while saccharin cannot. So cyclamates, made from coal-tar derivatives, came into common use, usually in combination with saccharin (the usual ratio was one part saccharin to ten parts cyclamate, each contributing one-half the sweetening effect).

Both saccharin and the cyclamates were originally intended for use by diabetics and other people whose doctors had told them not to use sugar. For normal people, especially for active, growing children, sugar is a valuable source of calories and carbohydrates. Saccharin and the cyclamates have absolutely no nutritional values. To point that out, federal regulations used to require a cyclamate to be labeled as a "nonnutritive, artificial sweetener which should be used only by persons who must restrict their intake of ordinary sweets." The wording was later softened.

But weight-conscious Americans saw the artificially sweetened foods and beverages as a way out of their conflict between the sweet tooth and the waist line.

An estimated 175 million Americans were taking cyclamates in 1969, in liquid form, in tablets, in a crystalline form that resembled granulated sugar, in preserves, puddings, canned fruits, salad dressings, baking goods mixes, powdered fruit flavor "ades," liquid meal substitutes, gelatin desserts, candies, bacon, ice cream, yogurt and other forms—but mostly in soft drinks.

More than 20 *billion* pounds of sugars were used in American foods in 1969 (sugar is a $2 billion industry in the U.S.), only about 20 *million* pounds of cyclamates (seventy per cent of them in soft drinks), up from 5 million in 1963. But cyclamates were still a big business, and growing—in 1955, Americans had consumed only 250 *thousand* pounds of artificial sweeteners.

Four per cent of soft drinks (100,000 cases of twenty-four eight-ounce bottles each) sold in 1963 were in the "low-calorie" cyclamate-sweetened category; in 1968 the percentage was up to an estimated fifteen per cent (490,000 cases), though sugar consumption remained undiminished.

Disquieting rumors had circulated for several years about the hazards of cyclamates. "Worse than thalidomide," [7] said one early rumor. In 1966 two Japanese researchers had found that certain people convert cyclamate into cyclohexylamine, which industrial chemists call CHA and use for curing rubber and as a rust inhibitor. But while CHA is quite irritating when inhaled or rubbed on the skin, and while feeding CHA to laboratory animals raised their blood pressure and heartbeat rates, no adverse reactions were shown by humans, even humans who convert cyclamate physiologically or, if you like, metabolically, into CHA.

Other studies suggested cyclamates caused bone marrow damage to laboratory test animals.

If the FDA was not troubled by this, the British were. They restricted the use of cyclamates in soft drinks and banned their use in ice cream. Three major British retail food chains in 1968 stopped sales in their 300 outlets of all private label products sweetened with cyclamates.

Late in 1968 the Albany, New York, Medical College released results of a three-month study of thirty-two prisoners at Clinton Prison in Dannemora. Of twenty-four prisoners who took cyclamates, nine developed severe diarrhea; seventeen converted the cyclamates into CHA. Some of the cyclamate-using prisoners were found to have an elevated level of protein-bound iodine in their blood, usually a sign of hyperthyroidism.

At about the same time as the Dannemora prison study, an FDA research team headed by Dr. Marvin Legator reported that injecting small amounts of CHA into laboratory mice had produced chromosome breaks.

Chromosomes are rodlike cellular structures that contain the genes and transfer all genetic information from parent to unborn child; if CHA could cause chromosome damage in humans, it could conceivably lead to hereditary defects.

---

[7] A sleep-inducing drug sold widely from 1957 to 1961, especially in Europe, which is generally thought to have produced an epidemic of dysmelia (deformities) among infants born to mothers who had taken the drug. The thalidomide scandal sharpened scrutiny of all drugs and food additives.

Like thalidomide? Yes, and also like X-rays which are well known to cause chromosome damage. What everyone does not know is that one can irradiate mice, and really break chromosomes, and—if care is taken not to inbreed or even crossbreed them—there will be no significant increase in birth defects. A cell with broken chromosomes, in the view of many biologists, simply dies.

Various chemicals, possibly even salt, sugar and caffeine, do routinely produce some human chromosome damage, though as of this writing CHA has not been shown to cause chromosome damage in humans.

Still, while chromosome damage had been found only in test animals, not in humans, and while the tests were based on CHA, not cyclamates, the FDA in December, 1968, read an interim report by a committee of the nongovernmental National Academy of Sciences and concluded that there were still some unanswered questions about cyclamates.

More than five grams a day gave adults a mild but unpleasant laxative reaction. And according to some reports, cyclamates could possibly interfere with the absorption and effectiveness of an antibiotic, lincomycin.

More importantly, concern was expressed about the long-term effects of cyclamates. Extra-large doses damaged the kidneys and livers of test animals. Again, other commonly used substances did similar damage, and daily doses of five to ten grams administered to humans disclosed no adverse effects. Nonetheless, the FDA cautiously suggested that adults confine their intake to five grams of cyclamates a day.

In April, 1969, the agency announced its intention to remove cyclamates from its list of substances "generally recognized as safe," the GRAS list (Chapter 11), and said it would require manufacturers to label all cyclamate-sweetened foods and beverages with a statement that adults should not consume more than 3500 milligrams of cyclamates a day, and children not more than 1200 milligrams.

The labels proposed by the FDA would also list products' cyclamate content in milligrams. (A ten-ounce bottle of Diet Pepsi or

Fresca at the time contained 600 milligrams, Tab 450, Wink and Diet Rite 380, Trim 330, Like 300.)

The soft drink companies said they would accept the FDA's plan, at least in principle. The cyclamate producers were less agreeable. A vice-president of Abbott Laboratories, Inc., of North Chicago, which produced more than half of all U.S. cyclamates (and used them in its "Sucaryl" line of consumer products), said he was afraid "consumers will be misled by the very fact an announcement . . . was made. Current use levels are well below the levels recommended by the National Academy of Sciences or the FDA, so in no way should these proposals be interpreted as an attempt to reduce consumption."

Abbott's chairman and chief executive officer said, "Regrettably, I must point out that what we have here is an economic question, masquerading as science. The FDA's disregard for scientific evidence constitutes an endorsement of a campaign designed to raise false fear."

"Sugar interests" were said to be behind the campaign.

For Abbott, Charles Pfizer and Co., and Union Starch and Refining Co. (a division of Miles Laboratories), the three U.S. manufacturers of cyclamates, the FDA ruling was a bitter pill. Nor did it please several hundred companies that made or distributed cyclamate-sweetened products, either. About $1 billion worth of low-calorie food and drink items were sold in the U.S. in 1968 and most of these contained at least some cyclamates; many also contained saccharin, produced chiefly by Monsanto Chemical Co., but saccharin was not considered a hazard (it has a different chemistry and is used in much smaller quantities than were the cyclamates).

Total U.S. cyclamate production in 1968 was about 17 million pounds, worth some $9 million at fifty-two cents a pound; 1970 production was projected at 21 million pounds, a figure which was probably reached in 1969. But 1970 production will not, in fact, come anywhere near the projected figure.

Concern had been expressed in the summer of 1969 that the FDA's April action had not been strong enough. It was said that grocers should not be permitted to display low-calorie beverages alongside sugar-sweetened ones, but should be obliged to keep them separate in "diet departments" at supermarkets. This would certainly avoid confusion. Since two twelve-ounce bottles of Fresca or Diet Pepsi would exceed the recommended daily limit of cyclamates for a child, many children were exceeding the limit. They should, it was urged, be protected from overexposure to cyclamates.

As a matter of convenience, most families eat and drink the same things. If one member of a family is a weight watcher, especially if that member does the family marketing, everyone in the family is likely to be on at least a relatively low-calorie diet, which in 1969 may well have included artificially-sweetened products, even though reliance on low-calorie beverages is no way to lose weight.

By the fall of 1969, some labels were warning people that cyclamates were potentially dangerous, something never imagined by Michael Sveda.

On September 30, Dr. Jacqueline Verrett of the FDA's Bureau of Science, appeared on NBC television and reported that her studies of chicken embryos given normal doses of cyclamates revealed that the artificial sweeteners produced deformities at a rate of fifteen per cent. She advised pregnant women not to use cyclamates, or any other chemicals, without consulting a physician. She also urged that studies be made with other animals.

Pregnant women had been advised for years by the American Medical Association and by the Department of Health, Education and Welfare to avoid chemicals except on the advice of their physicians. The chicken embryo studies seemed to introduce a note of hysteria to the cyclamate controversy.

FDA Commissioner Herbert L. Ley, Jr. said after the Dr. Verrett telecast that the unrestricted use of cyclamates could not continue. An announcement of new restrictions was expected at any time.

HEW Secretary Robert H. Finch criticized the FDA, which is an agency of his HEW Department. "I am not at all satisfied with the present situation there," he told an interviewer. "I think it's just inevitable that we're going to have some rather substantial reorganization of procedures and personnel in the Food and Drug Administration."

On Saturday, October 18, Finch announced that cyclamates were being removed from the GRAS list and that cyclamate-sweetened products would be removed from stores.

The action, it was stated, was not based on any birth defect studies (Finch was testy about Dr. Verrett's telecast; he claimed she had not cleared it with her supervisor, though she stated that he and two FDA press officers and an HEW undersecretary had all given her clearance).

The Finch move, ironically, was based on rather dubious studies which Abbott Laboratories, the major cyclamate producer, had conducted on rats. Fed massive doses of cyclamates, proportionately fifty times the limit recommended for humans by the National Academy of Sciences, and fed those doses for most of their adult life spans, the rats developed bladder cancers.[8] But Secretary Finch made it clear there was no evidence of cyclamates having caused cancer in humans.

Use of cyclamates in the production of general purpose foods and beverages was ordered discontinued immediately. All soft drinks containing cyclamates were to be recalled by their bottlers by January 1, 1970. All other artificially sweetened food products were to be phased out of the market by February 1.

Worst hurt by the order were canners who had already packed the summer '69 crop with cyclamate sweetening, had labeled the cans and had shipped them to market for sale in the winter and spring of 1970. So loud were their cries of distress that in mid-November Secretary Finch announced that cyclamate-sweetened processed fruits and vegetables, said to represent less than five per cent of cyclamate consumption, would not have to be withdrawn until September 1, 1970. It may be true that cyclamates are dangerous, at least at high levels of use, but

---

[8] Other study reports released on the heels of the bladder cancer report said hamsters developed coronary disorders and death within three months of being subjected to large doses of cyclamates (Cambridge Bio-Research Institute) and that rats fed with cyclamates produced offspring which seemed more nervous and active than normal (Worcester, Massachusetts, Foundation of Experimental Biology).

Finch's announcement tacitly conceded that there was more to be feared from the wrath of the food processors than from cyclamates themselves.

In both the U.S. and abroad (other countries quickly followed the U.S. ban on cyclamates), the FDA action and inaction, and the Finch bombshell with its subsequent concession to commercial pressures, produced a field day for food faddists (Chapter 10), at least those who oppose all food additives other than "natural" substances.

Cyclamates and saccharin are not the only sugar substitutes. Another is sorbitol, an alcohol sugar used in sugar-free candy; but sorbitol is only sixty per cent as sweet as ordinary sugar and it has just as many calories, four per gram, as ordinary sugar, though it may be used differently in human metabolism. Glycine, an amino acid, is the main ingredient of another sugar substitute.

Even sweeter than cyclamates is ammoniated glycyrrhizin, or A.G., a licorice root derivative that is low in calories and is 100 times sweeter than sugar. But A.G. has a licorice taste that may be masked in coffee but will be detected in tea or a fruit drink.

There is also neohesperidin dihydrochalcone, derived from the neohesperidin in the peel of Seville oranges. Neohesperidin itself is very bitter, but the compound derived from it is 2400 times sweeter than sucrose, 800 times sweeter than saccharin (which, along with sugar, is itself now undergoing a critical re-examination) and eighty times sweeter than cyclamates.

One company is experimenting with a sweetener that is a blend of saccharin, dextrose, sodium gluconate and sodium citrate. Another combines lactose, saccharin and potassium bitartrate, or cream of tartar. A third, 150 times sweeter than sugar, is aspartyl-phenylalanine methyl ester, derived from several plants, including soybeans.

A fourth is naringin dihydrochalcone, which is like neohesperidin dihydrochalcone except it is derived from grapefruit peel instead of from orange peel.

Ordinarily, the testing required for FDA approval of an additive as the laws now stand becomes uneconomic in terms of potential profit;

in the circumstances of the cyclamates' fall from grace (or from GRAS), testing of other surrogate sugars may be expedited, perhaps even subsidized.

Meanwhile, at least so long as saccharin is permitted (spherical pellets of saccharin implanted in the urinary bladder of female mice have produced cancerous tumors, but the significance of this is not yet known), diet drinks will contain about thirty calories per eight-ounce bottle, versus one or two calories in cyclamate-sweetened drinks, 105 in sugar-sweetened drinks.

Synthetic additives like saccharin and the cyclamates figure importantly in our modern foods. They are little understood by the general public and have been the subject of considerable controversy. We will examine further episodes of the controversy later in this chapter and in Chapter 11; we will examine many of the additives themselves in this chapter and in an appendix.

But while almost all food additives affect flavors by adding tartness, by delaying flavor losses, by enhancing colors that influence people's perception of taste, actual flavoring ingredients account for little of the total volume of additives used in our foods. And most of these flavoring ingredients are natural: concentrated natural flavor essences are used more widely than synthetic food flavors, though in some cases, ironically, some natural flavors like sassafras and calamus have been ruled hazardous by the FDA.

If root beer does not taste quite like it used to, perhaps it is because root beer makers can no longer use safrole, a naturally occurring flavoring material extracted chiefly from a South American tree, *Ocetea cymbarus*, though from ten to twenty per cent of it used to be extracted from sassafras bark. Safrole was found in the late 1950's to produce cancer in the small intestines of test rats. The FDA rule against it has been in effect since 1960. Sassafras tea, which grandma brewed for medicinal purposes (as a stimulant, to produce perspiration or as a diuretic), was made by boiling the bark and roots of the sassafras tree (*Sassafras albidum*); the active ingredient in grandma's "spring tonic" was safrole. Sassafras leaves, ground into the *file* used in Louisiana's gumbo as adapted by Creole cooks from the Choctaw Indians, and the extract of sassafras bark (if it is free of safrole) can still be used.

Coumarin, derived from tonka beans and used for almost seventy-five years in synthetic vanilla flavors and in chocolate, has been banned since 1954, four years before the 1958 Food Additives amendment (Chapter 11). It could, paradoxically, be re-instated today. Tonka beans themselves, the fragrant seeds of the South American *Dipteryx odorata*, are also banned from food use, though they may still be used in snuff and perfume. Coumarin, it was found, causes liver damage in dogs and rats: at high levels of use it has anti-clotting properties.

Some flavoring materials are "naturally occurring additives"; the common spices would be included among these. Then there are "natural identicals," which occur in nature only in limited amounts but can be synthesized in the laboratory; vanilla extract does not have *all* the flavor principles of natural vanilla, but it reproduces the most important, the most desirable principles accurately enough to satisfy most people's taste buds.

Some natural flavors are simply not available in large enough quantities to supply world demand. Natural vanilla is a good example. All the natural vanilla produced in the world [9] would not be enough to flavor the vanilla ice cream eaten in the U.S. alone. A minor but essential ingredient of natural vanilla is vanillin (accent on the first syllable), now produced from lignin, which is extracted from wood pulp in the sulphite pulp and paper making process, the process now polluting so many rivers and seas (Chapter 5). One ounce of vanillin is roughly the flavor equivalent of a gallon of natural vanilla extract.

But the technology of flavor is so complex that to say the food industry uses vanillin as well as natural vanilla only begins to tell the story. Fritzsche-D&O, a leading producer of oleoresins, essential oils and flavor compounds, offers food processors a whole list of vanilla

---

[9] Madagascar, Reunion Island and Mexico are the major producers of *Vanilla planifolia* L. (*Orchidaceae*), the source of most natural vanilla. Tahiti produces the less widely used *Vanilla tahitensis* L. Vanilla's original home (Chapter 2) was Mexico.

products, ranging from "Pure Vanilla Extract Tenfold Bourbon Select" down to "Essence Vanilla Bouquet Imitation."

In addition to all the natural flavor extracts, the food industry does use a good many synthetics. This dismays a lot of people. It should, more realistically, be one of the more encouraging evidences that ways can be found to feed the world's growing populations.[10] For a nutritional substitute fed to newly-weaned Algerian infants, chemists at New York's International Flavors and Fragrances, Inc., developed an artificial flavor closely resembling that of mothers' milk.

Closer to home, if the whole U.S. strawberry crop this year were turned into natural flavoring for all the strawberry desserts, candies and beverages we consume, there would be enough to satisfy the needs and appetites of just one medium-sized U.S. city. Everybody else would have to settle for chocolate or vanilla. And they would not be natural flavors, either.

Flavor technicians have, fortunately, been able to reproduce strawberry flavoring pretty faithfully with such chemicals as ethyl methylphenyl glycidate, benzyl valerate, ethyl malonate and benzyl acetate.

Natural grape flavor is made up of nineteen chemicals, but a synthetic grape flavor acceptable at least to children is made from just five of them.

Ethyl acetate is used in artificial strawberry, banana, apple, pineapple and mint flavors; ethyl butyrate in blueberry, pineapple, butter and eggnog flavors; benzaldehyde in cherry, peach, coconut and almond flavors; isoamyl acetate in raspberry, strawberry and caramel flavors; methyl salicylate in wintergreen, mint, walnut and grape flavors.

Acceptable cheese flavors are made from caproic acid, orange flavor from decyl aldehyde, butter flavor from diacetyl and, to a

---

[10] From less than 500 million in 1665, 870 million in 1800 and 1 billion in 1850, world population has grown to 3.5 billion today, will probably be 4 billion in 1975 and, according to a three-year study by a committee of the National Research Council, will be 30 billion by the year 2070 unless multiplication rates of the human race are controlled.

lesser degree, from butyric acid, the one that produced the odor the Japanese found offensive in "butter-stinkers" (Chapter 7).

The aroma that greets you when opening a jar of instant coffee is not a chemical. It comes from real coffee oils. But those oils are sprayed into the jar before it is capped and the aroma does nothing for the flavor of the coffee in the cup (which, you will notice, has no aroma while fresh-brewed coffee does). This "plating" of instant coffee powders, widespread since Instant Maxwell House originated it in the mid-1950's, is done purely for the psychological effect it has on consumers.

Today's flavor magicians, if it is any comfort, are merely carrying on a tradition as old as history. Accomplished cooks in ancient times were able to make salt pork, olives, onion, parsley, condiments and stuffing taste like quail. The Hellenistic King, Nicomedes, had a cook who reputedly could disguise a turnip with oil, salt, poppy-seeds and other seasonings and make it taste like anchovies. The deceits of the Elizabethans' "cooked dishes" (Chapter 2) may be recalled in this connection, too.

Today we make mock turtle soup from veal and go on from there to the enrichment of our diets.

To make good tastes more so

Aside from actual flavoring ingredients and sweeteners, the additives most directly concerned with taste properties are the flavor enhancers, or "flavor potentiators," used so widely in dry soup mixes, canned foods, frozen foods containing meat or fish, cheese spreads and frozen vegetables with sauces.

MSG (monosodium glutamate) is a term much better known to consumers than most of the terms used in the food additive business, and more acceptable. (We will talk about the "Chinese Restaurant Syndrome" shortly.) In the same way that sugar can make grapefruit taste more grapefruity, MSG and other flavor enhancers intensify the flavors of many foods.

Nobody knows exactly how they do this. It used to be thought that MSG increased the sensitivity of the taste buds, making them more responsive to specific flavors. A more recent theory holds that MSG works by stimulating the formation of saliva. Some people, observing that MSG in large doses has a meaty taste (while in small doses it is tasteless), suggest that the meaty flavor makes foods taste better, appealing perhaps to an instinctive human taste for meat.

MSG, as it happens, is not too effective in intensifying the flavors of foods like fruits, cereals and candies which are rich in carbohydrates, but it is great with a wide variety of high-protein foods.

A Japanese, Dr. Kikunae Ikeda of Tokyo University, first demonstrated the effectiveness of MSG in 1908, and a Japanese company, Ajinomoto, is still the world's leading producer of MSG, accounting for about forty per cent of world output. Per capita consumption of MSG in Japan, where Ajinomoto has fifty-five per cent of the market, is more than three times the per capita consumption in the U.S. The big users here are food processors.

Dr. Ikeda isolated MSG while looking for the flavor-enhancing ingredient in a dried seaweed (known variously as kombu, sea tangle, Japanese tangle and, to botanists, as *Laminaria japonica*) which the Japanese had used for centuries to improve the flavor of soups and other foods.

What Dr. Ikeda isolated from the seaweed was glutamic acid, an amino acid found in highest concentrations in high-protein foods but more cheaply extracted from wheat protein. Tokyo University still preserves Dr. Ikeda's first sample of glutamic acid from seaweed.

The physical chemistry professor at that university converted glutamic acid, or glutamate, into MSG, and then developed a method for processing wheat flour or other flour to obtain gluten, a protein mixture. The gluten is hydrolized with hydrochloric acid to produce glutamic acid, which is then treated with sodium hydroxide to form monosodium glutamate.

Commercial production of MSG in the United States did not start until 1934. The biggest American producer, International Minerals and Chemicals Corporation, did not market MSG under its trade name Ac'cent until 1947. Millions of people who may never have heard of MSG are quite familiar with Ac'cent, which accounts for about ninety per cent of retail sales of MSG. But far more people have heard of neither, and yet consume MSG in processed foods.

Most MSG is now produced by a fermentation process from sugar beet molasses. America's use of MSG has increased from less than 6 million pounds a year in 1946 to somewhere between 42 and 60 million pounds today (IMC produces 30 million pounds; Merck & Company and Commercial Solvents Corporation most of the rest). World consumption is between 180 and 220 million pounds (Asians average about 8 ounces of MSG a year, four times the U.S. average).

Some other flavor-enhancers are the 5'-nucleotides and maltol. Disodium 5'-inosinate and disodium 5'-guanylate (about three times more potent than the inosinate) were discovered by a colleague of Dr. Ikeda, the MSG man. Again, the basis of the research was a traditional Japanese taste-intensifier, in this case dried bonito, a type of tuna. The Japanese had used dried bonito for this purpose for centuries, just as they had used crushed kombu seaweed. Dr. Shintaro Kodama at Tokyo University sought to find out why dried bonito did what it did. His investigations in 1913 resulted in the discovery of 5'-inosinic acid, which is somewhere between ten and twenty times more powerful than MSG, though it has some effects different from MSG and cannot therefore be directly compared.

The 5'-nucleotides, first offered commercially in Japan in 1959 and approved for use as food additives by the FDA in the U.S. in 1962, are used to increase the meatiness of soups, gravies, bouillons, sauces and meat products. They reduce the amount of beef extract required. A by-product of the process that produces corned beef, beef extract has in recent years become increasingly scarce and increasingly expensive, partly because people believe (mistakenly) that beef bouillon is a rich source of protein. (It does contain some iron and vitamins, but its chief effect is to stimulate the gastric juices and make one hungry.)

The use of 5'-nucleotides is expected to grow rapidly in years to come as their price declines. They are often used in combination with MSG because they are not merely more powerful than MSG as flavor enhancers but are more effective in giving liquid foods body, or viscosity.

Maltol, introduced in 1942, is primarily a fruit taste enhancer. It can intensify or modify the flavors of jams, gelatin desserts, soft drinks, fruit drinks and other foods with high carbohydrate content. Maltol is used primarily to intensify strawberry and raspberry flavors, though it can also be used with pineapple, black cherry, orange and other fruit flavors.

Way out on the horizon is another substance that can affect taste buds. It is called glutathione, and it may one day develop into a sort of universal flavoring agent, one that will make *anything* appetizing. (And we may need it.)

At the University of Miami, scientists are experimenting with the hydra, a tiny aquatic creature which is practically covered with taste buds. The hydra cannot see or hear; it uses the tiny taste-budlike cells on its tentacles to locate food. Glutathione, a chemical which exists in most animal flesh, attracts the hydra's perceptor cells. A hydra has been seen trying to eat a laboratory instrument covered with glutathione.

As for the here and now, some flavors are not intensified at all by present flavor enhancers and frustrated researchers continue to seek out new enhancers that will work on the hold-out flavors.

Meanwhile, MSG is far and away the dominant flavor enhancer. It was put on the FDA's GRAS list in 1960 (after all it had been used one way or another by cooks for centuries).

But some people have an allergy or intolerance for MSG, or at least to excessive amounts of it. This received some publicity in the spring and summer of 1968 when the "Chinese Restaurant Syndrome" was tracked down to a heavy-handed use of MSG in the kitchens of Chinese restaurants.

Researchers reported that it took two teaspoons of MSG in a six-ounce glass of tomato juice to produce symptoms of headache, dizziness, facial pressure, chest pain, burning sensations in the back and neck, and numbness. That was the dosage for susceptible females; males required twice the amount. There was a certain tongue-in-cheek quality to the studies, which were not considered conclusive.

Early in 1969, four medical researchers at the Albert Einstein College of Medicine in New York published a report that as little as a quarter of a teaspoon of MSG could produce the symptoms in some subjects.

A few months later, a U.S. Senate Committee on Nutrition and Human Needs, headed by George S. McGovern of South Dakota, heard testimony that MSG injected into baby mice at three times the level found in human baby food caused brain damage. Said a doctor from Albert Einstein, "It may well be that babies get the Chinese Restaurant Syndrome and don't know what hit them."

But FDA Commissioner Herbert Ley cried foul: subcutaneous injection of MSG, he said, was not comparable to ingestion of MSG. Besides, the amount injected was not realistic.

Baby-food makers protested, too. The head of H. J. Heinz said a fifteen-pound baby would have to eat twenty-six jars of baby food at one sitting to get as much MSG as the mice got. Gerber Products Company, leading producer of U.S. baby foods since 1928 (it has about half the market) testified it had been adding salt to its products since 1931 and MSG since 1951. Gerber cited its slogan, "Babies are our business, our only business." A company representative actually stated, "We're in the business of feeding babies, and profit is only secondary."

Industry sources said no company in the $340 million baby-food business could afford to disregard the tastes of mothers who buy baby foods, and who evidently did not buy them in the early days before salt was added. Disinterested parties observed that today baby foods were well established, and that advertising could reassure mothers on baby foods' lack of flavor.

Late in October an assistant professor of psychiatry at the Washington University School of Medicine in St. Louis announced that he had fed (not injected) mice with MSG, in amounts greater than the amounts used in baby foods, and had produced damage in the rodents' hypothalamus area, the part of their brains which, among other things, controls desire for food and water.

Dr. Jean Mayer, the Harvard nutrition scientist who was in Washington to direct a White House Conference on Food, Nutrition and Health, told a Women's National Press Club audience that with "even the slightest presumption of guilt [he] would take the damn stuff out of baby food."

Gerber, Heinz and Beechnut thereupon immediately announced they would stop using MSG in their baby foods pending further study of the chemical. The New York City Health Department ordered Chinese restaurants to go easy on MSG; some of them, it turned out, had been routinely adding a teaspoonful, and even a tablespoonful, of MSG to their wonton soup. Epidemiologists in the Department revealed that they had first heard about the Chinese Restaurant Syndrome in 1965, and found then that two pounds of MSG had been added to 1500 egg rolls. Some French restaurants, too, were found to be using too much MSG.

By the fall of 1969, all 680 items on the GRAS list were being looked on with suspicion, including salt, pepper, cinnamon, cloves, sugar and hundreds of other common herbs, spices and seasonings. "What we really need," said Senator McGovern, "is to change the name of the GRAS list to the PAS list instead—Proven As Safe."

It sounded like an abandonment of the basic rules of Anglo-Saxon jurisprudence. It certainly seemed an over-reaction. Banning MSG from baby foods, where they served no valid purpose, is one thing; casting doubts on the whole spectrum of food additives, natural and synthetic, as used by adults as well as children, mostly in minuscule amounts, is something else.

In addition to the 680 food ingredients on the GRAS list, another 2000 additives are used in our foods, though these must meet minimum federal standards arrived at after long testing procedures.

If they are all eliminated from our foods for "even the slightest presumption of guilt," our taste buds will pay for what may well prove a ridiculous excess of caution.

Right on the tip of your tongue

In announcing its retreat on the MSG question, H.J. Heinz said it was acting "in full confidence that industry practice will be vindicated by scientific findings of a more valid order than those [11] that have been used to promote the current controversy."

New studies are sure to be forthcoming. The U.S. food industry uses too many additives for the attacks on additives to go unchallenged.

To restore to processed foods what processing removes from them, additives are imperative, say industry leaders. Without additives, canned peaches would taste like vulcanized rubber, said one expert quoted in the *New York Times*.

Emotional responses to what should be scientific questions have exacerbated the problems of processors, of grocers and of consumers, who can be deprived of reasonably safe products, or have to pay more for them, because of possible over-reaction by lawmakers or administrators.

As the chief economist of the U.S. Chamber of Commerce told the Grocery Manufacturers of America in November, 1969:

> Commercial food processing is hardly half a century old, a mere blink of experience. The science of epidemiology, which allows study among masses of people of long-range side effects of regularly ingested substances, is barely twenty-five years old.

---

[11] The dose of MSG that produced nerve cell death in seven of nine baby mice was a half gram per one kilogram of body weight, about five times the proportionate amount in a four-and-a-half-ounce jar of baby food. The ten-day-old mice, tube fed because they were not yet weaned, were equivalent to three-month-old human infants. Since MSG is used primarily in vegetable and meat mixtures, it is rarely fed to babies under five months of age. More serious, perhaps, than the mice studies was a report that a relatively heavy dose of MSG injected into a rhesus monkey (a primate, like man) damaged nerve cells in the newborn monkey's brain. But the case against MSG is still not altogether convincing.

It is true that we do not know all the long-term synergistic effects of all the additives in our foods, but neither do we know all the ultimate effects of salt, sugar, caffeine and scores of other naturally occurring food substances.

Some of the less natural additives now go to make palatable the increasing numbers of isolated soy protein foods many companies are producing. Soybeans are high in protein, though it is a kind of protein lacking in some of the qualities of animal protein. Vegetarians (Chapter 10) have for years eaten simulated turkey, ham, sausage and other "meats" made of soybeans.

Companies like General Mills, Worthington Foods, Archer Daniels Midland and Ralston Purina are now using a process which dissolves soy protein isolate in an alkaline medium, turns it into filaments, coagulates the filaments in an acid salt bath and creates fibers, called "tow," which are virtually without color or taste.

The fibers can be, and are being, spun like textile fibers into foods which look and taste like almost anything consumers want: scallops, chicken, pecans, pork, beef, bacon—anything.

One of the initial mass-marketed soy protein isolate products has been General Mills' Bac*Os, baconlike bits which can be used in place of fried and crumbled bacon in salads, omelettes, soups, in bacon, lettuce and tomato sandwiches and in other ways. A jar of Bac*Os is not cheap, but it is usually cheaper than a pound of bacon (to which the amount in the standard Bac*Os jar is equivalent, according to the label) and it will not dissolve into grease as does so much of a pound of real bacon. It is even kosher!

The labeling of products like Bac*Os has been the subject of much legal maneuvering, cases of Bac*Os being seized by the FDA in at least one area. General Mills would like to avoid having to use the word "imitation" or even the term "soybean." The present label calls Bac*Os "crispy Bontrae bits with a flavor like bacon," and Bontrae is described as a registered trademark for a vegetable protein product.

This raises questions of deceptive labeling, and certainly soybean isolates lend themselves beautifully to many deceptions, especially when they are used in combination with real meat.

Labeling laws do not require the amount of real meat to be specified in some cases. A pound of isolated soy protein, which costs a producer as little as thirty cents dry, can be tripled in bulk by hydration and used to stretch the real (and expensive) meat in a product.

Restaurants do not usually have to say anything on their menus about the contents of the food they serve—at least there is no federal law which compels such disclosure. Some restaurants now buy from Swift & Company items like Salisbury steak, chili, canned meat loaf and sloppy joes, all extended with soy protein at the packing house.

The process employed by General Mills, Worthington and Ralston Purina is licensed by Robert Boyer, its inventor, who patented it in the early 1950's. Boyer was a protégé of Henry Ford, who for many years promoted the uses of soybeans for plastics and other purposes.

Next to corn, soybeans are now America's largest agricultural crop, though most of the crop now goes into products like margarine and is not used to extend meat products or imitate them. That use, however, is growing. Between 250 and 300 million pounds of soy flour were used in U.S. food products in 1969. The greatest potential for soybean protein is in the so-called "analogs," the meatless meats that are analogous to beef, pork, poultry and seafood. Sales of such analogs in 1969 were only an estimated $10 million, up from about $3 million in 1964. But a West Coast research firm predicts that sales of analog products will reach $1.5 billion to $2 billion by 1980 and will equal five to six per cent of meat and poultry sales.

How close do the analogs come to tasting like meat loaf, corned beef hash, bacon, hamburger, fried chicken, breakfast sausages and the other foods they pretend to? Close enough in some cases to worry livestock feeders and other meat industry elements.

To be successful impostors, soybeans depend on the skills of food technicians in using properly designed flavor additives. Their technology will be called upon more and more in years to come, not only in this country but more especially perhaps in developing synthetic foods to help feed the world's growing populations.

Is it kosher?

For Jews observing dietary laws (Chapter 7), and for kosher food inspectors, the new food technology has made life complicated. "Non-dairy" coffee lighteners, for example, are not necessarily made without milk derivatives (Chapter 4).

The Joint Kashruth division of the Union of Orthodox Jewish Congregations of America [12] sends out almost 500 inspectors to about 500 companies, spot-checking 3000 products. Rabbi Alexander S. Rosenberg, rabbinic administrator of the division, has suggested some of the latter-day difficulties attendant to bestowing the little circled "U" on approved kosher foods:

> Glycerine is a fat derivative [he told a *New York Times* reporter], but what fat? It's non-kosher if it derives from tallow or lard, but it is kosher if it's from vegetable oil. But the Government permits a pure vegetable product to contain glycerine, no matter what the derivative.

The shortening used in bread, cookies, potato chips and such must not be lard or animal fat. And products to be used at Passover must be made without leavening. To non-Jews and to the non-Orthodox, these appear to be unnecessary extremes, but at the large food companies, to whom kosher certification means extra sales, the complexities of religious dietary requirements are not taken lightly.

Orthodox Jews are by no means the only people thrown into a tizzy by the hazards, real or imaginary, of food additives. Some of the outcry has come from alarmists we will discuss in the next chapter; it

---

[12] The U.S. has some 5.9 million Jews, about half of them Orthodox. There are less than 14 million Jews in the whole world, about 2.6 million of them in the Soviet Union, 2.4 million in Israel, 535,000 in France. Less than three per cent of the U.S. is Jewish, but New York state is about 14 per cent Jewish, New Jersey 5.5 per cent, California, 3.6 per cent, Connecticut 3.5 per cent and Florida three per cent.

is, of course, impossible to say that *all* their anxieties are exaggerated, but it should be said that "engineered" flavoring has wide potential for good. Virtually all the new foods which are proposed as partial solutions to world hunger—artificially grown yeasts, fish protein flour or whatever—will need flavor additives and other additives if they are to pass the organoleptic tests of the consuming public in any country.

⁖[10]⁖

Nuts in the fruitcake

Americans are so concerned with their health that our foods are advertised at least as much for their nutritional values as for their qualities of taste and pleasure. Much of our nutrition consciousness has developed in the past quarter-century.

People who never knew a calorie from a vitamin, if indeed they had ever heard those words, learned in the mess halls of World War II —or from young men returned from military service—that there is more to good eating than corn pone, fried pork and hot biscuits.

Millions of Americans in the 1940's shifted from fats and carbohydrates to foods with higher protein content. More grown men drank milk and orange juice and ate leafy green vegetables, even if they did not go on eating creamed chipped beef (made from cured, smoked, dehydrated chip-sliced beef round) on toast, a dish well remembered by servicemen for its earthy nickname.

This awareness of good nutrition has been a useful thing for the country. But America's interest in the health aspects of food has had its less fortunate side.

The country has often been swept by the campaigns of food faddists. We have no monopoly on such faddists. In their own ways, Confucius, Lao-Tze, Zoroaster, Siddhartha Gautama (the Buddha) and Moses all promulgated extreme views about food and nutrition.

Vegetarians past and present

One of the earliest and most persistent food mystiques has been vegetarianism, which can be based on the sort of sensibilities that prevent Hindus from killing any living thing (Chapter 7) or from attitudes about health.

Hindus are vegetarians, many of them because they believe it is healthier to live on a vegetarian diet. Trappist monks are vegetarians, too, and so are various occult groups and small Protestant sects like the Seventh Day Adventists, some of whose members operate Worthington Foods, a U.S. corporation active in producing meat-substitute analogs (Chapter 9).

The poet Percy Bysshe Shelley published a treatise in 1813 which claimed the human digestive system was suited only to plant foods, a pseudo-scientific idea we looked at in Chapter 1. Shelley's thesis was taken quite seriously by George Bernard Shaw, who gave up eating meat when he was twenty-five. Some of Shaw's statements suggest, however, that he was more motivated by conscience than by science. "A man of my spiritual intensity," said GBS, "does not eat corpses."

Shaw maintained a vegetarian diet for the remainder of his ninety-four years [1] and claimed he was "seldom less than ten times as well as an ordinary carcass eater."

Another long-lived vegetarian, eighty-two when he died in 1910, was Leo Tolstoy. The Russian novelist and social critic proclaimed a new religion when he was forty-eight; it rejected sexuality, war, violence, drinking, smoking and the eating of animal flesh.

A few years earlier, in 1872, Samuel Butler in England had pub-

---

[1] "I don't like to peach on a pal," said H. G. Wells to Alexander Woollcott, "but Shaw cheats. He takes liver extract and calls it 'those chemicals.'" Mrs. Patrick Campbell, in a stormy rehearsal of *Pygmalion*, cried out, "Shaw, some day you'll eat a pork chop and then God help all the women." But the day never came.

lished a satirical novel, *Erewhon*, which kidded the vegetarians. Butler's fictional Erewhonians became vegetarians for reasons of moral
scruple; one of them wrote a thesis on "The Rights of Vegetables."
He went to some lengths to prove that vegetables, like animals, are
alive and have feelings. Driven by logic to eat only such things as
cabbages certified to have died of natural causes, the Erewhonians in
the end gave up vegetarianism altogether.

Marston Bates, who recalls the Butler satire in his own book,
Gluttons and Libertines, reminds us that we cold-bloodedly eat some
things alive:

> In general, [he says] only mute things are eaten alive—plants and
> invertebrates. If oysters shrieked as they were pried open, or
> squealed when jabbed with a fork, I doubt whether they would be
> eaten alive. But as it is, thoughtful people quite callously look for
> the muscular twitch as they drop lemon juice on a poor oyster, to
> be sure that it is alive before they eat it.

At the other extreme of the question are food extremists, like
Gayelord Hauser whom we will discuss presently, who maintain that
we should eat "living" foods and not "dead" ones.

Some vegetarians insist on eating raw vegetables, not cooked ones.
Some call themselves "fruitarians" and eat only fruit. More permis-
sive are the "lacto-vegetarians" who include milk, eggs and cheese in
their diets, but other vegetarians say these are forms of meat and will
not touch them.

One vegetarian argument has been that meat produces "necrones"
and harmful deposits of uric acid in the body. An increase of uric acid
in the blood is associated with diseases like gout; the body itself produces more uric acid when these diseases are present. But uric acid
in the diet is not a *cause* of such diseases. As for necrones, no reputable
doctor can tell you what they are.

Sensitivities aside, there are no convincing nutritional justifications
for vegetarianism. Some vegetarians have, it is true, lived to ripe ages,
but so have many meat eaters; more than one food fad, in fact, has
recommended eating great quantities of meat. A 1948 book by Daniel
C. Munro, *You Can Live Longer Than You Think*, claimed that

Methuselah lived 969 years because he ate mostly meat. And then there was Dr. Salisbury (Chapter 3) of Salisbury steak fame.

No real correlation has ever been established between either a meat diet or a vegetarian diet and long life. Much of the world is forced by economic circumstance or religious law to subsist almost entirely without the primary sources of high-quality protein. Some amino acids and vitamin B_{12} are particularly hard to come by without animal protein.

But food fads and diet dogma tend to be simplistic and only dimly related to facts or realistic interpretations of facts. Some cultists have taken the fact that various bodily ills are accompanied by loss of appetite as evidence that long fasting has therapeutic value ("the body is trying to tell us something"). Upton Sinclair, whose novel *The Jungle* helped bring about the Pure Food and Drug Law, fell for this fasting nonsense. (He also defended vegetarianism, which his meat-packing exposés encouraged, and a number of other fads.) *The Fasting Cure*, which Sinclair wrote in 1911, claimed that prolonged fasting would be effective against tuberculosis, syphilis, asthma, cancer, the common cold, Bright's disease and liver trouble.

Graham, the cracker-barrel evangelist

One of America's first home-grown food faddists, and this country has had more than its share, was the Reverend Sylvester W. Graham, whose name survives in Graham flour and the Graham cracker.

Graham, a former Presbyterian preacher, was a temperance lecturer, vegetarian, dietetic "expert" and self-styled doctor of medicine. Born in West Suffield, Connecticut, in 1794, he launched an attack in his mid-thirties on meats and fats (which, he said, heated people's tempers and led them to sexual excesses). Condiments like mustard, catsup and pepper, he charged, could cause insanity.

Mostly he propagandized for a regimen of eating based on bread made from coarse, unbolted or unsifted flour and eaten slightly stale. The important thing was to keep the bran in the bread. Graham declared war on white bread, which had long been a symbol of good living and of Western civilization. He had no knowledge of the vitamins and minerals in bran, but like so many of his successors he was obsessed with bowel regularity; bran has laxative effects.

Graham neglected the fact that refined flour keeps better than whole grain flour in storage, and that it is easier to digest (bran irritates many people's intestines).

Indigestion, even the severe extremes of it called dyspepsia, were so common in early nineteenth-century America (Adams, Cooper and Volney all remarked about it, as we saw in Chapter 3) that Graham's teachings fell on fertile ground. Graham hotels sprang up around the country; and Graham followers, indoctrinated with ideas about eating more fruits and vegetables and less salt, shellfish and pork (Graham opposed them violently and barely tolerated milk, eggs and honey), included the founders of Oberlin College, John J. Shipherd and Philo Penfield Stewart; they included also Bronson Alcott (father of Louisa May who wrote *Little Women*), Joseph Smith who founded the Mormon Church, Amelia Bloomer the fashion revolutionary and, from time to time, the inventor Thomas Edison and the journalist-editor-politician Horace Greeley.

Graham's philosophies of nutrition led, by way of the Adventist Church (whose spiritual leader, Mother Ellen Harmon White, promised God-given health and happiness to all who eschewed tobacco, salt, spices and spirits, drank only water and ate two meatless meals a day) to the whole modern breakfast food industry.

Mother White founded the Western Health Reform Institute at Battle Creek, Michigan, in 1866. Some years later, Dr. John Harvey Kellogg was hired to manage the Institute, whose name he changed to the Battle Creek Sanitarium, or the San, as it was called.

Patients at the San ate lots of bran in the Graham tradition. If they had high blood pressure, they were fed nothing but grapes—up to fourteen pounds of grapes a day. If thin, they were fed twenty-six times a day and forced to remain motionless lest they waste calories: they were not even allowed to brush their teeth.

Dr. Kellogg, with his brother Will K., developed a dry cereal called Granose; it sold 100,000 pounds its first year and went on from there.[2] And as we saw in Chapter 8 a patient at the San, C.W. Post (whose nine months' stay did him no good) went on to invent Postum and Grape-Nuts.

Sylvester Graham, while he helped in a positive way to make America aware of the health aspects of food, unfortunately prepared the way for ensuing waves of food faddism and quackery.

Dietary apostles have appeared on the American scene regularly ever since. No doubt some of them have made valid contributions, if only by spurring scientists to find solid refutations to their claims. Many have also piled up sizable fortunes.

"Chew every bite"

Britain's nineteenth-century Prime Minister William Gladstone, near the end of his career, said rather self-righteously, "I have made it a rule to give every tooth of mine a chance, and when I eat, to chew every bite thirty-two times. To this rule I owe much of my success in life."

An American businessman, Horace Fletcher, digested this pap and developed it into a system he called "Fletcherism." His book, *The ABC of Nutrition*, went into six editions between 1903 and 1905. "Nature will castigate those who don't masticate," was one of its precepts. Only five foot six, Fletcher weighed 217 pounds at age

---

[2] Today the breakfast food business is a $670 million industry and is highly competitive. There are some sixty-five nationally advertised brands (Kellogg has over forty per cent of the business), about twenty-five per cent of them less than eight years old. Health claims have always been effective in promoting cereal brands; one health claim in the future may involve dental health—some experimental work is being done to find cereal additives that will reduce tooth decay. For years, advertising was pitched strongly to children ("they're going to be with us longer," said the head of Kellogg) even though half the breakfast cereal output is eaten by adults. Lately, with the U.S. birth rate lower, the emphasis has been swinging to the geriatric market. Biggest seller is still Kellogg's Corn Flakes, with about ten per cent of the market.

forty when he read Gladstone's statement. He went on a strict diet, chewed vigorously [3] and lost sixty-five pounds. He also overcame shortness of breath, but it was what he ate rather than how he ate it that made the difference.

Nevertheless, Fletcherism was a huge fad by the time Horace Fletcher died in 1919. It was taken up by Thomas Edison, John D. Rockefeller, the cadets at West Point, scientists at Harvard, Yale, Johns Hopkins, Cambridge University and the Sorbonne—and, of course, by Upton Sinclair, who met Fletcher at the Battle Creek Sanitarium.

The philosopher William James was a Fletcherite for three months. "I had to give it up," he said later. "It nearly killed me."

Many food fads have been based on the idea that some foods should not be eaten together. If you avoid mixing pickles and milk, or fruit and milk or milk and potatoes, it may be a hangover of a food fad that influenced your mother or grandmother and was handed down in the family.

Did someone warn you in childhood that the acid in the fruit or the pickle would curdle the milk? What about the acid the milk will encounter in the stomach?

Hayism and other myths

The milk-and-potatoes injunction goes back to Dr. William Howard Hay whose 1933 book, *Health Via Food*, alleged that almost all bodily ills came from "acidosis." This, he said, was caused by eating too much protein, too much adulterated food like white bread, retention of food in the bowels more than twenty-four hours after eating and the combining of protein and carbohydrate.

Proteins, said Hay very solemnly, need acid for their digesting and carbohydrates require alkaline; "no human stomach can be expected to be acid and alkaline at the same time."

---

[3] Chewing is useful (it stimulates the digestive juices), but Fletcher and Gladstone went off the deep end.

The fact is, most foods contain mixtures of proteins and starches. Facts, however, have never stood in the way of fads. Such, to echo Fabre, is human folly.

Hay also preached the gospel of frequent fasting, though fasting really *does* cause acidity, or "acidosis" as Hay called it.

Some widely believed food myths are less easily traced, but there are so many of them that almost everybody believes at least some of them. *None* of the following is true:

"Feed a cold, starve a fever."
Sweets cause adolescent acne.
Sugar in the diet causes diabetes.
Grapefruit, cottage cheese, yogurt, lemon juice and protein bread have positive powers to take off weight.
Sour cream is less fattening than sweet cream.
Honey is less fattening than sugar.
Diets high in red meats cause high blood pressure and kidney disease.
Avoid salt when trying to lose weight.
Ice cream or milk should not be taken at the same meal as shell-fish.
Butter is rich in protein.
Bread and potatoes are fattening.
Brown eggs are more nutritious than white eggs.
White eggs are more nutritious than brown eggs.
Gelatin desserts are low in calories.
Beets make the blood rich.
Lemons make the blood thin.
Citrus fruits and tomatoes make the blood acid.
Eating big meals late in the day puts on more weight than eating heavily earlier in the day.
Veal is less nutritious than mature beef.
Toasting bread reduces its calorie content.
Hard-cooked eggs are hard to digest.
Thunderstorms curdle milk.
Applesauce served with greasy food absorbs excess grease.
Searing meat seals in the juices.
Basting meat with is own juices keeps it from drying out.
Black coffee is "stronger" than coffee with milk or cream.
Fish is brain food.
An apple a day keeps the doctor away.

We repeat: *none* of the above statements is true, no matter what you were brought up to believe.

While some people religiously avoid meat during the Lenten period, or religiously avoid serving meat and dairy products at the same meal, many more "religiously" follow unfounded beliefs like the ones we have listed.

Look deeper, live smarter

Perhaps the most prominent diet and health mythologist in recent years has been Gayelord Hauser, whose book *Look Younger, Live Longer* was third on the nation's non-fiction bestseller list in 1950 and led the list in 1951.

Hauser, born Helmut Eugene Benjamin Gellert Hauser in Tübingen, Germany, in 1895, sold his dietary ideas to the Hollywood movie colony in the late 1920's and 'thirties. He had no medical or nutritional education, but Hauser charmed such deep thinkers as Lady Elsie Mendl, the Duchess of Windsor, Queen Alexandra of Yugoslavia, Baron Philippe de Rothschild, Cobina Wright, Sr. and Paulette Goddard into endorsing his views. And he no doubt had an influence on the influential Gloria Swanson (Chapter 11).

Hauser's book cited a medical journal which claimed that "seventy-five per cent of the senior half of our population suffers from malnutrition." To overcome "a number of nutritional deficiencies" which lead to "premature aging," Hauser campaigned not only for large intakes of vitamins and minerals, but also for such food factors as yeast nucleic acid, which—along with pyridoxine (vitamin B6) and pantothenic acid—can be found, Hauser said, in such "wonder foods" as brewers' yeast.

Other wonder foods on Hauser's list include powdered skim milk, yogurt, wheat germ and blackstrap molasses, the dark sticky dregs left by the sugar refining process. Blackstrap molasses, said Hauser, will help cure insomnia, menopause troubles, nervousness, baldness and low blood pressure. It will aid the digestion, help restore gray hair to its original color, strengthen the heart, help the glands to function properly and prevent many changes associated with old age.

The geriatric set has always been most susceptible to such promises, largely because older people tend to have digestive troubles (the musculature of their stomachs, small intestines and colons often loses some of its tonus; their gastric juices often lose some of their volume, acidity and pepsin content). Older people often fail, too, to maintain proper diets; they eat too many carbohydrates (which are cheap, easy to chew and require no preparation). They are misguided by myths into avoiding milk (they think it is gassy, or constipating) and fruits (regarded as "acidy"). Or they get the idea they do not need much food because they are inactive. Often they follow quack diet ideas and take unnecessary vitamin supplements (which they can ill afford) beyond the point where medical advice and sound nutritional practices can help them.

Some food faddists prescribe grape juice for cancer, honey and vinegar for arthritis, garlic for high blood pressure, alfalfa powder for diabetes. Gelatin, they say, will give you strong fingernails, beets will give you red blood. It is all baloney.

The preachings of men like Hauser, abetted by confidence-weakening government actions (the recent "chickenfurter" decision is a case in point), have given rise to a health food business which, according to the *Wall Street Journal*, is a billion-dollar business in the U.S.

Part of this craze is based on the "soil depletion" myth. The nutritional values of the foods we eat, according to this apocrypha, have been depreciated as the fertility of the soil has been exhausted.

Farm animals, it is true, are sometimes affected by deficiencies or excesses of certain elements in the soil; this is because farm animals are so often fed on such a limited number of plant species grown on soil in a very confined area. Even with those limitations, the calcium content of cows' milk remains essentially the same no matter what the level of calcium in the cow's diet. The truth of this has been repeatedly documented.

Most people, certainly in the United States, have such a variety of meats, fish, cereals, fruits and vegetables in their diets that examples of human malnutrition due to soil deficiencies are virtually non-existent.

Soil fertility will determine how many plants will grow in a given area of land and how large the plants will grow, but for all practical purposes of human nutrition, the content of the soil will have little if any effect on the composition of plant foods grown on that soil.

In the case of vitamin C in tomatoes, in fact, poor soil may be a positive blessing. The vitamin C content depends mostly on how much sunlight strikes the fruit just before it is picked, and how intense the sunlight is. If the soil is too fertile, the tomato plants will produce large leaves that will shade the fruit with the result that it will be lower in vitamin C.

That "organic" baloney

There are unquestionably dangers of contamination from insecticides in foods, and the run-off of fertilizers into streams may jeopardize fishlife, but while some pesticide and herbicide residues may indeed be carcinogenic it is hardly true, as claimed by "organic farming" exponents, that the use of "artificial" fertilizers, weed killers and insect sprays are behind the majority of America's health disorders, including cancer. As we saw in Chapter 5, DDT has not yet been shown to have harmful effects for humans except as it affects fish and wildlife. More and more curbs are being imposed on the use of DDT, and on some herbicides as well. Use of the weed-killer 2,4,5-T was limited in late October, 1969, by the federal government after it was shown that relatively large doses of it, fed during pregnancy to mice and rats, evidently cause the animals to produce offspring with more than the usual percentage of birth defects.

But the opposition to chemical herbicides and pesticides is not the central issue with the organic farming crowd.

Their leading spokesman has been a manufacturer of electrical wiring devices in Emmaus, Pennsylvania, one Jerome I. Rodale, whose 1948 book, *The Organic Front*, contained the arguments echoed in three monthly magazines Rodale now edits: *The Organic Farmer, Organic Gardening* and *Prevention*. The last is concerned with preventing diseases and disorders through organic agriculture.

Rodale is a raw food fanatic. "No animal eats cooked foods," he has written. "Man is the only creature that does." It is hard to argue with that, but Rodale's campaign against chemical fertilizers finds little support from the scientific community.

Health food shops nevertheless get healthy prices for "organically grown" foods. The only acceptable fertilizers for health food fans are green manures and animal manures. But in South Korea, where "night soil" is the time-honored fertilizer and seventy per cent of human excrement is used for the purpose, the Health Ministry is campaigning for chemical fertilizers. Some ninety-five per cent of South Korea's 30 million people suffer from parasites like roundworm, whipworm, tinworm and hookworm; the Ministry blames this on the country's traditional organic agriculture. Vegetables produced by such methods, time-honored in the Orient, spread the parasites; the Health Ministry now bans the use of "night soil" on fields surrounding eleven major South Korean cities.

It may be, as Barry Commoner says, that artificial nitrates added to the soil not only run off into rivers and promote an overgrowth of algae, but also tend to reduce the soil's natural ability to produce nitrogen compounds. But efficient agriculture depends on chemical fertilizers for all their hazards to our environment; the developing countries are in desperate need of them to increase food production and avert famine; food grown with them is every bit as good as food grown organically.

Yet "organically grown" remains a magic phrase in the health food shops of America and Great Britain, shops whose proprietors thrive on the credibility gap which exists on many levels of modern society but which comes closest to home when it concerns what people eat.

Exploiters of doubt

Preachers of wild-eyed gospels continue to find willing listeners, medical and nutritional advances notwithstanding.

Nutrition is still a young science, but it has come a long way and is going farther all the time to sort out mysteries of nutrients and their functions in human physiology. The gaps in nutritional knowledge are still filled by false prophets whose credentials are little better than those of Horace Fletcher, William Howard Hay or Gayelord Hauser.

One reason the purveyors of irresponsible misinformation about foods find such a rich seedbed for their Mickey Mouse products and proclamations is the communications problem which confronts the FDA, the Department of Agriculture and other responsible bodies. The pronouncements of the legitimate authorities, based on solid research and careful evaluation of the best possible relevant data, are not as a rule sensational. They do not make large headlines. They do not appear over and over again in various ways in various underground media as do the wilder assertions of the iconoclasts.

Not every research finding issued by the "Establishment" is necessarily the final and absolute truth. All "truths" are subject to constant re-examination. Yet one error, or one reversal of position, on the part of an official agency is taken by millions of people as evidence that nothing the agency says can be trusted—which somehow gets turned round to mean that whatever is published by irresponsible sources *can* be trusted.

The uproar over cyclamates (Chapter 9) helps to illustrate the point. The removal of cyclamates from the FDA's GRAS list and from the market should not shatter the credibility of all FDA rulings or confirm the notions of the extremists. Unfortunately, it will have that effect for some people.

The undercover sniping by health food elements at the medical

Establishment and at official government agencies falls within the sanctuary of freedom of speech. But it poses a dilemma. Occasional reassurances by public officials are no match for the virulence of inadequately documented assertions which appeal to popular emotions.

Carlton Fredericks, who has built a career as a "nutrition authority" with a radio program, a publication, lectures and several popular books, is a paramount example of the foodlore extremists who see "betrayal" in every supermarket.

It was Fredericks who crusaded so vociferously against the use of BHT as an antioxidant (Appendix); he remains unconvinced by the judgment of the World Health Organization and the FAO, a judgment based on opinions of men with better credentials than Carlton Fredericks'.

Fredericks rests his arguments heavily on the idea that each of us is an individual and the "average" established requirement of any vitamin or mineral or other nutrient may not be adequate in our particular health circumstances.

No one can argue with that. Tolerances, allergies and bodily needs are all very individual things. The fact of individual variations, however, does not justify assertions that boosting intake of certain vitamins and minerals, some of which have not been recognized as having any nutritional value at all, can ward off gray hair, prevent cancer, cure sterility or hypothyroidism or arthritis.

Fredericks was arrested back in 1945 and charged with practicing medicine without a license. He pleaded guilty in Special Sessions Court in New York City and paid a $500 fine. It was either that or spend three months in jail.

A more flagrant case of quackery is that of Adolphus Hohensee as related in James Harvey Young's book, *The Medical Messiahs.* Like Gayelord Hauser, Hohensee gave health lectures to promote health foods, but he was less of a charm boy than Hauser. He put an M.D. after his name, even though he had had only one semester of high school. A big, balding man with a waxed black moustache, Hohensee was a caricature of a pitchman. But his partisans were fierce in their adherence to his claims.

The normal diet, said Hohensee, eroded the kidneys, stagnated the blood, corroded the blood vessels, clogged the intestines. His diet, on the other hand, could rebuild all the body's organs except the kidneys, could dissolve incrustations in the brain that prevented clear thinking and could dissolve incrustations between the laminations of the eyeballs, thus making eyeglasses unnecessary.

This last claim is reminiscent of Stan Freeburg's crack about the advertising slogan used for some years by the Tea Council. "Take tea and see," said the Council. "You mean I can throw away my glasses?" asked Freeburg.

Hohensee revived the old myth that aluminum cooking utensils poisoned food. Milling cereals, pasteurizing milk and canning foods destroyed the natural nutrients, he said. He quoted the Bible freely and used big scientific words to impress his listeners. But once he got going, he promised people they could live to 180 by using his products and invited them to join him on man's first trip to the moon.

After five years of coining money at this game, Hohensee was arrested and tried in Phoenix in 1948. The foreman of the jury was a local merchant named Barry Goldwater. Hohensee paid an $1800 fine. Six years later he was convicted again, this time in Scranton, Pennsylvania. While his lawyers were appealing his case, Hohensee was caught by newspaper photographers at a back table in a Houston restaurant. He was eating fried red snapper (he had often said that frying destroys the good qualities of food) and slices of white French bread (he had said white bread "knots in a ball in your stomach and stays there in a big lump") and guzzling beer.

This modern medicine man finally went to jail in the spring of 1957 and served a year and a day. In 1962 he was sentenced by a California judge for selling honey, which he called "ambrosia of the gods" and promoted with his usual curative promises. The judge suggested Hohensee be put in charge of the prison's beehives. But after eighteen months behind bars Adolphus' conviction was reversed on an appeal that the evidence in the case had been falsely secured. Hohensee was soon back in business, frightening people with talk about the "Marble Orchard," teasing them about their sex lives

("The sex act," he declared, "should last for one hour."), and spreading the myths that most diseases stem from improper diet, that modern foods are lacking in vitamins and minerals because the soil is depleted, that foods are poisoned by chemical fertilizers and that everyone needs diet supplements to be healthy.

Tiger's Milk, honey, cider vinegar and vitamin pills

As we shall see in Chapter 11, it is hard to stop the sale of "magic" foods and nostrums. One mixture of alfalfa, parsley and watercress was sold door-to-door under the name "Nutrilite" by 15,000 salesmen as a cure for fifty-seven different diseases, the number being suggested, I imagine, by the success of H. J. Heinz with his "57 Varieties" of pickles, relishes, sauces and soups (the company now produces more than 1250 food varieties). After four years of trying, the FDA was able to make Nutrilite's manufacturer soften his claims, but it could not stop him from selling his product.

Claims of high protein, high vitamin and low fat content suffice for some health food items; trade names and packaging accomplish the rest. Consider "Tiger's Milk," a powder which, when water is added, makes a costly beverage (almost twenty-four cents a serving based on ninety-five cents for an eight-ounce package) widely sold to masochists. It tastes like the barium "milk shake" a radiologist has a patient drink before he takes a G.I. series (X-rays of the gastrointestinal tract).

Available in either vanilla or carob bean flavor, a two-ounce serving of Tiger's Milk (nonfat dry milk, raw sugar, sodium caseinate, yeast, tri-calcium phosphate, emulsifier and natural and artificial flavors, to quote the label) mixed with water contains over seventeen grams of protein, 120 per cent of the minimum daily requirement of calcium, 100 per cent of the mdr of iron, eighty-six per cent of the mdr of phosphorus, some potassium, and some choline, inositol and biotin, whose needs have not been established—all in just 196 calories. The Los Angeles manufacturer advises the purchaser to drink Tiger's Milk ice cold, presumably so he will not taste it. But even ice cold, it is hard to take.

Claims by health food missionaries are also hard to take. Their acceptance is undoubtedly a skeptical reaction to the "unnatural" additives, the processing and the packaging of foods in general distribution today.

As Dr. Robert F. Olson at the University of Pittsburgh's School of Public Health has noted, "The food faddist appreciates the symbolic value of food better than those of us concerned with nutrition. . . . The blandishments of the 'health' food educator may be based solely upon emotional responses to food as a symbol."

The facts about most food additives, and about chemical fertilizers, do not support the scare stories of these "educators," but their alarms beguile people into trying "good old-fashioned *natural*" foods like royal queen bee jelly, honey, apple cider vinegar, peppermint tea and, as urged by men like Hauser, yogurt, wheat germ, brewers' yeast, powdered skim milk and blackstrap molasses.[4]

Another basis for the success of health foods is the credibility gap atmosphere of our skeptical society, an atmosphere created in some degree by the excesses of advertising.

What makes faddists dangerous, at least to themselves and their families, and one reason they are so stoutly opposed by the health establishment, is that they encourage self-medication. Too much vitamin A or D, to cite a specific danger, can lead to serious medical complications, but many people proceed on the premise that if vitamins are good, more vitamins are better.

One "authority" who has not endeared himself to his colleagues is the Vermont doctor, D.C. Jarvis, whose 1958 book, *Folk Medicine*, advised people to test their urine for acidity. Alkalinity, said Dr. Jarvis, was dangerous; he told readers to guard against it by avoiding

---

[4] The blackstrap molasses story was started by a pianist. Crude, dark molasses contains sugar, iron and some B vitamins (so do many other foods) but it cannot cure arthritis or do any of the other things claimed for it.

meat, wheat foods, citrus fruits, white sugar and maple sugar. He recommended eating corn, oat and rye cereals, and rye bread rather than wheat bread. Follow the natural animal instincts, he suggested, and eat acid vegetation which prevents "infestation of the body with pathogenic microorganisms" which, he said, grow on alkaline soil.

Jarvis railed against the lack of potassium in Vermont soil, and the removal of potassium from food by processors. The deficiency, he said, kept Vermonters from growing tall, hardened their arteries, decayed their teeth, made them lose their hair and break their fingernails.

Among the natural foods this Green Mountain medic recommended were honey and apple cider vinegar because they were rich in potassium (though wheat contains four times as much potassium as apple cider vinegar, and potassium is an element plentifully supplied by the average diet anyway).

Dr. Jarvis does mention many of the wild "weeds" espoused by Euell Gibbons, but Gibbons does not pretend to medical expertise.

It is quite true that pasteurizing milk does destroy most of its vitamin C. Milling white flour does remove all the B vitamins and iron of the wheat berry. But relax. There is not too much vitamin C in milk to begin with; citrus fruits, strawberries, spinach, cabbage, tomatoes and liver are much better sources. Fortifying white flour restores the most important nutrients lost in milling; besides, we get enough of those nutrients if we eat dairy products, eggs, meat, liver, fish and poultry.

The idea of "natural" vitamins rather than synthetic can always be calculated to win consumers, but the fact is that there is no difference between the two, chemically, nutritionally or any other way. Vitamin capsules are no way to make up for deficiencies caused by crash reducing diets or doughnut-and-coffee breakfasts, but most Americans get all the vitamins they need from even a minimal diet. For all but a relatively few Americans, vitamin capsules are a waste of money. The molecular structure of vitamins in such capsules, however, is exactly the same as the structure of vitamins found in any food.

While most of the complaints about modern foods are based on their being "unnatural" or "denatured," exactly the opposite feeling determines the position which prevails among some of the caviar cognoscenti. The word "malossol" on a caviar label means "lightly salted." Among certain effete connoisseurs, the complaint is that while good Russian and Iranian *beluga* caviar, taken from the sturgeon of the fast-shrinking inland Caspian Sea, is washed and preserved in a weak solution of boric acid, American laws do not permit importation of food products containing boric acid. Fresh caviar [5] is imported by air and sells for close to $50 for fourteen ounces in New York, but seventy-five per cent of the sixty-five tons of caviar affluent Americans eat in a year is sold vacuum-packed for less than a dollar an ounce. In both kinds of caviar, say gastronomic critics of U.S. caviar policy, the salt used for the American market takes away something of the flavor (and limits the amount of caviar a rich old man with hypertension can eat). Too much boric acid is a hazard, they concede, but so is too much benzoate of soda, a common enough preservative for soft drinks, cider and the like.

It is probably human nature, or plain cussedness, that makes people want to believe their health is threatened by the food-processing interests and the big-money interests, that they are being exploited and must find far-out ways to defend themselves against the inhuman machine age and the evil forces of change.

The quality of food served in vending machines, and at the impersonal feeding stations that appear in the "service areas" along major U.S. highways, may tend to support these doom criers, but many of

---

[5] According to FDA regulations, only dark caviar, or sturgeon eggs, can be labeled caviar. Red caviar is technically not caviar at all, but merely salmon roe. The costliest caviar is the large grain gray *beluga*. Next is *osetra*, last is *sevruga*. Few people know that Amagansett, Long Island, fishermen and whalers years ago used to ship unprocessed sturgeon roe to Persia (Iran); the Persians processed it and shipped it back to America. Some caviar is now made at Amagansett (it takes about two and a half pounds of sturgeon eggs to make a pound of caviar), but it is not up to the standard of Russian and Iranian caviar, customarily eaten with lemon juice, buttered toast and vodka. Chopped hard-boiled egg, chopped onion and sour cream are served with Amagansett caviar, which sells for a modest $6 or $7 a pound.

the changes in modern foods are in fact genuine improvements, certainly in convenience and in economic practicality, and often in nutritional values, if not always in taste qualities.

In any case, it is in vain to think in terms of turning the clock back to some halcyon time of "natural" goodness in foods. Will Rogers used to say that things "ain't what they used to be, and what's more, they probably never were." In the "good old days," brown sugar turned hard as rock on the pantry shelf. The peanut butter at the bottom of the jar was so dry nobody wanted to eat it. Out of every pack of potatoes bought, a lot had to be thrown away because they were rotten.

Intentional additives have solved many such problems. Unintentional additives have posed new problems. While we may no longer have to cut off more of an ear of corn than we are able to cook, and while half the farmer's apple crop is no longer wormy, doubts are being raised as to the price we have had to pay for these blessings. The dangers of pesticides have not yet been fully explored.

But it is not the "health food" evangelists and diet careerists who are leveling the questions here; they are still peddling their old doctrines and nostrums.

Instead of sounding alarms about additives and fertilizers, it might be more appropriate to devote our efforts to improving the eating qualities of modern foods, however "unnatural" they may at first blush appear. We have an obligation to ourselves and to the future to be vigilant against the devaluation of foods, against "improvement" at the expense of flavor. Change is inevitable. But the obsession with health values in food is obscuring the decline of other values.

It is beyond the province of this book to pursue the complexities of protein, with all its varying amino acid components, or of protein metabolism by the body. Nor can we examine here such issues as cholesterol, its relation to saturated fats in the diet, and its effects on fat deposits in the arteries. But the idea that our food is not what it used to be, or that honest consumers are the dupes of cunning merchants, is nothing new. We shall deal with it in our final chapter.

Here let us merely observe that today's food alarmists, who, with little or no scientific documentation, declare that the public is constantly being victimized, ignore matters of degree. Of course fluorine is poisonous—in large enough quantities; so is theobromine (present in cocoa and in tea), oxalic acid (found in rhubarb) and arsenic (present in many natural foods). The small amounts of such "poisons" in our commercially available foods are perfectly safe, at least so far as anyone knows. Controlled fluoridation of community drinking water has reduced tooth decay in children dramatically in the U.S. and Canada. Other questions of food safety are constantly being studied; but the food alarmists seldom produce new, sound information.

England probably has even more food worriers than the U.S. The extremes to which they go over there can be illustrated best by quoting an AP dispatch cited by David Sanford in a *New Republic* article:

> Canterbury, England (AP)—a 23-year old woman starved to death because she believed nearly all human food was produced by the suffering of animals, the Canterbury coroner's court was told.
>
> Miss Brenda Holton, an office secretary, had a horror of meat and of other foods that she thought had been tainted by chemical sprays. She tried to live on a diet of honey, cereals and dandelion coffee, but her appetite faded and she wasted away.

Miss Holton's hang-ups were evidently all her own; to the extent that diet evangelists produce such hang-ups they are a public menace.

They can get people upset about any food substance; to some of them, as it was to Brillat-Savarin, caffeine is as hazardous as anything else. Mrs. Ruth Winter, in *Poisons in Your Food*, cites research linking caffeine (in large amounts) to chromosome breakage in lower animals and cell breakage in mammals. She says "its destructive effect may be synergistic with other chromosome breakers, such as X-rays." Americans over fourteen consume caffeine at an average of 500 milligrams per person each day, in tea, cocoa, Coca-Cola and, most especially, coffee (Chapter 8).

Diets for lovers

Less menacing than the diet evangelists, though often overlapping them, are those "authorities" who specify this food or that as beneficial to virility, or as "aphrodisiacs."

Back in the Middle Ages, coffee was called the "black enemy of sleep and copulation." If copulation had an enemy in coffee, it had alleged allies everywhere else through history.

The Old Testament mentions the mandrake root, a cousin of the potato and the tomato. The Greeks used the carrot as "love medicine" and called it "Philtron." They credited the leek ("Storgethron") with powers of venery, too. Pliny echoed the Old Testament's mandrake root and also prescribed the snout and foot of the hippopotamus to increase sexual potency. Ovid listed a number of aphrodisiacs of his time:

> Pepper with biting nettle-seed they bruise
> With yellow pillitory wine infuse . . .
> Eat the white shallots sent from Megara
> Or garden herbs that aphrodisiac are,
> Or eggs, or honey on Hymettus flowing,
> Or nuts upon the sharp-leaved pine trees growing.

Horace spoke of dried marrow and liver as being popular love foods of his era. Petronius and others in the next century recommended the pitch from a branch of the pomegranate tree, the testicles of an ass, intestines of various birds and fish, oysters and other shellfish, frogs, parts of reptiles, mushrooms, fava beans, snails, onions and snails' heads with sauce.

The peoples of the Near East and the Orient have always been particularly susceptible to aphrodisiac claims; in 1907 the Kamashastra Society (Paris and Benares) published a translation by Sir Richard Burton of *The Perfumed Garden for the Soul's Delectation*, a celebrated work on the subject by the Shaykh Nafzawi.

Among other things, Nafzawi said, "he who boils asparagus, and then fries them in fat, and then pours upon them the yolks of eggs with pounded condiments, and eats every day of this dish, will grow very strong for coitus, and find in it a stimulant for his amorous desires."

Brillat-Savarin wrote in *The Physiology of Taste* that the truffle can "make women more tender and men more apt to love."

Ah, those Frenchmen! Absinthe, a liqueur made from wormwood and outlawed even in France since 1915 (it can cause blindness, insanity and death), was long prized by the French for its aphrodisiac powers, real or imagined.

But seafood probably has the most enduring reputation as an aid to lovemaking.

One story, retold by Brillat-Savarin, goes back to the days of the Crusades. The Sultan Saladin supposedly locked up some celibate dervishes to test their ascetic will power. He fed them well on a diet of meat and then presented them with "two odalisques of surpassing loveliness [but the] saints emerged from their soft ordeal as pure as the diamond of Visapoor." Then Saladin put the men on a diet of fish and exposed them once again to the temptations of the flesh, "and this time the two happy cenobites succumbed most marvelously."

In *Tableau de l'Amour*, written in the seventeenth century, Dr. Nicolas Venette put it this way: "We have observed in France that those who live almost entirely on shellfish and fish . . . are more ardent in love than others. In fact, we ourselves feel most amorously inclined during Lent."

Roy de Groot quotes the poet Monselet on the powers of *bouillabaisse*, that fish stew the Greeks call *psaro*, the Italians *zuppa di pesce* and the Belgians *Ghentsche waterzooie*. Wrote Monselet:

> And chilly beauties, not a few,
> Will do whate'er you wish,
> Partaking, tête-a-tête with you,
> Of this perfidious dish.

Some ancient cults encouraged their people to eat great amounts of fish, but forbade priests, who were supposed to be celibate, to eat any at all.

And in the United States today the Oyster Institute of North America distributes posters which read, "Eat Oysters: Love Longer."

Aphrodisiac powers have been ascribed to crabs, caviar, crayfish tails and shark fin soup, the last being a classic Chinese love potion.

Some of the most innocent foods have at various times been credited with remarkable powers—potatoes, for example. In seventeenth-century Europe, when the potato was eyed with such suspicion (Chapter 6), one writer said, "Eating of these roots doth excite Venus and increaseth lust." The idea is widely echoed in various surviving writings of the time.

What other foods have been alleged to have aphrodisiac effects? If we take seriously diverse claims made at different times in history, the list is endless.

To arouse Louis XV, Madame DuBarry is supposed to have used truffled sweetbreads, venison, pheasant cooked in white wine, capon in sherry broth and various vegetables, herbs and spices. James Boswell thought ambergris from whales was effective. The Dutch gynecologist Van de Velde (author of *Ideal Marriage*) favored celery, artichokes and asparagus on the ground that the acids they contain are filtered and eliminated separately by the kidneys and excite the urinary passages.

But all of the following, and more, have been cited at one time or another as aphrodisiacs: anise, avocados, beans, raw beef, white beets (named by Pliny along with asparagus, dill, licorice and hyena eyes), birds' nest soup, carrots, cheeses of various kinds (notably Parmesan), chocolates and cocoa (forbidden to their women by the Aztecs and to seventeenth-century monks by Jean Franco Raucher), chutneys, cloves, Coca-Cola, eels, eggs (especially raw eggs), fennel, garlic, honey, hot sauces, various kinds of mushrooms (particularly the morel), mutton with caraway seed, nutmeg, olives, peas, peppermints and peppermint oil (mentioned by Aristotle), pimentos, pistachio nuts, radishes, saffron, thyme, tomatoes (those dangerous "love apples") and vanilla.

Joseph Wood Krutch, who mentions capsicums (peppers), observes delicately that "the number of things credited with this characteristic suggests that a ready spontaneity is often attributed to some artificial stimulant."

The mandrake root of the Old Testament sometimes resembles in its outward appearance the human male genitalia. Its alleged powers as an aphrodisiac seem to be based more on its suggestive physical appearance than on anything else. The Chinese penchant for ginseng root [6] has the same foundation.

People who subscribe most to the idea of aphrodisiac foods and virility diets are people who live in countries where diet deficiencies are common. Their ordinary diets in many cases simply do not provide the normal animal energy and vitality required for healthy sexual activity—or any other kind of activity. One hesitates to cite Gayelord Hauser as an authority for anything, but he must be right in saying that "When nutritional deficiencies have been overcome, improved health and vigor will be reflected in greater virility and normal libido." Viva libido. In the absence of extraordinary physical or psychological factors to the contrary, Hauser has to be correct.

Livestock breeders, for whom sexual performance is a gut matter of dollars and cents, have noted that a low plane of nutrition limits sperm production in rams, boars and bulls. Severe restriction of protein, vitamin A or calorie intake impairs also the production of the male sex hormone testosterone, which is manufactured both by the testicles and by the adrenal glands, but the restriction has to be severe. Excessive calorie intake can be another deterrent to satisfactory male reproductive performance, animal breeders have found.

---

[6] When the first American ship to reach China, Major Samuel Shaw's *Empress of China*, arrived at Canton in 1784 (it had sailed out of New York in November, 1783, less than three months after the British evacuated the town), it carried a cargo of ginseng, an herb native to both China and North America and prized by Chinese doctors as an aphrodisiac.

As for females, heifers raised on protein-deficient diets do not go into heat (or, as the breeders put it, "show no symptoms of estrus"). Their ovaries and uterus remain infantile. Phosphorus deficiency, or reduced phosphate utilization due to a high calcium intake, can produce "irregular estrus" and eventually stop the heifer from going into heat at all. Vitamin A, B_{12} and E deficiencies can also interfere with female animals' sexual health.

Human sexuality is somewhat different from animal sexuality. As Dr. Paul Ehrlich points out in *The Population Bomb*, one reason for the world's present problems of over-population is that in humans, as we have evolved through natural selection, the female is, in effect, in heat the year round. (And the human female, says Desmond Morris—one wonders how he can be so sure—is the only female which experiences sexual orgasm.) Still, the effect of diet on sexuality cannot be too different for humans from what it is for livestock and other animals.

A final discrediting note about aphrodisiac foods is the very number and diversity of prescriptions for "sexually stimulating" comestibles. History, after all, can produce a similar list of items used with little success for purposes of contraception, including peas, asparagus, marjoram, rosemary, thistle (in North America), green coconut (in the Pacific islands) and pineapple (in Malaya). None did a thing to slow the multiplication of the human race.

Marijuana, LSD and Spanish fly,[7] all illegal under present laws, may all be effective aphrodisiacs, if in varying degrees dangerous, and the chemical drug PCA (p-chlorophenylalanine), or "steam," seems to have remarkable properties, but as to the efficacy of any food or bev-

---

[7] The fly, *Lytta vesicatoria*, found in Spain and southern France, is actually an iridescent blister beetle whose body is pulverized to make a preparation called cantharides (sometimes the powdered bodies are chemically treated to extract a drug cantharidin). Cantharides and cantharidin are used on farm animals, but for human females they are dangerously and maddeningly irritating to the point where they can be quite lethal. The Marquis de Sade was imprisoned partly for using cantharides.

erage in the cause of love-making, there has to be considerable doubt. As for contraception, Dr. David Reuben, in his new, enlightened manual, *Everything you always wanted to know about sex but were afraid to ask*, says the familiar six-and-a-half-ounce bottle of Coca-Cola (shake well before using) is the best available vaginal douche: its carbonic acid kills sperm and its sugar explodes sperm cells, says Dr. Reuben. But he points out that a Coke is far from being one hundred per cent effective because its application is invariably too late.

There are many books of aphrodisiac recipes, but one ingredient is conspicuously missing from them all: any "aphrodisiac" must certainly be taken with a grain, at least, of salt.

As the French gastronome and food columnist Robert Courtine says, "The mouth is not used only for eating, and a good meal puts you in the mood. They say wine is good for women when men drink it, and they say the same of eating artichokes."

Not only Frenchmen but all men (and women, too) have a basic appetite for sex as for food. The first appetite can hardly be satisfied without sufficient bodily nourishment. Thus does Marston Bates raise the familiar objection to Freudian psychology that "its emphasis on sex comes from its basis in Western culture where sex is scarce—or at least strictly controlled—while food is reasonably abundant and generally available."

Bates recalls the studies of a British anthropologist, Audrey Richards, who explored human relations in an African tribe where the sex-food balance was quite the reverse of the Western balance. She found that culture and tradition governed food behavior much more than they did sexual behavior, leading Bates to comment that "even in our own society food behavior is subject to all sorts of taboos and controls." The reason these have not been studied more thoroughly by psychologists and sociologists, Bates suggests, is that "we tend to find sex more fascinating than food—I suppose because we have more trouble with it."

No need to go to Africa to find a reverse in the relative importance of sex and food. Friends confined during the war to prisoner-of-war

camps under near-starvation conditions tell us their fantasies then re-
volved around food, not sex. As for sex being more fascinating than
food, M. Courtine reminds us that "cooking is the only area where
you can still invent. In sex we know all the positions—it's limited. But
in cooking there are unexplored regions—bitter-sweet, *chaud-froid*,
cold goose with hot sliced potatoes, texture."

At the rate the human race has multipled to crowd the earth—and
jeopardize its ability to feed itself (half the world even now is under-
nourished or actually hungry)—the last thing we would seem to need
is an aphrodisiac food. But nobody should be confused by the fact
that birth rates are highest in the starving countries of the world: a
couple need have sexual relations (Bates prefers the four-letter word;
Britisher N. W. Pirie suggests we revive the Chaucerian word,
"swyve") but once a year for the reproductive apparatus to operate
at close to maximum capacity.

The truth about aphrodisiac foods, however, is that their major
function is to serve as entertainment, like the fried grasshoppers sold in
cans at supermarkets. They are related, in a reverse way, to saltpeter,
a subject of schoolboy bull sessions for as long as anyone can remember.

Boys have long speculated that saltpeter was being added to their
food for the purpose of dampening their youthful lubricity. How the
rumor began is anybody's guess, but it has no basis in fact. Saltpeter,
or saltpetre, is potassium nitrate; it is a white salt used to some extent
as a meat preservative and used more widely in the manufacture of
gunpowder, fireworks and dynamite. But it does no more to cool a
young man's explosive sexual appetite than mandrake root, tomatoes,
cocoa, artichokes or oysters will do to inflame or sustain those
appetites.

Eating astrologically

There is no law against believing that "wonder foods" will keep you young, that aphrodisiac foods will prolong or reawaken your sexual vitality, or even that the zodiac sign of your birthday determines what you should eat.

Astrology is an ancient mystic "science," originally Egyptian and Middle Eastern; it is based on the questionable premise that people born in different calendar periods share certain qualities and characteristics. We are all governed, say the astrologists, by different planets, the calendar periods of our birthdays being represented by such symbols as a ram, a bull, twins, a crab, a lion, a virgin, a balance scale, a scorpion, an archer or centaur, a goat, a water bearer and two fish.

Anyone born under a certain zodiac sign is said to have tendencies toward certain diseases. And just as a person is "ruled" by a given planet (e.g., Mars in the case of Aries, Venus in the case of Taurus, Uranus for Aquarius), various foods are also "ruled" by these planets (e.g., Mars controls most of the spices, Venus controls apples, almonds, apricots, grapes, figs, peaches, wheat and sweet-smelling spices, Uranus controls—well, that is the general idea).

According to this elaborate design, the best vitamin A sources for an Aries are milk, cheese, butter, fish oils, green leaf vegetables (especially escarole), yellow vegetables (sweet potatoes, carrots), okra pods, watercress, alfalfa herb, lettuce and fruits with yellow flesh.

But for an Aquarius in this Age of Aquarius, the best vitamin A sources are whole milk products, seafoods, fish liver oils, liver, lamb, green leaf vegetables, kale, yellow vegetables and fruits with yellow flesh, and salad greens.

It is perfectly possible, however, to be an Aries who is allergic to vegetables in the carrot family, or an Aquarius with an intolerance for milk products. The astrologists no doubt have glib answers to those problems, but their "science" is as modern as Hippocrates, who required his fourth-century B.C. students to study astrology because no science at the time was any better.

In this anti-rational age too many people still prefer to avoid the truths established by science and to pursue any food fad that comes along, however discredited its proponents, however unlikely its claims. It is the Age of Aquarius.

∘⟦ *11* ⟧∘

The cops on the food beat

The Bishop of Carthage wrote early in the Christian Era to the Roman proconsul in Africa, a certain Demetrius, that "the world itself now bears witness to its failing powers. There is not so much rain in the winter for fertilizing the seeds, nor in the summer is there so much warmth for ripening them. The springtime is no longer so mild, nor the autumn so rich in fruit."

There is no doubt more basis for hand-wringing in a world that is overcrowded and polluted, but it is well to remember that gloom and doom are not twentieth-century inventions.

Today we are told that our food is inferior, possibly unsafe and unwholesome. It may be that today's foods are increasingly tainted with potentially harmful residues of chemical insecticides and herbicides, or have been selectively bred for qualities other than taste qualities, or that health and taste values have been sacrificed to efficiency and to sales appeal (the poet e.e. cummings called U.S. processed foods "Battle Creek seaweed"), but any falling off in the quality of our food in general has been marginal. As for laments about intentional adulteration of food, they are old news. Only in years past they had more merit.

Costly spices were stretched with so many foreign substances in the fifteenth century that the English had to pass an ordinance against

fraudulent adulteration of spices in 1447; it was probably the original pure food law.

Two hundred years ago, when forty-eight was an old age in England, the Scottish surgeon and novelist Tobias Smollett, a man of just that cantankerous age, wrote his last novel, *Humphry Clinker*. There appears in it a letter written by fictional Matthew Bramble to his friend Dr. Lewis:

> The bread I eat in London [writes Bramble] is a deleterious paste, mixed up with chalk, alum, and bone-ashes; insipid to the taste, and destructive to the constitution. The good people are not ignorant of this adulteration; but they prefer it to wholesome bread, because it is whiter than the meal of corn: thus they sacrifice their taste and their health, and the lives of their tender infants, to a most absurd gratification of a mis-judging eye; and the miller, or the baker, is obliged to poison them and their families, in order to live by his profession. . . . As they have discharged the natural colour from their bread, . . . so they insist upon having the complexion of their pot-herbs mended, even at the hazard of their lives. Perhaps, you will hardly believe they can be so mad as to boil their greens with brass half-pence in order to improve their colour; and yet nothing is more true—Indeed, without this improvement in the colour, they have no personal merit. They are produced in an artificial soil, and taste of nothing but the dunghills, from whence they spring.

On and on he goes, sounding very much like the voices raised today in the "health food" shops and publications—except that Smollett wrote at a time when there *was* wholesale and unpoliced adulteration of foods. He was a muckraker long before Upton Sinclair. Nearly a century elapsed between *Humphry Clinker* and Britain's first Adulteration of Foods Act, passed in 1860. (A much stricter law, the Adulteration of Food, Drink and Drugs Act, came in 1872, thirty-four years before the U.S. Pure Food and Drug Act.)

Foods and beverages in those "good old days" were unbelievable. Milk and beer were watered, there was chicory in coffee and barley meal in oatmeal, common cheats that enriched merchants and reduced the nutritional value of foods. Other eighteenth- and nineteenth-century additives were more dangerous: there was sulphate of copper in pickles, bottled fruits and preserves; mustard contained lead chromate; sugar confectionery contained mineral dyes that killed some people every year. Bread contained boiled potatoes, magnesium and ammonia carbohydrates, potato flour, pipe clay, gypsum, whiting and ground Derbyshire stone along with the "chalk, alum, and bone-ashes" mentioned by Matthew Bramble.

Bitter almonds were used to flavor wines, vermilion and red lead to color the rind of Gloucester cheese. Exhausted tea leaves were bought from hotels, coffee houses and charwomen and mixed in factories with a gum solution. Redried, they were colored with black lead, Prussian blue, indigo, Dutch pink, turmeric and poisons like copper carbonate and lead chromate and sold as new tea.

Gunpowder tea is a fine variety of green China tea in which each leaf is rolled into a tiny ball; in Victorian England merchants sold "tea" that was actually gunpowder mixed with gum, pale Prussian blue dye, turmeric and sulphate of lime. Other "tea" was made from ash, elder and sloe leaves picked from English hedgerows and curled and colored on copper plates.

Little credence was given to revelations like Smollett's. When a reputable analytical chemist, Frederick Accum, published his *Treatise on Adulterations of Food and Culinary Poisons* in 1820, many of the frauds mentioned above were made public. The book was a great success; it was widely reviewed in newspapers and periodicals and, within a few months, it enraged the vested interests to the point where Accum was forced to leave the country (he went to Berlin) to avoid disgrace and public trial.

Accum's book had no immediate constructive effect. When another analytical chemist, John Mitchell, published *A Treatise on the Falsifications of Food, and the Chemical Means Employed to Detect Them*, in 1848, it was clear that adulteration had increased enormously in the years since Accum's book.

John Burnett, who discusses the history of English food adultera-tion in his 1966 book, *Plenty and Want*, ascribes the trouble to "a doctrinaire belief in the efficacy of free competition to ensure the best interests of the consumer."

Today we have learned to temper the advice of Adam Smith, as the English learned long before us.[1]

Britain enacted Food and Drug laws in 1860, amended them in 1870. But until Theodore Roosevelt signed the Heyburn Act, our first federal Pure Food and Drug Act, into law in 1906, and even for some years after, many foods sold to U.S. consumers contained alarming ingredients with little or no restriction.

This tampering with foods had existed in America for a long time. Amelia Simmons, in her *American Cookery* more than a century before the Heyburn Act, had warned readers against cheeses colored with "hemlock cocumberries, or saffron, infufed into the milk," and against fish whose gills were painted—or at least peppered or moistened with blood—to make them look fresh.

The prime mover beyond the Heyburn legislation was Dr. Harvey M. Wiley who, as chief chemist of the U.S. Department of Agriculture in the 1880's and nineties, stumped the country crusading against the "creative" chemistry that modified almost every item of food Americans ate.

In 1889, a Nebraska senator was inspired by Wiley to present a pure food law to Congress; his proposal met with ridicule. Wiley did not quit; an energetic bachelor with wit and style, he aroused such ardent loyalty that the public was stirred to petition Congress to hold public hearings on food. Some 10,000 such petitions were filed in 1892. Ten years later, Wiley formed what a newspaperman called a "Poison Squad" to study the physiological effects of preservatives and colorings used in foods. These included boric acid and borax, salicylic acid and salicylates, benzoic acid and benzoates, sulphur dioxide and

---

[1] Some of England's food reform was concededly voluntary. In 1855, for example, Thomas Blackwell, of Crosse & Blackwell, announced that his firm had stopped coppering pickles and fruits and using *bole armenian* to color sauces. Other "respectable" merchants stopped, too, though it took advertising to persuade the public to accept brown pickles instead of bright green and to give up insisting that anchovy sauce be a brilliant red.

sulphites, sulfate of copper and saltpeter, all of them widely used preservatives.

In those days of weak federal control, the food manufacturers were able to exert pressure and prevent publication of Wiley's findings, which found all the common preservatives dangerous and would have ruled out use of a common food coloring as well.

For all their censoring of Wiley, the food interests could not suppress Upton Sinclair with his *Jungle* (Chapter 3). That got the public up in arms. It led to the passage by Congress of what was often called Dr. Wiley's law, legislation the *New York Times* hailed by saying, "the purity and honesty of the food and medicines of the people are now guaranteed."

The rejoicing was somewhat premature. The Heyburn Act's enforcement provisions were weak; commercial forces mobilized to cripple the new Pure Food and Drug Law. Before long, Dr. Wiley was locked in battle with the alum baking powder interests, corn syrup manufacturers, the oyster industry, users of sulfate of copper for greener vegetables, and the Coca-Cola Company. Most of the cases brought to trial ended in compromise.

Now the Federal Department of Agriculture and the state agriculture departments [2] have more authority and more power. It is well they do. And it is well we have the FDA, no longer a part of the Agriculture Department, and local consumer protection bodies, too. The public is almost completely dependent on these agencies of government to protect it from irresponsible use, deliberate or innocent, of food additives. The more "engineered" our foods become, the more important is the role of these watchdog agencies in safeguarding the public.

---

[2] Strictest of the state departments in its requirements for small grain products (made of wheat, rye, oats or barley) is the Pennsylvania department, whose acceptance is often indicated on bakery products.

The top watchdog

All intentional [3] food additives, whether natural or synthetic, are given close scrutiny by the FDA, which in 1940 was taken out of the Department of Agriculture and put under the Federal Security Agency, which became the Department of Health, Education and Welfare in 1953.

The FDA's powers were expanded by the Federal Food, Drug and Cosmetic Act of 1938, and further expanded by the Food Additives Amendment, containing the so-called Delaney clause, enacted in September, 1958.

Under this amendment, which took effect in March, 1960, no additive other than additives which had been used widely for many years and were "generally recognized as safe" (GRAS) could be used in foods unless the FDA, after a thorough review of test data, agreed that it was safe at intended levels of use.

Called the White List until its acronym was adopted, the GRAS list originally contained about 190 chemical compounds and natural spices. It was circulated among about 900 pharmacologists, toxicologists and other experts, 350 of whom responded and 200 of whom agreed that all the items were safe at intended levels of use. The list included baking powder, cinnamon, citric acid, cyclamates, monosodium glutamate and pepper.

The 1958 amendment served a useful purpose. Before it, the FDA had been unable to act against a possibly harmful food additive

---

[3] Unintentional additives, usually pesticide or herbicide residues, are the province of the Department of Agriculture. For some the tolerance limits are zero. They are often detected by gas chromotography, thin-layer chromotography, atomic absorption spectrophotometry and other sophisticated techniques. Residues of heptachlor, a chlorinated hydrocarbon like DDT used to control chiggers, kept 4 million pounds of turkey meat and 150,000 live turkeys off Thanksgiving tables in 1969 when discovered at a Minnesota processing plant.

until some food including that additive was sold in interstate commerce.

One of the amendment's fathers was Representative James J. Delaney, a Democrat of Queens County, New York City. As chairman of the Select Committee to Investigate the Use of Chemicals in Food, Delaney had held extensive investigations into additives from 1950 to 1952. He introduced his amendment bill to Congress five times after that and got nowhere.

But in 1956 a health food advocate, movie actress Gloria Swanson, addressed a group of congressmen's wives in Washington and evidently mesmerized them. They spoke to their husbands and the husbands voted for Delaney's pet bill. Delaney credited Miss Swanson for the success he had two years later in having his bill enacted. "I was screaming at the wind until she came along," he said.

In the first six years after the amendment took effect, the number of intentional food additives permitted by the FDA dropped off by about fifteen per cent, despite acceptance in 1964 and 1965 of more than 850 synthetic and natural flavor additives.

Under the stewardship of Dr. James Goddard, who served as Food and Drug Commissioner from January, 1966, until the spring of 1968, the FDA became especially zealous in its administration of the laws concerning food additives. Too zealous, said some critics. But the law itself has come in for more attack than its administrators.

What has been questioned most is the Delaney "cancer clause" in the 1958 amendment. Under this clause, which departs from the rest of the amendment in its acceptance of GRAS list ingredients at safe levels of use, *no* amount of any chemical may be added to foods if *any* amount of that chemical, when ingested by humans or animals, produces cancer.

The test rats that got bladder cancers from cyclamates were ingesting what amounted, in proportion to their size, to fifty times the amount of cyclamates recommended for humans. An adult would have to drink 388 bottles of Tab, a child 133 bottles of Tab each day to reach that level. But even if it took 100 times or 200 times the recommended usage level for cyclamates to be carcinogenic, if they produced cancer they could not legally be used in human foods.

Being against cancer is like being against sin and in favor of motherhood. It always wins votes, though the world might be better off these days in terms of feeding itself if it had more sin and less motherhood. And fewer pieces of legislation like the Delaney cancer clause in the 1958 Food Additive amendment.

Even before the cyclamates uproar, many scientists felt the cancer clause was an exaggerated precaution. They said the law should be changed to ban the use of any chemicals "found to induce cancer when ingested by man or animals in amounts and under conditions related to its intended use."

Inject enough table salt or glucose, say the critics, and animals will get cancer as readily as if injected with massive amounts of cyclamates or other substances. Shall we therefore ban the use of salt and sugar in our foods? There must be levels at which carcinogens have no ill effects; otherwise we would all get cancer, since we are all exposed to so many foodstuffs (as opposed to additives, a semantic distinction) and to a certain amount of background radiation, sunlight, natural estrogens and other "environmental" carcinogens.

Besides, it is argued, why single out cancer? What about the heart, the liver, the kidneys? Why not prohibit the use of any amount of any additive that in high dosage may damage these organs?

On the other side of the argument, the points are made that sixteen per cent of all deaths in the U.S. are due to cancer, which is second only to cardiovascular disease as a major cause of death, and that no threshold levels, no safe tolerances for carcinogens have ever been established.

The controversy is sure to go on for years until more is known about cancer and its causes. If something produces cancer in animals there is serious presumption that it may be hazardous to humans; nobody can ask the public to serve as guinea pigs (or test rats) for something that can be dangerous. We can all live without cyclamates; perhaps it is just as well to err on the side of over-caution. It is well to remember, however, that there is no real proof that cyclamates and some other outlawed substances are dangerous to humans, certainly at the levels at which they could conceivably be ingested.

We do open a can of worms when we start banning this food additive or that on the basis of present testing. While we have well-established animal tests for determining potential carcinogens, experimental models for diseases like hypertension and atherosclerosis are less well-developed, hence the exaggerated emphasis on cancer. As our testing becomes more sophisticated and covers more hazards, we may find the list of safe foods drastically diminished and we may have to revise our criteria. What would the food faddists say if bonemeal, wheat germ, honey, blackstrap molasses or cider vinegar were found hazardous?

One thing is certain: the cyclamate ban has made more people aware of the questionability of the cancer clause in the 1958 amendment.

That amendment puts the burden of proof that a chemical is harmless squarely on its manufacturer; this explains why Abbott Laboratories sponsored the tests which finally knocked cyclamates off the GRAS list. But while cyclamates have possible harmful effects on chromosomes, on the kidney, the liver and on bone marrow, knowledgeable authorities generally think the cyclamates got what the underworld calls a bum rap; even taken at the rate of a dozen bottles of diet cola a day, cyclamates are probably no more likely to produce cancer in humans than, say, the char on charcoal-broiled meat, rumored to be carcinogenic until the rumor was quashed a few years ago.

This is not to say that additives are all perfectly splendid. They should all, individually, be open to question; they should be banned from our foods when they are found to be true health hazards in the amounts used. Our watchdogs should have sharp teeth; but the hand on the leash should be guided by reason and not by political panic.

The private investigator,
the public interest

Passed in the same year as the 1906 Pure Food and Drug Act was a federal Meat Inspection Act, the more direct result of Upton Sinclair's *The Jungle*. While the Heyburn Act was concerned with food ingredient standards, inspection acts are concerned more with the conditions under which food commodities are handled and packed.

An enterprising muckraker in the great tradition of Sinclair is consumer crusader Ralph Nader, who has been credited with the passage of more than one federal food inspection law.

In the spring of 1969, Nader called for a "basic cleaning up" in America's food-processing industry; he cited a Consumer's Union report which showed that one eighth of federally inspected sausage was found in a survey to contain insect larvae or other contamination. A few months later, more than 100 of "Nader's raiders"—law, medical and engineering students and undergraduates, subsidized by foundation grants—fine-tooth-combed a dozen or so federal agencies, including the FDA and the Agriculture Department's meat and poultry inspection apparatus, the latter "with special attention to evidence of favoritism to food industry groups," to quote the influential Mr. Nader.

There is, no doubt, room for concern. Federal and local inspectors in 1968, says the *New York Times*, refused entry to New York City of enough food to fill a sixty-car freight train. The barred and condemned food included more than a million shrimp, twelve tons of frogs' legs, every other kind of meat (including crab meat), enough cheese to supply nearly half a pound to every family in the city (141 tons of New York state cheese was found to be contaminated by rodent and insect filth, and cheese in general was the main item rejected), along with dates, liquid eggs, powdered milk, canned tomatoes, pickles, mushrooms, raspberries and pigeon peas.

Three quarters of the 6 million pounds of rejected food were imported products described by inspectors as "unfit for human consumption." About sixty-five per cent of all U.S. food imports enter the
country through the port of New York.

Food inspection is not easy. It is easier to pass laws than to implement them. The *Times* quoted the head of the operations analysis
group of the Agriculture Department's Consumer Protection Program:

> In meat we've got a product not only subject to easy contamination
> but extremely amenable to adulteration and to concealment of
> adulteration. Partially spoiled meat can be subjected to cooking and
> curing operations and chemicals that make it look fine.

The *Times* the same day reported a crack-down by the city's
Department of Consumer Affairs on so-called "hamburgers" (Ralph
Nader calls them "shamburgers") served at some city restaurants and
luncheonettes. In 156 of 421 such places the Department investigated,
the meat came from boxes labeled "meat patties"; these contained such
nonmeat ingredients as cereal, starch, soy protein concentrate, gluten,
vegetable flour, hydrolized plant protein, chemical additives and other
substances. (One Department official joked, "The hamburgers I buy
are O.K.—they're too small to contain all that.")

City and state laws say hamburgers can only be "chopped fresh
beef with or without the addition of beef fat or seasoning."

Hot dogs, too, were in the national spotlight in 1969. Department
of Agriculture regulations (Chapter 3) have said that hot dogs,
frankfurters, wieners or bologna sausage may be sold as such only if
they consist of beef, mutton, pork or goat meat, fat, and no more
than three-and-a-third per cent cereal or similar filler.

Fat content of hot dogs in the 1930's averaged eighteen per cent;
by World War II the average was nineteen per cent; but in 1969
it averaged thirty-three per cent and some franks ("fatfurters," Ralph
Nader called them) contained as much as fifty-one per cent fat.
There was no legal limit, and no required label statement on fat
content.

The Johnson Administration had proposed a thirty per cent limit. The Amalgamated Meat Cutters and Butcher Workmen's Union favored a thirty per cent limit. Virginia H. Knauer, President Nixon's Special Assistant for Consumer Affairs, said in her first testimony before a Congressional Committee in June, 1969, that she was in favor of a thirty per cent limit, maybe less,[4] but said her position was "personal" and tentative. (Later she said she had been "speaking for the White House.")

Secretary Hardin's Agriculture Department had proposed a thirty-three per cent fat limit, in keeping with the average, though a thirty per cent fat hot dog is fourteen per cent protein and a thirty-three per cent fat hot dog only twelve per cent protein.

The thirty per centers won. On September 19, 1969, the Agriculture Department announced that effective October 23, all federally inspected cooked sausage, including frankfurters, bologna and knockwurst, would have to conform to the limitation of thirty per cent fat content.

Despite its lower nutritional content, the hot dog has increased in per capita consumption by seventy-five per cent since World War II, while annual per capita consumption of all meat has increased by only twelve per cent. Meat industry sources say the public wants a high fat content; a return to the eighteen per cent fat limit, they say, would not be acceptable because it would make hot dogs taste "rubbery."

The public took less interest in the fat debate than it took in the matter of "chickendogs" or "chickenfurters." For years, the poultry industry tried to get the Agriculture Department to permit up to twenty-five per cent chicken content in hot dogs without any mention of the fact on labels. The American National Cattlemen's Association battled the proposal.

---

[4] The Consumer Federation of America and the National Consumer's League advocated a twenty-five per cent fat limit and establishment of a minimum protein level. So did Bess Myerson Grant, the former Miss America who was New York City's Commissioner of Consumer Affairs. Nutritionists have urged a reduction in U.S. fat consumption because of Americans' high rate of atherosclerosis, an artery condition that leads to coronary attacks.

In April, 1969, the Department suggested a compromise: a fifteen per cent poultry meat content in frankfurters. It proposed public hearings to test consumer reaction, the first time consumer testimony had ever been invited. The White House dumped the hearing idea, saying it would "unnecessarily delay" a decision. Instead, forty-five days were allowed for consumers and other interested parties to submit written comments.

"Franks are so bad now that nothing could hurt them," wrote a Bakersfield, California, woman. "What unsavory items fall under the 'all meat' category on their labels, I would shudder to think."

A Washington, D.C., baseball fan wrote, "Any relaxation of the traditional ground rules for making and marketing something as inherently suspect as a frankfurter makes even more vulnerable the ball park consumer who already is at the seller's mercy."

"Although we may not object to chicken meat in hot dogs we do definitely object to the new proposal making it possible to deceive the public," wrote a South Washington, Illinois, woman.

Another woman wrote, "I don't eat feather-meat of no kind." Most of the correspondents opposed changing the regulations.

But on August 28, 1969, the Nixon Administration okayed the fifteen per cent chicken content rule. The Agriculture Department announced that the rule would take effect in early November and would apply to the use of chicken and other poultry products in federally inspected cooked sausages, including frankfurters, knockwurst and bologna. Labels would have to mention the chicken or other poultry in their ingredient lists, but no percentages would be required. Up to one per cent bone residues in deboned poultry would be allowed, but poultry kidneys and sex glands would be banned from cooked sausage products.

The consumer letters (more than 1000 of them, the largest number ever received on a proposed change in meat and poultry inspection regulations) had been to no avail.

In addition to issues of poultry meat content and fat content of our hot dogs, the use of paprika to season processed meat has come under fire. The tangy seasoning, it is argued, can cover the taste of bad meat and make nonmeat substances look like meat, a boon to the analogs.

Senator Frank E. Moss, a Utah Democrat and new chairman of the Senate Subcommittee for Consumers, has spearheaded the airing of controversial consumer issues in Washington. He and the Ralph Nader forces have their work cut out for them.

Agriculture Department meat inspection officials, before the ban on cyclamates, had proposed using sodium cyclamate in place of the sugar now employed in vinegar solutions packed with some pickled meats; the synthetic sweetening, it was said, would reduce the growth of yeast when jars of pickled meats were left standing for long periods of time.

It has also been proposed that higher levels of an acid-promoting chemical be permitted in processing Genoa salami; this would eliminate one of the steps in traditional aging methods, a step during which mold sometimes forms on the salami.

Agriculture Department positions on some of these matters seem at first glance to be inimical to consumer interests. But the Department has an interest in keeping consumer prices low, and many of its stands can be explained on that basis.

The explanation will never appease the alarmists (Chapter 10) who are quick to cry panic, to impute evil consequences to fluoridation of drinking water, and in other ways to inflame the emotional response of consumers to every move the FDA or Agriculture Department makes.

When the ingredients are chemical, the reaction is emotional

Much of the panic, as we have seen in the previous two chapters, has gyrated around chemicals, which now play such a large part in the food industry that a high percentage of our foods would not exist without their help.

An important share of the morning orange drink market is held by products made for the most part of ingredients which have never been anywhere near an orange grove. And there are other foods, or fabricated foods if you prefer, that are almost completely artificial.

A popular unrefrigerated breakfast drink contains, according to its label, "sugar, citric acid, gum arabic, natural orange flavor, cellulose gum, calcium phosphate, sodium citrate, vitamin C, hydrogenated vegetable oil, vitamin A, U.S. certified color, BHA, a preservative." The Appendix following this chapter will clear up any mysteries the uninitiated may find in that listing. No indication is given as to what percentage of natural orange product is used; none is required by law, though ingredients must be listed in order of percentage of use.

Although natural orange juice contains more than a hundred chemicals, the chemical names on the labels of processed products seem to make people extremely uncomfortable, and susceptible to products with reassuring names like Aunt Jemima, Log Cabin, Pepperidge Farm and the like. Restaurants with names like Yankee Kitchen or Old Homestead find ready acceptance; so do basic homespun advertising appeals along the lines of "just like grandma used to make."

The facts do not jibe with popular sentiment. Most of our grandmothers were no great shakes in the kitchen. They spent more time there than women do today, but what came out of their hard work was often no match for what a new bride today can turn out easy as pie. The pie-crust may be made from a mix, but even die-hards admit that cakes and pie-crusts made from mixes are every bit as good as those made from scratch, and much less prone to failure.

Food companies, if they could, would avoid using terms like citric acid, calcium phosphate, sodium citrate and BHA on their labels. They are quite aware of the stigma attached to "food chemicals" and "food additives." But while formidable chemical names are disquieting to housewives, the ladies have no reluctance about using chemicals like sodium chloride and disaccharide, which are respectively table salt and sugar.

We discussed briefly in Chapter 5 some of the problems of food contamination by pesticides, herbicides and fungicides, the "incidental" chemicals (like DDT, endrin, dieldrin, aldrin, chlordane, heptachlor, benzine hexachloride and toxaphene) that in many cases do present real hazards. It is not quite cricket, however, to lump these together with "intentional" additives and call them all "poisons" as Robert and Leona Rienow did in their 1967 book, *Moment in the Sun.*

There is no question but that some qualities of taste have been sacrificed in modern American foods. Rolled oats are not the same as oatmeal. Sulphured molasses, hams injected with smoke, ice cream made from commercial mixes, artificially cultured buttermilk, processed cheese, reconstituted orange juice, bleached flour, bananas ripened in gas chambers—some people prefer them to the old foods, but there is some justice on the side of traditionalists who say we are all victims of a kind of Gresham's Law in which good food is being driven out by shoddy.

We pay a premium price for homogenized milk, which was originally invented to solve a marketing problem. When cream was separated from whole milk, the skimmed milk did not sell well. So sweet butter was brought into the East from Midwestern dairy states, which had a surplus butter problem, and this fat was put back into the skimmed milk under high pressure. Homogenized milk—and in most places it is now almost impossible to find any other whole milk—is in most cases reconstituted milk, changed somewhat in molecular structure so its particles will not separate. But instead of costing more than the plain old milk that had to be shaken, it should cost less.

Luther Burbank's Russet Potato solves problems for the potato farmer, but critics who say it does not taste as good as some unimproved potatoes may be right. As we saw in the case of the California grapes (Chapter 6), many fruits and vegetables have been developed not for improved flavor but for eye appeal; or for larger yields, better average size, better keeping qualities in storage, resistance to insect pests or fungus diseases, or so they can be shipped with fewer losses. Taste and eating qualities have received short shrift.

One can get misty-eyed at this decline and fall of taste values. Some have questioned the moral fiber of a people who will accept such exploitation, declaring that the beginning of the end of the American Republic came with the submission to cake mixes.

One can get choked up listening to accounts of the old days when Americans stewed their own hens, smoked their own hams and bacons, churned their own butter, baked their own bread, fished pickles out of barrels at the store with dippers and bought peanut butter ladled by the pound into cardboard containers.

Self-service stores, where food must be pre-packaged to get shelf space and where more attention is paid to merchandising than to qualities of taste, may indeed be inventions of the devil. But to look at *all* additives with a fishy eye, to be stampeded by "even the slightest presumption of guilt," to damn indiscriminately, encouraging distrust of the protective powers of the FDA and other consumer agencies, does little or no service to the public.

As an FDA official has said, "Our knowledge is not static. We must continually make changes, where necessary, on the basis of reliable new information—information that in many cases may result from new or improved experimental methods."

Thus, the actions, actual and proposed, taken against cigarette smoking after the Surgeon General's Report should reassure us that we are not victims of commercial interests immune from government control and all out to exploit us. Some people will only be convinced by outright prohibition of smoking. And some people make no distinction between questions of nutritive content and safety on the one hand, and questions of food flavor and other eating qualities on the other; they tar with too wide a brush.

As for our watchdogs, they sometimes overreact as wildly as the forces that provoke them to overreact.

Cranberries and capons

For all their vigilance in protecting the consumer, the FDA and the U.S. Department of Agriculture sometimes move in ways that shake public confidence far out of proportion to any reality. A classic instance is the infamous cranberry panic of 1959. While Easterners tend to associate cranberries with the bogs on Cape Cod, a certain percentage of the U.S. cranberry crop is produced in Washington state and Oregon. In 1958 and 1959, growers in those states went against regulations and used a weedkiller, aminotriazole, in the cranberry bogs before harvest instead of after. Cranberry shipments were found to be contaminated with aminotriazole, which can produce thyroid cancer in test rats.

Immediately, a temporary embargo was clamped on the cranberry crop, specific lots were banned, and a tiny 0.25 per cent of the crop was seized. Government officials and industry leaders made reassuring noises, but millions of Americans ate their Thanksgiving turkey in 1959 without cranberry sauce. Many are probably still suspicious of all "bounceberries"; doubts once raised are not easily allayed.

Another brouhaha of 1959 was the capon caper. For about ten years, a synthetic female sex hormone, diethylstilbestrol, had been used to turn young male chickens into capons (the ancient Romans had used a more elementary method, but using the hormone saved expensive manpower) and thus make them fatten faster. Diethylstilbestrol, it turned out, is a weak carcinogen; it can produce cancer in some cases. So in 1959 the FDA prohibited its use in poultry after small residues were found in the livers and skin fat of chickens treated with the compound. Rumors circulated that eating capon could make a man sterile. No residues have been found in slaughtered beef, so some beef cattle are still treated with diethylstilbestrol to make them fatten faster.

An organic chemistry expert in England in the spring of 1969 warned a conference of vegetarians in Lincoln that men who ate lots of chicken were endangering their virility; diethylstilbestrol again. The chemist had no proof, but he said, "It may take years to establish medical proof just in the same way that it took time to link cigarettes with cancer. There could be a cumulative effect. It is a risk not worth running. Already one chain of shops will not sell chicken which have been treated in this way."

As we saw in the previous chapter, the English in their anxiety about food sometimes starve to death.

Americans, by and large, still have more confidence in the powers of their FDA,[5] Agriculture Department and other consumer agencies to safeguard the nation's food. Most of us shrug off the inconsistencies of these agencies as easily as we shrug off the alarms of the food faddists.

---

[5] The Agency's strength and reputation, it would sometimes seem, depends on the charisma and personality of its leader. On July 1, 1968, FDA was put under a new Consumer Protection and Environmental Health Service (CPEHS) in the Department of Health, Education and Welfare. Dr. Herbert Ley, who succeeded the charismatic Dr. James Goddard as FDA chief the day of the HEW reorganization, had no direct contact with the Secretary of Health, Education and Welfare. The "rather substantial reorganization of procedures and personnel" in FDA which HEW Secretary Finch called "inevitable" in October, 1969, after the cyclamate "waffle," followed two months later: Dr. Ley and two other top FDA officials were ousted, a Chicago management specialist being named to succeed Ley. Dr. Charles C. Edwards, the new FDA chief, had been assistant to Dr. Roger O. Egeberg, HEW's assistant secretary for health and scientific affairs; he continues to report to Egeberg. The shake-up in FDA management, which came December 10, was accompanied by a Finch statement that the Agency would be reorganized "along product rather than functional lines," with a bureau of foods, pesticides and product safety and a bureau of drugs replacing the previous bureaus of science, medicine and compliance.

The innocent frauds

Some small food deceits we accept as being harmless. Oranges, for example, are often exposed to ethylene gas to improve their color.[6] What gives an orange its orange color is not ripeness but cold weather. The green chlorophyll in the orange's outer skin is protected by a thin membrane that breaks down in chilly weather, destroying the chlorophyll and turning the orange orange. It has nothing to do with ripeness.

Where oranges are not exposed to any cold weather, as in Thailand, they never turn orange. In a warm season, many Florida oranges do not turn orange, either. Much of the fruit used for concentrate is harvested green.

But oranges marketed for eating or home squeezing must be orange or they will not sell. So they are gassed. Ethylene is a gas given off naturally by bananas and by McIntosh apples. It can turn a green orange into an orange orange—unless the orange is not ripe. Ethylene will not work on an unripe orange, nor will it work on an orange that has turned orange on the tree in cold weather but then turns green again.

In any case, putting oranges into gas chambers has no bad effect on them. It is done in Florida, California and in Arizona, too, often just to improve the color of oranges that are already orange.

Florida oranges are sometimes bathed in a dye permitted by the FDA and known in the trade as Citrus Red No. 2. The oranges must be stamped with the words, "Color Added," in purple letters and, according to Florida law, they must have ten per cent more juice than the minimum required for undyed oranges. The oranges are not

---

[6] Tomatoes are gassed with ethylene, too, but there it is not so innocent. The tomatoes are picked before they are fully ripe, at the expense of both taste and nutritional qualities; they travel better green, and the gas turns their pinkening color into a richer, more marketable red.

dyed in winter, when there is no color problem, but only for a few weeks in the autumn. New England housewives will not touch "Color Added" oranges, but in the Midwest consumers actually prefer them. The stores in Chicago advertise color-added oranges and buyers come a-running.

Oranges are often coated with an edible Johnson's Wax. This is to replace natural wax lost when the fruit is cleaned with soapy water and fiber brushes, and then dried with hot air and foam rubber squee-gees. Without surface wax, oranges shrivel. Adding the Johnson's Wax is quite harmless, though if too much wax is applied, the orange, which ordinarily breathes for a month or so after picking, will suffocate and lose some of its taste.

Raisins are commonly treated with lye and sulphur before drying.

Egg producers feed marigold petals to their laying hens. The flower petals contain a yellow chemical compound, xanthophyll, and the yellow color carries over into the egg yolks to make them look good sunny side up.

These and similar artifices improve the appearance of foods and thus enhance their consumer appeal. Appearance may not be everything in life, but people do judge by appearances. Some improvements for appearance sake may be innocent enough, but it is well to take care lest we be gulled into accepting foods like those good-looking California grapes that do not taste as good as they look.

Not that Californians, or Americans in general, have any monopoly on food frauds. Every country has its food scandals.

Germany, in the late 1950's, had its nitrite scandal. Chopped meat, somebody noticed, stayed fresh and red longer than it normally should have. It turned out to contain a dangerous amount of nitrite, which above a certain point can turn the blood's hemoglobin into methemoglobin, rob it of its function of providing the cells with nitrogen and produce headaches, nausea, paralysis of the circulatory muscular system and ultimately death. A certain amount of nitrite is harmless; the body can reduce the methemoglobin quickly if it is just a small percentage of the total hemoglobin.

Using brine to which 0.5 to 0.6 per cent nitrite has been added speeds up the pickling process, which otherwise takes weeks. It is a common practice, but it must be policed carefully lest too much nitrite be added.

There had been an incident of mass nitrite poisoning in Leipzig during World War I. Forty years later, nitrite made headlines in Germany again, though the butchers who used it were evidently ignorant of its dangers. Sodium nitrite and sodium nitrate are among the ingredients listed on U.S. processed meats, but the amount used is rigidly controlled.

The not-so-innocent frauds

Italy, until 1962, had no federal law enforcement at all to combat the "sophisticators" (a Victorian nice–Nellyism for adulterators) who made "olive" oil out of animal fats (or out of whale or dolphin grease); "butter" out of cow, horse and donkey hooves (and also out of a mixture of whey, soy oil, coconut oil and fish oil); "wine" out of old wine dregs mixed with beet sugar, potassium ferrocyanide, well water, ox blood and ethyl chlorocarbonate; "Parmesan cheese" out of cheese residue mixed with fish oil, soy oil, coconut oil, palm oil, margarine and carotene (they also made "cheese" out of banana peels).

Outside the U.S., Canada and England, food regulation tends to be rather arbitrary. While antistaling agents, dough conditioners and the like are used in U.S. bread, they are not permitted in French and Italian bread. The U.S., on the contrary, does not permit coloring of peas, whereas France, to quote George R. Grange, "colors the hell out of green peas."

Grange, a U.S. Department of Agriculture official, is the American delegate to an international food body called the Codex Alimentarius Commission which has been meeting since 1962 to set food standards for its fifty-two member nations. The standards it sets are not binding on any country but they do attempt to keep food products in international commerce consistent with safety standards, and to maintain a certain uniformity of essential properties in such foods.

As for Italy's food and wine "sophisticators," Robert Daley titillated the readers of *Life* magazine with an exposé of their activities in an article which appeared early in 1968.

Some of the Italian deceptions brought to light by Daley and others have involved putting illegal additives in pasta to improve its texture (and up its price); injecting meat with additives (like the Germans' nitrite) to keep it looking young and fresh, even when not refrigerated; and "netting" *frozen* fish out of the Bay of Naples and other fished-out waters.

Adulterated foods are called *"migliorato"*—improved—by the cynical Italians. Thanks to a little improving, Italy in recent years has produced more wine than France, though it has fewer vines. The wine "sophisticators" used well water because it was cheaper than tap water and, perhaps more important, because it was unmetered, nobody could ask any questions about the use of extraordinary quantities. Ox blood was used to clear up the sediment and ethyl chlorocarbonate, a bactericide, to kill off the natural microorganisms which produce fermentation,[7] thus controlling the degree of the "wine's" fermentation.

The Italian press estimated that a third of Italian wines, mostly cheap table wines, had never been anywhere near a whole, fresh-squeezed grape.

One brand of *vino migliorato* was promoted with television commercials showing a tired businessman being revitalized by a glass of the "wine." When the scandal first made headlines, Italians turned away for a while from all wine, even French wine, and drank beer and soft drinks instead. Many are still drinking beer and soft drinks instead.

And the case of the adulterated wine is still making headlines. The latest episode in this *opéra bouffe* came in May, 1969, when it was

---

[7] Ethyl chlorocarbonate breaks down in solution to produce ethyl alcohol, which gives "wine" more kick, and carbon dioxide, which gives a sparkling wine its fizz.

discovered that about two thirds of the material evidence—875,000 gallons of suspected *vino migliorato*, confiscated and stored under official seal in the town of Ascoli Piceno (where 217 Italians, including vintner Bruno Ferrari, were being tried in one of the longest, costliest and most complex trials in Italian history)—had vanished. The "wine" had been replaced with casks of water.

Extremists would have us believe that all our foods today, unless they are "natural, organically grown" health foods, are little better than the products of Italy's sophisticators.

And because most of us are so unsophisticated in what we believe, the extremists find plenty of listeners. (So do the tobacco companies, who relate fears of cigarette smoking to the old fears of tomatoes and say, "Within a few years we will look back and laugh about 'the great tobacco scare of the 1960's.' ")

To protect ourselves from such blandishments, and from those who would endanger our foods with unpoliced adulterant additives, are two separate matters.

More and more countries have laws, and not just economic laws, against adulterated foods. The Italians learned, probably from us Americans, what we learned from the English: if the laws of supply and demand worked perfectly, people would refuse to buy doctored "cheese" and gibberellic grapes and butter *migliorato*. The producers of such articles would fail in their deceit.

Unfortunately, the experience of history shows that those who can distinguish good food from bad are not in the majority, any more than are those who can distinguish sense from nonsense.

Samuel Johnson, as recorded by his amanuensis James Boswell, said back in 1763, "Some people have a foolish way of not minding, or pretending not to mind, what they eat. For my part, I mind my belly very studiously and very carefully, for I look upon it that he who does not mind his belly will hardly mind anything else."

While half the world today suffers from visible or invisible hunger, and while at least 10 million red, white and black Americans go to bed hungry at night, and ten times that many eat too much of the wrong things, more and more of us are aware of the wrongs of society and the decline of human values.

Nothing is more universally human than the need to eat. Few wrongs are greater than hunger, especially the needless hunger that is rooted in apathy, ignorance and misunderstanding.

The governments of the world are concerned with protecting citizens against communism (or imperialism), against pornography, against marijuana, cancer and crime, but they offer very little protection against the terrors of overpopulation, of environmental decay, of rubber chicken or cardboard cantaloupe, of steadily mounting prices for food whose basic values are in so many cases diminished and declining.

While "consumerism" is a novel concept viewed in high places with surprise and suspicion, some of us consumers occupy ourselves with gourmet preciosities, some of us haunt the health food shops, few of us connect the quality and safety of what we eat with those threats to our environment that put the future of all eating in jeopardy. Except to complain about the rising cost of steak and to panic about cyclamates and MSG, we give matters of food too low a priority on our agenda of political issues.

In the climate of the 1970's, where the dominant philosophy, the Zeitgeist, tends to be apocalyptic despair, the horrors of technology, of the dynamo Henry Adams visualized in his *Education*, make many of us susceptible to the appeal of the virginal, the simple, the unspoiled. If the sentiment motivates meaningful efforts to police our environment and not just talk about it, to clean things up to whatever extent is possible in the face of runaway population growth in societies with high consumption levels, the fear of the dynamo may save some of our natural food resources as it saves other values and pleasures of life.

But the history of man is an arrogant history; our hubris shows itself as much in health food cult as in gourmet coterie—the cultist could not care less about his neighbor.

We may be so obsessed with anxieties about our weight (a concern less related to mortality statistics than to fashion) that for many the pleasures of the table are as guilt-ridden as those of the bedroom, but still we put away enough food to make half of us overweight and a sixth of us obese; whether for reasons of happy self-indulgence or of excessive distrust of artifice, in our various ways some of us still echo Rome's obscenities, the feasting at Versailles, and those callous poverty socials of old New York.

Americans, even educated Americans, know little more about the basics of food than do the malnourished Hottentots for whom we show so little concern. This book, it is hoped, has illustrated the need for a broader understanding of these basics, a keener appreciation of the forces that threaten our sustenance, and a more active interest in the taste values of our foods—and not simply their health values. To preserve the gustatory joys that figure so largely in the quality of life at all levels of society, pleasures that make life worth living and that today are in danger of fading into fond memory, is part of the survival crisis that now challenges mankind.

°𝕀 Appendix 𝕀°

A multiplication of additives

In Chapter 9 we discussed saccharin, cyclamates, flavorings and flavor enhancers which directly affect the taste of what we eat and drink.

The U.S. food industry in 1969 used more than 90 million pounds of flavor and flavor enhancing additives. In addition it used close to 800 million pounds of additives to improve the color, texture and keeping qualities of foods. This figure was up from 661 in 1965, 419 in 1955. Experts predict a rate of 1.03 billion pounds by 1975.

From 2500 to 3000 food additives are now used in U.S. foods, including several leavening agents, nine emulsifiers, thirty-one stabilizers and thickeners, eighty-five surfactants, seven anti-caking agents, twenty-eight anti-oxidants, forty-four sequestrants, perhaps a dozen coloring materials, at least eight acidulants, more than thirty chemical preservatives and over 1100 flavoring ingredients.

The great bulk of these additives affect flavor only indirectly; actual flavor ingredients, as noted in Chapter 9, are mostly "naturally occurring additives" like the common spices, or at least are "natural identicals." But a great many of the other additives in foods fall into a third group made up of entirely synthetic compounds which have no exact counterparts in nature.

A certain number of new additives are introduced each year, but one effect of the 1958 Food Additives Amendment (Chapter 11) has been to increase the costs of developing new additives, lengthen the time it takes to get them cleared for use, and generally reduce the number of such new—and possibly better and safer—additives. Fewer companies can afford to work on additives; the companies are mostly chemical companies, since food companies work on profit margins too small to permit much research and development activity.

Délicieux, Delizioso, Kerkou, Oishii, Köstlich, Geshmecht!

Making foods taste good is the underlying purpose of food additives, however indirectly they achieve this purpose.

[515]

It may be, as biologist Barry Commoner has said, that we would not need so many additives if we delivered our foods from producer to consumer with more speed. Other countries, he suggests, beat the U.S. at this. The *New York Times* in November, 1969, quoted the Washington University (St. Louis) professor as saying, "In Paris you can get fresh fish from the Mediterranean with no trouble. But in Pittsburgh, just try to get fresh fish from the Atlantic Seaboard."

Dr. Commoner's point would be better made if he used bread and other baked goods as examples; our inland cities do get pretty good air delivery of fresh seafood. But given the realities of today's smaller family units—which demand foods that will keep longer—and of U.S. transportation troubles, produced by our automobile-age prosperity and our overpopulation, we could hardly feed our urban populations without chemical food additives.

Such additives are continually being tested; they are used only with the approval of the Food and Drug Administration; they are often beneficial in terms both of health and of eating qualities; and they are obviously safer than the formaldehyde, salicylic acid and boric acid used in grandma's—and great-grandma's—food before the 1906 Pure Food and Drug Act.

Few foods use more chemical additives than our daily bread.

The bread stuffs

America's bread industry uses over sixteen million pounds of chemicals a year, mostly leaveners, preservatives and anti-staling compounds.

If standards of identity [1] were not so strict, bakers would use a recently-invented additive with the impossible name of 1,4,5,6-tetrahydro-2-acetopyridine to impregnate the paper wrapping on bread so it would give off an aroma of newly-baked bread. (The "fresh" loaves sold in packages at supermarkets are often baked weeks before they are sold; their natural aroma disappears within twenty-four hours of leaving the oven.)

So many chemicals are added to bread itself that a British scientist in the summer of 1969 patented a new additive that would make bread taste like bread; or at least like the bread made fresh daily, even several times a day, in small batches in local bakeries in the non-industrialized societies of the world but rarely now in countries like Britain and the U.S.

This use of chemicals in bread is as old as the Egyptian's leavened bread. American bakeries today use over 65 million pounds a year of leavening agents to release carbon dioxide from sodium bicarbonate and similar compounds used in baking.

---

[1] Rigid federal standards have been established for bakery products, cereal flours, canned fruits and juices, cocoa and cocoa products, all kinds of cheeses, frozen desserts, eggs and egg products, macaroni and noodles, margarine, milk and cream, nut products, salad dressings, shellfish and tomato products.

Until the end of the eighteenth century, the only way to make baked goods light was to beat air into the dough, along with eggs, or to add yeast or spirits. Then, in the 1790's, pearlash was discovered in America; produced by burning wood, it was responsible for some of the wholesale destruction of American forests; but it revolutionized baking methods.

Pearlash is potassium carbonate; it produces carbon dioxide in baking dough and makes it rise. The fledgling American republic exported some 8000 tons of pearlash to Europe in 1792. Four years later, Amelia Simmons' *American Cookery* contained several recipes calling for pearlash.

An improvement on pearlash, and on saleratus, or baking soda, was baking powder, first produced commercially in the 1850's by Preston & Merrill of Boston.

More sophisticated than any of these are the phosphates; monocalcium phosphate, dicalcium phosphate, sodium acid phosphate and sodium aluminum phosphate comprise the major group of leavening agents used today. Cream of tartar (potassium acid tartrate) and sodium aluminum sulfate are also used. Used singly or in combination, such leavening agents release carbon dioxide as a bakery product is mixed or baked, and release it at any rate the baker desires.

To inhibit the growth of mold on bread and other baked goods, bakers use calcium propionate and sodium propionate. To retard mold growth on some breads and cakes, and also on pie crusts, they use sodium diacetate, also used to kill rope bacteria, which makes bread slimy, or "ropy." Bakers used to add vinegar to their dough to resist rope bacteria.

The main problem with bread is staling. An average American eats ninety-two pounds of bread a year—ninety-two sixteen- or twenty-slice loaves. Nearly seven per cent of the average grocery dollar goes for the staff of life. Bread prices have risen steeply since World War II, price increases for bread being more than three times greater than the average increase for other food products. Nearly one-fifth of the rise in grocery bills since 1945 has been accounted for by higher bread prices.

One reason is that over ten per cent of U.S. bread is returned to bakeries because it is stale; its starch has crystallized. To retard this crystallization, bakers use what are widely called "bread emulsifiers" but are actually antistaling or antifirming agents. The compounds used are also emulsifying agents, which we will get to presently and which led to the confusion in terms. Mono- and diglycerides, diacetyl tartaric acid esters of mono- and diglycerides, and succinylated mono- and diglycerides are the most commonly used antistaling agents.

Glycerides are used also in cakes, doughnuts and other baked goods, where they not only retard staling but help produce desirable volume and textures as well. Such compounds as sorbitan monostearate and polyoxyethylene (20) sorbitan monostearate are used in foods where federal government standards permit.

To produce uniformly high-quality bread, despite variations in flour characteristics, bread bakers now use dough conditioners such as calcium stearyl-2-lactylate and sodium stearyl fumarate. The compounds make bread dough drier, more extensible and easier to machine. They are often used in combination with the glycerides, which are dough conditioners themselves, though not such good ones.

Distribution and marketing costs are the big factors behind the spiralling of bread prices; without the additives that reduce staling, bread prices in our industrialized urban societies would be even higher.

Emulsifiers

Used in even greater volume than leavening agents in U.S. foods are emulsifiers, or dispersing agents. Our food industry employs over 150 million pounds of these "surface-active agents" in a typical year.

Emulsifiers disperse one liquid in another, usually an oil in water or vice-versa, and they perform other functions.

Synthetic emulsifiers, the so-called mono- and diglycerides, now dominate the emulsifier business, accounting for about eighty per cent by weight of all emulsifiers. Shortenings, margarines, ice cream, baked goods and many other food products are made with mono- and diglycerides, first used commercially in the U.S. food industry by Swift in 1928.

Mono- and diglycerides emulsify water in oil. So does a sorbitan ester called sorbitan monostearate, introduced in the food industry in the early 1940's.

To emulsify oil in water, food processors generally use polysorbates (poly-oxyethylene sorbitan fatty acid esters), introduced at about the same time as sorbitan monostearate. If there is a name like polyoxyethylene (20), polysorbate (60) or polysorbate (80) on a label, it is a compound used to emulsify oil in water—a flavoring in a soft drink, perhaps, or the dill oil in pickles or flavor oils in a sherbet.

Polysorbates are also used to enhance the freezing qualities of ice cream and to improve the texture of cake mixes. They are sometimes used in combination with other emulsifiers to obtain a desired degree of hydrophilic or lipophilic properties and to get the most effect from the smallest concentration of total emulsifier.

In addition to synthetic emulsifiers, many natural dispersing agents are still used. Lecithin is the leading example; contained in egg yolks, lecithin was the original emulsifier in mayonnaise, the dressing invented in the 1750's by France's Duc de Richelieu, the *bon vivant* whose dinner guests sometimes ate their truffled turkey and quaffed their champagne in the nude.

Egg yolks containing lecithin (pronounced with a soft 'c' and a hard 'th') are still the major emulsifier in mayonnaise, though lecithin from soybeans is permitted in cake mixes and other foods for which there are no federal standards of identity.

Stabilizers and thickeners

Well over 100 million pounds of food additives used each year in American foods are stabilizers and thickeners.

These tend more often to be natural substances than chemical compounds. The leading one is gum arabic from the stem and branches of acacia trees. Next is gum tragacanth. Third is guar gum from the ground-up seeds of a leguminous plant, *Cyamopsis tetragonoloba* (the gum is used also as a sizing material in the paper and textile industries). Fourth and fifth in order of use are sodium carboxymethylcellulose and gelatin.

Sixth is carrageenin, extracted from a foul-smelling green and purplish North Atlantic seaweed called Irish Moss, or carrageen, after a town by that name in the southeast of Ireland, near Waterford (though more than eighty per cent of Irish Moss now comes from Canada's Maritime region, especially from Prince Edward Island). Carrageenin, which is also an emulsifier (used in beer and pie fillings), retards the settling of particles, as in liquid diet foods, so we do not have to "shake well before using."

In ice cream, stabilizers absorb or bind some of the water to prevent it from freezing into grainy crystals; they keep the ice cream smooth and creamy. Stabilizers minimize the settling of cocoa particles in chocolate drinks and pulp particles in orange drinks.

Three other stabilizers used for such purposes are carob bean gum, from the seeds of a Mediterranean tree (Chapter 7), agar-agar, from certain seaweeds, and methylcellulose.

Thickeners give added body to soft drinks made with artificial sweeteners. They also help create any desired consistency in cheese spreads, gravies, icings, pie fillings, salad dressings and syrups. Vegetable gums can act both as stabilizers and thickeners, one reason they are used more often than the synthetic products.

Like leavening agents and emulsifiers, stabilizers and thickeners are used to improve the physical properties of foods. Physical properties, at least psychologically, affect taste properties.

A number of other additives are used for the same purposes as firming agents, anticaking compounds, surfactants or moisture-retaining agents.

To increase the firmness of canned tomatoes (regulated by standards of identity), canned sliced apples and canned potatoes, packers add calcium chloride, calcium citrate and mono- and dicalcium phosphate. Calcium salts are also added to pickles to keep them crisp. The salts produce a calcium pectate gel in some foods that keeps the food tissues from collapsing.

To keep baking powder from caking, calcium silicate is used. It is also used (along with magnesium silicate, tricalcium phosphate, sodium aluminosilicate, silica gel and the like) to keep table salt free-pouring. Malted milk powders, nondairy coffee creamers and garlic salt also employ anticaking compounds.

Some foods face an opposite problem: moisture retention. To keep shredded coconut and candies from drying out, food and confectionery companies use sorbitol. Glycerol is added to marshmallows, propylene glycol to candies.

Color it delicious

Until the mid-nineteenth century, all food colorings were of natural origin and many still are. Annatto, from the seeds of a tropical American tree, is still used for its yellowish-red coloring. Saffron is used for its orange coloring. The dried bodies of the females of a Central American cactus scale insect are used to make cochineal, a red dye. A brown coloring, caramel, is made from sugar. An East Indian aromatic herb of the ginger family is ground into a powder, turmeric, which is used in curry and also for its yellow coloring principle.

Back in the eighteenth century, the French village of Gallargues made a dye out of sunflowers that was sent to Holland to color Edam cheeses.

But about ninety per cent of the colors used in foods today are synthetic. The synthetics are more uniform, more stable, more effective and usually cheaper than natural vegetable colorings. Only seven synthetic colors were approved for use in foods when the Federal Food and Drug Act was passed in 1906; the number had grown to nineteen by 1950, but has since been reduced to less than a dozen as a result of government restrictions, including a recent one on the red coloring used for maraschino cherries.

Producers of food colors will need to search for new colors to replace those banned by the government or approved for limited use only. Their customers in the food industry would like a bright red, and not just for maraschino cherries. They would also like an inexpensive oil-soluble yellow to replace the B-carotene now used to color butter and margarine.

Preservation

As we saw in the case of bakery products, a major function of chemical additives is to control molds, yeasts, rope bacteria and other organisms, to keep food from getting stale or rancid, to extend its shelf life.

Housewives always react uneasily to the word "chemical," though the "natural" process of preserving meats by smoking them, a process used since prehistoric times, is effective because it imparts chemicals—phenols, and pyroligneous acids and some aldehydes—to the meats.

Some other chemical preservatives are quite natural. Swiss cheese contains propionic acid by nature; various berries (and some fruits, like plums) contain benzoic acid; both act as effective preservatives.

Sodium benzoate, or benzoate of soda as it may be listed on a label, has long been employed to preserve acidic foods such as apple cider, soft drinks and fruit cocktail. It is a synthetic chemical but it is closely related to the natural benzoic acid in cranberries.

Less natural, but no more harmful, are sorbic acid and potassium sorbate used to inhibit molding of cheese, chocolate syrups, jellies, dried fruits and some cakes.

To control yeasts, molds and bacteria in dried fruits, spices, nuts and other foods, ethyl formate, methyl formate, ethylene oxide and propylene oxide are commonly used.

But the great enemy of food processors is not mold, yeast or bacteria; it is oxygen.

The oxygen fighters

Oxygen makes iron rust and food spoil. Oxygen activates enzymes which tend to discolor cut fruits and vegetables. To prevent browning, processors treat apple slices, peeled potatoes and other fruits and vegetables with sodium sulfite, ascorbic acid and sulfur dioxide.

Browning is detrimental to the appearance of foods. More serious is the way oxygen breaks down fats and oils in food, turning them rancid, and the way it diminishes essential fatty acids and certain vitamins, notably vitamin C.

To minimize such losses and hazards, the food industry uses great quantities of antioxidants, mostly BHA and, to a lesser extent, BHT.

Tocopherol, or vitamin E, which occurs naturally in vegetable oils, is still used a little; so is ascorbic acid and its salts and erythorbic acid and its salts; but nordihydroguaiaretic acid, obtained from creosote bushes in the deserts of the Southwest, has been banned for several years. BHA (butylated hydroxyanisole) and BHT (butylated hydroxytoluene) have, along with propyl gallate, largely supplanted gum guaiac, which was the first commercial antioxidant but which does not hold up in frying and baking.

Antioxidants can be found in breakfast cereals, cooking oils, chicken pot pies, dehydrated soups, potato chips, shortenings, salted nuts and a great many other food items. Their effectiveness can be judged by the results of an accelerated test in which potato chips were subjected to 145° heat. After three days, potato chips containing no antioxidant turned rancid; potato chips treated with a mixture of antioxidants remained rancid-free for twenty-six days.

BHA, the most widely used antioxidant, was first produced commercially for food uses in 1947. It withstands the effects of high temperatures in food processing (processors call this "good carrythrough"); it is very effective even at low concentrations in animal fats and it works well in combination with other antioxidants.

BHT, the subject of much agitation in the past ten years, does not have quite the carrythrough of BHA, but since it is produced in large volume for use as an antioxidant in such nonfood products as gasoline, lubricating oil and rubber, it is much cheaper than BHA—less than one-sixth the cost.

The FDA approved the use of BHT in foods in 1954. Five years later, some Australian scientists fed BHT in very high doses to rabbits and concluded it wasn't safe for use in foods. In 1963, England's Food Standards Committee recommended that BHT be banned from British foods, but the Committee later reversed itself. In late 1965, a joint committee of experts from the World Health Organization and the UN's Food and Agriculture Organization made a thorough review of all the research on BHT. Used at recommended levels in foods, they declared, BHT was perfectly safe.

In her book, *Poisons in Your Food*, Ruth Winter mentions the case of a young woman who was allergic to both BHA and BHT. Other allergies are far more common. Mrs. Winter levels no further charge against BHT.

But BHT has been banned in Germany and it is not unlikely that some reason will be found before long to ban it in U.S. foods as well.

About five times costlier than BHT, though cheaper than BHA, is propyl gallate, which is more effective than any other antioxidant in highly unsaturated fats. But propyl gallate has very poor carrythrough under alkaline conditions, and in the presence of iron or copper and small amounts of moisture it can produce disturbing blue or green colors in foods. It is frequently used in combination with BHA and BHT, the combination having a synergistic effect.

Producers of antioxidants are less vulnerable to attack than producers of artificial sweeteners because their products are so much more necessary. They are constantly looking for compounds still more effective than those now used and less likely to produce off-colors or undesirable odors. They are on the look-out especially for antioxidants that will be water-soluble and oil-soluble. In solution, these might extend the shelf life of hams, sausages, fish fillets, bacon and other foods vulnerable to oxidative attack.

The war against oxygen's allies

Trace metals like iron and copper, which limit the use of propyl gallate, can serve as catalysts to speed the oxidative breakdown of foods, especially of fats and oils. To deactivate these metals, food processors use forty-four different compounds called sequestrants, chelating agents or metal scavengers.

The leading ones include citric acid, sodium hexametaphosphate, sodium tripolyphosphate and the salts of EDTA (ethylenediaminetetraacetic acid).

They often improve the flavor, color and texture of margarine, cheese, salad dressings, cooked clams, canned beans and frozen peaches.

The two EDTA salts, calcium disodium salt and disodium dihydrogen salt (sometimes called simply disodium salt) are used to sequester trace amounts of iron in beer and prevent the sudden gushing of the suds as the can or bottle is opened and the carbon dioxide is released. EDTA salts, which react with copper, lead, zinc and other metals as well as iron, are also used to inhibit off-taste, discoloration or rancidity in canned shrimp, sandwich spreads, potato salad, mayonnaise, canned beans, soft drinks and other items.

Acidulants, for that sharp, sour taste

Next to emulsifiers, the additives most widely used in U.S. foods are acidulants, which give foods a desirable tartness.

Over 120 million pounds of acidulants a year go into candies, fruit juices, gelatin desserts, carbonated soft drinks, instant soft drink mixes, desserts, sherbets and other foods.

Citric acid, which occurs naturally in almost every fruit, is the most widely employed acidulant; it accounts for about sixty per cent by weight of the total market. Until 1923, citric acid was obtained almost entirely from the juice of lemons, limes and pineapples; natural citric acid has now largely been replaced by citric acid produced from sucrose or dextrose by a fermentation process.

Its attractive flavor, high solubility in water, long history of use and reasonable price make citric acid the standard against which other food acids are judged.

Phosphoric acid, present in the human body, is preferred over citric, however, for cola drinks: its sharp, quick-acting sourness brings out the flavor of these drinks more effectively. The cheapest of the acidulants, phosphoric acid accounts for about twenty-five per cent of total acidulant use. It is used a lot by brewers and cheese makers.

Other acidulants are fumaric acid, malic acid and adipic acid. The first of these, the only acidulant not found in nature, is more economical than citric acid; it is also less hygroscopic, which means it is less likely to absorb water from the air, making it especially useful in dry gelatin powders, puddings and pie fillings. Fumaric acid used to dissolve too slowly in cold water to be used in powdered soft-drink mixes, but a fast-dissolving variety is now available which dissolves in ice water in less than thirty seconds, so do not be surprised if you see fumaric acid is listed on packages of belly-wash mix.

Malic acid, the major acid in apples and the one that gives white wines their sprightly sharpness (it also occurs in rhubarb), has been in use as a food additive for more than forty years. It once cost more than twice as much as citric acid, but not any more: a new process has brought its price down to the same level, and it can be used more economically than citric acid to produce the same degree of tartness. It is somewhat less hygroscopic than citric acid, too. Various fruit-flavored soft drinks, candies, apple drinks, cocktail mixes and newer products are now being made with malic acid.

Also less hygroscopic than citric acid is adipic acid, which may be found listed on packages of gelatin desserts, among other things. It has a blander flavor than citric acid, though pound for pound it is just as acidifying and costs the food processor about the same as citric or malic acid.

Less widely used acidulants are tartaric acid (sometimes used in grape-flavored soft drinks, jellies and candies), lactic acid and succinic acid.

The material in this appendix has been isolated from the body of the book simply because it makes difficult reading for anyone but a chemist. There is no denying that chemical names are forbidding; but the substances they identify should not be forbidden simply because people react to their fear of everything that is unfamiliar to them, as so many people in years past reacted to iodized salt and fluoridated drinking water, whose blessings are now beyond serious dispute.

Hopefully this appendix will have removed some of the mystery from the mysterious words that appear on so many package ingredient lists. There are truly more worrisome things in the world in this final third of the twentieth century.

ᵒ₀⟦ *Bibliography* ⟧₀ᵒ

Chapter 1

Aresty, Esther B. *The Delectable Past.* New York: Simon and Schuster, 1964.

Bates, Marston. *Gluttons and Libertines.* New York: Random House, 1967.

Chamberlain, Narcissa G. *A Vintage Food Sampler.* New York: Vintage Books, 1962.

Clor, Harry M. *Obscenity and Public Morality.* Chicago: University of Chicago Press, 1969.

Craveri, Marcello. *The Life of Jesus.* New York: Grove Press, 1967.

de Groot, Roy Andries. *Feasts for All Seasons.* New York: Knopf, 1966.

Editors of Time-Life Books, Great Ages of Man Series. New York: Time-Life Books, 1965–1968.

Editors of *Woman's Day. Woman's Day Encyclopedia of Cookery* (12 vols.). New York: Fawcett, 1965.

Farb, Peter. *The Land, Wildlife, and Peoples of the Bible.* New York: Harper and Row, 1967.

Frazer, Sir James. *The Golden Bough,* third edition. London: Macmillan, 1951.

Hale, William Harlan and the Editors of *Horizon* Magazine. *The Horizon Cookbook and Illustrated History of Eating and Drinking Through the Ages.* New York: American Heritage, 1968.

Hill, Albert F. *Economic Botany.* New York: McGraw-Hill, 1952.

McCully, Helen. *Nobody Ever Tells You These Things About Food and Drink.* New York: Holt, Rinehart and Winston, 1967.

Mendelsohn, Oscar A. *A Salute to Onions.* New York: Hawthorn, 1966.

Montagne, Prosper. *Larousse Gastronomique.* New York: Crown, 1961.

Morris, Desmond. *The Naked Ape.* New York: McGraw-Hill, 1967.

Orr, John Boyd. *The Wonderful World of Food, the Substance of Life.* Garden City, N.Y.: Garden City Books, 1958.

Osborn, Fairfield. *Our Plundered Planet.* Boston: Little, Brown, 1948.

Perl, Lila. *Rice, Spice and Bitter Oranges.* Cleveland: World, 1967.

Sauer, Carl O. *Agricultural Origins and Dispersals.* Cambridge, Mass.: The M.I.T. Press, 1969.

Sebrell, William H., Jr., Haggerty, James J. and the Editors of *Life. Food and Nutrition.* Life Science Library Series. New York: Time-Life Books, 1963.

Ward, Artemus. *The Encyclopedia of Food.* New York: Number Fifty, Union Square, 1923.

Wason, Betty. *Cooks, Gluttons and Gourmets, a History of Cookery.* Garden City, N.Y.: Doubleday, 1962.

Webster, Hanson Hart and Polkinghorne, Ada R. *What the World Eats.* Boston: Houghton Mifflin, 1938.

Wechsberg, Joseph. *The Best Things in Life.* Boston: Little, Brown, 1964.

Chapter 2

Appleby, John T. *John, King of England.* New York: Knopf, 1959.

Cannon, Poppy. *Eating European* (2 vols.). New York: Award Books, 1968.

Chamberlain, Narcissa. *op. cit.*

Crone, Gerald R., translator and editor. *The Voyages of Cadamosto.* London: Hakluyt Society, 1937.

de Gramont, Sanche. *Epitaph for Kings.* New York: G.P. Putnam's Sons, 1967.

Editors of Time-Life Books. Great Ages of Man Series. *op. cit.*

Editors of *Woman's Day. op. cit.*

Ellwanger, George H. *The Pleasures of the Table.* London: William Heinemann, 1903.

Erlanger, Philippe. *The Age of Courts and Kings, Manners and Morals, 1558–1715.* New York: Harper and Row, 1907.

Evelyn, John, F.R.S. *Diary and Correspondence.* London: Henry Colburn, 1850. Vol. II, page 34.

Fernandez, A.M. de Ybarra, A.B., M.D. *Reprint from Smithsonian Miscellaneous Collections,* Vol. 48, part 4, No. 1698, page 434. Washington, D.C.: Smithsonian Institute, 1907.

Fisher, M.F.K. *With Bold Knife and Fork.* New York: G.P. Putnam's Sons, 1969.

Glover, T. R. *The Ancient World.* Harmondsworth, Middlesex, England: Penguin, 1944.

Guy, Christian. *An Illustrated History of French Cuisine.* New York: Bramhall House, 1944.

Hale, William Harlan and the Editors of *Horizon* Magazine. *op. cit.*

Heilbroner, Robert L. *The Quest for Wealth.* New York: Simon and Schuster, 1956.

Hill, Albert. *op. cit.*

Krutch, Joseph Wood. *Herbal.* New York: G. P. Putnam's Sons, 1965.

Laver, James. *Manners and Morals in the Age of Optimism, 1848–1915.* New York: Harper & Row, 1966.

Lewis, W. H. *The Splendid Century*. Garden City, N.Y.: Doubleday Anchor, 1957.

Martin, Jane Weeks. *Cooking As You Like It*. New York: Macmillan, 1963.

McCully, Helen. *op. cit.*

McMillen, Wheeler. *Land of Plenty, The American Farm Story*. New York: Holt, Rinehart and Winston, 1961.

McPhee, John. *Oranges*. New York: Farrar, Straus & Giroux, 1967.

Melikian, K. Cyrus and Rudd, Lloyd K. *The Wonder of Food*. New York: Appleton-Century-Crofts, 1961.

Montagne, Prosper. *op. cit.*

Morison, Samuel Eliot. *Admiral of the Ocean Sea*. Boston: Little, Brown, 1942.

———. *Christopher Columbus, Mariner*. Boston: Little, Brown, 1942.

Oliver, Raymond. *Gastronomy of France*. Cleveland: World, 1967.

Orr, John Boyd. *op. cit.*

Pan American Coffee Bureau. *Annual Coffee Statistics, 1969*. New York: Pan American Coffee Bureau, 1970.

Penrose, Boies. *Travel and Discovery in the Renaissance*. New York: Atheneum, 1962.

Perl, Lila. *op. cit.*

Radford, Erwin. *Unusual Words and How They Came About*. New York: Philosophical Library, 1946.

Root, Waverley. *The Food of France*. New York: Vintage Books, 1966.

——— and the Editors of Time-Life Books. *The Cooking of Italy*. New York: Time-Life Books, 1968.

Sauer, Carl. *op. cit.*

Savage, George. *Porcelain Through the Ages*. Baltimore: Penguin Books, 1954.

Sebrell, William H. *et. al. op. cit.*

Seranne, Ann and Tebbel, John. *The Epicure's Companion*. New York: David McKay, 1962.

Soyer, Alexis. *The Pantropheon, or History of Food, and its Preparation, from the Earliest Ages of the World*. Boston: Ticknor, Reed and Fields, 1853.

Thomas, Gertrude Z. *Richer Than Spices*. New York: Knopf, 1965.

Trevelyan, G.M. *English Social History, A Survey of Six Centuries, Chaucer to Queen Victoria*. Harmondsworth, Middlesex, England: Penguin, 1967.

van Saher, Lilla. *Exotic Cookery*. Cleveland: World, 1964.

Ward, Artemus. *op. cit.*

Wason, Betty. *op. cit.*

Webster and Polkinghorne. *op. cit.*

Wechsberg, Joseph. *op. cit.*

White, T.H. *The Age of Scandal, An Excursion Through a Minor Period*. Harmondsworth, Middlesex, England: Penguin, 1962.

Williams, Jay. *Life in the Middle Ages*. New York: Random House, 1966.

Chapter 3

Adams, Henry. *History of the United States During the First Administration of Thomas Jefferson.* New York: Antiquarian Press, 1962.

Allen, Durward L. *Our Wildlife Legacy.* New York: Funk & Wagnalls, 1954.

Allen, Frederick Lewis, *Only Yesterday, An Informal History of the Nineteen-Twenties.* New York: Harper & Bros., 1931.

Aresty, Esther. *op. cit.*

Audubon, John James. *The Birds of North America.* New York: Macmillan, 1937.

Barbour, Philip L. *The Three Worlds of Captain John Smith.* Boston: Houghton-Mifflin, 1964.

Beebe, Lucius. *The Big Spenders.* Garden City, N.Y.: Doubleday, 1966.

Boorstin, Daniel J. *The Americans. The Colonial Experience.* New York: Vintage Books, 1964.

———. *The Americans. The National Experience.* New York: Vintage Books, 1967.

Borgstrom, Georg. *The Hungry Planet.* New York: Collier, 1967.

Brogan, D.W. *The American Character.* New York: Vintage Books, 1956.

Brown, Dale. *American Cooking.* New York: Time-Life Books, 1968.

Brown, John Hull. *Early American Beverages.* Rutland, Vermont: Charles E. Tuttle Co., 1968.

Cannon, Poppy. *op. cit.*

Chamberlain, John. *The Enterprising Americans: A Business History of the United States.* New York: Harper & Row, 1963.

Cooper, James Fenimore. *The Travelling Bachelor, or Notions of the Americans.* New York: Stringer and Townsend, 1856.

———. *The Chainbearer, or The Littlepage Manuscripts.* New York: D. Appleton and Co., 1873.

de Crèvecoeur, Michel Guillaume St. John. *Letters from an American Farmer.* New York: Fox, Duffield & Co., 1904.

———. *Sketches of Eighteenth Century America.* New Haven: Yale University Press, 1925.

de Kruif, Paul. *Hunger Fighters.* New York: Harcourt, Brace & World, 1928.

DuPuy, William Atherton. *Our Animal Friends and Foes.* New York: Dover, 1969.

Editors of *American Heritage. American Heritage Cookbook and Illustrated History of American Eating and Drinking.* New York: American Heritage, 1964.

Editors of *The National Observer. The Consumer's Handbook.* Princeton: Dow Jones Books, 1968.

Farb, Peter and the Editors of *Life. Ecology.* Life Nature Library. New York: Time, Inc., 1963.

Fisher, Dorothy Canfield. *Vermont Tradition.* Boston: Little, Brown, 1953.

Fodor, Eugene, editor. *Guide to Europe, 1967*. London: MacGibbon & Kee, Ltd., 1967.

Frome, Michael. *Whose Woods These Are: The Story of the National Forests*. Garden City, N.Y.: Doubleday, 1962.

Furnas, J.C. *The Americans, a Social History of the United States, 1587–1914*. New York: G. P. Putnam's Sons, 1969.

Gates, Paul W. *The Farmer's Age: Agriculture, 1815–1860*. (Vol. III of *The Economic History of the United States*). New York: Harper & Row Torchbooks, 1968.

Goodwyn, Lawrence and the Editors of Time-Life Books. *The South Central States*. Time-Life Library of America Series. New York: Time, Inc., 1967.

Gould, John. *Monstrous Depravity*. New York: William Morrow, 1963.

Hale, William Harland and the Editors of *Horizon* Magazine. *op. cit.*

Handlin, Oscar. *Immigration as a Factor in American History*. Englewood Cliffs, N.J.: Prentice-Hall, 1959.

Heilbroner, Robert. *op. cit.*

Lankford, John. *Captain John Smith's America. Selections from His Writings*. New York: Harper & Row, 1967.

Lindsay, Vachel. *Collected Poems*. New York: Macmillan, 1923.

Mahoney, Tom. *The Great Merchants, The Stories of Twenty Famous Retail Operations and the People Who Made Them Great*. New York: Harper & Bros., 1955.

Marryat, Captain Frederick. *A Diary in America with Remarks on Its Institutions, Part Second*. London: Pans. Baudry's European Library, 1840.

Matthiessen, Peter. *Wildlife in America*. New York: Viking, 1964.

McLaughlin, Robert and the Editors of Time-Life Books. *The Heartland*. Time-Life Library of America Series. New York: Time, Inc., 1967.

Mencken, H.L. *The American Language*, Supplement One. New York: Knopf, 1945.

———. *Happy Days*. New York: Knopf, 1940.

O'Hara, John. *A Rage to Live*. New York: Random House, 1949.

Orr, John. *op. cit.*

Ortiz, Elisabeth Lambert. *The Complete Book of Mexican Cooking*. New York: Bantam, 1968.

Parkes, Henry Bamford. *The American Experience*. New York: Vintage Books, 1959.

Purchas, Samuel. *Hakluytus Posthumus, or Purchas His Pilgrimes*. Extracts "of Captaine Smiths Transylvanian Acts, out of Fr. Fer. his Storie." Vol. VIII, pages 326 ff. Glasgow: James MecLehose & Sons, 1905.

Roueché, Berton, editor. *Curiosities of Medicine*. Boston: Little, Brown, 1958.

Sinclair, Upton. *The Jungle*. New York: Viking, 1946.

Sloane, Eric. *The Seasons of America Past*. New York: Wilfred Funk, 1958.

Udall, Stewart L. *The Quiet Crisis*. New York: Holt, Rinehart and Winston, 1963.

Volney, Comte de, Constantin François Chasseboeuf. *Tableau du climat et du sol des Etats-Unis d'Amérique*. Paris: 1803.

Von Haller, Albert. *The Vitamin Hunters*. Philadelphia: Chilton, 1962.

Walden, Howard T. 2nd. *Native Inheritance, The Story of Corn in America*. New York: Harper & Row, 1966.

Webster and Polkinghorne. *op. cit.*

Wechsberg, Joseph. *op. cit.*

Wolfe, Thomas. *Of Time and the River*. New York: Scribner's, 1935.

Woodward, William E. *The Way Our People Lived*. New York: Washington Square Press, 1965.

Chapter 4

Abernethy, Robert G. *Introduction to Tomorrow*. New York: Harcourt, Brace & World, 1966.

Brown, Dale. *op cit.*

Brown, Joe David and the Editors of *Life*. *India*. New York: Time, Inc., 1961.

Bundy, Clarence E. and Diggins, Ronald V. *Livestock and Poultry Production*. Englewood Cliffs, N.J.: Prentice-Hall, 1968.

Burnett, John. *Plenty and Want, A Social History of Diet in England from 1815 to the Present Day*. Harmondsworth, Middlesex, England: Penguin, 1966.

Calder, Ritchie. *Science in Our Lives*. New York: New American Library, 1962.

Davis, Adele. *Let's Cook It Right*. New York: Harcourt, Brace, 1947.

de Groot, Roy. *op. cit.*

DuPuy, William. *op. cit.*

Editors of Time-Life Books. *Kitchen Guide*. New York: Time, Inc., 1968.

Farb, Peter. *op. cit.*

Field, Michael. *Michael Field's Cooking School*. New York: M. Barrows and Company, 1965.

Fisher, Dorothy Canfield. *op. cit.*

Furnas, J.C. *op. cit.*

Gates, Paul W. *op. cit.*

Hafez, E.S.E. *Reproduction in Farm Animals*. Philadelphia: Lea and Febiger, 1968.

Hogner, Dorothy Childs. *Farm Animals*. New York: Oxford University Press, 1945.

Holthausen, Henriette. *Chicken Cookery Round the World*. New York: Paperback Library, 1967.

Institut National de la Statistique. *Annuaire Statistique de la France*. Paris, 1967.

Margolius, Sidney. *The Consumer's Guide to Better Buying*. New York: Pocket Books, 1963.

Matthiessen, Peter, *op. cit.*

McCoy, J.J. *Animal Servants of Man.* New York: Lothrop, Lee & Shepard, 1963.

McCully, Helen. *op. cit.*

Melikian and Rudd. *op. cit.*

Mencken, H. L. *The American Language.* New York: Knopf, 1936.

Moryson, Fynes. *An Itinerary containing his Ten Years Travell through the Twelve Dominions of Germany, Bohmerland, Sweitzerland, Netherland, Denmarke, Poland, Italy, Turky, France, England, Scotland & Ireland, written by Fynes Moryson, Gent.* Vol. IV, page 171. New York: Macmillan, 1907.

Odum, Eugene P. *Ecology.* New York: Holt, Rinehart and Winston, 1966.

Pellegrini, Angelo. *The Unprejudiced Palate.* New York: Macmillan, 1948.

President's Science Advisory Committee. *The World Food Problem* (3 vols.). Washington, D.C.: U.S. Government Printing Office, 1967.

Roberson, John and Marie, *The Meat Cookbook.* New York: Holt, Rinehart and Winston, 1953.

Sanford, David, editor. *Hot War on the Consumer.* New York: Pittman/New Republic, 1969.

Sherman, Margaret. *The Wine and Food Society's Guide to Eggs.* Cleveland: World, 1968.

Smith, Anthony. *The Body.* New York: Avon, 1968.

Trevelyan, G.M. *op. cit.*

Vail, Gladys E., Griswold, Ruth M., Justin, Margaret M. and Rust, Lucile O. *Foods, An Introductory College Course.* Boston: Houghton Mifflin, 1967.

Waldo, Myra. *The Complete Round the World Meat Cookbook.* Garden City, N.Y.: Doubleday, 1967.

Webster and Polkinghorne. *op. cit.*

Winter, A. R. and Funk, E. M. *Poultry Science and Practice.* Philadelphia: Lippincott, 1960.

World Almanac, The. New York: Newspaper Enterprise Alliance, 1969.

Wright, Carlton E. *Food Buying.* New York: Macmillan, 1962.

Chapter 5

Barnett, Harriet and James. *Game and Fish Cookbook.* New York: Grossman, 1968.

Bolitho, Hector, editor. *The Glorious Oyster.* New York: Horizon, 1961.

Boorstin, Daniel. *The Colonial Experience. op. cit.*

Borgstrom, Georg. *op. cit.*

Boyle, Robert H. *The Hudson River, a natural and unnatural history.* New York: W.W. Norton, 1969.

Brown, Dale. *op. cit.*

Carson, Rachel. *The Sea Around Us.* New York: Oxford University Press, 1951.

Clark, Eleanor. *The Oysters of Loqmariaquer.* New York: Pantheon, 1964.

Coker, R.E. *This Great and Wide Sea, an Introduction to Oceanography and Marine Biology*. New York: Harper & Row, 1962.

de Crèvecoeur, Michel. *Letters. op. cit.*

de Groot, Roy. *op. cit.*

Editors of *American Heritage, op. cit.*

Editors of Time-Life Books. Great Ages of Man Series. *op. cit.*

————. *Kitchen Guide. op. cit.*

Farb, Peter and the Editors of *Life. op. cit.*

Furnas, J.C. *op. cit.*

Gibbons, Euell, *Stalking the Blue-Eyed Scallop*. New York: David McKay, 1964.

Hale, William Harlan and the Editors of *Horizon* Magazine. *op. cit.*

Lewis, W. H. *op. cit.*

Lyon, Ninette. *Fish for All Occasions*. New York: Rand McNally, 1967.

Marine, Gene. *America the Raped*. New York: Simon and Schuster, 1969.

Marx, Wesley. *The Frail Ocean*. New York: Ballantine, 1969.

Matthiessen, Peter, *op. cit.*

McCully, Helen. *op. cit.*

Morris, Dan and Moore, Matilda. *The Savor of the Sea, A Complete Seafood Cookbook*. New York: Macmillan, 1966.

Radford, Erwin. *op. cit.*

Sauer, Carl O. *Land and Life*. Berkeley and Los Angeles: University of California Press, 1967.

Thoreau, Henry David. *A Week on the Concord and Merrimack Rivers*. Boston: Houghton Mifflin, 1881.

Trevelyan, G. M. *op. cit.*

Webster and Polkinghorne. *op. cit.*

Chapter 6

Angier, Bradford. *How To Stay Alive in the Woods* (originally published as *Living Off the Country*). New York: Collier, 1968.

Beaty, John Y. *Luther Burbank, Plant Magician*. New York: Julian Messner, 1943.

Bevona, Don. *The Love Apple Cookbook*. New York: Funk & Wagnalls, 1968.

Boy Scouts of America. *The Boy Scout Handbook*, 7th edition. 1965.

Bundy and Diggins. *op. cit.*

Coon, Nelson. *Using Wayside Plants*. New York: Hearthside Press, 1960.

Crispo, Dorothy. *The Story of Our Fruits and Vegetables*. Dorex, 1968.

Cruess, W.V. *Commercial Fruit and Vegetable Products*. New York: McGraw-Hill, 1958.

de Groot, Roy. *op. cit.*

Editors of *American Heritage. op. cit.*

Editors of Time-Life Books. *Kitchen Guide. op. cit.*

Editors of *Woman's Day. op. cit.*

Elliott, Lawrence. *George Washington Carver, The Man Who Overcame.* Englewood Cliffs, N.J.: Prentice-Hall, 1966.

Farb, Peter. *op. cit.*

Field, Michael. *op. cit.*

Furnas, J.C. *op. cit.*

Gerard, John. *Herball.* London: 1597, pages 345–46.

Gibbons, Euell. *Stalking the Wild Asparagus.* New York: David McKay, 1962.

———. *Stalking the Healthful Herbs.* New York: David McKay, 1966.

Gordeon, Elizabeth. *Cuisines of the Modern World.* New York: Golden Press, 1965.

Hale, William Harlan and the Editors of *Horizon* Magazine. *op. cit.*

Hill, Albert. *op. cit.*

Institut National de la Statistique. *op. cit.*

Lankford, John. *op. cit.*

Launay, Andre. *Posh Food.* Baltimore: Penguin Books, 1967.

Lawson, John Howard. *The Hidden Heritage.* New York: Citadel Press, 1968.

Lehner, Ernst and Johanna. *Folklore and Odysseys of Food and Medicinal Plants.* New York: Tudor, 1962.

Lévi-Strauss, Claude. *The Savage Mind.* Chicago: University of Chicago Press. 1966.

Lewis, W.H. *op. cit.*

Martin, Jane. *op. cit.*

McCully, Helen. *op. cit.*

McMillen, Wheeler. *op. cit.*

McPhee, John. *op. cit.*

Melikian and Rudd. *op. cit.*

Miller, John C. *The First Frontier: Life in Colonial Virgina.* New York: Dell, 1966.

Miller, Philip. *The Gardeners Dictionary.* 7th edition. London: 1759.

Nesbitt, Paul H., Pond, Alonzo W. and Allen, William H. *The Survival Book.* Princeton, N.J.: D. Van Nostrand, 1959.

Pellegrini, Angelo. *op. cit.*

Prentice, E. Parmalee. *Hunger and History.* Caldwell, Idaho: Caxton Printers, 1951.

Sauer, Carl. *Agricultural Origins. op. cit.*

———. *Land and Life. op. cit.*

Webster and Polkinghorne. *op. cit.*

Went, Frits W. and the Editors of *Life. The Plants.* Life Nature Library. New York: Time, Inc., 1963.

Wells, George S. *Garden in the West, A Dramatic Account of Science in Agriculture.* New York: Dodd, Mead, 1969.

Wilson, Charles Morrow. *Roots: Miracles Below.* Garden City, N.Y.: Doubleday, 1968.

Woodham-Smith, Cecil. *The Reason Why*. London: Constable, 1955.
————. *The Great Hunger*. New York: Signet, New American Library, 1962.
Wright, Carlton. *op. cit.*

Chapter 7

Angier, Bradford. *op. cit.*
Borgstrom, Georg. *op. cit.*
Brasch, R. *How Did It Begin?* New York: David McKay, 1965.
Christensen, Clyde M. *Common Edible Mushrooms*. Minneapolis: University of Minnesota Press, 1943.
Cook, Captain James, F.R.S. *A Voyage to the Pacific Ocean*. London: Wit A. Strahan and T. Cadill in the Strand, 1784. Vol. II, page 249.
de Groot, Roy. *op. cit.*
De Mente, Boye and Perry, Fred Thomas. *The Japanese As Consumers*. New York and Tokyo: Weatherhill/Walker, 1968.
Dresner, Samuel H. and Siegel, Seymour. *The Jewish Dietary Laws*. New York: Burning Bush Press, 1966.
Editors of Time-Life Books. Great Ages of Man Series. *op. cit.*
Ellwanger, George. *op. cit.*
Farb, Peter. *op. cit.*
Fodor, Eugene. *op. cit.*
Graves, Robert. *Food for Centaurs*. Garden City, N.Y.: Doubleday, 1960.
Harris, Townsend. *The Complete Journals of Townsend Harris, First American Consul General and Minister to Japan*. Garden City, N.Y.: Doubleday, Doran, 1930.
————. *Some Unpublished Letters*, edited by Shio Sakanishi. New York: Japan Reference Library, 1941.
Hill, Albert. *op. cit.*
Kavaler, Lucy. *Mushrooms, Molds and Miracles*. New York: Signet, New American Library, 1966.
Krieger, Louis C.C. *The Mushroom Handbook*. New York: Dover, 1967.
Krutch, Joseph. *op. cit.*
Lankford, John. *op. cit.*
Mead, Margaret, editor and World Federation for Mental Health. *Cultural Patterns and Technical Change* (UNESCO). New York: Mentor, New American Library, 1955.
Mencken, H.L. *American Language. op. cit.*
Montagne, Prosper. *op. cit.*
Montaigne, Michel Eyquem de. *Essays*. (John Florio's translation.) Boston: Houghton Mifflin, 1904.
Moorehead, Alan. *The Fatal Impact*. New York: Harper & Row, 1966.
Nesbitt, Pond and Allen. *op. cit.*

Parmelee, Alice. *All the Birds of the Bible*. New York: Harper and Bros., 1959.

Pellegrini, Angelo. *op. cit.*

Pineau, Roger, editor. *The Japan Expedition, 1852–1854, The Personal Journal of Commodore Matthew C. Perry*. Washington, D.C.: Smithsonian Institution Press, 1969.

Pirie, N.W. *Food Resources, Conventional and Novel*. Harmondsworth, Middlesex, England: Penguin, 1969.

Rawson, Jeffrey. *Bligh of the Bounty*. London: P. Allen Co., 1930.

Rosten, Leo. *The Joys of Yiddish*. New York: McGraw-Hill, 1968.

Roussinov, Spass. *A Race Against Time*. Sofia, Bulgaria: Foreign Language Press, 1962.

Rudofsky, Bernard. *The Kimono Mind*. Garden City, N.Y.: Doubleday, 1965.

Sauer, Carl O. *Agricultural Origins. op. cit.*

Steiner, Franz. *Taboo*. Baltimore: Penguin Books, 1967.

Thomas, William S. *Field. Book of Common Mushrooms*. New York: G.P. Putnam's Sons, 1948.

Went, Frits. and the Editors of *Life. op. cit.*

Woollcott, Alexander. *Long, Long Ago*. New York: Viking, 1943.

Chapter 8

Boorstin, Daniel. *The National Experience. op. cit.*

Borgstrom, Georg. *op. cit.*

Brillat-Savarin, Jean-Anthelme. *The Physiology of Taste, or Meditations on Transcendental Gastronomy*. New York: Boni and Liveright, 1926.

Brown, Dale. *op. cit.*

Brown, Robert Carlton. *The Complete Book of Cheeses*. Introduction by Clifton Fadiman. New York: Random House, 1955.

Bruce, James. *An Interefting Narrative of the Travels of James Bruce, Esq. into Abyssinia to Discover the Source of the Nile*. Second American Edition. Boston: Samuel Etheridge, 1798, pages 233, 236.

Burnett, John. *op. cit.*

Clark, Sidney. *All the Best in Central America*. New York: Dodd, Mead, 1967.

Cooper, James Fenimore. *The Travelling Bachelor. op. cit.*

Cruess, W.V. *op. cit.*

de Crèvecoeur, Michel. *Sketches. op. cit.*, pages 102–103.

de Groot, Roy. *op. cit.*

Editors of *The National Observer. op. cit.*

Field, Michael. *op. cit.*

Forbes, R.J. and Dijksterhus, E.J. *A History of Science and Technology*, Vol. 2. Baltimore: Penguin, 1963.

Furnas, J.C. *op. cit.*

Institut National de la Statistique. *op. cit.*

Jacob, Dorothy. *Cures and Curses*. New York: Taplinger, 1967.

Kahn, E.J. *The Big Drink*. New York: Random House, 1960.

Launay, Andre. *op. cit.*

Layton, T.A. *The Wine and Food Society's Guide to Cheese and Cheese Cookery*. Cleveland: World, 1967.

Lévi-Strauss, Claude. *The Raw and the Cooked, Introduction to a Science of Mythology*. Vol. I. New York: Harper & Row, 1969.

Margolius, Sidney. *op. cit.*

Marquis, Vivienne and Haskell, Patricia. *The Cheese Book*. New York: Simon and Schuster, 1964.

McCully, Helen. *op. cit.*

McHenry, E.W. *Foods without Fads*. Philadelphia: Lippincott, 1960.

McPhee, John. *op. cit.*

Moorehead, Alan. *The Blue Nile*. New York: Harper & Row, 1962.

Stimson, George. *A Book about a Thousand Things*. New York: Harper and Bros., 1946.

Thoreau, Henry David. *Walden, or, Life in the Woods*. Boston: Houghton Mifflin, 1893, pages 455–59.

Von Haller, Albert. *op. cit.*

Webster and Polkinghorne. *op. cit.*

Went, Frits. and the Editors of *Life. op. cit.*

World Almanac, The. op. cit.

Wright, Carlton. *op. cit.*

Chapter 9

Brown, Dale. *op. cit.*

Comfort, Alex. *Nature and Human Nature*. Harmondsworth, Middlesex, England: Penguin, 1969.

Cuppy, Will. "Some Royal Stomachs," from *The Decline and Fall of Practically Everybody*. New York: Holt, Rinehart, Winston, 1950.

de Gramont, Sanche. *op. cit.*

Dreicer, Maurice. *The Diner's Companion*. New York: Crown, 1955.

Frost, David and Jay, Anthony. *The English*. New York: Stein & Day, 1967.

Kirk-Othmer, *Encyclopedia of Chemical Technology*. Second Edition, Vol. I. New York: John Wiley & Sons, 1963.

Martin, Lawrence and Sylvia. *England!* New York: McGraw-Hill, 1963.

Morris, Desmond. *op. cit.*

Rienow, Robert and Leona T. *Moment in the Sun*. New York: Dial, 1967.

Sanders, Howard J. Food Additives, in *Chemical and Engineering News*, October 10 and 17, 1966.

Sanford, David, *op. cit.*

Smith, Anthony. *op. cit.*

U.S. Tariff Commission. *Synthetic Organic Chemicals*. U.S. Production and Sales, 1966. Washington, D.C.: U.S. Government Printing Office, 1968.

Chapter 10

Belham, Dr. George. *The Virility Diet*. New York: Dell, 1965.
Bey, Pilaff, edited by Norman Douglas. *Venus in the Kitchen*, or *Love's Cookery Book*. New York: Viking, 1952.
Editors of *American Heritage. op. cit.*
Editors of Consumer Reports. *The Medicine Show*. Mount Vernon, N.Y.: Consumer's Union, 1963.
Ehrlich, Paul. *The Population Bomb*. New York: Ballantine, 1968.
Fredericks, Carlton. *Nutrition, Your Key to Good Health*. North Hollywood, Calif.: London Press, 1964.
—— and Bailey, Herbert. *Food Facts and Fallacies*. New York: ARC Books, Inc., 1968.
Gardner, Martin. *Fads and Fallacies*. New York: Dover, 1957.
Gould, John. *op. cit.*
Hafez, E.S.E. *op. cit.*
Hauser, Gayelord. *Look Younger, Live Longer*. New York: Farrar, Straus and Cudahy, 1951.
Jarvis, D.C., M.D. *Folk Medicine*. New York: Holt, Rinehart and Winston, 1958.
Krutch, Joseph. *op. cit.*
Reuben, David R., M.D. *Everything you always wanted to know about sex* * *but were afraid to ask*. New York: David McKay, 1969.
Righter, Carroll. *Your Astrological Guide to Health and Diet*. New York: G. P. Putnam's Sons, 1967.
Robinson, Corinne H. *Fundamentals of Normal Nutrition*. New York: Macmillan, 1968.
Rodale, J.I. *The Organic Front*. Emmaus, Penn.: Rodale Press, 1948.
Smith, Ralph Lee. *The Health Hucksters*. New York: Crowell, 1960.
Von Haller, Albert. *op. cit.*
Walton, Alan Hull. *Stimulants for Love, The Quest for Virility*. London: Tandem Books, 1966.
Winter, Ruth. *Poisons in Your Food*. New York: Crown, 1969.
Young, James Harvey. *The Medical Messiahs*. Princeton, N.J.: Princeton University Press, 1967.

Chapter 11

Burnett, John. *op. cit.*
Rienow, Robert and Leona T. *op. cit.*

Sanford, David. *op. cit.*
Smollett, Tobias George. *The Expedition of Humphry Clinker*. London: G. Routledge & Sons, Ltd., 1890.
Young, James Harvey. *op. cit.*

Appendix

Editors of *American Heritage*. *op. cit.*
Kirk-Othmer. *op. cit.*
Sanders, Howard J. *op. cit.*
U.S. Tariff Commission. *op. cit.*
Winter, Ruth. *op. cit.*

‰⟦ *Acknowledgments* ⟧‰

The help, encouragement and expertise of a number of people have contributed importantly to the book. I want especially to thank Joseph Baum of Restaurant Associates, the staff of the Brooklyn Botanical Garden, Gunnar Christiansson of Olle Hartwig A.B. in Johanneshov, Sweden, my sister Kathleen T. Cone, Roy and Jane Danish, William F. Dobbins, Acting Agricultural Attache to the American Embassy in Rome, Page Edwards of Grossman Publishers, Robert Doris and Robert J. Eiserle of Fritzsche Dodge & Olcott, Inc., the Fish and Wildlife Service of the U.S. Interior Department, David Greene of Greenway Meat Service in Jamaica, N.Y., Burton Hale, Florence C. Hodes, Helen Holmes, Sally Kuhn, Anthony Lewis of the *New York Times*, Kenneth Monfort of Monfort Packing Company, Greeley, Colorado, David P. Morgan of the USDA Agricultural Research Service at Beltsville, Md., George Mulgrue of FAO, Seymour Mann of Aceto Industrial Chemical Co., members of the New York Mycological Society, Professor Emil Negrutju and Dr. Ioan Puia of the Institutl Agronomic in Cluj, Romania, the staff of the New York State Agricultural Experimental Station at Geneva, N.Y., Chie Nishio of Tokyo, Donald Perry of Riegel Paper Co., Professor Nicholas Polyzopalous of Thessalonika University in Greece, Santha Rama Rau, Sydelle Shapiro, Marilyn Silverstone of Magnum Photos in New Delhi, Dr. Herman Steinberg, Bonny Thornton, Theresa Varvaris, Burton Watson, Associate Professor of Chinese at Columbia, K.T. Wu of the Library of Congress, and Eleanor Yarrow of the Bronx Botanical Garden. None of the above bears any responsibility for whatever errors the book may contain.

I also wish to express my gratitude to all authors, publishers and copyright owners for their cooperation in the preparation of this volume. Any errors or omissions that may have inadvertently occurred will be corrected in any subsequent printings.

Excerpt from *Our Wildlife Legacy*, by Durward L. Allen. Copyright 1954, by Durward L. Allen. By permission of the publisher, Funk & Wagnalls, N.Y.

Excerpt from *Gluttons and Libertines*, by Marston Bates. Copyright 1967, by Marston Bates. By permission of Random House, Inc.

540] ACKNOWLEDGMENTS

Excerpt from Clifton Fadiman's introduction to *The Complete Book of Cheese*, by Carlton Brown. Copyright 1955 by Carlton Brown. By permission of Random House, Inc.

Excerpts from *Science in Our Lives*, by Ritchie Calder. By permission of The New American Library.

Excerpt from *Vermont Tradition*, by Dorothy Canfield Fisher. By permission of Little, Brown and Co.

Excerpt from *The Golden Bough*, by James Frazer. By permission of Macmillan & Co.

Excerpt from *Stalking the Wild Asparagus*, by Euell Gibbons. By permission of David McKay and Co., Inc.

Excerpt from *Mushrooms, Molds and Miracles*, by Lucy Kavaler. Copyright © 1965 by Lucy Kavaler. Reprinted by permission of The John Day Company, Inc., publisher.

Excerpt from "The Ghosts of the Buffaloes" reprinted with permission of The Macmillan Company from *Complete Poems* by Vachel Lindsay. Copyright 1917 by The Macmillan Company, renewed 1945 by Elizabeth C. Lindsay.

Excerpt from "Profile: A Forager," by John McPhee, which originally appeared in the April 6, 1968, issue of *The New Yorker*, is reprinted by permission of that magazine.

Excerpt from *Happy Days*, by H. L. Mencken. Copyright 1940 by H. L. Mencken. By permission of Alfred A. Knopf, Inc.

Excerpt from *The Fatal Impact*, by Alan Moorehead. By permission of Harper & Row, publishers.

Excerpt from *The Clean Platter*, by Ogden Nash. From *Verses From 1929 On*. Copyright 1935, by Ogden Nash. By permission of Little, Brown and Co.

Excerpt from *Our Plundered Planet*, by Fairfield Osborn. By permission of Little, Brown and Co.

Excerpt from *Land and Life*, by Carl O. Sauer. Reprinted by permission of The Regents of the University of California.

Excerpts from *The Jungle*, by Upton Sinclair. By permission of The Viking Press, Inc.

Excerpts from *Of Time and the River*, by Thomas Wolfe. By permission of the publishers, Charles Scribner's Sons.

⋅∘⟦ Index ⟧∘⋅

This book was set on the linotype in Janson.
The display type is Goudy Old Style.
The composition is by Brown Bros. Linotypers, Inc.
The paper is Yarmouth Antique.
The printing and binding is by Halliday Lithograph Corporation.
Designed by Jacqueline Schuman.